CANTATE DOMINO

A COMMENTARY ON
THE HYMNS OF THE LITURGY
OF THE HOURS

VOLUME I

Proper of Time
Advent, Christmas, Lent, and Easter

CANTATE DOMINO

A COMMENTARY ON
THE HYMNS OF THE LITURGY
OF THE HOURS

VOLUME I

Proper of Time

Advent, Christmas, Lent, and Easter

Edited by Andrew Wadsworth, Cong. Orat.,
Nicholas Richardson, Peter Finn,
and Maria Kiely, OSB

The Catholic University of America Press
WASHINGTON, D.C.

Copyright © 2024
The Catholic University of America Press
All rights reserved
The paper used in this publication meets the minimum requirements
of American National Standards for Information Science—
Permanence of Paper for Printed Library Materials,
ANSI Z39.48-1992.
∞

Cover and interior design by Reflective Book Design

Cataloging-in-Publication Data available
from the Library of Congress
ISBN: 978-0-8132-3902-6
eISBN:978-0-8132-3903-3

CONTENTS

Foreword	ix
Acknowledgments	xi
Abbreviations	xiii
General Introduction	xv
Development and the Need for Reform *xvi*	
Complexities of the Tradition: An Example *xix*	
The Role of the Hymn in the Divine Office *xxxiv*	
General Characteristics of the Latin Liturgical Hymns *xl*	
The English Translations: ICEL Texts *xlv*	
Appendix I: Latin Meter	li
Fundamental Principles *li*	
Iambic Dimeter: Quantitative and Accentual *lvii*	
Meters in the *Liturgia Horarum* *lxiii*	
Appendix II: Assonance, Alliteration, and Rhyme	lxxi
A List of Terms *lxxi*	
Historical Development of Hymns *lxxii*	

Commentaries

Part 1. The Season of Advent

1

Seasonal Insert	Advent	Commentary #	Divine Office Hymnal #	Page #
	Conditor alme siderum	1	1	4
	Verbum supernum prodiens, a Patre	2	5	11
	Vox clara ecce intonat	3	7	17
	Verbum salutis omnium	4	15	24
	Veni, redemptor gentium	5	19	29
	Magnis prophetæ vocibus	6	21	37

Part 2. The Season of Christmas

45

Seasonal Insert	Christmas	Commentary #	Divine Office Hymnal #	Page #
	Christe, redemptor omnium, ex Patre	7	29	49
	Candor æternæ Deitatis alme	8	33	56
	A solis ortus cardine	9	35	62
	O lux beata cælitum	10	43	69
	Dulce fit nobis memorare parvum	11	45	72
	Christe, splendor Patris	12	47	77
	Corde natus ex Parentis	13	49	84
	Radix Iesse floruit	14	51	89
	Fit porta Christi pervia	15	53	93
	Hostis Herodes impie	16	55	97
	Magi videntes parvulum	17	59	102
	Quicumque Christum quæritis	18	61	106
	A Patre Unigenite	19	69	110
	Implente munus debitum	20	71	115
	Iesus refulsit omnium	21	73	119

Part 3. The Season of Lent & Holy Week

123

Seasonal Insert	Lent and Holy Week	Commentary #	Divine Office Hymnal #	Page #
	Audi, benigne Conditor	22	75	126
	Iesu, quadragenariæ	23	77	132
	Ex more docti mystico	24	83	136
	Nunc tempus acceptabile	25	85	142
	Precemur omnes cernui	26	87	147
	Iam, Christe, sol iustitiæ	27	89	152
	Dei fide, qua vivimus	28	91	160
	Qua Christus hora sitiit	29	93	164
	Ternis ter horis numerus	30	95	167
	Vexilla regis prodeunt	31	97, 501	169
	Pange, lingua, gloriosi proelium	32	99	175
	En acetum, fel, arundo	33	101	181
	Celsæ salutis gaudia	34	103	184
	O memoriale mortis Domini	35	105	190
	Christe, cælorum Domine	36	113	196
	Salva, Redemptor, plasma tuum nobile	37	107	202
	Crux, mundi benedictio	38	109	207
	Per crucem, Christe, quæsumus	39	111	211
	Tibi, Redemptor omnium	40	115	215
	Auctor salutis unice	41	117	220

Part 4. The Season of Easter
227

Seasonal Insert	Easter	Commentary #	Divine Office Hymnal #	Page #
	Ad cenam Agni providi	42	119	231
	O rex æterne, Domine	43	121	243
	Hic est dies verus Dei	44	125	248
	Lætare, cælum, desuper	45	127	255
	Aurora lucis rutilat	46	129	261
	Chorus novæ Ierusalem	47	131	267
	Iam surgit hora tertia	48	133	271
	Venite, servi, supplices	49	135, 155	275
	Hæc hora, quæ resplenduit	50	137, 157	279
	Iesu, redemptor sæculi	51	123, 147	283
	Iesu, nostra redemptio	52	139	288
	Æterne rex altissime	53	143	291
	Optatus votis omnium	54	145	296
	Veni, creator Spiritus	55	141	301
	Lux iucunda, lux insignis	56	149	310
	Beata nobis gaudia	57	151	317
	Iam Christus astra ascenderat	58	153	323

Bibliography	329
List of Contributors	347
Scriptural Index	349
Concordance of Hymn Numbers in the Commentary and the English *Divine Office Hymnal*	359

FOREWORD

"These compositions elaborated according to the classical metres or according to accent and rhythm, these sophisticated or simple outpourings of devotion and love, these songs full of enthusiastic praise or joy or lament—as long as they are pervaded by a noble and calm lyricism—constitute for the liturgy and by way of the liturgy an outstanding and enviable patrimony of the Church of which she continues to be the guardian and guarantor." So wrote Dom Anselmo Lentini, OSB, forty years ago of the hymnody of the post-conciliar Roman Divine Office. It is a patrimony formed by poets and saints, and it includes some 294 hymns reaching from the fourth century to the twentieth—Lentini himself contributed 43. It lives today on the lips of all who pray the Liturgy of the Hours.

We may safely say that Dom Anselmo would rejoice at the publication before us of this masterly five-volume Commentary on the Hymnody of the *Liturgia Horarum*, a joint project of the International Commission on English in the Liturgy and The Catholic University of America. These volumes, along with *The Divine Office Hymnal*, offer the first official and complete translation of the current corpus of the hymnody contained in the Liturgy of the Hours. The commentary, after a historical and technical introduction on Latin hymnody and the role it has played in the prayer of the Church, offers an analysis of each hymn and charts its history, leaving (or guiding?) the reader to draw his or her own theological, spiritual profit from it. Behind these five volumes lie ten years of study, directed by Msgr. Andrew Wadsworth and enriched by the contributions of other scholars. Their fruit will be, I am sure, a fuller understanding and deeper appreciation of this precious and considerable element of the Divine Office.

These hymns, says the general introduction to the Liturgy of the Hours,[1] "have a place in the Office from very early times, a position they still retain.... Indeed, they generally have an immediate effect in creating the individual characteristic of the Hour or individual feast, more so than other parts of the Office, and they are able to move and encourage the mind and heart to a devout celebration. Their literary beauty frequently

1. *GILH* no. 173

enhances their effectiveness." Thanks to this commentary that "place" will not only be on the page or in verbal recitation of the Office but in the grateful heart where believers, says St. Paul, "sing psalms, hymns and spiritual songs to God" (Col 3:16).

†Hugh Gilbert, OSB
Bishop of Aberdeen
Chairman of the International Commission for English in the Liturgy
Memorial of Ss. Basil and Gregory Nazianzen, January 2, 2024.

ACKNOWLEDGMENTS

In the sixty years of its existence, the International Commission on English in the Liturgy (ICEL) has served Catholics who worship in English by the presentation of English translations of the Latin liturgical texts. As a consequence of this work, ICEL has accumulated a wealth of scholarly commentary on these texts in archival resources that are unparalleled in their detail and depth, providing the narrative of how our current liturgical books were made, and how they have entered the Church's life in these years since the Second Vatican Council.

This present series of commentaries is the fruit of the preparation of the English translations and their accompanying melodies of the hymnody of the Liturgy of the Hours. The information contained here was compiled during the process of making the translations and is now made available to a wider audience who seek to deepen their knowledge and understanding of the way we pray the hours. In addition to all those whose individual scholarly contribution to the individual commentaries is acknowledged in the body of the text, it is only right that we immediately recognize our debt of gratitude to those who ultimately enabled this publication to come to light.

None of this would have been possible without the support at every stage of the bishops of the Commission, our colleagues at the ICEL Secretariat, and my successor as Executive Director, Rev. Andrew Menke. I, and my fellow editors feel honored to have been enabled to pursue this wonderfully interesting project, and we are conscious that it has been possible only through the generous collaboration of others. Trevor Crowell and the staff of The Catholic University of America Press have been of immense assistance to us in the process of redaction, and we have been very fortunate to have the collaboration of Anne Needham in the final stages of the preparation of the manuscript. We are also grateful to Br. Noah Sell, Cong. Orat. and Jane Maschue for their assistance in proof reading and in the compilation of the index and bibliography. Beyond these, our closest coworkers, we thank our families, our communities, and our many friends who have encouraged us in this work and assisted us in bringing it to publication.

Msgr. Andrew Wadsworth, Cong. Orat.

ABBREVIATIONS

Complete publication information for abbreviated works listed below is found in the bibliography.

(#, #)	Stanza number, line number within the stanza.
AAS (formerly *ASS*)	The *Acta Sanctae Sedis* was established in 1865 for the publication of official Vatican documents. In 1909, the name was changed to the *Acta Apostolicae Sedis*.
AH	Analecta Hymnica Medii Aevii, vols. 1–55.
Blaise	Albert Blaise, *Dictionnaire latin-français des auteurs Chrétiens*.
Britt	Matthew Britt, *Hymns of the Breviary and Missal*.
Bulst	Walther Bulst, *Hymni Latini antiquissimi LXXV; psalmi III*, 1956.
Cath	Prudentius, *Cathemerinon* 1–12. If stanza and line numbers are given in a particular hymn, it reads: *Cath* [hymn #]: [stanza #], [line #] (e.g., Cath 9: 3, 2–3).
CCC	*Catechism of the Catholic Church*. References are to numbers.
CCSL	Corpus Christianorum Series Latina.
Conf	Augustine of Hippo, *The Confessions*.
Connelly	Joseph Connelly, *Hymns of the Roman Liturgy*.
CSEL	Corpus Scriptorum Ecclesiaticorum Latinorum (Vienna Corpus).
DMLBS	*Dictionary of Medieval Latin from British Sources*. Online database from Brepols; previously R. E. Latham, *Revised Medieval Latin Word-List from British and Irish Sources*. Oxford.
DOH	*Divine Office Hymnal*: the printed edition of the ICEL English translation of the hymns of the *Liturgia Horarum*.
Fontaine	*Ambroise de Milan: Hymnes*, ed. Jacques Fontaine.
GILH	*General Instruction on the Liturgy of the Hours*: citations in this commentary are taken from the ICEL translation of 2021 for the revised edition of *The Liturgy of the Hours*.
H	References to single hymns as they are found in this commentary are given in parentheses (H followed by the hymn number). If a stanza and line are given in a particular hymn, it reads: H #: #, #. (e.g., H 45: 3, 2).

Abbreviations

HIBR	*Hymni instaurandi breviarii Romani*, 1968: the first edition of the revised hymnal, the final version of which is found in the *TDH*.
ICEL	International Commission on English in the Liturgy.
Julian	John Julian, *A Dictionary of Hymnology*.
Lewis and Short	Charlton T. Lewis and Charles Short, *A Latin Dictionary*.
LLT	Library of Latin Texts. An online database from Brepols Publishers containing Latin primary sources from antiquity to the present.
MGH	Monumenta Germaniae Historica, a multivolume collection of primary sources for the history and literature of Europe from the end of the Roman Empire until 1500 AD, available in print and online.
Milfull	Inge B. Milfull, *The Hymns of the Anglo-Saxon Church: a Study and Edition of the 'Durham Hymnal'*.
Norberg, *Introduction*	Dag Norberg, *An Introduction to the Study of Medieval Latin Versification*.
Norberg, *L'accentuation*	Dag Norberg, *L'accentuation des mots dans le vers latin du Moyen Age*.
Norberg, *Les vers*	Dag Norberg, *Les vers latins iambiques et trochaïques au Moyen Age et leurs répliques rythmiques*.
Norberg, *Manuel*	Dag Norberg, *Manuel pratique de latin médiéval*, Paris, 1968.
OLD	P. G. W. Glare and Roger A. B. Mynors, eds., *Oxford Latin Dictionary*.
Peristeph	Prudentius, *Peristephanon* (The Crowns of the Martyrs) 1–14. If stanza and line numbers are given in a particular hymn, it reads: *Peristeph* [hymn #]: [stanza #], [line #]. (e.g., *Peristeph* 9: 3, 2–3).
Pimont	S.-G. Pimont, *Les Hymnes du Brévière Romain: Études critiques, littéraires, et mystiques*.
SC	*Sacrosanctum Concilium*, Constitution on the Sacred Liturgy, Second Vatican Council, 1963.
SCh	Sources Chrétiennes. A bilingual collection of Patristic texts in the original language and French.
TDH	*Te Decet Hymnus: L'Innario della "Liturgia Horarum,"* ed. Anselmo Lentini, 1984.
TLL	*Thesaurus Linguae Latinae*. Deutsche Akademie der Wissenschaften, 1894–.
Walpole	Arthur S. Walpole, ed., *Early Latin Hymns*.
Walsh	Peter G. Walsh, ed., *One Hundred Latin Hymns*.

GENERAL INTRODUCTION

In the final verse of Psalm 148, we read: "His praise is above heaven and earth: and he has exalted the horn of his people, a hymn for all his saints: the children of Israel, the people who draw near to him."[1] In commenting on this verse, St. Augustine gives his celebrated definition of a hymn:

> Do you know what a hymn is? It is a song with praise of God. If you praise God, and you do not sing, you do not sing a hymn; if you sing, and do not praise God, you do not sing a hymn; if you praise something that does not pertain to the praise of God, even if you praise in song, you do not sing a hymn. A hymn, therefore, has these three: song, praise, and "of God." A hymn is praise of God in song.[2]

Continuing his commentary on the psalm verse, Augustine asks:

> What does this mean: "a hymn for all his saints"? Let his saints receive the hymn, let his saints proclaim the hymn, for this is what they are destined to receive in the end, an eternal hymn.[3]

According to Augustine, Christian Latin hymnody is a genre of poetry, which of its nature is made to be sung. It belongs to the liturgy, that is, to the common prayer of those who draw near to God; it belongs to the Christian faithful as they pray in this life and praise eternally in the next.

Augustine wrote these lines in the first generation after St. Ambrose of Milan had composed hymns that would define the genre of Christian Latin hymnody for centuries to come. Augustine sang Ambrose's hymns, and, as he says in the *Confessions*, he wept with joy and happiness as he sang.[4] Although St. Hilary of Poitiers had composed hymns before Ambrose, his content and meters were too complex for widespread congregational singing. His hymns fell into disuse and the greater part of them is now lost. Less than twenty years after Hilary's

---

1. *Confessio eius super cælum et terram, et exaltabit cornu populi sui, hymnus omnibus sanctis eius, filiis Israel, populo appropinquanti sibi* (Ps 148:14).
2. *Hymnus scitis quid est? cantus est cum laude Dei. si laudas Deum, et non cantas, non dicis hymnum; si cantas, et non laudas Deum, non dicis hymnum; si laudas aliud quod non pertinet ad laudem Dei, etsi cantando laudes, non dicis hymnum. Hymnus ergo tria ista habet, et cantum, et laudem, et Dei. Laus ergo Dei in cantico, hymnus dicitur* (Augustine, *Enarrationes in Psalmos*, Ps 148.17).
3. *Quid est ergo: hymnus omnibus sanctis eius? Accipiant sancti eius hymnum, dicant sancti eius hymnum, quia hoc est quod accepturi sunt in fine, hymnum sempiternum* (Augustine, *Enarrationes in Psalmos*, Ps 148.17, cont.).
4. *voces illæ influebant auribus meis, et eliquabatur veritas in cor meum, et exæstuabat inde affectus pietatis, et currebant lacrimæ, et bene mihi erat cum eis* (Augustine, *Conf.*, 9.6).

death, during the Basilica crisis of 386 AD, Ambrose introduced into the liturgy at Milan antiphonal psalmody, as it was practiced in the East, and hymns in a simple meter suited to choral singing.[5] As Augustine tells us, Ambrose introduced this new aspect of the liturgy in order to help the faithful endure their long vigil in the Basilica Nova and the Basilica Portiana, as they resisted the imperial soldiers of the Arian Empress Justina.[6] Ambrose's expedient was a success, and the use of hymns spread rapidly. In the sixth century, St. Benedict, in his Rule, included the use of hymns in his legislation for the Divine Office (*Divinum Officium*), or the Work of God (*Opus Dei*), using the terms *hymnus* and *Ambrosianum* interchangeably. Partly under the influence of Benedictine monasticism and the Carolingian reforms, cycles of hymns for the offices and seasons of the liturgical year, as well as for the commemoration of saints, developed throughout the Western Church in the early Middle Ages.[7]

DEVELOPMENT AND THE NEED FOR REFORM

Like English, Latin has long and short vowels and syllables, as well as stressed and unstressed syllables. For example, the English word "weaver" has a diphthong "ea" that makes the first syllable long; this is followed by a second syllable containing a short vowel "e." The long first syllable also has a stress accent; the short second syllable is unaccented when compared to the first. In classical Latin, poetic meters, modeled after Greek quantitative verse, were based in large measure on the placement of long and short syllables into various metrical patterns. As the language developed in the later years of the Empire and the early Middle Ages, the stress accent, native to Latin and never lost, gradually became the predominating factor in the pronunciation of the language, and the innate ability to hear differences between long and short syllables was diminished, even among the educated elite.[8] Thus, in the late fourth century, Augustine says that the patterns made by

---

5. Augustine says: *tunc hymni et psalmi ut canerentur secundum morem orientalium partium, ne populus mæroris tædio contabesceret, institutum est: ex illo in hodiernum retentum multis iam ac pæne omnibus gregibus tuis et per cetera orbis imitantibus.* "Then it was instituted that hymns and psalms should be sung according to the custom of the Eastern provinces, so that the people would not be worn down by the weariness of sorrow. From that time to this, it is retained by many—and indeed almost all—your congregations, [Lord], and by those imitating them through other parts of the world" (Augustine, *Conf.* 9.7). See the analysis of this text of the *Confessions* by Fontaine, 16–22. Fontaine points out that the verb *institutum est* implies an act of instituting new liturgical practices.

6. For an excellent and succinct account of the crisis, and the significance of the Basilica Portiana for the Non-Nicenes of Milan in 386, see Colish, "Why the Portiana?."

7. *GILH*, 173; *TDH*, xv. For an overview of the early history of hymnody, see Hiley, *Western Plainchant*, 140–46, 492–93; Walpole, x–xxi; Szövérffy, *Latin Hymns*, 32–41. Szövérffy comments: "By the middle of the eighth century, we see most essential aspects of medieval Latin hymnody more or less fully developed," 41; see also 73–109.

8. This paragraph is a brief summary of an extremely complex question. For a more detailed and nuanced presentation, see Allen, *Vox Latina*, 126–128 and Allen, *Accent and Rhythm*, 335ff. Allen says, "in late Latin it was precisely the loss of length distinctions [in vowels] that led to the independence of the stress accent," (81); and this is borne out by the loss of unaccented syllables in the transition from Latin to the Romance languages (152).

long and short syllables are no longer heard.[9] He knew the differences, of course, and students learned the rules of classical meter in the schools, but these no longer reflected a natural and spontaneously felt rhythm in the spoken language.[10] As a result of this linguistic shift, a double track developed in the composition of hymns. One could still compose hymns according to the rules that governed classical quantitative meter. One could, however, also compose them in a new style based on stress accent. Dag Norberg, who has studied the development of medieval poetic, accentual meter at great length, gives an example of this double track in two eulogies composed in honor of the ninth-century emperor Louis the Pious. The first was composed in 814 by Theodulf, Bishop of Orléans, and is in quantitative Sapphic meter. The second was composed four years later by Theodulf or someone familiar with his earlier poem for the emperor's visit to Tours. It is in the same Sapphic meter but wholly based on stress accent.[11] Throughout the Middle Ages, hymn writers continued to write both in quantitative meter and in rhythmical verse.[12]

In the Renaissance, however, with the revival of interest in ancient classical authors, humanists favored quantitative verse and considered the rhythmical meters of the Middle Ages to be ill-conceived and inferior. This infatuation with quantitative meter eventually led, in the early seventeenth century, to the reform of the Roman Breviary by Pope Urban VIII (1568–1644), the last of the humanist popes. Urban gathered a team of Jesuits—Fathers Strada, Gallucci, Sarbiewski, and Petrucci—to work under his direction. They were humanists with high classical sensibilities who forced the medieval hymns back into the quantitative meters of antiquity. Though they were animated by a sincere desire to improve the Roman Liturgy, their humanist ideals were foreign to the linguistic culture out of which early Christian hymns grew.

The Urbanite reform was criticized by many from its inception; contemporary assessment was summarized in the quip: *accessit Latinitas, recessit pietas* (Latinity entered; piety withdrew). Religious orders were not required to update their breviaries, and many never adopted the revised hymns. Finally, after roughly 250 years, the Second Vatican Council, in the Constitution on the Sacred Liturgy, *Sacrosanctum Concilium*, called for a restoration of the hymns in liturgical use to their authentic and original forms.[13]

We will discuss in greater detail questions related to meter in an appendix to this introduction. Here, we are concerned only with the developments in meter that led finally to the reforms of Pope Urban VIII.

9. See the appendix on meter.

10. There is an ongoing debate about how well the patterns of long and short syllables were felt even in the classical era. Virgil seems to have used effectively a "counterpoint" between stress accent and quantitative meter. See Allen, *Accent and Rhythm*, 346–47.

11. Norberg, *Introduction*, 89.

12. See in Norberg, *Introduction*, the whole of ch. 6, "The Beginnings of Rhythmic Versification: Rhythmic Versification and Metrical Poetry," 81–129.

13. *Sacrosanctum Concilium* (SC) states: "In revising the Roman office, its ancient and venerable treasures are to be so adapted that all those to whom they are handed on may more extensively and easily draw profit from them" (90), and "To whatever extent may seem desirable, the hymns are to be restored to their original form, and whatever smacks of mythology or ill accords with Christian piety is to be removed or changed. Also, as occasion may arise, let other selections from the treasury of hymns be incorporated" (93). Note that the first

The hymn texts in this commentary represent both restored and revised texts from the "ancient and venerable treasures" of the Church (SC, 90), as well as more recent compositions. They comprise the 294 hymns of the Latin *editio typica* of the *Liturgia Horarum* (Liturgy of the Hours). Responsibility for the restoration of the Latin hymns was entrusted to the *cœtus* under the direction of Anselmo Lentini, OSB (1901–1989).[14] He was a Benedictine monk from Montecassino, a fine Latinist, and himself a writer of Latin hymns. The hymns have been translated by the International Commission on English in the Liturgy (ICEL), and this text is found in *The Divine Office Hymnal*. In this commentary, each hymn is given in Latin and English followed by notes and commentary. General characteristics of the restored Latin texts and the ICEL translations will be discussed in greater depth below, but there are three points to be made here.

First, translations of the hymns of the Roman Breviary made by Catholic poets, such as Edward Caswall (1814–1878), and translations found in commentaries, such as those of Britt and Connelly, were translations of the Urbanite Latin texts.[15] Anglican poets and musicians, such as John Mason Neale (1818–1866), who translated hymns found in the Sarum use, produced texts that were closer to the original Latin hymn texts, but even they reflect changes brought about by the Urbanite reform. Although all of these translators hold a place of honor in the tradition of English hymnody, for reasons of accuracy and style their hymns are no longer considered to be standard translations of the Latin hymns.

Second, as *Sacrosanctum Concilium* recommended, "other selections from the treasury of hymns" have been incorporated, and they double the size of the hymnal. Ancient hymns never included in the Roman Breviary were added: for example, the Latin originals of beloved English-language Christmas hymns: Ambrose's "Redeemer of the Nations, Come" (*Veni redemptor gentium*) and Prudentius's "Of the Father's Love (Heart) Begotten" (*Corde natus ex parentis*). Hymns that might otherwise have been lost were reassigned or repurposed, for instance, where the Office of Prime was suppressed, the hymn for that Hour was moved to Lauds, on Thursday of Weeks II and IV. *Dies iræ*, no longer part of the Mass for the Dead, was divided into three parts and assigned to the last week of the liturgical year.[16]

Third, although the commentary that follows is restricted to the hymns of the Divine Office, these hymns are representative of a much larger corpus that stems from the poetic genius of the Western Church. Beginning with Ambrose (fourth century) and Prudentius (late fourth and early fifth century) and ending

---

statement above (90) addresses the fact that the sense and poetic coherence of the hymns had been obscured by the Urbanite reform.

14. The *cœtus* (the form is the same in the singular and plural), or teams, were established after the Second Vatican Council to work on various areas of the liturgical reform. Lentini was the head, or *relator*, of *cœtus* VII. He left a detailed account of the principles that guided their work.

15. Matthew Britt, *The Hymns of the Breviary and the Missal* (1936), and Joseph Connelly, *Hymns of the Roman Breviary* (1957). Both Britt and Connelly discuss the Urbanite reform and its consequences in the introductions to their commentaries.

16. For the Latin text, see the *Liturgia Horarum*, 34th Week of Ordinary Time, and vol. 3 of this commentary: H 136–38. For the English, see *The Divine Office Hymnal*, nos. 183, 185, and 187.

with new compositions in the twentieth century, hymn writers from every era have been inspired by the beauty and holiness of the Church at prayer. Poets such as Sedulius (fifth century), Rabanus Maurus (d. 856), Paul the Deacon (d. 799), St. Paulinus of Aquileia (d. 802), St. Thomas Aquinas (d. 1274), Girolamo Casanate (d. 1700), and Pope Leo XIII (d. 1903) have followed one another and built on the foundations provided by earlier poets. Finally, Anselmo Lentini added his own compositions. Thus, in a real sense, the hymns in this collection represent a living repertory in which the reception of earlier generations leads to and marks later compositions.

COMPLEXITIES OF THE TRADITION: AN EXAMPLE

The genre of liturgical hymnody is extremely complex. There is still much work to be done, so much so that the mass of detailed material concerning the manuscript tradition and variant readings collected in the fifty-five volumes of the *Analecta Hymnica* (*AH*), for example, seems at times overwhelming.[17] For this reason, and in order to have a point of reference for later analyses, it may be helpful to look at a particular example before proceeding to a more detailed and theoretical description of the role and characteristics of the hymns, as well the changes they have undergone during centuries of use.

The hymn we will examine here exhibits a rather wide range of the difficulties encountered by those who attempt to restore, revise, and translate. It is representative of many hymns of the Divine Office that have been edited, shortened, retouched, and substantially changed since their original composition. Because they were composed in regular meters, even minor changes often resulted in compensatory revisions elsewhere, in order to maintain the meter. Finally, they were changed and translated in centuries with conventions and tastes other than those of the original hymn writer. It is necessary to sort through all of this, in order to appreciate the original Latin texts of the hymns and to assess later modifications of them. As noted above, Lentini and his *cœtus* brought into the revision many existing hymns of beauty, spiritual depth, high literary quality, and historical interest. For various reasons, however, even Lentini and his *cœtus* introduced new revisions and changes, and in some instances extensive cuts, to the ancient hymns. The English texts produced by ICEL must reflect these changes, but some discussion of the revisions made will be included in the commentaries on individual

---

17. The *Analecta Hymnica Medii Ævi* (Leipzig, 1886–1922), henceforth abbreviated *AH* followed by volume number, is an inestimable resource. It was published over a period of more than 35 years in 55 volumes by Guido Maria Dreves, SJ (1854–1909) and Clemens Blume, SJ (1862–1932) with the help of Henry M. Bannister (1854–1919). Originally planned to include 58 volumes, it has remained incomplete. It contains the most extensive collection of medieval Latin hymns, sequences, and tropes available with manuscript information and critical apparatus. It covers the fifth through the fifteenth centuries. After the Second World War, Joseph Szövérffy attempted to retrieve the unpublished documents but without success. He continued their work in his *Die Annalen der Lateinischen Hymnendichtung*.

hymns. The example given here will show that even modest changes can alter the character and effect of a hymn.

The hymn chosen as an example, *Conditor alme siderum*, is one of the best known and loved hymns for Advent.[18] The original is an anonymous composition, found in at least seven manuscripts from the tenth century; the dating cannot be more precise. Lentini lists it as a ninth-century hymn. This would make sense, given the widespread use of it in the tenth century; we will consider it here as such.[19] After centuries of use, it passed through the Urbanite reform. It was also given a traditional nineteenth-century English rhyming translation by John Mason Neale. The table below shows three versions: the restored version after the Second Vatican Council, which is essentially the original hymn (differing in only three respects), the retroversion into classical meter by Urban VIII, and the English translation of J. M. Neale.[20]

This hymn, like many others from the period, is written in the Ambrosian iambic dimeter, reconfigured according to ninth-century standards. In an appendix to this introduction, we will discuss the essentials of Latin meter and trace the developments by which classical quantitative meter was transformed into medieval accentual meter. We will also describe the various types of meter found in the hymns of the Liturgy of the Hours. Before we begin here the analysis of *Conditor alme siderum*, an explanation of some basic principles may be helpful.

Unlike Greek or French, Latin does not require accent marks as part of the spelling of a word. They are added to liturgical books only as an aid to those who declaim or sing the texts in the context of the liturgy. A stress accent mark (an acute ´) is routinely placed over the syllable that bears a stress accent in a word of three or more syllables. Thus, *Dómine* has a stress on the third to the last syllable. *Redémptor* has it on the second to the last syllable. In the analysis of Latin hymnody, accent marks are used also in order to indicate more clearly the meter. They will be used for this purpose in this general introduction and in the appendices that follow.

Accentuation in Latin follows a pattern known as the "Penult Rule." Syllables are counted back from the end of the word. The final syllable is the *ultima*; the second to the last syllable is the *penult*; the third to the last syllable is the *antepenult*. In Latin of every period, the *penult* receives a stress accent if it is long. If it is short, the stress accent falls back onto the third to the last syllable, the *antepenult*. The final syllable of a Latin word never has a stress accent. It may have a secondary stress accent, however, if a word of three or more syllables has a stress accent on the antepenult and comes before a significant break in a discourse or

---

18. AH 51, no. 47, pp. 46–47; *TDH*, no. 71, p. 73; Walpole, no. 84, p. 299.

19. See Daniel, *Thesaurum*, 4:119. He infers from the fact that the hymn is added in an appendix to a group of fifty-five hymns included in a manuscript that dates from the tenth century that it is more recent than the others. Thus the hymn is certainly no later than the tenth century, but because the hymns in the main body of the manuscript are older, it may also date from the late ninth century.

20. A more detailed commentary on the hymn, with the ICEL translation, may be found in the main commentary, H 1.

at the end of a line of poetry. A secondary stress is indicated by a grave accent (`). For example, we saw above that *Dómine* has a stress accent on the first syllable. In the psalms, one often finds verses such as this: "Miserere mei, Domine, vide humilitatem meam de inimicis meis (Ps 9:14); "Have mercy on me Lord, see my humiliation from my enemies." Because there is a pause after *Domine*, signaled by the comma, when the line from the psalm is recited, it sounds like *Dóminè*. The final syllable is not accented in the same way as the first; nevertheless, the pause that follows gives it a slight weight; the syllable cannot be "swallowed up" by the following syllable.

In Latin, as in other languages, a syllable is long if it contains a long vowel or diphthong, or if it has a short vowel followed by two consonants. There is a practical logic to this: long vowels, diphthongs, and consonant clusters take longer to say. In the analysis of texts, long vowels or diphthongs may be written with a *macron* (straight line) over them (ā), and short vowels may be written with a *breve* (curved line) over them (ĕ). In Latin, syllable length and stress accent are intimately connected.

The meter of the hymn under discussion here is *iambic dimeter*, also known as "Long Meter" in modern hymnals. It consists of a line of eight syllables arranged as a series of four iambs, that is, four pairs made up of a short syllable followed by a long. The ideal iambic line looks like this: ĕā ĕā ĕā ĕā. This rhythmic combination may be made up of words of differing syllables and lengths. Exceptions are allowed at the head of a line. In the world of classical poetry the combinations were based on syllable length. In the world of medieval poetry, the combinations could be based on stress accent alone. When ancient hymns composed in quantitative iambic dimeter were read by later generations of medieval hymn writers who heard only stress accents, the resulting meter could be different from what it was when the hymn was originally composed and sung. This complex issue will be discussed in detail in the appendix on meter. Here, it is sufficient to understand that if one were to read quantitative iambic dimeter paying no attention to syllable length and hearing only the stress accents, various new combinations would arise. For example, in quantitative meter, the four-syllable phrase from a hymn by Prudentius, "Christus venit" reads: long, long, short, long. In accentual verse, it reads stressed, unstressed, stressed, unstressed. Without going into more detail here, we can see that the same phrase sounds different depending on whether it is read with attention to syllable length or with attention to stress alone. As a matter of fact, the phrase read with stress accents sounds like the opposite of iambic dimeter; one could argue that "Chrístus vénit" sounds long-short, long-short. With this general explanation, we may proceed to an analysis of *Conditor alme siderum*.

xxii General Introduction

Three Versions of *Conditor alme siderum*

Paul VI's Restoration[21]	*Urban VIII (1632)*	*John Mason Neale* (nineteenth century)
1. Cónditor alme síderum, ætérna lux credéntium, Christe, redémptor ómnium, exáudi preces súpplicum.	Creátor alme síderum, ætérna lux credéntium Jesu redémptor ómnium, inténde votis súpplicum.	Creator of the stars of night, thy people's everlasting light, Jesu, Redeemer, save us all, and hear Thy servants when they call.
2. Qui cóndolens intéritu mortis períre sǽculum, salvásti mundum lánguidum, donans reis remédium.	Qui dæmonis ne fraúdibus períret orbis, ímpetu amóris actus, lánguidi mundi medéla factus es.	Thou, grieving that the ancient curse should doom to death a universe, hast found the medicine, full of grace, to save and heal a ruined race.
3. Vergénte mundi véspere, uti sponsus de thálamo, egréssus honestíssima Vírginis matris cláusula.	Commúne qui mundi nefas ut expiáres; ad crucem e Vírginis sacrário intácta prodis víctima.	Thou cam'st, the Bridegroom of the bride, as drew the world to evening-tide; proceeding from a virgin shrine, the spotless victim all divine.
4. Cuius forti poténtiæ genu curvántur ómnia; cæléstia, terréstria nutu faténtur súbdita.	Cuius potéstas glóriæ, noménque cum primum sonat et cœlites et ínferi treménte curvántur genu.	At whose dread name, majestic now, all knees must bend, all hearts must bow; and things celestial Thee shall own, and things terrestrial, Lord alone.
5. (missing stanza)	(missing stanza)	(missing stanza)
6(5). Te, Sancte, fide quǽsumus, ventúre iudex sǽculi, consérva nos in témpore hostis a telo pérfidi.	Te deprecámur últimæ magnum diéi Iúdicem, armis supérnæ grátiæ defénde nos ab hóstibus.	O Thou whose coming is with dread to judge and doom the quick and dead, preserve us, while we dwell below, from every insult of the foe.
7(6). Sit, Christe, rex piíssime, tibi Patríque glória cum Spíritu Paráclito, in sempitérna sǽcula. Amen.	Virtus, honor, laus, glória Deo Patri cum Fílio, Sancto simul Paráclito, in sæculórum sǽcula.	To God the Father, God the Son, and God the Spirit, Three in One, laud, honor, might, and glory be from age to age eternally.

All three columns are composed of four-line stanzas. Each line has eight syllables. Columns 1 and 3 generally have a stress accent on every other syllable: the second, fourth, sixth, and eighth, though there is variation within the first four syllables. The middle column has a stress accent on the sixth and eighth syllables; elsewhere the stress accents are free. Each line in the middle column, however, is in a pattern based entirely on long and short syllables.

    21. Each version of the Latin text of *Conditor alme siderum* given here is identified by the pope responsible for the text. Urban VIII was responsible for the seventeenth-century reform. Paul VI (1897–1978) was responsible for the implementation of the reform of the liturgy mandated by the Second Vatican Council. He assigned to the monks of Solesmes the task of editing and printing the Gregorian chant books for the *Novus Ordo Missae* and Divine Office of the Latin rite. Eugène Cardine, OSB, from Solesmes, was named president of a joint council, *cœtus* XXV, for work on Gregorian chant. For more detailed information, see Batiffol, *History of the Roman Breviary*, 221–22, and Combe, *Restoration of Gregorian Chant*, 410–13.

THE TWO LATIN VERSIONS

We will begin the analysis with a comparison of the two Latin versions and then, in light of what we find there, comment on the English version of J. M. Neale. The first thing we notice is that every line in the two Latin texts is different, except for stanza 1, line 2. Many words are the same, but in the second column they are displaced. From one stanza to the next, the differences between the two columns become more pronounced. These differences are due in part to the fact that the texts are metrical, and the meter must be maintained if a hymn is to be sung. If changes are made in one place, the fabric of the poetic text unravels elsewhere because it is difficult to find replacements that fit both the sense and the meter.

As a result of this unraveling, the spontaneity and integrity of the original *Conditor alme siderum* was partially lost in the Urbanite revision. The text was compromised when elements in the medieval text were replaced by others that met the requirements of classical quantitative iambic dimeter. Since questions of meter were of great significance to the Urbanites, they were willing to sacrifice content in order to retrieve the ideal of correct classical form. Their desire to restore the hymn to what they perceived to be a higher linguistic standard, and thereby make it worthy of liturgical use, was the driving force behind their changes.

Stanza 1

Paul VI's Restoration
Cónditor alme síderum,
ætérna lux credéntium,
Christe, redémptor ómnium,
exáudi preces súpplicum.

Literal English Translation
Loving founder of the heavenly bodies,
eternal light for those who believe,
Christ, Redeemer of all,
heed the prayers of (your) suppliants.

Urban VIII's Revision
Creátor alme síderum,
ætérna lux credéntium
Jesu redémptor ómnium,
inténde votis súpplicum.

Literal English Translation
Loving Creator of the heavenly bodies
eternal light for those who believe,
Jesus Redeemer of all,
attend to the vows/prayers of suppliants.

In line 1, *conditor* was changed to *creator*. The Urbanites read *condi* as long-short, where quantitative iambic dimeter required either short-long or long-long. By changing the word to *creator*, they solved the problem, since the quantities of the first two syllables of *creator* are the required short-long. Or did they? The two terms *conditor* and *creator* may be considered synonyms, though they need not and often do not mean the same thing. *Conditor* does not signify a creator in the strict biblical sense. We will see the significance of this below, but first it is worth asking the following question.

Why did the ninth century hymn writer use as the first word in the first stanza of his hymn, composed in iambic dimeters, a three-syllable word with a stress accent on the first syllable? In light of what we know about the transition from quantitative meter to accentual meter, the answer is simple. The rules of meter he derived from a reading of ancient hymns in quantitative meter allowed him to do it. That is, if the hymn writer felt the stress accent to be on the first syllable, he was following the configurations he found as he recited with attention only to stress accent the quantitative meters of the ancient hymns of composers such as Ambrose and Prudentius.[22]

There is also another possibility. He may have heard the short syllable *di* as a stress accent.[23] There are two Latin nouns spelled *conditor*. One comes from the verb *condo, condĕre* (compose, establish, found, etc.) and has the accent on the first syllable. The other comes from the verb *condio, condīre* (to season, make savory dishes) and has the accent on the second syllable. If the length of syllables was no longer felt in the ninth century, can we be sure that the nouns derived from these two verbs were pronounced differently? Perhaps we cannot know the answer, but it is suggestive that the melodies in traditional use for this hymn that date from the Middle Ages tend to emphasize the second syllable.[24]

In Ambrose's hymns, lines of iambic dimeter often begin with two-syllable words (either a short syllable followed by a long syllable, or else two longs). According to the accent rule, the second to the last syllable, that is, the first syllable in a two-syllable word, has the stress accent. Thus, in quantitative meter, a line that begins with a two-syllable word may have a stress accent on the first (short) syllable but still be felt as short-long, that is, a line beginning in iambic dimeter. If the line begins with a three-syllable word, the iambic meter requires that the second of the three syllables, the penult, be long; and according to the accent rule, it will also have a stress accent. The ninth century hymn writer would have seen both possibilities in his models. Thus, if we look at the first word of each of the four lines of stanza 1, we see that the stress accent is placed on the first syllable in *cónditor* (line 1) and *Chríste* (line 3). The stress accent is placed on the second syllable in *ætérna* (line 2) and *exáudi* (line 4). Both schemas were seen to be correct. Consequently, in the ninth century, a hymn in iambic dimeter, which is based on stressed and unstressed syllables and not on an alternation between long and short syllables, may have a stress accent either on the first syllable of the line or on the second, and it is still considered to be "in meter." This shows just how far removed poetic instincts of the ninth century were from the classical norms, so admired by the Urbanites.

---

22. In a thirteenth-century Spanish breviary, we find the following Sapphic line: *Cónditor álme | sidérum qui pálme* (AH 16, no. 299, p. 175). See also note 75 and the appendix for details. It may be that the hymn writer thought of repurposing the opening line of this hymn because he felt an accent on the first syllable, though in other circumstances, Sapphics in accentual versification could have an accent on the second syllable. We cannot be certain.

23. The accentuation of words in the later centuries of the Roman Empire and the early Middle Ages could vary. Verbs and nouns with a recognizable prefix, such as *re-* and *con-* (from the preposition *cum*), had a tendency to shift the accent off of the prefix onto the verb or noun stem, or to other syllables. To cite an example of a verb beginning with *con*: *cóncrepo* became *concrépo*. Norberg, *L'accentuation*, 7, 9, n.30. See also Norberg, *Introduction*, 4–14, and Norberg, *Manuel*, 18–21, 50ff.

24. For examples see Stäblein, *Hymnen*, hymn no. 23, pp. 30, 170, 215; no. 4, p. 70, though no. 19, p. 70, would favor the first syllable.

In line 3, the Urbanites solved the problem of the opening *Christe*, which, as we saw, presents the same "difficulty" as *cónditor*, by replacing it with the smoother *Iesu* (long-long). Finally, in line 4, the phrase *exaudi preces* has proper iambic stress accents (on the second and fourth syllable) but the wrong quantitative metrical sequence. This was a more difficult fix for the Urbanites. Their solution shows the unraveling process that may ensue after even one word is changed in a stanza. Counting long and short syllables, the fourth line in each version reads as follows:

> Original hymn: *exaudi preces supplicum* (long, long, long, short, long, long, short, long)
> Urbanite hymn: *intende votis supplicum* (long, long, short, long, long, long, short, long)

The stress accents on *au* and *pre* are correct, but *exaudi* has three longs and *pre* has a short "e." The Urbanite substitution of *intende votis* has the right quantitative meter. The introduction of two slightly different synonyms, however, subtly alters the intensity and meaning of the text. *Preces* and *vota* (here dative: *votis*) are synonyms. In both classical and Christian Latin, *votum* is a rich, multivalent term. It comes from the verb *voveo*: to make a vow or solemn promise; to consecrate something to a deity; and so (considering the wish inherent in a vow) to wish, to desire. The noun signifies vow, solemn promise, prayer, desire. *Prex, precis*, on the other hand, is less complex but more intense. It is derived from the verb *precor*, which means beg, entreat, pray, supplicate, beseech, even curse or deprecate. The noun signifies petition, request, or entreaty. Thus the idea behind the use of it here is one of direct and intense prayer.

Similarly, *exaudi* and *intende* are synonyms, but the cases they take and their connotations differ: *exaudi* means to hear and answer, to heed; it establishes contact between the one asking and the one asked. *Intende*, on the other hand, means to direct the attention towards, to pay attention, without establishing a clear link between two persons. This lack of direct contact is reflected in the use of the dative case for the things heard (*votis*) rather than the accusative. The difference is subtle, but if the prayer for something is intense, *exaudi* with the accusative *preces* is more expressive than *intende* with the dative *votis*. In a poetic idiom where vocabulary and structure (here it is the cases) are weight bearing as far as the sense goes, the direct, intense quality of entreaty of the original has been subtly transformed into an elegant invitation to God to pay attention to what we say, rather than a petition entreating him to grant what we ask.

In stanza 1, by a happy coincidence, all four line endings were correct both in quantitative and accentual meter. So the Urbanites left them unchanged. In the following stanzas, however, they found most of the line endings unacceptable. As a result, in stanza 1, the two versions are relatively close; but the principle that one alteration leads inevitably to another and another until the text is subtly dismantled accelerates through the following stanzas.

Stanza 2

Paul VI's Restoration
Qui cóndolens intéritu
mortis períre sǽculum,
salvásti mundum lánguidum,
donans reis remédium.

Literal English Translation
Having compassion on the whole temporal order
seeing it perish in the ruin of death,
you saved the languishing world,
granting a remedy to the guilty.

Urban VIII's Revision
Qui dæmonis ne fraúdibus
períret orbis, ímpetu
amóris actus, lánguidi
mundi medéla factus es.

Literal English Translation
Who lest by the deceits of the devil
the world should perish, led by the impulse
of love, you became the healing cure
of a languishing world.

In stanza 2, all lines end in three syllable words with a stress accent on the sixth syllable. By the ninth century, this is standard practice; and it is correct, for the most part, in quantitative meter for the hymns, but some of the syllables are short where they should be long. The offending words are: *intéritu* (2, 1) and *remédium* (2, 4). The Urbanites saved the meter, but they rewrote the stanza.[25]

Notice, first, the motive of compassionate sorrow on the part of Christ (*condolens* at the ruin that has already happened and is continuing to happen *interitu ... perire*) is lost in the Urbanite revision. Instead, demonic deceits (*dæmonis fraudibus*) are introduced, in order to "repair" the sixth syllable of the line, *-ter-* (*interitu*), which is short. Second, the intensely personal *remedium* for the *reis* (only people, ourselves, are guilty) is lost. Third, the fact that out of compassion for a fallen world Christ has already accomplished our salvation (*salvasti* is second person singular, perfect indicative: "you have saved") has been subtly transformed into a teaching moment, to explain the motive for the Incarnation (*ne ... periret*: third person singular, imperfect subjunctive: "lest the world should perish"), where the interested party is the rather abstract *orbis* (the world) and no longer the intensely personal "we," the singers of the hymn, the *reis* (we who are guilty). The words are similar, the ideas are similar; yet the effect of the whole is profoundly different.

Stanza 3

Paul VI's Restoration
Vergénte mundi véspere,
uti sponsus de thálamo,
egréssus honestíssima
Vírginis matris cláusula.

Literal English Translation
As the world declined towards evening
like a bridegroom from his chamber,
you came forth from the most honorable
chamber of the Virgin Mother.

---

25. The only words in stanza 2 that are common to both the original and the Urbanite text are *perire* (2, 2) and *lánguidum* (2, 3); in the Urbanite text both are in a different case than in the original hymn.

Urban VIII's Revision
Commúne qui mundi nefas
ut expiáres; ad crucem
e Vírginis sacrário
intácta prodis víctima.

Literal English Translation
Who that you might expiate
the crime and sin common to all
from the Virgins sacred womb
came forth a perfect victim.

Stanza 3, line 2 ends with a word essential for the meaning of the text, but that has a short sixth syllable: *thálamo*. In line 3, *honestíssima* is also significant for the meaning of the stanza, but the fourth syllable of the line, *hon*, is short. The Urbanites had to find a substitute for a large five-syllable superlative. To complicate matters, lines 2 through 4 of the original hymn make an indirect but clearly understood allusion to Psalm 18 (19):6. The psalm verse in the Vulgate reads: *in sole posuit tabernaculum suum et ipse tamquam sponsus procedens de thalamo suo exultavit ut gigas ad currendam viam suam* (Ps 18:6): "He has placed his tabernacle in the sun: and he, as a bridegroom coming out of his bridal chamber, has rejoiced like a giant to run his way." This psalm verse has been traditionally seen as a prophetic image of the Incarnation. In the Urbanite revision, all of the rich and multivalent images of Christ as the Bridegroom—with subtle allusion to Psalm 18 (19) and the Sun going forth (in contrast to the world sliding down into darkness: *vergente vespere*, 3, 1) from the Bridal chamber, the most honored Virgin's womb, the enclosure (*clausula* alludes to Ez 44:1–2), in which the Word was married to human flesh, and finally the evocative juxtaposition *virginis matris*—all were changed.

Stanza 4

Paul VI's Restoration
Cuius forti poténtiæ
genu curvántur ómnia;
cæléstia, terréstria
nutu faténtur súbdita.

Literal English Translation
Before whose mighty power
all things (beings) are bowed at the *knee*; (*genu*)
both heavenly things (beings) and terrestial
confess that they are subject to your *will*. (*nutu*)

Urban VIII's Revision
Cuius potéstas glóriæ,
noménque cum primum sonat
et cœlites et ínferi
treménte curvántur genu.

Literal English Translation
The power of whose glory
and whose name: as soon as it sounds
both dwellers in heaven and in hell
with trembling are brought to their knee.

Stanza 4, line 3 cannot stand in quantitative meter because the first word, *cælestia*, ends in a short vowel (ă), which is the standard neuter plural ending. In quantitative iambic dimeter, the fourth syllable of a line must be long; that is, the first iamb may be long-long, but the second iamb (on syllables 3 and 4 of the line) must be short-long. This convention is required, in order to preserve a sense of the meter in the ear of the one listening or singing.²⁶ Reconfiguring this line required an overhaul of the entire stanza. Line 4 of the original is removed, along with the graphic syntax created between *genu* at the beginning of line 2 and *nutu* at the beginning of line 4.²⁷ Further, in the original each noun is followed by a verb ending in *-ntur*. Thus, in line 2 we have *genu curvantur* and in the same position in line 4 we have *nutu fatentur*. Finally, the lines both end in neuter plurals ending in "a", creating assonance on the final syllable. Again, although the final syllable here, "a", is short, it is counted long because of the pause at the line end. Thus, lines 2 and 4 are in perfect symmetry in the original. This resemblance strongly suggests a conceptual relationship between the two lines, but the Urbanites removed the parallel.²⁸ They inserted instead the word *nomen* into line two. This is a textual reference to Philippians 2:9–10, to which this stanza alludes. This insertion makes obvious a scriptural allusion that can stand without it; the allusion in the original is more evocative because it is more subtle.

The Missing Stanza 5

Stanza 5 of the original hymn was removed at some point during the Middle Ages, long before the Urbanite reform. This is one of the intriguing and challenging aspects of the study of the hymns in liturgical use. We will consider here the lacuna in *Conditor* as an example of the effect that omissions can have.

In this particular hymn, the omission of stanza five does not create a noticeable gap if one does not know that it is missing. Nevertheless, it does introduce a loss of clarity and depth. The original stanza is as follows:

Original Latin	*Informal Translation*
Occasum sol custodiens,	The sun remembers when to set,
luna pallorem retinens,	the moon retains her pallid light,
candor in astris relucens	light gleams in splendor from the stars:
certos observant limites.	all know and heed established bounds.

This stanza is an elaboration of the statement in the previous stanza 4, in which all the heavenly bodies (*cælestia*) confess and yield to the strong power (*forti potentiæ*) of Christ. Here, the sun keeps its orderly setting, the moon retains its reflected light, bright light shines forth from the stars: they all observe their proper limits (*observant limites*). Thus, all the *cælestia* of stanza 4 obey with perfect submission their loving Conditor who made them (*Conditor alme siderum*). This

---

26. In modern editions, there is a comma after *cælestia*, and in fact, one senses a slight lengthening due to the sense of the line, but this does not make the final "a" of *cælestia* count as a metrically long syllable.

27. "Graphic Syntax" is a term coined by Dr. Frank Mantello, professor emeritus of Greek and Latin at The Catholic University of America, to describe the frequent expansion of ideas and images achieved in Latin poetry of all periods by the juxtaposition of words and the strategic placement of them in the lines of a poetic stanza.

28. For a detailed explanation of the parallel, see the consideration of this stanza in the commentary on H 1. Here it is enough to say that as physical things bend the knee, so spiritual beings bend the will. Based on the likeness of form in the dative and ablative cases, there is a pun on the word "will" (nutu) which can refer both to the will of the one to whom they are subject and also to their own will by which they subject themselves.

stanza both elucidates the full significance of the first line of the hymn, and it establishes a contrast between stanzas 4 and 6 of the original hymn. It is part of the panorama of the hymn: Christ is *Conditor*, he is also compassionate Savior (stanzas 2–3) and dread Lord (stanza 4). Since both the *cælestia* and *terrestria* were introduced in stanza 4, one may remove stanza 5 without wholly losing the coherence of the hymn. Nevertheless, it seems that the intention of the medieval composer was to pause for a moment on the *cælestia*, in order to bring into sharper focus the contrast found in the *terrestria* of stanza 6, where the established order on earth has been compromised by sin, evil, and danger, all of which will lead inexorably to a moment of judgment at the end of time.

There are, of course, practical reasons for the omission of stanzas. The lengthy hymns of Prudentius for example, would be impossible to sing in the context of a single liturgical hour. Even the hymns of Ambrose, which always had eight stanzas, were considered too long. Many other early hymns also had stanzas removed. Historically speaking, there seems to have been a growing sense that in the context of a liturgical structure composed primarily of psalms and readings from Scripture, a shorter hymn was better proportioned to the whole. This appears to have been one of the guiding principles in the transition from what scholars call the "Old Hymnal" (of the fourth to the sixth centuries) to the New Hymnal, which developed over the course of the eighth to the tenth centuries. The older and longer hymns were either shortened or replaced by new compositions, most of which have four to six stanzas, rarely seven.[29]

The Liturgical Stanza 5

Paul VI's Restoration	*Literal English Translation*
Te, Sancte, fide quæsumus,	Holy One with faith we ask you,
venture iudex sæculi,	the judge of the world, you who will come,
conserva nos in tempore	preserve us in our temporal life
hostis a telo perfidi.	from the javelin of our perfidious foe.

Urban VIII's Revision	*Literal English Translation*
Te deprecamur ultimæ	We beg you the great judge,
magnum diei Iudicem,[30]	of the final day,
armis supernæ gratiæ	by the weapons of grace from on high
defende nos ab hostibus.	defend us from our enemies.

---

29. See Walpole, xi–xx, and Milfull, 5–24, with the appendices 1 and 2, 473–78. The Hymnal now known as the Durham Hymnal was produced at the beginning of the eleventh century. It is particularly useful, since it contains hymns that belong to the New Hymnal but predate changes introduced into the liturgy in England after the Norman conquest.

30. Lines 1–2: *ultimæ*, which modifies *diei* (line 2, fem. here), is placed at the end of line 1, so that it can rhyme with *gratiæ*. There is no enjambment (the continuation of a phrase across a line break) in the original hymn. The sense may continue from one line to the next, but the phrasing is self-contained in each line. Thus, the style is not convoluted as it is here in the Urbanite text.

In the original text, the first line contained a transliterated Greek word brought into the Latin vocative (*hagie*). It was deemed a misfit not only by the Urbanites; *Sacrosanctum Concilium* also directed that foreign and "exotic" words were to be excised.[31] Since it means "holy," Lentini had an easy fix in the Latin *Sancte*. *Sancte*, however, has only two syllables where we need three. In order to keep the meter, a restructuring of the line was necessary. Lentini opted for *quæsumus*, a somewhat weaker equivalent of the intense, four syllable, *deprecamur*;[32] but *quæsumus* can stand at the end of a line because it has the correct accentuation (three syllables with the major stress on the first syllable), whereas *deprecamur* has the accent on the second to the last syllable (the penult), which is never allowed in iambic dimeter. The beginning of lines may be irregular, but the endings need to be securely placed in the metrical schema, in order for a sense of the meter to be heard and preserved. These two changes gave Lentini two extra syllables to work with, and so he chose *fide*. The original *te deprecamur hagie* is swift—only three words in the line, with two syllables bearing a primary stress, *ca* and *ha*; the other two accents are clearly secondary. The new line *Te, Sancte, fide quæsumus* moves more slowly under the weight of consecutive words with the same rhythm (*Sancte, fide,* and *quæsu-*).[33] Also, more or less the same vowel sound is heard in *Te, Sancte, fide,* and *quæ-*. This gives a heaviness to the line. Apart from the doxology, the change to the first line of this stanza and the omission of the original stanza 5 are the only changes Lentini and his *cœtus* made to the original hymn; and, as we saw above, in omitting stanza five, they were maintaining a cut that had been made already.

The Urbanites, on the other hand, revised this stanza so extensively that it became a new composition, inspired by the original hymn but substantially different. The first words of line 1 remained the same as the original (*Te deprecamur*), but instead of finding an equivalent to the excised *hagie*, they opted for an enjambment created by *ultimæ … diei*, which caused a moment of confusion in the first line not cleared up until halfway through the second. While such a moment of suspense may be fine in classical poetry, it is not a common characteristic of Christian hymnody. The Urbanites must have known this, but it added a classical flair and facilitated a rhyme with *gratiæ*. As a result of this change, where the original hymn and the Lentini revision kept the stanza clearly focused on direct address in prayer (vocatives in 5, 1–2: *Sancte* and *venture*; imperative in 5, 3: *conserva*), the Urbanite text took out the vocatives of 5, 1–2, and moved the imperative down to 5, 4 (*defende*). Note that *venture*, standing at the head of a line, is intense and a perfect descriptor for the *Iudex* destined to come at the end of time, but a future active participle in the vocative is rare and mainly post-classical.[34] The

---

31. *SC*, 93; also *TDH*, 73, where he says that *hagie* is exotic (*esotico*) and easily replaced by another word with the same meaning, *sancte*.

32. See the discussion of this verb in the context of stanza 1, 4, above.

33. Note that the commas (a modern addition) also slow down the line, but they do not enter into a discussion of meter.

34. A brief look at the *Library of Latin Texts* (*LLT*) shows that this sort of construction is used primarily in medieval texts.

Urbanites seem to have wished to instruct those who sang this stanza that it was with the defensive weapons of grace (*armis supernæ gratiæ / defende*) coming from the great Judge (*magnum iudicem*) that they would be able to fend off their enemies (plural). This idea, however excellent, is not found in the original hymn. In the process of teaching us about the power and source of grace, the Urbanites lost entirely the vivid imagery that drives forward the stanza. The original hymn, on the other hand, aroused in the singer an awareness of his precarious existence in time (*tempore*) and the need for safety (*conserva* is a cry for help). To be hit by one deadly missile (*telo* is ablative singular) belonging to and thrown from one perfidious and hidden foe (*perfidi* and *hostis* are genitive singular), intent on hitting us who sing the hymn (*quæsumus*, like *deprecamur*, is first person plural) is far more intense than a phalanx of enemies where Satan is like a general fighting a pitched battle, with equal preparedness on both sides (*hostibus* is plural and lined up against *armis* (plural) *gratiæ*—not a very moving or effective poetic image, and in any case not the image intended by the original hymn.

To the Urbanites, it was more important to implant an idea about the arms of grace than to arouse a sense of dread at the thought of the menacing javelin of the devil. This change may reflect cultural sensitivities of the post-Reformation seventeenth century, but it spoiled the imagery of a good hymn. One cannot help but think of St. Augustine's delightful and whimsical comment when he asks in the *De doctrina Christiana* why a sermon on the entrance of the newly baptized into the Church for their first Mass pleases the hearer less than an image of the Church as the Bride of the *Song of Songs*, whose beautiful teeth are like lambs coming up from the water two by two? He says in essence: Does the sermon teach anything different from the image? Yet, somehow we view the saints with greater sweetness and delight when we see them as the beautiful teeth of the Bride.[35]

This analysis of the Urbanite reform may seem minute and austere, but it is inspired by a consideration of capital importance. The life-blood of the ancient hymns, and medieval hymns based on the early models, is metaphor and imagery. These are fundamental to the logic and coherence of the hymns. Especially in iambic dimeter, where the syllable count is restrictive, letting the metaphors and images work is not only good poetry, but it expands considerably the meaning of elements in the hymn.[36] Metaphors achieve their effect by a process of decoding

---

35. Why is it, I wonder that if someone should say ... that there exist servants of the true God, good and faithful men who, putting aside the burdens of this life, have come to the holy font of baptism, arise from it born again with the Holy Spirit, and then produce the fruit of a double love, that is love of God and love of their neighbor—why is it that someone who says this gives less pleasure to an audience than by expounding in the same terms this passage from the Song of Songs, where the church is addressed and praised like a beautiful woman: "Your teeth are like a flock of shorn ewes ascending from the pool, all of which give birth to twins, and there is not a sterile animal among them"? Surely one learns the same lesson as when one hears it in plain words without the support of the imagery? And yet somehow it gives me more pleasure to contemplate holy men, when I see them as the teeth of the church tearing men away from their errors and transferring them into its body, breaking down their rawness by biting and chewing. And it is with the greatest of pleasure that I visualize the shorn ewes, their worldly burdens set aside like fleeces, ascending from the pool (baptism) and all giving birth to twins (the two commandments of love), with none of them failing to produce this holy fruit (Augustine, *De doctrina Christiana* II.6, trans. Green).

36. The single word *hagie* is a case in point.

in the mind of the receiver.³⁷ Letting the imagery speak for itself has the effect, therefore, of a prolonged assimilation of the hymn in the mind and heart of the singer, often long after the hymn has been sung. When a hymn becomes too didactic, when the point of the imagery is explained fully, as in the Urbanite insistence on grace mentioned above and in the gratuitous but didactic introduction of the Cross and expiation in stanza 3, and, finally, in the insertion of *nomen* in stanza 4, while other imagery is neglected, the work of the hymn is in some mysterious way thwarted; it may seem finished as soon as it has been sung, whereas if the metaphors and images are allowed to work in the souls of those who sing, they may last long after and "instruct" in a spiritual and deeply personal way.

The Liturgical Stanza 6, the Doxology

Paul VI's Restoration	*Urban VIII's Revision* (1632)
Sit, Christe, rex piissime,	Virtus, honor, laus, gloria
tibi Patrique gloria	Deo Patri cum Filio,
cum Spiritu Paraclito,	Sancto simul Paraclito,
in sempiterna sæcula. Amen.	in sæculorum sæcula.

The last question to consider in connection with *Conditor alme siderum* is the doxology. The original hymn had the same doxology as in the Urbanite text given above and translated by John Mason Neale. This doxology was standard and movable in the ninth century when the hymn was composed. The practice of adding a doxology to a hymn is similar to that of appending the doxology to the psalms when they are recited during the liturgy. The original doxology for this hymn is found with variations in the Anglo-Saxon Hymnal (ca. 1000 AD)³⁸ and at the end of multiple hymns in the AH. Lentini and his *cœtus* addressed the question of doxologies and decided to create a closer bond between the person addressed in the hymn and the one(s) addressed in the doxology.³⁹ Accordingly, they chose a different doxology for this hymn because it begins by addressing

---

37. The decoding of a metaphor happens when a tension is established between an expected word and a metaphorical replacement. To use an example from Aristotle (*Poetics*, 1457b), Achilles is a man. When a poet says, "Achilles is a lion," there is an element—perhaps minimal—of dislocation or surprise. In a first step, we think, "Achilles is not really a lion." Then, as we *decode* the metaphor, by working out the proportion in our own minds, we *participate* in the imagery in some way. We conclude, "Achilles is a lion because he is raging and dangerous." The poet has said more through this image than he might have in a treatise on anger, because he has subtly appealed to our own experience of anger and the dangers involved. The ancient theorists classified a metaphor as apt or fitting, as opposed to ornamental, when *transfertur ergo nomen aut verbum ex eo loco, in quo proprium est, in eum, in quo aut proprium deest aut translatum proprio melius est; id facimus, aut quia necesse est aut quia significantius est aut, ut dixi, quia decentius*: "a noun or a verb is transferred from that domain in which it is proper, to that in which a proper meaning is lacking or in which the transferred term is better than the proper term. We do this either because it is necessary or because it is more meaningful" (Quintilian, *Institutio Oratoria*, 8.6.5, quoted by Lausberg, *Handbook of Literary Rhetoric*, no. 561). The use of metaphor to express in a veiled or better way, or in the only way possible, realities that are beyond the ordinary world of sense experience is the basis for much theological use of metaphor. It is also the indispensable basis for the liturgical use of metaphor in the hymns.

38. See Milfull, 398, 457 and AH 51 throughout.

39. *HIBR*, no. 64, xv; *TDH*, xxii. For a general account of the elements appropriate to a doxology see *HIBR*, nos. 65–71, xv–xvii.

Christ directly.⁴⁰ Though the provision is sound, it has resulted in an occasional awkward reworking of older texts.

This analysis of the Latin texts of *Conditor alme siderum* shows that the revision of hymn texts marked by the poetic vision of the original composer is a delicate task. Though motivated by a desire to improve the texts and make them more worthy of divine worship, the Urbanites significantly altered and weakened the content and coherence of the original texts. Their efforts stand as a cautionary tale for those who come after them who must balance considerations of culture, history, theology, and pastoral need in any endeavor to modernize or translate liturgical texts.

The work of Lentini and *cœtus* VII was largely successful. It has received high praise from Josef Szövérffy, one of the finest hymnologues of the twentieth century. He says that Lentini's is a work of extraordinary value and that it may prove to be a milestone in the history of liturgical reform.⁴¹ Nevertheless, Szövérffy rightly points out the difficulties and shortcomings apparent in some aspects of Lentini's selection and editing of hymns. Working under the directives of *Sacrosanctum Concilium*, motivated by the theological and pastoral program of the Second Vatican Council, and guided by his own cultural and literary tastes, Lentini introduced alterations into existing hymns and also introduced a large number of his own compositions. He is transparent in his editorial notes, noting changes carefully and often giving a short reason for the change. In addition to the periodic reports he made to the *Consilium* for the implementation of *Sacrosanctum Concilium*, he also left notes for each hymn in his two published collections, as well as complementary introductions in *Hymni Instaurandi Breviarii Romani* (*HIBR*), issued in 1968, and in *Te Decet Hymnus* (*TDH*), issued in 1984. The *HIBR* contains the preliminary edition of the revised hymnal that was subject to further review. The *TDH* is the final edition, containing changes suggested by the reviewers. The introductions to the two editions contain important indications of the principles that guided the revisions. English translations will be provided in an appendix to volume five of the commentary.

THE ENGLISH TEXT OF JOHN MASON NEALE

In light of the comments made on the two Latin versions of this hymn, it is clear that the English text of John Mason Neale, beautiful as it is as an English hymn, translates neither the Urbanite nor the original text. It drifts between the two, taking some elements from the one and others from the other. To give a few examples: in stanza 1, we have "Jesus" instead of "Christ"; the noun *supplicum*, found in both Latin texts, is translated as "servants," a word foreign to the thrust of the hymn at large, but it facilitates the rhyme between "all" and "call." Also, as a translation of *redemptor omnium* (line 2), Neale could have written "Jesus,

---

40. *HIBR* has, in an appendix, a list of standard doxologies that may be added to hymns according to divine Person addressed and meter. Interestingly, the original doxology to *Conditor* is not included on the list.

41. Joseph Szövérffy, "Hymnological Notes, 457–72, especially 467–72.

Redeemer of us all" instead of "Jesus, Redeemer, save us all"; but "of" is an ugly word on the important sixth syllable of an eight syllable line; "save" is a "weight bearing" solution. The ICEL translators have struggled with just such difficulties. Neale's stanza 2 is clearly a translation of the Urbanite text; *interitus* is not well translated by "curse," but it does rhyme well with "universe." Then, "full of grace" comes into Neale, though it is not found in stanza 2 of either Latin text, though *gratiæ* is in the Urbanite text. In stanza 5 (original 6), "dread" describes the state the original hymn aroused through images, but it rhymes with "dead," which is not in either Latin text; nor does "insult" translate *telo*. These are a few examples among others of the subtle compromise of the Latin text caused by the need to fit the text into an English rhyme scheme. The end result is a lovely English hymn recognizably inspired by the Latin text. It is not, however, by any stretch of the imagination a faithful rendering of the original text. Thus, for different reasons, Neale's version suffers from some of the same deficiencies as the Urbanite text.

This detailed analysis of *Conditor alme siderum* has been undertaken in order to provide a context for the following commentary and to simplify the process of commenting on individual hymns. It is our hope that the hymns, translated by ICEL and commented upon here, will launch a recovery of one of the magnificent treasures of the Church. Others will no doubt improve on these efforts, but through the commentary that follows, we hope to offer new insights into the long tradition of Christian hymnody. It is a world of beauty and grace that is central to the life of the Church; it is the timeless patrimony, the prayer "of all the saints, of those who draw near to God" (Ps 148:14).

THE ROLE OF THE HYMN IN THE DIVINE OFFICE

In order better to understand the nature of the hymns, we will consider briefly the role and purpose assigned to them in the liturgy. Then, we will look at some of their essential characteristics. The *General Instruction of the Liturgy of the Hours* (*GILH*) gives the foundation upon which the use of hymns is based. It opens with a statement of two fundamental principles that lie behind the prayer of the Church at large and the Divine Office in particular.

First, the primary duty of creatures is to adore, praise, thank, and supplicate the Creator. The *GILH* states:

> Since men and women depend totally on God, they must recognize and express this dominion of their Creator, as holy people of every age have in fact done by means of prayer. Indeed, prayer, which is directed to God, must be linked with Christ, the Lord of all people, the one Mediator[42] through whom alone we have access to God.[43] For he so unites to himself the whole human community,[44] that an intimate bond

---

42. 1 Tm 2:5; Heb 8:6; 9:15; 12:24.
43. Rom 5:2; Eph 2:18; 3:12.
44. *SC*, 83.

develops between the prayer of Christ and the prayer of the whole human race. For in Christ and in him alone human religion achieves its redemptive value and its end. (*GILH*, 6)

We are "totally dependent on God": contingent beings living in the presence of Necessary Being. God once said to St. Catherine of Siena, "'Do you know, Daughter, who you are and who I am? You are she who is not, whereas I am He who is.'"[45] Through a continuous sequence of hours and seasons of prayer, the Church acknowledges God's sovereignty and recognizes her entire dependence upon him. She knows that her prayer is intimately bound to the prayer of Christ and that all Christians may approach the throne of God's grace and mercy through the one Mediator, Christ (Heb 4:16). This attitude of dependence and hope is the foundation of the prayer of the Church. It leads to a liturgy marked by praise, thanksgiving, and supplication. These three actions permeate the Divine Office and effect the salvation of those who pray. A "dialogue" is established between God and the soul; the soul listens to the words of Scripture and responds with hymns, prayers, and petitions. This "divine commerce" hour after hour, season after season, gradually builds up in the soul the effects of salvation.

These are the terms used by the *GILH* to describe the Divine Office: it is a *divinum commercium seu dialogus* (a "divine commerce or a dialogue, an exchange"):

> In this way, moreover, the sanctification of man is accomplished (SC, 10), and the worship of God is achieved in the Liturgy of the Hours, since, in it, it is as if an exchange is established, namely that dialogue between God and man by which "God speaks to his people ... and the people reply to God both by song and prayer." (SC, 33)[46] Those participating in the Liturgy of the Hours have in fact access to sanctification of the very richest kind through the life-giving word of God, to which it gives such great importance. For it is from Sacred Scripture that the readings are drawn, God's words in the Psalms are sung in his presence, and the intercessions, prayers, and hymns are infused with its inspiration and force. Thus, not only when things are read which "have been written for our instruction" (Rom 15:4), but also when the Church prays or sings, the faith of those taking part is nourished, and their minds are stirred up toward God, so that they may offer him their spiritual and rational worship (*rationabile obsequium*; Rom 12:1) and more abundantly receive his grace. (*GILH*, 14)

This paragraph makes an observation of particular significance for the hymns. There are moments in the Divine Office that appeal to the mind. These are the readings "that are for our instruction," and generally whatever informs and strengthens our faith. This instruction, however, takes root in the soul when it leads to prayer: "when the Church prays or sings." It is this "prayer or song" that establishes the divine commerce between God and the soul. God dwells in the innermost recesses of our souls, and one of the primary purposes of the liturgy

---

45. Raymond of Capua, *The Life of Catherine of Siena*, 62.
46. The Latin text of the first sentence of *GILH*, no. 14 reads: *Ita autem sanctificatio hominis efficitur et Dei cultus exercetur in Liturgia Horarum, ut in ea quasi commercium instituatur seu dialogus ille inter Deum et homines, quo "Deus ad populum suum loquitur, ... populus vero Deo respondet tum cantibus tum oratione"* (SC, 33, cited by *GILH*, in no. 14)

is to put us in contact with our own interior depth, so that we may recognize the presence of God there and enter into communication with him. All that is affective in the liturgy, all that appeals to our senses, to our personal experiences, to our conscience before God, our sense of beauty and the grandeur and mercy of God: all of this must be part of the liturgy, in order for it to be life-giving. Hymns that are based on Scripture and theologically rich are an essential element of this life-giving commerce, since they appeal to the whole person at prayer. They are privileged vehicles of the *rationabile obsequium* (Rom 12:1) offered to God in the liturgy.

The second fundamental principle is that the Eucharistic sacrifice is the heart of the life of the Church, the "center and culmination of the whole life of the Christian community"[47] and that the hours of prayer in the Divine Office are a necessary complement to this central act of worship.

> The Liturgy of the Hours extends[48] to the different hours of the day the praise and thanksgiving, the commemoration of the mysteries of salvation, the petitions and the foretaste of heavenly glory, that are present in the Eucharistic mystery.... The Liturgy of the Hours is also an excellent preparation for the celebration of the Eucharist itself, for it stirs up and nourishes in a fitting way the dispositions necessary for the fruitful celebration of the Eucharist, such as faith, hope, love, devotion, and a spirit of self-denial. (*GILH*, 12)

Thus, the recitation of the hours diffuses the divine light of the Eucharist throughout the hours of the day. It also prepares the hearts of those who pray to participate more deeply and more fruitfully in the Eucharist. To take from Genesis a rather whimsical image, the Eucharist is the greater light to rule the day; the hours of the Divine Office are the lesser lights to rule the night, that is, the hours before and after the Eucharist. Both together reflect and diffuse divine light throughout the day and night. Day after day, they form the natural rhythm of the life of the Church. Again, the *GILH* explains:

> Since Christ taught that we "ought always to pray and not lose heart" (Lk 18:1), the Church, faithfully obeying this admonition, never ceases to offer prayer and exhorts us in these words: "Through him (Jesus) then let us continually offer up a sacrifice of praise to God" (Heb 13:15). The Church satisfies this requirement not only by celebrating the Eucharist but in other ways also, especially through the Liturgy of the Hours, which is distinguished among other liturgical actions by ancient Christian tradition, in that through it the entire course of the day and night is consecrated.[49] (*GILH*, 10)

The Divine Office consecrates the hours of day and night and the seasons of the liturgical year by continual repetition and, more significantly, by its

---

47. *In perficiendo opere sanctificationis, curent parochi ut celebratio Eucharistici Sacrificii centrum sit et culmen totius vitæ communitatis christianæ*: "In discharging their duty of sanctifying their people, pastors should see to it that the celebration of the Eucharistic Sacrifice is the center and culmination of the whole life of the Christian community" (*Christus Dominus*, 30.2).
48. *Presbyterorum ordinis*, 5.
49. *SC*, 83–84.

adaptation to the different hours, needs, and events that take place in time. Compline, or Night Prayer, for example, is ordered to a preparation for silence, sleep, and the peace that comes from handing over all the affairs of the day at its end to God. Hymns for Lauds evoke images of dawn and sunrise; they speak of the transformation of the world at the coming of light and of dawn as the privileged hour for the encounter with God; they ask for the graces needed to live the day under the light of the true Sun, Christ. Hymns for Vespers speak of the day that is past, the coming of darkness, the light of faith that persists through the night. Hymns for the Little Hours often evoke events in the history of salvation that happened at that hour (e.g., the descent of the Holy Spirit at the third hour and the death of Christ on the Cross at the ninth) or themes appropriate to that time of day. Similarly, the Mass and the hours are configured to the seasons of the liturgical year and to particular feasts. One has only to think of all the *alleluias* that are sung throughout Easter Time. In this way, the liturgy, including the Mass and the hours, sanctifies the entire economy of our temporal existence, "the totality of human activity" (*GILH*, 11). The liturgy sanctifies time.[50]

These fundamental principles, the communication of the soul with God through the prayer of the Church and the sanctification of the whole of human life through the rhythm of the Mass and the Divine Office, are expressed by Cardinal Robert Sarah, former Prefect of the Dicastery for Divine Worship and the Discipline of the Sacraments. In *The Day Is Now Far Spent*, he speaks of reform in the Church as brought about primarily through the close connection between a living faith and the experience of God, the *divine commerce*. He says that the daily liturgy plays a pivotal role in the formation of this connection:

> What we need more than words is to re-experience God. This is perhaps the heart of all reform. Benedict XVI said in his address to the clergy of Rome on February 22, 2007, "Only if there is a certain experience can one also understand." We must therefore ask ourselves the question: How can we have the experience of God? We must therefore re-experience the Church as the place where God gives himself.... There *is* a place where we can have this experience of God and of the Church: the Liturgy. There, it is not possible to hide from God.... The existence of the Church draws its life from the correct celebration of the Liturgy.[51]

"Only if there is a certain experience can one also understand": Cardinal Sarah indicates that without an interior sense of the truths of the faith as true and good for each one of us, we cannot penetrate them and see them as real. Where do we find this interior experience? Ideally, in the liturgy.

The primary action of the liturgy to which Cardinal Sarah refers in this passage is the celebration of the Eucharist, but he goes on to ask where else one may

---

50. Since the purpose of the Liturgy of the Hours includes the sanctification of the day and of the whole range of human activity, the sequence of the hours has been revised in such a way that, as far as possible, each Hour might once again be celebrated at the proper time of day. Hence, "that the day may be truly sanctified, and that the hours themselves may be recited with spiritual advantage, it is best that each of them be prayed at a time which most closely corresponds with its true canonical hour" (SC, 94).

51. Robert Cardinal Sarah, *The Day Is Now Far Spent*, 111.

encounter God. His answer, which may seem surprising, is, in the monasteries. "God dwells there: he fills the hearts of the monks and nuns with his silent presence, and all of life there is liturgical. It is nourished by faith and the Divine Office and on fire with love and the burning bush of the Divine Presence."[52] Why is it that "all of life there is liturgical"? Because the Divine Office is celebrated day after day, season after season, without interruption.

After the general principles laid out in the opening paragraphs, the *GILH* goes on to explain the particular role and purpose of the hymn in the individual hours of the liturgy. It mandates that every hour of the liturgical day begin with a hymn.[53] The character of the hymn is determined by the hour it introduces, and so it sets the tone for the liturgy that follows. Hymns suited for liturgical use introduce themes and images appropriate to and illustrative of the particular hour, season, or feast.

> The hymn is composed in such a way as to give a certain color to the Hour or the feast, and, especially in celebrations with the people, to form a simple and pleasant beginning for the prayer.... Different hymns and prayers are given for each of the Hours so that they may, in keeping with received tradition, correspond to the actual time of day and thus sanctify the Hours in a more appropriate way (*horarum sanctificatio procuretur*) ... they generally have an immediate effect in creating the individual characteristic of the Hour or individual feast, more so than other parts of the Office, and are able to move and encourage the mind and heart to a devout celebration. Their literary beauty frequently enhances their effectiveness. Furthermore, in the Office the hymns are the chief poetic element created by the Church. (*GILH*, 42, 80, 173)

The last line of *GILH*, 173, is significant. It refers to a long tradition of reflection in the Church on the divine commerce; in the recitation of the Divine Office, the Church prays with Christ, in Christ, and to Christ,[54] and if "the hymns are the chief poetic element created by the Church," in an exchange in which the Church both listens and speaks, the hymn is her chief poetic response. Where the order of the Office of Readings is outlined, the *GILH* says this:

> Prayer should indeed accompany "the reading of Sacred Scripture so that there may be a conversation between God and man, for 'we speak to God when we pray, we hear God when we read the divine words.'"[55] For this reason the Office of Readings consists also of psalms, a hymn, a prayer and other formulas, so that it has the character of true prayer. (*GILH*, 56)

GILH 56 reminds us that the Office of Readings is not a time for study; the hymn at the beginning of the Hour and the prayer at the end show its character. The passage also references two other texts: the Council document *Dei Verbum*,

---

52. Sarah, *The Day is Now Far Spent*, 112–13.
53. The Liturgy of the Hours is ordered according to its own laws, while combining in a special way those elements that are found in other Christian celebrations. It is so arranged that, after a hymn, there is always psalmody, then a longer or shorter reading of Sacred Scripture, and finally intercessions (*GILH*, 33). Cf. *HIBR*, 4, and *TDH*, xiii.
54. *GILH*, 2, 6, and 148.
55. St. Ambrose, *De officiis ministrorum*, I; 20, 88: PL 16, 50; *Dei verbum*, 25.

25, and St. Ambrose's *De Officiis*, 1.20.88. In *Dei Verbum*, we read, "And let them [priest, religious, all the faithful] remember that prayer should accompany the reading of Sacred Scripture, so that God and man may talk together; for 'we speak to Him when we pray; we hear Him when we read the divine saying.'" And in the *De Officiis*, St. Ambrose says: "Why not employ those periods, when you are free from church responsibilities, in reading? Why not go to see Christ again, speak to Christ, listen to Christ? We speak to him when we pray, we listen to him when we read the divine oracles."

In Lentini's *HIBR*, published in 1968 before the promulgation of the revised liturgy, the hymns for Lauds and Vespers were still sung after the psalmody. He says:

> Hymns, which are human compositions, are also joined to the divinely inspired psalms and canticles, not that they are placed on an equal footing with them; but they rise as a humble and grateful response that rebounds to heaven in song for the words that have been sent forth from heaven for mortals to sing.[56]

Even after the place of the hymn has been changed, it is still the humble and grateful prayer of the Church raised to heaven, not divinely inspired in the same way as the Scriptures, but nevertheless filled with the unction of the Bride of Christ. By placing a hymn at the head of each hour of the Divine Office, the Church takes her children by the hand, so to speak, and guides them into the richness and beauty of the hour that follows, to provide a context appropriate to the time, season, or feast celebrated during that hour.

The function of the hymns, therefore, is twofold. It introduces the hour in such a way that the recitation of the rest of the Office falls under its light and inspiration; and as the voice of the Church, it helps us to make our own the particular mark of holiness proper to the hour.[57] The fact that the hymns are often literary compositions marked by lyricism and beauty makes them all the more effective in this role.[58] One might say that, joined to psalms and prayers, they are like our tutors in the art of prayer. They say well what we would wish to say to God in praise and prayer. They are also made to be sung with others (*GILH*, 173), and when together we praise and ask God for his gifts, we are the Church at prayer.

In the *Summa theologiæ*, St. Thomas says that the normal effect of the reception

---

56. *Conditi ab hominibus, hymni etiam in Opere Dei psalmis misti sunt canticisque divinitus inspiratis, non quidem ut illis pares efficerentur, sed ut verbis quæ de cælis missa erant mortalibus decantanda, humilis quædam ipsi evaderent et grata responsio, quæ de terra ad cælos cantibus resiliret* (*HIBR*, 4).

57. See *HIBR*, 6. *Neque illud prætereundum est eorum* [*hymnorum*] *officium, quo uniuscuiusque Horæ canonicæ vel mysterii individuam specialemque notam statim et expresse exhibent, iustamque singulis celebrationibus condicionem mentium cordiumque suppeditant.*

58. The entire no. 173 of the *GILH*, parts of which have been cited in separate places, is as follows: "Hymns have a place in the Office from very early times, a position they still retain. Indeed, as their name implies, they are not only destined for God's praise because of their lyrical nature, but they also provide participation for the people. Indeed, they generally have an immediate effect in creating the individual characteristic of the Hour or individual feast, more so than other parts of the Office, and are able to move and encourage the mind and heart to a devout celebration. Their literary beauty frequently enhances their effectiveness. Furthermore, in the Office the hymns are the chief poetic element created by the Church."

of the Eucharist is spiritual joy and delight, analogous to the delight we experience with physical nourishment: "Every effect that material food and drink have with respect to the life of the body—that is, that they sustain, augment, repair, and delight—this same and entire effect the Sacrament has with respect to the life of the soul."[59] The delight that comes naturally from the Eucharist is a joy deeper and more permanent than the ebb and flow of feeling on the surface of one's life. It comes from the awareness of the presence of Christ in the depths of the soul. The recitation of the Liturgy of the Hours, as a sacrifice of praise, is an echo of the celebration of the Eucharist. Often there is a commonality of scriptural texts, which means that what is heard in the Mass finds an echo throughout the rest of the day. The natural effect of the recitation of the Hours is often a quiet and sustaining joy and delight lesser than but similar to the delight that comes from the reception of the Eucharist. The hymns of the liturgy bring us this delight.

GENERAL CHARACTERISTICS OF THE LATIN LITURGICAL HYMNS

The description of the general qualities of the hymns of the revised Liturgy of the Hours is presented under five headings.

1. A Preliminary Note
2. Praise and Petition
3. Metaphorical Language and Imagery
4. The *Romanitas* of the Hymns: Sobriety of Style and Rich Theological Content
5. Scriptural Allusions

1. A PRELIMINARY NOTE

Some of the Latin hymns in this collection are literary poems of the highest quality, and as such they have a life of their own, independent of liturgical use. Such are the hymns of Ambrose, Prudentius, Venantius Fortunatus, and others. When they appear in the *Liturgia Horarum*, their original purpose is subsumed under their intended use in the liturgy. The hymns of Prudentius, for example, which easily run to a hundred lines or more, have been cut down to a mere twenty-four to twenty-eight lines, the approximate length for a hymn sung at the beginning of a liturgical office.[60] Excerpts from one of Prudentius's hymns, *Cathemerinon* 2, serve as hymns for Lauds on both Wednesday and Thursday

---

59. *omnem effectum quem cibus et potus materialis facit quantum ad vitam corporalem, quod scilicet sustentat, auget, reparat et delectat, hoc totum facit hoc sacramentum quantum ad vitam spiritualem* (*ST* III, q. 79, a. 1, c).

60. "The liturgical hymns which it has been our responsibility to work with, are not to be treated as literary texts … but as texts to be inserted in the breviary, that they may become the choicest instruments of prayer, song, and elevation of the mind and heart in the Lord…." (See *HIBR*, 28–29).

of Weeks I and III of the Psalter. Inevitably, changes such as this affect, to some degree at least, the full signification and logical order of the original hymn. Some of these abridgements, as in the case of Prudentius, are centuries old; others have resulted from the revision after the Second Vatican Council. These hymns, entire or abridged, are part of the living treasure from which the Church continually draws forth the new and the old (Mt 13:52), in order to enrich the liturgy. This commentary will treat of the texts as they are received into the liturgical books, while taking into consideration their original form and context.

2. PRAISE AND PETITION

The hymns as they appear in the Divine Office are generally divided into three parts. The first consists of the praise of God for his glory, for his beauty and mercy, for his providential ordering of hours, days, and seasons, for the gift of salvation, or for the holiness of martyrs and other saints. The second part applies the elements of praise to those who sing and pray the hymn. Thus, the glory of God and the desire of the soul are aligned.[61] In some hymns the division is clearly drawn; in others it is more diffuse. The petition, however, grows out of the contemplation of the attributes presented in the first part of the hymn.[62] Thus, in *Conditor alme siderum*, stanzas 1–4 present the condition of the universe, governed and saved by Christ. In stanza 5, we ask Christ to preserve in us, as we live our present life, the good he has given by the governing and saving of the world: *conserva nos in tempore*. Finally, in the third part, the hymn ends with a recapitulation of the praise with which it began. This is the role of the doxologies and one reason why the decision was made during the revision process to integrate the doxologies more closely into the particular context of individual hymns (*GILH*, 174).

Striking examples of the relation between praise and petition may be seen in the creation hymns attributed to Gregory the Great.[63] On the first day, God created light and brought the world out of chaos; as evening falls—the hymn is sung at Vespers—we pray that we may not fall back into the formless dark through sin and end by suffering the effect of chaos, which is to be heedless of eternal good (H 72).[64] Again, on the fifth day, God said: "Let the waters produce creeping things having life and flying things upon the earth and under the firmament of

---

61. *Come canta un bell'inno, sulla terra è* supplex gloria (*TDH*, xiii): "As a beautiful hymn sings, on the earth there is glory that supplicates." (*supplex gloria* is a phrase taken from the hymn H 100; *TDH*, no. 41).
62. *Infine la 'petitio': non strettamente necessaria, poiché la lode, specialmente se rivolta a Dio, basta a sé stessa. Ma l'inno è quasi sempre, come dicevamo a principio, una 'gloria supplex': una celebrazione di Dio e dei santi, ai quali l'anima cristiana volentieri indirizza anche l'invocazione di aiuto per camminare verso il Regno* (*TDH*, xxiii): "Ultimately, the petition is not strictly necessary, since the praise, especially if it is directed to God, is sufficient in itself. But the hymn is almost always, as we said from the beginning, a *gloria supplex*: a celebration of God and of the saints to which the Christian soul also willingly directs a prayer for assistance on her journey towards the Kingdom."
63. *Divine Office Hymnal*, nos. 197, 205, 213, 221, 229, 237. In the volumes of this commentary, they are: H 72, 76, 80, 84, 88, 92 (all in vol. 2).
64. *Ne mens graváta crímine / vitæ sit exsul múnere, / dum nil perénne cógitat / seséque culpis ílligat.* (H 72, stanza 3).

the sky."⁶⁵ The hymn writer picks up the idea that the waters brought forth both fish and fowl. Accordingly, he asks that we who are born in the waters of baptism neither fly up to heaven in pride, nor sink down into the depths of despair (H 88).

3. METAPHORICAL LANGUAGE & IMAGERY

In the examples given above, metaphor drives the logic of the hymns. As chaos is to the pristine light, so is dull and heedless sin to the light of salvation. Similarly, as water is a source of burgeoning life, so is baptism the source of spiritual life and equilibrium (picking up the spatial imagery of sinking into water and rising up into the sky). As we said earlier, metaphor is the poetic idiom par excellence of these hymns. Some metaphors come from the genius of the particular composer of the hymn. Others are standard scriptural and Christian images that reflect a shared view of the world, of nature, of salvation, and of the origin and destiny of the human race, all of which were more or less taken for granted during the centuries when these hymns were first written and sung. The image in *Conditor alme siderum* of the devil as a fierce and wily enemy roaming about and throwing darts is typical. It is based in part on the often repeated verse from the First Letter of Peter: "Be sober and watchful because your adversary the devil like a roaring lion prowls around seeking someone to devour."⁶⁶ In the analysis and liturgical use of these hymns, the reader and the singer are well served if they let their imaginations enter into this metaphorical and poetic language.

A magnificent example of the exploitation of a scriptural image comes from Ambrose's *Æterne rerum conditor* (H 71). The primary image in this beautiful hymn is the cockerel. He performed a number of lowly but essential duties in the Roman world of Ambrose; the last watch of the night was named for him, and during this hour, still pitch black, his crowing was thought of as a herald of the dawn (the first light). By means of a layering effect, this hymn builds up, as do many others patterned after it, a composite picture of progressively deeper meaning. Beginning with an image derived from common experience, the implications of the image in conjunction with the liturgical function of the hymn unfold. This "unfolding" may be thought of in terms of the literal, moral, and mystical senses, so common during the patristic and medieval periods, though a hymn need not progress strictly from one sense to the next. They are rather built up together in a rich and beautiful multivalent whole.⁶⁷

---

65. *Dixit etiam Deus: Producant aquæ reptile animæ viventis et volatile super terram sub firmamento cæli.* (Gn 1:20).

66. *Sobrii estote et vigilate quia adversarius vester diabolus tamquam leo rugiens circuit quærens quem devoret* (1 Pt 5:8).

67. For a detailed description of the layering of images in *Æterne rerum conditor*, see the commentary on H 71.

4. THE *ROMANITAS* OF THE HYMNS: SOBRIETY OF STYLE AND RICH THEOLOGICAL CONTENT

Sobriety, simplicity, and elegance of style combined with theological and spiritual depth are the hallmark of the early Christian Latin hymns. They say all that is needed with feeling but without excess. This character of restraint defines the Roman Rite as a whole. It is often called the *Romanitas* of the entire tradition of prayer and hymnody. It is seen, for example, in the ancient collects for the temporal cycle and Sundays in Ordinary Time. It is also present in the prefaces and Eucharistic Prayer I (Roman Canon) of the Mass.

The result of this *Romanitas* in the Latin hymns is a density of theological expression that is, on the whole, more intense than what is generally found in English hymnody. Ambrose's well-known *Veni, redemptor gentium* (H 5) or the great Ascension hymn *Jesu, nostra redemptio* (H 41) are prime examples. The English translations of these hymns attempt to communicate to the fullest extent the meaning of the Latin text and its rich theological content. Furthermore, since many of the Latin hymns were composed for canonical hours and seasons, these translations reconnect the hymns with the particular hours and feasts for which they were originally composed. The ICEL translations have sought to bring to the English recitation of the hours the native *Romanitas* of the Roman Rite.

Ambrose of Milan's signature phrase *sobria ebrietas* captures the ethos of the hymns of the Roman Rite: *sobria* (sober) *ebrietas* (intoxication).[68] It is an oxymoron that signifies in one short phrase the raising of the mind and heart to God through the hymn, the appropriation of the truths of the faith as one's own truth, and the interior joy that is the natural fruit of this appropriation of the truth. The hymns have a sobriety that precludes sentimentality; yet they are a source of an interior joy.

Economy of expression is also a mark of *Romanitas*. In the hymns, as in earlier Latin poetry, a minimum of words is combined with the use of images and multivalent terms as well as the suggestive juxtaposition of words and phrases; this is the "graphic syntax" mentioned earlier in connection with stanza 4 of *Conditor alme siderum*. The result is a connection of images and ideas that goes beyond the literal signification of the text. This enlarged syntax created by the rhetorical, poetic, even visual association of images, elements of structure, and words gives the hymns greater richness and depth without the multiplication of words.

When Ambrose instituted the singing of hymns at Milan, he drew criticism from the Arian bishop Auxentius. In his response to Auxentius, Ambrose describes the effect of his hymns on his congregation. His comments make use of a pun on the Latin *carmen*, which means both song or hymn and charm, incantation, enchantment. He says:

---

68. This phrase comes ultimately from Greek sources: Plato's myth, in the *Symposium*, of the birth of Eros (202d–203e) and Plotinus's commentary on this myth (in *Ennead* III.5). It passed through Philo into the Christian tradition. Parallels are also found in Scripture, both in the Old and New Testaments. Ambrose uses it in his hymn *Splendor paternæ gloriæ* (H 75).

They say that the people are deceived by the enchantments (songs) of my hymns; nor indeed do I deny it. This is a great charm (incantation), and nothing could be stronger. What indeed could be more powerful than the confession of the Trinity, which the whole congregation celebrates daily? They vie with one another to confess their faith; they know how to preach in verses the Father, the Son, and the Holy Spirit. And in this way, all have become masters who scarcely had been disciples.[69]

Ambrose likens the hymns to a "charm," a delight, an enchantment; they make theologians out of the singers. It is the confession of faith in song that effects the charm. This too is *Romanitas*.

5. SCRIPTURAL ALLUSIONS

Scripture is the idiom out of which the hymns grow. Often, they are based substantially on passages from the Scriptures: the creation hymns, for example. Even when they do not refer to particular passages from Scripture, they are marked by the language of the Vulgate and by allusions to words and phrases from the Vulgate. Scripture was read and memorized. It was understood to be the inspired word of God and revered as the revelation God made of himself to the world. As St. Basil once famously remarked, "To say there is an idle word in Scripture is a terrible blasphemy."[70] The early Church considered the Old Testament to be in its entirety a prophecy of Christ. St. Hilary of Poitiers has this to say about the Book of Genesis:

> There are many ways in which to interpret Scripture ... [but] every work contained in the Holy Books proclaims by word, announces by event, establishes by example the coming of Our Lord Jesus Christ who, sent by the Father, became Man by being born of the Virgin Mary, through the Holy Spirit. It was Christ, in effect, who throughout the entire history of the created world, in the Patriarchs, by figures that are both true and clearly seen, begets, cleanses, sanctifies, chooses, separates, or redeems the Church.[71]

When St. Hilary began to write hymns, he brought all of his acumen and his experience of the Eastern Church, gained in exile, to his compositions. Ambrose took his inspiration from Hilary, and Ambrose, schooled in the Latin classics, was a master of allusion. The direct quotation is often seen as superfluous and

---

69. *Hymnorum quoque meorum carminibus deceptum populum ferunt, plane nec hoc abnuo. Grande carmen istud est quo nihil potentius; quid enim potentius quam confessio trinitatis, quæ cotidie totius populi ore celebratur? Certatim omnes student fidem fateri, patrem et filium et spiritum sanctum norunt versibus prædicare. Facti sunt igitur omnes magistri, qui vix poterant esse discipuli* (Ambrose, *Contra Auxentium*, ep.75a, 34). Note that the phrase "they vie with one another" seems to indicate that the whole congregation sang the hymns antiphonally. Ambrose's hymns always had eight stanzas, often divided into pairs.

70. Basil, *Hexameron* 10.15. There is some question concerning the authorship of Homily 10. Even if Basil did not write it, his remark is representative of his thought and the thought of others in the early centuries of the Church. See Basile de Césarée, *Sur l'origine de l'homme*, 24–26, 50–52. See also Hildebrand, *The Trinitarian Theology of Basil of Cæsarea*, 110.

71. *Omne autem opus, quod sacris voluminibus continetur, adventum Domini nostri Jesu Christi, quo missus a Patre ex Virgine per Spiritum homo natus est, et dictis nuntiat et factis exprimit et confirmat exemplis. Namque hic per omne constituti huius sceculi tempus veris atque absolutis præfigurationibus in patriarchis ecclesiam aut generat aut abluit aut sanctificat aut eligit aut discernit aut redimit.* (Hilaire de Poitiers, *Traité des Mystères*, 72–75).

unnecessary in an age and in environments where scriptural literacy was high. This deft handling of the scriptural heritage is the legacy of Ambrose and the indispensable foundation for the spiritual logic and message of the hymns that were modeled after him.

THE ENGLISH TRANSLATIONS: ICEL TEXTS

The ICEL translators have made every effort to produce English translations of the Latin hymn texts that are both faithful to the Latin and usable in the liturgy. It is to be hoped that the translations fully reveal the Latin hymns. Inevitably, however, compromises have been necessary in order to keep the text both in the original meter and coherent as an English text. Still, far fewer changes have been introduced than are required by an English rhyming text (cf. the treatment of *Conditor alme siderum*, above). The ICEL translators themselves are keenly aware that they have entered, like many before them, into the dangerous arena of passing on a tradition and making it useful in a particular time and place.

ICEL has been guided throughout the translation process by three goals: first, to translate accurately the Latin texts; second, to produce texts that read well, for those who say the Divine Office individually; third, to produce texts that sing well, for those who recite or sing the Divine Office in community and for those who may wish to adapt this repertoire to other liturgical uses.

1. To translate accurately the Latin texts

The English hymns in this collection are translations of Latin hymns; they are not English hymns inspired by Latin models. Every effort has been made to capture as much as possible of the meaning, syntax, and theological content of the Latin hymns. This does not mean, however, that the English hymns are interlinear, word for word translations. ICEL has rendered them into the English idiom. They are true liturgical texts that may be recited or sung as an integral part of the Divine Office.

ICEL has avoided transforming these Latin texts into rhyming English hymns, in order to achieve a more accurate translation of the Latin text. As we saw above, in the case of John Mason Neale's translation of *Conditor alme siderum*, the process of seeking words that rhyme has two unfortunate consequences. First, the meaning of the Latin text may be compromised by extraneous words introduced for the sake of rhyme. Second, awkward inversions may be introduced, in order to line up rhyming words at the end of the lines in a stanza; for example, "and things celestial Thee shall own" (Neale, *Conditor*, stanza 4, line 3). By this inversion, "own" in line 3 rhymes with "alone" in line 4, though the syntax of line 4 ("and things terrestrial, Lord alone") is perhaps even more awkward than the third. Together the two lines read: "and things celestial Thee shall own / and things terrestrial, Lord alone."

Further, although rhyme has traditionally been a prominent feature of English hymnody (hymns composed originally in English), it is not a dominant feature of Latin hymnody. Even where Latin hymns do rhyme, the likeness of word endings does not predominate when a Latin hymn is recited or sung, as it does in an English rhyming hymn.[72] Indeed, at times Latin hymns rhyme by accident, merely because the language is inflected, and so words of the same case may end with the same or similar endings. Even where rhyme is deliberate and intended by the Latin hymn writer, the natural patterns of Latin accentuation that avoid an accent on the final syllable of a word soften the effect.[73] By preserving the original meters of the Latin hymns, without the extraneous addition of rhyme, ICEL has tried to preserve the poetic nature of the originals, without distorting the texts or losing content.

2. To produce texts that read well when the Divine Office is celebrated individually

Many who recite the Hours of the Divine Office do so alone or without music. ICEL has made every effort to make these English hymns easy and comfortable to recite. The translations offer a language and register that is consonant with the other elements of the liturgy as it is currently configured. The diction is less florid than some may wish, but it is simple, elegant, and contemporary, and the absence of inversion and rhyme scheme allows the themes of the hymns to unfold, as the stanzas are recited, into a pleasing, unified, and logical whole; the theological message and the spiritual imagery have pride of place and influence the poetic form. On the other hand, when hymns containing inversion and rhyme are recited rather than sung, the regularity of line endings and unusual word order distract from other more subtle elements of the hymn.

3. To produce texts that sing well, for those who recite the Divine Office in community, and for those who may wish to adapt this repertoire to other liturgical uses

Because the meters of the original Latin hymns have been preserved, the translations may be sung both to the chant melodies assigned to them in the *Liber Hymnarius* and to metrical tunes. In order to prepare the vocabulary and syntax of the texts for musical production, ICEL has carefully evaluated the sonority

---

72. A telling case in point is St. Thomas's *Sacris solemniis* (H 128), a hymn with a double rhyme. In the first three lines, the last syllable rhymes. In the first two lines the sixth syllable rhymes. In the third line the sixth syllable rhymes with the eighth syllable of the last line. The third line, therefore, navigates two rhymes, one on the sixth syllable, the other on the twelfth. The rhymes are noticeable but not pronounced as they would be in English, because in Latin rhyming syllables seldom bear a heavy accent. Here is a stanza from *Sacris solemniis*:

Dedit fragílibus córporis férculum,
dedit et trístibus sánguinis póculum,
dicens: "Accípite quod trado vásculum;
  omnes ex eo bíbite."

73. The question of rhyme in the Latin hymns will be discussed in greater detail in the appendix on rhyme and assonance at the end of this general introduction.

and the position of words. To the degree possible, words that do not sing well have been eliminated. One particular difficulty arises from the need in English to use a large number of prepositions and the article "the" because the language is not inflected. As noted earlier, in the context of Neale's translation of *Conditor alme siderum*, the placement of prepositions and articles is a delicate task; these little words, "of," "the," "at," and so forth, on the sixth syllable of a line of iambic dimeter may be awkward and jarring to the ear. When the meaning of the text allows a change, connecting words have been moved to a different place in the line or eliminated. As much as possible, metrical sequences of words that may be adequate for recitation but awkward when sung have also been adjusted to make a smoother and more coherent line.

It may be helpful to mention here one final challenge for translators from Latin into English. The English language is not only uninflected; it is in its pre-Norman foundations an Anglo-Saxon tongue. The core of the language is radically different from the Latin core; and when English becomes intense, the core resurfaces in the form of one-syllable words. Latin, on the other hand, maintains a structure based on two or more syllables; the first syllable (or syllables) gives the meaning of the word and the last syllable (or syllables) expresses the inflection: case, number, person, tense, and so on. As a result, adjustments need to be made, in order to arrive at a line or stanza in English that fits the meter of the same line or stanza in a Latin hymn. A particularly eloquent example of this phenomenon is H 33, one of the hymns in honor of the Cross by Venantius Fortunatus. It describes actions, instruments, and images surrounding the Crucifixion and so is filled with names for physical, concrete things. Most are two or thee-syllable words in Latin, but they are one-syllable words in English. In this single hymn, sixteen or more one-syllable words in English have multiple-syllable counterparts in Latin: words such as reed, nail, blood, tree, wood, lamb, weight, earth, sea, sky, world, and so forth.

The general presentation above and this example in particular make it clear that the poetic richness of these hymns is inevitably tied to the Latin idiom. At every turn, there have been sacrifices required of the translators, even without the added burden of rhyme. Over the course of these commentaries, many of these sacrifices will become apparent. Consequently, the reader should be aware that, in order to understand the depth of content and poetic language in these hymns, and to taste fully the scriptural language and allusions woven into every verse, one must consult the Latin texts. The Latin hymn, therefore, is the primary text on which the individual commentaries in this series are based.

An additional reason for focusing on the Latin texts arises out of the tradition itself. Each new hymn grew out of a living family of hymns. The first commentators were the hymn writers of the next generation. Thus, when one looks at the reception of the hymns of Ambrose, one finds any number of imitations that range from the overall theme and structure to significant words and phrases. Whole lines have been taken from earlier hymns, in order to draw liturgical and thematic connections. Thus, St. Thomas Aquinas began his hymn on the Last Supper and the Eucharist, for the feast of Corpus Christi, with the opening line of Venantius Fortunatus's hymn in honor of the Cross.[74] Lentini's new hymns are filled with Ambrosian words and phrases. The tradition has never become static or relegated to a historical past. It is living and still expanding. All of this is like an echo chamber reminding us of the manifold connections the hymn writers themselves delighted to make. Many imitations are subtle, reminiscent of the borrowing and expansion made by the great poets of antiquity. In the later Middle Ages, centos became popular,[75] in which new hymns were composed out of lines taken from well-known hymns; such is the Sapphic hymn from a Spanish breviary, mentioned earlier. It begins: *Cónditor álme síderum qui pálme....* and then ends with the line: *ut queant laxis* (taken from the hymn for the Nativity of St. John the Baptist).[76]

Finally, many commentators have preceded us in this endeavor, beginning with the Benedictines of Anglo-Saxon England, who transcribed liturgical hymns into prose in order to instruct their pupils. Dionysus the Carthusian, in the fifteenth century, wrote commentaries on his favorite hymns. The nineteenth and twentieth centuries saw a renewed interest in the tradition of commenting on the hymns found in the breviary and other sources. We have benefited from their insights and scholarship.

The following commentaries on individual hymns begin with the text in Latin and in the ICEL translation.[77] The hymns are followed by notes that pertain to the editing of the Latin texts now found in the *Liturgia Horarum*. These are followed by a historical, liturgical, and spiritual commentary. Unless indicated otherwise, all references to Scripture are to the Vulgate, since this is the biblical text upon which the hymns are based. English translations of the Vulgate are either made by the individual commentators or taken from a standard English version, for instance, New American Bible, Revised Edition (NABRE), or the like. If a standard English version is used, it will be acknowledged.

The commentary has been divided into five volumes. The numbering of hymns in the commentary differs from numbering in *The Divine Office Hymnal*, in part because in the hymnal, each hymn is given twice on facing pages, one page has a modern hymn tune and the other has the Gregorian melody as it is found in the *Liber Hymnarius*. Consequently, each hymn has two numbers. Concordances at the end of each volume of the hymn commentary give the corresponding number and title for each hymn in the commentary and in the *Divine Office Hymnal*. The

---

74. Venantius Fortunatus: *Pange, lingua, gloriosi proelium certaminis* (H 32). Thomas Aquinas: *Pange, lingua, gloriosi corporis mysterium* (H 127).

75. The Latin word *cento* (*centonis*, m.) means patchwork. It is used for poems and musical compositions that in whole or part are made from previously written works. T. S. Eliot's *Wasteland* is an eloquent example.

76. Norberg, *Introduction*, 57; Szövérffy, *Annalen*, 2:278; for other adaptations see *Annalen* 2:231, 257, 290.; AH 16, nos. 299–301, hymns in honor of Saint Indaletio, have verses from well-known hymns throughout.

77. The Latin text is taken from the *Liturgia Horarum*, editio typica, 2004.

full name of the commentary is *Cantate Domino: A Commentary on the Hymns of the Liturgy of the Hours*. The volumes of the *Commentary* are as follows:

1. Proper of Time: Advent, Christmas, Lent, and Easter (H 1–58).
2. Proper of Time: Ordinary Time (59–123). These include hymns for the daily offices of Terce, Sext, None, and Compline, followed by those assigned to the Office of Readings, Lauds, and Vespers during alternating weekly cycles in the Four-Week Psalter.
3. Solemnities of the Lord in Ordinary Time, Commons, and the Office for the Dead (H 124–188).
4. Proper of Saints, January through August (H 189–252)
5. Proper of Saints, September through December, followed by an appendix containing the hymns for Our Lord Jesus Christ, The Eternal High Priest (H 253–297).

NOTE

The following appendices are offered to those who may wish to deepen their knowledge of the literary aspects of the varied styles of hymnody contained in this series. They present more detailed accounts of the meters used in the hymns of this collection and the historical development of meter as it applies to the hymns, as well as a discussion of the developments that led from quantitative, non-rhyming hymns to the late Medieval rhyming sequences. These appendices may be consulted as supplementary resources independent of the General Introduction.

APPENDIX I

Latin Meter

In order to sing and even to understand Latin hymnody, it is essential to have a basic knowledge of the conventions of classical and medieval Latin meter. In this appendix we will review some fundamental principles. Then, using *iambic dimeter* as a model, we will analyze the shift from classical meter based on the quantities of syllables to medieval versification based on the spoken stress accent. Finally, we will present the meters found in the *Liturgia Horarum*, giving examples of both quantitative and accentual versions.

FUNDAMENTAL PRINCIPLES

A LIST OF TERMS[1]

1. *Foot*: a term in modern use that signifies a group of two or three syllables, the smallest unit in a line of poetry.

2. *Meter*: two senses are in common use. (1) English for the Latin *metrum* (pl. *metra*; from the Greek μέτρον): a measure, like a musical measure, made of one or two feet. It is the building block of poetry. (2) A general term used to signify the entire range of poetic pattern and structure.[2]

3. *Long syllable*: a syllable containing a long vowel, a diphthong, or a short vowel followed by two consonants, or the double consonants *x* or *z*. The "i" in "bite" is long; "bite" is a long syllable. The diphthong "oa" in "boat" is also long, the equivalent of a long "o" as in "note"; "boat" is a long syllable. The "i" in "blitz" is short, but it is followed by a consonant cluster "tz"; the syllable "blitz" is long—it takes some time to say all the consonants—even though it contains a short vowel.

---

1. The definitions and explanations given here are sufficient for the following appendix and for the commentary. Much that is pertinent to Latin accentuation and poetic practice is beyond the scope of this presentation. Latin writers applied Greek terminology to their own different language, and this resulted in some ambiguity, since classical Greek was a tonal language and Latin had a native stress accent. For more information, see the works by Sydney Allen, *Vox Latina* and *Accent and Rhythm*. See also Allen and Greenough, *Latin Grammar*, nos. 12–13, 607–29.

2. Allen and Greenough, *Latin Grammar*, no. 608; Lausberg, *Handbook of Literary Rhetoric*, nos. 977–79.

    a. A syllable having a long vowel or diphthong is *long by nature*.
    b. A syllable having a short vowel followed by two consonants or a double consonant is *long by position*.
    c. By convention, long vowels are indicated by a *macron* (a straight line) over the vowel: ā.

4. *Short syllable*: a syllable containing a short vowel and either open (followed by no consonant) or closed by one consonant. A short syllable is sometimes also called a *mora*, meaning "delay" and quantifying the time it takes to say one short vowel or syllable. The "i" in "bit" is short; "bit" is a short syllable. It takes less time to say "bit" than it does to say "bite," "boat," or "blitz." Note that "bit" followed by a word that begins with a consonant turns "bit" into a syllable that is long by position, for example, "bit by bit": the first "bit" has become long. By Latin metrical convention, two short syllables are the equivalent of one long syllable.[3] This alternation between long and short syllables is the foundation on which all classical quantitative poetry is based.

    d. Short vowels are indicated by a breve (a small curved line) over the vowel (ă).

5. *Heavy syllables* and *light syllables*: strictly speaking, vowels are long or short. Syllables containing long vowels, or the equivalent, are heavy; syllables containing short vowels are light. The distinction between heavy and light signifies the stress and change of pitch that marks syllables in real speech better than the distinction between long and short. As useful as this distinction is, it is sufficient for our purposes to use the conventional names and refer to syllables as long or short depending on the sort of vowel or vowel-consonant combination they contain.[4]

6. The following is a short list of standard poetical feet, symbols, and terms.

Syllables:	Metrical Feet:	*Metrum* (pl.: *metra*):
⏑ : short syllable	Iamb: ⏑ –	2 iambic feet
– : long syllable	Trochee: – ⏑	2 trochaic feet
⏓ : long or short syllable (*anceps*)	Spondee: – –	1 dactyl
macron (ā): long vowel	Pyrrhic: ⏑ ⏑	1 choriamb
breve (ă): short vowel	Dactyl: – ⏑ ⏑	
	Choriamb: – ⏑ ⏑ –	

7. *Penult*: the second to the last syllable of a word of two or more syllables.
8. *Antepenult*: the third to the last syllable of a word of three or more syllables.[5]
9. *Enclitic*: a word that, in the context in which it is used, "leans" back upon the

---

    3. To some degree at least, the distinction between long and short syllables is perceived by the ear in any language based on a vowel system. In real speech, however, there are many variations and changes in vowel length depending on context: "through" is a bit longer than "though," even though both are long syllables.
    4. See Hanson, "Quantitative Meter" 42, n. 2.
    5. In conventional accounts of grammar and meter, a penult that bears an accent is *paroxytone* (e.g. amáz-ing); an antepenult that bears an accent is *proparoxytone* (e.g. illústrious)

word to which it is connected. Examples of Latin enclitics are *-que, -met, -ne* (in a question) and *-cum* after a personal pronoun, as in *Dominus vobiscum*.

10. *Quantity*: the length of a syllable, long or short.

11. *Quantitative meter*: poetic form based on patterns of long and short syllables.

12. *Accent*: an ambiguous term used in discussions of both Greek and Latin poetry. With regard to Latin poetry, it signifies a stress or a slight increase in volume that may occur on either a long or a short syllable. In this appendix and the commentary, the stress is called a *stress accent*, or simply an *accent*. This is the same as the normal spoken word accent in English. A primary stress accent is signified by an acute accent (´); a secondary stress by a grave accent (`).

13. *Accentual meter, accentual versification, rhythmic versification*: terms that signify poetic form based on patterns of stressed and unstressed syllables. Scholars may distinguish between *quantitative meter* and *rhythmic* or *accentual versification*. Here we will use the term *meter* in the general sense for both quantitative and accentual poetic structure.

14. *Ictus*: the "beat" that results from the repetition of regular patterns in poetry, similar to the musical patterns signified by a time signature; for example, a waltz has a time signature of ¾. There are three quarter notes to a measure and the beat, or ictus, is: "<u>One</u>-two-three, <u>One</u>-two-three" where "One" is stressed and determines the steps of the dance. In Shakespeare's iambic pentameter, the *ictus* is on every second syllable: "un<u>ea</u>sy <u>lies</u> the <u>head</u> that <u>wears</u> a <u>crown</u>" (*Henry IV*, Part 2, Act 3, scene 1, line 31).

15. *Iamb* and *trochee*: these terms will be considered in detail later, but briefly, since they are used throughout the discussion, an *iamb* is made from a short or unstressed syllable followed by a long, and in various combinations it makes *iambic* meter; a *trochee* is the opposite, a long or stressed syllable followed by a short, and in various configurations it makes *trochaic* meter.

THE PENULT RULE

In Latin of all periods for which we have historical sources, most words receive some sort of stress accent. The accent never falls on the last syllable unless an enclitic follows. Thus, two-syllable words always have a stress accent on the first syllable, whether it is long or short. Words of more than two syllables have a stress accent on the penult if the penult is long (*deféndo*). If the penult is short, the stress accent slips back onto the antepenult (*aúdio* and *sócius*). Note that the antepenult may be long or short; it receives a stress accent not because of its own length but only because the penult is short. "The position of the accent in words of 2 or more syllables is thus governed by *syllabic quantity* (of the penultimate); and very similar rules may be found in some other dynamically accented languages."[6] This is

---

6. Allen, *Accent and Rhythm*, 155; emphasis added. In this passage Allen is making a comparison of Greek and Latin accentuation. In Greek the vowel alone is significant for the placement of accents. In Latin the whole syllable is significant. Greek has a tonal accent, similar to Chinese; Latin has a stress accent, similar to English, though less pronounced.

the *Penult Rule*. Here are a few examples of the rule; the accent is indicated by an acute over the vowel or over the diphthong: cǽlum, cǽlites, but cælέstibus; píus (ĭ), ímpius; vírum, virúmque, sócius, sociúsque, refúlge, refulgémus (because "e" here is long by nature: ē).

The essential point is that the Penult Rule brings the native Latin stress accent into the arena of quantitative meter; in the last three syllables of a word, syllabic quantity, and the spoken stress accent are closely related. Native Latin speakers would not necessarily be aware of this relation, but they maintained it as long as they remembered where to put the stress accent in a word. Evidence of this relation is seen in the fairly regular coincidence of metrical *ictus* (or beat) and spoken stress accent in the final syllables at the end of the line in classical epic poetry. The tension between *ictus* and stress accent at other points in the line may be pronounced, and this creates interest and vividness, what the Roman rhetoricians called *varietas*.[7] The balance between variety and regularity gives movement and life to a line of poetry. The meter is remembered from line to line if there is enough of a return to the pattern at the end. The opening line from Hamlet's first soliloquy is an interesting case in point: "O that this too, too solid flesh would melt." Notice that if one says this line naturally and with feeling, the meter is not wholly apparent at the beginning. The line begins with five one-syllable words, each of which takes time to say; all are long syllables. The long "O" feels as long as, even longer than, "that"; the repetitions of "th" and "t" require each word to be slowly articulated, and the repetition of "too" keeps one from slurring them together. From "solid flesh" to the end of the line, however, we sense a definite alternation between stressed and unstressed syllables. The effect of this tension at the beginning with resolution into the meter in the second half creates a certain weight, the line drags. Combined with the meaning of the words, this heavy beginning gives intensity and anxiety to Hamlet's speech. This is *varietas*. If we always felt the regular rhythm, or beat, of the iambic pentameter, it would become tedious. Latin poets throughout the classical period exploited the effects of tension between *ictus* and stress accent and the resolution of it in the meter at the line-ending.[8] In the felicitous phrase of A. S. Gratwick, the non-reconciliation of *ictus* to word accent in lines of metrical poetry is "the salt to the meat."[9] This artistic and rhetorical discordance is of particular significance to the study of hymns, because tension and resolution are fundamental principles of musical texts, and the hymns were composed to be sung. Tension and resolution also contributed to the shape of early medieval accentual versification as it developed out of classical quantitative meter.

---

7. *Variatio* or *varietas*, which appears throughout rhetoric, counteracts the audience's *tædium* by alternations in the direction of thought (intellectual *ornatus*) and in linguistic expression (linguistic *ornatus*) —Even *voluptas* itself, if it lacks *variatio*, can become *fastidium*. See Lausberg, *Handbook of Literary Rhetoric*, no. 257.2b, 115–16, quoting Cicero, Quintilian, and others.

8. Allen, *Vox Latina*, 92; see also the entire discussion on pages 82–94. See also Gratwick, "Origins of Roman Drama," 87–92.

9. Gratwick, "Origins of Roman Drama," 90.

The hymns of Ambrose, and of Prudentius and Sedulius after him, were the models followed by succeeding generations as the new forms developed. Ambrose's hymns were masterpieces of quantitative verse, but they were also composed for liturgical use, to be sung by the congregation at large. The meter was simple, easy to sing, easy to memorize. Line-endings in particular were composed in such a way that the natural Latin stress accent coincided with the long sixth syllable required by the meter. This regularity suggested clearly identifiable patterns that transferred well into rhythmic versification.[10] Later hymn writers felt these patterns as based on stress accent, even when they did not hear the quantities of syllables, and as a result, his hymns quickly became the norm, recited, analyzed, copied, and transformed by succeeding generations.

The history of nearly a thousand years of transformation is complex and largely beyond the scope of this appendix. The daunting array of texts to be analyzed, the lacunæ that mark the early years before the Carolingian reform, the absence of musical notation, all render a continuous account difficult.[11] In general, however, there is evidence suggesting that over the course of the later Roman Empire the native Latin stress accent had a stronger influence, and differences in syllable length became progressively harder to hear and less significant to native Latin speakers.[12] This does not mean that all distinction between long and short syllables was lost, nor does it mean that the stress accent was actually growing stronger. The balance between the quantity of syllables and the stress accent, however, was shifting. Some idea of the change may be seen in comments made by Cicero at the end of the first century BC and then by St. Augustine at the end of the fourth century AD. In his treatise *Orator* (written in 46 BC), Cicero describes the reactions of the average theatregoer in his day:

> In a line of verse, the whole theater shouts, if one syllable has been either too short or too long. Nor indeed, does the multitude know about feet or grasp the meter, nor do they understand what offends, or why, or in what it offends. And yet, nature herself has established in our ears a power to judge in speech all long and short (syllables), just as all high and low pitches.[13]

---

10. Norberg, *Les vers*, 19–21.

11. The following presentation of the development during late antiquity and the early Middle Ages of accentual verse is largely based on the magisterial work of Dag Norberg. In his introduction to Dag Norberg's *Introduction to the Study of Medieval Latin Versification*, Jan Ziolkowski says of Norberg: "He holds fast to facts as he develops the case ... that, partly under the influence of the music, medieval poets often created rhythmic verse by reading ancient meters as prose, without maintaining the lengths of syllables or *ictus* demanded by classical prosody, but while retaining the number of syllables, placement of cæsuras, and cadences before the cæsuras and line endings. In making his case, Norberg avoids espousing any single theory to account for the origins of all rhythmic poetry" (xiv).

12. The strengthening of the stress accent and the subsequent loss of the perception of syllable length led to transformative changes by the end of the fourth century. See, for example, Dag Norberg, "A quelle époque a-t-on cessé de parler latin en Gaule?" Citing the calculations of M. Hagendahl, Norberg concludes from a comparison of texts from Cicero with texts from Minucius Felix, Cyprian of Carthage, and Arnobius that over the course of the third century, preferences for clausulæ similar to those found in Cicero, based on vowel quantity and found in Minucius Felix, shift to others that favor a stress accent, found in Arnobius.

13. *In versu quidem theatra tota exclamant, si fuit una syllaba aut brevior aut longior; nec vero multitudo pedes novit nec ullos numeros tenet nec illud, quod offendit, aut cur aut in quo offendat intelligit; et tamen omnium*

In his treatise on music (*De musica*, finished in 389 AD), St. Augustine presents a dialogue between master and disciple, and from their exchange, it is evident that at the end of the fourth century "nature herself" no longer provided the ability to distinguish between long and short syllables. The distinction had long since passed into the domain of the grammarians. The disciple says to the master:

> Just the same, you do not seem to me to remember you have already sufficiently distinguished the difference between the grammarian and the musician when I told you I did not possess the knowledge of long and short syllables, a knowledge passed down by grammarians. Unless, perhaps, you let me show the rhythm in beats and not in words. For I do not deny I am capable of ear-judgments for regulating the values of times. But as to what syllables are to be pronounced long or short, since it is a matter of authority, I am altogether ignorant.[14]

In another passage, Augustine implies, first, that the authority of the grammarians is what preserves the art of distinguishing between long and short syllables and, second, that their teaching is based on books left behind by earlier generations; it is based "on those who came before us and whose books survive.... And so whatever is valid here, has been made valid by authority."[15]

Even as the schools taught the traditional techniques of quantitative poetry, the spoken language changed, and in some cases this change destabilized the pronunciation of vowels.[16] Thus, vowel lengths changed: accented short vowels lengthened, and unaccented long vowels weakened, for example, in classical Latin the verb *cano* had a short but accented penult followed by a long but unaccented final syllable (*căn̄o*). In later Latin, the short "a", which had the stress accent, lengthened, and the unaccented but long "o" became short (*cānŏ*).[17] Unaccented vowels were also lost; grammarians needed to remind Latin speakers that correct spelling required *oculus*, not *oclus*.[18] In some cases stress accents moved to new syllables; *récipit* became *recípit*; the original vowels of simple verbs resurfaced

---

longitudinum et brevitatum in sonis sicut acutarum graviumque vocum iudicium ipsa natura in auribus nostris collocavit (Cicero, *Orator*, 173). The Latin text is cited with commentary by Norberg, "La récitation du vers Latin," 501–2.

14. *videris mihi non recordari iam te satis discrevisse, quid inter grammaticum et musicum intersit, cum ego tibi respondissem syllabarum longarum et brevium cognitionem me non habere, quæ a grammaticis traditur, nisi forte si permittis, ut non verbis, sed aliquo pulsu rhythmum istum exhibeam. Nam iudicium aurium ad temporum momenta moderanda me posse habere non nego, quæ vero syllaba producenda vel corripienda sit, quod in auctoritate situm est, omnino nescio* (Augustine, *De musica*, 3.3). See also Norberg, *Introduction*, 81, n. 1.

15. *Itaque verbi gratia cum dixeris 'cano' vel in versu forte posueris, ita ut vel tu pronuntians producas huius verbi syllabam primam vel in versu eo loco ponas, ubi esse productam oportebat, reprehendet grammaticus, custos ille videlicet historiæ, nihil aliud asserens, cur hanc corripi oporteat, nisi quod hi, qui ante nos fuerunt et quorum libri exstant tractanturque a grammaticis, ea corrupta, non producta usi fuerint. Quare hic quidquid valet, auctoritas valet* (Augustine, *De musica*, 2.1). See also Nicolau, "Les deux sources de la versification latine accentuelle," 57–58.

16. The emblematic example of this shift is in the change of "æ" to an open "e" eventually reflected in the spelling of words in medieval manuscripts and in the Romance languages; Latin *cælum* becomes Italian *cielo*. In hymns from the fifth and sixth centuries, we find *teter* for *tæter*, *adheret* for *adhæret*, etc. (Norberg, *L'accentuation*, 20–22).

17. Norberg, *Les vers*, 7–9. St. Augustine mentions this example in the same passage of the *De musica*, 2.1. See note 16 above. Differences such as that between *veni*, present tense, and *vēni*, perfect tense, were weakened; similarly the meaning of nouns could no longer be differentiated by case; *rosa*, nominative, was not easily distinguished from *rosā*, ablative.

18. Allen, *Accent and Rhythm*, 152–53.

in compound forms: *displicet* became *displácet*.[19] As a result of such changes, in the later years of the Roman Empire, the quantity of syllables was no longer felt strongly enough for it to stand as a natural basis for prose rhythm or for poetic meter.[20] The educated elite still learned the rules of quantitative meter in the schools, but those who sang and recited the hymns of Ambrose, Prudentius, and Sedulius naturally and spontaneously heard stress accents, not quantity. They composed as they heard. In the case of liturgical hymns the results were similar to though different from the old quantitative verse.[21] As poets experimented with new forms, developments in accentual meter flowered in the rise of new genres, and finally in sequences and hymns based on syllable count and two-syllable rhyme.

It is important to remember that any account of the development of accentual meter is complicated by a variety of influences. Some of these are differences in education received in the schools, though throughout the provinces of the former Roman Empire, schools largely ceased to function by the end of the sixth century. The evolution and use of the language was also affected by geographical region, social standing of the poets and the audience for which they wrote,[22] the ecclesiastical culture of poet and audience (monastic or clerical), and the function for which the hymns and other poetry were composed. In this regard, Bede's comments in his *De arte metrica* are significant. When he discusses rhythmical versification, he notes that normal use of language could provide an instinctive sense of the right combination of sound and rhythmical beat, but that common (unlearned) poets often missed the mark.

> You will commonly find measured quantities by chance in rhythmic verse, not because the regular artistic arrangement has been preserved, but from the influence of the sound and the rhythmical beat itself. The common poets inevitably do this awkwardly, and the learned poets skillfully.[23]

IAMBIC DIMETER: QUANTITATIVE AND ACCENTUAL

Latin iambic dimeter, as it was developed by Ambrose, has weathered centuries of change in language and custom so well that after more than 1600 years, it is still the meter most often used for English as well as Latin hymnody. Modern hymnals often refer to it as Long Meter. The majority of the hymns in the *Liturgia Horarum* are in iambic dimeter, both quantitative and accentual. The accentual versions of other more complex meters found in the tradition developed out of

---

19. Norberg, *L'accentuation*, 5–9.
20. See Norberg, "La récitation du vers latin," 501–2.
21. See Norberg, *Les vers*, 25–27. He analyzes rhythmical hymns based on stress accent from 5th and 6th c. Gaul, Milan, and Visigothic Spain, p. 27ff.
22. As early as 475, Auspicius, Bishop of Toul, wrote a letter to Arbogast, Count of Trier, entirely in accentual meter. A copy is extant. See Norberg, *Introduction*, 101–2.
23. Bede, *Libri II De Arte Metrica*, I, 24.

their quantitative counterparts in much the same way as the accentual versions of iambic dimeter developed out of the old quantitative meter. We will look at iambic dimeter here, and explanations of the other meters will be given when the individual meters are introduced.

The term *iambic* signifies that the feet in the poetic line are made of *iambs*; as the table above shows, each *iamb* is a short syllable plus a long syllable, or in terms of accent, an unstressed syllable followed by one that is stressed. One iamb is a foot; one meter is made up of two feet. The term *dimeter* signifies that there are *two meters* to a line. Again, *meter* is the Anglicization of *metrum* (the plural is *metra*). Iambic dimeter has two *metra* per line, and the type of *metrum* is iambic. The basic pattern of a line of iambic dimeter looks like this: ᴗ – ᴗ – | ᴗ – ᴗ – .[24]

In all types of quantitative meter, substitutions are allowed at strategic points in a line. This means that a long syllable may be substituted for one or two shorts, two shorts may substitute for a long, and more complex patterns are allowed, depending on the type of meter, the time period, and the stylistic preferences of the poet. Hymns in quantitative iambic dimeter commonly allow one type of substitution: in each half of an eight-syllable line, the first short syllable may be replaced by a long; in an eight-syllable line, these are syllables 1 and 5.[25] Where ᴗ̱ is a syllable that may be either short or long (*anceps*), an adjusted pattern looks like this: ᴗ̱ – ᴗ – | ᴗ̱ – ᴗ – . In quantitative iambic dimeter, therefore, the first and the fifth syllables may be either short or long. Since Latin has a preponderance of long syllables, they are often long.

Taking as an example the hymn of St. Ambrose, *Splendor paternæ gloriæ* (H 75), we will analyze several lines that show different patterns arising out of the alternation of long and short syllables in conjunction with word length (number of syllables) and the natural stress accent. Beginning with the first line, *Splendor paternæ gloriæ*, we find substitutions on syllables 1 and 5. Syllable 1 of *splendor* is long because, even though the vowel *e* is short, the syllable ends in *n* and is followed by the *d* of *dor*: they are in separate syllables, but *n* plus *d* form two consonants back-to-back. Syllable 5, *næ*, is also long because it contains a diphthong. Looking at the other syllables in the line, *dor* is long before *p*, *pa* is short before *t*, *ter* is long before *n*, *glo* is long because the *o* is long by nature (*ō*), *ri* is short because it has a short vowel, *æ* is long, both because it is a diphthong and because it ends the line. There is always a slight pause at the line end, and this causes the last syllable to feel long regardless of syllable length. In quantitative iambic dimeter, the last syllable of a line is always counted as long.

In the following table and in the others below, long syllables are underscored; natural, primary stress accents are marked with an acute accent; secondary stress accents, as in syllable 8, are marked with a grave accent. The line looks like this:

---

24. Note that iambs and trochees have two feet in each metron. Longer feet (dactyls and choriambs) have only one foot per metron.

25. Other types of substitution are allowed, but they are relatively few. In H 5: 4, 3, for example, we find an anapest (two shorts plus one long) in the first foot: *gĕmĭnæ gigas substantiæ*. See Norberg, *Les vers*, 18.

Iambic Dimeter: Quantitative and Accentual

<u>Splén</u>-	<u>dor</u>	pa-	<u>tér</u>-	<u>næ</u>	<u>gló</u>-	ri-	<u>æ̀</u>
1	2	3	4	5	6	7	8

If one recites this line simply but slowly in natural speech, giving each syllable time, one gets a sense of the alternation between long and short syllables; the first, second, fourth, fifth, and sixth are clearly long; they feel longer than the third and the seventh. The eighth syllable is long because here it is a diphthong, but also because it incorporates the pause at the end of the line. None of the differences in length are great; they are just enough to make us feel a difference. It is a subtle, "undulating" rhythm based on the fact that it takes slightly longer to say syllables 1, 2, 4, 5, 6, and 8 than it does to say syllables 3 and 7. Note, also, that the sixth syllable, *glō-*, has a stress accent because it is the first of a three-syllable word; since the penult is short, the stress accent has moved back onto the antepenult, *glō-*. The Penult Rule does not require *glō-* to be long, but the function of the sixth syllable in quantitative iambic dimeter does. It also requires the fourth syllable to be long. Here it is the penult of a three-syllable word and long by position (e before r + n). Hence, in this line it too has a stress accent.

In this line a substitution was made on the first syllable. A long syllable *splen-* was used where one would expect a short. If a substitution is not made on the first syllable, the iambic pattern is felt more strongly. Thus, in the line *iubárque Sancti Spíritus* (2, 3), the first *metrum* of four syllables has no substitutions. Syllable 1 is short, followed by a syllable long by position before the short enclitic *-que*. Syllable 5 is long, but it follows an especially large syllable 4 (ending in a cluster of three consonants). Syllable 5 is thus a legitimate substitution, but it feels relatively short when compared to 4. In this line, *ictus* (the beat) and stress accents coincide. It reads well accentually. It looks like this:

iu	<u>-bár</u>	-que	<u>Sánc</u>	-tī	<u>Spí</u>	-ri	-tùs
1	2	3	4	5	6	7	8

In the line: *fides velut meridies* (7, 3), there are also no substitutions. The first, third, fifth, and seventh syllables are all short: It looks like this:

fí-	<u>des</u>	vél-	<u>ut</u>	me-	<u>rí-</u>	di-	<u>ès</u>
1	2	3	4	5	6	7	8

Again, if we say this line naturally but slowly enough not to slur the consonants, we sense that the second, fourth, sixth, and eighth syllables last a little longer. The first, third, fifth, and seventh syllables are a little shorter. The first and third syllables have a stress accent, however, even though they are short. The "conflict" between stress accent and vowel length in the first half of the line adds variety and interest, like the first half of the line from Hamlet analyzed above.

The analysis thus far has shown three different ways in which stress accent and metrical beat may line up in quantitative meter. All three lines end in a three- or four-syllable word with a stress accent on the requisite long sixth syllable. In these examples, metrical beat and the stress accent of a multisyllable word coincide on the sixth syllable. Since the Penult Rule allows a stress on the antepenult only if the penult is short, this arrangement assures a short vowel on the seventh syllable, the proper long-short-long sequence for iambic dimeter. If one recites these lines without paying attention to syllable length, the last three syllables are still heard as an iambic sequence: stressed, unstressed, stressed. When it comes to line endings, therefore, the Penult Rule in a three-syllable word allows a transition from quantitative meter to accentual verse without an appreciable change. This type of ending quickly became the norm.

In many ancient hymns, however, and in later hymns consciously written in quantitative meter, lines of iambic dimeter may end with two-syllable words. The sixth syllable is always long, but it may be followed by a separate two-syllable word on syllables 7 and 8. The two-syllable word may be composed either of two short syllables (a pyrrhic), or one short syllable followed by a long (an iamb). As long as syllable 6 is long and syllable 7 is short, the quantitative iambic meter is maintained, since, again, syllable 8 before a pause is always counted as long regardless of vowel length. Lines such as *potúsque noster sit fides* (6, 2) and *et tótus in Vérbo Páter* (8, 4) are impeccable quantitative iambic dimeter. The sixth syllables are long by position (*sit* before *fi-*) or long by nature (*-bō* of *Verbō*); *fidēs* is an iamb—it has a first short syllable followed by a long—and *Pater* is a pyrrhic—it has two short syllables. The lines look like this:

a)	po	-tús	-que	nós	-ter	sit	fí	-dès
	1	2	3	4	5	6	7	8
b)	et	tó	-tus	in	Vér	-bō	Pá	-tèr
	1	2	3	4	5	6	7	8

The hymns of Ambrose have a large proportion of two-syllable endings similar to both (a) and (b) above. If one recites both (a) and (b), however, with attention only to natural stress accent, the line endings have a different cadence from each other and from the three-syllable endings above. Each line, taken as a whole, does not seem to fit well into iambic dimeter. This is especially true of the (b) ending in *Verbo Pater*. The line ending in (a) has a large one-syllable word on syllable 6 followed by an iamb (*sit fides*) that suggests a loose sort of unity between *sit* and *fides*; that is, *fides* has an "enclitic effect," so to speak, that leads it to coalesce to some degree with *sit*.[26] This makes a functional three-syllable line-ending, even if it is made up of two separate words. This type of ending remains

---

26. Norberg, *L'accentuation*, 46–50. The long sixth syllable in combination with a two-syllable word on the seventh and the eighth syllable forms a single "metrical word." See also Norberg, *Introduction*, 14–20; see especially 19.

in use throughout the Middle Ages. Type (b), however, is irremediably awkward, and it drops out of use. In Ambrose's hymns more than 30 percent of his lines end in two-syllable words; in Prudentius, it is 25 percent; in Sedulius, 9 percent; in Venantius Fortunatus and Bede, 7 percent.[27]

In addition to factors that arose directly out of new ways of reading the old quantitative verse, other more indirect influences were also at work. Musical practice, preexisting hymn tunes, and liturgical melodies,[28] liturgical poetry and prose, such as antiphons and responsories: all of these contributed to the development of new literary forms. As vernacular languages developed, they too influenced religious poetic practice. In some cases, there also seems to be a conscious blending of quantitative and accentual meters. This phenomenon has been studied in connection with Paulinus of Aquileia by Norberg, though it is more widespread than one might think;[29] it would be a mistake to attribute it solely to incompetence on the part of the composers. The hymns themselves show artistic evidence of this blending. For example, the Easter hymn, *Aurora lucis rutilat* begins in quantitative meter (*au-*, *ro-*, and *lu-* are long), but the *ru-* of *rutilat*, the all-important sixth syllable, though accented, is short; it hardly matters, because the rhyme it establishes with *iubilat* and *ululat* (*ul-* is also short) is intentional and magnificent. A surprising number of hymns also have an irregular number of syllables or variations in rhyme schemes that seem to indicate the influence of melody rather than textual poetic norms.[30] In the passage cited above from his *De arte metrica*, Bede continues his discussion by giving a stanza of a hymn he considers to be an excellent example of Ambrosian iambic dimeter. Interestingly, the first line has only seven syllables, *Rex æterne Domine*. Bede, an accomplished poet, surely knew there were only seven. He is not concerned; it is a beautiful hymn, ancient even for Bede, with irregularities in other lines throughout. Norberg sees the influence of music here, perhaps a preexisting melody, that would account for missing syllables and irregularities in the rhyme scheme.[31] The sequences of the twelfth and thirteenth centuries are the final result of the creativity of the medieval mind and centuries of experimentation, all based on the original quantitative Latin meters. The entire range of this development is seen in the hymns of the *Liturgia Horarum*.

Before looking at individual meters, it might be helpful to compare briefly the

---

27. Norberg, *Les vers*, 19–21. Again, there are exceptions, but the trend toward standard three-syllable endings was unmistakable and is easily seen in the majority of early anonymous hymns. Norberg comments: "A part cette combinaison [monosyllable + dissyllable, as in *sit fides*, above], la tendance à éviter les dissyllabes en fin de vers est tout-à-fait claire. Mais il s'agit ici aussi d'une tendance et non pas d'une règle obligatoire" (Norberg, *Les vers*, 20): "With the exception of this combination [as in *sit fides*, above], the tendency to avoid two-syllable combinations at the end of the line is entirely clear. But we are dealing here also with a tendency and not an obligatory rule." See the entire discussion on pp. 18–24, and Norberg, *L'accentuation*, 49–50.

28. For example, the early sequences originated in strict dependence on music. The form of a text was derived from the musical "sequences" to which it was set. See Norberg, *Introduction*, 159–60 and 165n23; see also Bower, *Liber Ymnorum*, 54.

29. Norberg, *Introduction*, 128–29. See also the final paragraphs of appendix 2 on assonance and rhyme.

30. Norberg, *Introduction*, 130ff.

31. Bede, *De arte metrica*, I, 24. *Rex æterne Domine* is included in the *Liturgia Horarum* (H 43). Lentini added an *O* before *Rex*, which resolves the irregular seven-syllable line.

lines from Ambrose's *Splendor paternæ gloriæ* analyzed above without the complication of long and short syllables. This is how they look with stress accents alone:

1, 1: Spléndor patérnæ glóriæ
2, 3: iubárque Sáncti Spíritùs
7, 3: fídes vélut merídièrs
6, 2: potúsque nóster sit fídès
8, 4: et tótus in Vérbo Pátèr

Stanza 2, 3 is clearly recognizable as a pattern of unstressed-stressed (accentual iambic dimeter). Stanza 1, 1 also fits the pattern, since even though *splen-* has the accent, *-dor* before *pa-* is large enough to balance *splen-*. Stanza 7, 3 ends with a clear iteration of the stressed-unstressed-stressed line ending typical of iambic dimeter. *Fides* and *velut* are trochaic, clearly not in the meter, but they remind us of the variation found in the line from Hamlet above; the second half settles well into the meter. Stanza 6, 2 begins in the meter, and the ending is close enough to the pattern of stressed-unstressed-stressed to stay within the general range of the meter; that is, the phrase *sit fides*, beginning with a large one-syllable word followed by a two-syllable iambic word with a light penult, is pronounced as enough of a verbal unit to qualify as Norberg's single "metrical word." Finally, 8, 4 has a trochaic sequence of stressed-unstressed at the end of the line, on the two final words. This clearly cannot fit into iambic dimeter. As we saw above, this last schema was gradually eliminated. The other four and others like them were retained.[32]

In conclusion, the accentual reconfiguration of quantitative iambic dimeter that admits of variation in the first half of the line is both flexible and stable. The transition from quantitative to accentual meter was made possible largely by Ambrose's careful alignment of the length of the sixth syllable, and to a lesser extent the fourth, to the natural stress accent of Latin words. Thus, in his own hymns, Ambrose satisfied the requirements of quantitative meter but at the same time provided the foundation for the development of accentual iambic dimeter.

We see the same flexibility and stability in modern English hymns in Long Meter. Here are a few examples. For the most part, the second half of the line is stable, the first half may contain variation. Accented syllables are underlined.

1. "I <u>know</u> that <u>my</u> <u>Redee</u>mer <u>lives</u>" (the second, fourth, sixth, and eighth syllables are stressed).

2. "(<u>On</u>) <u>Jor</u>dan's <u>bank</u> the <u>Bap</u>tist's <u>cry</u>" (the third, fifth, and seventh syllables are unstressed; Is the first stressed or unstressed? It feels heavy because the juxtaposition of "n" of "on" with "j" of "Jordan's" requires one to pronounce "on" fully; this takes time, and so it receives a certain secondary stress accent. Also notice that "Jordan's bank" has large syllables, again *varietas*, whereas the last four

---

32. See Dag Norberg, "La Récitation," 503–4.

syllables are well within the meter. This arrangement is an accentual equivalent of quantitative iambic dimeter with a substitution on syllable 1.

3. In the hymn "All <u>people</u> that on <u>earth</u> do <u>dwell</u>," the first line is well within the meter. At stanza 4, 3, however, we find the following: "His <u>truth</u> at all <u>times</u> <u>firmly</u> <u>stood</u>." On the fifth syllable, "times" is stressed; "all" on the fourth syllable is unstressed and so "out" of the meter: *varietas*. The end, "firmly stood" is back in the meter. The effect of *varietas* here is to emphasize the abiding universality of God's truth.

4. "<u>Jesus</u> my <u>Lord</u>, my <u>God</u>, my <u>All</u>" (again the first syllable is stressed; the second, third, and fifth are unstressed. The line opens with a dactyl (long-short-short).

5. Two lines from the hymn "All Creatures of our God and King" show again that the last four syllables are set in two sequences of unstressed followed by stressed syllables, but the first four syllables are free. In (a), the first and the fourth syllables are stressed; syllable 5 feels short, as it should. In (b), the primary stress is on the third syllable; because of the stress on syllable 3, syllable 4 feels unstressed. This weak syllable 4 causes momentary uncertainty in the metrical pattern.

a) <u>Waiting</u> to <u>hush</u> our <u>final</u> <u>breath</u>
b) Let all <u>things</u> their Cre<u>a</u>tor <u>bless</u>.

METERS IN THE *LITURGIA HORARUM*

Five meters are used frequently enough in the *Liturgia Horarum* and consequently in the English *Divine Office Hymnal* to be included in a general presentation here. After a description of each meter, examples will be given from the *Hymnal*. References to the standard accounts of the individual meters for further consultation are given in the notes. The five meters are *iambic dimeter, Sapphics, iambic trimeter, trochaic tetrameter catalectic*, and *Asclepiads*.

As we have seen, Greek meters were based on long and short syllables combined with a tonal, melodic accent. The resulting meters were supple, variable, and often complex. By contrast, Latin, as we have also seen, always had a native stress accent, more or less strongly felt, linked, at a fundamental level, to the length of syllables. It also had many more long syllables than Greek. Owing to these differences and to what D. S. Raven calls the "tidy Roman mind," and perhaps to differences in function and performance,[33] Greek meters became simpler and more regular when used by Latin poets, and many of the more complex schemas of the Greek tragedians and lyric poets were never brought into Latin. The result was a poetic idiom with differing rules and more predictable metrical

---

33. Raven, *Latin Metre*, 20. See pages 19–21 for Raven's brief comparison of Greek and Roman metrical practice. See also Gratwick, "Origins of Roman Drama," 87–90.

schemas, though the basic forms and names were the same. The more regular Latin stanzas made from meters based on iambs, trochees, Sapphics, and some forms of Asclepiads became standard as they were used by Catullus, Horace, Statius, Ausonius, and others.

Hilary, Ambrose, and Prudentius adapted classical meters to Christian use, especially as they found them in Horace, and handed on a supple and living tradition of Latin quantitative verse.[34] When syllable length no longer represented a natural, instinctive use of language, hymn writers still revered the ancient models and poetic practice as they developed the new accentual versification. As a result, both quantitative and accentual meter have been in continuous use throughout the tradition of Latin hymnody. Both are found in the *Liturgia Horarum*. Examples of both will be given here.

The list below indicates symbols and metrical terms used in the following discussion and throughout the commentary. Some of these are found in the list at the beginning of the appendix. They are given here again for convenient reference.

Syllables:

⏑ : short syllable

– : long syllable

⏑̱ or x : a syllable that may be long or short, named *anceps*.

a : any syllable in a schema based on stress accent

á : a syllable that bears the stress accent

| : *cæsura*: here it indicates a small break between feet or meters, not necessarily a word break. In classical usage, it indicates a word break in the middle of a foot, or meter.

‖ : *diaresis*: here it indicates a word break in the middle of a line. In classical usage it indicates a word break that coincides with the end of a foot, or meter.

Metrical Feet and Terms:

Iamb: ⏑ –

Trochee: – ⏑

Spondee: – –

Dactyl: – ⏑ ⏑

Choriamb: – ⏑ ⏑ –

Catalectic: the final syllable of a line in a particular meter is left off.

Metrum (pl. *metra*): 2 iambic or trochaic feet, one dactyl, or one choriamb.

The numbers that appear after the name of each meter refer to the number of syllables per line and the number of lines per stanza: e.g., 8 8 8 8 signifies that each line has eight syllables and that there are four lines per stanza.

---

34. Charlet, *La Création poétique*, 37–38. See also the helpful overview of Prudentius's meters and the comments on the transition from quantitative to accentual meter in Richardson, *Hymns*, 22–26, and O'Daly, *Days Linked by Song*, 23; for an example of his evocative use of Horace, 28; for the classical sources of Prudentius's meters, 30–31.

1. **Iambic Dimeter (8 8 8 8)**

The metrical scheme is as follows:

> quantitative: ⏑ – ⏑ – | ⏑ – ⏑ –
> accentual: a á a á | a á a á
> accentual variation: á a a á | a á a á [35]

Examples of quantitative meter, from H 71 and H 80:

> regular iambs: fletuque culpa solvitur (H 71: 5, 4)
> iambs with lengthening: Telluris ingens conditor (H 80: 1, 1)

Example of accentual meter, from H 7:

> accentual: Salútis aúctor, récole (3, 1)
> variation: Chríste, redémptor ómnium (1, 1)

Ambrose used exclusively this simplest and, in a sense, most restrictive of meters. In classical Greek and Latin poetry, iambic meter was commonly used in the form of iambic trimeter (three metra of four syllables each: 12 syllables) in tragic dialogue and lyric poetry.[36] Horace used iambic trimeter alternating with iambic dimeter in couplets in his first ten epodes. Seneca used iambic dimeter alone in some passages of his plays. Ausonius, a contemporary of Ambrose, used it in letters and in his *Ephemeris* II.2.[37] The meter, therefore, was well known to Ambrose, but he transformed it into a series of uniform four-line stanzas. Each line admitted of no substitutions except for a long syllable in place of a short syllable for the first and fifth syllables of each line. There was also a break at the end of each line; enjambment (continuing a syntactic unit from one line to the next) is not a feature of this style. Stanzas of iambic dimeter, so unique to Ambrose that it was named after him, have several advantages. Hymns in this meter are easy to adapt to different melodies, clearly felt as metrical, and easy to memorize. In the hands of a good poet, the meter has a sobriety and simplicity that makes it appropriate for frequent use.[38] Since the majority of hymns in this collection are from the early centuries of the tradition, iambic dimeter is the most widely used meter in the *Liturgia Horarum*.

2. **Sapphics (11 11 11 5); named for the Greek poet Sappho, ca. 630–ca. 570 BC**

During the Carolingian renaissance, erudite members of Charlemagne's entourage began to write hymns in Sapphic meter. It represented a retrieval of the

---

35. This is only one possible variation among others. See the table of accentual versions of lines from the hymns of Ambrose given above. See also Norberg, *Introduction*, 103–104.
36. Raven, *Latin Metre*, 46–60; Allen and Greenough, *New Latin Grammar*, no. 618–19.
37. Symmachus used it also. For a discussion of the use of iambic meter by contemporaries of Ambrose, see Fontaine, 82–85.
38. Fontaine, 63–67. See also 82–92.

classical poetic heritage and was an alternative to the Ambrosian iambic dimeter. Sapphics were widely used by the Greek lyric poets and copied by Horace, Catullus, Statius, and Seneca. Prudentius also uses them in *Cathemerinon* 8 and *Peristephanon* 4. For the most part, Sapphics consisted of four-line stanzas: three lines of eleven syllables (Sapphic) and a fourth line of five syllables (Adonic).[39] In his adaptation of Greek Sapphics to Latin, Horace imposed certain restrictions that were carried over into Christian hymnody. The fourth syllable in the eleven-syllable line was always long, and the break was generally after the fifth syllable, less often after the sixth.[40] The first three lines were clearly separated, but the third and the fourth lines were regarded as closely related, and the syntactical separation between them might be slight. Horace wrote twenty-five odes in this meter as well as the *Carmen Sæculare*. The quantitative form is:

>lines 1–3: – ᴗ – – || ᴗ ᴗ – ᴗ – – (Sapphics in Horace much of the time)
>line 4: – ᴗ ᴗ – – (Adonic).

Example, from H 114:

>lines 1–3: Ecce iam noctis tenuatur umbra (1, 1)
>line 4: gloria mundum (3, 4)

The regularity of the meter inherited from Horace caused Sapphics to make the transition simply and naturally from metrical into rhythmical schemas.[41] Since the break came after the fifth syllable and since the fourth syllable was always long (and again the native Latin stress accent is never found on the final syllable of a word), more often than not the fourth syllable was read by the Carolingians and later poets as a stress accent. Similarly, the tenth syllable, the penult, was always long in quantitative Sapphics, and it would naturally have had a stress accent as well (Penult Rule). The process of reading Sapphics with a stress accent resulted in the following schema in rhythmical verse:

>lines 1–3: á a a á a || á a á a á a
>line 4: á a a á a

Example, taken from H 106:[42]

>lines 1–3: Déus, inclína pìetáte sóla (106: 1, 2)
>line 4: fámuli túi (106: 1, 4)

---

39. Allen and Greenough, *New Latin Grammar*, no. 625.6–7 and 626.2; also Raven, *Latin Metre*, 143–45, no. 139; Garrison, *Horace: Epodes and Odes*, 379–80; Allen, *Accent and Rhythm*, 347–50.

40. Statius and Seneca always had a break after the fifth syllable. Christian hymns imitated this fixed placement, Raven, *Latin Metre*, 145; Allen and Greenough, *New Latin Grammar*, 625.7; Richardson, *Hymns*, 24 and 133.

41. See Norberg, *Introduction*, 89–91.

42. A second option might arise if a line began with a one syllable word, such as in the hymn that begins "O sator rerum, reparator ævi" (H 109). The initial "O" might be felt as short, leading into "sator." The rhythmical schema would then be: a á a á a || á a á a á a. See Norberg, *Introduction*, 90.

Careful attention to the number of syllables and a regular line break after the fifth syllable led to an accented fourth syllable before the break. Similarly, the long tenth syllable in metrical Sapphics led to a stress accent on the tenth syllable at the end of the line in accentual Sapphics. The short second syllable in metrical Sapphics led to the placement of words of two or three syllables at the head of the line with a stress accent on the first syllable. Other accents readily fell into place in such a way that, for the most part, accentual Sapphics imitated strictly the structure of metrical Sapphics.[43]

3. Iambic Trimeter: 12 12 12 12; some hymns have an additional fifth line of 12

Iambic trimeter, as we saw in connection with iambic dimeter, is also a classical meter, used for dialogue in classical drama and in the Latin poets both alone and in combination with other meters.[44] Prudentius uses it in *Cathemerinon* 7. It consists of three sets of iambic *metra*. The metrical scheme is as follows:

$$\text{quantitative:} \;\; \underset{\smile}{\;\;} - \smile - \;|\; \underset{\smile}{\;\;} \;||- \smile - \;|\; \underset{\smile}{\;\;} - \smile -\;\;^{45}$$
$$\text{accentual: a á a á } | \text{ a } || \text{ á a á } | \text{ a á a á}$$
$$\text{variation: á a a á } | \text{ a } || \text{ á a á } | \text{ a á a á}$$

Lines of iambic trimeter are longer than iambic dimeter by a third. The standard practice was to place a word break in the middle of the third iamb, that is, after the fifth syllable.[46] This regularity, combined with the transition to stress accent, changed slightly the feel of the meter. The first half of the line has an accent on the fourth syllable, before the word end on the fifth. The line ends aways with a three-syllable word having the accent on the antepenult, and the final syllable. Thus, the accents on the fourth, tenth, and twelfth syllables were stable. This yields the rhythm indicated above. More often than not the sixth syllable bore either a primary or secondary accent depending on the number of syllables in the word. This gives the last half of the line a slightly trochaic feel. The salient characteristic of the accentual version of this meter is the recurring break after the fifth syllable, and the slight impression of two meters combined.[47]

In the *Liturgia Horarum*, hymns in this meter, including the hymns of Paulinus of Aquileia in stanzas of five lines, are all in a quasi-accentual configuration of this meter. Paulinus's hymns regularly combine quantitative meter with accentual meter. He was a versatile Carolingian poet. It seems that in his hymns in honor of Saints Peter and Paul he may be combining what he considers to be the best of both metrical systems.[48]

---

43. Ibid.
44. Raven, *Latin Metre*, 46–54.
45. Norberg, *Introduction*, 65–66.
46. Raven, *Latin Metre*, 52, no. 36A.
47. For a full discussion of the complexities of this meter with examples, see Norberg, *Introduction*, 105–06.
48. One may perhaps infer this from the analysis of Dag Norberg, *L'œuvre poétique de Paulin d'Aquilée*, 78–80.

Examples, taken from H 222:

    accentual meter: O Róma félix, quæ tantórum príncipùm (3, 1)
    variations : Aúrea lúce ét decóre róseò (1, 1)

4. Trochaic Tetrameter Catalectic: 87 87 87

Trochaic tetrameter catalectic was an ancient and popular meter.[49] The metrical schema is based on the *trochee*, the opposite of an iamb. As the name *tetra* indicates, there are four meters to a line, the last of which has lost the final syllable because the line has stopped one syllable short (*catalectic*). It reads: $-\cup-\cup\ |\ -\cup-\cup\ ||\ -\cup-\cup\ |\ -\cup-$. The look and feel of this meter is in general the opposite of iambic meters. Also, in a mirror image of iambic meters, a long may be substituted for the second short syllable in each group of four. The pattern looks like this: $-\cup-\underset{\smile}{-}$. Because the lines are long, they are often divided halfway through, after the eighth syllable (||) and placed on two lines. Hymns in this meter usually come in stanzas of three lines, though the division in the middle, which results in three lines of eight syllables alternating with three lines of seven syllables, gives the appearance of a six-line stanza. This is how the hymns are presented in the *Liturgia Horarum* and explains the metrical indicator: 87 87 87.

    quantitative: $-\cup-\underset{\smile}{-}\ |\ -\cup-\underset{\smile}{-}\ ||\ -\cup-\underset{\smile}{-}\ |\ -\cup-$
    accentual: á a á a | á a á a || á a á a | á a á[50]

Examples from H 32 and H 141:

    quantitative: Crux fidélis inter omnes, || arbor una nóbilis! (H 33: 3, 1–2)
quant. with extra longs: et sŭper crucis trŏpæo || dic trĭumphum nobĭlem (H 32: 1, 3–4)[51]
    accentual: Urbs Ierúsalem beáta, || dícta pácis visiò (H 141: 1, 1–2)
    variations in accent: pláteæ et múri éius || ex aúro puríssimò (H 141: 2, 5–6)

The metrical schema is such that a stress accent normally coincides with long syllables.[52] This yields a clearly defined rhythmic quality, reinforced by the strong division coinciding with a word ending halfway through. The result is a regular, rhythmic binary meter, well suited to movement, as in marching and processions. The meter was used in Roman comedy, imperial triumphs (*carmina triumphalia*), in military marching songs, and later by Christian poets for processional hymns. Venantius Fortunatus's *Pange, lingua, gloriosi prœlium certaminis* (H 32), composed for the procession that brought the relic of the true cross—a triumphal procession—into the city of Poitiers, is a prime example. Two hundred years earlier, Hilary of Poitiers had used this meter to celebrate the triumph of Christ over death. Prudentius used it in *Cathemerinon* 9 to recount the glorious deeds

---

49. Raven, *Latin Metre*, 74–82; Norberg, *Introduction*, 67–71.
50. Norberg, *Introduction*, 106–11. For variations in the accentual versions, see the examples on page 109. Again, it is the first part of the line that tends to vary.
51. Most syllables in this line are long. Short syllables have a breve (ă) over them.
52. Norberg, *Introduction*, 68; Fontaine, "Quelques vicissitudes," 351.

(the *res gestæ*) of Christ and to celebrate his victory over sin and hell. Prudentius also opens his *Peristephanon*, a collection dedicated to the martyrs, with this same meter to tell the story of two soldiers who, leaving the standard of Cæsar for the Cross of Christ, triumphed through their sufferings over Satan and death just as Christ had done.[53]

5. Asclepiads: 12 12 12 8 (named for Asclepiades of Samos, ca. 300 BC)

The Asclepiads represent a "family" of Greek meters, which were adapted to Latin and used by Horace. Prudentius, in turn, followed Horace and brought them into the tradition of Christian hymnody. *Cathemerinon* 5 is in this type of meter. All Asclepiads are based on the *choriamb*, the nucleus to which syllables were added before and after.[54] The *Glyconic* (named after the fourth-century Greek lyric poet) had one choriamb, a head of two longs and a tail of one short plus one long. The lines properly named *Asclepiad* added extra choriambs. A lesser Asclepiad adds one choriamb; a greater adds two. The schema used in the hymns of the *Liturgia Horarum* is a four-line stanza based on three lesser Asclepiads followed by one Glyconic.

+ Lesser Asclepiad: two choriambs preceded by two longs and followed by one short plus one long. It has a regular word break after the sixth syllable:

$$-\,-\ |\ -\,\cup\,\cup\,-\ \|\ -\,\cup\,\cup\,-\ |\ \cup\,-\,{}^{55}$$

+ Glyconic: one choriamb preceded by two longs and followed by one short plus one long:

$$-\,-\ |\ -\,\cup\,\cup\,-\ |\ \cup\,-$$

+ The meter of our hymns is as follows: three lines of lesser Asclepiads followed by one Glyconic:

$$\begin{array}{l} -\,-\ |\ -\,\cup\,\cup\,-\ \|\ -\,\cup\,\cup\,-\ |\ \cup\,-\ \text{(lesser Asclepiad)} \\ -\,-\ |\ -\,\cup\,\cup\,-\ \|\ -\,\cup\,\cup\,-\ |\ \cup\,- \\ -\,-\ |\ -\,\cup\,\cup\,-\ \|\ -\,\cup\,\cup\,-\ |\ \cup\,- \\ -\,-\ |\ -\,\cup\,\cup\,-\ |\ \cup\,-\ \text{(Glyconic)} \end{array}$$

Example, from the *Liturgia Horarum*, H 154: 1, lines 2 and 4:

twelve-syllable line: <u>pangá</u>mus (3 longs) soci<u>ī</u> gés<u>ta</u>que <u>fór</u>tia[56]
eight-syllable line: <u>victó</u>rum (3 longs) genus <u>optí</u>mum

---

53. Fontaine, "Quelques vicissitudes," 352–53; Richardson, *Hymns*, 24–25.
54. "Nucleus" is Raven's term, *Latin Metre*, 133ff. Dane, in *The Long and the Short of It*, 31ff., gives a good summary of Raven. Note that numbering systems differ. See also Gildersleeve and Lodge, *Latin Grammar*, nos. 801–03; Nisbet and Hubbard, *Commentary on Horace*, xxxviii–xxxix. Please note that these lines are divided differently by scholars. Here, the divisions are added to show clearly the rhythmical structure based on the *choriamb*.
55. In the Greek meters the leading syllables, the "head," could be resolved in various ways. Horace stabilized it into two longs.
56. *pangámus* (3 longs), *sociī* (short, short, long), *géstaque* (long, short, short), *fórtia* (long, short, long)

Asclepiads, both quantitative and rhythmic, were commonly used throughout the Middle Ages and beyond.[57] Five hymns in the *Liturgia Horarum* have this meter. Four of them are in quantitative verse. One is a medieval adaptation in accentual meter. These hymns span the centuries from the Carolingian era through the twentieth century. They are as follows:

1. *Sanctorum meritis* (attributed to Rabanus Maurus, d. 856), H 154.
2. *Sacris solemniis* (St. Thomas Aquinas, d. 1274), H 128.
3. *Custodes hominum* (St. Robert Bellarmine, d. 1621), H 269.
4. *Te Ioseph celebrent* (Girolamo Casanante, d. 1700), H 200.
5. *Festiva canimus* (Anselmo Lentini, d. 1989), H 266.

Four of the hymns (nos. 1, 3, 4, and 5 above) represent the unbroken tradition of writing hymns in quantitative meter. They are a reminder that throughout the corpus of the *Liturgia Horarum* one will find hymns from every era composed, partially or wholly, in quantitative meter. The structure of the English language and the heavy stress accent native to English make it difficult to transfer quantitative meter into English. Experiments were made during the Renaissance by poets such as Thomas Campion, Philip Sidney, and others; but the effort was abandoned, in part because syllable length or weight is too ambiguous in English.[58] In the four hymns in quantitative Asclepiads, the ICEL translators have endeavored to preserve to the degree possible the "feel" of the quantitative meter. Aquinas's adaptation is based on stress accent alone and has been translated in accentual meter, essentially a series of four dactyls per line: á a a á a a ‖ á a a á a a (*panis angelicus fit panis hominum*). This accentual adaptation resulted from the same process of attending only to stress accents when one recited quantitative Asclepiads. Because there was always a break in the middle of the line, and the two halves of the line had the same number of syllables, the two halves gradually coalesced into two iterations of the same pattern.[59] In this way, through a process of repeated aural recitation, the quantitative form was transformed into the regular schema we find in Aquinas. Aquinas emphasizes the break after the sixth syllable with an elaborate double rhyme scheme.

6. Other Meters in the *Liturgia Horarum*

Other meters found in the *Liturgia Horarum* represent, for the most part, variations on the meters considered in this appendix. For example, two hymns, *Christe, splendor Patris* (H 12) and *Ave, maris stella* (H 145), have lines consisting of three *trochees* in four-line stanzas. Others that originated as sequences but are used as hymns in the *Liturgia Horarum* will be explained in detail in the commentaries on individual hymns.

---

57. Norberg, *Introduction*, 74–75; 93–95.
58. Hanson, "Quantitative Meter in English" 51.
59. For details, see Norberg, *Introduction*, 94–95.

APPENDIX II

Assonance, Alliteration, and Rhyme

A LIST OF TERMS

1. *Alliteration*: the repetition of a sound (a letter or syllable) at the beginning of successive words or phrases. An English example is the sound "sh" in the following lines from A. E. Housman (*The Oracles*, 7–8):

> And from the cave of oracles I hear the priestess shrieking
> That she and I should surely die and never live again.

2. *Assonance*: the practice of repeating similar vowel sounds either in prose or poetry for rhetorical effect. An English example is the long "ee" sound in the following lines from Emily Dickenson (no. 162, *My River Runs to Thee*, 1–2, 7):

> My River runs to thee—
> Blue Sea—Wilt welcome me? ...
> Say Sea, take me.

3. *Consonance*: the practice of repeating similar consonant sounds either in prose or poetry for rhetorical effect. An English example is the sound of "s" in the following line: "Increasing store with loss and loss with store" (Shakespeare, Sonnet 64.8).

4. *Rhyme*: the repetition of syllables at the end of a phrase or line of poetry. Rhymes may be of one or of two or more syllables. In the following example, "leaping" and "sleeping" are a two-syllable rhyme; "laid" and "fade" are one-syllable (A. E. Housman, *A Shropshire Lad*, no. 54):

> By brooks too broad for leaping
> The lightfoot boys are laid;
> The rose-lipt girls are sleeping
> In fields where roses fade.

5. *Melisma*: a group of more than five or six notes sung to a single syllable. The term is used primarily with reference to Gregorian chant to designate long series of notes sung on one syllable of a text, such as the final "a" of Alleluia. Melismatic song is the opposite of syllabic (one note to one syllable).

6. *Iamb*: a metrical foot consisting of two syllables in which the first syllable is short, or weak, and the second long, or stressed. An English example is the word *revolt*.

7. *Trochee*: a metrical foot consisting of two syllables in which the first syllable is long, or stressed, and the second short, or weak. An English example is the word *glory*.

8. *Pyrrhic*: a metrical foot consisting of two short, or weak, syllables. It is fairly common in Greek and Latin poetry. In English, it refers more often to syllables and words in a line of verse alternating with other types of meter; for example, "To a green thought in a green shade" (Andrew Marvel, "The Garden"): "to a" and "in a" are pyrrhics. Another example might be the word "edit"; though there is a slight stress on the first syllable, both are short.

9. *Cretic*: a metrical foot consisting of three syllables in which the first is long, or stressed, the second is short, or weak, and the third is long, or stressed. An English example is "Over hill, over dale" (Shakespeare, *A Midsummer Night's Dream*, act 1, scene 2).

10. *Hiatus*: a pause or break in sound caused in a line of verse by two adjacent vowels pronounced separately. An English example is the word "cooperate."

11. *Elision*: the opposite of hiatus. It consists in the removal of sounds or vowels in speech or in a line of poetry. An English example is the reduction of the three-syllable word "every" to two syllables (pronounced and written "ev'ry" or "every"). In texts and translations of liturgical hymns, both forms may be found. In this commentary, since hymn texts are given without musical notation, italics are used. In notated English hymnals, apostrophes are generally preferred.

HISTORICAL DEVELOPMENT OF HYMNS

The Latin hymns in the *Liturgia Horarum* span seventeen centuries of poetic composition. Although music and poetry changed dramatically over the course of these centuries, the genre of liturgical hymnody composed for and consistently used in the Divine Office displayed a high level of continuity. The purposes for which these hymns were written and sung, as well as the liturgical life of monastic communities and cathedrals, helped to maintain this continuity. These hymns are some of the finest examples of the thousands of hymns produced from the fourth century onward. They tell the story of the development of the hymn from the quantitative iambic dimeters of St. Ambrose to the rhyming sequences of the thirteenth century, and finally they tell of the return to a preference for quantitative meter in the modern era.

This evolution is extremely complex, marked by differences in function, region, cultural priorities, musical innovations, and other factors that partially escape the historical record. The Middle Ages was a time marked by an effort to conserve the culture received from classical antiquity and the models received from the early centuries of the Church; but it was also marked by magnificent innovation. Both of these influences require careful consideration on the part of the modern historian. This appendix can only briefly describe some of the historical developments as they pertain to the hymns of the *Liturgia Horarum*. These hymns, however, open doors onto a world about which many questions remain to be answered. It will be helpful to divide the consideration of this long development into external and internal factors and influences. External factors are the historical developments that were more or less parallel to the development of hymns and that had a collateral effect on them. The internal factors are literary and textual developments as well as precedents from the past that influenced the composition of the hymn texts.[1]

EXTERNAL FACTORS

In 751 Pepin the Short, father of Charlemagne, became King of the Franks with the support of Pope Zachary (d. 751). In 752, the new pope, Stephen, appealed to Pepin for help against the Lombards. This inaugurated an exchange of protection and privileges that created the foundation of the Papal States and led to Charlemagne's coronation as Holy Roman Emperor at St. Peter's in Rome on Christmas Day, 800. In 754 Pope Stephen visited Pepin's court bringing with him a retinue of clergy, liturgical books having texts only, and chant masters who could pass on the oral chant tradition as it was practiced at Rome. As a result of this visit, Pepin implemented the use of Roman chant throughout his kingdom, and Charlemagne continued his father's policies.[2] Charlemagne (d. 814) and his successors surrounded themselves with intelligent, well-educated, and able advisers. The Carolingian reforms of liturgical and monastic life, both of which had an effect on the hymns, originated in court and monastic circles, and they were implemented in a deliberate manner; this was not a grass-roots movement.

The century between 750 and 850 is marked both by reverence for the received tradition and by immense creativity. The Franks profoundly assimilated, integrated, and transformed the Roman chant they had received.[3] By the second half of the ninth century, in both East and West Francia, a region covering roughly France, Belgium, Germany, and Switzerland, they had begun to develop new musical forms based on the chants of the Mass and the Divine Office. For the feasts

---

1. This account is based on numerous resources. Some of the more general sources are Norberg, *Introduction*, 81ff.; Sedgwick, "The Origin of Rhyme," 330–46; Caldwell, "Rhythm and Meter," in *The Cambridge History of Medieval Music*, 718–46; chapters on "Medieval Chant" and "Monophony" by Crocker, in *Oxford History of Music*, 2:121–307, especially 225ff. More detailed resources include Fassler, *Music in the Medieval West* and *Gothic Song*; and Bower, *Liber Ymnorum*. Bower gives a magisterial presentation of Notker's sequences, with analysis, translation, and musical settings.

2. The continuity between the Old Roman Chant, as it was later called, and Gregorian (Frankish) Chant is real and visible in the underlying structure of the melodies, as well as in the choice of texts set to music. The two traditions have been called "dialects" of the same language. Nevertheless, what the Franks received were books containing texts accompanied by chant masters from the Roman *schola cantorum*. It was an oral tradition. By the late 8th c. the legend of Gregory the Great had grown to such an extent that he was the established authority for liturgical texts (and music, though there is lithe evidence for this); a Roman antiphoner and sacramentary appear to have been brought from Rome into Gaul under his name. (See Hiley, Western Plainchant, 503–23). The fidelity of the Franks to the tradition received from Rome was remarkable, but creative, and subject to variation and change. "Old Roman Chant" is a misnomer, since the written sources for the Roman chant date from the eleventh to the thirteenth centuries, over three hundred years after its importation into the Frankish kingdom. The written versions of the Old Roman Chant bear the marks of a longstanding oral tradition.

3. Crocker, "Medieval Chant," 227–28.

of the liturgical year, they embellished the chants with melismatic passages and with supplementary Latin texts either added between elements of liturgical texts or set to the melodies of elaborate melismas.

Thus, over the course of the Middle Ages, the core of liturgical texts for the Mass and the Divine Office became the trunk of a great tree that prospered into a proliferation of forms that began as commentaries on the venerable host texts; but eventually took on a musical and textual life of their own. Many terms were used to describe these new compositions: *sequence, prosæ, prosulæ, trope,* and *versus* all signify varied compositions of text and music brought into the liturgy as an elaboration of the traditional chants. The wealth of this textual and musical commentary on the liturgy is astonishing; it is the reflection of a culture deeply and creatively rooted in the Scriptures and the distillation of sacred texts through a profound and shared liturgical life. Some of these developments will be presented here to the degree that they contribute to the hymns in the *Liturgia Horarum*.

Tropes (additions of both text and music) were inserted into or added to the chants, and *prosulæ* (little *prosæ*: textual additions to preexisting music)[4] were attached to melismatic passages in chants, such as the *Kyrie, Sanctus,* and *Agnus Dei*. They were like a running commentary or gloss on the texts to which they were attached.[5] Whole sections of *tropes* are found in medieval manuscripts. The Marian antiphon *Salve, Regina* received tropes on the final verses, some of which are included as a hymn in the *Liturgia Horarum* for the feast of the Presentation of Mary. *Salve, mater misericordiæ* (H 282) begins:

Salve, mater misericórdiæ,	Hail, O Mother, gracious and merciful,
mater spei et mater véniæ,	Mother of hope, Mother of clemency,
mater Dei et mater grátiæ,	Mother of God, Mother of every[6] grace,
mater plena sanctæ lætítiæ.	Blessed Mother, filled with all holy joy.
(O María.)	(O María.)

The term *versus* had a number of meanings; but it seems to refer to tropes that were marked by clearly discernible patterns of stress accents and regular rhyme schemes. In an eleventh-century manuscript from St. Martial, in Aquitaine, there is a rhythmical *versus* that ends: *ergo nos puro animo / Benedicamus Domino*.[7] This versus would have been inserted at the end of the Office to embellish the normal conclusion: V. *Benedicamus Domino*, R. *Deo gratias*. Notker Balbulus (d. 912), a monk of St. Gall, now in Switzerland, also uses the term for poetic lines he found in a manuscript from Jumièges (Normandy). It may be synonymous with *prosa*, a term used in other manuscripts.[8]

Sequences (the standard name used by modern scholars and liturgists) were texts set to the long "sequences" of notes at the end of the *Alleluia* in what is called

---

4. This distinction is from Fassler, *Music*, 67.
5. See Dag Norberg, *Manuel*, 62–67; also Fassler, *Music*, 70–71.
6. Elided syllables are in italics when the hymn text appears without music. With music, an apostrophe is generally used.
7. "Therefore, we with a pure soul / let us bless the Lord"; quoted by Crocker in the article on "Versus," *New Grove Dictionary of Music*.
8. Bower, *Liber Ymnorum*, 3–4.

the *jubilus*. Some of those used for special feasts could be long and elaborate; and, according to the account given by Notker, they were difficult to remember. Though sequences existed before Notker, he is considered the "father" of the genre that developed after his immensely creative work. Margot Fassler comments:

> A Notkerian sequence is a magnificent liturgical song by one of the greatest poets of the Middle Ages, rich with Biblical allusions and festive resonance. The poetry is expressed in a kind of heightened prose and unfolds with a single line of text followed by couplets of varying lengths.[9]

The genre of sequences proliferated from the ninth century onward. In the twelfth century, in the wake of the Gregorian reforms (Gregory VII), sequences developed into regular compositions set to newly composed melodies and organized into regular metrical stanzas of varying lengths; every group of two stanzas was sung to the same melody. This pattern of aa bb cc, etc., was similar to the old Notkerian sequences, and they retained their association with the *Alleluia* at Mass; but the overall structure of late sequences began to resemble that of hymns.[10] Several late sequences are found in the *Liturgia Horarum*: *Lux iucunda, lux insignis* (H 56) and *Salve dies, dierum gloria* (H 98), both by Adam of St. Victor, d. 1146; *Dies iræ, dies illa* (H 136–38); and *Stabat mater dolorosa* (H 259–61).[11]

Following are two examples, one taken from an early sequence by Notker, the other from a late sequence by Adam of St. Victor. Though they are both recognizable as sequences, the difference between them is marked. The lines given below are from Notker's sequence, *Psallat ecclesia*, set to the *jubilus* after the *Alleluia* for the Dedication of a Church. Notker considered it to be the mature and refined culmination of his earlier efforts.[12] It is marked by parallelism, assonance, alliteration, and the rhetorical use of rhyme.

Alleluia	**Alleluia**[13]
Psallat ecclésia,	Let the church sing psalms,
mater illibata…	mother unblemished…
8a. Hic novam prolem grátia párturit	8a Here grace brings forth new offspring
8b. fœcúnda Spíritu Sancto:	8b made fruitful by the Holy Spirit.
9a. Ángeli cives vísitant hic suos	9a Angels visit their fellow-citizens,
9b. et corpus súmitur Iesu.	9b and the body of Jesus is received.
10. Fúgiunt univérsa córpori nócua:	10 All things noxious to the body flee;
11. Péreunt peccatrícis ánimæ crímina.	11 The crimes of the sinful soul perish.
12. Hic vox lætítiæ pérsonat:	12 Here the music of gladness resounds;
13. Hic pax et gaúdia rédundant.	13 Here peace and joys overflow.
14a Hac domo Trinitati laus et gloria	14a In this house praise and glory
14b semper resultant.	14b re-echo to the Trinity without end.

---

9. Fassler, *Music*, 73, and 71–74.
10. See Fassler, *Gothic Song*, 69–73, and the entire discussion of ch. 4, 58–82.
11. These two sequences are both divided into three separate hymns in the *Liturgia Horarum*.
12. See Bower, *Liber Ymnorum*, no. 37, pp. 252–54; see also Notker's reference to this sequence in his *dedicatio*, p. 130, with Bower's commentary, pp. 14–16.
13. The translation given here is from Bower, *Liber Ymnorum*, 162–63, with light editing, in order to make it more literal for our purposes here, at the cost of smooth English word order.

Lines are paired into couplets of varying lengths, but each couplet has the same number of syllables, the same rhythmical meter, and the same melody. A couplet may or may not have subdivisions. Thus, 8a and 8b with 9a and 9b form a couplet, while 10 and 11 form a couplet but without internal subdivisions into parts a and b. Though regular rhyme schemes are absent, there is a fair amount of assonance, and even some one-syllable rhyme (*nocua* and *crimina*), at the end of lines 10 through 14b. Lines 12 to 14a also have alliteration (*anaphora*) on *Hic* and *Hac* and consonance on the syllables *vox* and *pax*.

This sequence is a work of high art and filled with many of the same rhetorical features one finds in contemporary hymns. Later sequences had regular meter and rhyme throughout; these became fixed structural principles of poetic composition, rather than rhetorical and poetic ornament. The sequences continued to be sung in couplets, where hymns were always sung in repeating stanzas, and the melodic range in sequences was greater than in hymns. In many respects, however, poetic technique is similar in both.[14] A brief look at stanzas from Adam of St. Victor's *Salve dies, dierum gloria* (H 98) will show the difference between Notker and Adam:

Resurréxit liber ab ínferis restaurátor humáni géneris, ovem suam repórtans úmeris ad supérna.	He is risen, free from the power of hell, great restorer of the whole human race, on his shoulders bearing his wayward sheep up to heaven.
Angelórum pax fit et hóminum, plenitúdo succréscit órdinum, triumphántem laus decet Dóminum, laus ætérna.	Peace of angels graces the human race; ranks of heaven grow and fill up again; praise is fitting to our triumphant Lord, praise eternal.
Harmóniæ cæléstis pátriæ vox concórdet matris Ecclésiæ, "Allelúia" frequéntet hódie plebs fidélis.	Let the Church our Mother now raise her voice with the choirs of heaven in harmony. Let the faithful cry out with joy this day: Alleluia!
Triumpháto mortis império, triumpháli fruámur gáudio; in terra pax, et iubilátio sit in cælis. Amen.	Death is conquered, vanquished and powerless; with delight let all sing in victory: Peace on earth, and let jubilation ring in high heaven. Amen.

Four stanzas of the sequence as it is found in the *Liturgia Horarum* are given here, in order to show the double rhyme scheme that joins couplets set to the same melody. Each half of a couplet has a series of three (or more) long lines of ten syllables made of two trochees and two dactyls: $-\cup-\cup-\cup\cup-\cup$. These are followed by a short line of four syllables made of two trochees: $-\cup-\cup$. The first

---

14. See Fassler, *Medieval Song*, 72–73.

three lines end with a three-syllable word having strict two-syllable rhyme; the final syllables of fourth line differ from the other lines of the stanza but match the fourth line of its musical pair in the couplet. Thus, *superna* (line 4 above) rhymes with *æterna* (line 8), and *fidelis* (line 12) rhymes with *cælis* (line 16). Again, rhyme is no longer an ornament; it has become a structural element of the sequence.

During the Middle Ages, the sequence was never more than one form among others, but its alignment of accentual rhythm with regular rhyme influenced late medieval hymnody.[15] A comparison of two of the finest liturgical hymns is instructive. *Pange, lingua, gloriosi prœlium certaminis*, by Venantius Fortunatus (d. ca. 600), and *Pange, lingua, gloriosi corporis mysterium*, by St. Thomas Aquinas (d. 1274), are in the same meter, and by using the same opening line St. Thomas consciously created a link between his own hymn (on the Eucharist) and that of Fortunatus (on the Cross). The earlier hymn has beautiful rich meter and imagery but no rhyme whatever; the later hymn is in strict two-syllable rhyme throughout. Here is the first stanza from each hymn:

Venantius Fortunatus (H 32)	*St. Thomas Aquinas* (H 127)
Pange, lingua, gloriósi	Pange, lingua, gloriósi
proélium certáminis,	córporis mystérium,
et super crucis tropǽo	sanguinísque pretiósi,
dic triúmphum nóbilem,	quem in mundi prétium
quáliter redémptor orbis	fructus ventris generósi
immolátus vícerit.	Rex effúdit géntium.

The use of assonance and rhyme throughout the Middle Ages was a much wider phenomenon than what we can see in liturgical sequences, tropes, and other forms of verse.[16] There seems to have been a general delight in formal elements that come from the sound and color of words both in Latin texts and in the rising vernaculars. It culminated in the late sequences and then in the works of poets such as Dante (d. 1321) and Chaucer (d. 1400). These elements will be points of interest throughout the volumes of this commentary, but it is necessary to remember that often these techniques are subtler and more organic to the texts than clear and pronounced structural rhymes. There is a tendency among English speakers to think that if a hymn does not rhyme, it is not a good hymn. The medieval poets would not necessarily agree. They knew only too well that Bede was right when he said that the common poets inevitably do it poorly.[17] Before we look at the internal factors that influenced the tradition of hymnody, it might be helpful to look briefly at several hymns that use the techniques under discussion freely but exceptionally well.

---

15. See Raby, *History of Christian Latin Poetry*, 20–28.
16. This discussion is beyond the scope of this appendix, but Old English and Irish hymns and texts generally are filled with the elements under discussion here.
17. See the excerpt from Bede's *De arte metrica* at the end of this appendix.

In the fifth-century rhythmical hymn for Easter, *Aurora lucis rutilat* (H 46), the strong assonance in the first stanza on *rutilat*, *iubilat*, and *ululat* encapsulates the essence of Easter morning. The disciples awake with the ruddy dawn (*rutilat*) to the news of the resurrection; they exult (*iubilat*) with joy, and the devil howls in hell (*ululat*). The tenth-century hymn for Lent, *Nunc tempus acceptabile* (H 25), has no appreciable rhyme scheme, though it has rhetorical alliteration, assonance, and consonance; for example, *dum corda culpis saucia* "while hearts wounded by faults…" (2, 3). The eighth-century hymn for the Ascension *Iesu, nostra redemptio* (H 52) has a fair amount of assonance and rhyme that adds color without forming a consistent pattern. Lines 3–4 in stanza 1 are striking in their structure, which is reinforced by a one-syllable rhyme at the end:

> Deus creátor ómnium,   true God, Creator of all things,
> homo in fine témporum   true Man beyond the end of time,

The hymn is addressed to Christ at the moment of his Ascension into Heaven. These two lines are vertically balanced in a way that emphasizes by graphic syntax the mystery of the feast. *Deus* is at the beginning of line 3; *homo* is placed directly under it at the beginning of line 4. At the end of each line, *omnium* and *temporum* are also stacked one above the other, and, finally, stacked in the middle we have *creator* and *in fine*. The two lines have exactly the same rhythm: two-syllable words at the head of the line, followed by rhythmical units with the stress accent on the middle syllable ("a" of *creatore* and "fi" of *in fine*), and finally three-syllable words with the accent on the first syllable. Christ is both God and Man. As God, he is *creator of all things*, and as Man, he comes *in fine temporum*, that is, in the last age of the temporal order. The two natures of Christ are beautifully expressed by the structure and resonance of the lines in a hymn for the feast commemorating the moment when at the Ascension, Christ as our Shepherd and Forerunner unites forever and definitively, with immense consequences for us, his divine nature with our humanity. This mystery is captured by the structure and content of lines 3–4 of the hymn. Finally, a hymn by Peter Damian (d. 1072), *Excelsam Pauli gloriam* (H 193), has a mix of alliteration, assonance and one-syllable rhyme that builds up vivid imagery of sowing and reaping that fills up the barns and granaries of heaven:

> Dum verbi spargit sémina,   Then, as he sowed the word in seed,
> seges surgit ubérrima;   the harvest grew with richest grain,
> sic cæli replent hórreum   and so the barns of heaven filled
> bonórum fruges óperum.   with fruit of good and holy works
>   (H 193: 4, 1–4)

Engaging as these rhetorical features are, one must bear in mind that in every epoch, Latin hymns have line endings that look alike merely because Latin is an inflected language. These are cases of "accidental" assonance or rhyme. Words ending in the same case, or infinitives of the same conjugation, and many other similar forms necessarily have like endings. In the following stanza from a hymn attributed to Gregory the Great, *Lucis creator optime* (H 72), there are two sets of "rhyme." In lines 1 and 2 the rhyme is the result of two ablatives and governed by the sense. In lines 3 and 4, it is the result of two verbs in the third person singular, again governed by a singular subject (*mens*) and required by the sense.

Ne mens graváta crímine	Let not our soul, weighed down by faults,
vitæ sit exsul múnere,	be exiled from the gift of life
dum nil perénne cógitat	and, heedless of eternal good,
seséque culpis ílligat.	ensnare itself in bonds of guilt.

The examples above show that the various literary devices included under the general headings of assonance, consonance, alliteration, and rhyme could be used with great skill and finesse by the poets who composed hymns, sequences, and the ever-expanding musical and poetic repertoire of the Middle Ages. They also show the immense variety and subtlety that could mark these compositions, as well as elements of delight and humor often characteristic of medieval artistic endeavor. Liturgical hymns remained a conservative genre, tied as they were to the formal prayers and celebrations of the Church, but within this framework, as a genre, they remained free of restrictive literary conventions. As we shall see, this is due in part to the nature and suppleness of the Latin language. It is due also to questions of taste.

INTERNAL FACTORS

There are also elements internal to the literary tradition of Western hymnody that led to or at least invited the use of assonance and rhyme. As with other questions surrounding the growth of early and medieval hymns, an account of this development is difficult in part because many early texts have been lost, information about the music to which they were set is mostly lacking, and medieval treatises dealing with music are primarily concerned with it as a liberal art and thus too theoretical to provide much detailed information about the development of composition techniques and performance practice.[18] There are some factors, however, that partially explain why and how the rhyming hymn developed. Three of them will be considered here: (1) the legacy of the ancient poets, who were read in the schools and used as models throughout the Middle Ages; (2) the close connection between native stress accent and quantity of syllables (the Penult Rule) even in accentual versification; and (3) traces in the hymn texts and comments of theorists that may signal the importance of sound in the composition of hymn

---

18. Since music was one of the liberal arts, it was presented in a highly theoretical manner; see, for instance, the discussion of mathematical ratios and proportions of intervals in Boethius's *De institutione musica*, a canonical text throughout the Middle Ages. See Thomas Christensen, "Music Theory," in *The Cambridge History of Medieval Music*, 59–61.

texts—they were composed to be sung. Musical structure based on cadences and on what the ear hears, in the absence of a native instinct for quantitative meter, would perhaps invite assonance and rhyme, a greater focus on what the fourteenth-century anonymous author of *Tria Sunt* may mean when he speaks of *colores verborum*, "the colors of words."[19]

1. The Legacy of the Poets

The first internal factor is the legacy of the ancient poets. Classical authors continued to be read throughout the Middle Ages. Virgil and others were studied, analyzed, and revered. What may have been an occasional use for the ancients could become a precedent for the medieval poet. There are plenty of instances of assonance and rhyme in the classical authors. To take one of the greatest examples, in Virgil's fourth Eclogue, we find lines such as this:

> ipsæ lacte domum referent distenta capellæ
> ubera, nec magnos metuent armenta leones.
> ipsa tibi blandos fundent cunabula flores.
>
> Of their own accord, the she-goats shall bring home udders swollen with milk
> nor shall the flocks fear the monstrous lions.
> Your very cradle shall pour forth flowers to charm and delight you.[20]

The same vowel sounds are repeated in line 1; in lines 2–3, the same sounds are stacked on top of each other, at the same place in each line. R. G. Austin, who quotes these lines, argues that in this Eclogue, Virgil intends to prophesy in the manner of the Sibylline oracles; hence the subtle and elegant hint of an incantation in the repetitive assonance.[21] Without an excessive uniformity that would cause annoyance, the same vowel sounds are repeated in each line and at the same position in successive lines. Generations of Christians read this Eclogue throughout the Middle Ages, since they considered it to be a prophecy of the Messiah. It is no surprise, therefore, to find the same type of assonance in Christian hymns; for example, the first stanza from the Advent hymn *Vox clara ecce intonat* (H 3). Lentini opted for the Urbanite reworking of the third line, which removed the assonance. The original line 3, restored here, shows the intention of the tenth-century author:

Vox clara ecce íntonat,	Behold a voice resounding, clear,
obscúra quæque íncrepat:	rebuking hidden fears and deeds:
pellantur eminus sómnia;	Let dreams be driven far away,
ab æthre Christus prómicat.	for Christ shines forth from heaven's height

In lines 1–2, there is a series of four assonances at identical positions in each line. In lines 3–4, there is a series of two assonances in the same positions in each line.

---

19. *Tria Sunt: An Art of Poetry and Prose*, 13.4, p. 378.
20. Virgil, *Eclogues* 4.21–23; see the commentary of Coleman, *Virgil, Eclogues*, 136–37.
21. Austin, "Virgil and the Sybil," 101.

This is the same procedure as in Virgil above.[22] Finally, lines 1, 2, and 4 have a simple one-syllable end rhyme. Line 3 ends slightly differently but is in assonance with the others.

Here is a magnificent example of a subtle use of assonance and rhyme worthy of the fourth Eclogue. It is found in the fifth stanza of Ambrose's *Splendor paternæ gloriæ* (H 75):

Mentem gubérnet et regat	May he direct and rule our minds,
casto, fidéli córpore;	in bodies faithful, chaste, and pure;
fides calóre férveat,	may faith enkindled never know
fraudis venéna nésciat.	the deadly poison of deceit.

The subject of the verbs in line 1 is God the Father, mentioned in an earlier stanza. The subject of the verbs in lines 3 and 4 is *fides*, in line 3. Notice that lines 2 and 3 have three words each, and they form an interlocking alliteration on c-f-c and f-c-f. Line 4 begins with another f. The assonance (and consonance) comes from the repetition of *ca* and *fi*; *fr* and *fer*; multiple repetitions of *the* same consonantal sounds. Finally, lines 1, 3, and 4 end with *at*. The rhetorical use of alliteration and assonance establishes a close and multivalent relationship between words and ideas, which adds intensity to the prayer. This stanza will be discussed in greater detail in the body of the commentary, but consider here that *casto corpore* makes sense, but does *fideli corpore*? *fideli* is inserted between *casto* and *corpore*, and also linked by sense to *fides*. Perhaps it is *fides* that in the final analysis gives chastity and integrity to our bodies. The words beginning with *c* read: *casto, calore, corpore*, and the word beginning with *f* read: *fides, fideli, ferveat*. The verbs *ferveat* and *nesciat* stand in identical metrical positions and they evoke some kind of opposition; *venena* (poison) cools *calor* (both are in the same metrical position in lines 3 and 4). *Splendor paternæ gloriæ* is not a rhyming hymn; but Ambrose has spun a beautiful, evocative web by the rhetorical use of alliteration, assonance, and simple end rhyme.

Austin concludes his article on Virgilian assonance with this comment:

> [Virgil] is in reality the most rhetorical of all the classical Latin poets because he uses rhetoric in the best way, having the skill to avoid the monotony and blatancy of excess in a manner for which neither Ovid nor even Lucan had the power. And it is that skill which points the way to all that is best in the work of the Christian poets in a later age: they stand at one end of the history of Latin verse, Virgil is pre-eminent at the other, and between them is a real link.[23]

In the verse of both Virgil and Ambrose assonance and rhyme are present without becoming a commanding element in the poetic structure. As Austin notes, their poetry never degenerates into anything the ear would find annoying

---

22. See also Stevens, *Words and Music in the Middle Ages*, 88, where he shows multiple assonances in pairs of stanzas in a sequence.

23. Austin, "Virgilian Assonance," 55.

or even particularly regular. As the new literary and musical forms created in the ninth and tenth centuries came to maturity in the later Middle Ages, however, the use of assonance and rhyme in prose as well as poetry became standard and ubiquitous. In the great poets and writers, it could be fresh and vigorous. Mary Carruthers offers an interesting insight into this cultural propensity to rhyme in her analysis of the prayers of St. Anselm of Canterbury (d. 1109). She says, "This common feature of medieval Latin seems almost to embarrass even sympathetic scholars.... But exactly this deconstructive word play ... makes pieces of prose text readily memorable. And without memory there is no meditation."[24]

2. The Connection between Native Stress Accent and the Quantity of Syllables

The second factor is the connection between stress accent and syllable length, or the lack of it. Accentual meter based on stress seems to have opened the way to a regular use of assonance and rhyme, and there seem to be two reasons for this. First, where quantitative meter was based on the subtle differences in vowel length and the variety caused by the interplay of *ictus* with stress accent, the loss of an awareness of syllable length introduced a measure of uniformity that was new. Syllables were perceived as more or less the same. *Ictus* and stress accent did not necessarily coincide, but they were caused by the same phenomenon, a rise in intensity and perhaps pitch on stressed syllables. The three-syllable line endings so evident in iambic dimeter became the standard in iambic trimeter, trochaic tetrameter catalectic, and even Asclepiads. The only meters where this ending would not fit are those that require a weak syllable at the end of the line, such as in a trochaic line (e.g., <u>A</u>ve, <u>ma</u>ris <u>stel</u>la, H 145). In accentual meter, there are no substitutions to speak of, since time caused by syllable length is no longer significant. The greater regularity in meter would invite new ways of adding variety to a line of verse that would come from the sound or "color" of the syllables rather than length. Hence assonance and rhyme.

Second, it may be that in hymns composed in accentual meter where the sixth syllable of the line is no longer felt as long, but only as stressed, the finishing effect of the secondary stress on the eighth syllable (the final syllable in the line), is more evident if the syllables bearing the secondary stress all end with the same vowel sound or in a recurring pattern. The fact remains that Latin rhyme schemes in iambic dimeter do not stand out to the ear; unless one is looking for them, one often hardly notices them when they are there, and one hardly misses them when they are absent. This may be one reason why hymn writers would freely abandon rhyme in stanzas where it did not fit the sense. Throughout the formative period when many hymns of the *Liturgia Horarum* were composed, rhyme did not much matter, from a metrical point of view. From a rhetorical point of view of course it could, as the examples above show. It was not until poets established rhyme schemes in trochaic or dactylic meters in which the first of a two or three-syllable

---

24. Carruthers, *The Craft of Thought*, 308–9n128.

unit received a primary stress accent that Latin rhyme schemes were fully felt. Thus, the syllable with a stress accent, governed by the old penult rule, either belonged to the rhyme scheme or, if it were on the antepenult, it led to a two syllable rhyme directly after it. Examples from the *Liturgia Horarum* are *Dies iræ, dies illa / solvet sæclum in favílla, / teste David cum Sibýlla* (H 136) where the first syllable of a trochee receives the primary stress. In sequences such as that of Adam of St. Victor viewed above, the final dactyl has a two-syllable rhyme after the primary stress or the stressed antepenult is included in the rhyme. This happens in the first stanza of the sequence of Adam of St. Victor, mentioned above (H 98). Here below is the first stanza, where *gloria* and *victoria* show three-syllable rhyme:

> Salve dies, diérum glória, Hail, O day, of all days most glorious,
> dies felix Christi victória, blessed day of Christ's noble victory,
> dies digna iugi lætítia, day of gladness, worthy of endless joy,
> dies prima first and foremost

We may define *rhyme* in Latin hymnody as full syllable likeness, including vowels and consonants on two or more syllables, at the end of the line in two or more lines. The likeness includes a stress accent if the stress is on the penult, as in *illa, favílla*, and *Sibýlla* above. If the stress accent is on the antepenult, the rhyme will either include it, as in *gloria* and *victoria*, or be on the two following unstressed syllables, as in *victoria* and *lætitia* above. If it is on the two unstressed syllables only, it will still be felt though perhaps not as strongly. Further, if the lines in a hymn have many syllables (e.g., 12 or 15 [or 8x7]), the end rhyme may be reinforced by internal rhyme. This is the case in *Pange lingua* by St. Thomas given above (H 127): *gloriosi, pretiósi*, and *generósi* all rhyme at the midpoint of the line, and *mysterium, prétium*, and *gentium* rhyme at the end of the line.

The hymn below, in Asclepiads (12 12 12 8) also by Thomas Aquinas, *Sacris sollemniis iuncta sint gaudia* (H 128), has two-syllable rhyme both at the end of the line and at the cæsura halfway through. Lines 1–3 have end rhyme on *-minum*; lines 1 and 2 have internal rhyme on *-licus*; lines 3 and 4 have rhyme on *-ilis*, internal in line 3 (syllable 6) and at the end in the shorter line 4. This rhyme scheme continues through all the stanzas of the hymn.

> Panis angélicus fit panis hóminum;
> dat panis cælicus figúris términum.
> O res mirábilis: mandúcat Dóminum
> servus pauper et húmilis.
>
> Bread of the angel hosts now is made bread for us,
> heavenly bread from God, truth of all prophecies,
> O marvel, wondrous gift! Who may consume the Lord?
> Lowly servants and poor of heart.

This is not to say that likeness in the final syllable at the end of a line in Latin hymnody is not rhyme in any sense of the word, but only that such likeness does not command our attention in the same way as two and three syllable rhyme, because Latin cannot have a primary stress accent on the final syllable of a word. Rhyming syllables that are either unstressed or bear a secondary stress remain in the background. The rhyme may be felt, but as an ornament, not as a structural element. This is in stark contrast to English hymnody, where one-syllable rhyme at the end of a line is a major structural device.

The development and quality of rhyme in Latin hymnody show that the Penult Rule is still operative at a fundamental level in the Latin language as it developed and changed throughout the Middle Ages. Scholars have tended to say that during the medieval period, syllable count was the main requirement for poetic meter with stress accents superimposed. This is not incorrect, but it does not give a nuanced and complete picture.[25] Where, after all, do the stress accents come from? As we have seen, the function of three-syllable words at the end of the line of iambic dimeter and related meters is not an accident. Calvin Bower has also noticed that even in the sequences of Notker Balbalus, where the rhythm of the text is all-important but the meter is not as regular as in later sequences, lines end regularly with three-syllable words with a primary stress on the third to the last syllable (the antepenult). When they do not, Notker seems to be deliberately using unusual line endings to make a poetic or theological statement.[26] That is, his instincts tell him that some line endings are normal and unemphatic and some are not.

To summarize: a three-syllable word with a stress accent on the antepenult syllable is either a *dactyl* (long-short-short or stressed-unstressed-unstressed) or a *cretic* (long-short-long or stressed-unstressed-stressed). Every *dactyl* before a line ending in prose or poetry is a functional *cretic* because the pause that follows lengthens the syllable somewhat as it is perceived by the ear. In medieval liturgical hymns, these functional *cretics* at the end of each line have a pleasing and rather unobtrusive secondary stress on the last syllable. Again, this is due to the old Penult Rule, which does not allow a strong stress on the final syllable of a word. Again, it should be noted that this is markedly different from the English language which often does have a strong stress accent on the final syllable of a

---

25. Crocker seems to imply this: "The early medieval cantor seems to have adopted a characteristically simple, reductionist view: he ignored the quantities and, finding the accents formed no regular pattern, he ignored those too, and took into account only the number of syllables. For him, this verse form consisted of eight syllables in each of four short lines; or of sixteen syllables with a cæsura in the middle in each of two long lines. He would, of course, be aware of the word accents, and might even observe one or another in his melodic setting; *but they provided no regular basis for structure*" (emphasis added, Crocker, "Medieval Chant," 286). Norberg, however, brings much needed clarity to the analysis of accentual versification. He comments, "St. Augustine, Master Stephen, and others distinguish between, on the one hand, the *carmen*, composed of *pedes metrici*, which one learned with difficulty in the school of that time period, and on the other hand, rhythmic poetry, which was much simpler; but they do not say that the structure of rhythmic verse does not matter" (*Introduction*, 88); and "Rhythmic verse had ... exactly the same [stress] accents as the corresponding quantitative verse" (*Introduction*, 85).

26. Bower, *Liber Ymnorum*, 6–7, 12, 27–29.

word. This causes a radical difference in the perception of rhyme in Latin and English hymns. It is instructive to contrast the English hymn "All People that on Earth do Dwell" by William Kethe (d. 1594) with a twelfth-century Latin hymn by Peter Abelard in which rhyme is present. Here are the first two stanzas of the English hymn:

1. All people that on earth do dwell,	2. Know that the Lord is God indeed;
Sing to the Lord with cheerful voice;	Without our aid He did us make;
Him serve with mirth, His praise forth tell,	We are His folk, He doth us feed,
Come ye before Him and rejoice.	And for His sheep He doth us take.

Here are the first two stanzas of *Adorna Sion* (H 195), Abelard's hymn for the feast of the Presentation:

Adórna, Sion, thálamum,	O Zion, waiting for the Lord,
quæ præstoláris Dóminum;	adorn and trim the bridal room,
sponsum et sponsam súscipe	keep watch with burning lamps of faith,
vigil fídei lúmine.	receive the Bridegroom and the Bride.
Beáte senex, própera,	O blessed Simeon, come forth,
promíssa comple gáudia	and, late in life, find promised joy;
et revelándum géntibus	reveal to all the nations Light
revéla lumen ómnibus.	that comes to be revealed to all.

Both hymns are in iambic dimeter, but how different they are. Notice that every line in the English hymn ends with a strongly stressed syllable. One cannot construct the hymn otherwise without changing the meter. Note also the inversions introduced to accommodate the rhyme: "Him serve with mirth, His praise forth tell." The Latin hymn is more subtle.

It is fair to say that in the hands of skilled composers with a musical ear, stress accent was still linked to the Penult Rule. The stress was either on a long penult, or it was pushed back onto a long or short antepenult; if it was on the antepenult, the last syllable could have a secondary stress. Thus, accent and quantitatively long syllables together still produced intuitively felt patterns.[27] These felt patterns in conjunction with fixed line lengths created an environment favorable to rhyme, though liturgical hymns of the finest sort remained supple and flexible.

3. Traces of Musical Composition

The third internal factor comes from traces of the music for which these hymns might have been composed and from comments made by Bede. We know little about the music of the early hymns beyond the facts that they were arranged in stanzas and made to be sung. Norberg observes that in some hymns, the third line of a stanza either does not rhyme or has a conflicting rhythmic structure,

---

27. Bede points this out in his *De arte metrica*. See the quotation given below in the main text. Norberg also cites this passage from Bede (*Introduction*, 127–28).

sometimes it is the second line. *Vox clara ecce intonat* (H 3), cited above, is an example: lines 1, 2, and 4 all end in *at*, but line 3 ends in *a*. The same irregularity is found in other ancient hymns.[28] Is this an indication that musical structure sometimes, at least, determined poetic structure? Lines 3 and 4 may have formed a single musical unit, as they do in modern English hymns.[29] Other irregularities abound that may reflect the adjustment of the text to a preexisting melody; for example, the ancient hymn *Rex æterne, Domine* (H 43), mentioned above in appendix 1,[30] is given by Bede in his *De arte metrica* as a celebrated hymn beautifully composed in iambic dimeter, but it has only seven syllables in the first line; it has other irregularities in 1, 3 and 5, 3.[31] Would a preexisting musical line with repetitive patterns determine to some degree at least corresponding textual patterns?

A clear indication of the significance of sound for the composition of hymns comes from the same passage in the *De arte metrica*, where Bede says:

> Rhythmic verse seems similar to metrical verse; rhythmic verse is the measured-out composition of words not according to a system of meter, but according to the number of syllables weighed according to the judgment of the ears. Such are the songs of the common poets. And in fact, rhythm can exist by itself without [quantitative] meter, but meter cannot exist without rhythm. This can be defined more clearly thus: meter is rule and art with measure, and rhythm is measure without rule and art. Yet, for the most part, by some chance you will find rule and art even in rhythm, not preserved by artistic arrangement, but the sound and the measure itself are the guide. Common poets must of necessity do this awkwardly; learned poets do it skillfully.[32]

Bede's "learned poets" had artistic sense and well-trained ears, which qualified them as learned. He says, in essence, that their composition of rhythmic verse based on a skillful appraisal of sound and rhythm leads them to a result that is similar to or has significant elements of quantitative meter. He says that this

---

28. In the original text of the complete *Aurora lucis rutilat* (now H 42, H 114, and H 115), stanzas 4, 8, 9, 10, and 11 have an irregular third line. See Bulst, 114–15; see also Milfull, 293. The original *Christe, cæli Domine* (now *Christe, cælorum Domine*, H 36), which is a metrical paraphrase of the *Te Deum*, has multiple irregularities in syllable count and line structure, most of which have been removed from the hymn as it stands in the *Liturgia Horarum*. Most of the irregularities are in odd-numbered lines, which may indicate long lines of 15 to 16 syllables. See Walpole, no. 49, p. 234ff., and the commentary on the hymn (H 36) in this volume.

29. Norberg, *Introduction*, 133–35. *Vox clara ecce intonat* is given with melody 402, version 1, in Bruno Stäblein, *Hymnen*, 171; lines 1 and 4 of the melody are the same, line 2 ends as lines 1 and 4, line 3 moves up into a new register before returning to the tonic in preparation for line 4. See also Crocker's analysis of *Verbum supernum prodiens*, "Medieval Chant," 241–42.

30. See appendix 1, note 32. See also the entry for the hymn in the commentary (H 43).

31. Dag Norberg, *La poésie latine*, 28. See also Norberg, *Les vers*, 36, where he suggests that the form of the hymn may be stanzas of two lines of sixteen syllables; also *AH* 51, no. 2, p. 5; *TDH*, no. 110, pp. 114–15, and no. 114, p. 119.

32. The first sentence of the quotation above is taken from the English translation by Calvin Bower, *Liber Ymnorum*, 4–5. The remainder is a new translation based in part on Bede, *De arte metrica*, 160. Also note that Bede mentions syllable count only in conjunction with the "weight" (i.e., accentual rhythm) of the syllables as perceived by the ear. The Latin *plerumque* does not mean "often" but "very often, for the most part." The Latin text is as follows: *Videtur autem rithmus metris esse consimilis, quæ est verborum modulata conpositio, non metrica ratione, sed numero syllabarum ad iudicium aurium examinata, ut sunt carmina vulgarium poetarum. Et quidem rithmus per se sine metro esse potest, metrum vero sine rithmo esse non potest. Quod liquidius ita definitur: metrum est ratio cum modulatione, rithmus modulatio sine ratione. Plerumque tamen casu quodam invenies etiam rationem in rithmo, non artifici moderatione servata, sed sono et ipsa modulatione ducente, quem vulgares poetæ necesse est rustice, docti faciant docte* (Bede, *De arte metrica*, 1.24).

happens by chance, but it happens very often, and it can happen at all only because even with all the changes that resulted from the language shift away from quantity to stress, enough of the foundation of the language was left intact to produce verse that was, to some degree at least, acceptable even by the standards of traditional quantitative meter. This means that when poetry is "measured by the judgment of the ear," the two methods of reading texts, though they may not have produced exactly the same results, were in a harmonious relationship at a deep level.[33]

With the Renaissance there was a renewed interest in the more subtle and sophisticated quantitative meter.[34] Rhyme did not cease, of course, just as quantitative meter had not been lost in previous centuries, but there is a shift away from the exuberance and commanding regularity of rhyming stanzas and sequences toward the older forms.[35]

In conclusion, an analysis of the long tradition of Latin hymnody shows that alliteration, assonance, and rhyme belong to the tradition as tools used variously in different periods and regions, and subject to the stylistic preferences of individual poets. A host of Latin hymns do not rhyme in a systematic way; rhyme is not a primary structural device in Latin hymnody as it is in much of English hymnody. Since the ICEL mandate has been to translate the Latin hymns in such a way that the sense and theological depth is faithfully conveyed while providing texts that can be used in the liturgy, the decision was made to keep the original meters of the Latin hymns but to avoid the inevitable compromises caused by seeking English rhyme. This may be a disappointment to some, but it has allowed the Latin hymns to speak with greater theological fidelity and liturgical effect to those who sing them in English. It is hoped that the English texts of the *Divine Office Hymnal* in conjunction with this commentary may guide the reader into the rich content and heritage of the Latin hymns.

---

33. Looking at the blend of quantitative and accentual meter in the hymns of Paulinus of Aquileia, Norberg concludes that "the boundaries between rhythmic and quantitative poetry are sometimes quite vague" (*Introduction*, 127–29). See also Norberg, *Les vers*, 29–30.

34. The following are examples of hymns in iambic dimeter, composed without regular, consistent rhyme schemes, from the sixteenth century onward and included in the *Liturgia Horarum*. In an individual stanza, two lines may rhyme, but they are not the same from stanza to stanza, and some stanzas have no rhyme at all. The result is a rhyme scheme that is casual or accidental. They are listed by the number assigned to them in this commentary: H 285: *Fortem piumque præsulem*, G. Battista Amalteo (d. 1573); H 181: *Fortem virili pectore*, Silvio Antoniano (d. 1603); H 286: *Præclara custos virginum*, anon. seventeenth c.; H 292: *Cohors beata seraphim*, Carlo Rosa (d. 1781); H 166: *Sacrata nobis gaudia*, Pietro Piacenza (d. 1919); H 247 *Rerum supremo in vertice*, Vittorio Genovesi (d. 1967); H 147: *Quæ caritatis fulgidum*, Anselmo Lentini (d. 1989).

35. Raby, *History of Christian-Latin Poetry*. For a brief overview of the efforts to recover medieval hymns that resulted in the *Analecta Hymnica* and other collections, see pp. 456–57.

Part 1

THE SEASON OF ADVENT

The liturgical year presents to those who pray the Liturgy of the Hours the entirety of human history from the creation of the world to the Last Judgment. The principal goal of this linear presentation of salvation history is to renew and strengthen us, as we progressively contemplate the mysteries of salvation year after year, until that day when we grow into the full stature of Christ (Eph 4:13). Our minds are formed by the truths of the faith, our hearts are enlivened with hope, and we are transformed by the light and the love of Christ offered to us through seasons of grace.

The first season is Advent. Unlike other seasons in which a particular mystery is celebrated, Advent opens before us the panorama of God's saving intervention in the life of the world. It is an invitation to enter into the divine economy of salvation, an invitation to desire the inestimable good that God proposes to give us. Thus, it is a time of seeking and waiting for the coming of the Lord. St. Bernard tells us that the Lord's coming is threefold: "In the first coming, he comes in the flesh and in weakness; in the second, he comes in spirit and in power; in the third, he comes in glory and in majesty; and the second coming is the means whereby we pass from the first to the third."[1] The first coming is in the Incarnation, humble and hidden; the second is in our soul, mysterious, filled with truth and love; the third is in the Last Judgment, majestic and terrible.[2] A complex matrix of sentiments, therefore, pervades the season of Advent. With the prophets of old, we long for the birth of the Messiah. With all those who thirst for holiness and righteousness, we long for a renewed presence of Christ in the life of the Church and in the world. With the Church, the Bride, we await the definitive Advent of

---

1. St. Bernard, *Sermones in adventu Domini, sermo* 5.1 : *In priore quidem [adventu] in terris visus est et cum hominibus conversatus est, quando, sicut ipse testatur, et viderunt, et oderunt* (Jn 15:24). *In posteriore vero videbit omnis caro salutare Dei nostri,'* (Lk 3:6) *et videbunt in quem transfixerunt* (Jn 19:37). *Medius occultus est, in quo soli eum in seipsis vident electi, et salvae fiunt animae eorum. In primo ergo venit in carne et infirmitate, in hoc medio in spiritu et virtute, in ultimo in gloria et maiestate.... Adventus siquidem iste medius, via quaedam est per quam a primo veniatur ad ultimum*: "In the first [Advent] he (Christ) is seen on earth and he lived with men, at which time, as he himself testified, "they saw and they hated," (Jn 15:24) In the latter [Advent], however, "all flesh shall see the salvation of our God" (Lk 3:6), and "they will look upon him who they have transfixed" (Jn 19:37). The middle [Advent] is hidden, in which only the elect see him within themselves, and their souls shall be saved." The rest of the text from St. Bernard follows as it is given above and quoted by Prosper Guéranger, *Liturgical Year* 1:28.

2. See Guéranger, *Liturgical Year*, 1:16–17.

the Bridegroom, who will come in power and glory to judge the living and the dead and then lead faithful souls into the joy of eternal life.[3]

During the weeks of Advent, the liturgy presents to us the intense longing of the whole of creation for the coming of Christ: At First Vespers we sing: "Behold, the name of the Lord comes from afar, and his glory fills the whole world."[4] Then, at the Office of Readings, the magnificent responsory of Advent follows: "Looking from afar, behold, I see the power of God coming.... Tell us if you are the One.... Let every earth-dweller and child of men, rich and poor, go forth to meet him...."[5] As we participate in the liturgy, the Church invites each of us to enter personally into this longing for a Savior; she invites us to enter into the interior chamber of the heart and to recognize there our innate longing for God of which St. Augustine speaks so eloquently.[6] Only when we discover, through our need, the fundamental reality that our hearts are made for God, can we fully rejoice in the immense gift of the Incarnation. This intimate participation in the longing for Christ and for the joy he brings by his presence, both in the Incarnation and in his final return at the end of the world, this is St. Bernard's second Advent that leads us from the first coming of Christ to the last.

The liturgy exhorts us both to cleanse our hearts, so that we may walk worthily before Christ when he comes, and to rejoice because he is our Great King, who will not delay[7]: God, our Savior, will come with great power; he will come with all the saints, and on that day there will be great light.[8] We must be vigilant for we know not the day on which he shall come.[9] And, "behold, I come quickly," says the Lord, "to render to each according to his works."[10] Yet, when he comes, the mountains will drip with sweetness and the hills will flow with milk and honey.[11] John the Baptist is the living sign of and guide to the spiritual good of Advent. He is "the voice of one crying in the desert: 'Prepare the way of the Lord'" (Is 40:3). He is also one who "leapt with joy" in his mother's womb (Lk 1:41); and he described himself as the friend of the Bridegroom (Jn 3:29).

---

3. Mt 25:6ff. The three great parables of the Christ's return follow without a break in ch. 25: the Bridegroom returning in the middle of the night, the Master who returns to bring in revenue from the talents entrusted to his servants, the Judge of the sheep and the goats. All three belong to the thematic imagery of Advent.

4. *Ecce nomen Domini venit de longinquo, et claritas eius replet orbem terrarum* (Vespers I, First Sunday of Advent, Magnificat antiphon, Year B). This ancient and well-known antiphon is composed of three texts of great significance for the liturgical year (Is 30:27 for Advent; Lk 2:9 for Christmas and Wis 1:7 for Pentecost). See Kennedy and Bakker, "The Charterhouse Antiphonal Fragment," 175–86.

5. "R. Aspiciens a longe, ecce video Dei potentiam venientem, et nebulam totam terram tegentem. * Ite obviam ei, et dicite: * Nuntia nobis, si tu es ipse, * Qui regnaturus es in populo Israel. V. Quique terrigenæ, et filii hominum, simul in unum dives et pauper, * Ite obviam ei, et dicite: V. Qui regis Israel, intende, qui deducis velut ovem Ioseph, * Nuntia nobis, si tu es ipse. V. Tollite portas, principes, vestras, et elevamini, portæ æternales, et introibit Rex gloriæ. * Qui regnaturus es in populo Israel. R. Aspiciens a longe ..." Responsory, Office of Readings, First Sunday of Advent.

6. Augustine, *Conf.*, 1.1: *quia fecisti nos ad te et inquietum est cor nostrum, donec requiescat in te*: "for you have made us for yourself, and our heart is restless (unquiet), until it rests in you." The Latin *inquietum* has been traditionally translated as "restless." A better translation would be "unquiet, anxious." Maria Boulding, OSB, and others have preferred "unquiet" because it captures the deep, often half-hidden anxiety that marks the life of one whose heart has no anchor in God.

7. Office of Readings for the Sundays of Advent, antiphons 2 and 3.
8. Antiphon 2, Vespers I, First Sunday of Advent.
9. Magnificat antiphon, Vespers I, First Sunday of Advent.
10. Antiphon 3, Vespers II, First Sunday of Advent.
11. Antiphon 1, Lauds, First Sunday of Advent.

Part 1. The Season Of Advent

The Church clothes the liturgy in purple, the color of penance and, one might say, of dissatisfaction with our worldly ways. At Mass, she suppresses the *Gloria in excelsis Deo*, as if to remind us, "Not yet. Repent and wait for the Lord. If he seems to tarry, know for certain that he will not delay."[12] As the Solemnity of the Nativity of the Lord approaches, she intensifies her focus on the immediate appearance of the Savior. Finally, on December 17, she begins the great preparatory novena. A new set of hymns is introduced, each day has individual antiphons for the psalmody of the hours, and she calls upon the Lord using the solemn Messianic titles of the ancient *O Antiphons*; she begs Christ to come and bring her gifts that correspond to the title by which she addresses him in the antiphon. The pattern of each antiphon may be seen in the first one for December 17: "O Wisdom, who have come forth from the mouth of the Most High, reaching from end to end, strongly and gently ordering all things: O come to teach us the way of prudence."[13]

The hymns of Advent occupy a privileged place in the liturgy as the theological setting where the interwoven images of the season meet. Each of the six hymns presents to us the threefold coming of the Lord, though with varied emphasis. The first three, *Conditor alme siderum*, *Verbum supernum prodiens*, and *Vox clara ecce intonat*, were composed during a period of reform and stabilization of the ancient hymnal. All are found in the "New Hymnal" that grew out of the Carolingian and English Benedictine reforms of the ninth and tenth centuries.[14] They have been in continual use ever since, in both the monastic and Roman offices.[15] As a result of the liturgical reform after the Second Vatican Council, three additional ancient hymns were added for the period between December 17 and the Nativity of the Lord (Christmas Day). The newly added hymns retain the themes of Advent, but they lead more directly to the mystery of Christmas: *Verbum salutis omnium* (tenth c.), *Veni, redemptor gentium* (St. Ambrose), and *Magnis prophetæ vocibus* (Mozarabic, seventh c.?).

The hymns for the season of Advent are as follows:

No.	Name	Liturgical Hour
1	Conditor alme siderum	Vespers, through December 16
2	Verbum supernum prodiens	Readings, through December 16
3	Vox clara ecce intonat	Lauds, through December 16
4	Verbum salutis omnium	Vespers, after December 16
5	Veni, redemptor gentium	Readings, after December 16
6	Magnis prophetæ vocibus	Lauds, after December 16

---

12. *Ecce apparebit Dominus, et non mentietur; si moram fecerit, exspecta eum, quia veniet et non tardabit, alleluia*: "Behold, the Lord shall appear, and he shall not deceive; if he tarries, wait for him for he will come and not delay, alleluia" (Antiphon 2, Vespers II, Second Sunday of Advent; Heb 2:3; Is 46:13; Heb 10:37).

13. *O Sapientia, quæ ex ore Altissimi prodisti, attingens a fine usque ad finem, fortiter suaviterque disponens omnia: veni et docendum nos viam prudentiæ* (Magnificat antiphon, 17 December). Translation taken from the ICEL Index of Antiphons: revised Liturgy of the Hours, in production.

14. For a discussion of the development of the liturgical hymnal from the earliest sources (fourth to seventh centuries) to the appearance of the "New Hymnal," see Walpole, xi–xx, and Milfull, 5–24, with the lists in appendices 1 and 2, 473–78. See also the lists in *AH* 51, xx–xxvii.

15. This is true as a general principle, though there are of course variations among different religious communities and among the ancient rites.

Conditor alme siderum 1

9th c.
8 8 8 8 (LM)

Advent to 16 December
Vespers

Cónditor alme síderum,	1. O loving Maker of the stars,
ætérna lux credéntium,	believers' everlasting light,
Christe, redémptor ómnium,	O Christ, Redeemer of us all,
exáudi preces súpplicum.	with kindness hear our humble prayer.
Qui cóndolens intéritu	2. With pity, you beheld the fate
mortis períre sǽculum,	that death imposed on ages past;
salvásti mundum lánguidum,	you gave the guilty healing grace
donans reis remédium,	and saved a weak and fallen world.
Vergénte mundi véspere,	3. When evening fell upon the earth,
uti sponsus de thálamo,	as bridegroom from the bridal room,
egréssus honestíssima	from honored cloister forth you came,
Vírginis matris cláusula.	born from the Virgin Mother pure.
Cuius forti poténtiæ	4. Before your strong and steadfast might,
genu curvántur ómnia;	on earth and in the heavens above
cæléstia, terréstria	all knees bend low, all hearts confess
nutu faténtur súbdita.	submission to your sovereign will.
Te, Sancte, fide quǽsumus,	5. With faith we beg you, Holy Lord,
ventúre iudex sǽculi,	the Judge of ages still to come,
consérva nos ín témpore	that in our time you keep us safe
hostis a telo pérfidi.	from snares of our deceitful foe.
Sit, Christe, rex piíssime,	6. To you, O Christ, most loving King,
tibi Patríque glória	and to the Father, glory be,
cum Spíritu Paráclito,	one with the Spirit Paraclete,
in sempitérna sǽcula. Amen.	from age to age for evermore. Amen.

Text found in *TDH*, no. 71; AH 51, no. 47; Walpole, no. 84. Changes in *TDH*: stanza 5, 1: *Sancte* for *Hagie*, with adjustments required by the meter; the original stanza 5 has been omitted.

COMMENTARY

The grandeur, simplicity, and spontaneous movement of the text beautifully reflect the hope and the rising joy of Advent. Each line of the first stanza presents in quick succession the full panorama of the salvation we await: the One who rules and orders an entire universe of brilliant, heavenly lights is the eternal light of the spiritual universe of those who believe. Who is he in the context of this hymn?

God Incarnate, Christ, the Redeemer, our compassionate Savior attentive to our humble prayer, but also the dread Lord and Judge who will return to close the age.

Conditor alme siderum has been assigned to Vespers during Advent since the tenth century.[16] Because the cycle of each liturgical year begins with the First Vespers of the First Sunday of Advent, this hymn is our first taste of Advent and of the liturgical economy of the year ahead. Walsh points out that references to evening and to night falling on the world (3, 1) as well as references to sunset, the moon, and stars (in the missing stanza 5) make this hymn an appropriate choice for Vespers.[17] Historically speaking, seasonal hymns have been assigned to different hours in various hymnals and breviaries; but Walsh's comments reflect the age-old liturgical practice of linking the hours of the day at which an Office is said to the spiritual hours and seasons of the lives of those who say the Divine Office. This is essentially the Church's understanding of the sanctification of time. The liturgical use of physical imagery to speak of spiritual reality is of the greatest significance because it anchors the truths of salvation in the here and now of the lives of those who pray. Thus, as we sing *Conditor* at the end of the day, as darkness is falling around us, we enter more fully into the metaphor of spiritual darkness that has fallen on the world through sin and through the evening of life that is death.

STANZA 1

The Latin term *conditor* refers to one who founds something, a city or state, bringing it into existence and giving it order and governance. It does not mean "creator," though when it refers to God, it is often used as a synonym for "creator."[18] Here *conditor* is invoked as *alme*, a Latin word of such richness, it defies translation. It signifies: nurturing, kind, loving, fruitful, and in connection with God and the saints, holy.[19] Long ago, the *alme Conditor* brought forth and ordered the *sidera*, not just the stars, as in modern translations,[20] but the planets also, the sun, and the other heavenly bodies.[21] In the fullness of time, he himself shone forth, as eternal light for those who believe and receive him. And so, the well-ordered constellations (Bar 3:34–35), are an image of the spiritual light of the faithful. The word *conditor* is used only once in the Vulgate, at Hebrews 11:9–10, where Abraham is presented as a model of faith, living in tents in the Promised Land, as he waited in faith for a city with foundations that are designed and founded by God, the *Artifex et Conditor*. Abraham entered into the *lux æterna*

---

16. Milful, 9, 183. It is found in all the early Anglo-Saxon hymnals as well as in contemporary continental hymnals. See AH 51, xxv ff.

17. Walsh, 445.

18. Please see the discussion of this hymn in the introduction; topics treated there will not be considered in detail here.

19. The Marian antiphon for Advent begins: *Alma Redemptoris Mater*. Christ is the *alme Redemptor*.

20. The Latin *sidus, sideris* n., refers to all heavenly bodies, the sun, moon, constellations, planets, as well as the stars. Latin has another word for "star" in particular, *stella, stellæ* f.

21. See Dante, *The Divine Comedy, Paradise*, Canto 33, 145.

credentium (1, 2) by believing in the promises, and we, his descendants, wait by the same light of faith during Advent for the one who will redeem us (*redemptor omnium*) and build the eternal city. When he comes, the faithful will be like burning torches, the new heavenly bodies (*sidera*), in the celestial firmament of heaven: "Then the righteous will shine like the sun in the kingdom of their Father" (Mt 13:43).[22] The first two lines of the hymn have brought together multiple images inspired by texts from Scripture. The role of the hymn is to turn the truths of Scripture into a mosaic of contemplation and prayer.

Line 3, *Christe, redemptor omnium*, is an example of the idiom of Latin hymnody transmitted throughout the tradition. Iconic lines such as this figure in hymns composed both before and after this one. To mention only those found in the *Divine Office Hymnal*, it is the opening line in an early hymn for Christmas day (ca. sixth century; H 7) and in a ninth-century hymn for All Saints (H 276); finally, it is an internal line in an eighteenth-century hymn in honor of the Sacred Heart (H 130).

In line 4, we ask Christ to hear our prayers. The verb, *exaudi*, is often translated in the litanies as "graciously hear," as opposed to *audi* ("hear") without the prefix. What is the prayer we ask him to hear graciously? It comes only in stanza 5. Stanzas 2 through 4 recount the *res gestæ* (the mighty deeds) of our Redeemer and God. These mighty deeds bring us to our knees in supplication in stanza 5.

STANZA 2

Pimont says that stanzas 2 and 3 form one of the most beautiful pieces of Latin hymnody. The inspiration of the Scriptures that passes through it has imprinted on it a mark of brilliance.[23] Stanza 2 opens with the transitional relative pronoun *qui*, which links what follows to Christ, named in stanza 1. *Qui* is modified by the present participles *condolens* in line 1 and *donans* in line 4; this makes a tight construction for the stanza as a whole. Notice that the stanza has no prepositions or conjunctions, little words that can clog up a line of poetry and which English cannot do without. This compact structure is typical of Latin hymnody. *Condolens* comes from *doleo*: to feel pain, ache, suffer, and then: to grieve, feel sorrow, lament; *con* is *cum* ("with") used as a prefix. Christ grieves with us because he is compassionate. The cause of grief is that the world and the age (*sæculum* can mean both) is perishing (*perire*) in the ruin (*interitu*) of death (*mortis*). The Latin *interitu* is a colorful synonym for death; it comes from *inter* + *eo*: to collapse, decay, be undone; the noun signifies destruction, ruin, annihilation. The phrase *interitu mortis* is pleonastic, based on the Hebrew idiom, preserved in the Vulgate, in which phrases are made emphatic by repetition.[24] It is an allusion to the solemn warnings and punishments of God in Genesis. He says to Adam: "for

---

22. Pimont, 2:17.
23. Pimont, 2:21.
24. In Latin, one of the two terms may be in the genitive, as in the well-known examples: *sæculum sæculi* (ages without end); *cæli cælorum* (the heights of heaven); *Sancta Sanctorum* (Holy of Holies).

on the day that you eat of it, you shall surely die," or literally: "die by the death" (*morte morieris*).[25]

Line 3 begins with the main verb of the stanza, in the past tense, second person singular: *salvasti*. It is addressed to Christ and signifies that we celebrate Advent knowing well that he has already accomplished our salvation. During the liturgical year, we re-enact, so to speak, the mysteries of salvation, in order to understand them more deeply and to draw near to Christ as we contemplate all that he has done for us. We live by the grace of an accomplished fact, yet we wait for him to come at Christmas and to come again at the end of time. These are St. Bernard's three Advents.[26] The past tense here is a moment of self-awareness that is a precious element in the economy of liturgical life.

In line 2, *sæculum* has connotations of time, in line 3 *mundus* has connotations of space; it signifies the world with all that is in it, the universe. The whole economy of time and space is in need of salvation, the *mundus* is *languidus*. In classical Latin, the primary meaning of *languidus* is faint, weary, languid. In the Christian idiom, the meaning shifts slightly to focus on the idea of sickness or infirmity. Again, the language of the Vulgate has shaped Christian thought and sensitivities.[27] This sense is reinforced by line 4: *donans reis remedium*. The sickness here is the guilt of sin (*reus*), and all the tragic consequences of it that lead to ruin. Note the alliteration on *reis* and *remedium*, which gives these final words a certain weight. In classical usage, *reus* signifies one who is bound, accused, subject to penalty. In the idiom derived from Scripture, it normally has the connotation of personal guilt for sin.[28] Thus, sickness and sin are closely aligned in this stanza. One thinks of the healing of the paralytic by the pool of Bethsaida (Jn 5:2–14). Jesus finds the man lying among the *languentium* (Jn 5:3); the Gospel then refers to him simply as the *languidus* (Jn 5:7). Later, when Jesus finds him in the Temple, he says: "Sin no more, that nothing worse may happen to you" (Jn 5:14). In his commentary on this hymn, Denis the Carthusian says that to perish by the ruin of death is to perish by the guilt (*reatu*) of original sin and by the lethal wound of each mortal sin.[29]

---

25. Gn 2:17, 20:7; Ex 19:12 and 21:12ff.; Lv 20:2ff.; 2 Sm 12:14; Ez 3:18; and elsewhere in the Old Testament.

26. See the introduction to the season of Advent that precedes the commentary on this hymn.

27. A discussion of this shift is beyond the scope of this commentary, but when one examines the use of *languor* in the Vulgate, one sees clear evidence of it. To give two examples only: Is 53:4 says of the suffering servant: *vere languores nostros ipse tulit et dolores nostros ipse portavit*: "Truly, he bore our infirmities (*languores*), and he himself carried our sorrows." The LXX has ἁμαρτία (sin; error, failure; spiritual sickness, and in any case something worse than weariness). Similarly, in the New Testament, Christ heals illnesses (*languores*) and infirmities (e.g., Mt 4:23, 9:35; Lk 7:21, 9:1).

28. Lv 17:4; Nm 35:16, 21, 31; Mt 5:21–22; Jas 2:10.

29. Denis the Carthusian, *Expositio hymnorum*, 21: *perire.... id est, damnationem incurrere, spiritualiter mori, æternam salutem amittere, "interitu mortis," id est, reatu originalis peccati, læsione etiam propriæ culpæ peccantium, letalique vulneratione cuiuscumque peccati mortalis*: "to perish (2, 3): that is to incur damnation, to die spiritually, to lose eternal salvation, by the ruin of death (2, 2–3), that is by the guilt of original sin, also by the injury of the particular fault of those who sin and the lethal wound of each and every mortal sin." See also Pimont, 1:20.

STANZA 3

Stanza 3 opens with an ablative absolute: *vergente mundi vespere*. The Latin *vergo, vergere* means to incline, turn: the evening of the world is on "the verge" of darkness, it is at the end of its strength and life. The image—the world spiraling down into darkness—sets the stage for lines 2–4. In Scripture and in the mind of the early Church, Christ came in the last age of the world; the moment of the Incarnation was the end of the fifth age of the world, and Christ in his coming would inaugurate the sixth and final age.[30]

As the world grows old and dark, Christ, the Light, bursts forth like a Bridegroom (*sponsus*) from the bridal chamber of the nuptials of the Word with human nature. He goes forth (*egressus*) from the most honorable room (*honestissima clausula*) of the Virgin. The pronounced and regular rhythm of line 3 evokes the stride of the Bridegroom as he comes forth: *egressus honestissima*. Without quoting the psalm directly, these lines allude to the imagery of Psalm 18 (19):6, that speaks of the sun rising and traversing the sky. The Septuagint and the Vulgate have: "He placed his tent in the sun and he like a bridegroom proceeding from his bridal chamber exulted like a giant to run his course."[31] For the early Church, this verse was understood to be a transparent image of the Incarnation. St. Ambrose had already used it in his hymn *Veni, redemptor gentium* (H 5: 4, 1–4) where Christ is a giant (*gigas*) with a twin substance or nature (*geminæ substantiæ*). Ambrose's hymn was included in the Old Hymnal and the Frankish and Anglo-Saxon Hymnals.[32] It would have been known to the composer of this hymn. St. Augustine also commented on the psalm verse in the same vein as St. Ambrose.[33] For the ninth-century Christian, the prophetic nature of this stanza was evident.

Line 4, *Virginis matris clausula*, discreetly alludes to Scriptural imagery long used in the Church to symbolize the virginity of the Blessed Virgin Mary and the Virgin birth of Christ. The Bride of the Song of Songs at 4:12 is a garden enclosed (*conclusus*); Mary is a new Paradise from which the new Adam goes forth. Ezekiel says at 44:2: "And the Lord said to me, 'This gate shall remain shut (*porta hæc clausa erit*); it shall not be opened, and no one shall enter by it, for the Lord, the God of Israel, has entered by it. Therefore, it shall remain shut (*eritque clausa*).'"[34] Ambrose wrote: "This door is Mary, of whom it is written that the Lord shall

---

30. Augustine, *De catechizandis rudibus*, 22. See also Heb 1:2 "in these last days he has spoken to us by his Son."

31. *In sole posuit tabernaculum suum et ipse tamquam sponsus procedens de thalamo suo exultavit ut gigas ad currendam viam suam* (Ps 18 [19]:6).

32. See Milfull, 474.

33. St. Augustine: *naturæ coniunctus humane, tamquam de castissimo procedens cubili, humilis misericordia infra omnes, fortis maiestate super omnes. Hoc est enim, gigas....* (*Enarrationes in psalmos*, no. 2. on Ps 18 [19]:6). "Once wedded to human nature he came forth from that purest of all rooms, humbler in mercy than all others, stronger than all in majesty. [This is] what is meant by *he leaps up like a giant*...." From Boulding, *Exposition of the Psalms 1–32*, 209

34. *et dixit Dominus ad me porta hæc clausa erit non aperietur et vir non transiet per eam quoniam Dominus Deus Israel ingressus est per eam eritque clausa* (Ez 44:2).

pass through her, and she shall be closed."³⁵ Only Christ shall come forth from the womb of the Virgin Mother, and he will come as light into a darkened world, at the end of time. Note the juxtaposition of *Virginis* with *matris*.

STANZA 4

Stanza 4 is, in part, a paraphrase of Philippians 2:10–11, itself a meditation on Isaiah 45:23. The stanza reminds us that the merciful savior and bridegroom of stanzas 2 and 3 also comes with power and might so great that all created beings fall on their knees before him. The stanza is divided into two parts separated by a semi-colon and beautifully balanced by parallel constructions and rhythm in lines 2 and 4. Though the infernal regions St. Paul evokes are not mentioned, they are implied by the *omnia* of line 2: all things bend the knee before his strength and might. We gather from the *omnia* that the bending of the knee in lines 1–2 is an obligatory homage. By contrast, in lines 3 and 4, the rational beings in heaven and on earth willingly confess (*fatentur*) their submission to his will (*nutu*). The primary meaning of *nutus* is a nod or gesture of beckoning; then, "will," command (indicated by a gesture). The contrast between the absolute subjection of the universe to Christ's power and might, on the one hand (4, 1–2), and the willing submission to his rule and authority, on the other (4, 3–4), is reinforced through graphic syntax created by the placement of *genu* ("knee") and *nutu* ("nod") at the head of lines 2 and 4.³⁶ Both Latin nouns are of the fourth declension; *genu* is ablative, and we would expect *nutu* to be ablative as well. In the language of poetry, however, the fourth declension dative, normally *nutui*, may also be *nutu*.³⁷ The result of this poetic license is that *nutu* in line 4 may be understood as both dative and ablative. Each case adds a different dimension to the signification. The primary meaning of lines 3–4 requires the dative: creatures of heaven and earth confess that they are subject *to* his will. The secondary meaning sees in the ablative a nod, a gesture, which is the rational equivalent of bending the knee; it signifies the gesture (a consent of the will) *by* which rational creatures submit to his divine will. By the use and placement of *nutu*, the hymn writer has considerably expanded the meaning of the stanza.

STANZA 5

As the verbs in stanzas 1 and 2 attest (*exaudi* and *salvasti*), the hymn is addressed directly to Christ. In stanza 5, we return to this direct form of address with the imperative (*conserva*). As in many other hymns, this final stanza before the doxology gathers the ideas of the preceding stanzas into a petition for those who sing the hymn.

---

35. *Hæc porta est Maria de qua scriptum est quia dominus pertransibit eam et erit clausa* (Ambrose, *Epistulæ extra Collectionem*, 15.6).
36. For an explanation of the term "graphic syntax", see the general introduction, note 27.
37. See Walpole, no. 84, l. 16, p. 301, who cites Virgil, *Æn.* 7.592.

In stanzas 1–4, Christ, whose coming we await, is presented as the *Conditor*, the Redeemer, the Bridegroom, the Lord of heaven and earth. He is also for us who are still bound by time the Judge, who is holy (*Sancte*) and certain to come: *venture* is a vocative future active participle; it implies something more deliberate than the simple future, as if to say, "he *is about* to come," and when he does, he will judge the world and end the age. This image brings vividly to mind the phrase of the Nicene Creed (*venturus est*) as well as the biblical parables and prophecies of the Last Judgment.[38]

The vision of the Judge brings into poignant relief the petition of line 3: preserve us as we live our lives in the world and in time (*conserva nos in tempore*). Note the juxtaposition of *sæculi* and *tempore* at the end of lines 2 and 3. Yet, we do not stop at a request for generic protection. We know all too well the enemy, whose sole aim is to keep us from appearing before the Judge with a clean conscience. In line 4, we identify him as a single foe (*hostis* is singular). He is a liar and the father of lies (*perfidus* signifies one who breaks faith, who is dishonest and treacherous). Finally, he strikes from afar (*telum* signifies a thrown weapon, a dart, javelin, missile). He does not declare himself and give us a fair fight. It is Christ's protection that will save us from the evil one and bring us safely to the Last Judgment. Again, our personal victory in this life-long struggle under the protection of Christ is the realization of St. Bernard's second Advent.

STANZA 6

For a discussion of the role of the doxology at the end of each hymn, please see the General Introduction. The doxology typically brings the hymn full circle, so that it ends on a note of praise. During the Middle Ages, generic doxologies were composed, which differed in meter, person addressed, and subject matter in such a way that they could be attached to a variety of hymns. The same doxology might appear at the end of many hymns, and one finds different doxologies attached to one and the same hymn. This practice is continued in the revised hymns of the Divine Office. The doxology found here is placed at the end of nineteen different hymns.

This doxology was chosen because it begins by addressing Christ directly (*Sit, Christe, rex piissime, tibi...*), and so it fits the euchology of the hymn, which is addressed directly to Christ. Lines 2–3 bring in the other Persons of the Trinity. In line 3 the Holy Spirit is given the title *Paraclitus*, the Greek name for an advocate or legal assistant, someone who comes to the aid of another as counselor, guide, intercessor. Through liturgical use, we have become accustomed to this title, but it is worth noting that it is found only in the Gospel of John in Christ's discourse at the Last Supper.[39] There, he uses the word, referring indirectly to himself and to the Spirit as "another Paraclete" whom the Father will send (Jn 14:16).

---

38. See Niceno-Constantinopolitan Creed. *Et iterum venturus est cum gloria, iudicare vivos et mortuos.* See also Ps 97(98):9; Mt 25:31–46; Acts 10:42; Rv 20:11–15.

39. Jn 14:16, 26; 15:26; and 16:7.

Verbum supernum prodiens 2

10th c.   Advent to 16 December
8 8 8 8 (LM)   Office of Readings

Verbum supérnum pródiens,   1. O Word proceeding from on high,
a Patre lumen éxiens,   light coming from the Father's light,
qui natus orbi súbvenis   by birth you came to save the world
cursu declívi témporis: when time's appointed course had run.

Illúmina nunc péctora   2. Now come and fill our hearts with light,
tuóque amóre cóncrema;   consume them in your love's bright heat,
audíta per præcónia   and when the herald's cry is heard,
sint pulsa tandem lúbrica.   may all deceit be put to flight.

Iudéxque cum post áderis,   3. So when at length you come as Judge
rimári facta péctoris,   to probe our hearts in thought and deed,
reddens vicem pro ábditis   to weigh the guilt for hidden sin
iustísque regnum pro bonis,   and crown the just for deeds well done,

Non demum artémur malis   4. Let not the nature of our sins
pro qualitáte críminis,   detain us in the evil throng,
sed cum beátis cómpotes   but let us with the blessed share
simus perénnes cælites.   the life of heaven evermore.

Sit, Christe, rex piíssime,   5. To you, O Christ, most loving King,
tibi Patríque glória   and to the Father, glory be,
cum Spíritu Paráclito,   one with the Spirit Paraclete,
in sempitérna sæcula. Amen.   from age to age for evermore. Amen.

Text found in *TDH*, no. 72; AH 51, no. 48; Walpole, no. 85. Changes in *TDH*: stanza 1, 2: *lumen* for *olim*; 3, 3: *per* for *ut*; 4, 4: *cælites* for *cælibes*.

COMMENTARY

Like *Conditor alme siderum* (H 1), *Verbum supernum prodiens* (H 2) is found in tenth-century manuscripts. As such it belongs to the oldest group of hymns found in the "New Hymnal" of the Carolingian and Benedictine reforms.[40] These two (H 1–2) with *Vox clara ecce intonat* (H 3) all refer to Christ's return at the end of time, but *Verbum supernum*, assigned to the Office of Readings, focuses primarily on the Last Judgment. Christ is presented to us as the eternal Word, coming

---

[40]. See the lists in AH 51, pp. xxiiff., esp. no. 10 on p. xxxvi (a manuscript from Canterbury, now in London with the no. Ad. 37517). This manuscript shows all three hymns together in liturgical use for Vespers, Matins, and Lauds in Advent. See also Milfull, 9ff. and 41–43. This manuscript is named B in Milfull's edition.

forth from the Father, born in order to come to the aid of the world (stanza 1). We ask him to prepare our hearts (stanza 2). After a description of the Judgment (stanza 3), we pray for a blessed outcome (stanza 4).

As with other ninth- and tenth-century hymns, *Verbum supernum prodiens* is composed in a combination of quantitative and rhythmical meter; sequences of long and short syllables are for the most part observed, but exceptions are found at *declivi* (1, 4), *aderis* (3, 1), and *rimari* (3, 2), and the hiatus at *pro abditis* (3, 3). In these examples, stress accents are well observed. One senses that the author acknowledges the rules of meter and follows them where it is convenient. Where it is not, he follows the accentual conventions of his day.

STANZA I

This hymn is rich in allusions that suggest passages and concepts familiar from Scripture without referring to any one passage in particular but often echoing multiple passages. Thus, the hymn draws the singer into a realm of meaning far larger than the text itself. Line 1 is an example of this poetic richness. The word *prodiens* (*prodeo*) is found in a handful of passages in Scripture, one of which is Sirach 24:5. Chapter 24 of Sirach contains the well-known praise of wisdom, from which the first of the Advent O Antiphons, *O Sapientia*, is taken. The O Antiphons were in liturgical use during Advent when *Verbum supernum prodiens* was composed.[41] Those who knew the O Antiphon and Sirach 24 would have had no trouble associating both with the opening words of the hymn, *Verbum supernum prodiens*. Other references also come to mind; for example, at John 8:23, Jesus says, "You are from below; I am from above" (*Vos de deorsum estis, ego de supernis sum*).[42] Thus, a range of nuances and associations open as the hymn begins. This first line is a beautiful example of the way in which the liturgy works, by forming a vast web of meaning that is based on Scripture but also on the different uses of Scripture in the liturgy itself.

Not only was *Verbum supernum prodiens* drawn from other liturgical sources, but it entered into the tradition and became a source for later hymns. St. Thomas Aquinas used the first two lines of stanza 1 to begin one of his hymns for the feast of Corpus Christi. His lines read: *Verbum supernum prodiens / nec Patris linquens dexteram*. The first line is entirely the same, the second line has the name *Pater* (in a different case) in the same position (syllables 2–3), preceded by the one syllable *nec* instead of *a*. The hymnologist H. A. Daniel remarks on the manifest affinity between the Incarnation, in which the Word came down from on high to become flesh and dwell among us, and his abiding presence among us in the Eucharist.[43]

---

41. *O Sapientia, quæ ex ore Altissimi prodisti, attingens a fine usque ad finem, fortiter suaviter disponensque omnia: veni ad docendum nos viam prudentiæ* (Magnificat antiphon, Vespers, December 17).

42. Jn 3:31; cf. Lk 1:78 and Jn 1:1–2, 14, 18.

43. *Aptissime S. Thomas carmen suum hymno fecit simile notissimo de Nativitate Domini (LXXIV), nam festivitas S. Eucharistiæ, qua per omnia sæcula Verbum caro factum habitabit in nobis, quid habeat affinitatis cum Nativitate Domini non est quod fusius explanemus. Ecclesiam idem sentire id perspicue docet, quod in sollemnitate corporis Christi et per totam Octavam cantatur Præfatio de Nativitate:* "Very appropriately did Aquinas make his

By his appeal to this well-known Advent hymn, Aquinas draws the singer of both hymns into a contemplation of the full theological truth of the Eucharist as an extension of the Incarnation.[44]

In line 1, *supernum* is an adjective standing between *Verbum* and *prodiens*; syntactically, it modifies *Verbum*, but the sense of the line seems to require that it be felt as adverbial modifying the participle *prodiens*: "proceeding forth on high." In the original hymn, this was balanced both in form and content by the adverb *olim* in line 2: *a Patre olim exiens*. The Latin *olim* indicates time (usually past time), where *supernum* indicates space (height); lines 1 and 2 are parallel and create a unit; line 1 refers to the supernatural origin of the Word, line 2 tells us "where" he came from (*a Patre*) and "when"; that is, he came forth long ago, eternally, from the Father. In a similar way the letter to the Hebrews begins: "In times past (*olim*), God spoke in partial and various ways to our ancestors through the prophets."[45] The passage continues: "but in these last days he [God] has spoken to us by his Son." In the hymn (1, 4), the last days are signified by the *cursu declivi temporis*, the declining course of time.[46] At this appointed end of time, Christ the Son is born (in the flesh), to come to the aid of the world. Line 3 forms a balanced and vivid contrast to lines 1–2; *qui natus* occupies the same place in line 3 as *a Patre* in line 2. The idea in lines 2–4 seems to be that by his birth, Christ comes from the Father to the aid of the world. To borrow a line from Aquinas's hymn, Christ was *natus ad hoc* ("born for this"). The verb *subvenis* (1, 3) literally means: "you rescue / relieve / come to the aid of the world."

Returning to line 2, *olim* was considered problematic by Lentini and his team of revisers, *coetus* VII. They thought that, since *olim* is a word that signifies time, it should not be used to indicate the eternal generation of the Word from the Father, since those who sing the hymn might fail to understand the poetic image of a long stretch of time as a symbol of eternity. We regularly use such an image in expressions such as "world without end" or "from age to age." In the context of the opening phrases of a hymn, however, it might indicate an Arian tendency to think of Christ as less eternal and less divine than the Father. Inserting *lumen* ("light") in place of *olim* is wholly unambiguous. It refers the singer to the Creed: *lumen de lumine* ("Light from Light").[47]

---

hymn similar to the one that is most well-known for the Nativity of the Lord; for the affinity between the feast of the Holy Eucharist by which through all ages the Word made flesh dwells among us needs no explanation from us. The Church herself knows this and teaches it clearly." (Daniel, *Thesaurus* 1:254).

44. A striking analogue to the association between the two hymns is found in the fifteenth-century Portinari Altarpiece by Hugo Van der Goes in the Uffizi Gallery, Florence. It depicts the adoration of the Shepherds. The Christ child is lying naked on the ground, just born; in the foreground parallel to him is a sheaf of wheat. The angels in attendance are all clad in the liturgical attire of those who assist the priest at a Solemn High Mass: cope, dalmatic, alb, stole. The chasuble, the garment reserved for the officiating priest, is conspicuously absent. Christ is High Priest "offering the Mass" of his birth. See McNamee, "Further Symbolism in the Portinari Altarpiece," 142–43.

45. *Multifariam et multis modis olim Deus loquens patribus in prophetis* (Heb 1:1).

46. The Latin *declivi* is ablative singular modifying *cursu*. It signifies sloping downwards, that is, the sun or the day is going down towards evening; "the age is compared to a day" as at *Conditor* 3, 1. See Walpole, no. 85, l. 4, p. 303.

47. In *HIBR* (1968), *summo* was substituted for *olim*. This was later changed in the *TDH* (1984) to *lumen*.

STANZA 2

Stanza 2 contains three petitions we make to Christ at his coming in the flesh. First, we ask that he bring light (*illumina*), not to our minds, but to our *pectora*. Literally, *pectus, pectoris* n., signifies the chest, breast, both in humans and animals. It may also mean "soul, spirit, mind, understanding," but at a depth that precludes mere intellectual knowledge. The ancients saw the *pectus* as the seat of emotion, moral conviction, prophecy, and deep understanding. The light we seek in line 1 is of the sort that brings conversion and purification. Second, we ask that Christ might burn up completely, as in a burnt offering, these same enlightened *pectora* with his love. The Latin *concrema* is a second person singular imperative. It does not signify "to warm," but rather "to burn up and turn into ashes." The verb is also found in the *Dies iræ* (H 138: 2, 3) and refers there to the souls burning in hell.[48] Christ himself said, "I have come to cast fire on the earth, and would that it were already kindled!" (Lk 12:49). Here, we ask him to light a fire of love in our hearts, to burn up the dross, and to consume our hearts. In this stanza, one senses the weight of long centuries of waiting for deliverance: the intensity of line 2 is mirrored in the use of *tandem* in line 4.

The third petition comes in 2, 3–4. In line 3, we find the second change Lentini made to the text. The ancient hymn had: *Audita ut præconia*: *ut* means "that" and goes with *sint pulsa*, "may be expelled." The line was soon changed in medieval manuscripts to *audito … præconio*.[49] Both Blume and Walpole say that the original *audita … præconia* is a nominative or accusative absolute, a *lectio difficilior*, changed by later copyists to a regular ablative absolute (*audito ut præconio*). In his additions and revisions to his earlier text, Daniel proposes the replacement of *ut* by *per*, and Lentini followed him. There is no manuscript precedent for this change. It resolves the hiatus and simplifies the syntax in line 3, but it weakens the connection between lines 1–2 and 3–4. In the medieval hymn, *ut* nestled between the members of the absolute clause creates a direct link between the action of God *concrema* (2, 2) and *sint pulsa* (2, 4); it also creates an indirect link between the action of the absolute clause and the clause, *ut … sint pulsa*, of line 4. *Ut* implies purpose, but also result; God's purposes are always accomplished. In the context of the hymn, *ut* is a more expressive and coherent word than *per*.[50] It is God who melts our hearts (*concrema*), in order to drive away all slippery things (*lubrica*). In the revised text, the slippery things are driven away through the herald's cry heard by us. This may appear to be a subtle difference, but it may be seen as separating the effect in us from the agency of God and so flattening the meaning of the stanza. This change necessitates the semicolon placed now after line 2.

Here Lentini comments: "se s'intende della generazione eterna, l' *olim* temporale è parso teologicamente poco esatto. *Lumen* suggerito da *lumen de lumine*": "If eternal generation is intended, the temporal interpretation of olim is inexact, *Lumen* is suggested by *lumen de lumine*" (Nicene Creed), *TDH*, no. 72.

48. The Latin *concremo* is a synonym of *uro*, the more usual verb signifying "burn." See H 93 (3, 1): *lumbos adure*; H 109 (4, 1): *ure cor nostrum* …

49. Daniel, *Thesaurus* 1:77; AH, 51, no. 48; see also Walpole, 303, no. 85, p. 303.

50. Daniel, *Thesaurus* 4:144. See also Walpole, no. 85, l. 7, p. 303.

The Latin *præconium* refers to the message delivered by a *præco*, a herald. It is translated by the somewhat archaic "tidings." In a world where news spread largely by word of mouth, the herald was an important person who "brought tidings." Here, in the neuter plural, *præconia* refers to the proclamations of the long line of prophets foretelling the Incarnation. The greatest prophet of them all was John the Baptist, to whom the Evangelists apply the prophecy of Isaiah: "The voice of one crying in the desert, 'Prepare the way of the Lord.'"[51] The present hymn is for the Office of Readings, which was traditionally said during the night or before Lauds. This stanza leads directly to the hymn for Lauds, which opens with the clarion voice of John, crying from the desert and delivering his message of repentance and mercy: *Vox clara ecce intonat*. Finally, the long centuries of *præconia* herald not only the coming of the Messiah, but also his Second Coming at the end of time; they are the prophetic trumpets preparing for and sounding the Last Judgment. This will be the theme of the next stanza.

In line 4 of stanza 2, *tandem* means "finally, at last"; it may also be an intensifier, in questions or commands (or prayers, as here) expressing impatience or insistence.[52] It echoes the verses and antiphons of the Divine Office during Advent that ask the Lord not to delay in his coming.[53] To what does it refer here? To the casting out (*pulsa*, from *pello*) of *lubrica* from our hearts and souls (2, 4). *Lubricum* is a colorful scriptural and Ambrosian word.[54] The literal meaning of the adjective *lubricus* is "slippery, smooth, slimy." Moving into the moral sphere, it means "uncertain, dangerous, deceitful," what, in rather colloquial language we call the "slippery slope." It describes the perils of sin in general, and sexual sin in particular. The petition asks that these sins may be rejected (*pulsa*) finally and definitively (*tandem*) before the Judge returns. It also refers to the expressive "digging up" (*rimari*) of stanza 3, 2, below.

STANZA 3

Stanzas 3 and 4 present the Last Judgment in its grandeur and terror, as it is presented in Matthew 25:31–46. Together the stanzas form one complete sentence. In stanza 3 we see the judgment unfold; in stanza 4 we ask for mercy and for a blessed outcome. Notice the preposition *post* in line 1 of stanza 3. The series of time words, one per stanza, through a rather subtle form of graphic syntax, provide a kind of historical context to the unfolding drama of the hymn; this is not merely an interior, spiritual progression, it is also external, historical: the greatest drama the world has ever known.[55] It began in eternity (*olim*, in the original form of stanza 1), it proceeds through Christ's intervention on our behalf, in our lives

---

51. Is 40:3; Mt 3:3; Mk 1:3; Lk 3:4.
52. Walpole, l. 8, p. 303. He refers to Quintilian, who says, "it is used for the sake of insistence" (*Institutes* 9.2.6–7). *OLD*, s.v. *tandem*.
53. *Veni, Domine, et noli tardare*: "Come Lord, and do not delay." Short Responsory at None in Advent.
54. See St. Ambrose, *Splendor paternæ gloriæ* (H 75: 3, 4), and Prudentius, *Sol ecce surgit igneus* (4, 3). *Tandem* appears in a long line of hymns after them. Uses of *lubricum* in the Vulgate include Ps 34:6; Prv 26:28; Jer 23:12 and 38:22. Note the connection between *lubricum* and darkness: one slips and falls out of the light.
55. See Walpole's note on line 9, p. 303.

now (*nunc*, stanza 2), it will draw to a close at the Judgment (*post*, stanza 3), and as a result of this judgment, it will bring us finally (*demum*, stanza 4) into eternal life for good or for evil. We are part of a history of divine intervention that began long ago and will lead to a future rendering of accounts and finally back into eternity.

In line 2, *rimari* (present infinitive of the deponent *rimor*) is a colorful word. The hymn writer might have used *scrutari* (a synonym and deponent), equally suited to the meter and the idea of careful examination. By choosing *rimari*, however, he introduced the idea of physical, even agricultural activity: "to root out, turn over the soil." The word is said of animals—to rummage and dig looking for food—then in a secondary sense—to pry into, examine thoroughly, find out. And where does the Judge rummage? In the same *pectora* he came to enlighten and inflame in stanza 2. This turning over and examining the deeds of the heart will bring to light the hidden things (*abditis*) that have been lurking there until the Last Judgment.[56] The contrast between *pro abditis* at the end of line 3 and *pro bonis* at the end of line 4, combined with the similarly placed *vicem* ("requital, recompense", 3, 3) and *regnum* ("kingdom", 3, 4) implies that the *abditis* are indeed the hidden sins that will be fully revealed at the end of time. There is, however, a note of ambiguity here. Many good deeds will also have been hidden; they too will be revealed at the Last Judgment. Each will receive a due recompense, but the righteous (*iustis*) will receive the Kingdom.

STANZA 4

Finally, in stanza 4, we are not so bold as to ask to be free of all sin but rather that the quality or nature of our sin may not be such as to condemn us to be pressed and crowded together, encompassed by evils; *arto* is another colorful verb meaning to draw or press tightly together, squeeze, hem in, crowd, curtail. The image brings to mind paintings of the Last Judgment, where demons prod and torment sinners on their way to hell. The *malis* may be evils of every sort pressing in, though here it is used in contrast to the *beatis* of line 3, the blessed. The balance and contrast between lines 1 and 3 is seen also in *artemur* and *compotes*. We ask that we be *compotes* with the blessed (*cum beatis compotes*). *Compos* is an adjective that signifies "in possession of, or control of, having a share in." It is often used with *voti* (*voti compotes*) and means having been granted one's prayer, having attained one's wish. Here *voti* is understood; we ask to attain all that we long for and to enjoy it, blessed for ever (*perennes*; adjective modifying *cælites*). The final word of the stanza is the third emendation made by Lentini. The original was *cælibes* (unmarried, celibate); it alludes to Matthew 22:30: "For in the resurrection

---

56. "Nothing is covered up that will not be revealed, or hidden that will not be known" (Lk 12:2); "who will bring to light the things now hidden in darkness and will disclose the purposes of the heart" (1 Cor 4:5). See also Rom 2:16; Heb 4:12–13.

they neither marry nor are given in marriage, but are like angels in heaven."[57] The minor substitution of "t" for "b" gives a beautiful and more readily understood name; they are those who dwell in heaven, in the communion of saints.

STANZA 5

The Doxology is the same as in H 1.

Vox clara ecce intonat	3
10th c.	Advent to 16 December
8 8 8 8 (LM)	Lauds

Vox clara ecce íntonat,	1. Behold a voice resounding, clear,
obscúra quæque íncrepat:	rebuking hidden fears and deeds:
procul fugéntur sómnia;	Let dreams be driven far away,
ab æthre Christus prómicat.	for Christ shines forth from heaven's height.
Mens iam resúrgat tórpida	2. Now let the weary soul arise,
quæ sorde exstat sáucia;	infirm and wounded by her sin;
sidus refúlget iam novum,	a new star now sends forth its light
ut tollat omne nóxium.	to rid the world of every harm.
E sursum Agnus míttitur	3. The Lamb is sent from realms on high
laxáre gratis débitum;	to free us from our mortal debt.
omnes pro indulgéntia	Let every voice give thankful praise
vocem demus cum lácrimis,	and weep for tender mercy shown,
Secúndo ut cum fúlserit	4. That when he comes like lightning flash
mundúmque horror cínxerit,	and terror grips the world in dread,
non pro reátu púniat,	he need not punish us for guilt
sed nos pius tunc prótegat.	but with compassion shield us then.
Summo Parénti glória	5. Praise to the Father, God most high,
Natóque sit victória,	all victory to his only Son,
et Flámini laus débita	due honor to the Spirit blest,
per sæculórum sǽcula. Amen.	through endless ages evermore. Amen.

Text found in *TDH*, no. 73; AH 51, no. 49; Walpole, no. 86. Changes in *TDH*: stanza 1, 3: *procul fugentur* for *pellantur eminus*; 5, 1–4: a doxology of St. Alfanus (d. 1085), PL 147, 1227–28, for the original but common doxology found in AH 51:49.

---

57. Lentini, *TDH*, 74, no. 72 says of *cælibes*: "vocabolo che nell'uso ecclesiastico medievale significa lo stesso che *cælestem vitam agens, cæles*": "A word which in medieval ecclesiastical usage has the same meaning as *cælestem vitam agens, cæles*. See also Daniel, *Thesaurus* 1:77–78.

COMMENTARY

This hymn is difficult to date. It is found in many of the earliest extant manuscripts, one of which is the complete hymnal from the tenth century, originating in Canterbury, now in the British Library (BL, Add. MS 37517). Helmut Gneuss says of this manuscript, "We no longer have before us the initial stages of the New Hymnal but a more fully developed form."[58] Lentini indicates that the hymn was composed "at least" (*almeno*) by the tenth century. Certain characteristics of the text may indicate that it is considerably older. As a general rule, in classical quantitative meter and post-Carolingian accentual verse, hiatus and elision are treated carefully, either reduced to a minimum or avoided altogether. This hymn makes no attempt whatsoever to avoid either. It has seven instances of hiatus, two in the first line, as well as quantitatively incorrect syllable lengths on several third syllables (long for short) and two sixth syllables (short for long). In the original version, after three instances of hiatus in the first two lines, it had an elision; *eminus* would need to be pronounced *em'nus* (1, 3).[59] The instances of hiatus were left by Lentini, but he opted for the Urbanite emendation of the elision. As a result of irregularities in syllable length, the hymn seems to "float" between quantitative and accentual meter.[60] It is probable that it was composed during the interim between the fifth and ninth centuries; this is a judgment about the date of composition, not about the quality of the hymn.[61]

Although the hymn was sung at Matins, and even at Vespers in the Mozarabic liturgy[62], it has been generally assigned to Lauds. The imagery of the first two stanzas makes it eminently suited to the early morning hour when light returns, and one is encouraged to shake off sleep and the obscure deeds that thrive at night under cover of darkness. There is more to this hymn, however. The rich layering of metaphors, so typical of the hymns of St. Ambrose, the vocabulary found in both Ambrose and Prudentius, and finally the strong rhythm of the poetic lines make this hymn a magnificent and powerful expression of the spiritual and liturgical message of Advent. Images of the voice that cries out, the *sidus* (both star and sun), the saving Lamb, the just Judge: all come together in four short stanzas to show us the vast range and significance of the divine plan of salvation. Equally intense, the earthly counterpart to God's divine intervention is darkness, sleep, vain dreams, torpor, and sin. These themes allude to Romans 13:11–14, the text

---

58. Gneuss, "Latin Hymns," 413. For a discussion of the Old Hymnal, the Frankish Hymnal, and the New Hymnal, see Gneuss, "Latin Hymns," 408–11. See also the discussion in the general introduction, note 29.

59. Hiatus is a slight pause or break created by the pronunciation of two separate and adjacent vowels in consecutive syllables or words, as in the English word *naïve*. Hiatus occurs in this hymn at 1, 1: *clara ecce intonat*; at 1, 2: *quæque increpat*; at 2, 2: *sorde exstat*; at 3, 3: *pro indulgentia*; at 4, 1: *secundo ut*; finally, at 4, 2, because the "h" is silent: *mundumque horror*. See Norberg, *Introduction*, 26–27.

60. In *TDH* Lentini calls it metrical; Milfull calls it rhythmical, 187. The combining of elements from quantitative and accentual meter is not necessarily due to mistakes on the part of the hymn writer. It may be intentional in an environment where both are acceptable.

61. Connelly, 53, and Albin, *La poésie*, 115, both place the hymn in the fifth century.

62. Mozarabic generally implies the Christian liturgy in Spain during the time of Muslim rule. As a liturgical rite, however, its antecedents predate the Mozarabic period and represent an ancient patrimony of Hispanic liturgical texts.

used for the short readings at Lauds and Terce for the Sundays of Advent and for the second reading at Mass on the First Sunday of Advent: "Now is the hour for us to rise from sleep; For our salvation is nearer now than when we first believed. The night is far spent and the day is at hand. Let us then cast off the works of darkness and put on the armor of light."[63]

STANZA 1

Vox clara: a voice resounds (*intonat*). It is loud and clear, unambiguous, illustrious, honorable; *clara* can mean all of these. Alluding to the prophecy of Isaiah (40:3–4), John the Baptist identifies himself as the voice: *ego sum vox clamantis in deserto...*, "I am the voice of one crying in the desert..." (Jn 1:23).[64] Note that where the Scriptures say *vox clamantis*, the hymn says *vox clara*. John is clear in his message; he is also the greatest of all the prophets; he is *clarus* in the fullest sense.[65] He is the subject of the verbs in lines 1–2; he speaks line 3. John's voice rebukes and censures (*increpat*) the dark and hidden deeds of the night, the sins committed in secret, in "hatred of the light" (1, 2).[66] He bids all who come to hear him to chase away the idle dreams that breed in sleep and the obscurity (1, 3) that overcomes the mind and leads to sin and death. Pimont comments, "Dreams signify here that state of spiritual somnolence that leads inevitably to sin, if it is not already sin, and also the vanities of the world, true dreams, which, alas, all too often in this life trap us in the forgetfulness of God."[67]

One may wonder whether John speaks line 4 or whether it is merely a statement of fact. The best course seems to be to take the first two and a half stanzas of the hymn as belonging to John. At 3, 3 *we* the singers are introduced by the verb *demus*, "let us give...." This is in keeping with the general structure of liturgical hymns, in which the first part is devoted to praise or to certain events or persons connected with salvation history; then in a second part, the singers are brought into the hymn by means of a prayer or exhortation linked to the praise of the first part; finally a third part returns to praise, usually in the doxology.

Thus, line 4 is part of John's message. He pauses in his exhortations, which he will take up again in stanza 2, to fulfill his mandate as precursor.[68] He announces that Christ is close at hand, already gleaming, shining forth (*promicat*) from the brightness (*æthre*) above.[69] John is not named in the hymn. He is merely a

---

63. The Latin is given here to show the close connections with the Latin of the hymn. *Hoc scientes tempus quia hora est iam nos de somno surgere nunc enim propior est nostra salus quam cum credidimus nox præcessit dies autem adpropiavit abiciamus ergo opera tenebrarum et induamur arma lucis sicut in die honeste ambulemus* (Rom 13:11–13).

64. All four gospels record the prophecy of Isaiah in reference to John the Baptist. See Mt 3:1–3; Mk 2:2–4; Lk 3:3–6; and especially Jn 1:23: *Ait*: "*ego vox clamantis in deserto: dirigite viam Domini, sicut dixit Isaias propheta*": "He [John] said: I am the voice of one crying out in the desert, "Make straight the way of the Lord," as Isaiah the prophet said."

65. Connelly, 53.

66. *Omnis enim qui mala agit odit lucem et non venit ad lucem ut non arguantur opera eius; qui autem facit veritatem venit ad lucem ut manifestentur eius opera quia in Deo sunt facta*: "For everyone who does wicked things hates the light and does not come to the light, lest his works should be exposed. But he who does what is true comes to the light, that it may be clearly seen that his deeds have been wrought in God" (Jn 3:20–21).

67. Pimont 2:44.

68. Cf. Lk 7:24–28.

69. The Latin *æthre* is an elision from *æthere*, the ablative, after the preposition *ab*, of *æther*. It signifies the

voice; Christ is named, and he is light. In the next stanza the light will be named; Christ is a star (*sidus*). In both the first and second stanzas, there is a close association between sound and light. The voice exhorts and rebukes, the light uncovers the darkness. Thus the role of John, the voice, and the work of Christ, the light, are simultaneous and superimposed, so to speak, in the hymn. This blending of sound and light is reminiscent of Ambrose's hymn *Æterne rerum Conditor* (H 71), where at the darkest hour of the night the cock by his crowing is herald of the dawn. Pimont comments, "In the ancient hymns, as in the Holy Scriptures, senses abound and superimpose; one sense does not exclude the other, all recommend themselves to our respect and meditation."[70] The end of line 1, *intonat*, balances the end of line 4, *promicat*.

Assonance marks the line endings of this hymn in stanzas 1, 2, and 4. Stanza 1, however, is also a masterpiece of internal and external rhetorical rhyme. It mimics the clarion voice of line 1 and gives it the look and feel of a public proclamation.[71] In his notes, Lentini says that he chose the version of line 3 revised by Urban VIII and found in the Roman breviary, *procul fugentur somnia*, in order to avoid the elision on *eminus* since it makes the line more difficult to sing.[72] In the original version, *eminus* on the fifth syllable of line 3 forms an internal one-syllable rhyme with *Christus*, also on the fifth syllable, in line 4. In the first two lines, there is a series of four assonances at identical positions in each line. The effect is a light "sing-song" feel to the stanza as a whole, as one might find in a true prophetic utterance.

Vox clara ecce intonat,	Behold a voice resounding, clear,
obscura quæque increpat:	rebuking hidden fears and deeds:
pellantur eminus somnia;	Let dreams be driven far away,
ab æthre Christus promicat.	for Christ shines forth from heaven's height

The Latin adverb *eminus* comes from *e manus* (away from the hand). It means "at a distance" or "from a distance." It is a military technical term used for fighting with thrown weapons, as opposed to "hand to hand" combat. The rhyming parallel established between *eminus* and *Christus* reinforces, by a subtle graphic syntax, the idea of line 4 that he shines in the heavens, still far away. The idea is found elsewhere in the Advent liturgy. Christ has been announced through the ages and long awaited. The great response for the Office of Readings on the First Sunday of Advent begins: "Looking from afar, behold I see the power of God coming...." The Magnificat antiphon (Year B) at First Vespers on the First Sunday of Advent also begins: "Behold, the name of the Lord comes from afar...."[73]

---

upper, pure, bright air. The English word "ether" comes from it. The Latin verb *mico* means "to move rapidly to and fro, glitter, gleam"; with the prefix *pro*, it signifies "gleam forth" (of light) or "spring forth" (of liquids or plants, etc.).

70. Pimont 2:42.
71. This passage was discussed in appendix 2, on assonance and rhyme, under "Internal Factors," "The Legacy of the Poets."
72. Lentini, note on 1, 3, *TDH*, 75.
73. *Aspiciens a longe, ecce video Dei potentiam venientem ...* and *Ecce nomen Domini venit de longinquo ...*

STANZA 2

The *vox clara* of stanza 1 returns to the work of conversion and preparation in stanza 2. Here, the examination of the interior heart is even more intense than in stanza 1. The star, named in 2, 3 is also brighter than the light of stanza 1. There the verb was *promicat*, "sparkle" (1, 4), here it is *refulget* (2, 3): "be radiant with brightness."

The obscure and hidden dreams of stanza 1 have rendered the mind and heart lethargic; they have wounded and weakened the soul with the filth of sin.[74] John, the voice, exhorts the mind (*mens*) to rise up; *resurgo* means "to rise or get up again" (*re-*) and to shake off the torpor caused by dreams (*somnia*) and sin (*sordes*). A numb and jaded heart asks why, what is the point? The answer at 2, 3 is that a new star (*sidus novum*) is shining, a star whose light is fresh and able to renew, a light that can remove every harmful, evil, injurious, noxious thing (*omne noxium*). The Latin *sidus* is properly "a heavenly body, a constellation," not a single star (*stella*). Said of Christ, *sidus* refers to "the star that shall rise out of Jacob" (Nm 24:17), "the sun of justice that shall arise" (Mal 4:2), and to the offspring of David, "the bright morning star" (Rv 22:16). *Sidus* here is an icon of all of these prophecies. The hymn would have been sung at the hour of Lauds, and soon the Benedictus would be sung: the sun of Justice and the bright morning star shall dawn upon us from on high, to give light to those who sit in darkness and in the shadow of death, to guide our feet into the way of peace (Lk 1:76–79).

STANZA 3

At the end of stanza 2, John says that the new star is shining in order to take away (*tollat*) harm. The implication seems to be that the light of the star will shed light upon and so remove all harmful things (2, 3–4). In stanza 3, John introduces another prophetic icon when he identifies the star as the Lamb sent from on high.[75] The star is *the* Lamb of sacrifice to which all the prophetic lambs sacrificed under the old covenant have led. He will undo, dissolve our debt (*laxare*); he will pay for us at great cost what we ourselves owe (*debitum*); finally, he will release us from our debt gratuitously (*gratis*).[76] The gift is pure *indulgentia*. This word can mean anything from "kindness, indulgence, gentleness" to "remission, pardon." We have only to ask, in order to receive Christ's *indulgentia* in all its forms. The infinitive *laxare* ("to stretch out, slacken, ease, relieve, undo") is somewhat unusual, though it fits well the range of meanings in *indulgentia*. It also resonates with the antiphon, used as a verse and response in the Advent

---

74. The Latin *mens* signifies the deep-seated source of thought, understanding, and disposition. It may be variously translated as mind, heart, soul, even conscience; the adjective *torpidus* signifies "benumbed, stupefied, torpid." The adjective *saucius* signifies "wounded, hurt, or sick." Finally, *sorde*, ablative of *sordes*, signifies "squalor, filth, baseness." The English adjective "sordid" captures much of the Latin.

75. References in the New Testament to Christ as the Lamb: Jn 1:29, 1:36; Acts 8:32 [quoting Is 53:7]; Rv 5:6–7:17, 21:22–23.

76. *Omnes enim peccaverunt et egent gloriam Dei, iustificati gratis per gratiam ipsius per redemptionem quæ est in Christo Iesu*: "Since all have sinned and fall short of the glory of God, they are justified by his grace as a gift, through the redemption that is in Christ Jesus." (Rom 3:24).

liturgy: *Veni, Domine, et noli tardare; Relaxa facinora plebi tuæ Israel.* The antiphon is found in all of the ancient manuscripts, including the royal antiphoner of Compiègne, written between 860 and 880.[77]

At 3, 3 either the *vox clara* is still speaking, in which case he identifies himself with those who have received the gift,[78] or, as was suggested earlier, the hymn now begins to speak with the voice of those who sing. In either case, the response to such a great gift of mercy can only be another voice (*vocem*), here a liturgical voice, with tears: *vocem* of 3, 4 at the head of the line corresponds to *vox* of 1, 1. Those who sing now find their own interior voice with tears.

Tears are a liturgical trope in early hymns. They are seen as a gift of the Holy Spirit. They may of course be real physical tears, but they are an icon of the interior disposition that leads to tears. This is named *compunction* in the monastic literature. In a series of retreat conferences, Gabriel Morin considers the significance of the conclusion of Peter's first sermon on Pentecost: the listeners were "cut to the heart" (*compuncti sunt corde*). He concludes: "Compunction, therefore, is the first fruit which the Holy Spirit produces in the souls of those whom He calls to the Christian Faith."[79] In his lapidary summary of John Cassian's teaching on compunction, Gregory the Great associates it with more than sorrow for sin. It also encompasses reverential fear at the prospect of judgment, lucidity about our sins and failures, sorrow at the condition of the world in which we live now, and longing for the joys of heaven.[80] Thus, it represents the restless dissatisfaction with oneself and the ways of the world that is at the heart of Advent. In this regard, it is significant that in the Roman Missal (2011), there is a "Mass for the Forgiveness of Sin (B)" in which the gift of tears is implored in all three proper prayers of the Mass. The collect is as follows:

> Almighty and most gentle God, who brought forth from the rock a fountain of living water for your thirsty people, bring forth we pray, from the hardness of our heart, tears of sorrow, that we may lament our sins and merit forgiveness from your mercy. Through our Lord …

By the simple phrase *cum lacrimis*, the hymn draws the singer, *hic et nunc*, into a world of repentance, longing, and hope that is at the heart of John's message and of the liturgy of Advent.

STANZA 4

In stanza 4, the hymn finishes the prayer begun in stanza 3. The Latin text opens with *ut* (4, 1) signifying both purpose and result: "that, so that, in order that, with the result that." See also 2, 4. The invitation of stanza 3 is that we respond with our own voice to the *vox clara* that heralds Christ and that we speak from the

---

77. V. "Come, Lord, and do not delay." R. "Free your people from their sinfulness." See Hesbert, *Corpus antiphonalium officii*, 1, 14. The Compiègne Antiphoner appears to have belonged to Charles the Bald (d. 877), grandson of Charlemagne.
78. Connelly, 53.
79. Morin, *Ideal of the Monastic Life*, 2.
80. Gregory the Great, *Moralia in Job*, 23, 41; Cassian, *Conferences*, 9.26–29.

heart with compunction, signified by tears (3, 4). If we respond in this way, then when the merciful Lamb returns at the end of time as the just Judge, we shall be able to weather the lightning that reveals all and the horror that will bind and engulf the world.[81] The Lamb as Judge will not need to punish us according to our guilt (*pro reatu*) because we will have already placed ourselves by our lives under the protection of his love and pity.[82] The verbs in the first two lines, *fulserit* and *cinxerit*, are in the Latin future perfect tense, the past in the future. This is a strong and vivid tense carrying the nuance that the actions signified will surely come to pass and that they will be swift, in the sense that they will be fully accomplished before something else happens in the future; here it is the judgment of our actions by the Lamb who is Judge; *fulserit* means "he shall have flashed like lightning," and *cinxerit*, "he shall have girded, encompassed."

Conditor alme siderum (H 1) and *Verbum supernum prodiens* (H 2) both present the Last Judgment as the decisive hour for the sake of which Christ has intervened in human history. *Vox clara ecce intonat* goes farther and draws a vivid picture of the scene both in the contrast between the Lamb and the Judge and in the choice and placement of vocabulary. The scene as it unfolds in stanza 4 is an allusion to the liturgy in the Book of Revelation in which saints and elders adore the Lamb and angels destroy the world. The inhabitants of the earth desire in vain to hide from the "wrath of the Lamb" (Rv 6:16).

The vocabulary used in this hymn is rich and traditional. Varying forms of words such as *mico*, as in *promicat* (1, 4), *vox* (1, 1) and *vocem* (3, 4), *refulgens* (2, 3) and *fulserit* (4, 1), *somnia* (1, 3), *obscura* (1, 2), and *reatus/reus*, (4, 3) appear at significant places in the hymns of Ambrose and Prudentius, and others. Thus they entered into the traditional imagery of the liturgical hymns. To give only one example: *obscura* (1, 2), associated with what is dark and sinful and with activity that takes place under cover of night, appears in Prudentius's hymn *Cathemerinon* 2, where *obscuritas* is present in a heart that is vaguely aware of its own fraud; the darkness and confusion clear when the clouds are torn away (stanza 3) and God's reign becomes visible.[83] Later, at stanza 25 of the same hymn, the singers pray that they may be involved in no dark thought or deed (*nihil obscurum*). This same hymn that had a great influence on later hymn writers also references tears as a sign of compunction and sorrow for sin.[84]

---

81. Lk 17:24: *nam, sicut fulgur coruscans de sub cælo in ea quæ sub cælo sunt, fulget: ita erit Filii hominis in die sua*: "For just as lightning flashes and lights up the sky from one side to the other, so will the Son of Man be in his day"; see also Mt 24:17.

82. In his note on line 16, p. 305, Walpole comments that *pius* (gracious, kind, benevolent, loving) in this context is close to the English "pity."

83. *sic nostra mox obscuritas / fraudisque pectus conscium / ruptis retectum nubibus, / regnante pallescet deo*: "Thus soon the darkness in our souls, / the heart that's conscious of deceit, / discovered as the clouds are rent, / will pale before the reign of God," (*Cath* 2: 3, 1–4; trans. Richardson, *Hymns*, 35). Prudentius's iconic morning hymn is sung at Lauds in Weeks I and III on Wednesday (H 83). Another cento of the same hymn by Prudentius is sung at Lauds on Thursday of Weeks I and III (H 87). Examples from Ambrose included in the *Liturgia Horarum*: H 71: 6, 2; H 75: 5, 4; H 83: 3, 3.

84. H 83: 4, 3–4: *rogare curvatu genu / flendo et canendo discimus*. See also Ambrose, H 71: 5, 4; H 80: 3, 3; H 93: 2, 2; H 174: 3, 2; H 244: 4, 2; H 290: 4, 1.

STANZA 5

In the notes to the original hymn as it is given in AH 51, no. 48, the opening lines of several standard doxologies are listed as they are found attached to the hymn in different manuscripts. Rather than use one of these, Lentini took a doxology from a collection of hymns composed by Alfanus I, Archbishop of Salerno (d. 1085). Alfanus was a medical doctor, a patron of the arts and renowned theologian. He was a friend of Abbot Desiderius of Montecassino (later Pope Victor III) and of Hildebrand of Sovana (later Pope Gregory VII). Lentini says in his notes (*TDH*, 75) that he used this doxology because it has assonance on "a" at the end of each line. The doxology is addressed to all three Persons of the Trinity.

Verbum salutis omnium	4
ca. 10th c.	Advent after 16 December
8 8 8 8 (LM)	Vespers

Verbum salútis ómnium,
Patris ab ore pródiens,
Virgo beáta, súscipe
casto, María, víscere.

1. Receive, O Mary, Virgin pure,
within your chaste and blessed womb
the saving Word proclaimed for all,
proceeding from the Father's mouth.

Te nunc illústrat cælitus
umbra fecúndi Spíritus,
gestes ut Christum Dóminum,
æquálem Patri Fílium.

2. The fruitful Spirit's shadow comes
and fills you now with heaven's light,
that you may carry Christ the Lord,
the Father's own co-equal Son.

Hæc est sacráti iánua
templi seráta iúgiter,
soli suprémo Príncipi
pandens beáta límina.

3. She is the sacred temple gate,
for ever sealed and barred to all;
yet for the heavenly Prince alone
the blessed threshold opens wide.

Olim promíssus vátibus,
natus ante lucíferum,
quem Gábriel annúntiat,
terris descéndit Dóminus.

4. Foretold by prophets long ago
and born before the morning star,
the one proclaimed by Gabriel
is Christ the Lord come down to earth.

Læténtur simul ángeli,
omnes exsúltent pópuli:
excélsus venit húmilis
salváre quod períerat.

5. Rejoice together, angel hosts!
Let all the peoples sing for joy.
The Most High comes, a humble child,
to save and ransom what was lost.

Sit, Christe, rex piíssime,
tibi Patríque glória
cum Spíritu Paráclito,
in sempitérna sæcula. Amen.

6. To you, O Christ, most loving King,
and to the Father, glory be,
one with the Spirit Paraclete,
from age to age for evermore. Amen.

Text found in *TDH*, 74; AH 14, nos. 1–2. The text is adapted from two medieval Advent hymns: stanzas 1–3 are from *Verbum salutis omnium* (AH 14, n. 2); stanzas 4–5 are from *Sol astra terra æquora* (AH 14, n. 1). Changes in *TDH*: stanza 2, 2: *fecundi* for *sacrati*; 4, 4: *annuntiat* for *prædixerat*.

A. *Verbum salutis omnium*: The first three stanzas are taken directly from this hymn. Stanzas 4–5 and the doxology of the original hymn are omitted. In line 2, 2, *sacrati* is replaced by *fecundi*.[85] In line 2, 4, the original *Patri æqualem filium* is inverted to *æqualem Patri filium*.

B. *Sol astra terra æquora*: The fourth and fifth stanzas of the revised hymn are adapted from the sixteen stanzas of *Sol astra*. Stanza 4 is a centonization of four lines of *Sol astra*:[86] line 4, 1 of the revised hymn is taken from the first line of the original stanza 3 (with *promissum* changed to *promissus*); line 4, 2 from the third line of the original stanza 3; line 4, 3 from the first line of the original stanza 2;[87] and line 4, 4 from the fourth line of the original stanza 8 (with *terras* changed to *terris*, a variant found in one AH source). Stanza 5 of the revised hymn is stanza 7 of *Sol astra*.

The doxology is not taken from either of the two source hymns but corresponds to the doxology used in the *Liturgia Horarum* for H 1, *Conditor alme siderum*.

COMMENTARY

The revised *Verbum salutis omnium* comes from two hymns that appear in hymnals from southern and central Italy beginning in the eleventh century.[88] The hymn is assigned for Vespers in Advent after 16 December, that is, for the eight days leading up to Christmas. The hymn's focus on the Annunciation parallels the focus on the events leading up to the birth of Jesus recalled in the Lectionary for Mass from December 16 to 23.

---

85. Lentini comments that *sacrati* is "less fitting for the Holy Spirit and is repeated in line 9" (*TDH*, 76).

86. To centonize is to select elements from more than one original text, in order to form a new text made out of them, with or without the addition of new material.

87. Lentini explains that *prædixerat* is changed to *annuntiat*, in order to emphasize the moment of the Annunciation (*TDH*, 76)

88. The *Divine Office* hymn was adapted by Lentini from Guido Maria Dreves's AH 14, which is based primarily on two mid-eleventh-century manuscript sources: Vatican City, BAV, Vat. lat. 7172, and Paris, BnF, Latin 1092. Dreves designated these sources as the *Hymnarius Severianus* because of a purported connection with the Abbey of Santi Severino e Sossio in Naples, but recent scholarship suggests that the two manuscripts in fact come from Narni in central Italy, although they have important connections with hymnals from Benevento in southern Italy; see Vergine, "Hymns of Medieval Southern Italy", 231–44. The two hymns appear together in a slightly earlier source, Vatican City, BAV, Ott. lat. 145, likely copied at Santa Sofia in Benevento in the first half of the eleventh century. Although *Sol astra* and *Verbum salutis* appear in sequential order in the AH edition, they do not form a pair in the manuscript sources, but are separated by other Advent hymns (*O quam beatus nuntius* and *Vox clara ecce intonat* in Ott. lat. 145, and *Verbum supernum prodiens*, *Vox clara ecce intonat*, and *Conditor alme siderum* in Vat. lat. 7172 and BnF, Latin 1092). In addition to the three manuscripts that provide both hymns, fourteen other manuscripts give *Verbum salutis* and five other manuscripts give *Sol astra*; see Vergine, "Hymns of Medieval Southern Italy," pp. 459, 465, 737–38.

STANZA 1

The first stanza focuses on the Word of God, who eternally proceeds from the Father and has become flesh in the chaste womb of the blessed Virgin Mary. In the Latin text, the opening lines emphasize Jesus, while the English translation reverses the order of the lines to begin by addressing Mary, a choice that reflects natural English word order and syntax. Lines 1–2 resonate with the opening words of *Verbum supernum prodiens* (H 2), sung at Office of Readings in the opening period of Advent. Both *Verbum salutis* and *Verbum supernum* were transmitted together in eleventh-century Italian sources, which suggests that the verbal similarity is intentional and would have been appreciated by medieval singers.[89] Line 1 recalls the Gospel of John's identification of Jesus as the "Word made flesh" (Jn 1:14: *Verbum caro factum est*). Line 2 evokes the concept of the Trinitarian "procession" of the Son from the Father, likening the eternal generation of the Son to the speaking of a word by the Father's mouth (see Heb 1:1–2). Lines 3–4 hint at the relationship between the eternal generation of the Word from the Father's mouth and the temporal generation of the Word-Made-Flesh at the word of the Annunciation of the Angel Gabriel. Line 4 uses the somewhat unusual *viscus, visceris* ("inner parts, internal organs, uterus") in place of the more familiar *venter* ("belly, womb"), used in the Vulgate version of Elizabeth's exclamation "blessed is the fruit of thy womb" (*benedictus fructus ventris tui*) (Lk 1:42) and subsequently incorporated into the *Ave Maria*. Not only does the three-syllable ablative form *viscere* fit the meter better than *ventre*, the author of the hymn was likely familiar with the use of the same word in *A solis ortus cardine*, a fifth-century hymn by Sedulius in which the third verse includes the phrase *Clausæ parentis viscera / cælestis intrat gratia* (translated in H 9 as "Pure grace from heaven entered then / the Mother's womb, both sealed and closed").

STANZA 2

Stanza 2 continues the Annunciation narrative, with the words *umbra* and *Spiritus* evoking the language of Luke 1:35, where the Angel Gabriel declares that "The holy Spirit will come upon you, and the power of the Most High will overshadow you": *Spiritus Sanctus superveniet in te, et virtus Altissimi obumbrabit tibi*. Lines 1–2 contrast the temporary darkness caused by the shadow (*umbra*) of the Holy Spirit with the heavenly illumination (*cælitus illustrat*) that results from the Incarnation. Line 3 uses the word *gesto, gestare* ("bear, carry"); while the word is typically used in a more external sense (e.g., to carry an object), the poet seems to be using it here to refer to the act of carrying within the womb (cf. the English word "gestation"). The use of this word recalls Deuteronomy 1:31 (*portavit te Dominus Deus tuus, ut solet homo gestare parvulum filium suum*) and Isaiah 46:3 (*qui portamini a*

---

89. The Advent hymn *Verbum supernum prodiens* also supplied the opening line for H 129, St. Thomas Aquinas's Corpus Christi hymn *Verbum supernum prodiens nec Patris*.

meo utero, qui gestamini a mea vulva), verses in which God uses language of carrying and giving birth to children as images of his love for his people. Complementing the mention of Trinitarian processions in 1, 2 and 2, 4, this emphasizes the equality of the Divine Persons.

STANZA 3

Stanza 3 shifts from narrating the Annunciation to contemplating the mystery of the virgin birth, in a sense providing a response to Mary's question to Gabriel in Luke 1:34: "How shall this be done, because I know not man?" Although it uses the term *ianua* rather than *porta*, the stanza seems to be a paraphrase of Ezekiel 44:2–3, a text used by Church Fathers such as Ambrose[90] and Jerome[91] to describe the mystery of Mary's perpetual virginity. The text from Ezekiel is as follows:

> And the Lord said to me: "This gate shall be shut, it shall not be opened, and no man shall pass through it: because the Lord the God of Israel has entered in by it, and it shall be shut; it is for the prince. The prince himself shall sit in it, to eat bread before the Lord: he shall enter in by the way of the porch of the gate, and shall go out by the same way."[92]

Although the hymn uses slightly different language, it is noteworthy that both the hymn and the Vulgate version of Ezekiel 44 use the word *princeps*. The use of *ianua* rather than *porta* may draw on language from 2 Chronicles 28:24 (*clausit ianuas templi Dei*). The reference to the thresholds (*limina*) in line 12 recalls Ezekiel 10:18: "And the glory of the Lord went out from the threshold of the Temple": *Et egressa est gloria Domini a limine templi*.

STANZA 4

Stanza 4 is centonized from four lines of a different hymn, *Sol astra terra æquora*.[93] Line 1 presents Christ as the fulfillment of the prophets of Israel (see Lk 24:27: "Then beginning with Moses and all the prophets, he interpreted to them what referred to him in all the scriptures"). Line 2 links one example of an Old Testament prophecy of Christ, given in Psalm 109 (110):3—"From the womb before the dawn, I have begotten you": *ex utero ante luciferum genui te*—with the theme

---

90. Ambrose, *De Institutione Virginis*, 8:52: *Quæ est hæc porta, nisi Maria? Ideo clausa quia virgo. Porta igitur Maria, per quam Christus intravit in hunc mundum, quando virginali fusus est partu, et genitalia virginitatis claustra non solvit*: "Who is this gate, if not Mary? It is closed because she is a virgin. Thus Mary is the gate through which Christ entered into this world, when he was brought forth by a virginal birth, and did not loosen the seals of virginity."

91. *Pulchre quidam portam clausam per quam solus Dominus Deus Israel ingreditur et dux cui porta clausa est, Mariam Virginem intellegunt, quæ et ante partum et post partum virgo permansit*: "It is beautiful that some understand the Virgin Mary as the *shut gate* through which *the Lord God of Israel alone goes in* and the leader for whom the gate is shut, because she remained a virgin both before and after his birth." Jerome, *In Hiezechielem*, 13.44.

92. *Et dixit Dominus ad me: Porta hæc clausa erit: non aperietur, et vir non transibit per eam, quoniam Dominus Deus Israël ingressus est per eam: eritque clausa principi; princeps ipse sedebit in ea, ut comedat panem coram Domino: per viam portæ vestibuli ingredietur, et per viam eius egredietur* (Ez 44:2–3).

93. For details, see the analysis of the text at the beginning of this commentary, section B.

of the Son's eternal birth from the Father articulated in line 2. Line 3 recalls the Annunciation to Mary by the Angel Gabriel (Lk 1:26–38) which was the focus of the first two stanzas. Line 4 has resonances with Micah 1:3: "For behold, the Lord is coming out of his place, and he will come down and tread upon the high places of the earth": *quia ecce Dominus egreditur de loco suo, et descendet, et calcabit super excelsa terræ.*

STANZA 5

Stanza 5, taken directly from *Sol astra terra æquora*, serves as a sort of pre-doxology, inviting both angels and humans to rejoice and give praise to God for the Incarnation. Lines 1–2 have strong resonances with various Psalm verses, for instance, Psalm 69 (70):5: *Exsultent et lætentur in te omnes qui quærunt te:* "Let all those who seek you exult and rejoice in you"; Psalm 116 (117):1: *Laudate Dominum, omnes gentes; laudate eum, omnes populi:* "Praise the Lord, all you nations, praise him all you peoples"; Psalm 148:2: *Laudate eum, omnes angeli eius:* "Praise him, all you his angels." In addition to adapting language directly from the Psalms, these verses also anticipate the Christmas story of the angels praising God in the presence of the shepherds, as recounted in Luke 2:8–21. Line 3 contrasts the divine title *excelsus*, "Most High," with the humility of the Incarnation, *humilis*. In addition to being used as a title for God in the Vulgate, for instance in Genesis 14:20 (*benedictus Deus excelsus*), the pairing of *excelsus* and *humilis* recalls the Most High's concern for the lowly in Psalm 137:6 (138:8) (*quoniam excelsus Dominus, et humilia respicit:* "since, although the Lord is exalted, he has regard for the humble") and anticipates the pairing of glory on high with peace on earth proclaimed by the angels in Luke 2:14 (*Gloria in altissimis* [= excelsis] *Deo, et in terra pax hominibus bonæ voluntatis:* "Glory to God in the highest, and on earth peace to men of good will"). The word *venit* in line 3 and the entirety of line 4 are taken directly from Matthew 18:11: *Venit enim Filius hominis salvare quod perierat.*[94] The poet evidently recognized that the Vulgate text *salvare quod perierat* comprises exactly eight syllables in addition to following a regular stress-pattern. By choosing this particular stanza from *Sol astra* to conclude the Divine Office version of *Verbum salutis*, the editors in effect give Jesus the last word, allowing him to remind us of the reason why he has become man: to save those who had gone astray.

STANZA 6

For a discussion of this doxology, see the commentary on H 1, *Conditor alme siderum*.

---

94. In the *Nova Vulgata*, as well as some contemporary English translations, such as the *New American Bible Revised Edition* and the *English Standard Version*, Mt 18:11 is omitted from the main biblical text and included only in the apparatus. As the *New American Bible Revised Edition* explains, "Some manuscripts add, 'For the Son of Man has come to save what was lost'; see Mt 9:13. This is practically identical with Lk 19:10 and is probably a copyist's addition from that source." Prescinding from the context of Greek New Testament textual criticism, it seems clear that the original author of *Sol astra* was drawing on Mt 18:11 rather than Lk 19:10. In the Clementine Vulgate, Lk 19:10 appears in a slightly different version than Mt 18:11, with the addition of *quærere* and with *salvum facere* in place of *salvare*: *Venit enim Filius hominis quærere, et salvum facere quod perierat*. According to the Oxford Vulgate, most Latin sources present distinct versions of Mt 18:11 and Lk 19:10, although a few sources give *salvare* instead of *salvum facere* in the Lukan version.

Veni, redemptor gentium 5

St. Ambrose, d. 397
8 8 8 8 (LM)

Advent after 16 December
Office of Readings

Veni, redémptor géntium, ostténde partum Vírginis; mirétur omne sǽculum: talis decet partus Deum.	1. Redeemer of the nations, come; reveal yourself by virgin birth. Let every age with wonder know that such a birth befits our God.

Veni, redémptor géntium,
osténde partum Vírginis;
mirétur omne sǽculum:
talis decet partus Deum.

1. Redeemer of the nations, come;
reveal yourself by virgin birth.
Let every age with wonder know
that such a birth befits our God.

Non ex viríli sémine,
sed mýstico spirámine
Verbum Dei *factum* est caro
fructúsque ventris flóruit.

2. Conceived not from the seed of man
but by the Spirit's wondrous breath,
the Word of God is now made flesh,
as Mary's womb brings forth its fruit.

Alvus tuméscit Vírginis,
claustrum pudóris pérmanet,
vexílla virtútum micant,
versátur in templo Deus.

3. The Virgin's womb grows great with child,
this cloister is for ever pure;
the banners of her virtues gleam,
for in this temple God resides.

Procédat e thálamo suo,
pudóris aula régia,
gémínæ gigas substántiæ
alácris ut currat viam.

4. From bridal chamber let him come,
from royal Virgin, palace chaste,
with twofold nature God and man,
a champ*io*n swift to run his course.

Æquális ætérno Patri,
carnis tropǽo cíngere,
infírma nostri córporis
virtúte firmans pérpeti.

5. The eternal Father's Equal, come,
bind on the trophy of our flesh,
and strengthen with your lasting power
the weakness of our mortal frame.

Præsépe iam fulget tuum
luménque nox spirat novum,
quod nulla nox intérpolet
fidéque iugi lúceat.

6. Your manger now with splendor shines
and night breathes forth new rad*ia*nt light,
which no night may corrupt or dim:
so let it shine through constant faith.

Sit, Christe, rex piíssime,
tibi Patríque glória
cum Spíritu Paráclito,
in sempitérna sǽcula. Amen.

7. To you, O Christ, most loving King,
and to the Father, glory be,
one with the Spirit Paraclete,
from age to age for evermore. Amen.

Text found in *TDH*, no. 75; *AH*, 50, no. 8; Walpole, no. 6; Fontaine, no. 5. Changes in *TDH*: stanzas 1 and 6 of the original hymn are omitted; 1, 4: *Deo* for *Deum*; 5, 2: *cingere* for *accingere*.

COMMENTARY:

This hymn is taken from the one composed by St. Ambrose for the Nativity of the Lord, as attested by several early sources. Later it was also known as a hymn for Advent. It was not included in the *Breviarium Romanum* but remained in that of Milan and in several monastic breviaries.

In its original form it consists of eight stanzas (as in the case of the other hymns by Ambrose). Two of these are omitted in this version. The first stanza, beginning *Intende, qui regis Israel*, is addressed to God as the ruler of Israel, and is an almost word-for-word adaptation of Psalm 79:2–3 (80:1–2).[95] It asks God to hear, to appear, to rouse up his might, and to come. The last word of this stanza, *veni*, is then repeated as the first one of the following stanza, *Veni, redemptor gentium*, in a way typical of Ambrose, and "come, Redeemer" also echoes the psalm, which says "come to save us." Moreover, the first two stanzas are balanced in the original, as God is invoked first as King of Israel, and then as Redeemer of the nations, that is, the Gentiles. This would have suited the antiphonal singing of the hymn.

In fact, the whole hymn, in its original form with the first and sixth stanzas included, can be analyzed as consisting of four pairs of stanzas.[96] The first pair asks God to reveal himself in human form for our salvation, balancing an Old Testament formulation of this in the first four stanzas with a New Testament one in the second four. The second pair (H 5, stanzas 2 and 3) celebrates the birth of Christ as the Word born of the Holy Spirit and the Virgin Mary. In the third pair the focus is on Christ coming forth to accomplish the task set before him. The first of these (H 5, stanza 4) again echoes the Old Testament, Psalm 18:6 (19:5), asking him to come forth as a bridegroom and also a giant with twofold nature. The second of this pair of stanzas (which is omitted in our version) elaborates this in terms drawn from the early Christian Creeds, describing how he comes forth from the Father and returns to the Father, even descending to hell, and returning "to the seat of the Father." In the final pair (H 5, stanzas 5 and 6), Christ is asked to "bind on the trophy of our flesh," and the result of this is the radiant light shining from the manger of his birth, which continues to shine in the faith of the believer. Thus, there is a progression in the hymn, from the expectation of the Messiah in the Old Testament, through the Incarnation, to the actual birth or Epiphany of Christ.

Throughout the hymn Ambrose is concerned to express the orthodox doctrines formulated in the Nicene and Constantinopolitan Creeds in opposition to the Arians, about the divinity of Christ and his life, death, and resurrection. His

---

95. Psalm 79(80):1–2 was used in the *Missale Romanum* of 1962 in the Gradual for the Third Sunday of Advent, and the Collects for the First and Fourth Sundays. In the *Missale Romanum* of 1969 these verses are again used for part of the Psalm for the First Sunday (Year B) and Fourth Sunday (Year C) of Advent.

96. See Springer, "Ambrose's *Veni Redemptor Gentium*," 76–87, and Fontaine, 64–65, 268–69.

Veni, redemptor gentium

emphasis on the perpetual virginity of Mary and her role as the Mother of God (*Theotokos*) also anticipates the debates of the fifth century about these issues.[97]

The first stanza (*Intende, qui regis Israel*) is omitted in some of the early manuscripts, although it appears in those of Milanese origin. The probable reason is the number of elided words it contains, which would have made singing more difficult once elision fell out of use. Elision is rare in Ambrose's hymns, and the reason for it here is because Ambrose is so closely adapting the psalm.[98] He also replaces the usual iambic foot with an anapest (two shorts + long) in *regis Is-* in line 1. In H 5, stanza 4, we again find this in lines 1, *thalamo*, and 3, *geminæ*, where he is also quoting from a psalm. Again this is rare in Ambrose.[99]

STANZA I

In the Latin text the opening word is the urgent imperative *Veni* ("come"), parallel with the first word of the original hymn, *Intende* ("hear"), and repeated from the end of that opening stanza. Christ is urged to come as the Savior of the Gentiles, of all nations. In the Old Testament God is frequently addressed or referred to as *redemptor* in the Vulgate, but especially relevant are Isaiah 59:20, *Et venerit Sion redemptor ... dicit Dominus* ("And there shall come a Redeemer to Zion' ... says the Lord"), and Job 19:25, *Scio enim quod redemptor meus vivit* ("For I know that my Redeemer lives"). In line 3 of stanza 1 of H 1, *Conditor alme siderum*, Christ is likewise addressed by the same title (*Christe redemptor omnium*).

The Latin stanza is composed of four independent sentences of one line each, and each of the first three opens emphatically with a verb. Christ's advent is a revelation or epiphany (*ostende*), which in turn should evoke the human response of wonder (*miretur*). The final line explains the reason for this response. In line 2, *ostende* has a religious connotation. Fontaine notes that the noun *ostentum* was used in a sacred sense in classical Latin, denoting a portent or divine manifestation. The phrase *ostende partum Virginis* means literally "reveal the birth from the Virgin," a compressed way of asking Christ to reveal himself as offspring of a virgin. The prophecy in Isaiah 7:14, *Ecce virgo concipiet, et pariet filium* ("Behold, a virgin shall conceive and bear a son") is explained in Matthew 1:22–23 as referring to the birth of Christ.

In line 3 the response of wonder is typical in both ancient classical and Hebrew literature in accounts of a divine epiphany, and regularly leads to worship or the institution of a cult. Here this wonder is not confined to the actual time of the birth but will continue throughout human history (*omne sæculum*).

The final line was quoted by Pope Celestine I at the Council of Rome in 430 AD, as proof that Mary was the Mother of God.[100] Pope Leo the Great also echoed it: *talis nativitas decuit Dei virtutem et Dei sapientiam Christum*: "Such a

---

97. See Dunkle, *Enchantment*, 120–29, and Fontaine, 267.
98. See Norberg, *Introduction*, 26.
99. See Norberg, *Introduction*, 66.
100. Cf. Walpole, 50; Fontaine, 267, note 4.

birth was fitting for Christ, the power of God and wisdom of God" (*Serm.* 21.2). We find a similar statement already in St. Augustine (*Serm.* 186.1): *Deum sic nasci oportuit, quando esse dignatus est homo*: "It was right for God to be born in this way, when he condescended to be born as man." For *Deum* in this line there is a less-well attested variant *Deo*. The verb *decet* usually takes the accusative in classical Latin, but sometimes dative. The quotation by Celestine and the echo by Leo tend to favor the accusative.

STANZA 2

This stanza, for the most part, keeps closely to the words of the gospels on which it is constructed. The first two lines are related to Luke's account of the Annunciation, at 1:34–35, where Mary says "I have no relations with a man" (*virum non cognosco*), and the Angel tells her that "the Holy Spirit will come upon you" (*Spiritus Sanctus superveniet in te*). But the wording also reflects John's Prologue (1:13), where he describes all those who have received "the true light." They are those "who were born, not of blood nor of the will of the flesh nor of the will of man, but of God" (*Qui non ex sanguinibus, neque ex voluntate carnis, neque ex voluntate viri, sed ex Deo nati sunt*). The first part of the following verse in John is then repeated almost verbatim in line 3, "And the Word was made flesh" (*Et Verbum caro factum est*). After the Annunciation in Luke, Mary visits her cousin Elizabeth, who greets her with the words "Blessed are you among women, and blessed is the fruit of your womb" (*Benedicta tu inter mulieres, et benedictus fructus ventris tui*; 1:42), and this is echoed here in line 4.

There is an alternation in this stanza between the more prosaic language of the first and third lines and the more elevated wording of the second and fourth. In the first couplet, the two phrases are counterbalanced, with *spiramine* ("breathing") rhyming and in alliteration with *semine* ("seed"). The word *mystico* has connotations both of secrecy and sanctity. In line 3 there is an elision in *factum est*, again associated with the scriptural quotation. In his commentary on Luke Ambrose says of *fructus ventris* that "this is Christ, the flower of Mary, who now blossoms like the fruit of a good tree" (*qui veluti bonæ arboris fructus ... nunc floret*). He is probably also alluding to the prophecy of the Messiah in Isaiah: *Et egredietur virga de radice Iesse, et flos de radice eius ascendet* (literally, "And there shall come forth a rod from the root of Jesse, and a flower shall grow up from its root").[101]

STANZA 3

Like stanza 1, this stanza is composed of four independent sentences. Here each is a statement, and in each couplet the lines are balanced in terms of word length:

---

101. Ambrose, *Expositio evangelii secundum Lucam*, 2.24; Is 11:1.

in lines 1–2, a disyllable plus two trisyllables, in lines 3–4, two trisyllables (counting *in templo* as a unit) plus a disyllable. There is also an elegant variation in the position of the verb within the line, and alliteration in line 2 (*pudoris permanet*) and lines 3–4 (*vexilla virtutum ... versatur*).

The physical realism of the first line is again in contrast with the more poetic language of the other three, and there is a strong antithesis between the description of the pregnancy in line 1 and the emphasis on the continual virginity of Mary in line 2. Ambrose elsewhere supports the view that Mary's hymen remained unbroken not only at conception but also at birth.[102] This is echoed by later hymn writers (for example, H 9: 3, 1, by Sedulius). The word *claustrum* is used, in earlier Latin, of anything that keeps a door or gate closed or locked, or of a closed space, or a barrier, and so literally the line means "the barrier of her chastity remains constant."

Regarding *vexilla virtutum micant*, Ambrose writes elsewhere of Mary that she "raised up the signal of sacred virginity, and lifted on high for Christ the holy banner of immaculate purity" (*signum sacræ virginitatis extulit et intemeratæ integritatis pium Christo vexillum erexit*), and "in a single Virgin how great are the types of virtues that shine forth! The secret of modesty, the banner of faith, the obedience of devotion" (*quantæ in una virgine species virtutum emicant! Secretum verecundiæ, vexillum fidei, devotionis obsequium*).[103] The *vexilla* are military standards or banners. Here they also show the presence of Christ in his mother's womb, and so (3, 4) "God resides in his temple." *Vexilla* can also be used in relation to the Cross, as in Venantius Fortunatus's hymn *Vexilla regis prodeunt* (H 31). In Psalm 10:5 (11:4), "the Lord is in his holy temple," and Ambrose calls Mary "the wonderful temple of God and the heavenly court" (*admirabile templum Dei et aula cælestis*), anticipating line 2 of the next stanza, *pudoris aula regia*.[104]

STANZA 4

As in the omitted first stanza, Ambrose is here reworking a psalm text, 18:6 (19:5) "He has set his tabernacle in the sun; and he, as a bridegroom coming out of his bride chamber, has rejoiced as a giant to run the way": *In sole posuit tabernaculum suum; et ipse tamquam sponsus procedens de thalamo suo. Exsultavit ut gigas ad currendam viam*. This psalm text had already been applied to Christ by earlier Christian writers.[105] In the psalm the subject is the sun, and Ambrose may have in mind the fact that the Christmas festival probably replaced the pagan celebration of the Birthday of the Unconquered Sun, at the turning-point of the

---

102. Ambrose, *De institutione virginis*, 8.52, and other references in Walpole, 53, and Fontaine, 285. See also the passage of Ambrose quoted in the commentary on H 1: 3, 4, and cf. the Alleluia for the Mass *Salve, sancta Parens: Post partum Virgo inviolata permansisti* ("After birth you remained a Virgin entire").

103. Ambrose, *De inst. virg.* 5.35, *De virginibus* 2.15.

104. Augustine, *In psalm.* 45.13.

105. See Fontaine, 289 (Origen and Cyprian), and also Walpole, 55, on line 21ff. (Irenaeus and Justin). See also H 1, stanza 3, with the commentary on these lines.

year.[106] In line 1, Christ (the Bridegroom) is asked to come forth (or "proceed") from the bridal chamber (*thalamus*), the womb of Mary, which is explained in Ambrose's own words as "the royal court of chastity" in line 2. Ambrose often uses this phrase elsewhere of Mary. Particularly relevant is a passage commenting on 2 Corinthians 6:16, where he says: "you are the temple of God, in which the Lord Jesus should dwell, and from which he should proceed for the redemption of all, so that in the womb of the Virgin should be found the sacred court (*aula*) in which the king of heaven should dwell, and the human body should become the temple of God."[107]

Lines 3–4 adapt the psalm, in contrast to Arianism, to emphasize the dual nature of Christ as divine and human. The word *gigas*, translated here as "champion" (rendering the original Hebrew word), means literally "giant," and there may be a reference to the idea that the giants were the offspring of angels and human women mentioned in Genesis 6:2.[108] The word *substantia* ("substance") is a word used in theological contexts of the nature of a person or thing. Thus, in the Nicene Creed, Christ is descibed as "consubstantial with the Father." Several theologians in the fifth century (Leporius, Faustus, and Facundus) quoted this stanza in support for the orthodox view of Christ's dual nature.[109] The phrase *alacris ut currat viam* (either "keen to run his course" or "to run his course with eagerness") echoes the sense of joyfulness in the psalm (*Exsultavit ... ad currendam viam*).

There is alliteration in lines 1–2 (*procedat ... pudoris*, in the same position in the verse), and in line 3 (*geminæ gigas*). There are also variant readings in the stanza: *procedat* for *procedens* (4, 1) and *occurrat* for *ut currat* (4, 4).

After stanza 4 of H 5 comes the other missing stanza:

Egressus eius a Patre,	First from the Father he sets forth,
regressus eius ad Patrem;	then to the Father he returns;
excursus usque ad inferos,	he sallies to the realms below,
recursus ad sedem Dei.	then journeys back to God's abode.[110]

The first two lines are adapted from the next verse (7) of Psalm 18: *A summo cæli egressio eius, et occursus eius usque ad summum eius* ("His going out is from the end of heaven, and his circuit even to the end thereof"). But they also reflect the words of Jesus in John 16:28: "I came from the Father and have come into the world. Now I am leaving the world and going back to the Father." In line 3, Christ's descent to hell is stated, as in the Apostles' Creed. In his commentary on Psalm 43 Ambrose writes: "The Lord descended to hell so that those dwelling there should also be

---

106. See *Oxford Dictionary of the Christian Church*, s.v. "Christmas."
107. Ambrose, *Epist.* 12 = 30 Maur. 3.
108. See Dunkle, *Enchantment*, 124.
109. See Walpole, 50 and 54 (on line 19).
110. Translation from Walsh, 17.

loosed from their everlasting bonds."[111] Line 4 is again a credal statement. Literally the Latin means "his return is to the seat of God," as in "He ascended into heaven and is seated at the right hand of the Father" (*Et ascendit in cælum; sedet ad dexteram Patris*).

STANZA 5

The emphasis in the missing stanza on Christ's relationship with his Father is continued in the opening line of this one, and again Ambrose is stressing the orthodox doctrine of Christ's divinity, as "consubstantial with the Father." In Philippians 2:6 he is "equal to God" (*æqualem Deo*). *Æqualis æterno* also suggests that he is co-eternal with the Father. Here this is addressed to Christ, with the prayer that he will (literally) "gird on the trophy of flesh" or, in other words, put on the armor of our human nature, and "strengthen the weakness of our body" with his "lasting power." The military image (as in *vexilla virtutum* in 1, 3) reminds one of St. Paul's exhortation in Ephesians 6:13–14 to "put on the armor of God" and "stand fast with your loins girded in truth" (*succincti lumbos in veritate*). Christ's body (or "flesh") is a trophy, "because it is the everlasting monument of his Victory over Satan and death" (as Walpole puts it). St. Paulinus of Nola (*Carm*. 19.654) says, "he set the trophy of his body in its heavenly abode and implanted the banner of the Cross above all the stars."[112]

In line 2 it is possible that the verb is indicative, "you gird," but it has usually been taken as imperative, and the change from the third person in the previous stanza to second in this makes more sense if taken in this way. For *cingere* some editors have preferred *accingere*, which is a well-attested variant, and the compound verb is used elsewhere by Ambrose, whereas *cingi* is not. If this reading is correct, the elision of *tropæo* could have led to its being altered when the addition of the prefix led to its becoming difficult to sing.[113]

Lines 3 and 4 are beautifully balanced, each having the same structure of trisyllable, disyllable and trisyllable, with *infirma* answered by *firmans*. There is an echo of 2 Corinthians 12:9, where the Lord says to Paul "my power is made perfect in weakness" (*virtus in infirmitate perficitur*). These two lines are repeated in the hymn *Veni creator Spiritus* (H 55: 4, 3–4).

STANZA 6

After the build-up of expectation in the preceding stanzas, Ambrose switches emphatically, with *iam fulget*, to the present event, the actual birth of Christ and the divine radiance shining from the humble manger wherein he lies. Light is the theme in the opening two lines and the final one, with *fulget ... lumen ... luceat*. The first two lines have the same structure, of trisyllabic noun, monosyllable,

---

111. See Walpole, p. 55; Fontaine, 294.
112. Translation from Walsh, *Poems of St. Paulinus of Nola*, 153.
113. See Walpole, l. 16, p. 55. Fontaine prefers *cingere*, 295.

disyllabic verb and disyllabic adjective, ending with rhyme. The third line is similar, with *nox* again in the same position as in line 2. The last two lines end with two subjunctive verbs which again have similar endings (*interpolet, luceat*). The contrast expressed in these two lines is like that in Ambrose's hymn *Splendor paternæ gloriæ* (H 75: 5, 3–4): *fides calore ferveat, fraudis venena nesciat*.[114]

In the gospels the heavenly light is mentioned at the appearance of the Angel to the shepherds ("and the glory of the Lord shone around them") in Luke 2:9. In Matthew 2:9 the star seen by the Magi "came to rest over the place where the child was." Apocryphal versions of the Nativity also describe the light shining from the birthplace of Jesus.[115] In his commentary on Luke, Ambrose says: "in an earthly lodging he lies, but he is strong with heavenly light."[116] The newness of this light is also stressed by him elsewhere.[117] Night "breathes forth" light, much as earlier poetry used the verb in the context of exhaling fire, but here there may also be a suggestion of the divine Spirit filling the darkness with light. At any rate, night is seen as positive here through the presence of Christ, whereas in line 3 it is a potentially negative force.

The last two lines form a concluding wish or prayer. The verb *interpolare* in earlier Latin is sometimes used to mean "alter, spoil."[118] Ambrose is echoing John 1:5, "the light shines in the darkness, and the darkness has not overcome it." He uses the same word several times elsewhere in this context.[119] The final prayer in line 4 is that the effect of Christ's presence may continue to be seen through the constancy of faith. The word *iugis* ("constant, perpetual") is also frequently used by Ambrose.[120] The closing emphasis on faith is typical of Ambrose in his hymns, as in his other works. As Dunkle comments: "The notion of *fides* ... is especially frequent, appearing twenty-six times and in all but one of his fourteen hymns."[121] By implication, the orthodoxy of faith expressed throughout the hymn should also shine out in the life of Christ's followers.

STANZA 7

For this doxology see the discussion on H 1, stanza 6. It was added to the original hymn of Ambrose at a later date.

---

114. See the analysis of these lines in appendix 2, on assonance and rhyme, under the heading "Internal Factors," "The Legacy of the Poets."
115. See Fontaine, 298.
116. *In Luc.* 2.43; cf. *Isaac* 4.31, *In Psalm.* 118, 12.13 (quoted by Walpole, 56, and Fontaine, 298).
117. *In Psalm 38*, 18.
118. See Lewis and Short, *s.v. interpolare*.
119. See the passages of Ambrose quoted by Walpole, especially *In Psalm 118*, 12.13, *fulgoris perpetui claritatem, quam nulla nox interpolat* (Walpole, 56).
120. See Walpole, 57.
121. Dunkle, *Enchantment*, 116.

Magnis prophetæ vocibus	6
Anon., early Mozarabic 8 8 8 8r	**Advent after 16 December** Lauds

Magnis prophétæ vócibus veníre Christum núntiant, lætæ salútis prævia, qua nos redémit, grátia.	1. With mighty voice the prophets cry that Christ the Lord is drawing near; rejoicing, they foresee the grace by which he saves us and redeems.
Hinc mane nostrum prómicat et corda læta exæstuant, cum vox fidélis pérsonat prænuntiátrix glóriæ.	2. And so our morning sun shines forth, our hearts ablaze with rad*ia*nt joy; we hear the faithful voice resound, precursor of God's glor*iou*s gift.
Advéntus hic primus fuit, puníre quo non sæculum venit, sed ulcus térgere, salvándo quod períerat.	3. At that first Advent Christ our God came forth not to condemn the world, but came to cleanse our gaping wound, to seek and save what had been lost.
At nos secúndus præmonet adésse Christum iánuis, sanctis corónas réddere cælíque regna pándere.	4. Christ's Second Coming warns us all that he is standing at the gates to give to saints their glor*iou*s crowns and open wide the heavenly realm.
Ætérna lux promíttitur sidúsque salvans prómitur; iam nos iubar præfúlgidum ad ius vocat cæléstium.	5. Eternal light is now foretold, the saving star is shining forth, its rad*ia*nt splendor summons us and calls us to the heavenly court.
Te, Christe, solum quærimus vidére, sicut es Deus, ut perpes hæc sit vísio perénne laudis cánticum. Amen.	6. Christ Jesus, you alone we seek to see you face to face as God; may this unending vision be an everlasting hymn of praise. Amen.

Text found in *TDH*, no. 76; *AH* 27, no. 1; *Hymnodia hispanica*, 131ff. Changes in *TDH*: stanza 1, 1: *magnis prophetæ vocibus* for *voces prophetarum sonant*; 1, 2: *Christum* for *Iesum*; 1, 3: *lætæ salutis* for *redemptionis*; 4, 1: *nos* for *nunc*; 6, 3–4: *ut perpes hæc sit visio / perenne laudis canticum* for *ut læta nos hæc visio / evellat omni tartaro*. Stanzas 1, 4, and 9 of the original hymn have been omitted.

COMMENTARY

This hymn was composed during the Visigothic renaissance of the seventh century.[122] It belongs to the Hispanic, or Mozarabic, rite and is found in the *Gothic Breviary* of 1775, which is a revision of the sixteenth-century work of discovery and restoration carried out by Cardinal Ximenez of Toledo.[123]

In the seventh century, Advent lasted for six weeks in Spain; it began around the middle of November. The feast of the early fourth-century martyrs Acisclus and Victoria, sister and brother, was widely celebrated in Spain on November 17, usually during the first week of Advent. The hymn now known as *Magnis prophetæ vocibus* was a hymn in honor of them. The first stanza refers to their martyrdom, without mentioning them by name; it began: *Gaudete, flores martyrum*, a line formed after a well-known line from Prudentius's hymn *Cathemerinon* 12: 32, 1 (H 294: 4, 1): *Salvete, flores martyrum*. In this stanza, Prudentius greets the Holy Innocents, cut down by Herod like budding roses in a gale. Acisclus and Victoria were also young, cut down in the prime of life by the governor of Cordoba during the persecutions of Diocletian. This borrowing of familiar lines and phrases from Prudentius offers indirect evidence of the Spanish provenance of the hymn.[124] It is also a classic example of the use of an earlier hymn to expand and deepen the message of a later composition. Since the Spanish martyrs were celebrated each year at the beginning of Advent, the hymn composed in their honor was an Advent hymn. By removing the stanzas that concern the martyrs in particular (stanzas 1, 4, and 9), Lentini was able to use the remaining stanzas as a hymn for Lauds in the season of Advent.

STANZA 1

Lentini made changes to lines 1 and 3 in the first stanza.[125] He explains that he changed the first line in order to achieve a more lyrical (singable) rhythm. The original line was a fine quantitative line in iambic dimeter, but less pleasing to ears attuned to accentual rhythm.[126] The sense, however, remains essentially unchanged. The first line is an indirect allusion to John the Baptist, the voice crying in the wilderness.[127] The subject *prophetæ* is plural, as is the verb *nuntiant*. We

---

122. *Himnodia hispánica*, 102. Note that this is a reference to notes in the Spanish volume that is a companion to and translation of CCSL 167. It is entitled *Himnodia hispánica*, CCSL in Translation, 19.
123. *Breviarium Gothicum*, 320. See also Messenger, "The Mozarabic Hymnal," 103–26, esp. 103–4. The *Breviarium* was reprinted in Migne, PL 86. The terms Visigothic, Gothic, and Mozarabic are used of the liturgy in Spain from the rise of the Visigothic kingdom into the Arab occupation until the Spanish liturgy was replaced by the Roman Liturgy in 1089.
124. Messenger, "Mozarabic Hymns," 156–57. See also Messenger, *Mozarabic Hymnal*, 107.
125. Other changes have also been made from the text in AH 27. In line 2, *Iesum* has become *Christum*; in line 4 *cum* has become *qua*. There is manuscript evidence for these changes. See Neale, *Hymni Ecclesiæ*, 56; *Hymnodia hispanica*, 131.
126. The original version also made a one-syllable rhyme between lines 1 and 2. Assonance and rhyme are present throughout the hymn, though not in a regular way.
127. See Mt 3:1–3; Mk 1:2–4; Lk 3:3–6; and Jn 1:23: *Ait*: "*ego vox clamantis in deserto: dirigite viam Domini,*

think of John, but he is the last in a long line of prophets who have announced that Christ will come; they are all represented here in the *magnis vocibus*. In line 3, *redemptionis* is replaced by *lætæ salutis*.[128] Again, the meaning is nearly the same. The resonance between *redemptionis* and *redemit* is lost; the element of joy has been added.

Lines 3–4, in both the original text and in Lentini's adaptation, are a lovely piece of Latin syntax, nearly impossible to translate. Here are the lines:

> lætæ salútis prǽvia,
> qua nos redémit, grátia

The lines end with words in a near two-syllable rhyme. The placement and rhyme create graphic syntax that determines the sense; *gratia* is a noun in the ablative singular, *prævia* is an adjective in the ablative singular. Together they form an ablative absolute. Literally, they mean "grace going before, leading the way." The phrase *qua nos redemit* is set off in commas; it is a relative clause describing *gratia*. Note also that *redemit* is a verb in the past tense that needs a subject. The subject is Christ, understood, and the phrase indicates the instrumentality of grace: the grace by which he (Christ) saves us. Finally, the phrase *lætæ salutis* is in the genitive case; it must modify a noun, and the only candidate here is *gratia*. The entire phrase means something like: "the grace of joyous salvation, by which he has saved us, goes before, leading the way."[129]

This analysis may seem minute, but it reveals the precision and subtlety of Latin, and this is one of the reasons why Latin is such an effective liturgical language. It is possible to say much in few words. Here, there are three major ideas packed into these two lines. First, the verb is in the past tense. Christ has already saved those who sing the hymn; his grace has already been given, yet it is leading the way for us in Advent. This participation in the yearly repetition of the events of salvation that have already happened is part of our liturgical consciousness. Second, the unfolding of salvation has nothing uncertain about it. The prophets knew that what they foresaw would indeed happen. Their participation in the joy of salvation was to come first and show the way. For us, as we relive the period of waiting for the coming of Christ, we see the grace of a joyous salvation in the person of John the Baptist. He is the one who goes "before the Lord to prepare his ways" (Lk 1:76). He is not an empty voice; he leapt for joy in his mother's womb; he is as single-minded in that joy as any prophet could be, so much so that those who came out to him to be baptized wondered if he were in fact the Messiah

---

sicut dixit Isaias propheta": "He [John] said: 'I am the voice of one crying out in the desert: Make straight the way of the Lord,' as Isaiah the prophet said."

128. Lentini does not say why he made the change, but one may suspect that he found *redemptio* in line 3 too close to *redemit* in line 4 and thus awkward. This is a matter of taste, and the hymns have been adapted to modern use. Other times and places have enjoyed such repetition.

129. The phrase would have been stronger if Lentini had left *redemptionis* in place. It would signify "the grace of redemption."

(Lk 3:15). He continues his role as precursor and intercessor. He is the only saint, after Mary the Mother of God, whose birth we celebrate with a Solemnity, and in the collect for the day, the Church prays: "grant to your people the grace of spiritual joys, and direct the minds and hearts of all the faithful into the way of salvation and peace": *da populis tuis spiritalium gratiam gaudiorum, et omnium fidelium mentes dirige in viam salutis et pacis*.[130] Third, Christ himself, the Apostles, and the Fathers of the Church interpreted the events of the New Testament in terms of the Old: "Beginning with Moses and all the Prophets, he interpreted to them in all the Scriptures the things concerning himself" (Lk 24:27). The prophets lead the way into our reception of the grace of the joy of salvation.[131]

STANZA 2

The hymn is assigned to Lauds, the hour of the liturgical day that coincides with dawn (*mane*); early morning light is beginning to spread over the horizon and to shine forth (*promicat*). According to the structural logic of stanza 2, the morning light shines forth, and our hearts fill with light and heat (*exæstuant*), and they are joyous (*læta*) (line 2) when they hear the faithful voice (line 3) resound and announce future glory (line 4).

The first word of line 1, *hinc*, is an adverb that indicates place "from where"; in a figurative sense, with respect to cause, it can mean "from this cause or source." It connects the first line of this stanza to lines 3–4 of the first. The hymn works on two different levels here. It is the morning of the day that lies ahead; it is also *our* spiritual morning (*mane nostrum*) because the prophetic voice is announcing the dawn of our salvation. "Our morning" is, finally, Christ himself coming to dwell in our midst.[132]

This stanza is filled with vocabulary and imagery that belong to the tradition of liturgical hymnody. Hymns both before and after resonate with it. For example, the phrase *vox personat* (line 2) reminds the singer of the hymn of Ambrose *Æterne rerum conditor* (H 71), where the cock who keeps vigil through the darkness of night (*noctis profundæ pervigil*) is the herald of the day (*præco diei*); he bursts forth, making a loud noise (*iam sonat*) to usher in the dawn. In the final stanza of Ambrose's hymn, the same verb *sono* returns, this time in the subjunctive (*vox sonet*): we pray that our voice may also sing forth to Christ as the day begins (*te nostra vox primum sonet*). The theme of the cockcrow is reinforced by

---

130. Byzantine icons known as the Deësis show John the Baptist standing on one side of Christ and the Blessed Virgin Mary on the other, both interceding for us still, as we pray.

131. St. Ambrose insists on the need to read the Old and New Testaments together: "Drink each cup, that of the Old Testament and that of the New since in each you drink Christ. Drink Christ since he is the vine (Jn 15:1–5). Drink Christ, since he is the rock that pours forth water (Ex 17:6). Drink Christ since he is the fountain of life (Ps 35:9). Drink Christ, since he is the river, whose rushing waters rejoice the city of God (Ps 45:4) … the Old Testament is his word, the New Testament is his word. One drinks the divine Scripture, and one devours the divine Scripture, when the juice of the eternal Word descends into the veins of the mind and the faculties of the soul; indeed 'Man does not live by bread alone, but by every word of God (Mt 4:4)'" (Ambrose, *Explanatio psalmorum XII*, 1.33).

132. *Himnodia hispánica*, 102.

the use Prudentius makes of it in *Cathemerinon* 1, a hymn well known to later Spanish hymn writers. Prudentius followed Ambrose, and the seventh-century hymn writer followed them both, whether consciously or unconsciously. The tradition was etched into his poetic craft. In both Ambrose and Prudentius, as in this hymn, multiple layers are woven into the structure: the voice that cries out, the shining morning, and our personal spiritual dawn all symbolize and call forth the advent of Christ. Note the graphic syntax between *promicat* (line 1) and *personat* (line 3). In line 4 another nuance is added; the dawn is a herald of glory (*prænuntiatrix gloriæ*). This is the language of Prudentius, who in *Cathemerinon* 12: 1, 4 describes the star that the wise men see as a sign of eternal glory (*signum perennis gloriæ*).[133] The use of the phrase here prepares the following stanzas. The verb *mane* in stanza 2 also belongs to the tradition.[134].

STANZA 3

Stanzas 3 and 4 form a pair. They place us in "liturgical time," the time between the first and second coming of Christ. Stanza 3 summarizes the purpose and effects of the first coming; stanza 4 bids us to remember that Christ is still at work in our lives and will surely return.

His first coming was not for punishment, but for mercy. Lines 1–2 are an allusion to John 3:17: "For God did not send his Son into the world to condemn the world, but that the world might be saved through him": *Non enim misit Deus Filium suum in mundum, ut iudicet mundum, sed ut salvetur mundus per ipsum*. In normal prose, as with *non* and *sed* in the verse from John, adverbs precede the words they modify (*non* precedes the verb) and conjunctions come at the head of the clause or close to it. In the hymn, *quo* (functioning as a connector), *non*, and *sed* are all three in the "wrong" place. This causes them to stand out and emphasize the contrast between what might have been—that the world should be punished—and what did actually happen—Christ came to cleanse and heal an open wound and to save what had already perished. The imagery in lines 3–4 is expressive. Without Christ, the world was lost and badly wounded. The Latin *ulcus* signifies a sore, an ulcer, an open wound that needs to be wiped clean (*tergere*). Christ came to cleanse and restore to health (*salvando*) the world and

---

133. *Himnodia hispánica*, 102.

134. See Prudentius, *Cath* 1: 24, 4; *Cath* 2: 4, 3, and 2: 8, 1. For the use of *mane* in a hymn that postdates this hymn, see the *Iubilus* attributed to St. Bernard and divided into three hymns in the *Liturgia Horarum*, H 132, H 134, and H 238. The complete stanza of H 132 is: *Mane nobiscum, Domine, / Mane novum cum lumine, / pulsa noctis caligine / mundum replens dulcedine*: "Remain with us, O Lord, remain, / dispel the darkened gloom of night / and with your light renew the dawn; / with sweetness fill the world once more" (H 132: 5, 1–4). Does *mane* in line 2 mean "remain" or "morning" or both? The first *mane* is clearly an imperative of *maneo*: this is what the disciples of Emmaus said to Jesus, "Remain with us, Lord." The second *mane*, however, could be a verb, but it may also be a noun. This is rich multivalence. If it is a noun, it may be nominative, vocative, or accusative. In the vocative *mane* signifies that the Lord (*Domine*) whom they (and we who sing) have begged to abide with them, is in fact the "New Dawn with light." He is the true and lasting spiritual dawn, which is the spiritual reality behind the phrase *mane nostrum* of stanza 2, line 1 in this hymn. The full explanation may be found in the commentary on that hymn. Other examples of the multivalent use of *mane* in the *Liturgia Horarum* are H 72 and H 95.

the age (both are included in the meaning of *sæculum*). The verb *perierat* is third person singular, pluperfect of *perire*. The verb means "to come to nothing, disappear, perish, die"; in the pluperfect tense, it means "had been lost." Here, the pluperfect signifies that the world was not in danger of perishing, but it was already lost. In the Vulgate, this verb in the pluperfect is used to introduce the parable of the lost sheep (Mt 18:11; Lk 15:4). The father of the prodigal son also uses it as he tries to explain to the older brother why it is necessary to feast and rejoice. Finally, Christ uses it to justify to the Pharisees his acceptance of hospitality at the house of Zacchaeus: "For the Son of Man has come to seek and to save what was lost": *venit enim Filius hominis quærere et salvum facere quod perierat* (Lk 19:10).

STANZA 4

The western portals of medieval European cathedrals were traditionally decorated with scenes of the Last Judgment: Christ in majesty entirely surrounded by an aureole sits in judgment surrounded by angels and saints, while demons and sinners depart. The inside back wall might also be decorated with frescos, mosaics, or rose windows depicting Christ's Second Coming. These murals and windows were intended as warnings and reminders; the first line of stanza 4 is a poetic mural admonishing us in advance to be ready (*At nos secundus præmonet*).[135] It reminds us that throughout our lives lived in "liturgical time," Christ is always standing at the door of our souls (*adesse ianuis*), waiting: "Behold, I stand at the door and knock. If anyone hears my voice and opens the door, I will enter and dine with him, and he with me": *ecce sto ad ostium et pulso: si quis audierit vocem meam et aperuerit ianuam, introibo ad illum et cenabo cum illo et ipse mecum* (Rv 3:20). In his epistle, James also issues a similar warning: "Do not grumble, brothers, about one another, that you may not be judged. Behold, the Judge is standing before the door": *nolite ingemescere fratres in alterutrum ut non iudicemini; ecce iudex ante ianuam adsistit* (Jas 5:9). In this Advent hymn, the prophetic message is intensified by the repetiton of *præ*, indicating precedence in time: at 1, 3 (*prævia*), at 2, 4 (*prænuntiatrix*), and at 4, 1 (*præmonet*).

If we are faithful and remember the mercies received from Christ in his First Coming, if we revere him as he stands knocking, we will be able to open to him, and the reward will be great: he will crown us with glory and open wide (*pandet*) to us the Kingdom of Heaven. "When the chief shepherd shall be revealed, you will receive an unfading crown of glory": *et cum apparuerit princeps pastorum, percipietis immarcescibilem gloriæ coronam* (1 Pt 5:4).

---

135. There seems to be no manuscript evidence for the substitution of *nos* for *nunc*. The difference is not great, though there is an immediacy to *nunc*. It emphasizes our task here and now to pay attention to the fact that there has been a First and will be a Second Coming.

STANZA 5

In Stanza 5 the multiple layers of the hymn converge. This multivalence is emphasized by the rhetorical sonority of the lines. Assonance, alliteration, and rhyme as well as graphic syntax create a rich tapestry. Lines 1 and 2 end with near homonyms: *promititur* (promised) and *promitur* (sent forth). Though the third person singular endings must be the same grammatically, the likeness in form is intended here. The eternal light (*æterna lux*) that is promised (line 1) is identified with the star (*sidus*) that is sent (line 2).[136] From stanzas 3 and 4, it is clear that *salvans* (line 2) refers both to the merciful intervention of stanza 3 and to the final accomplishment described in stanza 4. Both the eternal light (*æterna lux*) and the star (*sidus*) refer without ambiguity to Christ himself.[137]

Lines 3 and 4 continue the same reference to the twofold coming of Christ but in the opposite order. The Latin *iubar* signifies the first ray of light in the morning as the sun comes over the horizon.[138] It is a bursting forth (*præfulgidum*) of light over the darkened world. The first light of day—the singers are at Lauds—beckons all peoples to the *ius cælestium*. At line 3, it beckons us (*nos*). Again, similar to lines 1 and 2, lines 3 and 4 are in assonance in the final two syllables (line 3 is an adjective, line 4 is a genitive plural). The stanza forms a *chiasm* between lines 1–2, on the one hand, and lines 3–4, on the other. Lines 1 and 4 refer to the Second Coming; lines 2 and 3 refer to the First Coming that is almost here: the *sidus* is the star of Bethlehem, the *iubar* is a ray from the star but also the first ray of the sun on the day that lies before us, this day on which we will be called to prepare for the twofold coming of Christ.

The phrase *ius cælestium* in line 4 is taken from Prudentius, *Contra Symmachum* 2.1036. As far as we know the phrase is unique to Prudentius.[139] In the *Contra Symmachum*, Prudentius mentions the parable of the sower and says that as Christ told the story, he gave instructions on how to sow: not on rocky ground, not among thorns, and so forth. Prudentius continues:

> By these laws or rules [*his legibus*], God strengthens [*confirmat*] the farmer [*agricolam*]. He, the farmer [*ille*], does not grasp the heavenly law with the highest part of his ear (i.e., he does not fully understand), but still, he orders at the same time both the crop of his heart and that of the field in such a way that his heart by an interior cultivation does not shine less than when his prosperous acres show forth their harvests.

---

136. There are many references to Christ in Scripture that combine the idea of light with eternity, either directly or by implication. In the book of Wisdom he (Wisdom) is named *lux æterna*: Wis 7:26: *candor est enim lucis æternæ*: "For she (wisdom) is the brightness of eternal light." See also Is 60:20 and Jn 1:4–5, 8–9; 8:12; 9:5; 12:46. Jesus appears to Saul on the road to Damascus as blinding light: Acts 9:3 and 22:6. Finally, John summarizes the gospel by saying that God is light with no place for darkness in him (1 Jn 1:5). See also the commentary on H 8, *Candor æterne deitatis alme*.

137. See Rv 22:16: *ego Iesus ... sum radix et genus David stella splendida et matutina*: "I, Jesus, ... am the root and offspring of David, the bright morning star."

138. See Ambrose's *Splendor paternæ gloriæ* (H 75: 2, 3).

139. *Himnodia hispánica*, 102. The phrase *ius cæleste* is the only instance of it in the Library of Latin Texts. The form of it in this hymn (*ius cælestium*) does not appear at all. At the very least this is a phrase to remember from Prudentius's *Contra Symmachum*.

> His Deus agricolam confirmat legibus. Ille
> ius cæleste patris non summa intellegit aure,
> sed simul et cordis segetem disponit et agri,
> ne minus interno niteant præcordia cultu
> quam cum læta suas ostentant iugera messes.[140]

In line 1035, Prudentius uses the term *lex* (*legibus*) or "law"; in line 1036, he uses *ius*, also "law." They are synonyms, but with differences. Without going beyond the scope of this commentary, the difference between *lex* and *ius* lies in the scope. Where *lex* is more closely tied to enactments by legitimate authority (positive law), *ius* can signify a law code beyond the scope of any written legal system. Thus, the *ius gentium* is a recognized code of behavior between nations, the *ius belli* is a moral code regulating conduct in war, especially the treatment of prisoners; the *ius naturale* is the natural law more fundamental and binding than any legal code. On the basis of these senses of *ius*, the meaning is extended to include certain rights and privileges belonging to those "under" the code, such as the *ius civitatis*, the right of citizenship; this sense is also found in expressions such as *in* or *pro suo iure*, within one's right, or *sui iuris*, of one's own right, that is, a law unto oneself, among others. Finally, the term also indicates the place where justice is served, the tribunal, the court; *in ius vocare*, to call someone to court. Line 4 of stanza 5 reads: *ad ius vocat cælestium*. In the context of the hymn, the *ius cælestium* refers to the Last Judgment, the "place" where divine justice will bestow crowns of glory on those who are worthy. It also signifies the right of citizenship in heaven (*ius civitatis cælestium*), the privileges of those who belong to the communion of saints.[141]

STANZA 6

The first two lines of stanza 6 belong to the original stanza 8 of the hymn. Lentini changed the last two lines, in order to create a doxology. The stanza is a prayer for the beatific vision in which we will see Christ as he is, as God. In his letter, John says: "Beloved, we are God's children now, and what we shall be has not yet been revealed; we do know that when he appears, we shall be like him, for we shall see him as he is" (1 Jn 3:2). This transforming vision will be the fruit and privilege of the *ius caelestium*: we pray that it may be unending (*perpes*) and an eternal (*perenne*) hymn of praise.

---

140. *Contra Symmachum* 2, 1035–39.
141. The translation attempts to include both senses with the word "court" as a place of justice and the palace of the kingdom of heaven with all its inhabitants.

Part 2

THE SEASON OF CHRISTMAS

Advent is a season of desire and waiting for the Lord. Christmas is a season of wonder and joy. The mystery of the Incarnation is so deep and the exaltation so great that we require time and leisure to contemplate and savor the multiple aspects of this greatest of gifts.

Christmas begins, therefore, with an entire liturgical day designated as a Vigil of the Solemnity of the Nativity of the Lord, the sole purpose of which is to invite us, like children waiting for Christmas, to anticipate the joy of Christ's arrival: "Today you will know that the Lord will come and save us; in the morning you shall see his glory."[1] The Martyrology for December 24 is a solemn proclamation of the entrance of the Lord of all ages into the economy of sacred and secular history: "... in the twenty-first century from Abraham ... in the ninety-fourth Olympiad ... in the forty-second year of the reign of Cæsar Octavian Augustus ... Jesus Christ, eternal God and Son of the eternal Father, desiring to consecrate the world by his most loving presence, was conceived by the Holy Spirit, and when nine months had passed since his conception, was born of the Virgin Mary in Bethlehem of Judah, and was made man."

On the evening of December 24, at First Vespers, we contemplate the King of peace, so long desired: "The King of peace is magnified, whose countenance all the earth desires."[2] In addition to the different hours of the Divine Office, there are four distinct Masses for the Solemnity of Christmas; each has a liturgy appropriate to the hour at which it is said: in the evening of the vigil, at night, at dawn, and during the day. At the Office of Readings and the Mass during the Night, the Church leads our hearts into the reality and wonder of the birth of the Savior: "The Lord said to me, 'You are my Son. This day I have begotten you'" (Ps 2:7); "As a bridegroom the Lord comes forth from his chamber" (Ps 18:6). The Office of Readings ends with the recitation of the human genealogy of Christ

---

1. *Hodie scietis quia veniet Dominus et salvabit nos, et mane videbitis gloriam eius*, Mass for the Vigil of the Nativity: Entrance Antiphon and Gradual. The same theme recurs throughout the Mass and Office for December 24 and in the response at Vespers I of the Nativity of the Lord.
2. Ant. 1: *Rex pacificus magnificatus est, cuius vultum desiderat universa terra*. Vespers I of the Nativity of the Lord.

(Mt 1:1–25). Then, at dawn, Lauds and the Mass at Dawn bring before us the joy and excitement of the shepherds and the beauty of the child they see: he is the true Light that shines forth upon us today, the child that is born for us. Finally, at the Mass during the Day, the Church recounts his divine generation (Jn 1:1–18) and contemplates the far-reaching consequences of his birth: "All the ends of the earth shall see the salvation of our God" (Ps 97 [98]:3).

One day, however, cannot suffice for us to enter into the mystery. Christmas and Easter are the only feasts during the liturgical year that have an octave, eight days in which to contemplate the magnitude of the divine gift. Within the Octave of the Nativity are included the Feasts of St. Stephen, St. John the Evangelist, and the Holy Innocents, as well as the Feast of the Holy Family of Jesus, Mary, and Joseph. The Octave of the Nativity ends with the Solemnity of Mary, the Holy Mother of God. The Solemnity of the Epiphany of the Lord follows, and the season closes with the Feast of the Baptism of the Lord. Epiphany, as we celebrate it, represents the manifestation of Christ to the nations through the Magi. Christ's Baptism represents the end of his hidden life and initiates the sacramental economy of salvation. Together, all of these feasts form a constellation emanating the light of the mystery of the Incarnation. Where Advent draws us into the divine economy of God's salvific intervention in the life of the world, Christmas invites us to focus our attention on the Person of Christ, the Incarnate Word, who is the full and gracious revelation of God to a thirsty and fallen world. As he lies in the manger, receives the gifts of the Magi, submits to the baptism of John, he is also God who governs and saves the world. Prosper Guéranger comments, "The splendor of this mystery dazzles the understanding, but it inundates the heart with joy. It is the consummation of the designs of God in time."[3]

The marks of the season are adoration, joy, confident hope, gratitude, and love: adoration of the infant in a manger ("eternity in a span")[4]; joy, "for unto us a child is given" (Is 9:6); confident hope because he is Emmanuel, God-with-us (Is 7:14 with Mt 1:23) until the end of time (Mt 28:20), and the government is upon his shoulders (Is 9:6); gratitude for our deliverance by one who is like us in all things but sin and all-powerful to accomplish his mission (Heb 4:15 and 7:25–26); finally, love for the most beautiful and lovable child the world has ever known. He has come "to seek our love and to sanctify us through our very love for him."[5]

Easter is also a time of peace and joy, yet how different are the seasons. At Christmas, it is the peace and joy of great promise; at Easter, it is the peace and joy of victory. One might say that the high feasts of Christmas and Easter are the poles of the liturgical year. Together they present the essential facts and truths of

---

3. Guéranger, *The Liturgical Year* 2:15–16.
4. "Welcome, all wonders in one sight! / Eternity shut in a span; / Summer in winter; day in night; / Heaven in earth, and God in man. / Great little one, whose all-embracing birth / Lifts earth to heaven, stoops heav'n to earth" (Richard Crashaw, *The Holy Nativity of Our Lord*, 79–84).
5. Guéranger, *The Liturgical Year*, 2:16.

salvation history: the Word became flesh, in order to die for our sins and to raise us, through his own resurrection, to eternal life.

Epiphany is an ancient feast.[6] In the early Church it celebrated the manifestation of the Incarnate Word as God. First in the East and later in the West, it was a feast of three miraculous theophanies. Christ's divinity was revealed to the world in his manifestation to the Magi (Mt 2:9–11), in the revelation of the Trinity at his Baptism (Mk 1:9–11), and in the revelation of his divine power at the wedding feast of Cana (Jn 2:11): a star sent from God led the Magi to the divine child in Bethlehem; the voice of the Father and the Dove proclaimed his divine Sonship within the Trinity; the miraculous transformation of water into wine at the wedding feast of Cana showed his divine power to the Apostles and inaugurated his public ministry. Traces of the ancient multidimensional feast remain in the fifth-century hymn for Lauds by Sedulius (H 16) and in the antiphons of the Divine Office. The antiphon for the Magnificat of Second Vespers is an ancient *hodie* antiphon that refers to all three miracles: "We celebrate this holy day adorned with three miracles: today a star led the magi to the manger; today wine was made from water at the marriage feast; today in the Jordan Christ willed to be baptized by John, in order to save us, alleluia."[7]

There are fifteen hymns included in the liturgy for the Christmas season (H 7–21). They are in five sets of three for each of the following periods or feasts:

No.	Name	Liturgical Hour
7	Christe, redemptor omnium	Vespers, Christmas before Epiphany
8	Candor æternæ Deitatis alme	Readings, Christmas before Epiphany
9	A solis ortus cardine	Lauds, Christmas before Epiphany
10	O lux beata cælitum	Vespers, the Holy Family
11	Dulce fit nobis memorare parvum	Readings, the Holy Family
12	Christe, splendor Patris	Lauds, the Holy Family
13	Corde natus ex Parentis	Vespers, the Solemnity of Mary, Mother of God
14	Radix Iesse floruit	Readings, the Solemnity of Mary, Mother of God
15	Fit porta Christi pervia	Lauds, the Solemnity of Mary, Mother of God

(Continues)

6. By the end of the fourth century both the feast of Christmas (originating in the West) and Epiphany (originating in the East) are clearly attested. Where both feasts were celebrated, Christmas commemorated the birth of Christ and Epiphany the multiple revelations of his divinity as they are recounted in Scripture. See the articles on Christmas and Epiphany in the *Encyclopedia of the Early Church*, 163, 282–83.

7. See the antiphon for the Vespers II of Epiphany, Magnificat antiphon: *Tribus miraculis ornatum diem sanctum colimus: hodie stella magos duxit ad presepium; hodie vinum ex aqua factum est ad nuptias; hodie in Iordane a Ioanne Christus baptizari voluit, ut salvaret nos, alleluia.* Both the text and the music of the *hodie* antiphons are based on Byzantine chants that begin with the same word, σήμερον. They were used as antiphons *ad Magnificat* for Vespers II of high feasts to summarize the significance of the feast. See Huglo, "Rélations musicales," 267–80.

(Continued)

No.	Name	Liturgical Hour
16	Hostis Herodes impie	Vespers, from Epiphany to the Baptism of the Lord
17	Magi videntes parvulum	Readings, from Epiphany to the Baptism of the Lord
18	Quicumque Christum quæritis	Lauds, from Epiphany to the Baptism of the Lord
19	A Patre Unigenite	Vespers, the Baptism of the Lord
20	Implente munus debitum	Readings, the Baptism of the Lord
21	Iesus refulsit omnium	Lauds, the Baptism of the Lord

To this group we may add hymns that belong to the great feasts of the Octave of Christmas. St. Stephen Protomartyr, December 26, represents Christ in his saving death for us and all those who will glorify Christ by witnessing to him before the powerful of this world in martyrdom (H 289–90). St. John the Evangelist, December 27, represents Christ in his divinity and all those who witness to him by their charity and purity of life (H 291–92). The Holy Innocents, December 28, represent Christ in his humanity and all the poor and the little ones who will suffer for his name's sake (H 293–94).

We should also briefly mention the hymns for the Feast of the Presentation of the Lord in the Temple (H 194–96). The account of the Presentation is also found in the Infancy Narratives (Lk 2:25–39), and for many centuries, this feast brought the forty days of Christmas to a close. We find a vestige of this liturgical tradition in the division of the Marian Antiphons, in which the first antiphon *Alma Redemptoris Mater*, designated for Advent and Christmas, is sung until February 2 inclusive. The hymns for the Presentation sing of Christ as the true Temple, of whom the Old Testament Temple was a figure: "the Lord whom you seek will suddenly come to his temple" (Mal 3:1); and "The Temple to the temple comes" (H 195: 3, 2). The Presentation of the Lord is the final revelation of the Infant Christ as expressed in the liturgical cycle. St. Thomas Aquinas observes that Christ was first made known to the poor and faithful, represented by the shepherds, then to the nations, represented by the Magi, and finally to the people of Israel, represented by Simeon and Anna in the Temple at Jerusalem.[8]

---

8. See St. Thomas Aquinas, *ST* III, q. 36, a 6.

Christe, redemptor omnium	7
6th c.	**Christmas Time before Epiphany**
8 8 8 8	**Vespers**

Christe, redémptor ómnium, ex Patre, Patris Unice, solus ante princípium natus ineffabíliter,	1. O Christ, Redeemer of us all, the Father's Sole-begotten Son, in mystery born alone from him, so wondrously before all time,
Tu lumen, tu splendor Patris, tu spes perénnis ómnium, inténde quas fundunt preces tui per orbem sérvuli.	2. The Father's splendor and true Light, O everlasting hope for all, bend low to hear your servants' prayers poured forth to you throughout the earth.
Salútis auctor, récole quod nostri quondam córporis, ex illibáta Vírgine nascéndo, formam súmpseris.	3. O Author of all saving grace, recall that once you took our flesh and from the Virgin pure and chaste assumed by birth our human form.
Hic præsens testátur dies, currens per anni círculum, quod solus a sede Patris mundi salus advéneris;	4. This feast today now testifies, within the cycle of the year, that you as Savior of the world alone came from the Father's throne.
Hunc cælum, terra, hunc mare, hunc omne quod in eis est, auctórem advéntus tui laudat exsúltans cántico.	5. The sky above, the earth, the sea, and all creation held therein extol with joyous hymns of praise the Author of your advent here.
Nos quoque, qui sancto tuo redémpti sumus sánguine, ob diem natális tui hymnum novum concínimus.	6. We also, whom you came to save and by your holy blood redeem, all sing a new and joyful hymn to celebrate your day of birth.
Iesu, tibi sit glória, qui natus es de Vírgine, cum Patre et almo Spíritu, in sempitérna sǽcula. Amen.	7. To you, Lord Jesus, glory be, the Virgin Mother's newborn Son, with God the Father, ever blest, and loving Spirit, ever one. Amen.

Text found in *TDH*, no. 77; *AH* 51, no. 50; Walpole, no. 87. Changes in TDH: stanza 1, 1: *omnium* for *gentium*; 2, 4: *tui servuli* for *tuis famulis*; 3, 1: *Salutis auctor, recole* for *Memento salutis auctor*; 4, 1: *hic* for *sic*; 5, 4: *laudat exsultans* for *collaudans canit*; 6, 2: *redempti sumus sanguine* for *redempti sanguine sumus*.

COMMENTARY:

The hymn for Christmas teems with language and imagery drawn directly from the deposit of the faith. We find expressions drawn directly from Scripture, especially the Psalms, and the conciliar tradition, especially the Niceno-Constantinopolitan Creed. The effect is to stress the doctrinal commitments that are foundational to a proper celebration of the humanization of the Savior at Christmas. The text is ancient—appearing already in the sixth century—and reflects a period when hymn writers were quite attuned to the technical terms that acquired orthodox status over the course of the Christological controversies of the fourth century.[9] Similar to Byzantine hymns of the same period, this hymn celebrates the dogmatic accord that the Church had achieved through a period of highly contentious dispute.[10] The communal song, then, renders otherwise abstract wrangling about doctrinal precision into the object of collective celebration and praise. Moreover, the profound concern for doctrinal orthodoxy is elegantly integrated with a psalmist's invocation of the shared praise of all creation.

The hymn exhibits stylistic features characteristic of the early *Ambrosiana*, or those compositions that imitate the form and content of St. Ambrose's originals. We find many terms and stylistic features, including frequent verbal repetition, that appear in the authentic corpus of Ambrose. In addition, the author employs certain features that characterize later hymnody, including alliteration, assonance, and rhyme, which would have influenced the musicality of the performance.

STANZA I

The opening stanza offers a theologically dense and credal celebration of Christ, the eternal Son of the Father. The first, "iconic" line appears as the third line of the more famous (but probably later) Advent hymn *Conditor alme siderum* (H 1).[11] Addressing Christ for his role in redemption (as in the Nicene Creed: "for us men and for our salvation"), the hymn proclaims his procession from the Father with the key terms *ex* ("from") and *Unice* ("unique").[12] As the hymn celebrates the orthodox conclusions of the Christological disputes of the fourth century, it proclaims Christ's eternal birth from the Father as transcending all speech and existing before all ages. The specific terms occur frequently in fourth-century

---

9. For background, see Ayres, *Nicaea and Its Legacy*, 85–104.
10. See Louth, "Late Patristic Developments," 138.
11. See the contemporaneous H 40, for Holy Saturday, which opens addressing Christ, *Tibi, Redemptor omnium*. The hymn from the eighteenth century in honor of the Sacred Heart, H 130, *Auctor beate seaculi*, repeats line 1 of H 7 as line 2 of stanza 1. The Lord is referred to as *redemptor* seventeen times in the Vulgate text; forms of the verb *redimo* are also numerous. See for instance, Jb 19:25: *Scio enim quod redemptor meus vivat*: "I know that my redeemer lives"; Ps 18 [19]:15: *Domine adiutor meus et redemptor meus*: "O Lord, my help and my redeemer"; Is 54:8: *In misericordia sempiterna misertus sum tui dixit redemptor tuus Dominus*: "with everlasting mercy I take pity on you, says the Lord, your redeemer"; Is 63:16b: *Domine, pater noster, redemptor noster, a sæculo nomen tuum*: "You, Lord, are our father, our redeemer, from eternity is your name."
12. See Jn 1:14, which announces that we have seen Christ, the "only-begotten" (*unigenitus*) of the Father.

Latin reflections on the Nicene faith and resonate for all listeners attuned to the legacy of the earlier doctrinal settlements.

The invocation of the first two lines (with Christ addressed in the vocative) stresses the Son as both agent of humanity's salvation and himself dependent on the Father. By specifying that the Son is from (*ex*) the Father, the Nicene Creed simultaneously ruled out that he is created, or "from nothing" (*ex nihilo*). The Son is also God's Only-begotten, distinguishing him as "unique" from the other figures in Scripture identified as "sons of God" (see Ps 81 [82]:6). Even before creation (*ante principium*) the Son was born of the Father. The term for that birth, in line 4, *natus*, likewise appears in the Nicene Creed.

The language of "ineffability" was crucial in the early doctrinal dispute on the Son's relationship to the Father. Early theologians, often drawing on Isaiah 53:8 ("Who shall declare his generation?")[13]; aimed to underscore the fundamental mystery of the Son's eternal birth.[14] Nicene Christians were especially concerned to distinguish such an eternal relationship from the biological birth that is known by human experience. Later in the hymn the "ineffability" of this eternal birth will be set in contrast with the Son's birth in time from the Virgin.

STANZA 2

Celebrating Christ as "light" (*lumen*), "brilliance" (*splendor*), and "hope" (*spes*; see 1 Tm 1:1), the stanza invokes his response to his attendants' prayers.[15] It is filled with language familiar from the Latin hymnodic tradition; indeed, virtually every term is attested in the authentic corpus of Ambrose, rendering all four lines a pastiche of familiar hymnodic terms. The ideas of light and brilliance relate closely to ancient themes of Christmas.

Christ as the Father's light and splendor is a familiar image in the New Testament (Lk 2:32: *lumen ad revelationem gentium*: "a light for the revelation to the gentiles"; and Heb 1:3: *qui cum sit splendor gloria, et figura substantia eius*: "who as he is the splendor of his glory and the figure of his substance") and also in the Niceno-Constantinopolitan Creed (*Et in unum Dominum Iesum Christum, ... Deum de Deo, lumen de lumine*: "And in one Lord Jesus Christ, ... God from God, light from light"). In a similar biblical register, Christ is "hope" (*spes*), recalling the language of 1 Timothy and Titus.[16] Ambrose had introduced the theme of Christ as light into the Latin hymnodic tradition with his hymn for the morning hour, *Splendor paternæ gloriæ* (H 75), which introduces Christ as *splendor* and *lucem* and *luminis* in its opening three lines; the same hymn uses the language of "everlasting" (*perennis*) to speak of the Father's glory.[17] This hymn, then, combines material from Scripture, dogmatic tradition, and the hymnodic archive to a noble and lofty effect.

---

13. *generationem eius quis enarrabit?*
14. See, e.g., Ambrose, *De fide* 14.89.
15. The alternative reading of *famuli* for *servi* may suggest "attendant" more than "slave"; see the *OLD*, under *famulus*, for potential links to "family." On Christ as *lumen*, see Lk 2:32.
16. 1 Tm 1:1 and Ti 2:13.
17. H 75: 2, 2.

The nobility of style appears also in the hymn's mode of address. In lines 1–2 the second-person address that is classical in hymnody (the *Du stil*) is evident in the repetition of *Tu* three times in sequence;[18] the address is reprised in line 4, with the reference to "*your* servants." The congregation places itself in a posture of supplication and adoration before God's effusive brilliance.

The final two lines of the stanza employ a similarly classical style. The first word of line 3, *intende*, recalls the opening line of the original version of Ambrose's hymn, *Intende, qui regis Israel* (see commentary on H 5), a request for God's response that is common in the Psalms.[19] The request for attention to the prayers that are poured out (*fundunt*) by the congregation is a frequent theme in the ancient corpus.[20] Likewise, the universality of the Church (*per orbem*) appears in Ambrose's hymn for Terce *Iam surgit hora tertia*.[21] Last, the identification of the congregation as praying servants (*servuli*) is found in the early Ambrosian hymn for all the saints *Æterna Christi munera*.[22]

STANZA 3

Invoking Christ as the author or agent of salvation, the stanza beseeches him to remember his own Incarnation. Informed by the language of Hebrews 2:10, where Christ is invoked as the "author of our salvation" (*auctor salutis*), and Philippians 2:7, where Christ is said to "take the form of a slave" (*forma servi*), the stanza presents the humanization of the Son in summary. Like the second stanza, the third abounds with language from the scriptural, credal, and hymnodic tradition, although it also employs distinctive language and imagery.

Some of the language adopts a more personal and intimate register than we find in the first two stanzas. The opening request that God "remember" (*recole*) his past actions is common in the Psalms.[23] The term for that remembering is frequent in Augustine's sermons (e.g., *sermo* 52.7.18; *sermo* 61.8.9), and, in some contrast to the elevated *intende* of the second stanza, may connote a certain familiarity with the addressee. While it is standard for hymns to praise the Virgin's purity (see lines 23–24 of Ambrose's *Iam surgit hora tertia*),[24] the hymn employs the somewhat technical term *illibata* ("untouched") in line 3 to underscore the miracle of Christ's human birth.

"Saving grace" translates *salutis* in line 1, itself a reference to Hebrews 2:10.

---

18. On the "Du-Stil" and the "Er-Stil," see E. Norden, *Agnostos Theos*, 143–66.
19. See, e.g., Ps 60 (61):2; 79 (80):2.
20. This use of *fundunt*, however, is somewhat unusual. In most instances from the hymns, terms signifying *fund-* describe the pouring out of God's actions on humanity: *refunditur* in Ambrose, *Æterne rerum conditor* (6,2; this stanza is omitted however in H 71); and *refundit* in *Hic est dies verus Dei* (H 44: 2, 1).
21. An abridged version of this hymn appears as H 48 in the *Liturgia Horarum*. For details, see the commentary on H 48.
22. See H 153 for the Common of Martyrs; the line in question is stanza 7, 3: *iungas precantes servulos*: "[we ask] that you join your praying servants" (line 31 in the original hymn).
23. See Ps 24(25):6; Ps 118(119):49.
24. H 48: lines 23–24: *ne virginis partus sacer / matris pudorem læderet*: "lest the holy offspring of the Virgin should injure the purity of his mother." The abridged version of this hymn in the *Liturgia Horarum* does not contain these lines.

There are many passages of Scripture that make a close association between salvation and grace; these passages state clearly that we are saved by grace and that it is by God's grace that we both receive the gift of faith and remain faithful to it (e.g., Eph 2:5: "By grace you have been saved").

STANZA 4

The fourth stanza locates the "remembered" day of the Incarnation in the cycle of time. Again, borrowing from the familiar hymnodic lexicon, the stanza brings the day of celebration to life, even attributing to it a certain agency in helping the congregation recall the moment of the Incarnation. Moreover, the stanza employs hymnodic strategies that further actualize the annual celebration by making it contemporaneous with the present-day celebration. Thus, we are drawn to identify the "then" of the first Christmas with the "now" of the liturgy.

The strategy is evident in the opening line. The reference to the present day (*hic præsens testatur dies*) is frequent in the hymns, actualizing the present moment.[25] In Ambrose's *Illuminans altissimus*[26], composed for Epiphany, the "present day" is likewise recalled as the moment of celebration (2, 4: *præsenti sacraris die*). As is typical in the hymn tradition, the moment celebrated itself becomes a focus. Moreover, line 2 describes the present day as running through the "cycle of the year" (*circulum anni*). Juxtaposed with "running" (*currens*) in line 2, the moment is presented as fleeting, recurring for but a day in the "circle" (*circulum*) of the year.[27] In Ambrose's morning hymn (H 75, stanza 8), the dawn, who is Christ, rides her course (*cursus*), creating an image that may be a source for the running of the annual course of the year that is evoked above. Moreover, like many of the early *Ambrosiana* that were composed for the liturgical hours, the hymn celebrates the cycling of time itself.[28]

The notion that the day "testifies" (*testatur*) attributes agency to the feast itself. Christmas day itself somehow gives witness to the events that transpire on the occasion of its recurrence. As in some of Ambrose's hymns, an otherwise inanimate or abstract figure is brought to life to add to the hymn's vibrancy.[29]

The final two lines of the stanza rehearse the scriptural and credal themes that were evoked in the opening stanzas, but in a distinctive register. Thus, Christ's "salvation" (*salus*), which we noted in stanza 3, 1, is again proclaimed in stanza 4, 4. Note, however, that in this second reference salvation is identical with Christ (rather than as coming from Christ). Furthermore, as Walpole notes, the identification of Christ "alone" (*solus*) as the source of salvation echoes Peter's

---

25. For discussion see Dunkle, *Enchantment*, 75–78.
26. *Illuminans altissimus* does not appear in the hymns of the Liturgy of the Hours.
27. See Jgs 11:40, which refers to the *anni circulum* after which the daughters of Israel gather to commemorate the daughter of Jephtha.
28. See Dunkle, "Here We Go Again", forthcoming.
29. See, e.g., *Illuminans Altissimus*, 5, 3: *mutata elementa stupent* (the changed elements of wine at Cana "marvel" [*stupent*] at themselves).

words in Acts 4:12: "Salvation is in no one else" (*non est in alio aliquo salus*).³⁰ But the Scripture's use of the third person is personalized with the second person *adveneris*. Likewise, the credal reference to the Son's "session" with the Father (*a sede Patris*) is noted, but also related directly to his descent to assume human form. The cumulative effect is to see Christmas less as the celebration of an abstract doctrine and a distant date when Christ's salvation is brought to us, and more as the present moment, when the infant Christ, of flesh and blood, whom we contemplate, is himself that salvation.

STANZA 5

As in biblical psalms and canticles, the sky, land, and sea, along with all that is in them, are invoked to praise God. Thus, the congregation's song is extended to all creation. As we approach the conclusion of the hymn, the circle of "exultant" participants (*exsultans*, line 4) widens.

Lines 1 and 2 recall familiar hymns of praise from Scripture, including the canticle of Daniel 3:56–88 ("All you works of the Lord, bless the Lord"). As Walpole notes, the most direct reference is Psalm 95 (96):11–12: "Let the heavens be glad and the earth rejoice; let the sea and what fills it resound."³¹ The singular *laudat* is used as the verb for sky, land, air, and all they contain, depicting the collective creation as an individual agent of song. Linking a song for the great Christian feast to the ancient language of psalmodic praise enmeshes the celebration with the congregation's regular liturgical prayer.

In lines 3 and 4 we should note the reference to the "coming" (*adventus*) of the one, and to his "author" (*auctor*), terms used earlier in the hymn (see 3, 1 and 4, 4). The reference to the "coming" may align with the season of "Advent," the liturgical time just concluded with Christmas.³² The referent of the term *auctor* is somewhat ambiguous, however, and has caused some confusion to copyists throughout the ages.³³ In the Divine Office version, the text indicates that we are recalling "this" (*hunc*) *auctor* of the Son's coming, which seems to shift the "author" from the Son to the Father. Both Father and Son, whose unity is stressed in the opening stanza, are "authors" of the Incarnation.

STANZA 6

The penultimate stanza shifts from direct address to the first person plural: we sing together (line 4: *concinimus*). As is somewhat common in the hymnodic tradition, we "too" (*quoque*) come to the conclusion by recalling the reason for the celebration itself. Moreover, even on the joyful feast of Christmas,

---

30. Walpole, no. 87, l. 15, page 307.
31. *Lætentur cæli, et exsultet terra; commoveatur mare et plenitudo eius* (Ps 95[96]:11–12). See also Walpole, l. 17, p. 307.
32. On the history of Advent, which emerges only in the Latin West, see Fassler and Baltzer, eds., *Divine Office in the Latin Middle Ages*, 15–47.
33. See Walpole, lines 17–19, pp. 307–8.

we anticipate the saving work of the Paschal Mystery by reference to Christ's "holy blood" (lines 2–3: *sancto ... sanguine*), a clear allusion to biblical accounts of salvation.

Lines 1 and 2 include a striking reference to the *Te Deum*, which dates most likely to the early fifth century and was long attributed to Ambrose.[34] Both hymns speak of the congregation redeemed by Christ's blood.[35] The reference thus links the memory of the Nativity with the events of the Passion, moving us forward in our liturgical sensitivities.

Lines 3 and 4 draw our attention closer to the mode and the motive for our singing. The verb "we sing together" (*concinimus*), which emphasizes the communal and participatory nature of the song, appears frequently in the hymnodic tradition.[36] In other contexts, the "birthday" (*dies natalis*), which calls to mind the start of Christ's earthly sojourn, refers to the saint's day of martyrdom (see Ambrose's hymn for Agnes, *Agnes beatæ virginis*, which, in stanza 1, 2, names the celebration her "birthday" with *natalis est*). Perhaps, then, along with the allusion to the Passion, the language of the stanza asks us to see that some sort of personal suffering is inevitably linked to the discipleship that is recalled on Christmas day. Celebrating not only Christ's birth but even his suffering, the singers join together in a "new hymn" (*hymnum novum*, line 4), recalling the references to the "new song" of the scriptural psalms and canticles.[37]

STANZA 7

See the introduction for a treatment of the doxologies. The final praise reinforces the link to the Nativity (*natus es*) before invoking the Father and the "nurturing" (*almo*) Spirit.[38] The reference to the Son's birth recalls the opening stanza's reference to the Son's ineffable birth from the Father (stanza 1, 4). While the epithet *almus* is typically applied to the Spirit in doxologies (see, e.g., H 46, H 47, and H 53), on the celebration of Christ's birth it may connote certain fostering, even mothering, aspects of the Spirit's agency.

Although this doxology is particularly well suited to the Christmas season, it is used seventeen times in the *Divine Office Hymnal* for feasts of the Blessed Virgin, virgins, and martyrs throughout the year. It seems to have been a common doxology by the time the Anglo-Saxon hymnal was in use (late tenth- or early eleventh-century).[39]

---

34. See Brian Dunkle, "Te Deum", in *Brill Encyclopedia of Early Christianity*.
35. Note also that the servants of the *Te Deum* are *famuli*, perhaps exerting an influence on the alternative reading of line 8 noted above.
36. See H 13: 4, 2; H 124: 6, 4.
37. See Ps 32(33):3; 39(40):4, 95(96):1, etc.
38. See commentary on H 1 for an extended discussion of *almus/alme*.
39. Milfull, 193.

Candor ætérnæ Deitátis alme	8

Anselmo Lentini, OSB, d. 1989
11 11 11 5

Christmas Time before Epiphany
Office of Readings

1 Candor ætérnæ Deitátis alme,
   Christe, tu lumen, vénia atque vita
   ádvenis, morbis hóminum medéla,
      porta salútis.

5 Intonat terræ chorus angelórum
   cælicum carmen, nova sæcla dicens,
   glóriam Patri, generíque nostro
      gáudia pacis.

9 Qui iaces parvus dóminans et orbi,
   Vírginis fructus sine labe sanctæ,
   Christe, iam mundo potiáris omni,
      semper amándus.

13 Násceris cælos pátriam datúrus,
   unus e nobis, caro nostra factus;
   ínnova mentes, trahe caritátis
      péctora vinclis.

17 Cœtus exsúltans canit ecce noster,
   ángelis læto sociátus ore,
   et Patri tecum parilíque Amóri
      cántica laudis. Amen.

1. Loving, eternal splendor of the Godhead,
   Life, Light, and Mercy, Christ you come among us,
   Healer of illness and all human weakness,
      Gate of Salvation.

2. Angels in chorus to the earth are singing
   tidings from heaven, telling of new ages:
   praise to the Father, to our human family
      joy, peace, and gladness.

3. Infant so lowly, Lord of all creation,
   born of the Virgin, holy, pure, and sinless,
   rule all the world now, Jesus Christ, our Master,
      ever beloved.

4. Born to give heaven, our eternal homeland,
   our flesh assuming, joined to us for ever;
   draw hearts that seek you, mind and soul renewing;
      by your love bind us.

5. Lord, see us gathered, filled with exultation,
   joined to the angels, singing hymns of gladness;
   joyous we praise you, one with God the Father,
      and Love, your equal. Amen.

Text found in *TDH*, no. 78.

COMMENTARY

This hymn is the first hymn in the *Liturgia Horarum* in the meter known as *Sapphics*.[40] After iambic dimeter, it is the most widely used meter in the *Hymnal*. Though the original Greek meter had more flexibility, the form of it used in the

---

40. See the section on "Sapphics" in appendix 1, on meter.

hymns is regular with patterns of long and short vowels that translate easily into accentual patterns. In metrical versions of this meter, as in this hymn, the second, sixth, and seventh syllable of every line is short. This gives the meter its distinctive rhythm. There is also a word break after every fifth syllable of the first three lines. The clear break halfway through each line causes the meter often to fall into a pattern of short phrases that may form a unified narrative but often gives the impression of a collage or mosaic of images. In this hymn the "collage effect" is marked; Lentini uses it to present clusters of scriptural images that reveal the wonder of Christ at his birth more effectively than a discourse could accomplish.

The hymn opens with the image of Christ in eternity and in heavenly glory. He comes as a cure for the sickness of sin and as the gate of salvation. In stanza 2, the angels sing his glory, which will bring peace to the earth. In stanza 3, the child lying in the manger governs the world, and now that he is here, let us address him and ask him to rule over us. We pray: one with us by your flesh, renew us and bind us with love. The final stanza joins us to the angels in their praise of the Trinity.

STANZA 1

In lines 1–2, the hymn gives us attributes of Christ in his divinity. The word *candor* is used sparingly in Scripture. Here, it is a reference to Wisdom 7:26: "For she [Wisdom] is the brightness of eternal light, the spotless mirror of the power of God, the image of his goodness": *candor est enim lucis æternæ et speculum sine macula Dei maiestatis et imago bonitatis illius*. This verse from the book of Wisdom is evocative of Hebrews 1:3: the Son is "the radiance of his (the Father's) glory and the exact imprint of his substance" (*splendor gloriæ et figura substantiæ*). The words *speculum*, *imago*, and *figura* express similar ideas.[41] The first line ends with the rich and beautiful word *alme*. It is in the vocative here, and so it signals to the singer that the hymn is addressed directly to Christ. The adjective *almus* has a wealth of meanings. It comes from the verb *alo* and signifies providing nurture, fostering, kind, gracious, loving. In this hymn, the brightness of eternity is not distant, uncaring, unaware of human suffering.

In line 2, the *candor* is named. He is Christ, *lumen*, "light," *vita*, "life," and *venia*, "mercy." He is *lumen*: at his presentation in the Temple, Simeon calls him "a light for revelation to the nations": *lumen ad revelationem gentium* (Lk 2:32). Long before, Isaiah had prophesied that God would give the suffering servant as a light to the nations: *Dedi te in lucem gentium ut sis salus mea usque ad extremum terræ*: "I will give you as a light to the nations, that you may be my salvation unto the end of the earth" (Is 49:6). Light is the defining quality of Christ in his

---

41. See Walpole, no. 3, l. 1, p. 35, where he speaks of the relation between *candor* and *splendor* in connection with Ambrose's hymn *Splendor paternæ gloriæ*.

transfiguration, when he manifests his divinity. His face shone like the sun and his garments were white as snow (Mt 17:2; Mk 9:4; Lk 9:29).⁴² The Gospel of John also dwells at length on the idea of light. Jesus says of himself: "I have come as light into the world" (Jn 12:46). References to Christ as *vita* are iconic and present throughout the New Testament: "For God so loved the world, that he gave his only Son, that whoever believes in him should not perish but have eternal life" (Jn 3:16), and "I am the way and the truth and the life" (Jn 14:6). In the Gospel of John the ideas of *vita* and *lumen* or *lux* come together in the Prologue where it is said of Christ: "In him was life, and the life was the light of men" (Jn 1:4); and later in the Gospel: "Jesus spoke to them again, saying, 'I am the light of the world. Whoever follows me will not walk in darkness, but will have the light of life'" (Jn 8:12).⁴³ Finally, Christ is *venia*, another rich Latin word. It signifies a favor, kindness; in religious language, it signifies a favor consisting of permission to do something. Then, it signifies allowance made for shortcomings, indulgence, mercy; and finally, forgiveness, pardon. The late Latin *venialis*, as in "venial," signifies "pardonable."

The titles in lines 1 and 2 give us some idea of what Christ is like when he comes. In lines 3–4, the hymn indicates that as *venia*, he will be *medela* (cure, remedy, healing). He is the cure for the multiple ills and sicknesses (*morbis*) that afflict the entire human race (*hominum*). In line 4, as light and life, he is the gate (*porta*) of salvation (*salutis*).⁴⁴

The first stanza is remarkable for the Marian overtones it contains. First, the verse from the book of Wisdom given above is traditionally applied to the Virgin in her Immaculate Conception, as it commemorates her in her sinless purity before God. Like Wisdom, she is *candor lucis æternæ et speculum sine macula Dei maiestatis*. *Alme* evokes the Marian antiphon for Advent, *Alma Redemptoris mater*. Finally, the Virgin is also *felix Cæli porta* in the hymn *Ave, maris stella* (H 145) and the *porta ex qua mundo lux est orta* ("the gate from which light has risen for the world") in the Marian antiphon for Lent, *Ave, Regina cælorum*. She is also the *porta* (the gate) that opens only to the Lord, the God of Israel, and then remains closed (see Ez 44:2, and *Fit porta Christi pervia* [H 15: 1, 1].

---

42. St. Thomas says that it was by a divine dispensation that the glory of Christ's soul united to his divinity did not overflow into his body from the first moment of conception, ST III, q. 45, a. 2.

43. The Latin of the quotations given above is as follows: *Ego lux in mundum veni* (Jn 12:46); *sic enim dilexit Deus mundum ut Filium suum unigenitum daret ut omnis qui credit in eum non pereat sed habeat vitam æternam* (Jn 3:16); *ego sum via et veritas et vita* (Jn 14:6); *in ipso [Iesu] vita erat et vita erat lux hominum* (Jn 1:4); *iterum ergo locutus est eis Iesus dicens ego sum lux mundi qui sequitur me non ambulabit in tenebris sed habebit lucem vitæ* (Jn 8:12). See also Jn 1:5 and 9; 12:35–36.

44. Jn 10:7–9: *Amen, amen dico vobis quia ego sum ostium ovium*: "Truly, truly, I say to you, I am the door of the sheep"; and (Ps 117 [118]:19–20): *aperite mihi portas iustitiæ ingressus in eas confitebor Domino; hæc porta Domini: iusti intrabunt in eam*: "Open to me the gates of righteousness, that I may enter through them and give thanks to the Lord. This is the gate of the Lord; the righteous shall enter through it".

STANZA 2

Stanza 2 is a colorful paraphrase of the angels' announcement of the birth of Christ in Luke 2:9–14:

Et ecce angelus Domini stetit iuxta illos et claritas Dei circumfulsit illos et timuerunt timore magno. Et dixit illis angelus, "Nolite timere; ecce enim evangelizo vobis gaudium magnum quod erit omni populo quia natus est vobis hodie salvator qui est Christus Dominus, in civitate David; et hoc vobis signum: invenietis infantem pannis involutum et positum in præsepio." Et subito facta est cum angelo multitudo militiæ cælestis laudantium Deum et dicentium: "Gloria in altissimis Deo et in terra pax in hominibus bonæ voluntatis."	And, behold, an angel of the Lord appeared to them and the glory of the Lord shone around them, and they were filled with great fear. The angel said to them, "Do not be afraid; for behold, I bring you good news of great joy that will be for all people. For today in the city of David a savior is born for you who is Christ the Lord. And this will be a sign for you: you will find an infant wrapped in swaddling clothes lying in a manger." And suddenly there was with the angel a multitude of the heavenly host, praising God and saying: "Glory to God in the highest and on earth peace among men of good will."

The first word of the stanza, *intonat*, literally means "to thunder; with regard to speech: thunder forth." Here it means something like "utter in resounding tones, proclaim loudly, shout"; it was a chorus that roused shepherds in the middle of the night and startled them. Scripture uses a milder expression. It was a chorus of angels *laudantium Deum et dicentium* ("praising God and saying"). It was a joyous chorus. The angels did not just say, "Peace to those of good will." In the hymn they go farther and announce the joy (*gaudium*) that peace would bring to the human race (*gaudium pacis*). Finally, the angels announce the arrival of new ages, new epochs of joy and peace. The birth of Christ inaugurates the definitive age of the new covenant, the last age of the world, the age in which the prophecies will be fulfilled, the age of the Church.[45] The New Testament is filled with a sense that the last age has arrived with the coming of Christ. "In many and various ways God spoke of old to our fathers by the prophets; but in these last days (*novissimis his diebus*, Nova Vulg.) he has spoken to us by a Son, whom he appointed the heir of all things, through whom also he created the world" (Heb 1:1–2). It is possible that Lentini is thinking here of Ambrose, who in his hymn for Terce, *Iam surgit hora tertia* (H 48) says: *Hinc iam beata tempora / Christi cœpere gratia*: "From this hour, now, already, blessed times have begun by the grace of Christ."[46]

---

45. See the commentary on *Conditor alme siderum* (H 1), stanza 3 and note 15. The theme of the last and golden age is essential to the imagery of Virgil's fourth Eclogue, read and treasured in late antiquity throughout the Middle Ages. See also Fontaine, 220.

46. Note that this hymn has been considerably shortened for inclusion in the *Liturgia Horarum*. The lines cited above are lines 3–4 of stanza 3 in the abridged hymn.

STANZA 3

In stanza 3, the hymn revels the paradoxes of the birth of Christ. He is a little child lying in a manger, yet he is sovereign Lord (*dominans*) of the universe. In the Old Testament, *Dominator* is a common title for God that expresses his absolute power and dominion over the world and events.[47] Jesus is lying in a manger in Bethlehem, which is not directly mentioned here, but the prophecy so deeply embedded in the Christmas tradition speaks of the sovereign Lord (*Dominator*) who will come from the little town of Judah: "And you, Bethlehem Ephratha, are little among the thousands of Judah: out of you he shall come forth from me who is to be the sovereign ruler (*Dominator*) in Israel: and his going forth is from the beginning, from the days of eternity" (Mi 5:2).[48] Christ is born "not of blood nor of the will of the flesh nor of the will of man, but of God" (Jn 1:13), conceived by the Holy Spirit (Nicene Creed), and born the fruit of a holy and immaculate Virgin (*Virginis fructus sine labe sanctæ*). Finally, in line 3 we speak directly to the child: "Now, be our Master, take possession of the world (*iam mundo potiaris omni*) into which you have come, you who are always lovable, ever to be loved."[49]

This stanza is reminiscent of Christmas sermons of St. Augustine in which he delights to juxtapose the contrasts that manifest the full reality of the Incarnation and that surpass our understanding:

> My mouth shall speak the praise of the Lord (Ps 144 [145]:21): of him, the Lord through whom all things were made, and who has been made among all things: who is the revealer of the Father, creator of his mother: ... Creator of the sun, created under the sun, ordering all ages from the bosom of the Father, consecrating the day today [Christmas] from the womb of his mother: remaining there, proceeding from here; maker of heaven and earth, born on the earth under heaven; unspeakably wise, wisely unspeaking; filling the world, lying in a manger, governing the stars, sucking at the breast, so great in the form of God and little in the form of a servant, that neither this littleness diminishes his greatness, nor does the greatness weigh upon his littleness.[50]

STANZA 4

Stanza 4 opens with a statement of what Christ will do for us and how he will do it; the stanza ends with an ardent prayer. The stanza is filled with allusions to scriptural texts and hymns Lentini no doubt heard many times over the course of

---

47. There are many examples in the Old Testament; e.g., *Dominator Domine Deus misericors et clemens patiens et multæ miserationis ac verus*: "Master, Lord, God, merciful and gracious, patient and compassionate and true" (Ex 34:5–6); *Ecce ego mittam angelum meum, et præparabit viam ante faciem meam et statim veniet ad templum suum Dominator quem vos quæritis, et angelus testamenti quem vos vultis ecce venit, dicit Dominus exercituum*: "Behold, I shall send my messenger, and he will prepare the way before me. And the Lord [*Dominator*] whom you seek will suddenly come to his temple; and the messenger of the covenant for whom you long, behold, he is coming, says the Lord of hosts." (Mal 3:1).

48. *Et tu Bethleem Ephrata parvulus es in millibus Iuda; ex te mihi egredietur qui sit dominator in Israel et egressus eius ab initio a diebus æternitatis* (Mi 5:2).

49. The Latin deponent verb *potior* signifies "gain possession of something and so own it, become master of it."

50. St. Augustine, *Sermones ad populum*, sermo 187, PL 38, 1285ff.

his life. In line 1, Christ is born to give us heaven (*cælos*) as a homeland (*patriam*). The future active participle indicates by its form that in the present, something is still to take place: *daturus* implies that at his birth Christ is going to give us a homeland in heaven. This sense easily acquires the nuance of intention, purpose, readiness to do or to happen. Venantius Fortunatus says the same succinctly in his hymn, *Pange, lingua, gloriosi prœlium certaminis* (H 32: 5, 3): *se volente, natus ad hoc* ("he willed it, he was born for this"). Line 2 says that he is one of us, made of our flesh: *unus e nobis, caro nostra factus*. This echoes John 1:14 ,"and the Word was made flesh and dwelt among us" (*et Verbum caro factum est et habitavit in nobis*); see also Philippians 2:7: "he emptied himself, taking the form of a slave, coming in human likeness; and found human in appearance" (*semetipsum exinanivit formam servi accipiens in similitudinem hominum factus et habitu inventus ut homo*).

Lines 3–4 ask Christ in his humanity, since he is one of us (*unus e nobis*) and made flesh of our flesh (*caro nostra factus*; see Gn 2:23), to renew our minds and draw our hearts to him by the bonds of charity. He will renew our minds by placing a law within them (Heb 8:10 and 10:16; both passages refer to Jer 31:31). He will draw us by the bonds of charity as the Bridegroom of the Church. The language used here is that of the Song of Songs and of the prophet Hosea. In the Song of Songs 1:3, the beloved says, "Draw me, we shall run after you" (*Trahe me: post te curremus*). This verse is used for the third antiphon at Lauds on the Solemnity of the Immaculate Conception. God says to Jeremiah (Jer 31:3), "I have loved you with everlasting love, therefore have I drawn you, taking pity on you": *in caritate perpetua dilexi te ideo adtraxi te miserans*.[51] At Hosea 11:4, God says of Israel: "I will draw them with the cords of Adam, with the bonds of love" (*in funiculis Adam traham eos, in vinculis caritatis*).

STANZA 5

Stanza 5 is a doxology addressed to Christ and then, in line 3, to the other Persons of the Trinity. The text presents something of a challenge to accommodate the placement of words in the metrical schema. Here is a version in prose word order: *Ecce exsultans, sociatus angelis læto ore, cœtus noster canit cantica laudis Patri tecum parilique Amori. Amen.*

In this final stanza of the hymn, we join the angels in their praise of the Trinity for the magnificent gift of the birth of Christ. With a joyous voice and heart we sing canticles of praise (*cantica laudis*). It is the new song, the *canticum novum*, of which the psalms and prophets sing. All may now join the great and thunderous chorus of praise.[52]

---

51. See also Jn 6:44; 12:32; Rom 8:35–39.
52. See, for example: Ps 32(33):3; 39:4(40:3–4); 95 (96):1; 97(98):149:1.

A solis ortus cárdine — 9

Sedulius, d. ca. 450
8 8 8 8

Christmas Time before Epiphany
Lauds

A solis ortus cárdine adúsque terræ límitem Christum canámus príncipem, natum María Vírgine.	1. From lands beneath the rising sun, through all the compass of the earth, now let us sing to Christ the Lord, the Virgin Mary's newborn Son.
Beátus auctor sǽculi servíle corpus índuit, ut carne carnem líberans non pérderet quod cóndidit.	2. The hallowed Author of the world a servant's body has assumed, that liberating flesh by flesh he should not lose what he has made.
Clausæ paréntis víscera cæléstis intrat grátia; venter puéllæ báiulat secréta quæ non nóverat.	3. Pure grace from heaven entered then the Mother's womb, both sealed and closed; the cloister of this maiden bride bore secrets she could not have known.
Domus pudíci péctoris templum repénte fit Dei; intácta nésciens virum verbo concépit Fílium.	4. The home of this pure heart became, with sudden power, the shrine of God; a virgin still, she knew not man and by a word conceived her Son.
Eníxa est puérpera quem Gábriel prædíxerat, quem matris alvo géstiens clausus Ioánnes sénserat.	5. She brought to birth her holy child, whose advent Gabriel proclaimed, whose presence John perceived with joy and leapt within his mother's womb.
Feno iacére pértulit, præsépe non abhórruit, parvóque lacte pastus est per quem nec ales ésurit.	6. He lay on straw with no complaint, not shrinking from a manger bed; an infant's share of milk he drank, while in his care he fed the birds.
Gaudet chorus cæléstium et ángeli canunt Deum, palámque fit pastóribus pastor, creator ómnium.	7. The hosts on high exult with joy and angels sing to God with praise; the shepherds wondrously behold the Shepherd, Maker of all things.
Iesu, tibi sit glória, qui natus es de Vírgine, cum Patre et almo Spíritu, in sempitérna sǽcula. Amen.	8. To you, Lord Jesus, glory be, the Virgin Mother's newborn Son, with God the Father, ever blest, and loving Spirit, ever one. Amen.

Text found in *TDH*, 79; *AH* 50, no. 58; Walpole, no. 31; Bulst, 71; Springer, *Sedulius*, 196. Changes in *TDH*: this hymn is composed of stanzas 1–7 of a longer hymn; stanza 2, 4: *non … quod* for *ne … quos* (Lentini adopts the better reading); 3, 1: *clausæ* for *castæ* in the Roman Breviary; 4, 4: *concepit* for *creavit* (modified in Breviaries to *concepit* in order to avoid a word that does not conform to a rigorously Scholastic theology); 5, 1: *enixa est* with hiatus, sometimes admitted by Sedulius. Stanza 7, 4: *creator* for *creatorque*.

COMMENTARY:

This Christmas hymn is part of a longer poem by Coelius Sedulius (*Pæan Alphabeticus de Christo*), the full text of which is found in an eighth-century manuscript in the British Library (MS Royal 2.A.XX, fol. 50), most probably written in the first half of the fifth century, which narrates Christ's life beginning from his nativity, through his earthly ministry, to his passion, death, and resurrection. The hymn is quantitative, although there are moments when it becomes accentual. It uses rhyme, but not throughout. Connelly observes that these two tendencies foreshadow later developments in Latin hymnody.[53]

The original text is an acrostic, or alphabetical hymn (*abecedarius*), its twenty three stanzas in iambic dimeter, each beginning with a consecutive letter of the Latin alphabet, taking up a format found in the Hebrew text of the Psalms.[54] Sedulius was not the first author to adopt this structure. St. Hilary of Poitiers had adopted it for two of his hymns a century earlier, as does St. Augustine in his *Psalmus contra partem Donati* (ca. 390).[55] The tradition continued to be popular into Late Antiquity and the early Middle Ages. The idea that the alphabet conveys the notion of completeness was already commonplace by the time of Sedulius. It is a notion that Christianity inherits from Judaism, where keeping the Torah is described in terms of the first and last letters of the Hebrew alphabet. Christ is frequently referred to as the Alpha and Omega, the first and last letters of the Greek alphabet.[56] Prudentius references this notion in *Cathemerinon* 9, where he speaks of salvation beginning and ending with Christ.[57]

Sedulius's text is received into the liturgy in the form of two hymns formed from the first seven, and four later stanzas of the poem. Alongside other texts of Sedulius, it enjoyed wide circulation in the Church, and in the schools, from late

---

53. Connelly, 57.
54. See, for instance, in the Hebrew Psalter: Ps 9–10:34, 37, 111, 112, 119, and 145. See also Prv 31:10–31, and Na 1:2–8.
55. St. Augustine mentions alphabetic psalmody in his commentary on Psalm 118 (119): *Quad autem de alphabeto Hebræo, ubi octoni versus singulis subiacent litteris atque ita psalmus totus contexitur, nihil dixi* (*Enarrationes in Psalmos*, 118.32.8): "I have said nothing about the Hebrew alphabet, which is used here in such a way that the stanzas of eight verses are headed by successive letters of the alphabet, so that the whole psalm is bound into a unity" (trans. Maria Boulding, *Exposition*, 495–96). See also Augustine, *Scripta contra Donatistas*, 3–15.
56. See Rv 22:13.
57. *alpha et Ω cognominatus, ipse fons et clausula omnium quæ sunt, fuerunt, quæque post futura sunt*: "named both Alpha and Omega, He the fount and closure too / of all things that are, and have been, all in future still to be" (*Cath* 9: 4, 2–3; trans. Richardson, *Hymns*, 63).

antiquity until the end of the seventeenth century. The opening words are cited by the Venerable Bede in his *De arte metrica*,[58] and were used without reference by medieval poets. The seventeenth verse of Sedulius's text, *Rivos cruoris torridi*, describing Christ's miraculous healing of a woman with an issue of blood, took on something of the character of a medieval charm against bleeding. The first seven stanzas, with a doxology by a different writer, were used from the early Middle Ages onward as a Christmas hymn. They treat of the striking contrast between the grandeur and omnipotence of the Word of God (the second person of the Trinity), and the vulnerable humanity of the child in whom the Word became flesh. In the Cistercian Breviary, the first four stanzas are ascribed to Terce of Christmas and Epiphany.

In 1589, Palestrina set the odd-numbered stanzas beginning with the letters A, C, E, G in his *Hymni totius anni secundum Sanctæ Romanæ Ecclesiæ consuetudinem, necnon hymni religionum*, a collection of hymn settings for use in Rome where the liturgical practice was for the even-numbered verses to be sung in Gregorian chant, with the odd-numbered verses in polyphony (faux bourdon). A four-part setting of *A solis ortus cardine*, with the Gregorian melody in the tenor line, is annotated at the bottom of two pages from an early sixteenth century collection of madrigals and hymns found in the Royal Library of King Henry VIII (London, BL, MS Royal, Appendix 58). In early Tudor England, the Latin hymn was sung in three parts with two voices added, one above and one below the plainchant. Polyphony of this kind became less common during the reign of Edward VI, when the increasing effects of the Protestant Reformation in England resulted in choirs being disbanded and organs dismantled.[59]

The popularity of the text is witnessed by a series of translations ranging from early monastic translations into Anglo-Saxon, and subsequently into other languages, most notably by Martin Luther (rendered into English verse by John Dryden). Luther translated the first seven verses into German as the hymn *Christum wir sollen loben schon*; it was also set by Bach in his chorale cantata of the same name, and referenced in his chorale prelude BWV 611. The text was furthermore set by various composers including Dufay, De Lassus, Praetorius, Scheidt, and de Grigny. Stanzas 8, 9, 11, and 13 of Sedulius's poem were also taken up into the liturgy, with an added doxology, as the Epiphany hymn *Hostis Herodes impie* (H 16). In the nineteenth century, eleven verses were translated into English by John Mason Neale ("From lands that see the sun arise"). The two hymns sourced from the text of Sedulius are among the oldest traceable non-scriptural texts to be found in the *Liturgia Horarum*.

STANZA I

The first stanza speaks of the Incarnation (the beginning of the "alphabet," if you will), and charts the spread of the news of Christ's birth throughout the world.

---

58. Springer, *Sedulius*, xii–xxii.
59. Dumitrescu, *Early Tudor Court*, 169.

Ortus is a genitive, and with *solis* forms a compound noun equivalent to the idea of "sunrise"; *cardo* conveys the idea of a "pivot" or "pole," upon which the earth turns. This stanza takes its character from the fourth Mass of Christmas (the Mass during the Day, *Puer natus est nobis*), which has as its gospel the Prologue of St. John (Jn 1:1–18), setting the significance of the birth in its cosmic context, and extending the news of Christ's birth throughout the earth.[60] There is a further scriptural and a liturgical allusion in lines 1 and 2 to *a solis ortu usque ad occasum* (Ps 112 [113]:3; see also Roman Missal, Eucharistic Prayer III), which speaks of the extent of the dominion of the newborn monarch (*principem*) across the lands of the world. *Princeps* or *Rex* is often used of Christ by both Fortunatus and Prudentius. Brian Dunkle observes Sedulius's conscious imitation of Ambrose in his choice of meter (iambic dimeter), and also in the use in this hymn of assonance and rhyme:[61] line 1 ends with *cardine*, which rhymes with *virgine* in line 4; *limitem* (line 2) and *principem* (line 3) likewise rhyme, giving the stanza an A-B-B-A structure. Dunkle also observes that Sedulius adopts a key word at the end of each stanza that "aligns with a particular event in the life of Jesus": in this stanza, *virgine*. Such artifice adds to the "mnemonic potential" of the rhyme, reinforcing the pedagogical aim of the abecedarians. The imperative *canamus* gives the stanza an invitatory quality in its exhortation.

STANZA 2

Sedulius expresses in this stanza something of the alphabetic completeness of his treatment of the mystery of salvation by recounting how Christ, who was in existence from all eternity, created the world and humankind in time, and in the course of time redeemed humanity.

The stanza begins with a bold Christological statement, immediately associating the Christ Child with the *auctor sæculi*, which once again picks up an allusion to the Prologue of the fourth gospel: *Omnia per ipsa facta sunt: et sine ipso factum est nihil, quod factum est*: "All things came to be through him and without him nothing came to be" (Jn 1:3). There are just three instances in the Vulgate where Christ Jesus is referred to as *auctor*: Acts of the Apostles 3:15: *auctorem vero vitæ interfecistis, quem Deus suscitavit a mortuis, cuius nos testes sumus*: "The author of life you put to death, but God raised him from the dead; of this we are witnesses;" Hebrews 2:10, where he is referenced as the *auctor salutis* ("author of salvation"); and Hebrews 12:2, in which he is called the *auctor fidei* ("author of faith").

In line 2, *servile* echoes the kenosis so evident in the hymn at Philippians 2:7: *sed semetipsum exinanivit, formam servi accipiens, in similitudinem hominum factus, et habitu inventus ut homo*: "Rather, he emptied himself, taking the form of a slave, coming in human likeness and found human in appearance". There may also be a conscious echoing here of a phrase of Prudentius, *mortale corpus induit*, found in *Cathemerinon* 11: 12, 1, also, interestingly, a Christmas hymn. There is also the theological reasoning that is found in the Roman Missal text for the adding of

---

60. For the idea of universal praise directed to God from sunrise to sunset, see Ps 112 [113]:3; Is 45:6; Mal 1:11.
61. Dunkle, *Enchantment*, 187.

the drop of water to the chalice in the Preparation of the Gifts, which itself owes its origin to a prayer of the Leonine Sacramentary for the Nativity:[62] *Per huius aquæ et vini mysterium eius efficiamur divinitatis consortes, qui humanitatis nostræ fieri dignatus est particeps* ("By the mystery of this water and wine may we come to share in the divinity of Christ who humbled himself to share in our humanity").

In line 3, Sedulius may have had Prudentius's words *sermone carnem glutinans* in mind when he wrote *ut carne carnem liberans*.[63] Christ frees mankind by becoming man (*carne carnem*). Finally, in his note on line 4, Lentini says that the best sources have *non ... quod*, although certain breviaries have *ne ... quos*.[64] Walpole notes that "*quod* gives a better, because wider, sense than the variant *quos*: the whole of creation is included."[65]

STANZA 3

The next two stanzas reflect on the significance of the Annunciation and seem somewhat reminiscent of the *Carmen Paschale* of Sedulius in which he describes Mary giving birth to Jesus. *Baiulat* here has the sense of bearing or carrying the child. The virgin birth, announced in Isaiah 7:14, is presented here by Sedulius invoking the image of the hidden or enclosed garden or cloister, a common medieval trope evoking the idea of a terrestrial Paradise, an earthly vision of the lost promised land of Eden. Walpole sees here an allusion to Ezekiel 44:2 "Then he [the Lord] turned me [Ezekiel] towards the way through the exterior gate of the sanctuary, which looks towards the East and it was closed. And the Lord said to me, "This gate shall be closed and it shall not be opened; no man shall pass through it because the Lord, the God of Israel has passed through it, and it shall be closed."[66] The Fathers of the Church often used this text as a prophetic announcement of the virgin birth of Christ.

Walpole also refers to a line from the poem of Venantius Fortunatus, written for his patron Agnes, when she assumed the responsibilities of abbess at the Holy Cross monastery in Poitiers (ca. 570 AD). He compares Mary, Mother of the Lord, to all the holy women of the Old Testament, who themselves were raised to the glory of the stars, but Mary outshone them all: "Mary remained closed as she gave birth to the Lord."[67] According to this thinking, the Virgin Mary is the New Eve. In his *Dialogue with Trypho the Jew* (ca. 150 AD), Justin Martyr explains that Christ destroyed Satan's work in the same way evil originally entered the world. Evil entered through Eve while she was still a virgin; so too salvation entered through Mary who was a virgin. In this way Mary "bore secrets she could

---

62. This prayer dates back to at least the sixth century. In the Leonine Sacramentary it opens section XL of the month of December. See the *Sacramentarium Veronense*, 157 (no. 1239).
63. See *Cath* 11: 12, 1–4, H 204: 5, 4 (for the Annunciation of the Lord).
64. *HIBR*, 73.
65. Walpole, no. 31, l. 8, p. 151.
66. *et convertit me ad viam portæ sanctuarii exterioris quæ respiciebat ad orientem et erat clausa, et dixit Dominus ad me porta hæc clausa erit non aperietur et vir non transiet per eam quoniam Dominus Deus Israel ingressus est per eam eritque clausa* (Ez 44:1–2).
67. *Dominum peperit clausa Maria manet* (Fortunatus, Poems 8.3.102, mentioned by Walpole, no. 31, l. 9, pp. 151–52. 8:3, 102).

not have known." (Justin Martyr, *Dialogue with Trypho*, 100). Lentini notes that certain breviaries have the stanza begin *Castæ* rather than *Clausæ*.⁶⁸ This removes the image of the enclosed garden and the gate that remains shut except to allow the Lord, the God of Israel, to enter (Ez 44:2). The next stanza continues the thought.

STANZA 4

From this point onward Sedulius takes up the Lucan narrative of the Annunciation, the Visitation, and the Nativity. The hidden garden suddenly becomes the temple of the Most High, by the power of the Holy Spirit (see Lk 1:35). The temple (*templum*) is invoked because it is the presence of God that makes a place holy, and here the womb of Mary is compared to the temple where God is present. Sedulius continues to follow the Lucan narrative, stating that Mary conceived *nesciens virum* (Lk 1:34). Lentini notes that line 4 originally read *verbo creavit Filium* which was changed in order to avoid a suggestion that is not consonant with Scholastic theology. The stanza calls to mind the *Carmen Paschale* of Sedulius, where similar vocabulary is adopted regarding the virgin birth: *nova virgo* (CP II, 31), *intacta* (CP II, 36).

This stanza is the source of the fifth and eighth responsories in the *Breviarium Romanum* for the Feast of the Circumcision (January 1). *Verbo* (by means of a word) in line 4 refers both to the word of the angel and the response of Mary. Springer notes that the doctrine of the perpetual virginity of Mary became increasingly popular during the second half of the fifth century, contemporary with the composition of this text.⁶⁹ For Sedulius, Mary is *semper virgo* (ever-virgin), and he states this here with a clarity of expression that became far less common in later hymnody.

STANZA 5

In this stanza, the fact of the Nativity is linked to the dialogue at the Annunciation (*quem Gabriel prædixerat*), and Mary's Visitation to Elizabeth, and the consequent leaping of John the Baptist in his mother's womb: *ut audivit salutationem Mariæ Elisabeth, exsultavit infans in utero eius*: "when Elizabeth heard the greeting of Mary, the baby leaped in her womb" (Lk 1:41). John the Baptist is described as *clausus*, which mirrors the treatment of Christ in stanza 3 "sealed and closed" within his mother's womb. Lentini observes that the stanza begins with a hiatus (*Enixa est*) after a short unaccented syllable, which, although rare, Sedulius did, on occasion, permit. In the *Breviarium Romanum* it was modified to *enititur*. Already in this stanza, by virtue of the Annunciation, the glory of God is seen as returning to his temple, *templum repente fit Dei* (see Mal 3:1) as Christ finds a home (*domus*) in the pure heart of Mary.

Mary describes herself as *intacta nesciens virum* (4, 3) in response to the angel (Lk 1:34). The Incarnation is effected by the means of a word, *verbo concepit Filium* (4, 4), in this case, the word of Mary, her *fiat*, by which she "agrees" to the

---

68. *TDH*, no. 79, 81.
69. Springer, *Sedulius*, 66.

Incarnation (Lk 1:38). The Visitation of Mary to Elizabeth and the joyful prenatal reaction of St. John the Baptist is narrated by the lines *quem matris alvo gestiens / clausus Ioannes senserat* (lines 3–4; Lk 1:41).

STANZA 6

This stanza offers three lines of a gloss on Luke 2:7: "And she gave birth to her firstborn son. She wrapped him in swaddling clothes and laid him in a manger, because there was no place for them in the inn": *et peperit filium suum primogenitum et pannis eum involvit et reclinavit eum in præsepio quia non erat eis locus in diversorio*. The gospel account makes no mention of hay (*Feno iacere pertulit*) but it is a reasonable addition, given the mention of the manger. Dunkle cites the use of *præsepe* here as a conscious imitation by Sedulius of the vocabulary of Ambrose.[70] Springer notes that in *parvoque lacte pastus est* Sedulius adds a detail that is not found in the scriptural narrative.[71] *Abhorruit* (line 2) is reminiscent of a line in the *Te Deum*: *non horruisti virginis uterum*.[72] In a departure from the Lucan narrative, the nursing of the infant is then developed into a Christological statement, in line 4, which expresses the notion that while the Christ child, in his humanity and humility, was being fed by his mother, he, at the same time, in his divinity, had care of the birds.[73] This trope reflects once again the Christology of the Johannine Prologue, in which the Incarnate Word is at work in creation: "All things came to be through him, and without him nothing came to be": *omnia per ipsum facta sunt et sine ipso factum est nihil quod factum est* (Jn 1:3).

STANZA 7

This stanza is based on the Lucan account of the shepherds (Lk 2:8–19). In some ways it mirrors the first stanza of the hymn, although here it is the angels exulting rather than ourselves. At line 2 some manuscripts have *Deo* rather than *Deum*, suggesting the idea of singing to the glory of God rather than singing of Christ's birth.[74] The shepherds behold the Shepherd (*palamque fit pastoribus pastor*), and yet the Shepherd they behold is also the Creator. The *auctor* of stanza 2 is now *creator* (line 4), leaving us in no doubt that the babe of Bethlehem is divine. Dunkle sees Sedulius's adoption of *creator omnium* here as an imitation of Ambrose's hymn *Deus creator omnium*.[75] In line 4, Lentini used *creator*, which is better both rhythmically and musically, rather than *creatorque* found in some manuscripts. He also notes that the assonance of this stanza is particularly characteristic of Sedulius in this text.[76]

---

70. Dunkle, *Enchantment*, 188.
71. Springer, *Sedulius*, 204 n. 23.
72. See Lk 2:12.
73. See Mt 6:26; also Ps 146(147):9, and Lk 12:6.
74. See Lk 2:13–18. For further references to God as shepherd, see Psalm 22:1, Sirach 18:13, Isaiah 40:11, Jeremiah 31:10, Ezekiel 34:11–16, Matthew 25:32, the account of Jesus as the Good Shepherd in John 10:1–18, and 1 Peter 5:4.
75. Dunkle, *Enchantment*, 188.
76. *HIBR*, 69.

STANZA 8

The doxology is not by Sedulius and is the generic medieval doxology for the Christmas season with slight adjustments by Lentini. It is also used for *Radix Iesse floruit*. It first appears as the doxology for *Christe Redemptor omnium* (see *TDH*, no. 77, 79). In line 2, *qui natus es de Virgine* is characteristic of doxologies that conclude hymns on Marian feasts.

O lux beata cælitum	10
Pope Leo XIII, d. 1903	The Holy Family of Jesus, Mary, and Joseph
8 8 8 8	Vespers I and II

O lux beáta cǽlitum et summa spes mortálium, Iesu, cui doméstica arrísit orto cáritas;	1. O blessed Light of saints above and highest Hope of mortal flesh, O Jesus, at your birth is seen the loving smile of family life.
María, dives grátia, o sola quæ casto potes fovére Iesum péctore, cum lacte donans óscula;	2. O Mary, Mother rich in grace, your purest heart alone can love and fondle Jesus on your breast with sweet caresses, nursing him.
Tuque ex vetústis pátribus delécte custos Vírginis, dulci patris quem nómine divína Proles ínvocat:	3. O Heir to Patriarchs of old, the Virgin's chosen guardian blest, with sweetest name, the child divine called you his father here on earth.
De stirpe Iesse nóbili nati in salútem géntium, audíte nos, qui súpplices ex corde vota fúndimus.	4. From Jesse's noble lineage sprung to save the nations lost in sin, with kindness hear the humble prayers our hearts pour forth with deep desire.
Qua vestra sedes flóruit virtútis omnis grátia, hanc detur in domésticis reférre posse móribus.	5. Your home was like a garden fair, with every virtue blest by grace. O grant that we may imitate such grace in family life at home.
Iesu, tuis obœdiens qui factus es paréntibus, cum Patre summo ac Spíritu semper tibi sit glória. Amen.	6. Lord Jesus, humbly you became obedient to your parents' will; to you eternal glory be with Father and with Spirit blest. Amen.

Text found in *TDH*, no. 80; Leo XIII, *Poems*, 104. Changes in *TDH*: stanza 1, 3: *Iesu cui* for *Iesu O cui*; 4, 4: *ex corde vota fundimus* for *vestras ad aras sistimus*.

COMMENTARY

The Feast of the Holy Family is of recent origin. In 1663 Barbara d'Hillehoust founded, in Montreal, the Association of the Holy Family; this devotion soon spread, and in 1893 Pope Leo XIII (1810–1903) expressed his approval of a feast under this title, and himself composed part of the office. The feast was welcomed as an efficacious means for bringing home to the Christian people the example of the Holy Family at Nazareth, and by the restoration of the true spirit of family life, curbing, in some measure, the evils of modern society. These motives led Pope Benedict XV to insert the feast into the universal calendar, and the Holy See instituted the Feast of the Holy Family in 1921, assigning it to the Third Sunday after Epiphany. In the modern Roman calendar, it is kept on the Sunday within the Octave of the Nativity of the Lord.

Pope Leo XIII, an able classicist, composed three hymns for the new feast in classical form: the hymns for Vespers, Matins (Office of Readings), and Lauds. The original hymn for the Matins (*Sacra iam splendent decorata lychnis*) contains nine Sapphic stanzas; stanzas 3, 5, 7, and 8 of this text now appear as the hymn for the Office of Readings, under the title: *Dulce fit nobis memorare parvum* (H 11). For Lauds, Leo XIII's original hymn, *O gente felix hospita*, has been replaced by a new hymn composed by Lentini, *Christe, splendor Patris* (H 12). It is composed in the "short" meter composed of six syllables per line, *trochaic brachycatalectic*, the same meter used for the Marian hymn *Ave maris stella* (H 145). The current hymn for Vespers (*O lux beata cælitum*) is taken from the original hymn by Pope Leo XIII; it has five of the original six stanzas (stanzas 1–4, 6), followed by a new doxology (*Iesu, tuis obœdiens*) composed by Lentini. It replaces Leo XIII's original doxology (*Jesu tibi sit gloria*). The hymn is in four-line stanzas of quantitative iambic dimeter.

All three of the original hymns by Leo XIII are expressive of the ideas contained in his encyclical *Rerum Novarum: On the Conditions of Labor* (1891), in his decision to found a pious association, under the patronage of the Holy Family, in order to promote family life, and in awareness of the conditions under which people must work. The first three stanzas of the hymn under discussion are addressed to Jesus, Mary, and Joseph in turn.

STANZA 1

In this stanza, the Incarnation is presented in terms of both light (*lux*) and hope (*spes*). The *lux* of line 1 refers to Jesus, as becomes clearer in the second half of this first stanza. There are references in the New Testament to Jesus as light from heaven. See, in particular, the striking testimony of St. Paul at Acts 22:6–8.[77] There is also a rich scriptural tradition of referring to God as our hope (line 2, *spes*) particularly expressed in the Psalms,[78] for example, Psalm 64 (65):6 reads: "Hear us, O God our savior, the hope of all the ends of the earth": *Exaudi nos,*

---

77. For example, see also Acts 9:3–4; Wis 7:26; Is 9:2; Jn 1:4–5, 8–9; 1 Jn 1:5.
78. See Ps 21:10 (22:9); 60:4 (61:3); 64:6 (65:5); 70 (71):5; 90 (91):9; and many others.

Deus, salutaris noster, spes omnium finium terræ. In line 3, Lentini simplified the original *Iesu, O cui*, removing the redundant elision of the *o*, which is found also at 2, 2.[79] The stanza expresses the single idea that the great hope of the Incarnation is that God comes to share our human lot, particularly in the *domestica* of family life.

STANZA 2

Line 1 evokes the angelic salutation of the Annunciation (see Lk 1:28–38) and the unique privilege of Mary in being called *gratia plena*, which, in the temporal realm, is reflected by the equally unique privilege she enjoys as the Mother of Christ to tend and nurse him. The chastity of Mary, and her perpetual virginity, *casto* (line 2), is contrasted with the intimacy of her very natural maternal care of the Christ Child. Once again, there is a juxtaposition of the theological notion of the unique privileges of Mary as the sole source of the humanity of her Son, and the deeply human experience of motherhood.

STANZA 3

In this stanza the hymn follows the account of the genealogy of Christ in Matthew 1:1–17, which enables a consideration of the role and importance of St. Joseph in the infancy narrative. In line 1, the reference to *vetustis patribus* seems to evoke an apocryphal legend concerning Joseph, by which his divine election was indicated by the miraculous flowering of his staff, reminiscent of the blossoming of Aaron's rod as a sign of his authority (Nm 16–17). Lines 3 and 4 also suggest that Joseph was responsible for the naming of the child.

STANZA 4

De stirpe Iesse nobili nati (line 1) expresses the idea that all three members of the Holy Family were of the line of David, and each has a role in the salvation of the nations (*salutem gentium*). Isaiah prophesies: "But a shoot shall sprout from the stump of Jesse, and from his roots a bud shall blossom": *Et egredietur virga de radice, et flos de radice ejus ascendet* (Is 11:1). Lentini removed the original line 4, *vestras ad aras sistimus*, which somewhat supposes the presence of a representation of the Holy Family before the altar; he used instead the final line of stanza 5 of the original hymn, which is omitted in the text of the *Liturgia Horarum*. The original stanza 5 is:

Dum sol redux ad vesperam	As sun is setting, evening comes,
rebus nitorem detrahit,	depriving us of all its light,
nos hic manentes intimo	yet we remain, and from the heart
ex corde vota fundimus.	pour forth our prayers throughout the night.

STANZA 5

Stanza 5 is the original stanza 6. Here the Holy Family is presented as a school of virtue for all family life. The "flowering" of virtue (*floruit*) picks up a trope found in several other hymns of this Christmas Season that speak of the Virgin

79. *TDH*, no. 80, 82.

Mary as a garden, or a cloister (see H. 15, *Fit porta Christi pervia*). It also strongly emphasizes that the Holy Family is presented as an exemplar for all families (a major theme in the magisterial writings of Leo XIII.)

STANZA 6

The doxology (by Lentini) is based on the account of the boy Jesus in the Temple in Luke 2:41–52, especially, verse 51, which reads: "He went down with them and came to Nazareth, and was obedient to them": *Et descendit cum eis, et venit Nazareth: et erat subditus illis.* This scriptural allusion also functions as a link that points from the season and feasts that narrate the years of Christ's infancy and childhood toward "the hidden years," which preface the inauguration of his public ministry.

Dulce fit nobis memorare parvum

Pope Leo XIII, d. 1903
11 11 11 5

The Holy Family of Jesus, Mary, and Joseph
Office of Readings

Dulce fit nobis memoráre parvum
Názaræ tectum tenuémque cultum;
éxpedit Iesu tácitam reférre
    cármine vitam.

Arte qua Ioseph húmili excoléndus,
ábdito Iesus iuvenéscit ævo,
seque fabrílis sócium labóris
    ádicit ultro.

Assidet nato pia mater almo,
ássidet sponso bona nupta, felix
si potest curas reveláre lassis
    múnere amíco.

O neque expértes óperæ et labóris,
nec mali ignári, míseros iuváte;
quotquot implórant cólumen, benigno
    cérnite vultu.

Sit tibi, Iesu, decus atque virtus,
sancta qui vitæ documénta præbes,
quique cum summo Genitóre et almo
    Flámine regnas. Amen.

1. Sweet is the memory of the child Christ Jesus,
his poor and humble life at home in Nazareth;
we raise our voices and do well to ponder
    his life of silence.

2. Through hidden seasons Jesus grew to manhood,
learning from Joseph, trained a humble craftsman,
freely embracing, as a willing helper,
    carpenter's labor.

3. Mother devoted to her child most loving,
wife good and holy caring for her husband,
happy to lighten burdens for the weary,
    kindly she serves them.

4. Family most holy, knowing work and labor,
conscious of evil, comfort the afflicted;
when they are seeking safety and assistance,
    show them your kindness.

5. Power and glory be to you, Lord Jesus,
holy exemplar of the life you give us,
one with the Father and the loving Spirit,
    you reign for ever. Amen.

Text found in *TDH*, no. 81; all the original hymns for the feast are found in Leo XIII, *Poems*, 104–15, 282–84. The original title of the hymn is *Sacra iam splendent decorata lychnis*; from the original stanzas, 1, 2, 4, and 6 have been omitted; stanza 8, 1–2, and stanza 9, 3–4, have been combined into a single stanza. The doxology is new. Changes in *TDH*: stanza 1, 1: *Dulce fit* for *Gratius*; 1, 3: *expedit* for *gratius*; 3, 3: *lassis* for *fessis*.

A NOTE ON THE TEXT

The original text of this hymn,[80] appointed for Matins in the *Breviarium Romanum*, has been shortened in the *Liturgia Horarum* to five stanzas, that is, by exactly half. In the *Liturgia Horarum*, the third stanza marks the beginning of the hymn, with the result that its opening words have had to be changed from *gratius nobis memorare* to *dulce fit nobis memorare*. That is because, in the preceding second stanza, the poet had asked the rhetorical question of whether it may not be fitting to sing of Jesus' royal lineage (*regios ortus*) from God, the supreme Father (*summo Parenti*), while singing also of the noble *Domus David*. But then, in the third stanza, the focus is turned to the simple life of Jesus in Nazareth, which explains the comparative *gratius* in the original version; the poet has chosen, in this hymn, to focus rather on the simple and modest circumstances of Jesus' life in the bosom of the Holy Family. For this same reason, *gratius* has been replaced by *expedit* in the third line of this stanza.

Furthermore, in the third stanza of the version in the *Liturgia Horarum*, the original *fessis* has been changed to *lassis*, since the former word is said to have a "negative ring" to it in certain regions.[81]

The fourth stanza in the *Liturgia Horarum* is a compilation of the first two lines of the original eighth stanza and the last two lines of the ninth stanza.

We are missing, in the *Liturgia Horarum*, in addition to the second stanza just mentioned, the opening stanza, which describes in general terms the joy of the feast; the fourth stanza, which refers to the flight into Egypt; the sixth stanza, which associates the pouring of Jesus' sweat as he worked with the shedding of his Blood for our salvation, and the ninth stanza, in which prayers are addressed to the Holy Family.

---

80. Leo XIII, *Carmina*, 77–78. The editor refers the reader to a number of variant readings of the hymn that differ from the text found in the *Breviarium Romanum*. Leo XIII must have revised the text once more before publication and, in particular, rewritten stanzas 2 to 4.

81. For the explanation, see *HIBR*, 75 fn. 3: ... *quod male sonat in aliquibus regionibus*. What is presumably meant is that, in Italian, *fesso* is colloquial language and means "stupid, dumb."

COMMENTARY

Pope Leo XIII (1810–1903) made a name for himself as a poet in both Italian and Latin, and his Latin poems far outnumber the Italian.[82] His poetic works cover a variety of topics:[83] in addition to writing poems with religious, ethical, historical, or autobiographical content, he also wrote various *carmina* addressed to friends and subjects, even singing the praises of the art of photography (*ars photographica*) in an epigram from 1867.[84] Included among his religious poems are three hymns for the feast of the Holy Family; the authorship of other hymns is uncertain or refuted.[85]

In terms of both language and style, Leo XIII aligns himself very closely to the forms of poetic expression from the golden age of Latin poetry, as developed by Virgil, Horace, and others.[86] Unlike the other two hymns found in the *Liturgia Horarum* for this feast, Leo's hymn is not composed in iambic dimeter, which is the most common meter in Christian hymnody, but rather in Sapphic meter, which was introduced into Roman poetry by Catullus and Horace, and which appears less frequently in Christian hymnody.[87] His links to the classical poets can be clearly seen also in this hymn; with the exception of biblical proper names, Leo XIII uses hardly any vocabulary that is typically Christian. Even the Holy Spirit is referred to in this hymn by the poetic term *Flamen*. Leo XIII's word choice and sentence structure convey a high degree of elegance and artistry, and thus testify to the author's intention to render Christian themes in a style of diction that is as classical as possible.

Leo XIII had a deep personal interest in the hymn's subject, since he very much promoted devotion to the Holy Family. In 1893 he instituted a proper feast in its honor, which initially could be celebrated locally on the Third Sunday after Epiphany and eventually was prescribed for the universal Church by Benedict XV. Leo XIII's Apostolic Letter *Neminem fugit* of June 14, 1892, is dedicated to the Holy Family and draws on certain tendencies of a devotional trend at the time, which sought to establish the Holy Family as a decisive model of

---

82. See Barthold, *Papæ poetæ*, 115–25, and Baumgartner, *Die lateinische Literatur*, 681–85.
83. See the summary in Leo XIII, *Carmina*, 5–25.
84. *Carmina*, 48.
85. In addition to the hymn discussed here, other genuine hymns by Leo XIII are the Vespers hymn for the Feast of the Holy Family, *O lux beata cælitum* (H 10), and the Lauds hymn for the same feast, *O gente felix hospita*, both in iambic dimeter. The latter was not incorporated into the *Liturgia Horarum*. In the *Liturgia Horarum*, one further hymn is listed with Leo XIII as the presumed author: *Te dicimus præconio* (H 287) in iambic dimeter. *Omnis expertem maculæ* in Sapphic meter was proposed by Lentini in *HIBR*, no. 211, but was not included in *TDH*. Additionally, Bach suggests that the hymns for the Feast of the Holy Rosary could also have been composed by Leo XIII, though it cannot be proven. In fact, these were written by the Dominicans Eustachio Sirena (d. 1769) and Tomaso Agostino Ricchini (1695–1779). See *HIBR* 217–20 (nos. 215–18).
86. A brief appreciation of the poetic language of Leo XIII may be found in Leo XIII, *Carmina*, 25–36.
87. Prudentius had already composed two of his, albeit literary, hymns in Sapphic meter, *Cath* 8 and *Peristeph* 4. See also, from a later period, the hymn attributed to Paul the Deacon for the Feast of the Nativity of John the Baptist, *Ut queant laxis* (H 219–21), the hymn *Virginis virgo venerande custos*, composed by Peter Damian (H 291), and finally, *Iste, quem læti colimus fideles* (H 201) and *Cælitum, Joseph, decus atque nostræ* (H 202), both composed for the Feast of St. Joseph by the Spanish Carmelite Juan Escalar Casanate (d. 1700).

Christian family life.[88] This letter of Leo XIII offers, in some passages, a key to understanding the hymn *Dulce fit nobis*.

STANZA 1

The first stanza begins by drawing our gaze to the simple life of the Holy Family in Nazareth.[89] *Tectum* properly means "roof" and can thus, by metonymy, often also in the plural, refer to the house as a whole.[90] By *tenuis cultus* is meant the Holy Family's simple, unpretentious way of life. In the original text of the hymn, the preceding stanza mentions the family's membership in the *Domus David*, which contrasts with their way of life in Nazareth. The last two lines more precisely specify the theme of the hymn; the *tacita vita Iesu* (the hidden life of Jesus) is introduced. The adjective *tacitus*, "hidden" or "unspoken," alludes to the fact that Jesus' childhood is mentioned only in passing in the gospels.

Leo XIII sees this way of life of the Holy Family as an example for those of all classes, an idea that he expounds more widely in the Apostolic Letter *Neminem fugit*: noblemen (*nobiles*) should learn how to show moderation in prosperous moments of life and how to bear misfortune with dignity; the rich (*dites*) might recognize that virtue is to be considered of higher value than wealth.[91] The great mass of workers (*operarii*) should look to the Holy Family in the afflictions and difficulties of their lives and learn to appreciate their status more than to lament it, since it has been sanctified, as it were, by the Holy Family.

STANZA 2

The second stanza first takes as its theme Jesus' training and subsequent work as a carpenter. While growing up (*iuvenescit*), he is trained (*excolendus*) in the same humble craft (*arte humili*) that his foster father Joseph practices (*qua Ioseph*).[92] The last two lines of this stanza denote Jesus' work as assistant (*socius*) to his father. It is specially emphasized that he took on this work voluntarily (*ultro*). Jesus performed this work as a carpenter before his public ministry (*abdito ævo*, that is, in his hidden years).

In this stanza, emphasis is placed on Jesus' great humility, as well as on his obedience to his foster father. Despite his origin from the Divine Father, which had been mentioned in the original second stanza, he is willing to be trained in

---

88. *ASS* 25 (1892/93), 8–10.
89. Leo XIII uses here the form *Nazara, -æ* f., instead of the indeclinable Nazareth, and thus is able to introduce the place name seamlessly into the Latin text, here in the form of the old locative.
90. *OLD*, s. v. *tectum*.
91. *ASS* 25, 9: *Qui nobiles nati sunt, discent a Familia regii sanguinis quomodo et in edita fortuna se temperent, et in afflicta retineant dignitatem: qui dites, noscent ab ea quantum sint virtutibus posthabendæ divitiæ*.
92. The incomplete relative clause *qua Ioseph* should be supplemented with a form such as *utitur* or the like: "In the simple art that Joseph practiced." The gerundive *excolendus* here takes on the function of the present passive participle ("being trained": one who is being trained), which does not exist in Latin, and expresses the incompleteness of a process or an action in contrast to the perfect passive participle. See Menge, *Lehrbuch*, 731–32 (§510.5).

the *ars humilis* of his foster father, as well as to practice this craft as his co-worker. Thus also the value of human work, through the example of Jesus, is highlighted and sanctified, since it was practiced even by the hands of the Son of God, as Leo XIII stresses in his Apostolic Letter *Breve Neminem fugit*.[93]

STANZA 3

In the third stanza, Mary is presented as an example for Christian mothers. She stands by (*assidet*) her son (*nato almo*) as a devoted mother (*pia mater*) and supportively by her husband as a good wife (*bona nupta*). Her happiness consists in being able to relieve the cares (*curas relevare*) of her family members, who are exhausted from work (*lassis*). This exemplary character of Mary, which is rooted in her unconditional care for her husband and her Son, also has a corresponding passage in the pope's Apostolic Letter *Neminem fugit*.[94]

STANZA 4

The fourth stanza formulates petitions, based on the living conditions of the Holy Family. They are familiar with the toils of human labor (*neque expertes operæ et laboris*) and have not escaped negative experiences (*nec mali ignari*). Given this background, Mary, Joseph, and Jesus are predisposed to help all those who are exposed to daily toils and burdens and to support them in the difficulties of their lives (*miseros iuvate*). To those who implore heavenly support (*implorant columen*[95]) they will show their grace and favor (*benigno cernite vultu*).

In this stanza, too, the exemplary character of the Holy Family is again echoed, at least indirectly: the Holy Family is united with all other families in the troubles and worries of everyday life. With this in mind, all families, likewise, should confidently follow the example of the Holy Family, praying to them, especially in times of trial.

STANZA 5

The concluding doxology places the praise of Jesus at the beginning and, in line 2, summarizes an important aspect of the entire hymn, namely the exemplary nature of Jesus' holy life in his family (*sancta qui vitæ documenta præbes*). Lines 3–4 then include the Father and the Holy Spirit (*cum summo Genitore et almo Flamine*[96]).

---

93. *ASS* 25, 9: *Imo ipsæ divinæ manus se fabrilibus exercuerunt*: "Indeed, those divine hands themselves were practiced in the arts of a carpenter."

94. *ASS* 25, 8: *Habent matres in Sanctissima Virgine Deipara amoris, verecundiæ, submissionis animi perfectæque fidei insigne specimen*: "In the most holy Virgin, Mother of God, mothers have an extraordinary model of love, modesty, submission of soul and of perfect faith."

95. See Schwering, "columen", in *TLL*, 3, 1735–37, at 1736, 37: *de summo cælo*.

96. On the term *Flamen* used for the Holy Spirit, see Blaise, *Dictionnaire*, 355; idem, *Le vocabulaire Latin*, 359 (§218).

	Christe, splendor Patris	12
Anselmo Lentini, OSB, d. 1989 6 6 6 6		The Holy Family of Jesus, Mary, and Joseph Lauds

Christe, splendor Patris,
Dei mater Virgo,
Ioseph, tam sacrórum
pígnorum servátor,

Nitet vestra domus
flóribus virtútum,
unde gratiárum
fons prománat ipse.

Angeli stupéntes
Natum Dei cernunt
servi forma indútum
servis famulántem.

Imus præes, Ioseph,
humilísque iubes;
iubes et María
et utríque servis.

Cunctis præstant aulis
hæc egéna sæpta,
salus unde cœpit
géneris humáni.

Iesu, Mater, Ioseph,
mansiónis vestræ
nostras date sedes
donis frui sanctis.

Tibi laudes, Christe,
spem qui nobis præbes,
tuos per paréntes
cæli adíre domum. Amen.

1. Christ, the Father's Splendor,
   Mary, God's own Mother,
   Joseph, blessed guardian
   of such holy pledges:

2. Your home shines in radiance,
   with the flowers of virtue,
   whence the Font of graces
   comes with mercy flowing.

3. Angels view in wonder
   God's own Son, an infant,
   clothed in servant's nature,
   serving us, his servants.

4. Joseph, humble leader,
   though the least, you guide him;
   Mary, you direct him,
   serving both with kindness.

5. This poor home surpasses
   every court and palace,
   harboring salvation
   for the human family.

6. Jesus, Mary, Joseph,
   grant us and our families
   joy and gifts most holy
   from your humble dwelling.

7. Praise to you, Christ Jesus,
   for to us you offer
   hope that through your parents
   we come home to heaven. Amen.

Text found in *TDH*, no. 82.

COMMENTARY

The meter of this hymn is the same as that of *Ave, maris stella*. It is called *trochaic dimeter brachycatalectic*. The base is a trochee, shown as – ᴗ; that is, long-short or stressed-unstressed. It is the opposite of an iamb. Like iambs, trochees come in pairs of *metra* (plural for *metron*), called a dimeter. Trochaic dimeter looks like this: – ᴗ – ᴗ | – ᴗ – ᴗ.[97] The last syllable of each *metron* may be either long or short: – ᴗ – ᵜ | – ᴗ – ᵜ. *Catalectic* signifies that one syllable is removed from the end of the line; *brachycatalectic* signifies that two syllables are removed. The result is a six-syllable line that looks like this: – ᴗ – ᵜ | – ᴗ. This meter was used in the Carolingian period and throughout the Middle Ages. The accentual form of it seems to have come from hymns and songs based on popular piety.[98] There are traces of it in old Visigothic prayers and tropes, such as the song with a refrain based on Psalm 50 (51): *Deus miserere, / Deus miserere / in peccatis eius*.[99] It was found joined to other meters in religious poetry from the fourth century onward, and it was the meter used in the second half of the line of some Goliardic verse in the later Middle Ages. Lentini is using the meter as it is found in *Ave, maris stella* (H 145). It is rhythmical based on stress accentuation, with an accent on the first, third, and fifth syllable of each six-syllable line. The impression given by this meter is one of short, intense, almost ejaculatory prayer.

The hymn celebrates the hidden life of the Holy Family at home in Nazareth. After an introductory invocation, it speaks of the virtues cultivated in the humble home, the wonder of the angels as they behold the service each member of the family offers to the others. No royal palace has such beauty. In stanza 6, the hymn asks the Holy Family to grant those who sing the hymn a share in the holy gifts from the home in Nazareth. The last stanza is a prayer of praise to Christ, and, in conformity to the practice of *cœtus* VII, it functions as a doxology.[100]

STANZA 1

In the first stanza, each person of the Holy Family is named by an epithet: Jesus is Christ, the anointed one and splendor of the Father,[101] Mary is *Dei mater Virgo* (Mother and Virgin). She is named by the paradox that expresses her divine privilege and her role in the history of salvation: mother and virgin.[102] In choosing

---

97. For a more thorough explanation, see appendix 1, on meter.
98. Lausberg, *Der Hymnus: Ave Maris Stella*, 26–27.
99. Norberg, *Introduction*, 144–46.
100. For a more detailed account of the role and structure of the doxology, see the general introduction: "The Liturgical Stanza 6, the Doxology." At *TDH*, xxii, Lentini appeals to the great Spanish hymnologist of the eighteenth century, Faustino Arevalo, who observes that the doxology may function with or without the mention of a particular Person of the Trinity, or with praise of Christ alone.
101. *Qui cum sit splendor gloriæ, et figura substantiæ eius*: "He [Christ] is the radiance of his [the Father's] glory and the exact imprint of his nature" (Heb 1:3); *et vidimus gloriam eius, gloriam quasi unigeniti a Patre plenum gratiæ et veritatis*: "and we have seen his glory, glory as of the only Son from the Father, full of grace and truth" (Jn 1:14).
102. See the *Communicantes* in the Roman Canon (Eucharistic Prayer I), where Mary is referred to as the *gloriosæ semper Virginis Mariæ, Genetricis Dei et Domini nostri Iesu Christi* ("the glorious ever-Virgin Mary,

an unusual meter for this hymn, Lentini has signaled a link between it and the only other hymn with the same meter in the collection of hymns in the revised *Liturgia Horarum*, for which he is largely responsible. This stanza clearly alludes to the opening stanza of *Ave, maris stella* (H 145), as the ancient and iconic hymn in honor of the Blessed Virgin Mary. Lines 2–3 of *Ave, maris stella* read:

> Dei mater alma,
> atque semper virgo

The visual arrangement of words in these two lines shows how easily one hymn writer may take another hymn and rework it into a new text. Lentini's second line is: *Dei mater Virgo*. Though the two hymns develop along different lines, similar verbal techniques appear in both; these will be discussed below in connection with individual stanzas. Finally, after Jesus and Mary, Joseph is introduced by name. He is the only one of the three named here. His epithet is *servator*, guardian of the holy pledges (*pignora*) entrusted to him. There is a pun here on the word *pignus*. It means, first, anything given as security: a guarantee, hostage, pledge, assurance, proof; second, it refers to offspring, children, as guarantees of the reality of a marriage. From this second sense, in later Latin the word was used to signify any person or thing especially valuable or dear. Joseph is the guardian or guarantor of the quiet beginnings of salvation, the "holy pledges" of the graces that will be given when Christ is grown to manhood and becomes the *fons gratiarum* (stanza 2, 3–4); he is also the guardian and guarantor of the honorable marriage of the Virgin Mother; finally he is guardian of the most lovable and holy people the world has ever known, Jesus and Mary.

In a homily on the genealogy of Christ, St. Augustine states clearly that Joseph is in the truest, though spiritual, sense the earthly father of Jesus:

> Just as Mary was a mother without carnal desire, so also Joseph was a father without carnal intercourse.... What the Holy Spirit achieved, he achieved in each of them, "since he [Joseph] was a just man" (Mt 1:19). The husband was righteous, the wife was righteous. The Holy Spirit came to rest in the justice of both and gave them both a son.... A son was born of the Virgin Mary, to the piety and love of Joseph, a son who was at the same time the Son of God.[103]

STANZA 2

In stanza 2, the home at Nazareth is described as a new garden of Eden, where all the flowers of virtue grow and where the fountain rises that will water the world with grace. It is a clear allusion to Genesis, chapter 2:

Mother of our God and Lord, Jesus Christ"). See also the twelfth-century Litany of Loreto, in which Mary is referred to as *Sancta Dei Genetrix* (Holy Mother of God).

103. *Sicut illa [Maria] sine carnali concupiscentia mater, sic ille [Ioseph] sine carnali commixtione pater.... Quod Spiritus sanctus operatus est, utrique operatus est, cum esset, inquit, vir iustus. Iustus ergo vir, iusta femina. Spiritus sanctus in amborum iustitia requiescens, ambobus filium dedit ... et tamen pietati et caritati Ioseph natus est de Maria virgine filius, idem que filius Dei* (St. Augustine, *Serm.*, 51.30). The translation is taken, with emendations, from *Sermons*, trans. Edmund Hill, 40–41.

In the beginning, the Lord God planted a garden of pleasure in Eden, in the east, and he placed there the man whom he had formed. Out of the ground the Lord God produced every tree that was delightful to look at and pleasant for food, with the tree of life in the middle of the garden and the tree of the knowledge of good and evil. And a river flowed out of Eden to water the garden (Gn 2:8–10).

Line 1 of the stanza opens with the verb *niteo*. This word has multiple senses that fit the hymn particularly well. It is a verb that has as a primary meaning "to shine, look bright, glisten, be radiant." It is said of heavenly bodies but also of polished surfaces. From this second application, it comes to signify a house that is clean and in order, and when said of people to be beautiful, youthful, shining with health. The house at Nazareth is spiritually radiant and is a household well-ordered.

The last word of the stanza is *ipse*. It modifies *fons* and shows that the fountain is no ordinary source of water. *Ipse* is an intensive demonstrative pronoun or adjective signifying "the very one, itself." By extension, it can also signify eminence: the main one, or the "one and only...." Here it means the fountain itself that waters the flowers of the virtues, the one and only fountain, the great fountain. Imagery concerning fountains, as sources of cleansing, inebriation, life (which is maintained by water), and grace as the water of supernatural life, is present throughout the Old and New Testaments and in the Patristic tradition based on them. Here are some examples: "They are inebriated by the abundance of your house and you give them to drink from the torrent of your pleasure; for with you is the fountain of life" (Ps 46:9–10); "With joy you will draw water out of the springs of salvation" (Is 12:3); "The water I shall give will become in him a fountain of water springing up into eternal life" (Jn 4:14); "Whoever believes in me, as the Scripture has said, 'Out of his heart will flow rivers of living water'" (Jn 7:38). The image entered into the hymn tradition with Ambrose and Prudentius, for example, in Prudentius's *Corde natus ex Parentis* (H 13: 1, 4–5): *ipse fons et clausula / omnium quæ sunt ... :* "He is the fount and closure of all things that are...."[104]

STANZA 3

Stanza 3 shows us the Nativity from the perspective of the angels. They have glorified God in the highest (Lk 2:13–14). Then, at 2:15, Luke says: "When the angels went away from them into heaven...." What did they do there? They fell into astonished and silent adoration as they looked upon their infant Lord. Again, St. Augustine gives a human voice to their amazement:

---

104. Examples from the *Liturgia Horarum* include, among others, H 74; H 104; H 132 for the Sacred Heart: *dulcoris fons et gratiæ*; H 238. See also Is 58:11, Rv 21:6, and many other references.

"In the beginning was the Word, and the Word was with God, and the Word was God" (Jn 1:1). O food and bread of angels! (Wis 16:20) From you angels are filled, from you they are satisfied, and they do not grow weary; from you they live and are wise. Where are you for my sake? In a cramped lodging, in swaddling clothes, in a manger. For whom? He who governs the stars, sucks at the breast; he who fills the angels and speaks from the heart of the Father, is silent on the breast of his mother. But he is destined to speak when he grows to the proper age, he is destined to fulfill for us the Gospel.[105]

They see their Lord clothed in the form of a servant, preparing to serve his servants. Note *servi* and *servis* placed at the head of two successive lines. He who "was in the form of God, thought it not robbery to be equal with God, but emptied himself, taking the form of a servant, being made in the likeness of men, and in habit found as a man."[106] Even in the manger, he was preparing to fulfill the prophecies. This preparation would come to fulfilment at the end of his life at the Last Supper: "knowing that the Father had given all things into his hands, and that he had come from God and was going back to God he rose from supper, laid aside his outer garments, and taking a towel, tied it around his waist. Then he poured water into a basin and began to wash the disciples' feet" (Jn 13:3–5).

STANZA 4

Stanza 4 names both Mary and Joseph and addresses them directly. The first two lines are devoted to Joseph, the second two to Mary. Notice the repetition of *iubes* (literally: "command"), back-to-back in lines 2 and 3. Joseph is the least of the three, yet he presides over the family: *imus*, "least," is the first word of the stanza and is juxtaposed with *præes*, second singular, present (*præesse* means "to be set over, preside, have charge of"). Joseph knows that he is the least, and he is humble in his directives (*humilisque*). Pope Leo XIII says of him:

> And Joseph shines among all mankind by the most august dignity, since by divine will, he was the guardian of the Son of God and reputed as His father among men. Hence it came about that the Word of God was humbly subject to Joseph, that He obeyed him, and that He rendered to him all those offices that children are bound to render to their parents. From this two-fold dignity flowed the obligation which

---

105. '*In principio erat Verbum, et Verbum erat apud Deum, et Deus erat Verbum.*' *O cibus et panis angelorum: de te implentur angeli, de te satiantur, et non fastidiunt; de te vivunt, de te sapiunt, de te beati sunt. Ubi es propter me? in diversorio angusto, in pannis, in præsepio. Propter quem? Qui regit sidera, sugit ubera: implet angelos, fatur in sinu Patris, tacet in sinu Matris. Sed locuturus est competente ætate, impleturus evangelium nobis....* St. Augustine, *Sermones ad populum*, 196, PL 38, 1020.

106. The Latin text of the Vulgate is: *qui cum in forma Dei esset non rapinam arbitratus est esse se æqualem Deo sed semet ipsum exinanivit formam servi accipiens in similitudinem hominum factus et habitu inventus ut homo* (Phil 2:6–7). The Greek word used in this passage, ἁρπαγμός ("robbery, rape"), is strong and clear: Christ is the equal of God / equally God. Some modern exegetes have sought a weaker meaning: "something to be grasped." This does not render fully the Greek text. St. Jerome translated the Greek with *rapina* ("robbery, prey, booty"). The Fathers of the Church took the terms ἁρπαγμός and *rapina* in this literal sense. The Latin is also clear in the use of the infinitive *esse*: he was *already* in the form of God. The translations here are based on the Vulgate.

nature lays upon the head of families, so that Joseph became the guardian, the administrator, and the legal defender of the divine house whose chief he was. And during the whole course of his life he fulfilled those charges and those duties. He set himself to protect with a mighty love and a daily solicitude his spouse and the Divine Infant; regularly by his work he earned what was necessary for the one and the other for nourishment and clothing; he guarded from death the Child threatened by a monarch's jealousy, and found for Him a refuge; in the miseries of the journey and in the bitterness of exile he was ever the companion, the assistance, and the upholder of the Virgin and of Jesus. Now the divine house which Joseph ruled with the authority of a father contained within its limits the scarce-born Church.[107]

Mary also commanded (*iubes et Maria*) even as she served both Joseph and Jesus. Jesus himself was docile and biddable, subject to them both (Lk 2:51–52). One can hardly fathom the depth of understanding that must have developed between them as Mary "kept all these things in her heart" (Lk 2:51) and Jesus obeyed (Lk 2:52). The wedding feast of Cana is the fruit of thirty years of bidding and guiding Jesus as he grew. There, Mary noticed the lack of wine, informed her Son, with steadfast faith instructed the servants to do whatever Jesus would tell them, and so she inaugurated both the public ministry of Christ and her own role as intercessor for all those Christ came to serve and save (Jn 2:2–5).

STANZA 5

In stanza 5, the contrast between *cunctis aulis* and *egena sæpta* is marked. The contrast is emphasized by the position of *aulis* and *sæpta* at the end of consecutive lines. An *aula* is a court before a house or a hall within it, an atrium. It is primarily used in association with nobility and power: a palace, royal court. In Scripture it is said exclusively of the palace of a king and is often modified by the genitive of king, *regis* or the adjective *regia*.[108] The Latin *sæptum*, commonly used in the plural *sæpta*, is as far as possible in meaning from an *aula regia*. Literally it signifies an enclosure: a fold for animals, paddock; in later Latin it could mean a refuge, a place of safety, a sanctuary. The adjective *egenus* that modifies it implies extreme poverty. The Latin *pauper* means poor, and *egenus* emphasizes the needy quality of poverty; it implies indigence, even destitution. The two are used together, *egenus et pauper*, in the psalms (Ps 69[70]:6; 108[109]:22). In Psalm 34[35]:10, these two with a third synonym, *inops*, are all found together: *Omnia ossa mea dicent, Domine, quis similis tui eripiens inopem de manu fortiorum eius, egenum et pauperem a diripientibus eum*: "All my bones shall say, 'O Lord, who is like you, delivering the destitute from the hand of those who are too strong for him, the poor and needy from those who rob him?'"

---

107. Leo XIII, *Quamquam Pluries*, 3.
108. The Latin *domus* is also used of royal palaces or of important public buildings, such as the house or palace of the High Priest (Lk 22:54). See Blaise, *Dictionnaire*. *Ecce qui mollibus vestiuntur in domibus regum sunt*: "Those clothed in soft garments live in the houses and palaces of kings." (Mt 11:8; Lk 7:25).

It might seem as if the hymn exaggerates the picture of the house at Nazareth, but if we understand the description in terms that resonate with the psalm mentioned above, it becomes clear that the little and poor house in which Jesus grew up was filled with the need for God and his righteousness that is the quintessential quality of a true Israelite; it was a place of refuge where the *anawim*[109] could live in peace under the gaze of God. The first line of the stanza says that it was more excellent (*præstant*) than all (*cunctis*) the royal palaces. When Jesus later told the crowds that Solomon in all his glory was not arrayed as one of these lilies (Mt 6:29), he might have been thinking of home.

STANZA 6

Stanza 6 expresses the prayer of those who sing the hymn. Notice the juxtaposition of *vestræ* ("your") and *nostras* ("our"). Notice also that the *sæpta* of stanza 5 has now become a *mansio* ("an abode, dwelling": synonym to *domus* and *sedes*). Finally, notice that the noun *mansio* and the verb *maneo* (both of which signify "dwell, abide in a permanent way") return again and again in the final discourse at the Last Supper. Jesus is bequeathing to his Apostles the joy and stability he gave to Mary and Joseph during the long years of preparation in Nazareth.[110]

All three members of the Holy Family are named in the first line, although the two-syllable *mater* is substituted for *Maria*, which has three syllables and would be too long for the line. We who sing ask the three to grant us the grace to have and enjoy (*frui*) in our own homes the holy gifts that are the fruit of their life together as the Holy Family.

STANZA 7

This stanza fulfills the purpose of a doxology as praise of God at the end of a hymn, but it is unusual in that it addresses Christ alone instead of the three Persons of the Trinity. It addresses him directly and praises him for the hope he has given us that through the intercession of Mary and Joseph we may enter into the definitive home of Nazareth, which awaits us in heaven.

---

109. *Anawim*, עֲנָוִים, a Hebrew term found in the Old Testament, especially in the Psalter, is rich in meaning. It signifies the remnant of Israel, who remain faithful to God in times of general apostasy or difficulty. They are often poor and oppressed, and wholly reliant on God for their salvation. They are the lowly of the *Magnificat*, the true Israel whom God remembers in his mercy. They live the first Beatitude: blessed are the poor in spirit, for theirs is the Kingdom of Heaven (Mt 5:3).

110. For use of *mansio* and *maneo*, see Jn 14:2, 14:23; 15:4 (twice), 15:6, 15:7 (twice).

Corde natus ex Parentis	13

Prudentius, d. ca. 405
87 87 87

January 1: Solemnity of Mary, the Holy Mother of God
Vespers I and II

Corde natus ex Paréntis
ante mundi exórdium,
Alpha et Omega vocátus,
ipse fons et cláusula
ómnium quæ sunt, fuérunt
quæque post futúra sunt.

Córporis formam cadúci,
membra morti obnóxia
índuit, ne gens períret
primoplásti ex gérmine,
mérserat quam lex profúndo
noxiális tártaro.

O beátus ortus ille,
Virgo cum puérpera
édidit nostram salútem
feta Sancto Spíritu,
et puer redémptor orbis
os sacrátum prótulit.

Ecce, quem vates vetústis
concinébant sǽculis,
quem prophetárum fidéles
páginæ spopónderant,
émicat promíssus olim:
cuncta colláudent eum!

Glóriam Patri melódis
personémus vócibus;
glóriam Christo canámus
matre nato vírgine,
inclitóque sempitérnam
glóriam Paráclito. Amen.

1. Of the Father's heart begotten
ere the dawning of the world,
he is Alpha and Omega,
ancient source and final end
of all things that are and have been
and shall be in years to come.

2. He assumed a mortal body,
frail and needy, fit to die,
that the race of Adam's children
might not perish, lost in death,
where sin's harmful law immersed them
in the hidden depths of hell.

3. O how blest that splendor rising
when the Virgin, giving birth,
fruitful by the Holy Spirit,
our salvation brought to light;
and the child, the world's Redeemer,
first revealed his sacred face.

4. Lo, the one whom through the ages
bards have sung with one accord,
whom the prophets in their writings
filled with faith had long foretold,
splendid child of ancient promise:
let creation sing him praise.

5. Praise and glory to the Father,
let our voices ring with song.
Praise and glory to Christ Jesus,
from the Virgin Mother born.
Endless glory to the Spirit,
high exalted Paraclete. Amen.

Text found in *TDH*, no. 83; AH 50, no. 25; Walpole, no. 23; Milfull, no. 136; Richardson, *Hymns*; O'Daly, *Days Linked by Song*. Changes in *TDH*: stanza 1, 3: *Alpha et Omega vocatus* for *Alpha et Ω cognominatus*; 2, 5: *quam* for *quem*; stanza 5 is the doxology for the feast of the Archangels (H 264; in the same meter) adapted to this hymn.

COMMENTARY

This hymn is composed of four stanzas taken from the a longer hymn composed by the Spanish poet Prudentius, who was writing around the turn of the fourth and fifth centuries. It is the ninth hymn in his collection entitled *Liber Cathemerinon*, which means "Book of daily (hymns)." To the hymn is added a doxology that has been adapted by Lentini from a later hymn in the same meter (H 264). The original hymn has thirty-eight stanzas, each having three long lines in trochaic tetrameter catalectic meter.[111] In the *Liturgia Horarum*, each stanza is set out in six shorter lines. The *Liber Cathemerinon* consisted of twelve long hymns, six for different hours of the day and the rest for other occasions. This one is entitled "Hymn for every hour" and is a poem in praise of "the glorious deeds of Christ" (1, 2). The meter was that of Roman triumphal songs and was used by St. Hilary in a hymn to which Prudentius is indebted,[112] and later by Venantius Fortunatus (H 32) and St. Thomas Aquinas (H 127) to celebrate the triumph of Christ.[113]

In the Mozarabic church of early medieval Spain, the whole hymn was sung during the Octave of Easter and after the Ascension. Later, various stanzas were selected by different churches as a Christmas hymn. Hymn 13 includes only stanzas 4, 6, 7, and 9 of the original poem. In this form its focus is on the nature of Christ as the eternal Son of the Father and Creator of all things, and his Incarnation as Redeemer of the world and as the fulfillment of all the prophecies.

STANZA 1

This stanza is a magnificent theological statement, with a rich texture of scriptural allusion, especially to St. John's Gospel and Revelation. Prudentius describes, in the first two lines, the relationship of Christ to his Father, as generated by him before the world began. He is "born from the heart of the Father." John's Prologue concludes (1:18) with the words (in the Vulgate version) *Unigenitus Filius, qui est in sinu Patris, ipse enarravit*: "the Only-Begotten Son, who is in the bosom of the Father, he has made him known." St. Ambrose writes "when we hear the words 'from the womb the Son, from the heart the Word,' let us believe that he is not made by hands, but born of the Father."[114] At the opening of his poem on the divinity of Christ (*Apotheosis*, Preface 1.2) Prudentius says: *corde Patris genita est Sapientia, Filius ipse est*: "From the heart of the Father, Wisdom was begotten: he is the Son" (see also below, 4, 5). In a hymn that was ascribed to Hilary, Christ is invoked as *tu Dei de corde Verbum*, "you who are the Word from the heart of

---

111. See appendix 1, on meter, "4. Trochaic Tetrameter Catalectic: 87 87 87." In the original hymn, each line consisted of fifteen syllables with a break after the eighth syllable.
112. Bulst, 34–35.
113. On Prudentius's *Cathemerinon*, see O'Daly, *Days Linked by Song*; and Richardson, *Hymns*; and on this hymn in particular, F. Lardelli, *Dux Salutis*. For the hymns of Hilary, see AH, 50:3–9; and Bulst, 31–35.
114. *Ergo et nos, cum audimus "ex utero filium", "ex corde verbum", credamus quia non plasmatus manibus, sed ex patre natus, non artificis opus, sed progenies est parentis* (*De fide* 1.82); the phrase *ex utero* refers to Ps 109 (110):3b, *ex utero ante luciferum genui te*: "from the womb before the day star I begot you."

God."[115] The Word was "in the beginning" (Jn 1:1–2). At John 17:5, Christ says: "Father, glorify me in your own presence with the glory that I had before the world was made"; and later, at John 17:24, "my glory that you have given me in your love for me before the foundation of the world."

The original reading of line 3 is *Alfa et Ω cognominatus*. Classical Latin did not have a separate letter to denote the Greek long O. In fact, the term 'o mega' was not used in Greek either until much later in the Byzantine period, to distinguish it from 'o micron' (short o). The first use of "omega" in English seems to be in Tyndale's Bible, in the early sixteenth century. Prudentius is echoing Revelation 1:8, *Ego sum A et Ω, principium et finis, dicit Dominus Deus*; "I am the A [Alpha] and the Ω [omega], the beginning and the end, says the Lord, God."[116] He is also alluding to Revelation 21:6: *ego sum A et Ω, initium et finis; ego sitienti dabo de fonte aquæ vivæ gratis*: "I am the Alpha and the Omega, the beginning and the end; to the thirsty I shall give freely from the font of living water." Line 4 again echoes Revelation 21:6, with the introduction of *fons* and *clausula*. The line reads: *ipse est fons et clausula*; "he is source and final end." Line 4 is a commentary on Revelation 21:6. *Clausula* ("conclusion") is an unusual word to be used of a person, although Tertullian called John the Baptist the *clausula* of the Law and the Prophets (*Scorpiace* 8.3). In lines 5–6, Revelation 1:8 is still in the poet's mind, as there God continues "who is, who was and who is to come." This is here transferred from the Creator to the creation, past, present and future.

This whole stanza could be a commentary on the words of the Niceno-Constantinopolitan Creed: *ex Patre natum ante omnia sæcula … per quem omnia facta sunt*: "born of the Father before all ages … through whom all things were made." In Colossians 1:16–17 Paul says: "all things were created through him and for him. He is before all things, and in him all things hold together." The missing stanza that follows in the original hymn elaborates this theme, describing how, at the command of Christ, all the different parts of the universe and all that live in it came into being.

STANZA 2

Lines 1–3 recall Philippians 2:6–8: "Christ Jesus, … though he was in the form of God, … emptied himself, taking the form of a slave, coming in human likeness and found human in appearance, he humbled himself, becoming obedient to death, even death on a cross." There is also an echo of the opening of Hilary's victory hymn (Bulst 1, hymn 3, lines 1–3): *Adæ carnis gloriosæ et caduci corporis / in cælesti rursum Adam concinamus prælia*: "Let us sing together of the battles of the glorious flesh and frail body of Adam in the second heavenly Adam." *Obnoxia* ("liable to, subject to") has a legal connotation, and this fits with the reference in line 5 to *lex*, the law of sin or death.

---

115. See Walpole, no. 1, l. 3, p. 5; Bulst, no. 12, line 3, p. 133.
116. See also Rv 22:13.

In line 3 *induit* literally means "he put on," like a garment. This image of Christ clothing himself in human flesh is often used by the Latin Fathers, especially Tertullian. In lines 3–4, *ne gens periret primoplasti ex germine* literally means "so that the race (sprung from) the seed of the first man should not perish." *Primoplastus* ("first-created") is a compound of Latin and Greek elements, instead of *protoplastus*, the more common form in early Christian literature.

In line 5 the reading *quam* seems better than *quem*, as it refers to the whole human race as affected by Adam's sin, rather than just to Adam. In line 6 *noxialis* ("harmful") may be a coinage by Prudentius. He uses it twice elsewhere (*Peristeph* 10.23, 4 and 10.221, 2).[117] Again it may have a legal aspect, as the similar term *noxalis* is a legal term ("relating to injury").

STANZA 3

After the negative emphasis in stanza 2 on human frailty, death, and damnation, with its legalistic language, this stanza is a complete contrast, expressed in the traditional form of a beatitude ("O how blest ... !"), and full of positive expressions. The birth of Christ is called a "rising" (*ortus*), which suggests a heavenly body like the sun. There is probably an echo of Isaiah 60:1–3, "Arise, be enlightened, O Jerusalem: for thy light has come, and the glory of the Lord is risen upon thee ... but the Lord shall arise upon thee.... And the Gentiles shall walk in thy light, and kings in the brightness of thy rising."[118] The last line of the stanza (*os sacratum protulit*) picks up the same imagery, as *os proferre* is applied in earlier Latin poetry to heavenly bodies like the moon and stars: for example in Horace, *Satires* 1.8.21–22; Ovid, *Fast.* 5. 419; and similarly Virgil, *Æn.* 8.591 of the morning star, *extulit os sacrum*. There is a paradox in the expressions *Virgo puerpera* ("Virgin giving birth") and *puer redemptor* ("child Redeemer") in lines 2 and 5. *Virgo puerpera* is another echo of Hilary, Hymn 1.8: *mundo te genuit Virgo puerpera*: "the Virgin great with child gave birth to you for the world."[119]

In line 3 Christ is called "our salvation": God is often described thus in the Old Testament. Line 4 recalls the words of the Angel to Mary in Luke 1:35: *Spiritus Sanctus superveniet in te... ideoque et quod nascetur sanctum vocabitur Filius Dei*: "The Holy Spirit will come upon you.... Therefore the child to be born will be called holy, the Son of God." For *redemptor* in line 5 see the commentary on H 5: 1, 1. In line 6 there is also a reminiscence of Old Testament passages where God is asked to show his face as a sign of his favor: for example, in the blessing at Numbers 6:25–26: "The Lord make his face to shine upon you.... The Lord lift up his countenance upon you...."

---

117. *Peristeph* 10 is a long poem of 1140 lines. Scholars speculate that it may have been published originally as an independent work. It is composed in iambic trimeter in 228 stanzas of 5 lines each. Some editions of the text give line numbers only. The lines cited above are 114 and 1107 respectively.

118. *Surge, illuminare, Ierusalem, quia venit lumen tuum, et gloria Domini super te orta est ... super te autem orietur Dominus.... Et ambulabunt gentes in lumine tuo, et reges in splendore ortus tui.*

119. Bulst, I.8, p. 31. See also *virginem puerperam* in the hymn ascribed to Hilary quoted on stanza 1, line 1: see Walpole, no. 1, l. 13, p. 7.

STANZA 4

Before this stanza in the original hymn there was a stanza, missing here, that responds to the exclamation in the previous lines by urging all in heaven and on earth to sing in praise of Christ. This stanza develops the theme of praise, opening with the dramatic *Ecce* ("Lo"), which calls attention to the statement that Christ is the fulfillment of all the ancient predictions of "bards" (*vates*) and "prophets." In Luke 1:70, Zechariah, the father of the Baptist, sings of God's redemption of his people Israel "as he promised through the mouths of his holy prophets from of old." Prudentius elsewhere uses *vates* of an Old Testament prophet (for example *Cath.* 4: 32, 4, and 7: 22, 4), as does Juvencus in his poetic version of the gospels (*Evangeliorum libri*, 1.122, and elsewhere). So lines 1–2 and 3–4 of this stanza could be two parallel expressions of the same idea. However, *vates* was also used to refer to those pagan poets who were believed to have anticipated the coming of Christ, especially Virgil, whose fourth *Eclogue* was interpreted as a Messianic prophecy. Lactantius used the phrase *veteribus sæculis* in the context of this convergence between classical and Jewish prophecy (*Institutiones Divinæ*, 7.24.10), as here with Prudentius's *vetustis sæculis*. Thus it seems reasonable to see *vates* as having a double reference, both to Jewish and to classical poets.[120]

In lines 1 and 6, the compound verbs *concinebant* and *collaudent* emphasize the universality of both prophecy and praise. In line 4 the verb *spondere* originally means "pledge," and hence "promise," with the idea of a solemn guarantee. In line 5 *emicat* is a vivid expression. It can refer to any sudden movement upward or outward, but it is also used to mean "emitting a sudden radiance." Prudentius applies it twice in his hymns to the light of the sun (*Cath.* 1: 4, 3, and 2: 14, 4), and here the notion of Christ's divine radiance is suggested (hence the version "splendid child"). In his *Apotheosis* (792–93) Prudentius says of Christ, *solus de corde Parentis / Filius emicuit*: "the Son alone flashed forth from the heart of the Father"); see also *Apotheosis*, 506: *gentibus emicuit, præfulsit regibus*: "he has flashed forth before nations, he has shone out before kings."

Cuncta collaudent eum is similar to the final verse of Psalm 150:6, *omnis spiritus laudet Dominum*: "Let everything that has breath praise the Lord." This invitation to praise closes the first part of Prudentius's hymn. What follows is a catalog of the miracles of Christ, culminating in his Resurrection, Ascension, and future Second Coming, with a reprise of the theme of universal praise in the final verses (*Cath.* 9: stanzas 37–38).

STANZA 5

The doxology is taken from H 254, a hymn to St. Michael the Archangel, with some adaptation. Lines 1–3 and 6 are from H 254. Lines 4–5 are new.

---

120. See Lardelli, *Dux Salutis*, 111, for this conclusion.

	Radix Iesse floruit	14

7–8th c.
8 8 8 8

January 1: Solemnity of Mary, the Holy Mother of God
Office of Readings

Radix Iesse flóruit	1. From Jesse's stock a bloom has sprung,

Radix Iesse flóruit
et virga fructum édidit;
fecúnda partum prótulit
et virgo mater pérmanet.

1. From Jesse's stock a bloom has sprung,
   the bough has borne its tender shoot;
   a fruitful maid has given birth,
   the ever-Virgin Mother blest.

Præsǽpe poni pértulit
qui lucis auctor éxstitit;
cum Patre cælos cóndidit,
sub matre pannos índuit.

2. Her Son endures a manger bed,
   though Source and Author of all light,
   who, swaddled by his Mother's hands,
   once with the Father made the skies.

Legem dedit qui sǽculo,
cuius decem præcépta sunt,
dignándo factus est homo
sub legis esse vínculo.

3. And to the world he gave the Law,
   the Ten Commandments are his own;
   becoming man, he deigned to live
   beneath the mandate of the Law.

Iam lux salúsque náscitur,
nox díffugit, mors víncitur;
veníte, gentes, crédite:
Deum María prótulit.

4. Salvation now and Light are born,
   as death is vanquished, night has fled;
   draw near, you nations, and believe
   that Mary bore for us our God.

Iesu, tibi sit glória,
qui natus es de Vírgine,
cum Patre et almo Spíritu,
in sempitérna sǽcula. Amen.

5. To you, Lord Jesus, glory be,
   the Virgin Mother's newborn Son,
   with God the Father, ever blest,
   and loving Spirit, ever one. Amen.

Text found in *TDH*, no. 84; AH 50, no. 71; pp. 85–86; Walpole, no. 38; Milfull, no. 135. Changes in *TDH*: the hymn is composed from stanzas 4, 5, 6, and 8 of the hymn *Agnoscat omne sæculum*, the hymn assigned to the Annunciation of the Lord (H 203); 1, 1: *Iesse* is a considered to be a three-syllable word; 1, 2: *fructum edidit* is not elided; 2, 1: *præsæpe* is considered to be ablative of *præsæpis*.

COMMENTARY

January 1 has undergone something of an evolution in terms of the naming of the liturgical day. It has been the Octave Day of the Nativity, the Feast of the Circumcision (the gospel at Mass on this day) and, more recently, The Solemnity of Mary, the Holy Mother of God. It is, of course, all these things, and reference to each of them abound in the liturgical texts. As befits the first day of the month named after the god, Januarius, the feast looks both backwards (to

Christmas Night), and forwards (to both the Epiphany and the Presentation in the Temple). The hymn is made up of a selection of stanzas (4, 5, 6, and 8) of the hymn *Agnoscat omne sæculum* (H 203), while stanzas 1–3 and 7 of the original hymn are used as a hymn for the Solemnity of the Annunciation of the Lord under the title of the original hymn.[121] Although it is generally regarded as an anonymous text of the seventh to eighth century, there have been suggestions by several commentators, the most insistent among them being Walpole,[122] that it may in fact be by Venantius Fortunatus (d. ca. 600). It appears in neither the Old nor the New Hymnal, nor is it to be found in extant manuscripts containing the collected works of Fortunatus, though Leo included it in his printed edition of the authentic works of Fortunatus.[123] The original text is clearly intended for Christmas, but in the more recent liturgical books it does duty (after some slight textual changes by Lentini) for the Solemnity of Mary, the Holy Mother of God, and also for the Solemnity of the Annunciation of the Lord.

STANZA 1

Jesse was the father of King David, and he lived in Bethlehem. Unusually, *Iesse* is here trisyllabic, in order to make the meter. The strophe draws heavily upon Isaiah's prophecy of the Virgin Birth.[124]

Lines 1 and 2 bear a strong resemblance to Prudentius's *Cathemerinon* 12: 13, 1–2, *iam flos subit Davidicus, radice Iesse editus*: "Now David's flower issues forth, from Jesse's root upsprung."[125] Prudentius cites the story in Numbers 17:1–11, where the flowering of Aaron's rod is seen as a sign of Divine election. There is a play on words between *virga* (line 2) and *virgo* (line 4), making it clear that the Virgin Mary (*virgo*) is the rod (*virga*) or branch from which the Messiah flowers. Walpole observes that a similar play on words is found in the *Laus Mariæ* (11),[126] which is generally placed among the *spuria* but likewise is considered by some to be by Fortunatus: *virgo hæc virga fuit*.... The stanza ends with a confident statement of the perpetual virginity of Mary, even after the birth of Christ: *et virgo mater permanet*, she remains a virgin.

STANZA 2

This stanza narrates the humility of the Savior's birth: Luke 2:7, "and she gave birth to her firstborn son. She wrapped him in swaddling clothes and laid him

---

121. For the complete original hymn, see AH 50, no. 71, 85 and Walpole, no. 38, 193–98.
122. Walpole, no. 38, pp. 193–98.
123. *Fortunatus*, MGH, vol. 4:1. Volume 1 contains the *Laus Mariæ* (See note 6 below). This and the hymns *Radix Iesse* and *Quem terra, pontus, æthera* (H 14 and H 143) are considered by many to be spurious. Nevertheless, they are printed under the title *Carmina Spuria* in the same volume as the poems considered authentic. Further references to this collection will be abbreviated "Leo" followed by the volume, page, and line number.
124. See Is 11:1: *Et egredietur virga de radice, et flos de radice eius ascendet*: "And there shall come forth a rod out of the root of Jesse, and a flower shall rise up out of his root." See also Is 7:14 and Mt 1:23.
125. Trans. Richardson, *Hymns*, 77, 169.
126. *radicis florem Iessea virga daret. / Virgo hæc virga fuit, de qua est flos Christus obortus*: "The branch of Jesse would give the flower from the root / this branch was the Virgin from whom the flower, Christ, blossomed." (Leo, p. 371, lines 10–11).

in a manger."¹²⁷ It brings an echo of the hymn of Sedulius, *A solis ortus cardine*, which is sung at Lauds of Christmas: *Feno iacere pertulit, præsepe non abhorruit* (H 9: 6, 1–2). The theme of the contrast between what might be expected as a reflection of the majesty of the Messiah's birth and the poverty of the birth of the Christ child, evident throughout this stanza, is a frequent trope in Fortunatus and is one of the features of this text that commentators cite in support of his authorship. In line 2, there is a further feature that points to Fortunatus, the use of the verb *exstare*, which he frequently adopts to mean little more than *esse* (to be). In line 2 Christ is referenced by the title *auctor*. There are just three instances in the Vulgate where Christ is referred to as *auctor*: in Hebrews 2:10, he is referred to as the *auctor salutis* ("author of salvation"); in Acts 3:15, he is called the *auctor vitæ* ("author of life"); and in Hebrews 12:2, he is called the *auctor fidei* ("author of faith"). Line 4 goes on to narrate the swaddling of the child, following the gospel account in Luke 2:7.

STANZA 3

The Law that is referenced here is not the Law of the First Covenant, as it might be understood later, but rather the understanding that we find in the Pauline corpus (see Gal 4:3, 4), which speaks of the human condition, which Christ accepts in his Incarnation, and which, in due course, occasions the "law" expressed in the Decalogue. Once again, Walpole observes that this echoes a trope found in the *Laus Mariæ* (255): *factor dans legem, factus sub lege minister*: "the Maker giving the Law is made a minister under the Law." It is also found in Sedulius: *rerumque creator, nascendi sub lege fuit*: "the Creator of all things was born under the Law."¹²⁸ In the unfolding of the infancy narratives, all that follows—the Circumcision, the naming of the Child, the Presentation in the Temple—is in fulfillment of the Jewish Law: "When the days were completed for their purification according to the law of Moses, they took him to Jerusalem to present him to the Lord, just as it is written in the law of the Lord, 'Every male that opens the womb shall be consecrated to the Lord,' and to offer the sacrifice of 'a pair of turtledoves or two young pigeons,' in accordance with the dictate in the law of the Lord" (Lk 2:22–24).

STANZA 4

The original text of lines 1–2 reads, *iam nata lux est et salus, / fugata nox et victa mors*. This is also the version found in the *HIBR*, no. 78. The text in *TDH* has been altered to *Iam lux salusque nascitur / nox diffugit, mors vincitur*. The meter of the new version is more pleasing; the sense has been subtly weakened. The balance between the content and the way the content is expressed is a perennial challenge for those who edit texts such as these ancient hymns. In the first version, night and death are totally banished and vanquished; in the second, they are

---

127. *Et peperit filium suum primogenitum, et pannis eum involvit, et reclinavit eum in præsepio. Præsæpe ... pertulit.*

128. See Walpole's comments in no. 38, on l. 21, p. 197; Sedulius, *Carmen II*, 38.

still in process; in the first, in addition to the past tense of the verb *nata est*, *lux* and *salus* are treated separately with emphasis given to light: "Light is born...." Walpole observes that Fortunatus often personifies abstract nouns such as light and salvation and associates them with Christ; for example, *illa utero lucem clausit*: "she [the virgin] enclosed light in her womb"; and, *concepit virgo salute*: "the Virgin conceived salvation."[129]

In stanza 4, the hymn turns to us who sing and to those who are invited to draw near to the light of salvation that is now shining upon the earth. It is through faith that all the nations may come. the verbs are imperative: *venite, gentes, credite* (4, 3). The primary foundation of faith is given succinctly in line 4: *Deum Maria protulit*: "Mary has brought forth God." There are numerous examples of *salus* in the Scriptures used in reference to the Lord as our light and our salvation; for example, he is light, as in Psalm 26:1, *Dominus illuminatio mea et salus mea*; and he is the all-wise and powerful source of our salvation, as in Psalm 3:9, *Domini est salus*.[130] The light dispelling darkness is a common theme, particularly in the Johannine corpus, for instance, in John 1:4–5: "What came to be through him was life, and this life was the light of the human race; the light shines in the darkness, and the darkness has not overcome it."[131] In the context of this hymn (especially 4, 3–4), the reference to light foreshadows the narrative of the Presentation in the Temple. The theme emerges more fully in the texts for February 2, which are the extension of the proclamation of Christ's birth and its significance to the nations.

The wonder and joy at the enormity of the gift of the Incarnation are given a voice in the iconic texts from Scripture for the season of Christmas and the feasts of the revelation of the incarnate Christ. Here are only two examples out of many. When the child is brought to the Temple, Simeon cries out: "Now, Master, you may let your servant go in peace, according to your word, for my eyes have seen your salvation, which you have prepared in the sight of all the peoples, a light for revelation to the Gentiles and glory for your people Israel."[132] The liturgy for the Epiphany can find no better hymn than Isaiah 60:1–3: "Arise! Shine, for you light has come, the glory of the Lord has dawned upon you. Though darkness covers the earth, and thick clouds, the peoples, upon you the Lord will dawn, and over you his glory will be seen. Nations shall walk by your light, kings by the radiance of your dawning."[133]

---

129. These examples are cited by Walpole, note on l. 19, p. 198. They are taken from the genuine poems of Fortunatus. The first is from Bk 1.15, line 58; the second is from Bk 10.10, line 5. For volume information, see note 3 above.

130. See also Ps 34:3; and especially 117:14, 21, and 28; see also Is 12:2; 46:13; Bar 4:24; Acts 4:12.

131. *In ipso vita erat, et vita erat lux hominum: et lux in tenebris, et tenebræ eam non comprehenderunt*. There are many other references throughout the Scriptures to the Lord as light; see, e.g., Wis 7:26; Mi 7:8; Mt 4:16 echoing Is 9:2; it was quite literally light from heaven that shone to Paul on the road to Damascus in Acts 22:6. Finally, St. John is at a loss for words at 1 Jn 1:5. The culminating statement of these five ecstatic verses is *Deus lux est*: "God is light."

132. *Nunc dimittis servum tuum Domine, secundum verbum tuum in pace:quia viderunt oculi mei salutare tuum, quod parasti ante faciem omnium populorum: lumen ad revelationem gentium, et gloriam plebis tuæ Israel* (Lk 2:29–32).

133. *Surge, illuminare, Ierusalem, quia venit lumen tuum, et gloria Domini super te orta est. Quia ecce tenebræ*

STANZA 5

Stanza 5 is a generic doxology for the Christmas season. For this doxology, see the commentary on *Christe, Redemptor omnium* (H 7: 7, 1–4).

Fit porta Christi pervia	15
9th c.	January 1: Solemnity of Mary, the Holy Mother of God
8 8 8 8	Lauds

Fit porta Christi pérvia
omni reférta grátia,
transítque rex, et pérmanet
clausa, ut fuit, per sǽcula.

1. The gate for Christ, so full of grace,
stands open that the King may pass.
When he comes forth, that gate shall close,
as in the past, for ever sealed.

Summi Paréntis Fílius
procéssit aula Vírginis,
sponsus, redémptor, cónditor,
suæ gigas Ecclésiæ:

2. The only Son of God most high
has left the Virgin's royal hall;
Creator, Spouse, Redeeming Lord,
he comes as champion of his Church.

Honor matris et gáudium,
imménsa spes credéntium,
lapis de monte véniens
mundúmque replens grátia.

3. His Mother's honor and her joy,
believers' true unbounded hope,
the stone hewn from the mountain side
now comes to fill the earth with grace.

Exsúltet omnis ánima,
quod nunc salvátor géntium
advénit mundi Dóminus
redímere quos cóndidit.

4. Let every soul with joy exult:
the Savior of the nations comes
as God and Lord of all the world,
to ransom those whom he has made.

Christo sit omnis glória,
quem Pater Deum génuit,
quem Virgo mater édidit
fecúnda Sancto Spíritu. Amen.

5. All glory be to Christ the Lord,
the Father's Sole-begotten Son,
born from the Virgin Mother's womb
made fruitful by the Spirit blest. Amen.

Text found in *TDH*, no. 85; AH 27, no. 82.2; Walpole, no. 88; *Hymnodia hispanica*, 309ff. Changes in *TDH*: 1, 2: *omni referta* for *referta plena* (or *referta omni*); 2, 1: *Summi Parentis Filius* for *Genus superni Numinis*; 3, 3–4: from an original stanza 7 in AH 27, lines 1–2 have been substituted for the original lines 3, 3–4; 4, 2–4: a clause beginning with *quod* followed by a finite verb *advenit* with an infinitive has been substituted for two infinitives in the original; stanza 13, 2 of the version in AH 27 has been partially incorporated into a new doxology as 5, 2.

---

operient terram, et caligo populos; super te autem orietur Dominus et gloria eius in te videbitur. Et ambulabunt gentes in lumine tuo, et reges in splendore ortus tui.

COMMENTARY

This hymn appears for the cycle of the year in the Mozarabic Breviary. Walpole says that the hymn "is a fragment of an alphabetic hymn, the rest of which is lost to us."[134] There has been a suggestion that the stanzas were originally excerpted from a longer version of the hymn of Sedulius, *A solis ortus cardine*, but although the rubrics of the Mozarabic Breviary suggest that the hymn is used on occasions when *A solis ortus cardine* is not sung, there is no further manuscript evidence for the connection of these two hymns. Walpole also notes that the Benedictine edition of St. Ambrose's hymns assigned authorship to him based on scanty evidence of the anonymous and undated Pseudo-Ildephonsus.[135] The hymn has been given for a number of Marian feasts arriving at its present assignation to January 1 only with the creation of the current liturgical books, and the newly-designated Solemnity of Mary, the Holy Mother of God.

STANZA 1

The stanza begins with the statement that Mary is made the gate for Christ (*fit porta Christi*)—Mary becomes the "gate" through which Christ enters the world. Ezekiel 44:1–3 records: "Then he brought me back to the outer gate of the sanctuary facing east, but it was closed. The Lord said to me: This gate must remain closed; it must not be opened, and no one should come through it. Because the Lord, the God of Israel, came through it, it must remain closed. Only the prince may sit in it to eat a meal in the presence of the Lord; he must enter through the vestibule of the gate and leave the same way." St. Ambrose, St. Augustine, and more recent authors including St. Louis de Montfort and St. John Henry Newman all draw a Christological inference from this text. Newman tells us that the title *Gate of Heaven* is given to Mary because "it was through her that our Lord passed from heaven to earth."[136] Psalm 23 (24):7 speaks of the gate which must be uplifted so that the King may enter: *Attolite portas, principes, vestras, elevamini, portæ æternales, et introibit rex gloriæ*: "Lift up your heads, O gates; be lifted, you ancient portals, that the king of glory may enter." For the tradition of referring to Mary as "gate" see also introduction to Mass 46, for the Blessed Virgin Mary, Gate of Heaven: "The metaphors of 'door' or 'entrance' or 'gate' or 'threshold' have been applied from patristic times to Our Lady to express her function as the second Eve, and to speak of her virginal motherhood, or her intercession for the faithful."[137] The image is used also in the Entrance Antiphon for the same Mass: "Maiden-Mother, bearing the Word of God, you are the gate of paradise; in bringing God into the world, you have unlocked for us the gate

---

134. Walpole, no. 88, p. 308. See also AH 27, 118ff.
135. Walpole, 308.
136. Newman, *Meditations and Devotions*, Meditation for May 13.
137. Mass 46 in *Collection of Masses of the Blessed Virgin Mary*, vol. 1.

of heaven." The Marian title *porta cæli* appears in the eleventh-century Advent and Christmas Marian anthem for Advent and Christmas *Alma redemptoris mater* (Loving Mother of the Redeemer, attributed to Hermannus Contractus, d. 1054). The title *Ianua cæli* ("Gate of heaven") is among the titles of Mary in the tweltfth-century Litany of Loreto, approved by Pope Sixtus V in 1587.[138] The fact that the gate is only momentarily open for the moment of the Incarnation, only to be closed thereafter, is a reference to the perpetual virginity of Mary: she was virgin both before and after giving birth to the Savior. The image of the gate through which Christ passes also has a resonance with this feast's falling on the first day of the first month of the civil year, named for the god Janus, who was god of doorways.

STANZA 2

In this stanza, three defining images are used of Christ as he comes forth from the Father to begin the work of salvation. He is *sponsus, redemptor, conditor* (2, 3).[139] In the Old Testament, the Lord God is compared to a *sponsus* (bridegroom), as in the Septuagint and Vulgate texts of Psalm 18:6 and also in Isaiah 62:5. Jesus compares himself to a *sponsus* (bridegroom) in Matthew 25:6, 10, and Mark 2:19–20; John the Baptist also compares Jesus to a *sponsus* (bridegroom) in John 3:29. References to the Lord as *redemptor* or as redeeming, using various forms of the verb, are numerous throughout the Scriptures.[140] See, for instance, Isaiah 63: "You, Lord, are our father, our redeemer you are named from of old."[141] The book of Job reads: "For I know that my Redeemer lives, and on the last day I shall rise from the earth."[142] In addition to the name *redemptor*, God is referred to by many other names related to the idea of redemption throughout the Old and New Testaments. Finally, in the description of the patriarchs and other great examples of faith from the Old Testament, recounted in Hebrews 11, God is called *conditor*: "for he [Abraham] was looking forward to the city with foundations, whose architect and maker is God";[143] it was to be an eternal city where all the promises would be fulfilled forever.

The stanza shares much in common with the antiphon *Adorna thalamum tuum Sion*, given for the Procession on the Feast of the Presentation of the Lord (February 2). This antiphon is ascribed to St. John Damascene (died December 4, ca. 749), and is one of the very few pieces that, text and music, have been borrowed by the Roman Church from the Greeks.

---

138. See also H 145, *Ave maris stella*.

139. Note that in this anonymous Mozarabic hymn the three names, one after the other, make a perfect line of iambic dimeter in classical quantitative meter. The first word, *sponsus*, has a stress accent on the first syllable, but the second is also long before another consonant.

140. In addition, the following references are particularly beautiful: Is 41:10–14; 44:23–24; 54:4–8.

141. *Domine, pater noster, redemptor noster, a sæculo nomen tuum* (Is 63:16b).

142. *Scio enim quod redemptor meus vivit, et in novissimo die de terra surrecturus sum* (Jb 19:25).

143. *Expectabat enim fundamenta habentem civitatem: cuius artifex et conditor Deus* (Heb 11:10).

Adorna thalamum tuum, Sion,	Adorn your bridal chamber, Sion,
et suscipe regem regum Christum	and receive Christ the King of Kings:
amplectere Mariam, quæ est cælestis porta:	welcome Mary, who is gate of heaven:
ipsa enim portat Regem gloriæ novi luminis:	she carries the King of glory, a new light:
subsistit Virgo, adducens manibus	she remains Virgin, bearing in her hands,
ante luciferum: quem accipiens Simeon	a Son begotten before the morning star:
in ulnas suas, prædicavit populis,	whom Simeon taking in his arms
Dominum eum esse vitæ et mortis,	proclaimed to the peoples as Lord of life
et Salvatorem mundi,	and death and Savior of the world.

See also Ps 18 (19): "He has set his tabernacle in the sun: and he, as a bridegroom, coming out of his bridal chamber, has rejoiced as a giant to run the way."[144] The New Jerusalem Bible translates *gigas* as "champion."

STANZA 3

All the privileges of Mary are in relation to her role in the plan of salvation as Mother of the Redeemer. Being the Mother of the Savior is *honor matris et gaudium* (line 1), his Mother's honor and her joy. As such, she becomes *immensa spes credentium* (line 2), the believers' true unbounded hope. Pope Benedict XVI wrote, "who more than Mary," archetype of the Church, "could be the star of hope for us?"[145] She, as this guide, brings certainty to human hope for life with the One who does not deceive. Line 3, *lapis de monte veniens*, the stone hewn from the mountain side, references Daniel 2:45: "According as you saw that the stone was cut out of the mountain without hands."[146] *Replens gratia* (line 4) echoes the angelic salutation at the Annunciation, when Gabriel addresses Mary as *gratia plena*, "full of grace" (Lk 1:28).

STANZA 4

This stanza is a florilegium of Christological tropes and seems very close in content and message to the opening stanza of the hymn of St. Ambrose, *Veni redemptor gentium* (H 5):

Veni, redemptor gentium;	Redeemer of the nations, come;
ostende partum Virginis;	reveal yourself by virgin birth.
miretur omne sæculum:	Let every age with wonder know
talis decet partus Deum.	that such a birth befits our God.

The Vulgate uses the title *Salvator* in numerous places: (a) in reference to the Lord God;[147] (b) in reference to the One sent to save his people, the people of Israel;[148] and (c) in reference to the Lord and Savior Jesus Christ.[149] The Savior

---

144. *In sole posuit tabernaculum suum; et ipse tamquam sponsus procedens de thalamo suo exsultavit ut gigas ad currendam viam.*
145. Pope Benedict XVI, *Spe salvi*, 49.
146. *Secundum quod vidisti de monte abscissus est lapsis sine manibus.*
147. For the Lord, the God of Israel, see 2 Kgs 22:1–4; 1 Chr 16:34–35; 1 Mc 4:30–34; Jb 13:15–16; Hos 13:4.
148. For the Messiah, Savior of God's people Israel, see Is 45:8; 62; 63; Zec 9:9.
149. For Jesus Christ, Lord and Savior in his Incarnation, see Lk 2:10–11; Jn 4:29–42; the multiple

comes to ransom (*redimere*) those whom he has made. Just so, the Son of Man came not to be served but to serve and to give his life as a ransom for many (Mt 20:28). See also 1 Timothy 2:5–6: "There is one mediator between God and the human race, Christ Jesus, himself sharing our human nature and flesh, who gave himself as ransom for all."

STANZA 5

The doxology is newly composed. The first line, *Christo sit omnis gloria*, is found in other doxologies addressed to Christ scattered throughout the *Liturgia Horarum*. Line 2, *quem Pater Deum genuit*, is taken partially from the version of the original hymn found in AH 27, where stanza 13, 2 reads: *Deus Deumque genuit*; *Pater* is substituted for *Deus*, in order to bring the other Persons of the Trinity into the doxology of the current hymn.

Hostis Herodes impie	16
Sedulius, d. ca. 450 8 8 8 8	Christmas Time from Epiphany Vespers

Hostis Heródes ímpie, Christum veníre quid times? Non éripit mortália qui regna dat cæléstia.	1. Why, wicked Herod, should you fear with hostile dread the Christ who comes? He gives us heaven, his own realm, and lays no claim to earthly rule.
Ibant magi, qua vénerant stellam sequéntes prǽviam, lumen requírunt lúmine, Deum faténtur múnere.	2. The Magi came, led by a star sent forth by God to show the way. By light they sought their way to Light; with incense they confessed him God.
Lavácra puri gúrgitis cæléstis Agnus áttigit; peccáta quæ non détulit nos abluéndo sústulit.	3. The Lamb of God came forth and touched the River Jordan's cleansing stream; to wash us clean he took away the sins for which he bore no guilt.
Novum genus poténtiæ: aquæ rubéscunt hýdriæ, vinúmque iussa fúndere mutávit unda oríginem.	4. At Cana, power fresh and new once made the jars of water blush; by his command new wine was poured, transformed from water at its source.
Iesu, tibi sit glória, qui te revélas géntibus, cum Patre et almo Spíritu, in sempitérna sǽcula. Amen.	5. To you, Lord Jesus, glory be, revealed to nations on this day, with God the Father, ever blest, and loving Spirit, ever one. Amen.

---

interpretations of the Scriptures in Acts as reaching their fulfillment in Christ, e.g., Acts 13:23; Phil 3:20; 2 Tm 1:10, etc.

Text found in *TDH*, no. 86; AH 50, no. 58; Walpole, no. 31; Bulst, no. 4, p. 71; Sedulius, *Paschal Song*, 198–99. Changes in *TDH*: stanza 1, 1: Lentini notes that the second syllable of *hostis* is counted as long before the following *h*; at 1, 3: he gives *eripit* where the manuscript tradition varies between *eripit* and *arripit*; at 2, 1: he gives *qua venerant* but notes that some manuscripts have *quam viderant*; and at 3, 3: he gives *peccata quæ non detulit* but notes that other sources have *peccata qui mundi tulit* (a line taken from Ambrose, *Iam surgit hora tertia*, 8, 3).

COMMENTARY

This Epiphany hymn narrates the triple manifestation of the Lord: to the Magi, at the River Jordan, and at the Wedding Feast of Cana. In this it evokes the text of the *Magnificat* antiphon (*Tribus miraculis*) of this Feast, which links the same three events. The hymn consists of four stanzas (8, 9, 11 and 13) of a longer text by Sedulius (*Pæan Alphabeticus de Christo*), the earlier part of which (the first seven stanzas) forms the Christmas hymn H 9, *A solis ortu cardine*. Since Sedulius's original hymn narrated the entire life of Christ, it was divided up into sections for various feasts and seasons.[150] This hymn consists of lines 29–36, 41–44, and 49–52 of the text by Sedulius, or in other words, the stanzas commencing with *h*, *i*, *l*, and *n* in the alphabetic system of the stanzas. In particular, stanzas 2, 3, and 4 treat of the three epiphanies, or manifestations (Kings, Baptism, and Cana) that are the subject of the feast. Julian observes that the hymn is found in the Sarum Use (*Hymnarium Sarisburiense*, London, 1851), for First and Second Vespers of the Epiphany, and daily throughout the Octave, at both Matins and Vespers; it is evidenced in other ancient uses as follows: of York (at First and Second Vespers, and Lauds on the Epiphany, and daily throughout the Octave), of Evesham and Worcester (through the Epiphany at Vespers), St. Alban's (Vespers and Lauds), St. Andrew de Bromholm, Norfolk (Lauds).[151] Daniel's *Thesaurus*, 4:148, 370, cites it as in a Rheinau manuscript of the ninth century, and a Bern manuscript, also of the ninth century.[152] The hymn was widely used in the Anglo-Saxon Church and is found in the Bosworth Psalter (ca. 970), the Durham Hymnal (ca. 1000) and others from the eleventh century.[153]

English translations of this beloved hymn have been preserved from the late Middle Ages. The Franciscan, William Herebert, who lectured in theology at Oxford between 1317 and 1319, produced an English translation as *Herod, thou*

---

150. The stanza *Katerva matrum* (the troop of mothers) occurs in a manuscript of the Harleian Library, of the eleventh century (London, BL, Harley, MS 2961, fol. 229v.), as a hymn for the Holy Innocents. In the Mozarabic Breviary, *Hostis Herodes impie* is the hymn at Lauds for the Epiphany, the stanzas h, i, l, n, q, r, s, t, u, x, y, z of the original being used, with doxology. Strophes k, m, o, p, with two additional, and a doxology, are used in this rite on the Feast of the Holy Innocents at Lauds; or *In allisione infantium, sive sanctorum innocentium*, "On the dashing to pieces of the Infants, or Holy Innocents" (see Ps 137:9).

151. Julian, 4–5.

152. See Gneuss, "Latin Hymns," 412.

153. Gneuss, "Latin Hymns," 413; Milfull, 217–19. For a detailed account of the manuscripts containing hymns used in the Anglo-Saxon Church, see Milfull, 9–55, and the tables on 474–78.

wicked foe, whereof is thy dreading? Herebert was a prolific translator of Latin hymns, mainly to enable them to be cited in preaching. The British Library holds, in addition to an eighth-century manuscript of the entire poem by Sedulius, a manuscript of an anonymous fifteenth-century English translation, *Thow cruell herode, thow mortall enemye* (London, BL, MS Add. 341993). Martin Luther made a translation of the hymn into German, as *Was fürchtst du, Feind Herodes, sehr.* In the 1632 *Breviarium Romanum* the first two lines were changed, as a result of the reform of Urban VIII, to *Crudelis Herodes, Deum Regem venire quid times.* This became the base for new English translations of the nineteenth-century. The nineteenth-century Anglican hymn writer, John Mason Neale, provided an English translation as *Why, impious Herod, vainly fear?*. In the twentieth century a translation by Percy Dearmer, *Why, impious Herod, shouldst thou fear?* appeared in *The English Hymnal.* These two have remained the most widely used versions of this hymn in English.

STANZA 1

Line 1, by which a hymn is traditionally identified, has been changed so many times that Lentini felt obliged to remind his reader that Hostis could in fact stand at the head of the line, since the second syllable -*tis* could be counted as long before a following *h*. Connelly notes that Erasmus changed line 1 to *Herodis hostis* in order to preserve with an unambiguous foreign name beginning with *He*- the alphabetical device of the text.[154] As noted above, the *Breviarium Romanum* reformed by Urban VIII changed the line yet again to *Crudelis Herodes Deum*, thus destroying the alphabetical sequence. The rather jarring initial reference to the slaughter of the innocents is a consequence of this hymn's being excerpted from a longer text that narrates the whole of the plan of salvation from the Incarnation to the Ascension. The liturgical feast of the Epiphany provides the context for the abrupt entry into the hymn in the first stanza. Herod's enmity sets the tone, by contrast, for the rest of the hymn. Messenger comments that while hymns in general do not emphasize one virtue in particular, in the Christmas season, humility is to the fore, taught by divine example.[155] This note is struck immediately by Sedulius in his reference to the humility of Christ, who lays no claim to earthly rule (*Non eripit mortalia qui regna dat cælestia*). The implication is that the slaughter of the Holy Innocents (commemorated during the Christmas season on December 28) is a direct consequence of Christ's implied challenge to earthly authorities. Messenger observes that "Herod is the chief figure in the story from the beginning and the enormity of his guilt increases as the story is taken up by the authors of sequences which were used at the feast."[156] In this hymn, it is something of a passing reference, but it is important to know that the Herod story is a major trope in the narrative.

---

154. Connelly, 67.
155. Messenger, *Ethical Teachings*, 82–83.
156. Messenger, *Ethical Teachings*, 84.

STANZA 2

This stanza comments on the significance of the visit of the Magi. Matthew 2:10–12: "They (the Magi) were overjoyed at seeing the star, and on entering the house they saw the child with Mary his mother. They prostrated themselves and did him homage. They then opened their treasures and offered him gifts of gold, frankincense, and myrrh." They were led by the star, *stellam sequentes præviam*, the star which had led them initially to Jerusalem led them on to Bethlehem. They are led by a light to the Light; they are led initially by a star but they are brought to the Light of the world, *lumen requirunt lumine*. Matthew 2:9: "And, behold, the star that they had seen at its rising preceded them, until it came and stopped over the place where the child was." The whole stanza is somewhat reminiscent, in its references to light, of the texts that will narrate the Presentation in the Temple, for example, Luke 2:32: *lumen ad revelationem gentium*: "a light for revelation to the Gentiles." Of all the gifts the Magi bore, frankincense most clearly confessed Christ's divinity and represented their worship of him as God.[157] The confession of the Magi's faith in Christ (line 4) is in the gifts they bear.[158] Lentini changed *quam viderant* (line 1), found in some breviaries, to *qua venerant*, which is the original reading and somewhat better from the point of accentuation.[159] Connelly notes that this is based on the gospel rendering in Matthew 2:9: *stella quam viderant*. The stanza that follows in the original hymn (*Katerva matrum personat*) is omitted in the *Liturgia Horarum*.

STANZA 3

This stanza narrates the Baptism of Jesus in the Jordan (line 1) and the words of John the Baptist on that occasion (line 2): "The next day he [John the Baptist] saw Jesus coming toward him and said, 'Behold, the Lamb of God, who takes away the sin of the world.'" (Jn 1:29).[160] In line 3 Lentini favors the majority reading *quæ non detulit* rather than *qui mundi tulit* found elsewhere and probably influenced by the same phrase in Ambrose's hymn *Iam surgit hora tertia* (8, 3).[161] Some manuscripts have a variation of line 3: *peccata qui mundi tulit* which would mean that *sustulit* of line 4 would then have the sense of "raised up." Sedulius copes deftly with the theological complexity of the fact that, while not in need of cleansing himself, by accepting baptism at the hands of John the Baptist, Christ begins his saving act by which we are washed from sin: *peccata quæ non detulit / nos abluendo sustulit*. The stanza that would follow in the original text (*Miraculis dedit fidem*) is omitted in the *Liturgia Horarum*.

---

157. See Walpole, no. 31, l. 36, p. 154: "*munere*, i.e. by the frankincense."
158. See Mt 2:10–12, quoted above
159. *HIBR*, 79.
160. *Ecce agnus Dei qui tollit peccatum mundi* (Jn 1:29). See also Acts 8:32 (quoting Is 53:7); 1 Pt 1:18–19; throughout Rv at 5:12; 7:17; 19:7; 21:22–23. For the Baptism of Jesus, see Mt 3:13–17; Mk 1:9–11; Lk 3:21–22.
161. *HIBR*, 79. This stanza is not included in H 48.

STANZA 4

The miracle at Cana occupies the whole stanza and follows the gospel narration in John 2:1–11, especially verses 7–10:

> Jesus told them, "Fill the jars with water." So they filled them to the brim. Then he told them, "Draw some out now and take it to the headwaiter." And when the headwaiter tasted the water that had become wine, without knowing where it came from (although the servers who had drawn the water knew), the headwaiter called the bridegroom and said to him, "Everyone serves good wine first, and then when people have drunk freely, an inferior one; but you have kept the good wine until now."

The idea of the water "blushing" in the act of turning into wine is found in an Epiphany hymn of Ambrose (*Inluminans Altissimus*): *aquas colorari videns, / inebriare flumina, / elementa mutata stupet / transire in usus alteros*.[162] Britt cites the epigram of Crashaw on the miracle at Cana: *Lympha pudica Deum vidit et erubuit*, the idea being that "modest water saw its God, and blushed."[163] Sedulius observes that in this transformation, water was changed in its nature, *mutavit unda originem*; he thereby alludes to the transformative nature of baptism by which an ontological change is brought about in the one baptized. In a sermon for the Epiphany, St. Augustine notes that "as soon as Christ was plunged into the waters, the waters washed away the sins of all."[164]

STANZA 5

The seasonal doxology expresses the particular nature of the Solemnity of the Epiphany in its second line, proper to this day: *qui te revelas gentibus*. As the name suggests, Epiphany is about revelation, God's self-revelation to humanity, which reaches its high point in the Incarnation. It is a fitting conclusion to this densely-ordered Christological hymn. Lines 1, 3, and 4 are the same as the doxology used for the Christmas season. See H 7.

---

162. "He [the servant] seeing the water change color, marvels that the floods inebriate and the elements are changed." Walpole, no. 8, lines 17-20, p. 67. The manuscript tradition is divided between *stupet* (singular) and *stupent* (plural). Both make sense. If the verb is singular, the servant marvels; if it is plural, the elements themselves marvel at the change. This second version (plural) has weightier manuscript support. The idea of physical elements in wonder at what has happened to them is present in Virgil and Ovid. Ambrose takes it up and then passes it on to Sedulius, who read and studied Ambrose's hymns; the idea was thus securely in the tradition and later used by Crashaw. This is a beautiful example, among many, of the reception of earlier hymns by later poets. Jean-Louis Charlet, who edits the hymn in the collection edited by Jacques Fontaine, also opts for the plural. See Fontaine, 347, 355.

163. Britt, 114. See also Springer, *Sedulius*, 205.

164. Augustine of Hippo, *Append. Serm.*, CLXXXV, cited by St. Thomas Aquinas, ST III, q. 66, a. 2, sed contra: *Augustinus dicit, in quodam sermone Epiphaniæ, ex quo Christus in aquis immergitur, ex eo omnium peccata abluit aqua*: "Augustine says in a sermon for Epiphany: from the moment when Christ is plunged into the waters, from that time the water cleanses the sins of all." See also from the *Catena Aurea*: Augustinus: *Salvator enim ideo baptizari voluit, non ut sibi munditiam acquireret, sed ut nobis fluentia mundaret*: "For this reason the Savior willed to be baptized, not in order to attain purity for himself but so that the flowing tides might cleanse us." (Thomas Aquinas, *Catena aurea in Matthæum*, cap. 3, lectio 6).

Magi videntes parvulum	17

Prudentius, d. ca. 405
8 8 8 8

Christmas Time from Epiphany
Office of Readings

Magi vidéntes párvulum
eóa promunt múnera,
stratíque votis ófferunt
tus, myrrh*am* et aurum régium.

1. The Magi, when they see the child,
draw forth their gifts from Eastern lands,
and falling down they worship him
with incense, myrrh, and royal gold.

Agnósce clar*a* insígnia
virtútis ac regni tui,
Puer, cui trinam Pater
prædestinávit índolem:

2. Receive and own, O holy Child,
clear tokens of your kingly power,
for which the Father preordained
a threefold nature, type, and plan.

Regem Deúmqu*e* annúntiant
thesáurus et fragrans odor
turis Sabǽi, at mýrrheus
pulvis sepúlcrum prædocet.

3. From Saba perfumed frankincense
and gold proclaim you God and King,
and fragrant dust of bitter myrrh
foretells the tomb where you will lie.

O sola magnár*um* úrbium
maior Bethlem, cui cóntigit
ducem salútis cǽlitus
incorporátum gígnere!

4. You stand alone, O Bethlehem,
more noble than the greatest towns,
for you brought forth in human flesh
the heavenly leader sent to save.

Hunc et prophétis téstibus
idémque signatóribus
testátor et sator iubet
adíre regn*um* et cérnere:

5. His Father, by the testament
that prophets witnessed, sealed, and signed,
now bids him to assume his reign,
receiving his inheritance:

Regnum quod ambit ómnia
di*a* et marín*a* et térrea
a solis ort*u* ad éxitum
et tárt*a*ra et cælum supra.

6. A kingdom that extends to all,
embracing earth and sea and sky,
from rising sun to evening star,
from netherworld to heaven above.

Iesu, tibi sit glória,
qui te revélas géntibus,
cum Patr*e* et almo Spíritu,
in sempitérna sǽcula. Amen.

7. To you, Lord Jesus, glory be,
revealed to nations on this day,
with God the Father, ever blest,
and loving Spirit, ever one. Amen.

Text found in *TDH*, no. 87; O'Daly, *Days Linked by Song*, 352–363; Richardson, *Hymns*, 76–81. Changes in *TDH*: 1, 1: *Magi videntes parvulum* for *videre quod postquam magi*; 2, 3: *Puer, cui trinam Pater* for *puer o cui trinam Pater*; 3, 3: *at* for *ac*.

Magi videntes parvulum

COMMENTARY

This hymn and H 18 should be considered together, since both are taken from the first half of Prudentius's hymn for Epiphany (*Cath* 12) and are about the star seen by the Magi and their response to this wonder. H 294, on the massacre of the Holy Innocents, is from the second half of the same poem. The original hymn had 208 lines (52 stanzas). It is in the Ambrosian meter (the iambic dimeter, in four-verse stanzas).[165]

H 17 is taken from stanzas 16–18, 20, and 22–23 of Prudentius's poem, and H 18 is from stanzas 1–2, 7, and 9–11. Thus H 18 precedes H 17 in the original, and is concerned with the star and its identification with Christ, whereas H 17 describes the worship by the Magi of the child Jesus and his universal Kingship.

The story of the Magi and the massacre of the Innocents is found only in Matthew's Gospel (chapter 2). The Magi (μάγοι in Greek) were originally a Median tribe, according to Herodotus (1.101), and in early Greek tradition the name was applied to wise men and interpreters of dreams in Persia. Later it was used more generally of experts in esoteric lore, astrology, or magic. Here they are the first Gentiles to worship Christ. Their number is not given in Matthew, but Origen in the third century already says that they were three. Tertullian called them "almost kings," and later (from about the sixth century) this idea of their kingship became general, influenced probably by association with Psalm 71 (72):10–11: "May the kings of Tarshish and of the isles render him tribute, may the kings of Sheba and Saba bring gifts! May all the kings fall down before him, all nations serve him!"

It was Pope Pius V who first introduced into the *Breviarium Romanum* four hymns taken from *Cathemerinon* 12: one for Epiphany (*O sola magnarum urbium*, a variant version of H 17), one for the Feast of the Transfiguration on August 6 (*Quicumque Christum quæritis*, H 18), and two for the Feast of the Holy Innocents (*Audit tyrannus anxius* and *Salvete flores martyrum*: see H 294).

STANZA 1

In the two stanzas preceding this one in Prudentius's hymn, the Magi follow the star until it hangs above the head of the child and, stooping down, reveals "the sacred head" (*caput sacratum*). This is picked up in the original by *videre quod postquam magi* ("after the Magi saw this"). In H 17, this is changed to *Magi videntes parvulum* to provide an object for the verb. Lentini also considered the original phrase difficult to sing.

The poet follows the account in Matthew closely here. He says (Mt 2:10–11): "and on entering the house they saw the child with Mary his mother. They

---

165. On Prudentius's original hymn, see O' Daly, *Days Linked by Song*, 352–80, and Richardson, *Hymns*, 166–73.

prostrated themselves and did him homage. Then they opened their treasures and offered him gifts of gold, frankincense, and myrrh." The significance of the gifts is explained in the following stanzas (2–3).

STANZA 2:

A literal translation of this stanza would read: "Recognize the clear emblems of your power and sovereignty, O Child, for whom the Father preordained a three-fold nature." The word *insigne* (here, plural: *insignia*) was often used of a symbol of royal status and also of a military mark of honor. The poet changes dramatically here from narrative mode to apostrophe, directly addressing the Christ Child. The "threefold nature" is not intended as a strictly theological statement about the human and divine natures in Christ. Rather, it refers to the threefold status of the incarnate Christ, as King, God, and Sacrifice, symbolized by the gifts, mentioned in the first stanza, of gold, frankincense, and myrrh.

In line 3 the original text was *puer o cui*. With this reading, the first iamb (short plus long syllable) is replaced by an anapest (two short syllables plus a long one). The word *cui* is scanned as two syllables (short plus long) often in later Latin.

STANZA 3

The threefold character of Christ is explained, as King and God, but also as mortal in his humanity. The frankincense is Sabaean, because Saba, in the southwest corner of the Arabian peninsula, was a prime source for this, as also of myrrh. Isaiah, in his Messianic prophecy at 60:5–6, says that "the wealth of the nations shall come to you ... all those from Sheba shall come. They shall bring gold and frankincense, and shall proclaim the praise of the Lord." There may also be an echo of Psalm 71 (72):10–11, quoted above.

Myrrh is a gum resin from the myrrh tree. In Egypt it was used in embalming. In the Old Testament myrrh could be used as incense in the Temple and also in oil for anointing priests or kings. In the gospels it is associated with the Passion and death of Christ. In Mark 15:23, Jesus is offered wine mingled with myrrh, as a narcotic to dull the pain, when he reaches Golgotha, although he does not take it. But myrrh "foretells the tomb," because in John's Gospel (19:39–40) Nicodemus brings "a mixture of myrrh and aloes, about a hundred pounds weight," and the body of Jesus is then "bound in linen cloths with the spices, as is the burial custom of the Jews." In the missing stanza that followed in the original poem, Prudentius picked up the word *sepulcrum*, adding that this is the tomb from which Christ rose again, and so "broke down the prison of death."

STANZA 4

As in stanza 2, the poet raises the tone again with this apostrophe of Christ's birthplace. In Matthew 2:6, Herod's chief priests and scribes tell him that the Christ will be born in Bethlehem, because of the prophecy of Micah (5:2), which in the version given by Matthew reads "And you, O Bethlehem, in the land of Judah, are by no means least among the rulers of Judah; for from you shall come a ruler who will govern my people Israel." Literally *O sola ... Bethlem* means "O Bethlehem, alone greater among great cities," an idiomatic way of saying "greatest of all great cities." Edward Caswall's version of this runs "Bethlehem, of noblest cities none can once with thee compare." In another poem (*Dittochaeon* 101) Prudentius calls Bethlehem "head of the world" (*caput orbis*).

The phrase *cui contigit ... gignere* (lines 2–4) means literally "to whom it has befallen to bring to birth in bodily form the heaven-sent leader of salvation." The verb *incorporare* ("to embody") is a late Latin word, used also by Augustine. Again there is a missing stanza, elaborating the praise of Bethlehem as the nurse of Christ, who is "the sole son and heir of the supreme Father, born of the breath of the Thunderer, yet also God in the flesh."

STANZA 5

The description of Christ as heir (*heres*) leads to a carefully worded sentence that occupies this whole stanza and is expressed in the technical language of the Roman law of inheritance. The Prophets are the witnesses and signatories to this testament, and the Father is the testator, who commands his Son to enter upon and formally accept (*adire et cernere*) the Kingdom, which is his inheritance. There is a play on the two senses of "testament." Christ is the one who fulfills all the prophecies of the Old Testament about the Messiah, as the "ruler who will govern my people Israel" (Mt 2:6). In Luke 1:68–72, Zechariah sings of how God "has visited and redeemed his people ... as he spoke by the mouth of his holy prophets from of old ... to perform the mercy promised to our fathers, and to remember his holy covenant...." The legal language is fitting for a poet who in his early life had practiced as a successful lawyer, as he says in his *Preface*, 13–15.

STANZA 6

This stanza emphasizes that the Kingdom is universal, embracing the whole created world. This is emphatically spelled out in three ways in lines 2–4: first the division into things of sky, sea, and earth, then the full geographical extent of the terrestrial world from east to west, and then the two other parts of the universe, heaven and the underworld. Compare Philippians 2:9–10: "Therefore God has highly exalted him and bestowed on him the name that is above every name, so that at the name of Jesus every knee should bow, in heaven and on earth and under the earth, and every tongue confess that Jesus Christ is Lord, to the glory of God the Father." In line 2 *dia* is used as a neuter plural adjective meaning "things of the sky."

STANZA 7

Line 2 of this doxology is *qui te revelas gentibus*, which fits the feast of the Epiphany. The wording echoes the Song of Simeon (Lk 2:32): *Lumen ad revelationem gentium, et gloriam plebis tuæ Israel*: "a light for revelation to the Gentiles, and the glory of your people Israel." Lines 1, 3, and 4 are the same as the doxology used for the Christmas season. See H 7.

Quicumque Christum quæritis	18
Prudentius, d. ca. 405 8 8 8 8	The Epiphany of the Lord, Vespers I and Lauds From Epiphany, Lauds

Quicúmque Christum quǽritis,
óc*u*los in altum tóllite:
illic licébit vísere
signum perénnis glóriæ.

1. All you who long to see the Christ,
 lift up your eyes to heaven's height,
 for there you will behold the sign
 of his eternal majesty.

Hæc stella, quæ solis rotam
vincit decóre ac lúmine,
venísse terris núntiat
cum carne terréstri Deum.

2. This star in light and beauty bright
 outshines the circle of the sun.
 It brings glad tidings to the earth,
 that God in mortal flesh has come.

En, Pérsici ex orbis sinu,
sol unde sumit iánuam,
cernunt perít*i* intérpretes
regále vexíllum magi.

3. Lo, Persian Magi from the East,
 the gateway of the rising sun,
 discern with wise and learned skill
 the royal standard of the King.

"Quis iste tantus — ínquiunt —
regnátor astris ímperans,
quem sic tremunt cælést*i*a,
cui lux et æthr*a* insérviunt?

4. "This great one, who is he?", they ask.
 "The sovereign ruler of the stars;
 cele*sti*al hosts before him quake,
 the light and skies obey his will.

"Illústre quiddam cérnimus
quod nésciat finem pati,
sublíme, cels*u*m, intérminum,
antíquius cælo et chao.

5. "Some noble wonder we behold
 that knows no limit, end, or death,
 sublime, exalted, boundless One,
 more ancient than the heights and depths.

"Hic ille rex est géntium
pop*u*líque rex Iudáici,
promíssus Abrahæ patri
eiúsqu*e* in ævum sémini."

6. "The King of nations, this is he,
 and sovereign King of Israel,
 pledged to their father Abraham
 and his descendants evermore."

Iesu, tibi sit glória,
qui te revélas géntibus,
cum Patre et almo Spíritu,
in sempitérna sǽcula. Amen.

7. To you, Lord Jesus, glory be,
 revealed to nations on this day,
 with God the Father, ever blest,
 and loving Spirit, ever one. Amen.

Text found in *TDH*, no. 88; for other sources, see the commentary on H 17.

COMMENTARY

This hymn is taken from stanzas 1–2, 7, and 9–11 of Prudentius's hymn for Epiphany (*Cath* 12: see commentary on H 17). The subject here is the star seen by the Magi and their interpretation of it as representing "the King of nations … and sovereign King of Israel" (6, 1–2).

A version of the hymn was traditionally sung at the Feast of the Transfiguration (*Cath* 12, stanzas 1, 10–11, and 22). The Transfiguration of Christ was another form of his Epiphany, and the reference in stanza 22 (= H 17: 5) to the Prophets also fits with the presence of Moses and Elijah at this event.[166]

STANZA 1

The opening of the hymn addresses "all you who long to see the Christ." The experience of the Magi, when they see the star, is extended to all believers. As Gerard O'Daly says "the poem's readers in some sense occupy the same time frame as the witnesses of the first Christmas."[167] We are asked to lift up our eyes to heaven's height (line 2)—as St. Paul says in Colossians 3:1: "If then you have been raised with Christ, seek the things which are above, where Christ is."

In line 2, *oculos* is an anapest (two shorts plus a long syllable) replacing the iamb, as in H 17: 2, 3. In 6, 2, the first iamb is again replaced by anapestic *populi*. In both cases, it is possible that the first two syllables were being pronounced as one by this period, by the process called syncope (*oc-los, pop-li*).[168]

In line 4, *signum* can be used of a constellation, and especially a sign of the zodiac. In Prudentius's poem on the divinity of Christ (*Apotheosis* 618–26), the astrologer sees the other constellations giving way in the sky for this new sign. It can also refer to a military standard, and in the present hymn, at stanza 3, 4, it is called a "royal standard" (*regale vexillum*). In stanza 1, it is "the sign of his eternal majesty" (1, 4). In the three stanzas following this one in the original hymn the poet says that it is not subject to change like other stars, but "remains for ever" (*æternum manet, Cath* 12: 5, 1), and later, in our stanzas 5–6, the *signum* is unlimited in time and space, because it is identified with Christ, "the King of nations" (6, 1).

STANZA 2

This star outshines the sun in its beauty and radiance. In his *Letter to the Ephesians* (19) St. Ignatius of Antioch writes: "A star shone forth in heaven brighter than all the stars before it.… All the other stars together with the sun and moon became a chorus for this star, but it surpassed them all in its radiance." Similarly, in Prudentius's hymn this stanza is followed by one describing how all the other

---

166. Philastrius of Brescia, writing ca. 385, says that some people associated the feast of Epiphany with the Transfiguration (*Diversarum hereseon liber*, 140).
167. O'Daly, *Days linked by Song*, 365.
168. On syncope, see Norberg, *Introduction*, 25–26. It is common in later hymns.

heavenly bodies gave way at the appearance of this star, and even the morning star dared not compete with it in beauty. In the passage about the constellations in *Apotheosis* the sun stands still, because it foresees the time when it will be eclipsed during the Crucifixion (626–30). Here, however, there is no such ominous reference, as the star is the messenger announcing the Incarnation.

The repetition in *terris … terrestri* stresses the miracle that God has come down to earth in earthly form. The message of the star is that of John 1:14: "And the Word was made flesh and dwelt among us and we beheld his glory, the glory as of the Only Begotten of the Father, full of grace and truth."

STANZA 3

Matthew's account of the Magi begins (2:1): "Now when Jesus was born in Bethlehem of Judea in the days of Herod the king, behold [*ecce*], wise men from the East came to Jerusalem…." In line 1, *En* ("Lo") echoes this, dramatically introducing these "skilled interpreters" (line 3), as they discern the new phenomenon. They come from "the heart of the Persian land" (*Persici ex orbis sinu*), in fact "from the place where the sun has its gateway" (1, 2), which suggests the eastern limit of the earth. So the message of Christ's birth has reached the very end of the world. The word *magi* is effectively postponed to the very end of this stanza, when we finally hear who these experts are. On *vexillum* in line 4, see the commentary on H 5, stanza 3.

STANZA 4

In the original hymn, this speech of the Magi continues over five stanzas. They discern at once that this star is something unique. It is not just a "royal standard," but actually the ruler of the stars, before whom all the heavens tremble, and whom the light and skies obey. In fact this radiant portent is unlimited in time, more ancient than the world itself (stanza 5). In what follows (stanza 6) they reveal their expertise also in Hebrew lore, as they declare that the star is the "King of nations" and "sovereign King of Israel," the one who was promised to "their father Abraham and his descendants evermore." So too in Matthew 2:2 they ask: "Where is he who has been born king of the Jews?" But here they go further, realizing that the star represents not only the King of the Jews but also the King of all nations.

STANZA 5

In this stanza the Magi are still searching for the right interpretation of what they see. They discern (*cernimus*) that this is "something brilliant" (*illustre*, with the double sense of "shining" and "illustrious"). Their language becomes increasingly elevated: line 2 literally means, "it knows not how to suffer ending." The phrase *sublime, celsum, interminum*: "exalted, lofty, lacking boundaries" (line 3), uses the rhetorical device of three parallel expressions, the third being longer than the first two. Finally, it is "more ancient than heaven and the realm of darkness"

Quicumque Christum quæritis

(line 4). The word *chaos* was originally used in Greek cosmology to denote the primordial state of things. It is related to the verb χάσκω, meaning "gape open, yawn," and so probably meant a yawning space, but a space with some substance and full of darkness.[169] Later, in both Greek and Latin, it came to be used also of the netherworld. Prudentius uses the word elsewhere in the context of God's existence "before the primeval darkness (*chaos*), without number or time" in his poem on the origin of sin (*Hamartigenia* 55), and in a similar way of God "who was without beginning and will be without end, who existed before the primeval darkness" in his *Reply to the Address of Symmachus* (2.96). So this is probably the intended sense here, too.[170]

STANZA 6

After the uncertainty of the previous two stanzas comes the realization of the truth. The star is not only the ruler of the Jews but also the King of the nations, the Gentiles of whom the Magi themselves are the representatives. The phrase *rex gentium* is found in relation to God in Jeremiah 10:7: "Who would not fear you, O King of the nations?" *Quis non timebit te, o rex gentium?* The identification of the star as the Messiah was thought to be foreshadowed in the oracle of Balaam in Numbers 24. Balaam has a "vision of the Almighty," and says that "a star shall come forth out of Jacob, and a scepter shall rise out of Israel," which shall destroy the enemies of the Jews (Nm 24:15–20). This was traditionally treated as a Messianic prophecy, and St. Ambrose, quoting Numbers 24:17, says "According to the mystery of the Incarnation, Christ is the star.... For he himself is the radiant and morning star."[171] Similarly, in Prudentius's *Apotheosis* (615) the Magi say: "we have seen this child moving through the stars."

Lines 3–4 echo the words of Mary in her *Magnificat* (Lk 1:54–55): "remembering his mercy, according to his promise to our fathers, to Abraham and his descendants for ever.[172]" The reference is to God's promise to Abraham at Genesis 22:15–18, that because Abraham was willing to sacrifice his son his descendants would be multiplied as the stars of heaven, "and by your descendants shall all the nations of the earth bless themselves." In his discussion of the faith of Abraham in Romans, Paul says that he was to become "the father of all who believe without circumcision," and "he is the father of us all, as it is written 'I have made you the father of many nations'" (Rom 4:11 and 17, quoting Gn 17:5). So the promise made to Abraham is not just for the Jews but for all believers. Prudentius echoes this in the stanza that followed this one (*Cath* 12: 12, 1–4): "For the first father of all

---

169. See the commentary of Martin West on Hesiod's *Theogony*, 192, on line 116.

170. The word "chaos" is used multiple times by Prudentius. Other examples include *Cath* 5: 1, 3; 9: 27, 3; *Apotheosis* 750 and 823; *Contra Symmachus* 1.96 and 2.903; *Peristeph* 3:11, 5. Sometimes it refers to hell, with the sense of the realm of eternal night.

171. Ambrose, *Expositio evangelii secundum Lucam*, 2, 634: *ergo stella hæc via est et via Christus, quia secundum incarnationis mysterium Christus est stella; orietur enim stella ex Iacob et exsurget homo ex Israel denique ubi Christus et stella est; ipse enim est stella splendida et matutina*; "This star, therefore, is the way, and the way is Christ, because according to the mystery of the Incarnation, Christ is the star; a star shall arise out of Jacob [Nm 24:17] and a man shall rise from Israel; in a word, where Christ is, there is the star; for he is the splendid star of morning."

172. *Recordatus misericordiæ suæ, sicut locutus est ad patres nostros, Abraham et semini eius in sæcula* (Lk 1:54–55).

believers (*primus sator credentium*), who offered his only son in sacrifice, learned that his progeny must one day be made equal to the stars."

The last stanza of the Magi's speech in the original poem (*Cath* 12: 13, 1–4) also recalls Hebrew lore about the Messiah. The star is identified as "the flower of David, sprung from the root of Jesse, and blooming along the rod of the scepter": an allusion not only to Christ as descendant of David, but also to Numbers 17:1–11, where the rod of Aaron blossoms as a sign that he is chosen by God.

The endings of lines 2–4 of this stanza rhyme. This may not be deliberate in the case of line 2, but the parallelism in the structure of lines 3–4 quite probably is, and this shows how easily rhyme could come to be used more generally in later hymns.[173]

STANZA 7

The doxology is the same as in H 17.

A Patre Unigenite	19
ca. 10th c.	The Baptism of the Lord
8 8 8 8	Vespers I

A Patre Unigénite,	1. The Father's Sole-begotten Son,
ad nos venis per Vírginem,	you came through Mary, Virgin chaste,
baptísmi rore cónsecrans	to hallow all who are baptized
cunctos, fide regénerans.	and born again by faith in you.
De cælo celsus pródiens	2. From highest heaven you go forth,
éxcipis formam hóminis,	assuming human form and flesh,
factúram morte rédimens,	to save creation by your death,
gáudia vitæ lárgiens.	bestowing all the joys of life.
Hoc te, Redémptor, quǽsumus:	3. Redeeming Lord, grant this, we pray:
illábere propítius,	Come down to us, with grace descend
clarúmque nostris córdibus	to show and offer to our hearts
lumen præbe deíficum.	your clear and deifying light.
Mane nobíscum, Dómine,	4. Remain with us, O Lord our God,
noctem obscúram rémove,	remove the darkness of our night,
omne delíctum áblue,	and wash away all sin and guilt;
pie medélam tríbue.	in mercy grant your healing balm.
O Christe, vita, véritas,	5. All glory be to you, O Christ;
tibi sit omnis glória,	the Father and the Spirit blest,
quem Patris atque Spíritus	in splendor from the heights of heaven,
splendor revélat cǽlitus. Amen.	reveal that you are Life and Truth. Amen.

---

173. See Norberg, *Introduction*, 31–47.

Text found in *TDH*, no. 89; AH 27, no. 6; Walpole, no. 89; *Hymnodia hispanica*, 143–44. Changes in *TDH*: stanza 1, 1: *Unigenite* follows the Mozarabic version, where other versions have *Unigenitus*; 1, 2: *venis* follows the Mozarabic version, where other versions have *venit*; 2, 1: *prodiens* follows the Mozarabic version, where other versions have *prodiit*; 2, 2: *excipis* for *excepit*; 3, 3: *clarumque* for *klarumque* (the "k" was solely for the sake of the alphabetical acrostic); original stanzas 5 and 6 have been omitted.[174]

COMMENTARY

This hymn dating from the tenth century or earlier is an alphabetical acrostic in accentual iambic dimeter. The original poem covered the whole alphabet in six stanzas. After the first line, each one starts with a new letter. The use of an alphabetic acrostic, involving as it does a hidden pattern that is comprehensive in scope, is fitting for the Baptism of the Lord, the feast that involves the revelation of the Trinity. It is also fitting for First Vespers that this hymn points to the larger meaning of Christ's Baptism in anticipation of the feast's fuller celebration. It thus incorporates many of the themes of Advent, Christmas, and Epiphany: the Incarnation (stanzas 1 and 2), light and redemption (stanza 3), the end of night and the cleansing from sin (stanza 4). The Mozarabic Breviary assigned this hymn to Advent, though other breviaries assigned it to Epiphany.[175]

STANZA 1

The alphabetic acrostic begins somewhat irregularly (*aabc*). The first line recalls John 1:14: "And the Word became flesh and dwelt among us, and we have seen his glory, the glory as of the only begotten from the Father, full of grace and truth."[176] The use of direct address and present tense makes this hymn more vivid.[177] There is a wonderfully balanced antithesis in the first two lines: Christ comes *from* the Father *to* us;[178] the Only Begotten comes *through* the Virgin.[179] Lines 3 and 4 point to the necessity both of baptism and of faith for the attainment of salvation.[180] There is also a subtle mirroring of lines 1 and 2 in lines 3 and 4: the Son, who eternally existed with the Father in holiness, makes holy all who are baptized,[181] and he who was born of the Virgin[182] gives new birth by faith.[183]

---

174. See *Hymnodia hispanica*, 143–44; 735–56; AH 27, no. 6, p. 66; AH 2, no. 107, p. 80; Walpole, no. 89, pp. 309–11.

175. See Julian, 172.

176. *Et Verbum caro factum est et habitavit in nobis et vidimus gloriam eius gloriam quasi unigeniti a Patre plenum gratiæ et veritatis.*

177. The present tense can be seen in the use of the vocative: *Unigenite* for *Unigenitus*, and of the second-person singular present tense verb: *venis* for *venit*.

178. *A Patre ... ad nos*.

179. *Unigenite ... per Virginem*.

180. *et dixit eis euntes in mundum universum prædicate evangelium omni creaturæ. qui crediderit et baptizatus fuerit salvus erit qui vero non crediderit condemnabitur*: "And he said to them: 'Going out into the whole world, preach the Gospel to the every creature. He who believes and is baptized shall be saved; he who does not believe shall be condemned.'" (Mk. 16:15–16).

181. *baptismi rore consecrans* (1, 3).

182. *venis per Virginem* (1, 2).

183. *fide regenerans* (1, 4); see Jn 3:5.

The "dew of baptism" (*baptismi rore*) in line 3 refers to Christ's Baptism. As Lactantius says, "When he first began to reach adulthood, he was plunged in the Jordan River by the prophet John so that he might wash away in a spiritual bath not his own sins, for he had none whatsoever, but the sins of the flesh that he bore, so that just as he saved the Jews by undergoing circumcision, so he might also save the Gentiles by undergoing baptism, that is, by the pouring forth of the purifying dew."[184] The "dew" can also refer to the baptism of those who follow Christ, for as Ambrose writes, "The hearts of the Gentiles, which beforehand had been dry, afterwards, through baptism, grew moist with the dew of the Spirit."[185] This "dew of baptism" is also suggestive of the refreshing dew foretold in Isaiah: "Your dead will live; my slain will rise. You who dwell in the dust, awake and give praise! For your dew is a dew of light."[186] Jerome understands this "dew" to refer to Christ: "For just as the Lord becomes for believers the light, the way, the truth, the bread, the vine, the fire, the shepherd, the lamb, the door, the worm, and so on, so also since we stand in need of his mercy, and are burning with the fever of our sins, for us he becomes dew, to whom Isaiah said, 'Your dew is their health.'"[187] Apponius links the "dew of light" expressly to the "dew" on the head of the Bridegroom in the Song of Songs: "Open to me, my sister, my love, my dove, my perfect one! For my head is covered with dew."[188]

STANZA 2

The alphabetic acrostic continues without any extraordinary word choices (*defg*). This stanza mirrors almost perfectly the structure and ideas of stanza 1. It thus provides a kind of variation on a theme. Stanza 1 begins "from the Father" (*A Patre*), stanza 2 begins "from heaven" (*de cælo*). The first line of each stanza thus begins with the eternal existence of the Son. The second line of each stanza indicates the Incarnation—the coming to us by the Virgin, the taking on of our human form. Lines three and four of each stanza end with present participles that indicate different aspects of the redemption Christ brings: consecrating us by the dew of baptism, giving us new birth by faith, redeeming creation by death and bestowing the joys of life. The mention of "creation" (*facturam*) in line 3 evokes Ephesians 2:10, and the mention of "death" (*morte*) looks forward to the Passion,[189] which is fittingly foreshadowed by Christ's descent under the waters

---

184. *Cum primum cœpit adolescere, tinctus est ab Iohanne propheta in Iordane flumine, ut lavacro spirituali peccata non sua, quæ utique non habebat, sed carnis quam gerebat aboleret, ut quemadmodum Iudæos suscepta circumcisione, sic etiam gentes baptismo id est purifici roris perfusione salvaret.* Lactantius, *Divinæ institutiones*, 4.15.2.

185. *pectoribus gentilium, quæ ante arida erant, postea per baptismum rore spiritus umescebant*, Ambrose, *Expositio evangelii secundum Lucam*, 7.95.

186. *Vivent mortui tui, interfecti mei resurgent. Expergiscimini, et laudate, qui habitatis in pulvere, quia ros lucis ros tuus*, Is 26:19.

187. *quomodo enim Dominus fit credentibus lumen, via, veritas, panis, vinea, ignis, pastor, agnus, ianua, vermis, et cetera; sic qui indigemus illius misericordia, et peccatorum febribus æstuamus, in rorem nobis vertitur, ad quem dicit Esaias: ros enim qui a te est, sanitas eorum est.* Jerome, *Commentarii in prophetas minores*, in Osee 3.14.

188. *Aperi mihi, soror mea, amica mea, columba mea, immaculata mea, quia caput meum plenum est rore*, Song 5:2; cf. Apponius, *In Canticum canticorum expositio* 8.96.

189. *facturam morte redimens* (2, 3).

of the Jordan at his Baptism. This provides another example of mirroring between stanzas 1 and 2: Christ consecrating us by the water of baptism (*baptismi rore consecrans*, 1, 3) foreshadows and parallels Christ redeeming creation by his death (*facturam morte redimens*, 2, 3). These parallels are strengthened by the fact that the third line of stanza 2 follows other versions (*facturam morte redimens*) over the Mozarabic Breviary reading (*fictor a morte rediens*), which is thematically plausible but requires an unusual spelling (*fictor* for *victor*) to fit the acrostic.

The use of second person and present tense in the second line of this stanza is in agreement with the first stanza and the vocatives in the third and fourth stanzas.[190] The hymn thus maintains its direct address to Christ throughout. By contrast, the Mozarabic version of this hymn mixes second person and third person, perfect and present,[191] while other versions maintain the third person perfect throughout stanzas 1 and 2,[192] only to shift to direct address in stanzas 3 and 4.[193]

Like stanza 1, stanza 2 has a well-balanced antithesis of the divine and the human between lines 1 and 2.[194] Line 2 is a clear echo of the Pauline canticle in the Letter to the Philippians: "But he emptied himself, taking on the form of a servant, made in the likeness of men, and being found in human form."[195] There is also in lines 3 and 4 an antithesis between death and life.[196] By including references to the Incarnation and the Passion, this stanza brings together the beginning and end of Christ's earthly life.

STANZA 3

Here the hymn becomes a prayer of petition in familiar liturgical language.[197] The request for the Redeemer to "come down"[198] and bring light to our hearts recalls both his coming down at his Incarnation[199] and the descent of the Holy Spirit at his Baptism.[200] It also echoes the second stanza of the famous hymn of Ambrose, "*Splendor paternæ gloriæ*" (H 75): "Descend into our soul, true Sun, / resplendent with eternal ray; / pour out upon our mind and heart / the Holy Spirit's radiant beam."[201] The more usual spelling of *clarum* is favored here at the slight expense of the acrostic (*hicl*). The request for Christ to shine a light into our hearts evokes several scriptural passages, especially 2 Corinthians 4:6: "For God,

---

190. Stanza 2: "you take on" (*excipis*, 2, 2) instead of "he took on" (*excepit*). Stanza 1: "you come" (*venis*, 1, 2) instead of "he came" (*venit*). Stanzas 3 & 4: "you, Redeemer" (*te, Redemptor*, 3, 1) and "Stay with us, Lord" (*mane nobiscum, Domine*, 4, 1).

191. *venis* at 1, 2; *excepit* at 2, 2.

192. *Unigenitus venit ... celsus prodiit ... excepit*.

193. *te, Redemptor* (3, 1); *mane nobiscum, Domine* (4, 1).

194. *prodiens ... excipis; de cælo celsus ... formam hominis*.

195. *Sed semetipsum exinanivit, formam servi accipiens, in similitudinem hominum factus, et habitu inventus ut homo*, Phil 2:7.

196. *morte ... vitæ*.

197. E.g., *quæsumus, propitius*.

198. Literally "drop down" or "flow down" (*illabere*, 3, 2).

199. Cf. *ad nos venis; de cælo celsus prodiens*

200. Mt 3:16; Mk 1:10.

201. *Verusque sol, illabere / micans nitore perpeti, / iubarque Sancti Spiritus / infunde nostris sensibus* (H 75: 2, 1–4).

who commanded light to shine out of the darkness, has shone in our hearts, to give the light of the knowledge of the glory of God, in the face of Jesus Christ."²⁰² Walsh notes that the reading *deificum* here follows the Mozarabic text, but he still finds it "an awkward second adjective after *klarum*."²⁰³ *Deificum* gives a clear echo of the *Rule of Benedict*: "you open our eyes to the deifying light."²⁰⁴

STANZA 4

Given the Trinitarian nature of Christ's Baptism, it is probably not accidental that this stanza consists completely (and the other stanzas generally) of three-word lines. The assonance of the first word of each line balances the assonance of the last word of each line.²⁰⁵ There is also considerable assonance in the middle word of each line.²⁰⁶ The letters of the acrostic (*mnop*) figure prominently in other places in the stanza.

As Walsh has noted,²⁰⁷ the first two lines of this stanza are fitting for a Vespers hymn, because line 1 quotes the petition of the disciples to the Lord in Luke 24:29: "Stay with us, for evening approaches,"²⁰⁸ and line 2 asks for the removal of "dark night" (*noctem obscuram*). The petition in line 3 echoes the admonition of Ananias to the Apostle Paul: "And now why do you delay? Arise, and be baptized, and wash away your sins, calling on his name."²⁰⁹ In line 4, we ask for the gracious "healing" (*medelam*) because "All healing is from God."²¹⁰

STANZA 5

The newly composed doxological final verse (cf. H 20 and 21) departs from the alphabetical acrostic. It maintains the direct address to Christ (*O Christe*) and recalls ideas found in earlier stanzas, most notably life (*vita*) and light (*gloria, splendor*). As in the original final verse of this hymn (*Vita, salus et veritas*), line 1 echoes the words of Christ: "I am the way, and the truth, and the life."²¹¹ The last line evokes the description of Christ in Hebrews: "He is the splendor of the glory of God, and the very imprint of his being."²¹²

---

202. *quoniam Deus, qui dixit de tenebris lucem splendescere, ipse illuxit in cordibus nostris ad illuminationem scientiæ claritatis Dei, in facie Christi Jesu*; cf. Lk 2:32; Jn 8:12; 2 Pt 1:19; cf. also Aug. *Serm.* 221.2.
203. Walsh, 471.
204. *apertis oculis nostris ad deificum lumen*, Benedict, *Rule*, Prologue, 9.
205. First words: *mane ... noctem ... omne ... pie*; last words: *Domine ... remove ... ablue ... tribue*.
206. *nobiscum ... obscuram ... delictum ... medelam*.
207. Walsh, 471.
208. *Mane nobiscum, quoniam advesperascit*.
209. *Et nunc quid moraris? Exsurge, et baptizare, et ablue peccata tua, invocato nomine ipsius* (Acts 22:16); see Cyprian, *Ep.* 25.1; Ambrose, *Expositio in Ps. 118*, 2.8.
210. Cf. *A Deo est enim omnis medela*, Sir 38:2; cf. Isidore, *Synonyma*, 1.72.
211. *Ego sum via, et veritas, et vita*, Jn 14:6; cf. Jn 1:4; 11:25.
212. *qui cum sit splendor gloriæ, et figura substantiæ eius* (Heb 1:3).

Implente munus debitum	20

ca. 10th c.	The Baptism of the Lord
8 8 8 8	Office of Readings and Vespers II

Impléne munus débitum
Ioánne, rerum cónditor
Iordáne mersus hac die
aquas lavándo díluit,

1. As John fulfilled his sacred charge,
Christ Jesus, Author of the world,
immersed this day in Jordan's tide,
by bathing, washed its waters clean.

Non ipse mundári volens
de ventre natus Vírginis,
peccáta sed mortálium
suo lavácro tóllere.

2. Born from the Virgin Mother's womb,
he did not need to be baptized,
yet by his washing, he desired
to take away our guilt and sin.

Dicénte Patre quod "meus
diléctus hic est Fílius,"
suménte Sancto Spíritu
formam colúmbæ cǽlitus,

3. The Father speaks, his voice proclaims:
This is my own beloved Son;
from heaven's height on him descends,
in dove-like form, the Spirit blest.

Hoc mýstico sub nómine
micat salus Ecclésiæ;
Persóna trina cómmanet
unus Deus per ómnia.

4. Beneath the mystery of this Name,
salvation shines within the Church;
the Trinity abides with her,
one God through every time and place.

O Christe, vita, véritas,
tibi sit omnis glória,
quem Patris atque Spíritus
splendor revélat cǽlitus. Amen.

5. All glory be to you, O Christ;
the Father and the Spirit blest,
in splendor from the heights of heaven,
reveal that you are Life and Truth. Amen.

Text found in *TDH*, 90; AH 14, no. 27; Walpole, no. 91. Changes in *TDH*: the hymn adapts stanzas 5 through 8 of the hymn *Illuxit orbi iam dies* and adds a newly composed doxological final verse (the same as in H 19 and H 21); stanza 1, 1–2 are inverted and slightly altered from the original: *implente munus debitum / Ioanne, rerum conditor* for *Ioanne baptista sacro / implente munus debitum*; 2, 4: *suo lavacro tollere* for *suo fugare lavacro*; 3, 3: *sumente sancto spiritu* for *sumensque sanctus spiritus*, and a comma replaces the period at the end of the stanza; 4, 2: a semicolon for a comma at the end of the line.

COMMENTARY

This is a quantitative hymn in iambic dimeter. Lentini dates it from "at least the tenth century."[213] Walpole says it is "certainly ancient."[214] It focuses on the details

---

213. *TDH*, 92.
214. Walpole, no. 91, p. 314.

of Christ's Baptism, with only occasional gestures to his past, whether the role of the Son at creation (*rerum conditor*, 1, 2), or the Incarnation (*de ventre natus Virginis*, 2, 2). In this way, the hymn provides a lightly contextualized reflection on the main event being celebrated. It offers an explanation of the Baptism that allows us to reflect throughout "this day" (*hac die*, 1, 3) on what it means for us that Christ was "immersed … in Jordan's tide" (*Iordane mersus*, 1, 3).

STANZA 1

Stanza 1 begins with John and ends with Christ. John is given an ablative absolute of eleven syllables, while Christ gets the main verb and twenty-one syllables. Thus John is both metrically and grammatically subordinated to Christ. This echoes the words of John: "The one who is coming after me is ahead of me because he was before me."[215] The reference to John fulfilling his "sacred charge" (*munus debitum*, line 1; literally "due service") also echoes his statement concerning Christ: "He must increase, and I must decrease."[216] The reference to what is "due" (*debitum*) further recalls John's objection to baptizing Christ: "John tried to prevent him, saying, 'I ought to be baptized by you, yet you are coming to me?' Jesus answered and said to him, 'Let it be so now, for thus it is fitting for us to fulfill all righteousness.' Then he consented."[217] John's "sacred charge" is to submit to Christ's will over his own objections, to allow himself to decrease as Christ increases, to consent to Christ's Baptism at his hands.

The reference to Christ as "Author of the world" (*rerum conditor*, line 2) is a clear echo of the famous Ambrosian hymn, *Æterne rerum conditor* (H 71). It thus points us back to the eternal existence of the Son of God, the Word of the Father who "was in the beginning with God" and through whom "all things were made."[218]

Line 4 introduces a central paradox of Christ's Baptism: normally water washes *us* clean, both physically in general and spiritually in baptism; but Christ, the spotless Lamb of God, "immersed this day in Jordan's tide, / by bathing, washed its waters clean" (*Iordane mersus hac die / aquas lavando diluit*, lines 3–4). Just as Christ, who by right should be baptizing John, is instead being baptized *by* John, so the water that normally washes others is itself being washed by Christ's immersion in it.

STANZA 2

Stanza 2 takes up the paradox indicated at the end of stanza 1 and explains the significance for us of Christ's receiving baptism. In this way, it answers the question raised by St. Maximus of Turin: "What sort of baptism is this, where the one who is immersed is purer than the font? Where the water, as it washes the one it receives, is not polluted with dirt but is honored with blessing? What sort of baptism, I ask, is the Savior's, in which the streams are purified more than they purify?"[219]

---

215. *Qui post me venturus est, ante me factus est: quia prior me erat* (Jn 1:15).
216. *Illum oportet crescere, me autem minui* (Jn 3:30).
217. *Iohannes autem prohibebat eum dicens, "ego a te debeo baptizari et tu venis ad me?" respondens autem Iesus dixit ei, "Sine modo sic enim decet nos implere omnem iustitiam." tunc dimisit eum* (Mt 3:14–15).
218. *Hoc erat in principio apud Deum. Omnia per ipsum facta sunt* (Jn 1:2–3).
219. *Quale hoc est baptismum, ubi purior ipso est fonte ille qui mergitur? ubi dum susceptum aqua diluit, non*

Line 1 of this stanza is taken from the words of St. Ambrose: "Therefore, the Lord was baptized, wanting not to be cleansed, but to cleanse the waters so that, washed in the blood of Christ who knew no sin, they might have the power to baptize."[220] The idea of Christ cleansing the waters of the Jordan goes back to St. Ignatius of Antioch: "He was born and baptized, so that by his Passion he might cleanse the water."[221]

Line 2 of this stanza echoes a passage of Fulgentius of Ruspe: "One person of the Trinity, Christ the only Son of God, in order that he might save us, was conceived in the flesh and born from the womb of the Virgin Mother, he who was the true and most high God from the bosom of God the Father."[222] The word used here for "womb" (*venter*) literally means "belly." It can bear the sense of "womb" and is sometimes used with that meaning in Scripture, for example in Psalm 70(71): "In you I have been upheld from birth; from my mother's womb you have been my protector."[223] Yet the more common Latin word for "womb", at least in the Vulgate New Testament, is *uterus*, as in Luke: "Behold, you will conceive in your womb, and you will bear a son, and you will call his name Jesus."[224] The use of "womb" (*venter*) here provides a point of connection with story of Jonah, even beyond the connection mentioned by Christ himself in Matthew: "For just as Jonah was three days and three nights in the belly of the whale, so the Son of Man will be three days and three nights in the heart of the earth."[225] As Jonah emerging from the belly of the whale prefigures Christ rising from the tomb, so also does Christ's own birth from the belly of Mary. As the tomb of Christ is a kind of womb, so is the womb of Mary a kind of tomb. At his Incarnation, the eternal Son of the Father has come down from heaven, emptying himself to take on the form of a servant.[226] His birth from the Virgin Mary thus involves a kind of death, just as his Passion and Death on the Cross lead to new life in his Resurrection. These associations are perhaps especially fitting on the feast of the Baptism, another moment of dying and rising, and one that, like Jonah's, takes place under water.

The reference to Christ taking away sin (*peccata ... tollere*, lines 3–4) echoes the words of John's confession of Christ: "Behold the Lamb of God, who takes away the sin of the world."[227] It also echoes the words of John: "You know that he appeared so that he might take away sins, and in him there is no sin."[228]

---

sordibus inficitur sed benedictionibus honoratur? quale, inquam, salvatoris baptismum est, in quo purgantur magis fluenta quam purgant? Maximus of Turin, *Sermo* 13a.

220. *baptizatus ergo est dominus non mundari volens, sed mundare aquas, ut ablutæ per carnem Christi, quæ peccatum non cognovit, baptismatis ius haberent*, Ambrose, *Expositio Evangelii secundum Lucam*, 2.83.

221. ὃς ἐγεννήθη καὶ ἐβαπτίσθη, ἵνα τῷ πάθει τὸ ὕδωρ καθαρίσῃ, Ignatius of Antioch, *Letter to the Ephesians*, 18.2.

222. *una ex Trinitate persona Christus dei filius unicus, ut nos salvos faceret, carne conceptus et natus est de ventre virginis matris, qui verus et summus Deus est ex utero Dei Patris*, Fulgentius of Ruspe, *Ep.* 17.18 bis.

223. *In te confirmatus sum ex utero; de ventre matris meæ tu es protector meus* (Ps 70 [71]:6).

224. *Ecce concipies in utero, et paries filium, et vocabis nomen eius Iesum* (Lk 1:31); cf. Mt 1:18, 22; Lk 1:15, 41, 44; 2:21.

225. *Sicut enim fuit Ionas in ventre ceti tribus diebus, et tribus noctibus, sic erit Filius hominis in corde terræ tribus diebus et tribus noctibus* (Mt 12:40); cf. Jn 2:1.

226. See Phil 2:7.

227. *Ecce agnus Dei, qui tollit peccatum mundi* (Jn 1:29).

228. *Et scitis quoniam ille apparuit, ut peccata tolleret, et peccatum in eo non est* (1 Jn 3:5).

STANZA 3

Stanza 3 follows most closely the Baptism account in Matthew: "When Jesus was baptized, he came up at once out of the water; and behold, the heavens were opened to him, and he saw the Spirit of God descending like a dove and coming upon him. And behold, a voice from heaven, saying: 'This is my beloved Son, in whom I am well pleased.'"[229] Here we have a succinct presentation of the first clear revelation of the Trinity: the voice of the Father declaring, "This is my Son," and the Spirit descending like a dove. This is the more public, third-person formulation ("This is my beloved Son"), rather than the more private, second-person declaration ("You are my beloved Son") in the Baptism accounts of Mark and Luke.[230]

The reference to the Holy Spirit "taking ... the form of a dove" (*sumente ... formam columbæ*, lines 3–4) is a particular Latin construction found only here and in Fulgentius of Ruspe, who clarifies in what sense the Holy Spirit takes the form of a dove: "For not in the same way as the Son took the form of a servant did the Holy Spirit take the form of a dove; nor in the same way as the Son was made in the likeness of men was the Holy Spirit made in the likeness of doves. Therefore, the Holy Spirit came in the appearance of a dove, not in any way taking the dove into the unity of his person."[231]

STANZA 4

Lines 1 and 2 continue from the previous stanza, with an opening ablative prepositional phrase to mirror the ablative absolutes of stanza 3 (*Dicente Patre*, 3, 1; *sumente Spiritu*, 3, 3). Thus, the actions of the Father and the Spirit (in stanza 3) are grammatically subordinate to the action of the "salvation of the Church" (or "salvation for the Church") that "shines forth" (*micat*, 4, 2) at the Baptism of Christ. It is possible to understand "salvation of the Church" to refer to Christ himself, in which case the grammatical structure of stanzas 3 and 4 is parallel to that of stanza 1, where the action of John (in the ablative absolute, *Implente ... Ioanne*) is subordinate to Christ (*rerum conditor ... diluit*). On this reading, the "mystery of this Name" would refer to the name of Jesus: "For this reason God also exalted him, and gave him the name which is above every name, so that at the name of Jesus every knee would bow, of those in heaven and on earth and under the earth, and every tongue confess, 'Jesus Christ is Lord!' to the glory of God the Father."[232] Yet it is also possible to understand the Trinity (or faith in the Trinity) as the "salvation of the Church" that "shines forth" (*micat*).[233] On this reading,

---

229. *Baptizatus autem Iesus, confestim ascendit de aqua; et ecce aperti sunt ei cæli, et vidit Spiritum Dei descendentem sicut columbam et venientem super se. Et ecce vox de cælis dicens: "Hic est Filius meus dilectus, in quo mihi complacui"* (Mt 3:16–17).

230. *Tu es filius meus dilectus* (Mk 1:11 and Lk 3:22).

231. *Non enim sicut formam servi accepit filius, ita formam columbæ accepit Spiritus sanctus; nec sicut factus est filius in similitudine hominum, ita spiritus sanctus factus est in similitudine columbarum. Venit ergo spiritus sanctus in specie columbæ, non utique columbam in unitatem personæ accipiens*, Fulgentius, *Incarn.*, 12; cf. *in columbæ specie cælitus adveniret*, Fulgentius, *Fid.*, 9.

232. *Propter quod et Deus exaltavit illum, et donavit illi nomen, quod est super omne nomen: ut in nomine Iesu omne genu flectatur cælestium, terrestrium et infernorum, et omnis lingua confiteatur, quia Dominus Iesus Christus in gloria est Dei Patris* (Phil 2:9–11).

233. For this interpretation, see Walpole, 316.

the "mystery of this Name" could still refer to Jesus, and each of the three ablative phrases would account for a different member of the Trinity: with the Father speaking (*Dicente Patre*), and with the Spirit taking the form of a dove (*sumente Spiritu*), and under the mystical name of Jesus, the salvation of the Church shines forth. It is also possible that "the mystery of this Name" refers to the Trinity, and not to any one person of the Trinity.

STANZA 5

This newly composed final stanza is the same as the other hymns for the Baptism (H 19 and H 21). See the commentary on H 19.

Iesus refulsit omnium	21
Anon.	**The Baptism of the Lord**
8 8 8 8	Lauds

Iesus refúlsit ómnium pius redémptor géntium; totum genus fidélium laudis celébret cánticum.	1. Christ Jesus, clothed in splendid light, redeems all nations by his love; let all the faithful everywhere extol him with a hymn of praise
Denis ter ævi círculis iam parte vivens córporis, lympham petit baptísmatis cunctis carens contágiis.	2. While thirty years have run their course, in human flesh he lives our life and, though he lacks all stain of sin, for us he asks to be baptized.
Felix Ioánnes mérgere illum treméscit flúmine, potest suo qui sánguine peccáta mundi térgere.	3. Then blessed John recoils in fear, to plunge him in the flowing tide, beholding him, who by his blood can cleanse the world of every sin.
Vox ergo Prolem de polis testátur excélsi Patris, fluítque virtus Spíritus sancti datrix charísmatis.	4. And so the Father's voice on high resounds in witness to his Son; the Spirit's mighty power pours forth, true source of every holy gift.
Nos, Christe, voce súpplici precámur, omnes prótege, ac mente fac nitéscere tibíque mundos vívere.	5. To you, O Christ, we lift our voice: Protect us all, we humbly pray, and fill our minds and hearts with light, that cleansed, we all may live for you.
O Christe, vita, véritas, tibi sit omnis glória, quem Patris atque Spíritus splendor revélat cælitus. Amen.	6. All glory be to you, O Christ; the Father and the Spirit blest, in splendor from the heights of heaven, reveal that you are Life and Truth. Amen.

Text found in *TDH*, no. 91; AH 51, no. 52; Walpole, no. 90. Changes in *TDH*: stanzas 2, 3, 8, and 9 of the original are omitted here, and a newly composed doxology is added as the final verse (the same as in H 19 and H 20); stanza 1, 4: *laudis ... canticum* for *laudes ... dra(g)matum*; 2, 1: *Denis ter ævi circulis* for *denum ter annorum cyclis*; 3, 4: *mundi* for *cosmi*; 4, 3: *fluitque virtus Spiritus* for *virtus adestque Pneumatis*; 5, 1: *voce supplici* for *supplici prece*; 5, 3–4: *ac mente fac nitescere / tibique mundos vivere* for *qui præcipis rubescere / potenter hydrias aquæ*.

COMMENTARY

This is a quantitative hymn in iambic dimeter with frequent rhyme. It appears to be "very ancient."[234] It has sometimes been attributed to St. Hilary of Poitiers.[235] It was originally assigned to Epiphany. It begins and ends with the theme of light (*refulsit*, 1, 1; *splendor*, 6, 4).

STANZA I

The first stanza opens with themes of light and the loving redemption of all nations. The reference to Christ as "compassionate" (*pius*, line 2) recalls Sirach: "For compassionate and merciful is God, and he will forgive sins on the day of tribulation and is a protector to all who call upon him in truth."[236] The reference to "all nations" (*omnium ... gentium*, lines 1–2) recalls the promise made to Abraham: "I will bless you, and I will multiply your offspring as the stars of heaven, and as the sand that is on the seashore. Your offspring will possess the gates of their enemies, and by your offspring all the nations of the earth will be blessed, because you have obeyed my voice."[237] It also recalls the fulfillment of that promise in the Gospel of Jesus Christ being preached to the Gentiles: "Now the Scripture, foreseeing that God would justify the Gentiles by faith, announced the gospel beforehand to Abraham, saying, 'In you all the nations will be blessed.' Therefore, those who are of faith are blessed with Abraham who had faith.... Christ redeemed us ... so that in Christ Jesus the blessing of Abraham might come to the Gentiles, that we might receive the promise of the Spirit through faith."[238] Just as the visit of the Magi (celebrated at Epiphany) represents the revelation of Christ to the nations, so the Baptism of Christ represents the first public revelation of the Trinity. It also sets the stage for the baptism of those who follow

---

234. *TDH*, 93.
235. See discussion in Walpole, 312.
236. *Quoniam pius et misericors est Deus et remittet in die tribulationis peccata et protector est omnibus exquirentibus se in veritate* (Sir 2:13).
237. *benedicam tibi, et multiplicabo semen tuum sicut stellas cæli, et velut arenam quæ est in littore maris: possidebit semen tuum portas inimicorum suorum, et benedicentur in semine tuo omnes gentes terræ, quia obedisti voci meæ* (Gn 22:17–18).
238. *Providens autem Scriptura quia ex fide iustificat gentes Deus, prænuntiavit Abrahæ: Quia benedicentur in te omnes gentes. Igitur qui ex fide sunt, benedicentur cum fideli Abraham. Christus nos redemit ... ut in gentibus benedictio Abrahæ fieret in Christo Iesu, ut pollicitationem Spiritus accipiamus per fidem* (Gal 3:7–14).

Christ: "Go, therefore, and make disciples of all nations, baptizing them in the name of the Father and of the Son and of the Holy Spirit."[239]

The reference to a "hymn of praise" (*laudis … canticum*, line 4) echoes Augustine's definition of a hymn as "a song of praise."[240] The hymn thus invites those who sing it to see themselves as part of the "whole race" of the "faithful" (*totum genus fidelium*, line 3), which is "a chosen race, a royal priesthood, a holy nation, a people for his own possession, so that you might proclaim the wondrous deeds of him who has called you out of darkness into his marvelous light."[241]

STANZA 2

This stanza opens with a reference to Christ's age at the time of his baptism and the start of his public ministry: "Jesus was beginning about thirty years of age."[242] It then references the paradox that Christ, who "lacks all stain of sin" (*cunctis carens contagiis*, line 4), should "ask to be baptized" (*lympham petit baptismatis*, line 3). It thus hints at the tensions, explored more fully in the Baptism hymn *Implente munus debitum* (H 20), that are inherent in this event in the life of Christ: the cleansing of one who is blameless, the servant administering Baptism to the Lord.

STANZA 3

This stanza opens with another indication of tension in the event of Christ's Baptism: John is both "blessed" (*felix*, line 1) to be chosen as the instrument through which Christ is baptized, and yet he "recoils in fear" (*tremescit*, line 2). This recalls John's objection to his appointed role: "John tried to prevent him, saying, 'I ought to be baptized by you, yet you are coming to me?' Jesus answered and said to him, 'Let it be so now, for thus it is fitting for us to fulfill all righteousness.' Then he consented (See note 217)." Here the tension is expressed as a matter of baptizing one "who by his blood can cleanse the world of every sin" (*potest suo qui sanguine peccata mundi tergere*, lines 3–4). By contrasting the water of Christ's Baptism with the saving blood of his Passion, this stanza points us forward to the saving Death and Resurrection of Christ. It also echoes the words of John the Baptist: "Behold the Lamb of God, behold him who takes away the sin of the world."[243]

STANZA 4

This stanza casts in poetic language the Trinitarian revelation at Christ's Baptism: "When Jesus was baptized, he came up at once out of the water; and behold, the heavens were opened to him, and he saw the Spirit of God descending like

---

239. *euntes ergo docete omnes gentes: baptizantes eos in nomine Patris, et Filii, et Spiritus Sancti* (Mt 28:19).
240. *hymnus est enim canticum laudis.* Augustine, *Enarrationes in Psalmos*, 39.4.
241. *Vos autem genus electum, regale sacerdotium, gens sancta, populus acquisitionis: ut virtutes annuntietis eius qui de tenebris vos vocavit in admirabile lumen suum* (1 Pt 2:9).
242. *Et ipse Iesus erat incipiens quasi annorum triginta* (Lk 3:23).
243. *Ecce agnus Dei, ecce qui tollit peccatum mundi* (Jn 1:29).

a dove and coming upon him. And behold, a voice from heaven, saying: 'This is my beloved Son, in whom I am well pleased.'"[244] The reference to the power of the Spirit "pouring forth" (*fluitque virtus Spiritus*, line 3) recalls the frequent scriptural association of water with the Spirit, especially the promise of living water: "Now on the last day of the feast, the great day, Jesus stood up and cried aloud, saying, 'If anyone thirsts, let him come to me and drink. Whoever believes in me, as the Scripture says: Out of his heart will flow living waters.' He said this about the Spirit, whom those who believed in him would receive; for the Spirit had not yet been given, since Jesus was not yet glorified."[245] The reference to the Holy Spirit as the giver of "every holy gift" (*sancti datrix charismatis*, line 4) echoes the words of St. Paul to the Corinthians: "Now there are varieties of gifts, but the same Spirit; there are varieties of service, but the same Lord; and there are varieties of works, but the same God who works them all in everyone."[246]

STANZA 5

Here the hymn adopts the liturgical language of a prayer of supplication: "To You, O Christ, we lift our voice: / Protect us all, we humbly pray" (lines 1–2). As the previous stanza began with the "voice" of the Father, so this stanza begins with the suppliant "voice" of the faithful. The request to "fill our minds and hearts with light" reiterates the idea of light that marks the beginning and end of this hymn (*refulsit*, 1, 1; *splendor*, 6, 4). The request that we might live "cleansed" connects this commemoration of Christ's Baptism with our own baptism and new life in Christ: "For if we live, we live for the Lord; if we die, we die for the Lord. Therefore, whether we live or we die, we are the Lord's."[247]

STANZA 6

This newly composed final stanza is the same as the other hymns for the Baptism (H 19, H 20). For details, see the commentary on H 19. This hymn ends where it began, with the image of Christ as "light", a fitting link to the Epiphany, the "Festival of Lights," the liturgical feast that commemorates three events: the visit of the Magi, the wedding feast at Cana, and the Baptism of the Lord.

---

244. *Baptizatus autem Iesus, confestim ascendit de aqua; et ecce aperti sunt ei cæli, et vidit Spiritum Dei descendentem sicut columbam et venientem super se. Et ecce vox de cælis dicens: "Hic est Filius meus dilectus, in quo mihi complacui"* (Mt 3:16–17); on "progeny" (*proles*) as a distinctly poetic word, see Cicero, *De oratore*, 3.153.

245. *In novissimo autem die magno festivitatis stabat Iesus, et clamabat dicens: Si quis sitit, veniat ad me et bibat. Qui credit in me, sicut dicit Scriptura, flumina de ventre eius fluent aquæ vivæ. Hoc autem dixit de Spiritu, quem accepturi erant credentes in eum: nondum enim erat Spiritus datus, quia Iesus nondum erat glorificatus* (Jn 7:37–39).

246. *Divisiones vero gratiarum sunt, idem autem Spiritus: et divisiones ministrationum sunt, idem autem Dominus: et divisiones operationum sunt, idem vero Deus qui operatur omnia in omnibus* (1 Cor 12:4–6). The word for *gratiarum* in the Greek is χαρισμάτων.

247. *Sive enim vivimus, Domino vivimus: sive morimur, Domino morimur. Sive ergo vivimus, sive morimur, Domini sumus* (Rom 14:8).

Part 3

THE SEASON OF LENT AND HOLY WEEK

During the season of Lent, the liturgy brings before us the deepest and most fundamental truths of the life of faith: we are creatures subject to the justice and mercy of God; all are in need of salvation; the loving and merciful intervention of Christ has saved us from the dire consequences of sin; and finally we have responsibilities in the economy of salvation. Lent is the season set aside each year for the contemplation and assimilation of these truths; it is an invitation to see ourselves as we are seen by God. This explains perhaps the uniformity and intensity of the Lenten liturgy at large, and of the hymns in particular.[1] The heart must go over the same ground again and again, in order to make progress through Lent.

During the first five weeks, the liturgy invites us to come face to face with the reality of sin and its remedy. St. Augustine famously said, "He who made you without you, does not save you without you."[2] We are called to participate in our own salvation, and Lent allows us to respond fully to this call. It is a season marked by austerity, but also by spiritual joy. In his *Rule*, St. Benedict speaks of joy twice, and in both instances, he is referring to Lenten observance. He says that real penance should be offered to God in the joy of the Holy Spirit, and that we may and should await the holy season of Easter with the joy of spiritual desire.[3] St. Benedict touches upon one of the most fundamental principles of the Lenten and Easter cycles: the fruits of Lent are a clean conscience and peace with God; the joy of Easter is directly proportioned to these Lenten fruits. The relation of Easter joy to Lenten observance is reflected in the hymns.[4]

Lent is the primary penitential season of the liturgical year. At Mass and

---

1. In the hymns sung at Lauds, Vespers, and the Office of Readings during the first five weeks of Lent, the same themes recur, with variations, in every hymn: the awareness of sin, the need of forgiveness, hope in God's mercy, and the healing power of fasting and penance.
2. *Qui ergo fecit te sine te, non te iustificat sine te*, from St. Augustine, *Sermo* 169.13, in Boodts et al., "Augustine's Sermon 169," 11–44.
3. Benedict, *Rule*, 49.6–7.
4. In the hymn for Lauds on the weekdays of Lent, we sing: "The day shall come, your holy day, / through which all things will flower again; / let us rejoice, for through this day / your grace will lead us back to you" (H 27: 4, 1–4). Note the ambiguity in "this"; does it refer to the day of the Resurrection or to the coming day of the one who sings the hymn at Lauds? See the commentary on H 27.

throughout the Divine Office, *alleluia* is suppressed, purple vestments are worn, and commemorations of the saints are kept to a minimum. At Mass on Ash Wednesday, the Church launches a public and solemn proclamation, a call to penance, prayer, almsgiving, and fasting. On the only ferial day of the year that has three readings, she begins with the prophet Joel: "Blow the trumpet in Zion! proclaim a fast, call an assembly; gather the people ... let the priests, the ministers of the Lord, weep, and say, "Spare, O Lord, your people" (Jl 2:15–17). Then, we sing the *Miserere* (Ps 50[51]) and listen to St. Paul as he tells us, "Behold, now is a very acceptable time; behold, now is the day of salvation" (2 Cor 6:2). Finally, in the gospel, Christ admonishes us to be sincere in our observance and avoid hypocrisy: When you give alms, do not blow a trumpet before you (Mt 6:2); when you pray, do not strive to be seen (Mt 6:5); when you fast, do not look gloomy like the hypocrites (Mt 6:16). The next day, in the verse before the gospel, we hear: "Repent, for the kingdom of heaven is at hand" (Mt 4:17). Similar admonitions continue like a drumroll throughout the first five weeks of Lent.

Although historically the length of the season has varied, for many centuries in the Western Church, Lent has lasted for forty days,[5] a number of the greatest significance in Scripture. For forty days, the waters of the flood rose to cleanse the earth (Gn 7:4). For forty days, Moses stayed alone on Mount Sinai, to receive the Law (Ex 24:18). For forty years, the Israelites wandered in the desert, to expiate their sin of disbelief (Num 14:32–34). For forty days and forty nights, Elijah, the greatest of the prophets, walked to Horeb, where he encountered the Lord (1 Kgs 19:8). Finally, Christ brought these Old Testament figures to fulfillment by fasting, himself, in the desert for forty days and forty nights, in order to be tempted and to prevail (Mt 4:2). All of these events—Noah on the waters, Moses on Mount Sinai, the Israelites in the desert, Elijah on the way to Horeb, and our Lord in the desert—are the great patterns presented to us as exemplars to imitate through the entire range of our lives, but most especially during Lent.[6]

The spiritual realities presented by the exemplars outlined above and reflected in the hymns pass before us from week to week during Lent. The first Sunday is dedicated to the temptations of Christ. He who entered into personal combat with Satan hears and answers our prayers when we are tempted.[7] The second Sunday of Lent commemorates the Transfiguration; Christ allows his native, divine glory to shine forth and be seen by his apostles, as Moses and Elijah converse with him; they "spoke of his exodus that he was going to accomplish in Jerusalem" (Lk 9:31).[8] Then, following the sequence of Year A, the third and fourth Sundays of Lent present Christ to us as the living water of salvation (the Samaritan

---

5. Although the Sundays of Lent are an important part of the liturgical season, they are not strictly speaking counted among the forty days of fasting and abstinence, which begin consequently on the Wednesday before the first Sunday of Lent.

6. "For forty days the circuit runs, / this holy season of renown; / by mystery and by number taught / let us observe our Lenten fast" (H 24: 1, 1–4). See also Guéranger, *Liturgical Year: Lent*, 5:20–21.

7. "and grant no room for ruthless power / to our deceitful, wily foe" (H 24: 4, 3–4).

8. "The day of our salvation dawns / resplendent with the light of Christ" (H 25: 2, 1–2). See also H 27, stanza 1: "O Sun of justice ... rend the darkness of our minds." The multiple images of light in the Lenten liturgical texts that reference the Transfiguration are expressive of the revelation of Christ's glory and divinity.

woman: Jn 4:5–42) and the true light of the world (John's account of the man born blind: Jn 9:1–41). The fifth Sunday of Lent tells of the raising of Lazarus, and this is the immediate preparation for Holy Week, both as a herald of Christ's Resurrection and as a proximate cause of his crucifixion. Also, in the fifth week, at the Office of Readings, we begin to read the Letter to the Hebrews, the long meditation on Christ the High Priest. The antiphons of the various hours begin to speak more directly of Christ in his suffering.

Finally, with the dawn of Palm Sunday, we enter into the holiest days of the liturgical year. Christ's triumphal entry into Jerusalem inaugurates the celebration of his Passion and death. The Greeks name Holy Week the Great Week; everything in the liturgy changes. We read the accounts of the Passion from the Synoptics and the Gospel of John, we sing two of the greatest hymns ever composed in honor of the Cross, *Vexilla regis* (H 31) and *Pange, lingua, gloriosi prælium certaminis* (H 32–33), and in addition to these, a constellation of lesser hymns is reserved for the Divine Office of Holy Week.

There are twenty hymns assigned to Lent and Holy Week. They are indicated here by the numbers found in this volume of the commentary on the hymns of the *Liturgia Horarum*. A concordance showing the relation between these numbers and those of the *DOH* may be found at the end of the volume.

The hymns for the Season of Lent and Holy Week are as follows:

No.	Name	Liturgical Hour
22	Audi, benigne Conditor	Vespers, Sunday
23	Iesu, quadragenariæ	Vespers, Weekdays
24	Ex more docti mystico	Office of Readings, Sunday
25	Nunc tempus acceptabile	Office of Readings, Weekdays
26	Precemur omnes cernui	Lauds, Sunday
27	Iam, Christe, sol iustitiæ	Lauds, Sunday
28	Dei fide, qua vivimus	Terce
29	Qua Christus hora sitiit	Sext
30	Ternis ter horis numerus	None
31	Vexilla regis prodeunt	Vespers, Holy Week
32	Pange, lingua, gloriosi … certaminis	Office of Readings, Holy Week
33	En acetum, fel, arundo	Lauds, Holy Week
34	Celsæ salutis gaudia	Terce, Palm Sunday
35	O memoriale mortis Domini	Vespers, Holy Thursday
36	Christe, cælorum Domine	Office of Readings, Holy Saturday
37	Salva, Redemptor, plasma tuum nobile	Terce, Easter Triduum
38	Crux, mundi benedictio	Sext, Easter Triduum
39	Per crucem, Christe, quæsumus	None, Easter Triduum
40	Tibi, Redemptor omnium	Lauds, Holy Saturday
41	Auctor salutis unice	Vespers, Holy Saturday

Dom Prosper Guéranger, first abbot of Solesmes, in his account of Holy Week, says:

Let us reflect upon the love and affection of the Son of God, who has treated His creatures with such unlimited confidence, lived their own life, spent His three and thirty years amidst them, not only humbly and peaceably, but in going about doing good (Acts 10:38). And now this life of kindness, condescension, and humility, is to be cut short by the disgraceful death, which none but slaves endured: the death of the cross.... God had said in the ancient Covenant: "Accursed is he that hangs on a tree" (Dt 21:23). The Lamb that saved us disdained not to suffer this curse; but, for that very cause, this tree, this wood of infamy, has become dear to us beyond measure.[9] It is the instrument of our salvation, it is the sublime pledge of Jesus' love for us.... This is the end the Church proposes to herself by the celebration of these solemn anniversaries. After humbling our pride and our resistance to grace by showing us how divine justice treats sin, she leads our hearts to love Jesus, who delivered Himself up, in our stead, to the rigors of that justice.... Let us say with the Apostle: "The charity of Christ impels us; that they who live, may not now live to themselves, but for Him who died for them" (2 Cor 5:14–15).[10]

Audi, benigne Conditor — 22

Attributed to St. Gregory the Great, d. 604
8 8 8 8 (LM)

Sundays of Lent
Vespers

Audi, benígne Cónditor,	1. O Loving Maker, hear the prayers
nostras preces cum flétibus,	we raise to you with sighs and tears,
sacráta in abstinéntia	as we observe these forty days
fusas quadragenária.	with holy fast and abstinence.
Scrutátor alme córdium,	2. You search all hearts with loving care
infírma tu scis vírium;	and know the weakness of our powers;
ad te revérsis éxhibe	show mercy, Lord, forgive the sins
remissiónis grátiam.	of those who turn to seek your grace.
Multum quidem peccávimus,	3. Though we, in truth, have greatly sinned,
sed parce confiténtibus,	yet spare us who confess our guilt;
tuíque laude nóminis	restore and heal our ailing souls
confer medélam lánguidis.	for praise and honor of your name.
Sic corpus extra cónteri	4. Grant us through corporal abstinence
dona per abstinéntiam,	to learn and practice self-control,
ieiúnet ut mens sóbria	that inwardly with sober mind
a labe prorsus críminum.	we fast from every stain of sin.
Præsta, beáta Trínitas,	5. Grant us, O Blessed Trinity,
concéde, simplex Unitas,	O Undivided Unity,
ut fructuósa sint tuis	to see this service of our fast
hæc parcitátis múnera. Amen.	bring forth your fruit within our hearts. Amen.

---

9. "O blessed tree whose branches bore / the price and ransom of the world!" (*Vexilla regis prodeunt*, H 31: 4, 1–2). See also stanzas 2–4 of *Pange, lingua, gloriosi prælium certaminis* (H 32).

10. Guéranger, *Liturgical Year*, 6:17, 20, and 23.

Text found in *TDH*, no. 92; AH 51, no. 54; Walpole, no. 93. Changes in *TDH*: stanza 1, 3–4: *sacrata in abstentia / fusas quadrageneria* for *hoc sacro ieiunio / fusas quadragenario*; 3, 3: *tuique laude nominis* for *ad laudem tui nominis* and its Urbanite revision *ad nominis laudem tui*; 5, 4: *hæc parcitatis* for *ieiuniorum*.

COMMENTARY

In this hymn, what most reflects our urgency and earnestness is the presence of imperative after imperative. Of the eleven verbs in this hymn, seven are commands to God that he listen to, heal, spare, and give us the various gifts and graces we need in this life. The hymn evokes much of the language of the Penitential Psalms, especially Psalms 6 and 50 (51), as well as the call, in Joel 2, for fasting and repentance before the coming of the Lord. Summarizing this hymn, Denys the Carthusian says that we "sing out this hymn with contrite hearts and healthy mourning in the soul, being devoted to prayer, devotion, compunction, and tears, and wisely directing the exteriors to interior improvement, the cleansing of the heart, and the growth of charity."[11]

STANZA 1

The hymn begins, like the cry of hungry children, with a simple imperative form (*Audi*). Only after requesting our needs do we address God as *benigne Conditor*. The title *Conditor*, although it appears once in Scripture (Heb 11:9–10), has been a common word in hymnody since the time of St. Ambrose (H 71, *Æterne rerum conditor*). It refers to the founder of a city or state, and, as one would speak of the continuing influence of the fathers or the founders, God's act of creation is not limited to a singular moment like begetting a child or bringing a city into existence, but rather God as *conditor* connotes creation, long-lasting influence, and governance, like rearing a child or governing a city.[12]

Benigne can be vocative, and therefore God is called *benigne*, but it can also be an adverb—we ask that the Father hear us graciously.[13] This calls to mind Psalm 50:20 (51:21): "Do good (*benigne fac*) to Zion in your good pleasure"; but also Psalm 68 (69):17: "Hear me, O Lord, for your mercy is kind"; Joel 2:13: "Return to the Lord your God, for he is gracious (*benignus*) and merciful"; and 1 Corinthians 13:4: "Love is patient, love is kind."[14] We address God, not in dread, but with a knowledge of his mercy and loving kindness.

Fasting and tears give prayer a character that God does not resist. In the book of Tobit, the Angel Raphael says, "Prayer is good with fasting ... when you were

---

11. Dionysius the Carthusian, *Expositio hymni*, 36 B.
12. See also the discussion of the word in H 1, *Conditor alme siderum*.
13. In the English translation of this hymn, the vocative is employed.
14. *Benigne fac Domine in bona voluntate tua Sion et ædificentur muri Hierusalem* (Ps. 50:20 [51:21]); *exaudi me, Domine, quoniam benigna est misericordia tua* (Ps 68 [69]:17); *Covertimini ad Dominum Deum vestrum quia benignus et misericors est* (Jl 2:13); *caritas patiens est, benigna est* (1 Cor 13:4).

praying with tears and burying the dead, and leaving behind your meal, I offered your prayer to God."[15] While this is true throughout our lives, it becomes all the more focused in the season of Lent. The *abstinentia* of the Church is not simply our going hungry, but rather it has been made sacred (*sacrata*) through the example of Christ, who fasted for forty days.

In line 4, *fusas*, a delayed modifier of *preces* in line 2, brings closer in sense the already juxtaposed *preces* and *fletibus*; the prayers are poured out through the tears of our weeping. The graphic syntax of *nostras* and *fusas* at the head of the lines 2 and 4 and *abstinentia* and *quadragenaria* at the end of lines 3 and 4 tightly unifies the actions of fasting, praying, and weeping into one holy action.

STANZA 2

The second stanza is divided into two parts, the first being another invocation of the Trinity and a reflection on God's omniscience, and the second being a further petition, this time a request for forgiveness. As in stanza 3 that follows, this twofold structure models the confession of the penitent and the absolution of God.

God is called the *Scrutator cordium*. This is a clear reference to Jeremiah 17:10: "I the Lord search the mind and try the heart"; Romans 8:27: "And he who searches the hearts of men knows what is the mind of the Spirit"; and Revelation 2:23: "I am he who searches mind and heart."[16] Moreover, we call God *alme*, a rather strange word in Latin hymnody. From the verb *alo*, from which the adjective *almus* is derived, refers to providing nourishment and sustenance. In the classical authors, the word is used primarily of women, goddesses, and objects of nature. The word never appears in the Vulgate, and extant use of *almus* to describe men is rare until St. Paulinus of Nola and St. Augustine.[17] The context in this hymn may evoke Prudentius (*Cath* 7: 42, 4), who calls the fast itself nourishing (*almo ieiunio*). In line 1 of stanza 2, *alme* suggests that the Father's examination of our hearts, however, is an act of love and provides strength to our souls. He is *Scrutator* not to chastise, says Pimont, but in order to heal.[18]

Line 2 evokes similar themes of the Psalms: Psalm 102: "As a father pities his children, so the Lord pities those who fear him. For he knows our frame; he remembers that we are dust"[19]; and Psalm 6: "Have mercy on me, O Lord, for I am weak."[20] Pimont notes that the phrase *infirma virium* not only presents an artful antithesis but is also theologically fitting:[21] original sin makes us weak and prone

---

15. *Bona est oratio cum ieiunio … quando orabas cum lacrimis et sepeliebas mortuos et derelinquebas prandium … ego obtuli orationem tuam Domino* (Tb 12:8, 12).
16. *ego Dominus scrutans cor et probans renes* (Jer 17:10); *qui autem scrutatur corda scit quid desideret Spiritus* (Rom 8:27); *ego sum scrutans renes et corda* (Rv 2:23). See also Ps 138 (139):1–3.
17. See H 1, *Conditor alme siderum*, with commentary.
18. Pimont, 3:5
19. *quomodo miseretur pater filiorum misertus est Dominus timentibus se, quoniam ipse cognovit figmentum nostrum. Recordatus est quoniam pulvis sumus* (Ps 102 [103]:13–14).
20. *miserere mei, Domine quoniam infirmus sum* (Ps 6:3).
21. Pimont, 3:5

to sin (*infirma*), but it does not annihilate the strength of our souls, and by means of God's grace, we recover our lost strength. We, moreover, appeal to God's love of the lowly, for as Paul says to the Corinthians: "God chose what is weak in the world to shame the strong."[22]

Ad te reversis in line 3 calls to mind the prodigal son, who returns to his father after first coming back to himself (*in se autem reversus*, Lk 15:17). St. Gregory the Great writes that the prodigal son would not have returned to himself if he were not poor and hungry, for "all the weak (*infirmi*) and those despised in this world for the most part hear the voice of God more quickly, the less they have with which to be delighted."[23] In the final line of this stanza, having recognized our weakness and come back to the Lord, we ask for the grace of forgiveness, and Christ will maintain our strength, just as he says to Paul: "My grace is sufficient for you, for my power is made perfect in weakness."[24]

STANZA 3

This stanza, the center of the hymn, begins with a confession. The first two lines call to mind Psalm 50 (51), where the Psalmist repeats with great fervor the extent of his sin ("wash me fully from my iniquity and cleanse me from my sin. For I know my iniquity, and my sin is always before me. Against you alone have I sinned and done evil in your presence").[25] Moreover, just as the Psalmist repeatedly asks for the forgiveness and healing power of God when he says, "turn your face from my sins, and blot out my iniquities. Create a clean heart in me, O God, and a right spirit renew within me,"[26] so too do we who confess our sins (*confitentibus*) ask for his mercy and forgiveness.

As the stanza begins with confession, so it ends with a request for absolution. The language of a remedy (*medelam*) for the weary (*languidis*) is a metaphor for the spiritual sickness of sin and the healing medicine of the sacraments.[27] The line *tuique laude nominis* is an emendation from Lentini;[28] the ablative *laude* could call to mind some instrumental use of the name of God to heal, as it does in St. Peter's healing of the lame man in Acts, "Silver and gold I have not; but what I have I give you: in the name of Jesus Christ of Nazareth, rise up and walk."[29] God himself is the source and end for all that he does; so here we ask that God

---

22. Pimont, 3:6; *infirma mundi elegit Deus ut confundat fortia* (1 Cor 1:27).

23. *infirmi quique atque in hoc mundo despecti, plerumque tanto celerius vocem Dei audiunt, quanto et in hoc mundo non habent ubi delectentur.* Gregory the Great, *Homiliæ in evangelia*, 36, 7.

24. *sufficit tibi gratia mea. Nam virtus in infirmitate perficitur* (2 Cor 12:9).

25. *amplius lava me ab iniquitate mea et a peccato meo munda me. Quoniam iniquitatem meam cognosco et peccatum meum contra me est semper. Tibi soli peccavi et malum coram te feci* (Ps 50[51]:4–5).

26. *Averte faciem tuam a peccatis meis, et omnes iniquitates meas dele. Cor mundum crea in me Deus, et spiritum rectum innova in visceribus meis* (Ps 50 [51]:11–12).

27. For more on *languidus*, see H 1, *Conditor alme siderum*, stanza 2.

28. The variants in the manuscripts include *ad laudem tui nominis*, a similar statement of purpose, and *sed cuncta qui solus potes*, an expression of God's omnipotence. *Ad laudem tui nominis* is given in Walpole, no. 93, p. 320, who also notes the second variant. Milfull, 239; gives *ad laudem tui nominis*. This seems to be the standard text for this line, though it is metrically irregular.

29. *Petrus autem dixit, "Argentum et aurum non est mihi; quod autem habeo hoc tibi do. In nomine Iesu Christi Nazareni surge et ambula."* (Acts 3:6)

draw the medicine out of the praise of his name as a source or cause. Pimont notes that God heals us and thus we shine with the glory of God.[30] This ablative of source may be seen in Isaiah, "for my praise (*laude mea*), I will bridle you, lest you perish."[31] The Lord also says in Isaiah, "I am, I am he who blots out your transgressions for my own sake."[32] Likewise the Lord says in Ezekiel, "It is not for your sake, O house of Israel, that I am about to act, but for the sake of my holy name."[33]

STANZA 4

This stanza, the final petition before the doxology, returns to the subject of fasting introduced in the first stanza, and places the hymn in its seasonal context. The stanza also speaks of fasting as a whole body and soul experience marked by the two words *sic* and *ut*: the body is crushed and bruised so that the soul may follow suit and fast. The Church, in her wisdom, proclaims this fast for the twofold mortification and sanctification of the body and soul. For Christ also stresses the interior fast when he tells us not to fast like the hypocrites, being focused too much on the external fast.

In line 1, *conteri* is the same verb found in Psalm 50 (51):19: *cor contritum et humiliatum Deus non spernet*; "A humbled and contrite heart God will not spurn." In the context of this hymn, this word connotes an intense image of fasting; the hymnodist asks that Lenten abstinence grind the body down. *Extra* appears with *sic* in this first line to highlight the exterior fast, but a corresponding *intra* is implied with *ut mens* below. Although *mens* is often understood through cognates and derivatives, such as *mind* or *mental*, this word is also used in antiquity to talk about the soul or, in the abstract sense, the heart.[34]

The object of *dona* in line 2 is *corpus conteri* above. Although anyone can by his own will forgo food and afflict the body, the fast is truly a gift sought from God. The *ut* in line 3 connects lines 3–4 to *dona*. Under the guidance of the *benigne Conditor*—the *Scrutator alme cordium*—the soul can fast in conjunction with the body. This calls to mind the precept from the *Rule of St. Benedict*: "Everyone should, however, make known to the abbot what he intends to do [for Lent], since it ought to be done with his prayer and approval. Whatever is undertaken without the permission of the spiritual father will be reckoned as presumption and vainglory, not deserving a reward."[35]

The phrase *ieiunet ut mens sobria* calls to mind St. Ambrose's similar phrase *ieiunium sobrietas mentis est*.[36] Denys the Carthusian, moreover, says that fasting

---

30. Pimont, 3:7
31. *Propter nomen meum longe faciam furorem meum et laude mea infrenabo te ne intereas* (Is 48:9)
32. *Ego sum, ego sum ipse qui deleo iniquitates tuas propter me* (Is 43:25).
33. *Non propter vos ego faciam domus Israel sed propter nomen sanctum meum* (Ez 36:22).
34. OLD, s.v. *mens*.
35. Benedict, *Rule*, 49.8–9.
36. Ambrose, *De Helia et ieiunio*, 8.23.

disposes one to prayer because it preserves a sober and vigilant mind and drives out the vices of the flesh, drowsiness, talkativeness, and laziness.[37]

Connelly remarks that the metaphor, used in the hymn, of fasting from sin (*ieiunet a labe criminum*) seems strange, but this idea goes as far back as Isaiah: "Is not this the fast that I choose: to loose the bonds of wickedness, to undo the thongs of the yoke, to let the oppressed go free, and to break every yoke?"[38] Moreover, Paul writes to the Galatians: "And those who belong to Christ Jesus have crucified the flesh with its passions and desires. If we live by the Spirit, let us also walk by the Spirit. Let us have no self-conceit, no provoking of one another, no envy of one another."[39]

STANZA 5

The doxology found here is placed at the end of three different hymns (H 22, H 24, H 26), all three of which are Lenten hymns attributed to St. Gregory the Great. The structure of the doxology is somewhat different from the average in that there is not much explicit praise, but like the abrupt imperative in the opening of this hymn, this stanza continues the unceasing petitions of the faithful to God, addressed as both Trinity and Unity with the imperatives *præsta* and *concede*.

The final two lines of this hymn are a prayer that this fast may be fruitful. The phrase is a very artful juxtaposition but also highlights a true paradox of asceticism, that fasting is a source of great strength. Consider Mark 9:28, where Christ himself says to his disciples after cleansing a man from an unclean spirit: "This kind can be put out by nothing, except by prayer and fasting" (*Hoc genus in nullo potest exire, nisi in oratione et ieiunio*).

The final word, *munera*, is difficult to translate. The word *munus* refers both to an office or service and to a gift given because of the service. The shared final position of *tuis* and *munera* also brings to light two possible meanings. In one sense, we ask that the service or gift of fasting be fruitful to God's children or servants, *tuis* [*famulis*], or we ask that our fasting as a gift or service to God be made fruitful by what he has to give in return, *tuis* [*muneribus*].[40]

---

37. Dionysius the Carthusian, *Enarratio in Evangelium*, art. 7, cap. 2, ver. 37: *Ieiunium autem ad orationem disponit, sobriam ac vigilem mentem præstando, vitia carnis, somnolentiam, loquacitatem, pigritiamque pellendo: quæ omnia ex edacitate nascuntur.*

38. *Nonne hoc est magis ieiunium quod elegi? Dissolve colligationes impietatis, solve fasciculos deprimentes, dimitte eos qui confracti sunt liberos, et omne onus dirumpe* (Is 58:6). See Connelly, 16.

39. *Qui sunt Christi, carnem suam crucifigunt cum vitiis et concupiscentiis. si vivimus spiritu spiritu et ambulemus, non efficiamur inanis gloriæ cupidi invicem provocantes invicem invidentes* (Gal 5:24–26).

40. OLD, s.v. *munus*

	Iesu, quadragenariæ	23
ca. 10th c.		Weekdays of Lent
8 8 8 8		Vespers

Iesu, quadragenáriæ dicátor abstinéntiæ, qui ob salútem méntiu præcéperas ieiúnium,	1. O Jesus, you have set apart these forty days for abstinence and you decreed a Lenten fast to heal and save our mind and heart.
Adésto nunc Ecclésiæ, adésto pæniténtiæ, qua supplicámus cérnui peccáta nostra dílui.	2. Now come, be present to your Church, be near and aid our penitence, as we bow down before you, Lord, and beg you wash away our sins.
Tu retroácta crímina tua remítte grátia et a futúris ádhibe custódiam mitíssime,	3. Remit and pardon with your grace misdeeds from which we turn aside; from future perils keep us safe by your most meek and gentle guard,
Ut, expiáti ánnuis compunctiónis áctibus, tendámus ad paschália digne colénda gáudia.	4. That, filled with sorrow for our sins and cleansed by yearly penitence, we may press on to celebrate the Paschal Feast with worthy praise.
Te rerum univérsitas, clemens, adóret, Trínitas, et nos novi per véniam novum canámus cánticum. Amen.	5. Let all your works adore you, Lord, O merciful and Triune God. Renewed by pardon, let us sing a new song to your holy name. Amen.

Text found in *TDH*, no. 93; *AH* 51, no. 58; Walpole, no. 96; Milfull, no. 57. Changes in *TDH*: stanza 1, 4: *præceperas* for *hoc sanxeras*; stanza 2 of the original hymn is omitted; 2, 3–4: *qua supplicamus cernui / peccata nostra dilui* for *quæ pro suis excessibus / orat profusis fletibus*; 4, 2: *compunctionis actibus* for *ieiuniorum victimis*.

COMMENTARY

The manuscripts of this hymn date from the tenth century onward. It was assigned in all of them to the period of Lent. The original text consisted of five stanzas and a doxology. The current version has undergone considerable changes, which were designed to suit a less strict Lenten regime, but tend to weaken the effect of the original.[41]

41. In his commentary on H 22, *Audi, benigne Conditor* (*TDH*, 92), Lentini says that, in view of the current ecclesiastical discipline on fasting, in this and the other Lenten hymns it has been necessary to make

Iesu, quadragenariæ

As it stands, the hymn invokes Jesus as the one who by the example of his fasting consecrated the forty days of Lent as a period of abstinence and fasting (see Mt 4:2 and Lk 4:2).[42] It asks him to assist his Church in fulfilling this duty, and to grant forgiveness for past sins and protection from future ones, so that she may be able to celebrate the joys of Easter worthily. These themes are recurrent ones in this group of Lenten hymns (H 22–27). The hymn also shows the influence of Prudentius's "Hymn for those who fast" (*Cath* 7). It is in rhyming couplets (mostly disyllabic), with the exception of the omitted stanza.

STANZA 1

Quadragenarius was used in classical Latin as a measurement of forty units or of someone who was forty years old. In Christian Latin it was applied to the forty days of Lent. In line 2 *dicator* means "consecrator." In H 24: 2, 2–4, Christ is said to have "consecrated" (*sacravit*) the law of fasting, and in the hymn given by Walpole as hymn 95 (*Clarum decus ieiunii*) Christ "consecrated (*dicavit*) the Lenten fast by abstaining from foods" (Walpole, l. 4, p. 324).[43] Likewise, in Prudentius's "Hymn for those who fast" (*Cath* 7: 36, 3), "Jesus fasted with consecrated heart" (*Iesus dicato corde ieiunaverit*), and so he is called "the master of the consecrated doctrine" (*consecrati ... magister dogmatis*), which "he has given to his followers" (*Cath* 7: 41–42). In line 4 of the present hymn the original reading was *sanxeras* ("you sanctified"). Lentini explains his change to *præceperas* by saying that the original text "seems to attribute to a divine institution the forty-day fast before Easter." This, however, is what Prudentius and the later hymns clearly do. Lentini perhaps intended *præceperas* to imply a strong encouragement, rather than a command. In line 3 the word *mentium* is an example of the fact that the hymns often use *mens* with a spiritual as well as intellectual sense: hence the translation "our mind and heart."

After this stanza the omitted one is:

Quo paradiso redderes	In order that you might restore to Paradise
servata parsimonia,	through the keeping of frugality,
quos inde gastrimargiæ	those whom the lure of gluttony
huc inlecebra depulit.	cast down into this world.

The absence of rhyme, together with the unusual language (*gastrimargiæ*) might suggest that this stanza was added to the original hymn. It reflects the view that the Fall of Man was caused by the sin of gluttony: *gastrimargia* is a

---

some modifications. This was because fasting was no longer required in Lent, except for Ash Wednesday and Good Friday, together with abstinence on all Fridays. See Paul VI, Apostolic Constitution *Pænitemini* (1966), chapter 3. On the history of fasting and abstinence in the Christian Church see also the *Oxford Dictionary of the Christian Church*, on "abstinence," "fast and fasting," and "Lent."

42. In addition to the reference to Christ's own period of fasting, the gospels give his advice on how to fast, in Mt 6: 16–18. See also Mk 2:20.

43. See also the original version of H 22: 1, 3: *in hoc sacro ieiunio*.

Greek word that means literally "madness or greed in the belly." Evagrius of Pontus (346–99) used it of gluttony in his account of the deadly sins. This was taken over by John Cassian (ca. 360–after 430), who was the first to use the word in Latin. The usual word in Christian Latin for gluttony was *gula*. In line 4 *depulit* ("cast down") suggests that Paradise was seen as above the present world, synonymous with heaven, as in Christ's promise on the Cross to the penitent thief, "today you will be with me in Paradise" (Lk 23:43).

STANZA 2

In lines 1–2 (*Adesto … adesto …*) the verb "be present" in the imperative is common in the invocation of a deity in classical Latin. From the sense "be present," *adesse* developed the meaning "be at hand with assistance," and then "give one's blessing to," "look favorably on." Here the repetition suggests the urgency of this prayer. In these lines there is probably another echo of the opening part of Prudentius's *Cathemerinon* 7: 1, 3: *adesto castis, Christe, parsimoniis* ("assist, O Christ, our chaste acts of abstinence"; which finds an echo also in *parsimonia* in line 2 of the missing stanza given above). *Cathemerinon* 7: 1, 5: *ieiuniorum dum litamus victimam* ("while we offer the sacrifice of our fasts"), and *Cathemerinon* 7: 2, 2: *quo fibra cordis expiatur vividi* ("by which the tissues of our lively heart are cleansed") are also echoed later in the original version of this hymn (stanza 5, 1–2), *Ut expiati annuis / ieiuniorum victimis* ("So that cleansed by the annual sacrifice of fasts").

In lines 3–4 of this stanza the original reading was *quæ pro suis excessibus / orat profusis fletibus* ("which on account of her transgressions / prays with copious tears"). Lentini justified his change by saying that it seemed better to make the expression simpler and closer to the current practice. The loss of reference to the transgressions (or "excesses") and tears of the Church weakens the force of the original expression. Prayer and fasting were traditionally associated in the Old Testament (and later by the Fathers of the Church) with the tears and sorrow of penitence, as in Joel 2:12–13, "'Yet even now,' says the Lord, 'return to me with all your heart, with fasting, with weeping, and with mourning.'" In the Lenten hymns in the *Liturgia Horarum* sorrow and tears are mentioned together with prayer in H 22 (*Audi, benigne Conditor*): 1, 2, and in H 26 (*Precemur omnes cernui*): 1, 1–3.

STANZA 3

The verb *retroagere* (or *retro agere*) normally meant "to drive or thrust back" or "reverse" in classical Latin. Seneca, for example, says *iram sæpe misericordia retrægit* ("mercy often thrusts back anger," *Dialogue* 3.17.4). So here the translation in the *DOH*, "misdeeds from which we turn aside," implies that we have made the effort of repentance for past sins and are resolved to avoid them in future. Walpole took *retro acta* (as two words) as meaning "done in the past," in contrast to *a futuris* (i.e., future sins) in line 3 (lines 13–15, p. 326). He commented that there were many other examples of *retro* meaning "in times past." In the Vulgate see, for example, Genesis 41:30 *cuncta retro abundantia* ("all past abundance"), and 1 Kings 3:13, *cunctis retro diebus* ("all past days"). Milfull also translates "the offences committed in the past" (245). This is a possible alternative way of taking these words.

In line 3 one can supply *criminibus* with *a futuris* ("from future sins"), or possibly take it more generally, as in the translation "from future perils." In line 4 *mitissime* could be either a vocative ("most gentle one") or an adverb ("most gently"). Walpole and Milfull both print a comma after *custodiam*, so taking it in the first way. This seems better in the context of prayer. *TDH* has no comma and so takes it as an adverb.

STANZA 4

Literally this stanza means, "So that cleansed by annual acts of compunction, we may press on to celebrate worthily the joys of Easter." The word *compunctio* ("sting of conscience") was first used in Christian Latin. The original reading of line 2 is *ieiuniorum victimis*. The lines then mean "so that, cleansed by annual sacrifices of fasts," as in the verses of Prudentius quoted on stanza 2. Lentini has no comment on his alteration, but presumably he found the idea of fasting as a sacrificial offering too demanding for current practice, and so substituted the softer expression. Lines 3–4 anticipate the Paschal mystery that will lead us into solemn liturgies of worthy and joyous praise throughout the fifty days between Easter and Penetcost. Thus, at Vespers every evening during Lent, the hymn reminds us that our goal throughout these forty days is joy and praise. The *colenda* ("to be celebrated") in the future of line 4 then will be transformed into a present participle *colens* ("celebrating") in the Easter hymn H 47 1, 3–4: *colens cum sobriis / paschale festum gaudiis*. See also H 150 1, 1: *claro paschali gaudio*.

STANZA 5

The doxology is repeated in H 25 and 27. It is original to the latter hymn. The phrase *universitas rerum* was used by Cicero in *De natura deorum* (1.120) of the totality of the world. In line 2 *clemens* is appropriate to the context of penitence and forgiveness. Lines 3–4 echo Revelation 14:3, where the souls of the redeemed "sing a new song before the throne," and those psalms that speak of singing a new song to the Lord.[44] The repetition *novi ... novam* is like that in H 47: 1, 1–3, *Chorus novæ Ierusalem / hymni novam dulcedinem / promat*.[45] For more details see the commentary on H 27.

---

44. *Et cantabant quasi canticum novum ante sedem* (Rv 14:3); *cantate ei canticum novum bene psallite in vociferatione* (Ps 32 [33]:3): "Sing to him a new song, sing well with loud acclamation"; *et inmisit in os meum canticum novum, carmen Deo nostro* (Ps 39 [40]:4): "and he put into my mouth a new song, a hymn for our God"; psalms that begin with *Cantate Domino canticum novum* (Ps 95 [96]:1; 97 [98]:1; 149:1): "Sing to the Lord a new song."

45. See also Walpole no. 87, lines 21–24, p. 308; *nos quoque, qui sancto tuo / redempti sanguine sumus, / ob diem natalis tui / hymnum novum concinimus*.

Ex more docti mystico	24

Attributed to St. Gregory the Great, d. 604 Sundays of Lent
8 8 8 8 Office of Readings

Ex more docti mýstico servémus abstinéntiam, deno diérum círculo ducto quater notíssimo.	1. For forty days the circuit runs, this holy season of renown; by mystery and by number taught let us observe our Lenten fast.
Lex et prophétæ prímitus hanc prætulérunt, póstmodum Christus sacrávit, ómnium rex atque factor témporum.	2. Christ, King and Maker of all time, has consecrated in due course this fast proclaimed and practiced first by prophets and the Law of old.
Utámur ergo párcius verbis, cibis et pótibus, somno, iocis et árctius perstémus in custódia.	3. So let us use with more restraint our speech, our sleep, our idle mirth, and, frugal in our food and drink, stand guard with heightened vigilance.
Vitémus autem péssima quæ súbruunt mentes vagas, nullúmque demus cállido hosti locum tyránnidis.	4. Let us avoid all wicked sin that undermines the heedless heart and grant no room for ruthless power to our deceitful, wily foe.
Præsta, beáta Trínitas, concéde, simplex Unitas, ut fructuósa sint tuis hæc parcitátis múnera. Amen.	5. Grant us, O Blessed Trinity, O Undivided Unity, to see this service of our fast bring forth your fruit within our hearts. Amen.

Text found in *TDH*, 94; AH 51, no. 55; Walpole, no. 94. Changes in *TDH*: stanza 1, 2: *abstinentiam* for *hoc ieiunium*; 1, 3: *deno* for *denum* (an archaic form of *denorum*); 2, 2: *hanc* for *hoc*; 5, 4: *hæc parcitatis* for *ieiuniorum*.

COMMENTARY

This hymn, which forms the first half of H 26, is a simple but artful reflection on the Lenten fast. After introducing the liturgical nature of the fast in stanza 1, and giving a brief history in stanza 2, the author gives in stanza 3 explicit details on what pertains to the fast (*Utamur ergo parcius* ...), and in the next stanza he reflects on the spiritual side of the fast (*Vitemus autem pessima* ...). Prudentius's lengthy hymn about fasting, *Cathemerinon* 7, seems to have influenced this hymn. Prudentius conveys in his own hymn similar aspects of the Lenten fast and narrates in detail the fasts of Elijah, Moses, John the Baptist, Jonah and the

Ninevites, as well as Christ's temptation in the desert. *Ex more docti mystico* is largely directed at the congregation, while the second half turns toward God. Sung every Sunday in Lent, the hymn serves as an exhortation to remain strong throughout the weeks of Lent.

STANZA 1

The hymn opens with an exhortation (*servemus*) to those who are singing. It asks that we maintain the fast we have just begun, or are continuing to keep throughout the weeks. The phrase *more mystico* alludes to past models and customs of fasting. To fast for forty days stems principally from the example of Christ, who fasted in the desert for forty days, but also from the examples of Moses, the Israelites, Elijah, Noah, and Jonah. *Mystico*, moreover, calls to mind Prudentius, who calls the fast itself *mysterium* (*Cath* 7: 2, 1). This practice is called *mysticus*, not only because it is mystical or mysterious, but because it is connected to the sacred mysteries, the sacraments. Fasting in this context always points to the feast. Thus, one fasts before Mass; Lent is the great fast that points to the mysteries of the Easter Triduum. The Church, moreover, is said to be taught (*docti*) by this custom, for seasonal rhythms of the liturgy teach us and shape our habits.

Lines 3 and 4 are surprisingly ornate. The fast is measured by forty laps of a *circulus*, a small race track or an orbit. This image calls to mind Prudentius's elaborate description of the sun looking down on Moses fasting as it rolls forty laps through the stars.[46] The distributive numeral *Deno* is a transferred epithet that grammatically agrees with *circulo* but properly modifies *dierum*. This numeral specifies groups (e.g., *deni advenerunt* "they arrived in tens"); such numbers are often used with a numeral to express multiplication (*ter septenis diebus* "thrice seven days," Pliny, *Natural History* 30.92). Although "ten times four" does not sound highly poetical to English ears, this is common in Latin verse (*bis denis Phrygium conscendi navibus æquor*, Virgil, *Æn.*, 1.381, "I navigated the sea with two times ten ships").

Ducto used in the context of time refers to something's being prolonged, stretched out, or, in mercantile language, calculated. The use of *ducto* to describe these forty days points to a passage in St. Gregory the Great: "Why in fasting is the number forty maintained if not because the power of the ten commandments is fulfilled through the four books of the Holy Gospel? A set of 10 calculated 4 times (*quater ductus*) increases to 40."[47] Franz Joseph Mone, in his *Lateinische Hymnen des Mittelalters*, argues that this reference is evidence for Gregory's authorship of the hymn, but it can also be evidence of an imitator.[48] The final line

---

46. *Cath* 7: 8, 1–5: *Non ante cæli principem septemplicis / Moses tremendi fidus interpres throni / potuit videre, quam decem recursibus / quater volutis sol peragrans sidera / omni carentem cerneret substantia.* "Moses, the faithful messenger of the awful throne, was not able to see the Lord of the sevenfold heavens till the sun in his passage through the constellations had rolled forty times on his returning path and beheld him lacking all sustenance." Translation from Thomson *Prudentius* 1:59–61.

47. Gregory the Great, *Homiliæ in evangelia*, 16, 5.

48. Mone, *Lateinische Hymnen*, I.95.

ends with *notissimo*, rounding out the stanza with internal and end rhymes (*deno ... circulo / ducto ... notissimo*).

STANZA 2

Fasting has been an integral part of the covenant between God and man from the beginning, and references to fasting in the Old Testament are numerous. In the book of Tobit, the Angel Raphael himself suggests fasting as a good practice: "Prayer is good when accompanied by fasting, almsgiving, and righteousness."[49] When Moses received the Law, he fasted for forty days on Mount Sinai (Ex 34:28); and the Lord commanded that the people afflict themselves for the Day of Atonement (Lv 23:26ff.). Walpole suggests that, in the context of this stanza, with the suggestive line endings *primitus* (line 1) and *postmodum* (line 2), the phrase "the law and the prophets" (2, 1) refers to the fast of Moses while receiving the Law and to Elijah's fast (1 Kgs 19:8).[50] Though references both to the law and to the prophets are found throughout the Old Testament, references in which both are found together in the same verse are common only in the New, for example, Matthew 22:37–40,[51] Luke 16:16,[52] and numerous other texts.

In the Old Testament, there are a few general reasons why the People of Israel fast: petition, mourning, and repentance.[53] Lent begins with these senses of fasting; in the liturgy for Ash Wednesday, we read Joel's proclamation of the fast, in order to prepare for the coming of the Lord's Day: "'Yet even now,' says the Lord, 'return to me with all your heart, with fasting, with weeping, and with mourning'... let the priests, the ministers of the Lord, weep and say, 'Spare your people, O Lord, and make not your heritage a reproach, a byword among the nations.'"[54] The sense of repentance is further emphasized by the singing of Psalm 50 (51), the archetypal psalm of repentance, and by the dramatic penitential sign of the imposition of ashes, accompanied by the words of the minister: "Remember that you are dust and to dust you shall return." Thus, the Lenten season of forty days is inaugurated by a solemn liturgy and consecrated (*sacravit*) by the forty days of Christ's fasting in the desert, as a fulfillment of the tradition established by the Law and the Prophets, that is, by Moses's fasting in the wilderness (Dt 9:9), and

---

49. *Bona est oratio cum ieiunio et elemosyna magis quam thesauros auri condere* (Tob. 12:8).

50. Walpole, no. 94, lines 5–6, p. 322.

51. "And he said to him, 'You shall love the Lord your God with all your heart, and with all your soul, and with all your mind. This is the great and first commandment. And a second is like it, You shall love your neighbor as yourself. On these two commandments depend all the law and the prophets.'"

52. "The law and the prophets lasted until John; since then, the kingdom of God is proclaimed, and everyone who enters into it does so with force."

53. Petition: "'Go, gather all the Jews to be found in Susa, and hold a fast on my behalf, and neither eat nor drink for three days, night or day. I and my maids will also fast as you do. Then I will go to the king'" (Est 4:16); see also Jgs 20:26; 2 Chr 20:3; Ezr 8:21–23; Neh 1:4; Jdt 4:8–12; Est 4:3; 9:31; 14:2; Ps 34 (35):13; 68 (69):11; 108 (109):24; 1 Mc 3:47; 2 Mc 13:12. Mourning: "And they took their bones and buried them under the tamarisk tree in Jabesh and fasted seven days" (1 Sm 31:13); see also 2 Kgs 1:12; 2 Kgs 12:16–23; 1 Chr 10:12; Jdt 8:6; Tb 2:3; Bar 1:5. Repentance: "And in the four and twentieth day of the month the children of Israel came together with fasting and with sackcloth, and earth upon them" (Neh 9:1); see also 1 Sm 7:6; Jer 36:9; Dn 9:3; Jon 3:5.

54. "Nunc, ergo," dicit Dominus, "convertimini ad me in toto corde vestro in ieiunio et in fletu et in planctu;... plorabunt sacerdotes ministri Domini et dicent, "Parce, Domine, populo tuo et ne des hereditatem tuam in obprobrium, ut dominentur eis nationes (Jl 2:12–17).

by Elijah's fast as he walked to the Mountain of God, Horeb (1 Kgs 19:8). See also, in this commentary, the introduction to the Season of Lent and Holy Week.

Prætulerunt offers here a double meaning from *fero*, "to carry," and *præ*, "in front or before," namely "to show" or "to anticipate." The Old Law carries or sets before us the fast as an example for our fasting today, and the Old Law anticipates the fast that Jesus transforms and teaches to us. The Old Testament is marked by warnings not to fast like hypocrites; Sirach says: "So if a man fasts for his sins, and goes again and does the same things, who will listen to his prayer? And what has he gained by humbling himself?" (Sir 34:26 [Vulgate 34:31]). The Lord says in Isaiah: "Behold, you fast only to quarrel and to fight and to hit with wicked fist.... Is such the fast that I choose, a day for a man to humble himself?"[55]

The original line 2 began with *hoc*, referring to *ieiunium*, but this has been changed to *hanc*, referring to *abstinentia*.[56] Christ in his fasting is not only an example for us (see Lk 4:1–13; Mt 4:1–11), but just as, by being baptized, he sanctified baptism itself, so also by fasting, he sanctified the fast (*sacravit*; line 3).

At the end of the stanza, Christ is called *rex* and *factor*. Although *factor* does appear in the New Testament, it refers to a doer of something.[57] The hymn refers to Christ here in a way that is typical of the Old Testament, where *factor* is used almost exclusively to refer to God the Creator; Proverbs says, "He who despises the poor, reproaches his Maker" (*factori eius*).[58] Ecclesiastes 2:12 uses both terms as they are applied to Christ in this stanza: "What is man, I say, that he can follow the King his maker (*regem factorem suum*)?"[59]

This use of *atque* (instead of *et*) denotes a closer unity of these two roles of King and Maker and their respective genitive modifiers, *omnium* and *temporum*. These forms agree, and they may be understood either together or as separate units: thus, Christ is King of all, Maker of times and seasons, and both King and Maker of all times. Pimont notes that *omnium* can refer to *omnium rerum* or *omnium hominum*.[60] Moreover, the graphic syntax in *Christus sacravit omnium* suggests subtly that Christ, King and Maker, sanctifies all things (*Christus sacravit omnia*); this is suggested by the placement of words in the stanza, not directly by the syntax.

---

55. *sic homo qui ieiunat in peccatis suis et iterum eadem faciens quid proficit humiliando se orationem illius quis exaudiet* (Sir 34:31); *ecce ad lites et contentiones ieiunatis et percutitis pugno impie ... tale est ieiunium quod elegi per diem adfligere hominem animam suam?* (Is 58:4–5). See also Zec 7:5ff.

56. On stanza 1, 3–4, of *Audi benigne conditor*, in *TDH* there is a note on the substitution of abstinentia for ieiunium. It reads: "3–4: orig. *in hoc sacro ieiunio* / *fusas, quadragenario*: data l'attuale disciplina ecclesiastica sul digiuno, in questo e negli altri inni della Quaresima si son dovuti modificare i versi relativi" ["given the current ecclesiastical discipline of fasting it has been necessary to modify the relative references"].

57. Rom 2:13; Jas 1:22–25; Jas 4:11.

58. *Qui despicit pauperem exprobrat factori eius*, Prv 17:5.

59. *Quid est, inquam, homo, ut sequi possit regem, factorem suum?* See also Job 4:17: *Numquid homo, Dei comparatione, iustificabitur? aut factore suo purior erit vir?*: "Shall man be justified in comparison of God, or shall a man be more pure than his maker?"; and Jb 32:22: *Nescio enim quamdiu subsistam, et si post modicum tollat me factor meus*: "For I know not how long I shall continue, and whether after a while my Maker may take me away." See also Wis 16:24; Is 17:7; and Is 51:13.

60. Pimont 3:16.

The harmony between the Old and New Testaments is also subtly marked by the structure of this stanza. At the beginning of the first and last lines, alliteration is found on *lex* from the Old Testament and *rex* from the New. Moreover, the last two syllables of each line have assonance on *primitus, postmodum, omnium, temporum* alternating between *i/u* and *o/u*. Unlike the other stanzas, which can be organized neatly into couplets, this stanza has enjambment at the end of lines 1–3. As a result, the depiction of the Old Testament flows smoothly into the New; fasting is a continuous practice received from the Law and the Prophets and consecrated by Christ for the age of the Church.

STANZA 3

This stanza shifts attention from a consideration of the Lenten fast to those who participate in it, the congregation itself (*Utamur ... perstemus*). It gives the details of a rather simple list of Lenten practices: fasting from food, drink, sleep, speech, and jokes. This stanza focuses more on external actions, while the following focuses on the internal fast.

Although fasting from food and drink may be found in any description of Lenten practice, all the items listed here from which we should fast are found in the *Rule of St. Benedict*, chapter 49: "let each one deny himself some food, drink, sleep, needless talking, and idle jesting, and look forward to holy Easter with joy and spiritual longing."[61] Pimont notes that foregoing material pleasures allows the soul, detached from earthly goods, to rise toward God; restraining one's words, he writes, and cultivating a discipline of silence allows one to hear the interior word of God.[62] These practices and more are also mentioned by Prudentius in his hymn on fasting: *Hinc subiugatur luxus et turpis gula, / vini atque somni degener socordia*: "Hence luxury and shameful gluttony are tamed and the degenerate sloth of wine and sleep" (*Cath* 7: 3, 1–2).[63]

The stanza is tightly constructed; the exhortations (*Utamur* and *perstemus*) serve as bookends to the examples of fasting in the center two lines.[64] These center lines are additionally unified by the internal rhyme with the ablatives *verbis, cibis*, and *iocis*, and the whole stanza is unified with the assonance on the end of the first three lines (*parcius, potibus, arctius*). The stanza ends with *custodia* pointing to the struggle against sin and the enemy described in the following stanza.

STANZA 4

Although the corporeal fast is important, it is ordered to a fasting from sin. This spiritual understanding of the fast is scriptural: the Lord says in Isaiah: "Is not

---

61. Benedict, *Rule*, 49.7: *id est subtrahat corpori suo de cibo, de potu, de somno, de loquacitate, de scurrilitate, et cum spiritalis desiderii gaudio sanctum Pascha exspectet.*
62. Pimont, 3:17.
63. Food and drink are repeatedly mentioned in this hymn by Prudentius; see *Cath* 7: 4, 1; 14, 2; 33, 1; 34, 3–4; 38, 3.
64. The slightest influence of St. Ambrose can be seen in the syntax of *Utamur ergo parcius*. In *Æterne rerum conditor*, St. Ambrose uses an exhortation, *ergo*, then an adverb: *Surgamus ergo strenue*. See H 86.

this the fast that I choose: to loose the bonds of wickedness, to undo the thongs of the yoke, to let the oppressed go free, and to break every yoke?"[65] Further, St. Paul writes to the Galatians: "And those who belong to Christ Jesus have crucified the flesh with its passions and desires. If we live by the Spirit, let us also walk by the Spirit. Let us have no self-conceit, no provoking of one another, no envy of one another."[66] He also tells the Thessalonians: "For this is the will of God, your sanctification; that you should abstain from immorality; that each one of you should know how to control his own body in holiness and honor."[67] In his *Rule*, before mentioning corporeal practices, St. Benedict writes that sacrifices in Lent "will then be worthily done, if we restrain ourselves from all vices."[68]

The first stanza described Lent as a contest or race (*circulo*) belonging to the whole economy of the universe. In stanza 3, the language evokes a spiritual battle. *Subruunt* is an uncommon word that has many senses. In its basic form the verb *ruo* can mean "to rush, fall, cast down, ruin," and in technical legal language, "to dig up."[69] The prefix *sub* may add to a verb that sense of the action's happening under something, movement up from underneath, or, rarely, it suggests that the action is subtle or covert.[70] Consequently, *subruo* can mean "to rush under, undermine, demolish," or even "uproot." The word appears in the works of Caesar, Livy, and Tacitus, often used to refer to an attack on city walls; in Lucretius and Horace it refers to some corruption or subversion.[71] In the context here, sins (*pessima*) are at war with our hearts (*mentes*), burrowing under our defenses or laying siege towers on them. The use of *mentes vagas* in the context of fasting calls to mind Prudentius's *Psychomachia*, in which *Luxuria*, the personification of excess, is said to have wandering eyes (*oculis vaga*, Psych. 312).

The second couplet of this stanza is a double reference—first to Ephesians 4:27, when Paul, exhorting that we put off the habits of the old man, says: *Nolite locum dare diabolo*, "Give no place to the devil". Secondly, the adjective *callido* is a reference to Genesis 3:1: "Now the serpent was more subtle (*callidior*) than any other wild creature that the Lord God had made". Walpole, moreover, suggests that *locum*, understood as a military term, is a "vantage ground."[72] The *hostis* in this passage also calls to mind Prudentius's hymn on fasting, when he depicts Christ's temptation in the desert; Christ is *inhospitali secretus loco* "withdrawn to

---

65. *Nonne hoc est magis ieiunium quod elegi? Dissolve colligationes impietatis, solve fasciculos deprimentes, dimitte eos qui confracti sunt liberos, et omne onus dirumpe* (Is 58:6).

66. *Qui sunt Christi, carnem suam crucifigunt cum vitiis et concupiscentiis. si vivimus spiritu, spiritu et ambulemus, non efficiamur inanis gloriæ cupidi invicem provocantes invicem invidentes* (Gal 5:24–26).

67. *Hæc est enim voluntas Dei, sanctificatio vestra : ut abstineatis vos a fornicatione, ut sciat unusquisque vestrum vas suum possidere in sanctificatione, et honore* (1 Thes 4:3–4).

68. Benedict, *Rule*, 49.4: *Quod tunc digne fit si ab omnibus vitiis temperamus.*

69. *OLD*, s.v. *ruo*

70. *OLD*, s.v.v. *ruo*, *sub-*, *subruo*,

71. Caesar uses the word *subruo* once in his *De bello Gallico* (6.27) to refer to the practice of hunters who, according to the received wisdom of the day, would chop the roots of a standing tree in order to catch the elk who lean on the trees to sleep and subsequently fall over.

72. Walpole no. 94, line 16, p. 322.

an inhospitable place" (*Cath* 7: 38, 1), and the enemy (*hostis*) is called *arte sciscitator callida*, "interrogator with cunning, or crafty, art" (*Cath* 7: 39, 3).

STANZA 5

The doxology found here is placed at the end of three different hymns (H 22, H 24, H 26), all three of which are Lenten hymns attributed to Gregory the Great. In order to understand the structure of this hymn, it is helpful to remember that the present hymn is composed of stanzas 1–3 of a longer hymn. The stanzas given here are a narrative followed by exhortation (*servemus … utamur … vitemus*). At the end, the doxology turns to God for help, addressed as both Trinity and Unity with the imperatives *præsta* and *concede*. See the commentary on H 22 for a more detailed account.

Nunc tempus acceptabile	25
ca. 10th c.	Weekdays of Lent
8 8 8 8	Office of Readings

Nunc tempus acceptábile fulget datum divínitus, ut sanet orbem lánguidum medéla parsimóniæ.	1. Behold, the accepted time has come: a holy gift from God shines forth to cure the sick and weary world with healing balm of abstinence.
Christi decóro lúmine dies salútis émicat, dum corda culpis sáucia refórmat abstinéntia.	2. The day of our salvation dawns resplendent with the light of Christ, as wounded hearts are freed from sin, restored by fasting and restraint.
Hanc mente nos et córpore, Deus, tenére pérfice, ut appetámus próspero perénne pascha tránsitu.	3. O God, perfect our firm resolve to fast with body, mind, and heart, that filled with longing we may seek and safely reach the eternal Pasch.
Te rerum univérsitas, clemens, adóret, Trínitas, et nos novi per véniam novum canámus cánticum. Amen.	4. Let all your works adore you, Lord, O merciful and Triune God. Renewed by pardon, let us sing a new song to your holy name. Amen.

Text found in *TDH*, no. 95; AH 51, no. 56. The text in *TDH* is the same as that found in AH 51, no. 56. The doxology is the same as in H 23 and H 27.

COMMENTARY

This hymn is a perfect ferial hymn in Lent: short, sober, and focused on essentials. Lentini says that it was composed in the tenth century at the latest. Since it is found in a number of manuscripts from the tenth and eleventh centuries, it may be considerably older. It did not have as wide a circulation as the other Lenten hymns in the *Liturgia Horarum*. It is eminently suited to the season of Lent, however, in the sobriety of the thematic content and the scriptural allusion with which it begins. It was traditionally assigned to the night office, the "Nocturns," and is now assigned to the Office of Readings during the week.

STANZA 1

From the earliest centuries in the Western Church, the passage from 2 Corinthians to which the first line alludes has been a scriptural icon of Lent. Referring to Isaiah, St. Paul says: "For it says, 'In an acceptable time I heard you, and on the day of salvation I helped you.' Behold, now is the acceptable time; behold, now is the day of salvation."[73] This verse reappears throughout Lenten offices in hymns, short readings at Sunday Vespers, verses, and other texts. As in the hymn for Lauds, *Iam, Christe, sol iustitiæ* (H 27: 2, 1), the acceptable time is presented as a gift of God (*datum divinitus*; line 2). The verb *fulget* (line 2) may seem surprising. It is a word used of bright light emanating from some source, as opposed to reflected light; it is said of stars and of lightning; it means "flash, glitter, gleam, shine, etc."[74] The first and literal meaning of the noun *fulgur* is "flash of lightning." At the resurrection, the Gospel of Matthew says of the angel, who came down from heaven and rolled back the stone: "his appearance was like lightning (*fulgur*), and his clothing was white as snow" (Mt 28:3).

The hymn says that the acceptable time shines or flashes forth as a gift from God. The theme of light will be developed in stanza 2. Here, at line 2, it is meant to surprise. It expresses a fundamental idea of the early Church: that fasting and abstinence bring light to the soul. Excess in food, drink, and in the suite of deadly sins that follow, clouds the intelligence and the spiritual senses of the soul. In the hymn *Æterne rerum conditor* (H 71), Ambrose prays to Christ: *Tu, lux, refulge sensibus / mentisque somnum discute*: "You, the light, shine brightly on our senses; scatter the sleep from our minds and hearts." The Latin *mens* is neither "mind" nor "heart" separately, but used together they approximate the idea of deep-seated conviction, disposition, and intention so often implied by the Latin *mens*. The hymns of Prudentius are also filled with variations on this theme. The following stanza from *Cathemerinon* 2 would have been well-known to generations of hymn writers after him:

---

73. *ait enim, "tempore accepto exaudivi te et in die salutis adiuvavi te"; ecce nunc tempus acceptabile, ecce nunc dies salutis* (2 Cor 6:2 with Is 49:8).

74. Scriptural references to *fulget* and related forms: Ps 96:4; Ez 1:13–14; Mt 13:43; Mt 24:27; Lk 17:24; Lk 10:18, etc.

Sol ecce surgit igneus:	Behold, the fiery sun appears!
piget, pudescit, pænitet,	Then shame, remorse, contrition come:
nec teste quisquam lumine	and with the witness of the light
peccare constanter potest.	none dares persist in sinfulness.[75]

The light of Christ, symbolized by the rising of the sun, opens up the murky reserves of the human heart. He bestows upon us the gift of Lent as a season of grace in which his light may heal and purify our wounded hearts (*corda saucia*) and a weary and languishing world (*orbem languidum*).[76] The hymn is filled with terms connected to health and healing. In line 3: *sano* (heal, cure) and *languidus* (feeble, languid; sick), in line 4: *medela* (remedy, medicine, cure); and in stanza 2, 3: *saucia* (wounded, sick). Other words, *parsimoniæ* in 1, 4 (frugality), *salutis* at 2, 2 (welfare, spiritual and physical safety), and *abstinentia* at 2, 4 (abstinence, self-restraint) are, in the context of the hymn, related to health and healing.

Line 3 begins with *ut*, signifying purpose here. We have been given the divine gift of Lent, in order that "the medicine of abstinence may heal the entire world (*orbem*) that is languishing (*languidum*) in sickness and sin." In stanza 2, it will be a question of healing the individual hearts of those who sing. Here the scope is universal. The implication is that we who sing and to whom Lent has been given are somehow engaged in the healing process of the whole world. As in the parable of the leaven, which a woman hid in three measures of flower, until all was leavened, we too may hide our Lenten observances as leaven in the endless measures of the world (Mt 13:33). We are in some way healing balm (*medela*). The Latin *medela* is found in many places throughout the corpus of hymns.[77]

Thus, in this hymn and in the other hymns for Lent, the remedy that fits the need is *abstinentia*, or *parsimonia*. If we remove the negative connotations often associated with this second term in English, "parsimony," we have a good idea of what the Latin means. It signifies frugality, the discipline of using the goods we have without excess or indulgence. In Christian usage, it is a synonym for fasting and abstinence. Prudentius uses it in his hymn for those who fast, *Cathemerinon* 7: 1, 3–5:

adesto castis, Christe, parsimoniis,	assist, O Christ, our pious abstinence:
festumque nostrum rex serenus aspice,	O King, with favor view this holy day,
ieiuniorum dum litamus victimam	on which we make the offering of our fast.[78]

---

75. Trans. Richardson, *Hymns*, 35. See H 87. In the Liturgy of the Hours, two hymns for Lauds are centos taken from Prudentius's *Cathemerinon* 2: H 83 and H 87. The stanza above is no. 7 in the original hymn, no. 1 in H 87.

76. See also *Conditor alme siderum* (H 1), 2, 3.

77. For example, in *Audi, benigne conditor* (H 22), the hymn for Sunday Vespers during Lent, the same connection is made between *medela* and *languidus*. Stanza 3, 1 and 4 are: *Multum quidem peccavimus ... confer medelam languidis*: "We have greatly sinned ... grant us (apply to us) your medicine for the sick." In stanza 4, the medicine and the regime are described as fasting for the body, with the result (in line 3) that the sober mind (*mens sobria*) may abstain from sin.

78. Trans. Richardson, *Hymns*, 55. The Latin hymn is in iambic trimeter. See appendix 1, on meter, no. 3,

"Abstinence" does not have exactly the same resonance as *parsimonia*, but it is a good translation here in the context of Lent. Note also the *victimam ieiuniorum*. The hymn asks Christ to look with a serene countenance (*serenus* modifies *rex*) upon the *victimam*, as in a sacrificial victim. Prudentius sees fasting as a liturgical act of expiation; such acts are beneficial to the one offering but also to others on behalf of whom the sacrifice is offered.[79]

A close parallel, *parcus*, (here the comparative: *parcius*), is in the hymn for the Office of Readings on Sundays during Lent, *Ex more docti mystico* (H 24, stanza 3):

> Utamur ergo *parcius*   So let us use with more restraint
> verbis, cibis et potibus,   our speech, our sleep, our idle mirth,
> somno, iocis et arctius   and, frugal in our food and drink,
> perstémus in custodia.   stand guard with heightened vigilance

Another form of the word, *parcitas*, is found in the hymn *Iam lucis orto sidere* (H 115, stanza 3) used on Thursday at Lauds in Weeks II and IV:

> Sint pura cordis intima,   Then let our inmost heart be pure
> absistat et vecordia;   and free of senseless ignorance;
> carnis terat superbiam   may sparing use of food and drink
> potus cibique parcitas;   wear down the lustful pride of flesh,

Both of these hymns reflect the principle that the self-control and abstinence from excess are the essential discipline of Lent and of daily life for a Christian. The purpose of *parsimonia / parcitas / abstinentia* is to free the soul from the tyranny of the body and the foolishness this engenders. The term *vecordia* (line 2 in the last example above) is the want of deep-seated reason, a lack that arises out of a disordered heart.

STANZA 2

Stanza 2 opens with an allusion to the first stanza of St. Ambrose's hymn *Deus creator omnium* (H 68). This hymn has been sung at Vespers from time immemorial. It is in the Old Hymnal, known to be in use in the sixth century.[80] In the *Confessions* 9.12, Augustine ascribes the hymn to Ambrose and gives the first two stanzas when he describes his sorrow at Monica's death and the solace this hymn

---

"Iambic Trimeter," under the section "Meters in the *Liturgia Horarum*." Richardson has rendered the hymn into English iambic pentameter.

79. The Latin *parsimonia* also appears in the original version of *Iesu, quadragenariæ* (H 23). Here it is the means by which we regain Paradise after the Fall. It is in direct opposition to a colorful name for gluttony (*gastrimargia*) known to the writer of this early hymn from monastic circles: *quo paradiso redderes / servata parsimonia, / quos inde gastrimargiæ / huc illecebra depulit* (stanza 2 of the original version). The doxologies of hymns for Sunday Offices during Lent also contain the word *parcitas*. It is a substitute introduced by Lentini for *ieiunium*.

80. For a discussion of the "Old Hymnal," see the historical accounts in Walpole, xi–xix; Gneuss, *Latin Hymns*, 408–13, with the tables on 418–21; and Milfull, 1–8.

gave him. Of all of Ambrose's hymns, this one was perhaps best known to later hymn writers. Here is stanza 1:

Deus, creator omnium	O God, Creator of the world
polique rector, vestiens	and Ruler of the sky above,
diem decoro lumine,	you clothe the day with splendid light
noctem soporis gratia,	and night with gracious gifts of sleep,

In Ambrose's hymn, God, the creator of all things and the one who governs and orders the vault of heaven (*polus*), clothes the day with beautiful, gracious, splendid light, and the night with the gift of sleep. The hymn is filled with praise and thanksgiving for God's provident care and a prayer that he continue to care for us at night, that the light of faith may know no setting but may cause night to be bright as day. The steps from day to faith and from faith to Christ himself are short. These images have been combined and reforged by the writer of this Lenten hymn into the first two lines of stanza 2. This is how the tradition lives. The beautiful radiant light belongs to Christ as it always has (*Christi decore lumine*); just as the physical day is filled with his splendid light, so also does the day of salvation shine brightly with the same light (*dies salutis emicat*). Lines 3 and 4 open with the conjunction *dum*: "while, as, during the time in which." The day of salvation gleams with the beautiful, splendid light of Christ, as *abstinentia* forms anew the hearts made ill and wounded (*saucia*) by sin.

STANZA 3

Stanzas 1 and 2 have described the *tempus acceptabile* and shown the conditions under which the day of salvation will shine forth for us in this life. Stanza 3 is a prayer. It opens with a demonstrative pronoun (*hanc*), which refers back to the healing work of abstinence described in stanza 2. The structure of lines 1 and 2 is stark and somewhat convoluted. The phrase *mente nos et corpore* fits the meter; it also emphasizes that our petition concerns the mind and heart as well as the body, spiritual as well as physical observance; *nos* (line 1) is an accusative subject of *tenere* (line 2) and *perfice* functions almost like the imperative *fac*, "make," except that it is more intense. Literally, these lines mean: "O God, make us hold fast to this regime in mind and body ..."

Lines 3 and 4 express the goal we seek. There are six words, three per line; all are weight-bearing and filled with richness. First, *ut* is a conjunction that introduces a purpose clause: "in order that": make us hold fast to our Lenten practices *so that* we may reach the goal. Here, however, as is often the case with the divine work of God, since "God accomplishes everything whatsoever he wills" (Ps 113 [115]:3), *ut* also signifies result: if we are faithful to the Lenten observance, we will surely reach the goal. Second, *appetamus* is the verb; it has a basic meaning of "seek, go after or toward, try to get." Then, it can mean "to strive after earnestly, desire eagerly, to long for." There are other senses as well. Here it means "earnestly long for, strive to reach, take all the appropriate means, etc."[81] As is often the case in the hymns, *prospero* at the end of line 3 and *transitu* at the end of line 4 form a pair. *Transitus* signifies, "going across, passing, transition," but also "passing away." A *transitus* is a passing through death to life after death, and this idea of "death" cannot be fully dissociated from the meaning; *prospero* is similar to its English cognate. The two are ablatives here and signify "by a prosperous passing," or "by a happy death." Finally, the goal is the *perenne pascha*, the eternal Pasch, in which the sacrifice of Christ will determine our eternal happiness.

STANZA 4

For discussion of this doxology, see the commentaries on H 23 and H 27.

Precemur omnes cernui	26
Attributed to St. Gregory the Great, d. 604	Sundays of Lent
8 8 8 8	Lauds

Precémur omnes cérnui,	1. Let all of us bow down in prayer,
clamémus atque sínguli,	let each with sorrow raise a cry,
plorémus ante iúdicem,	and let us weep before the Judge,
flectámus iram víndicem:	forestalling his avenging wrath.
Nostris malis offéndimus	2. O God, our faults and evil deeds
tuam, Deus, cleméntiam;	offend your loving clemency;
effúnde nobis désuper,	pour forth upon us from above
remíssor, indulgéntiam.	forgiveness and remission, Lord.
Meménto quod sumus tui,	3. Remember, we belong to you,
licet cadúci, plásmatis;	formed by your hand, yet prone to fall;
ne des honórem nóminis	do not bestow, O Lord, we pray,
tui, precámur, álteri.	on others honor due your name.
Laxa malum quod fécimus,	4. Forgive the evil we have done,
auge bonum quod póscimus,	increase the good for which we pray,
placére quo tandem tibi	by which we may be fit at last
possímus hic et pérpetim.	to please you here and evermore.
Præsta, beáta Trínitas,	5. Grant us, O Blessed Trinity,
concéde, simplex Unitas,	O Undivided Unity,
ut fructuósa sint tuis	to see this service of our fast
hæc parcitátis múnera. Amen.	bring forth your fruit within our hearts. Amen.

---

81. When speaking of Abraham and his descendants in the Promised Land, Heb 11:15–16 says: "If they had borne in mind the land from which they had come, they would have had the opportunity to return. But now they strive after a better homeland, a heavenly one. Therefore, God is not ashamed to be called their God, for he has prepared a city for them": *Si quidem illius meminissent de qua exierunt, habebant utique tempus revertendi. Nunc autem meliorem appetunt, id est cælestem; ideo non confunditur Deus vocari Deus eorum paravit enim illis civitatem.*

Text found in *TDH*, no. 96; *AH* 51, no. 55; Walpole, no. 94; this hymn is the second half of H 24. Changes in *TDH*: stanza 1, 1: *Precemur* for *Dicamus*.

COMMENTARY

This hymn is the second half of H 24. It was divided before the fourteenth or fifteenth century.[82] The first word of line 1 (*Dicamus*), which in the original hymn connected this half of the hymn to the first half, was changed to *Precemur*, in order to establish the tone of prayer at the beginning of the present hymn.[83] The first stanza continues the pattern of H 24; it is an exhortation addressed to those who sing the hymn. The second stanza begins a prayer to God, which from 2, 3 to the end is a succession of petitions organized into couplets. This hymn is strongly influenced by Prudentius's hymn on fasting (*Cath* 7). As in H 22, there is a focus on God the Creator, his fashioning of us, and his influence on our lives. The prayer of the Church begins and ends with a desire that God remember his creation and make it pleasing to himself.

STANZA 1

Looking back to the first half of the original hymn (H 24), the Church continues to exhort its members to prayer and repentance. While H 24 largely consists of encouragement to persevere in the fast, *Precemur* marks a shift toward prayer and a direct appeal to God.

The verbs in this stanza (*clamemus, ploremus*) evoke the language of the psalms: "this poor man cried and the Lord heard him": *Iste pauper clamavit, et Dominus exaudivit eum* (Ps 33 [34]:7); "and let us weep before the Lord who made us": *et ploremus ante Dominum qui fecit nos* (Ps 94:6).[84] Prudentius also writes: *Iesum ciamus vocibus / flentes, precantes, sobrii*: "To Jesus raise we now our voice / in tearfulness and sober prayer" (H 113: 4, 1–2).[85] Weeping (*ploremus*) appears frequently in the Lenten hymns (see H 22). In the book of Tobit, the Angel Raphael highlights this connection between praying, fasting, and weeping when he says, "Prayer is good with fasting ... when you were praying with tears and burying the dead, and leaving behind your meal, I offered your prayer to God."[86]

In lines 3 and 4, the hymn reminds us that God is our Judge and that he will surely punish sin: let us weep before the Judge (line 3) and so deflect his avenging

---

82. See Milfull, 242.

83. *TDH*, 98.

84. In the same verse, Jerome translates the Hebrew as follows: Ps. 94:6, *iuxta Hebraicum*: *Flectamus genua ante faciem Domini factoris nostri*: "Let us bend our knees before the face of the Lord our Creator."

85. Trans. Richardson, *Hymns*, 34. See also H 83: 4, 1–4, as well: *Te, Christe, solum novimus, / te mente pura et simplici / rogare curvato genu / flendo et canendo discimus*: "To Thee, with pure and simple mind, / Thee with our voice and pious chant,/ on bended knee we learn to pray, / and mingle singing with our tears" (trans. Richardson, *Hymns*, 36).

86. *bona est oratio cum ieiunio ... quando orabas cum lacrimis et sepeliebas mortuos et derelinquebas prandium ... ego obtuli orationem tuam Domino* (Tb 12:8, 12).

wrath (line 4). Scripture is filled with references to the Lord as *iudex*. In the Psalms, God is *iudex iustus* (Ps 74:8), who will come to judge all the earth: "The mountains shall rejoice at the presence of the Lord: because he will come to judge the earth. He shall judge the world with justice, and the people with equity."[87] St. Paul says to Timothy: "Henceforth, there is laid up for me a crown of justice, which the Lord the just judge will render to me in that day."[88] In the Acts of the Apostles, when Cornelius, the Roman centurion, requested that Peter come to Joppa, Peter gave a sermon that is recorded in Acts 10. After giving a brief account of the mission of Christ, Peter says: "and he commanded us to preach to the people and to testify that he is the one appointed by God to be judge of the living and the dead."[89]

God is also an avenger of evil. In response to one who boasts, Sirach says "God will surely take revenge."[90] At the beginning of the Book of Isaiah, the Lord says: "I will take vengeance on my enemies"[91]; when St. Paul writes to the Thessalonians that they should abstain from sins, he says that "the Lord is an avenger of all these things."[92]

In this stanza, there are also many echoes of Prudentius's hymn on fasting. He describes Moses as eating only his tears, with his face to the ground (*ore cernuo, Cath* 7: 9, 3). Jonah says to the Ninevites that the "wrath of the high avenger hangs overhead."[93] After they proclaim a great fast, Prudentius calls God the meek avenger (*mitis Ultor*), and Jonah knows that "the threatening Judge (*minacem Iudicem*) prefers to save rather than strike and beat."[94]

The rhyme and assonance of this stanza is artful; the three-syllable verbs at the head of each line create a succession of internal rhymes based on the repetition of the same third syllable "mus": *dicamus* (in the original) ... *clamemus* ... *ploremus* ... *flectamus*. The second syllable of each word, the penultimate, is long since it contains a long vowel, a, e, e, a, and as a result, it has a stress accent. Each line of the stanza also ends with a three-syllalble word having a stress accent on the first syllable. Thus, all lines in this stanza have exactly the same rhythm, based on a regular succession of a three-syllable word followed by a two-syllable word, followed by a three-syllable word. Each couplet also has end-rhyme. The first describes those who sing the hymn: *cernui* (line 1) and *singuli* (line 2). The second describes Christ: *iudicem* (line 3) and *vindicem* (line 4). Finally, assonance on *atque*

---

87. *Montes exultabunt a conspectu Domini: quoniam venit iudicare terram. Iudicabit orbem terrarum in iustitia, et populus æquitate* (Ps 97 [98]:8–9).

88. *In reliquo reposita est mihi corona iustitiæ, quam reddet mihi Dominus in illa die, iustus iudex* (2 Tm 4:8).

89. *et præcepit nobis prædicare populo et testificari quia ipse est qui constitutus est a Deo iudex vivorum et mortuorum* (Acts 10:42). See also the final judgment of the nations in Mt 25:31–46 and Rv 20:11–15 and the Niceno-Constantinopolitan Creed: *Et iterum venturus est cum gloria, iudicare vivos et mortuos*: "He will come again in glory to judge the living and the dead."

90. *Deus enim vindicans vindicabit* (Sir 5:3).

91. *vindicabor de inimicis meis* (Is 1:24).

92. *vindex est Dominus de his omnibus* (1 Thes 4:6).

93. *impendet, inquit, ira summi vindicis* (Cath 7: 27, 4).

94. *Mitis ultor... sed nosset [Iona] ... minacem iudicem / servare malle quam ferire ac plectere* (Cath 7: 21, 1, 3–4).

(line 2) and *ante* (line 3) in the middle of the lines joins the two couplets. Consequently, line 1 rhymes with 2 (at the end); line 2 rhymes with 3 (at the beginning and in the middle); line 3 rhymes with 4 (at the end); and lines 2–4 all have internal rhyme at the end of the first word.

STANZA 2

In the context of the whole hymn (including the first half, H 24), this stanza shifts from the Church's addressing its members to a series of prayers and petitions to God. These are arranged in couplets throughout stanzas 2–4.

This stanza seems to be influenced by a very ornate passage in Prudentius's hymn on fasting, in which he describes the beginning of God's anger at the Ninevites: *offensa tandem iugis indulgentiæ / Censura iustis excitatur motibus.*[95] The hymn writer here, however, inverts this passage of Prudentius to emphasize God's forgiveness rather than his slowness to anger.

The structure and syntax of this stanza presents dichotomies between God and us: in the first two lines, *nostris malis* is compared to *tuam clementiam*. Line 1 ends with *offendimus*; line 2 ends with *clementiam*: we are sinners who offend against God's mercy. Line 1 begins with *nostris* and 2 begins with *tuam*, both are possessive adjectives. Thus, even word order creates a contrast: God, who is good, is compared to our evil deeds, and our offense finds itself juxtaposed to his mercy. This interlocking word order creates a visual image as well, since there are pairs at the beginning (*nostris* and *tuam*), in the middle (*malis* describing us and *Deus*), and at end of the line (*offendimus* and *clementiam*).

The petition in lines 3–4 evokes a legal or financial image. The agent noun *remissor* is a late word, appearing only in Christian authors and almost never in poetry. The action of *remissio* refers originally to sending something back in general but later develops a sense of freeing something or someone—specifically cancellation of debts or penalties. This legal and financial sense is taken into the Christian idiom to explain the remission of sins: Christ frees us from our debts, as he teaches us to pray in the Lord's Prayer, *dimitte nobis debita nostra, sicut et nos dimittimus debitoribus nostris.*[96] In the passage here, Christ, whose mercy endures forever (see Ps 135 [136]), is the generous canceller of debts, pouring out pardon after pardon from heaven (*effunde nobis desuper, / remissor, indulgentiam*). The Lord also taught us to pray that he deliver us from evil (*Libera nos a malo*); so too in this hymn we ask for similar freedom, for our debts are none other than the evil we have done.

This stanza does not continue the complex rhyme scheme of the previous one; instead, only two lines rhyme (*clementiam ... indulgentiam*), and the other two lines both have internal assonance—*o* and *i* in the first line (*nostris malis offendimus*), and *e* in the third (*effunde nobis desuper*). Because of this lack of assonance

---

95. "The offended judgement of continual mercy was, at last, roused with righteous passions" (*Cath* 7: 19, 1).
96. "Forgive us our trespasses as we forgive those who trespass against us."; *OLD*, s.v. *remitto* 13 and *dimitto* 7.

and rhyme, Albin thought this stanza was an interpolation.[97] Absolute consistency, however, is not to be expected in the rhyming scheme of these Latin hymns.

STANZA 3

Pimont says of this stanza: "to soften the heart of God, we remind him that, though we are fragile, his creating hands kneaded us."[98]

Caduci and *tui* in the first couplet are both ambiguous—each being either nominative plural and the subject of *sumus*, or genitive singular and modifying *plasmatis*. It can be either "remember that we are yours, although we belong to a fallen creation," or "remember that we belong to your creation, although we are fallen."[99] The editors of the Latin text have inserted a comma after *caduci*, which favors the second interpretation.

The Greek loan word *plasma* simply means a figure or a molded image, but it takes on a sense, in the works of Christian authors, of God's creation. Surprisingly, this word appears in this hymn and often in the hymns of Prudentius in the context of the Fall.[100] The two words, *caduci* and *plasmatis*, moreover, echo two lines about Christ in Prudentius's hymn on fasting: Christ incarnate is said to be "weighed down with limbs liable to fall (*caducis artubus*)," and he is called the "Emancipator of enslaved creation (*emancipator servientis plasmatis*)."[101]

Pimont says the last couplet is a reference to Psalm 78 (79):9: "Help us, O God our Savior: and for the glory of your name, O Lord, deliver us: and forgive our sins for your name's sake."[102] Moreover, there is a reference to Isaiah 42:8 and 48:11: "I will not give my glory to another."[103] The stanza uses a weak, one-syllable rhyme scheme with the outer and inner lines (*tui—alteri, plasmatis—nominis*).

STANZA 4

The last stanza before the doxology continues the constant prayer and petition that we see in all of the Lenten hymns. The first two lines of this stanza quickly and simply restate the petitions of the previous two stanzas, and the second couplet describes our sanctification through a complex relative clause of purpose.

Sin (*malum*) enslaves us, and we ask God that he free us (*laxa*). In the context of this hymn, the good for which we pray is the forgiveness of sins and preservation of God's honor in us, but with the imperative *auge*, we ask for an increase in grace and divine life. We see this in the second couplet: that which makes

---

97. Albin, *La Poésie du Bréviaire*, 149.

98. Pimont, 3:20–21: "*En maintenant, pour attendrir le cœur de Dieu, nous lui rappelons que, tout fragiles que nous sommes, ce sont ses mains créatrices qui nous ont pétris.*"

99. Two other alternatives are less likely: "remember that we, your people, although fallen, belong to creation," or "remember that we belong to your creation, although it is fallen."

100. *Cath* 3: 37, 5; 9: 31, 2. A similar word, *protoplastus*, appears in Fortunatus to refer to fallen Adam. See H 32: 2, 1; and Fortunatus, *Opera Poetica*, 10.2.2.

101. *Cath* 7: 36, 2, and 37, 4. This is the earliest of only three attestations of the word *emancipator* in Latin, and the only use outside of legal language.

102. *Adiuva nos, Deus, salutaris noster; et propter gloriam nominis tui, Domine, libera nos, et propitius esto peccatis nostris, propter nomen tuum* (Ps 78 [79]:9).

103. *Gloriam meam alteri non dabo* (Is 48:11).

us more pleasing to the Lord is sanctifying grace, or *gratia gratum faciens* (grace making [us] pleasing). In this stanza grace is *quo tibi placere possimus*.

The first two lines have an identical four-word structure and maintain internal and end rhyme (*-um quod ... -imus*). The second couplet does not rhyme, but instead plays on the consonance of p's and t's (*placere quo tandem tibi / possimus hic et perpetim*). The syntactical structure of the second couplet is more complex than that of other verses in this hymn, with the exception of the opening stanza of H 24. The three adverbs *tandem ... hic et perpetim* seem to give the sense that this was originally the end of the hymn, to which the doxology below was added.

STANZA 5

The doxology found here is placed at the end of three different hymns (H 22, H 24, H 26), all three of which are Lenten hymns attributed to St. Gregory the Great. For a detailed account, see H 22.

Iam, Christe, sol iustitiæ 27

6th c. Weekdays of Lent
8 8 8 8 Lauds

Iam, Christe, sol iustítiæ,	1. O Sun of Justice, Christ our Lord,
mentis dehíscant ténebræ,	as you restore the day to earth,
virtútum ut lux rédeat,	now rend the darkness of our minds,
terris diem cum réparas.	that light from virtue may return.
Dans tempus acceptábile	2. In this, your favored time of grace,
et pænitens cor tríbue,	Lord, grant repentance from the heart,
convértat ut benígnitas	that your compassion may convert
quos longa suffert píetas;	all those your love has long endured.
Quiddámque pæniténtiæ	3. Grant us to bear the penances
da ferre, quo fit démptio,	that bring atonement for our sins:
maióre tuo múnere,	however great our faults and guilt
culpárum quamvis grándium.	yet greater is your gift of grace.
Dies venit, dies tua,	4. The day shall come, your holy day,
per quam reflórent ómnia;	through which all things will flower again;
lætémur in hac ut tuæ	let us rejoice, for through this day
per hanc redúcti grátiæ.	your grace will lead us back to you.
Te rerum univérsitas,	5. Let all your works adore you, Lord,
clemens, adóret, Trínitas.	O merciful and Triune God.
et nos novi per véniam	Renewed by pardon, let us sing
novum canámus cánticum. Amen.	a new song to your holy name. Amen.

Text found in *TDH*, 97; AH 51, no. 59; Walpole, no. 97. Changes in *TDH*: stanza 3, lines 2–4: *da ferre, quo fit demptio, / maiore tuo munere, / culparum quamvis grandium* for *da ferre, quamvis grandium / maiore tuo munere, / quo demptio fit criminum*.

COMMENTARY

This hymn is an ancient Lenten hymn in continuous use, dated by scholarly consensus to the sixth century and present in the earliest extant hymnals.[104] It has been traditionally assigned to the hour of Lauds. It is composed in accentual meter without regard for the quantities of syllables. The sixth syllable of the line often has a stressed short syllable. As a result, the hymn was extensively edited during the Urbanite reform; it is found in the *Breviarium Romanum* under the title *O sol salutis, intimis*. The original hymn has elements of rhyme, though it is irregular, and there are instances of hiatus in places where both accentual and quantitative meter would favor elision. These metrical irregularities make the hymn dateable to the period before the Carolingian reforms.[105]

The hymn is based on a layering of three different senses of dawn and light. In some hymns the composite picture is built up stanza by stanza; here all three senses are superimposed from the beginning. The first image is dawn: the morning as it brings back light into the world; second, grace: the new dawn of salvation; third, Christ: himself, the true day, on the day of his Resurrection.[106] The influence of Ambrose and Prudentius is marked.

STANZA 1

The opening *iam*, "now," places the singer in *medias res*, "in the middle of things." Those who sing the hymn witness the sun rise over the horizon as they sing the first line, and they address Christ directly (*Christe* is vocative), invoking him with the prophetic name "Sun of justice" (*Sol iustitiæ*), alluding to the prophecy of Malachi: *et orietur vobis timentibus nomen meum sol iustitiæ et sanitas in pennis eius*: "But for you who fear my name, there will arise the sun of justice with healing in its rays" (Mal 5:2).[107]

The foundational image in this stanza is the change wrought by the first appearance of the sun in the morning. It is helpful to remember that before the

---

104. The earliest hymnals date from the tenth century. If a hymn is in widespread use in these hymnals, it may be dated with some probability to the ninth or to an earlier century. *Iam, Christe, sol iustitiæ* is found in a hymnal from the Benedictine monastery of St. Marial in Limoges, now labeled Cod. Parisin. 1240. This manuscript was copied between 933 and 936 (see AH 51, pp. xxxii and 59). For the dating of the hymn, see *HIBR*, 99; Walpole, no. 97, p. 326; Szövérffy, *Annalen*, 2:452 (under the title from the Urbanite reform, *O Sol salutis intimis*); AH, 51, 60; Chevalier, *Repertorium*, no. 9205 and note, 552. All date it to the sixth century. Pimont, 3:25, dates it to the ninth century.

105. The sixth syllable is accented but short in every line of stanza 1, then at 2, 2 and 2, 4, and at 5, 3. The fourth syllable is accented but short at 3, 4. Hiatus occurs at 4, 3 and 5, 1.

106. See Connelly, 79.

107. Radiant light is one of the attributes of divinity; at the transfiguration Christ's face "shone as the sun" (Mt 17:2); see Heb 1:2; Rv 1:16.

advent of gas or electric lighting, the darkness of night was unmitigated, punctuated only by local and occasional sources of light. To be out of doors at night was to be subject to weighty darkness and to be exposed to all that lurks in darkness. At the first appearance of the sun all that was fearful and evil, all that lurked hiding under cover of darkness vanished, fled away in every direction. The light tore open the curtain of darkness to let life and goodness return once more. In this hymn, as in other early hymns, the image of the ray that scatters darkness and evil is rich and multivalent.

The colorful, poetic verb used in line 2 is *dehisco*; it is intransitive and signifies the action within the subject of "being split open, rent, divided asunder, burst or torn apart." Early Christian writers use it, as well as the more common *rumpo*, to describe the parting of the waters of the Red Sea (Ex 14:21), the gaping of the earth to swallow Korah, Dathan, and Abiram (Num 16:31), the bursting of old wineskins filled with new wine (Mt 9:17), or the breaking of the fishing nets under the weight of the great catch (Lk 5:6). In the hymn for None during Lent, *Ternis ter horis numerus* (H 30), *dehisco* is used with the same multivalence: "Death has died through the Cross, and after darkness, light returns; the bristling horror of sins has burst asunder, the splendor that fills minds and hearts shines forth."[108]

Prudentius is a source for the imagery of this stanza and for the hymn at large. *Cathemerinon* 1 and 2 are so filled with allusions to the advent of light and the scattering of evil and darkness that a full discussion is beyond the scope of this commentary. Here are several examples from Prudentius's hymns as they are found in the *Liturgia Horarum*.[109] Ambrose's hymns also have the same imagery, though because his hymns are short, the imagery is less expansive. The hymns from which these stanzas are taken are assigned to Lauds. In each, the physical level of the return of day, the moral level of the conflict with sin and darkness, and the spiritual level of Christ's intervention in human life are all superimposed. Christ is not named in the third example, but he is the Light that bears witness (*teste lumine*) to our sin and vanquishes it.

1) Tu, Christe, somnum disice,
   tu rumpe noctis vincula,
   tu solve peccatum vetus
   novumque lumen ingere.
     (H 113, stanza 5 and Prudentius,
     Cath 1: 25, 1–4)

O Christ, dispel and scatter sleep,
break through the bondage of the night,
release us from deep-rooted sin,
and with new light now flood our hearts.

---

108. *Mors per crucem nunc interit / et post tenebras lux redit; / horror dehiscat criminum, / splendor nitescat mentium* (H 30: 3, 1–4). A comparison of the verbs *dehisco* and *rumpo* in the Brepols Library of Latin Texts is revealing. The verb *rumpo* is used in all its forms approximately twelve times as often (3066 times) as *dehisco* (258 times), which is a poetic verb.

109. In addition to the examples given here, see *Cath* 1.10–12; H 71, stanza 6, 1–2; H 75, stanza 2 (Ambrose); H 95, stanzas 1–2; H 103, stanzas 1–3; and H 107, stanza 3.

2a) Nox et ten*eb*ræ et nubila,	O night and darkness, clouded gloom,
confusa mund*i* et turbida,	disturbed confusion of the world,
lux intrat albescit polus:	the dawn appears, the sky grows pale;
Christus venit; discedite.	disperse and go, for Christ comes forth.
2b) Caligo terræ scinditur	The veil of darkness, torn apart,
percussa solis spiculo,	is pierced by sharpened rays of sun;
rebusque iam color redit	now color is restored to earth
vultu nitentis sideris.	beneath the daystar's shining face.
(H 83, stanzas 1–2: Prudentius,	(see 2 Peter 1:19)
Cath 2.1–2)	
3) Sol ecce surgit igneus:	Behold the *fi*ery sun arise!
piget, pudescit, pænitet,	It troubles, shames, and brings remorse,
nec teste quisquam lumine	for no one can persist in sin
peccare constanter potest.	when light bears witness to our guilt.
(H 87, stanza 1: Prudentius,	
Cath 2.7, 1–4)	

In the hymn under discussion, *dehiscant* in line 2 is third person plural, subjunctive active. Lines 2 and 4 are in graphic syntax: *mentis* (line 2) and *terris* (line 4) both stand at the head of the line; they are in assonance and recognizable as a pair; they establish a bond between the advent of Christ, light for the mind, and the advent of day, light for the earth. The whole stanza is a prayer: when Christ, the sun of justice, rises, may the darkness and gloom of mind and heart be torn asunder, so that (*ut*, line 3) when he restores the physical day, or as he restores it, (*cum*, line 4), the light of virtue may flood the soul.[110] Pimont comments, "Jesus Christ is the source of all virtues, and these engender light just as vices accumulate darkness."[111]

STANZA 2

"For he [God] says: 'In an acceptable time I heard you, and on the day of salvation I helped you.' Behold, now is the acceptable time; behold, now is the day of salvation" (2 Cor 6:2). From the earliest centuries in the Western Church, this passage from 2 Corinthians has been associated with the Office and Mass during Lent.[112] Among other places, it is used as the short reading for the Second

---

110. Bastiaensen asks: "Is a given poetical text allegory or sacrament? Thus, with regard to the first stanza of the first hymn of the *Cathemerinon* the question must be asked: what connection is there between the figure of the crowing cock and the figure of the awakener Christ, both heralds of light? Is it referential only, the one evoking allegorically the image of the other, or is it a relationship at a deeper level, a kinship that makes us recognize the one in the other, the underlying assumption being that Nature's utterances are by way of being God's utterances, that in Nature's voice as in a sacrament it is the Creator of Nature who speaks?" (Bastiaensen, "Prudentius in Recent Literary Criticism," 129.)

111. Pimont, 3:12, 26.

112. The Latin text is *ait, enim: tempore accepto exaudivi te et in die salutis adiuvavi te; ecce nunc tempus acceptabile ecce nunc dies salutis* (2 Cor 6:2). St. Paul begins the verse with a shortened quotation from Is 49:8a: "Thus says the Lord: *hæc dicit Dominus in tempore placito exaudivi te et in die salutis auxiliatus sum tui et servavi te*: "In a time of favor I answered you, and on a day of salvation I helped you and saved you."

Vespers of the first five Sundays of Lent. Line 1 of stanza 2 is a clear allusion to this verse from St. Paul. It is another liturgical reminder that the acceptable time has come, and that it is a gift from God (*dans*). Recognizing the gift, we pray intensely (with an imperative rather than a subjunctive) that he give us also a heart that repents. Regret for sin and the desire to amend are a grace. We pray for a contrite heart so that his kindness may lead to conversion those whom his steadfast love has long endured. *Cor mundum crea in me Deus et spiritum rectum innova in visceribus meis*: "Create a clean heart in me, O God, and renew a righteous spirit within me" (Ps 50[51]:12). The Lord's reply comes to us each day during Lent at Sext: *Vivo ego dicit Dominus Deus nolo mortem impii sed ut revertatur impius a via sua et vivat*: "As I live, says the Lord, I take no pleasure in the death of the wicked, but rather that the wicked should turn back from his ways and live" (Ez 3:11).[113] God hates the sin, but loves the sinner. We recognize that we have tried his patience, but we pray with confidence.

STANZA 3

Stanza 3 has been significantly modified by Lentini and his team, primarily through the rearrangement of lines 2–4. The note in *TDH* after the hymn says, "We wanted to make the convoluted construction plainer and easier, preserving the same words." Here are the two versions:

Original	*Lentini's adaptation*
Quiddamque pænitentiæ	Quiddamque pænitentiæ
da ferre, quamvis grandium	da ferre, quo fit demptio,
maiore tuo munere,	maiore tuo munere,
quo demptio fit criminum:	culparum quamvis grandium.

The words are preserved; lines 1 and 3 remain unchanged. In the other lines, the only substitution is *culparum* for *criminum*, necessary in order to maintain the meter when words are placed differently in the line. The rhyme is lost on the final syllables of *grandium* and *criminum*. The syntax is simpler, but strangely, much of the message of the stanza is lost. In poetic texts, including liturgical hymns, content is not everything. The associations brought to mind as the hymn is sung are also part of the message. The hymn is a dialogue, in a sense, between the writer and the singer.

In the original hymn, the word order is slightly chaotic. The hymn writer intended a syntactical scramble, in order to expand the meaning of the stanza. He is making an emotional point, not a logical one. It is important to remember that these Latin hymns have the pathos of real prayer in time of need. Thus, the first phrase begins simply: "Grant us to endure to some degree at least, a measure—the

---

113. Stanza 2 is an indirect commentary on Rom 2:4: *An divitias benignitatis eius et patientiæ et longanimitatis contemnis, ignorans quoniam benignitas Dei ad pænitentiam te adducit?*: "Or do you hold his priceless kindness, forbearance, and patience in low esteem, unaware that the kindness of God would lead you to repentance?"

prescribed measure—of penance."[114] We know that our penance cannot be proportionate to the sins we are expiating, but it is the penance determined by the Church as part of the Lenten observance. In the middle of the second line, there is an intrusion: *quamvis grandium*, "though they are great." What things are great? We do not yet know what the hymn writer is referring to, only that they are great. It is a moment of emotional disarray. The eye is drawn down to the word below, at the end of line 4 where it sees *criminum*: sins, crimes. A *crimen* is a deed for which one may be condemned in court. A *culpa* may be as serious, but it may also be "fault, failure, defect." Thus, *culpa* may be a synonym for *crimen*, but it does not have the emotional weight of *crimen*. In between *grandium* and *criminum*, we find *maiore tuo munere*: "by your greater gift"; *grandium* and *maiore* are juxtaposed, one right after the other: our sins are great, but in the same breath we realize that God's gift is greater than the greatest of sins. *Ubi autem abundavit delictum superabundavit gratia*: "Where sin increased, grace overflowed all the more" (Rom 5:20). In this stanza of the original hymn, there are three instances of graphic syntax:

1. the interruption in the middle of line 2;
2. the vertical placement of *grandium* and *criminum*; and
3. the placement side by side, as the stanza is sung, of *grandium* and *maiore*.

These transform the stanza into a masterpiece of poetic genius. Walpole thinks that *quo* (3, 4) is an adverb signifying purpose, "in order that";[115] his reason is in part because it comes so late in the stanza. In Lentini's reworking, it comes before line 3 instead of after; is it a relative pronoun in the ablative referring to *quiddam* or *munere*? It is not entirely clear. In any case, *demptio* means "removal, taking away." The original hymn places it before *criminum*, which is what is removed. In Lentini's version, it is farther away from its complement.[116] When we arrive at line 4, we figure out that *demptio* goes with *culparum*, but then *quamvis grandium* is slipped in afterwards almost as an afterthought. The impact of the original is weakened in this respect.

STANZA 4

Stanza 4 is the counterpart to stanza 3. Stanza 3 presents the sustained effort of Lent in the face of the reality of our sinfulness. Stanza 4 presents the results of this effort that are beyond proportion to the Lenten observance. The greater gift (*maiore tuo munere*: 3, 3) that sustains us through Lent will show itself in the beauty of Easter morning. This hymn is sung at Lauds every weekday morning through the long weeks of Lent. The fourth stanza brings encouragement and consolation, a reminder that Lenten penance leads to Easter joy.

---

114. All of this qualification and hesitation is captured by *quiddam*.
115. Walpole, l. 12, p. 328.
116. The ancient, root meaning of the verb *emo* is " take." It is commonly used to mean "purchase" (take in exchange for money given). Redemption comes from the verb *redimo*: re + *emo*, "buy (take) back"; "d" is added between two vowels for ease of pronunciation. Christ has taken away our sins by making atonement for them; he has also bought us back. *Demptio* is a shortened form of *redemptio*.

In stanza 4, the hymn still addresses Christ directly, but here it is a reflection in his presence on the great work he will accomplish for us. The poet says in essence: "The day is coming that belongs to you as no other day; it is *dies tua*. Nature is reborn; grace is reborn. In you, we and all the earth are a new creation": *nova creatura*.[117] Again, nature (the physical morning), grace (redemption), and Christ himself are superimposed. The freshness of nature is an image of the freshness, newness, and beauty of grace. The blossoms of spring, the flowers of the field that are more beautiful than Solomon in all his glory are the fitting image of a new spiritual creation; the One who made Paradise has remade it yet more wonderfully.[118] The Church sings repeatedly throughout the liturgy of the Easter Octave: *Hæc est dies quam fecit Dominus; exsultemus et lætemur in ea*: "This is the day the Lord has made; let us rejoice in it and be glad" (Ps 117 [118]:24).

Finally, Christ himself is the day; he is the Sun of Justice risen definitively upon the world. He will perform the greatest of miracles in his own Resurrection, and he will bestow upon us and on the entire earth the fruits of his own life that will never die; he will be with us even "until the end of the age" (Mt 28:20). Pimont comments, "He will illumine the world forever. Just as flowers in Spring, so our souls bloom under the radiance of the divine Sun and recover from the cold and darkness of sin."[119] Ambrose puts it succinctly in his hymn *Splendor paternæ gloriæ* (H 75).[120] Not only is Easter Christ's day; he himself is the day.

Both Walpole and Connelly comment on the thematic resonances between this stanza and the magnificent poem for Easter by Venantius Fortunatus. The poem was originally sent as a letter to Bishop Felix of Nantes, in honor of his receiving into the Church a group of Saxons on Easter Sunday, sometime before the mid-570s.[121] The poem is in elegiac couplets. Lines 32–33 read:

Ecce renascentis testator gratia mundi omnia cum Domino dona redisse suo.	Behold, the loveliness of a world in rebirth testifies that all gifts return with her Lord.

Through many centuries, lines 39–40 have provided the refrain for countless processional hymns based on verses from this poem and used at Easter and other occasions:[122]

---

117. See 2 Cor 5:17: *Si qua ergo in Christo, nova creatura; vetera transierunt: ecce facta sunt nova*: "So whoever is in Christ is a new creation: the old things have passed away; behold, new things have come." See also Gal 6:15; Is 65:17–19.

118. "O God, who wonderfully created the dignity of human nature and still more wonderfully restored it, …" from the prayer after the first reading at the Solemn Easter Vigil (Roman Missal, 2011).

119. Pimont, 3:12, 28–29.

120. See stanza 1, 4: *diem dies illuminans*. This is the emendation accepted by Lentini because it is easier to sing. The original text, however, reads: *dies dierum illuminans*. An elision, commonly admitted in Ambrose's day, is required on *dierum illuminans*. The genitive *dierum*, placed between *dies* and *illuminans*, is multivalent. In the hymn, the phrase is addressed to Christ: you are the day of days shining forth, the day that illumines all days. *Dominus illuminatio mea et salus mea; quem timebo?*: "The Lord is my light and my salvation; whom shall I fear?" (Ps 26 [27]:1). See also, Walpole, no. 3, lines 3-4, p. 36; Bulst, 40; Fontaine, 189–90. See also Ambrose, *In Ps 118*, 12, 26.

121. See George, *Venantius Fortunatus*, 113–23. See also Connelly, no. 51, lines 13–14, p. 79 and Walpole, no. 97, lines 13–14, p. 328.

122. Walpole, p. 182.

Salve festa dies toto venerabilis ævo qua Deus infernum vicit et astra tenet.	Hail, festival day, revered for all time, when God has conquered hell and holds the stars.

Stanza 4 of the present hymn is built around three prepositional phrases, all referring to "day." The Latin *dies* is usually masculine in gender, but if the day is a particular day, an appointed day, it is often feminine. Here, this greatest of all days is feminine, as it is in Psalm 117[118]:24 (*hæc dies*) and in the poem of Venantius Fortunatus above (*festa dies*). The prepositional phrases are found in line 2, *per quam*: "through which (day)"; at line 3, *in hac*: "in this (day)"; and at line 4, *per hanc*: "through this (day)." The *per quam* of line 2 introduces the relative clause: "through which all things revive, rebloom." In line 3, we are invited to rejoice (*lætemur*) in or on this day (*in hac*): "Let us rejoice in this (day)" (see Ps 117[118]:24). The exhortation is followed by an *ut* clause. The Latin conjunction *ut* has many uses. Here it goes with a participle in line 4 (*reducti*), which is the past participle of the verb *reduco*, "lead back." Lines 3 and 4 end with *tuæ* and *gratiæ*; one must read them together and insert *per hanc*.[123] The Latin phrase *lætemur in hac ut tuæ / per hanc reducti gratiæ* in English word order means "Let us rejoice in this day since we are led back through this day to your grace."

STANZA 5

In the *Liturgia Horarum*, stanza 5 is the doxology for this hymn. It is found in most of the ancient versions and seems to have belonged to the original composition, perhaps as the doxology, but the manuscript tradition is unclear. Throughout the Middle Ages, doxologies were moved and shared. In AH 51, a doxology is added to this hymn beyond the present stanza. It is the same as the doxology now used in the hymns for Sundays during Lent. Lentini and his *cœtus* decided to use stanza 5 of this hymn as the doxology for weekdays during Lent.

Lines 1 and 2 are a prayer that the entirety of creation (*rerum universitas*) may be brought to adore the merciful Trinity. This is St. Paul's prayer: "that at the name of Jesus every knee should bend, of those in heaven and on earth and under the earth" (Phil 2:10). The phrase *rerum universitas* is found in the book of Tobit 8:19. Though various combinations of the words *rerum universitas* may be found elsewhere in Latin authors, the use of the phrase to signify the whole of what is, whether or not one thinks of it as a created whole, is primarily found in late Latin texts, most of them by Christian authors.[124] In the *City of God*, St. Augustine says: *sicut pictura cum colore nigro loco suo posito, ita universitas rerum, si quis possit intueri, etiam cum peccatoribus pulchra est, quamvis per se ipsos consideratos sua deformitas turpet*: "Just as a picture with the color black in the appropriate place, so also the universality of things, if one could see it, is beautiful, even with sinners, although

---

123. Notice that the line endings in the last two lines of this stanza (*tuæ, gratiæ*) correspond to the endings of lines 2 and 4 in stanza 3 (*grandium, criminum*). This seems to be a strategy favored by the author of this hymn. These two instances of graphic syntax are complementary in sense as well as in form. Great crimes (*grandium, criminum*) are healed by your grace (*tuæ gratiæ*).

124. One finds a few instances of the phrase used in a quasi-philosophical sense in Cicero (e.g., *De natura deorum*, I.39 and I.120) and elsewhere, but the overwhelming majority of uses come from Christian authors.

their deformity makes them ugly when they are considered by themselves."[125]

Venia may mean "kindness, permission, indulgence," but in line 3, it has the stronger meaning of "pardon, remission, forgiveness" in relation to a misdeed or sin. In the context of the hymn, we are led back to grace through the gift of pardon and remission of sin, either through baptism or through Lenten penance.[126] In lines 3–4, there is a typical Latinate play on the words *novi* (line 3) and *novum* (line 4). We who have received the grace of pardon are new creatures, recreated by the gracious gift obtained for us by our Lord Jesus Christ, and so we may sing a new song of praise to the Triune God. The phrase *canticum novum* is found throughout the Psalter, in Isaiah, and in the Book of Revelation.[127] At Revelation 5:9, those who have been redeemed by the blood of the Lamb sing a new song: "Worthy are you to receive the scroll and to break open its seals, for you were slain and with your blood you purchased for God those from every tribe and tongue, people and nation."[128]

Dei fide, qua vívimus	28
8th c. 8 8 8 8	Ash Wednesday until Good Friday Terce

Dei fide, qua vívimus, qua spe perénni crédimus, per caritátis grátiam Christi canámus glóriam,	1. With faith in God by which we live, by lasting hope that spurs on faith, and by the grace of charity we sing the glory of the Christ.
Qui ductus hora tértia ad passiónis hóstiam, crucis ferens suspéndia ovem redúxit pérditam.	2. Led forth at this third hour to die, he gave himself in sacrifice and suffered hanging on the Cross, to find his sheep and lead them home.
Precémur ergo súbditi, redemptióne líberi, ut éruat a sǽculo quos solvit a chirógrapho.	3. Made free by his redeeming blood, as humble servants, let us pray that he may save from worldly pride all those released from death's decree.
Christum rogámus et Patrem, Christi Patrísque Spíritum; unum potens per ómnia, fove precántes, Trínitas. Amen.	4. We ask the Father and the Son and beg the Spirit of them both: Sustain us with your loving care, who reign for ever Three in One. Amen.

---

125. St. Augustine, *De civitate Dei*, XI, 23.
126. Pimont says: "Yes, let us rejoice in this day (*in hac die*) of the resurrection of Our Redeemer; for it is by the mystery of this day (*per hanc diem*) that we have been reconciled to God and recalled to life: 'He who was handed over for our sins, and rose again for our justification' (Rom 4:25). The grace in question here is rightly called in the last stanza *veniam*; that is, pardon obtained in the holy season by virtue of the sacrament of penance" (3:12, 29).
127. *cantate ei canticum novum bene psallite in vociferatione*: "Sing to him a new song, sing well with loud acclamation" (Ps 32 [33]:3); *et inmisit in os meum canticum novum carmen Deo nostro*: "and he put into my mouth a new song, a hymn for out God" (Ps 39 [40]:4); *Cantate Domino canticum novum*: "Sing to the Lord a new song" (Ps 95 [96]:1). This is also opening verse for Ps 97 [98] and Ps 149.
128. *et cantant novum canticum dicentes: dignus es accipere librum et aperire signacula eius quoniam occisus es et redemisti nos Deo in sanguine tuo ex omni tribu et lingua et populo et natione.*

Text found in *TDH*, no. 98; AH 51, no. 63; Bulst, 113; Walpole, no. 99. Changes in *TDH*: stanza 1, line 2: *qua spe perenni* for *spe perenni qua*; 1, 4: *Christi* for *Christo*.

COMMENTARY

Dei fide qua vivimus is the first of three hymns that Lentini selected as a Lenten alternative to the hymns given for the Little Hours—Terce, Sext, and None—in the *Breviarium Romanum*. At Terce, with the single exception of Pentecost, the hymn in the Roman Breviary is *Nunc Sancte nobis Spiritus*. Lentini selected as an alternative for Terce *Dei fide qua vivimus*, together with *Qua Christus hora sitiit* for Sext, and *Ternis ter horis numerus* for None: three texts in iambic dimeter of an unknown author, probably written before the eighth century and found either singly or together in the earliest extant manuscripts.[129] These hymns serve to indicate at the beginning of each hour that the major purpose of the Liturgy of the Hours is the sanctification of time, often linking the hour of prayer with the events that brought about salvation commemorated at that particular time.

Terce is not Morning Prayer, as such—that would be Lauds—it is rather the office that indicates the start of the working day. In monastic communities, it often precedes the celebration of the Conventual Mass. Aemiliana Löhr, OSB (d. 1972), in her commentary on the hymns, says of the hour of Terce:

> It was with prayer that the Church received the newborn day from the womb of the night; prayer has accompanied the day in its steady growth; and now that the day has attained to its fullness, it is ready to receive its solemn consecration.[130]

By the ancient reckoning of time, the day was divided into four periods marked by the first, third, sixth, and ninth hours. The third hour (9 a.m.) was the high point of the morning, the hour of the first of the daily sacrifices in the temple at Jerusalem.[131] Christian tradition holds that it was the hour at which the disciples of Jesus went up to the temple to pray, and after the destruction of the Temple, the hour at which they gathered for prayer; it was the hour at which Christ was condemned by Pilate and ascended the Cross,[132] and the hour at which the Holy Spirit descended at Pentecost: all these commemorations add further resonances to this "consecration" of the third hour. The *Apostolic Tradition*, from the third century, elaborates on the duty of Christians to pray at the third, sixth, and ninth hours. It attributes the significance of the third hour to

---

129. *Dei fide qua vivimus* was already included in the Frankish Hymnal and was widely used in the Anglo-Saxon Church (Milfull, 232). The other two hymns are found together in a large number of tenth-century manuscripts (see AH 51, pp. 65–67, in particular the note at the top of p. 67).

130. Löhr, *Il y eut un soir*, 249.

131. Josephus in his *Antiquites* 14.4.3, refers to the continuous practice of offering a sacrifice in the morning at the third hour and in the afternoon at the ninth hour even as Jerusalem was under siege and eventually conquered by Pompey in 63 BC. See also Ex 29:39; Num 28:3; Ps 5:4–5.

132. See Mk 15:25: *Erat autem hora tertia: et crucifixerunt eum*: "And it was the third hour, and they crucified him." See also Acts 2:15.

the raising of Christ on the Cross and to the typology of Old Testament practices and sacrifices, which took place at this hour.[133]

STANZA 1

The hymn begins by laying out the project of the Christian life as being a life of faith (*fides*), hope (*spes*), and charity (*caritas*).[134] The *Catechism of the Catholic Church* (*CCC*) states that the theological virtues of faith, hope, and charity allow human beings, through grace, to share in God's nature.[135] The hymn suggests that this, in itself, is sufficient cause to sing of our life in Christ—*Christi canamus gloriam*.

STANZA 2

Löhr explains that the third hour is forever associated with the time of Christ's sentencing by Pilate, and that he was also led out with the Cross at this hour, and thus began his Passion. For this reason, it has particular significance as a time of prayer linked to Christ's saving sacrifice, which is itself the fulfillment of the morning sacrifice that was offered in the temple at this hour. While the sheep are being sacrificed in the temple, Christ, the Good Shepherd, is going out in search of his lost sheep to bring them home, or reconcile them, to the Father.[136] The sacrifice is carried out *crucis ferens suspendia*, by Christ hanging on the Cross, an evocation of the public and extreme nature of this manner of execution. That is, Christ is executed like a common criminal and by this ordeal he leads back the sheep who are lost (*ovem reduxit perditam*), and establishes a new and lasting priesthood by which this process of redemption may be carried forward by the Church.

STANZA 3

It is the salvific humility of Christ, in freely handing himself over to those who sought his life, that is the single notion in this stanza. It is by the shedding of Christ's blood in his perfect sacrifice that we are redeemed: "For you were slain and with your blood you purchased for God those from every tribe and tongue, people and nation" (Rv 5:9).[137] The greatness of this salvation should evoke in us a humility (*Precemur ergo subditi*) that in turn saves those redeemed from the

---

133. "If you are at home, pray at the third hour and praise God. If you are elsewhere at that time, pray in your heart to God. For at this hour Christ was displayed nailed to the wood. And for this reason also in the Old Testament the Law instructed that the shewbread be offered at the third hour as a type of the Body and Blood of Christ. And the slaughter of the speechless lamb was a type of the perfect Lamb. For Christ is the Shepherd, and he is also the bread which descended from heaven." Hippolytus, *Apostolic Tradition*, 41:5 ff., with modifications.

134. "The righteous shall live by faith" (Rom 1:17); "We become heirs in hope of eternal life" (Ti 3:6–7); "Love one another as I have loved you" (Jn 15:9, 12).

135. *CCC*, 1812–13.

136. See Luke 15:4–6: "What man among you having a hundred sheep and losing one of them would not leave the ninety-nine in the desert and go after the lost one until he finds it? And when he does find it he sets it on his shoulders with great joy and, upon his arrival home he calls together his friends and neighbors and says to them, 'Rejoice with me because I have found my lost sheep.'" See also Ez 34:11–16.

137. See also Eph 1:7.

Dei fide, quá vívimus

effects of the world (*ut eruat a sæculo*) who are also liberated from their death sentence (*quos solvit a chirographo*): "You were dead in your transgressions and sins in which you once lived following the age of this world, following the ruler of the power of the air, the spirit that is now at work in the disobedient" (Eph 2:1–2). *Chirographo* carries the sense of a handwritten bond or death sentence. The stanza seems to be based on a single text from Colossians 2:12–14:

consepulti in baptismo, in quo et resurrexistis per fidem operationis Dei, qui suscitavit illum a mortuis. Et vos cum mortui essetis in delictis, et præputio carnis vestræ, convivicavit cum illo, donans vobis omnia delicta: delens quod adversus nos erat chirographum decreti, quod erat contrarium nobis, et ipsum tulit de medio, affigens illud cruci.	You were buried with him in baptism, in which you were also raised with him through faith in the power of God, who raised him from the dead. And even when you were dead in transgressions and the uncircumcision of your flesh, he brought you to life along with him, having forgiven all your transgressions; obliterating the bond against us, with its legal claims, which was opposed to us, he also removed it from our midst, nailing it to the cross.

STANZA 4

The three hymns *Dei fide qua vivimus*, *Qua Christus hora sitiit*, and *Ternis ter horus numerus* all have the same doxology. It is stanza 8 of St. Ambrose's hymn *Deus Creator omnium*.[138] This hymn is firmly attributed to Ambrose from references to it by St Augustine in his *Confessions*, 9.12, and in the *De beata vita*, 35. In the *Confessions*, he cites two stanzas and says that he derived great consolation from the hymn after his mother's death. In the *De beata vita*, he cites the last line of the hymn (*fove precantes, Trinitas*) and says that his mother, St. Monica, was in the habit of reciting the hymn. Lentini used the stanza as a doxology for two further hymns that appear in the Four-Week Psalter: *Æterna lux, divinitas* (H 74), and *O lux, beata Trinitas* (H 100).[139] Walpole leaves it doubtful whether line 1 reads *rogamus* or *rogemus*.[140] Although *rogemus* would be the *lectio facilior*, Walpole notes that the indicative (*rogamus*) seems to offer the better sense. In line 2, St. Ambrose leaves no doubt in his belief in the *filioque*, for he uses the formulation *Christi Patrisque Spiritum*, with the Holy Spirit proceeding as the Spirit of both Father and Son.[141] Fontaine observes that the order of the divine Persons chosen by Ambrose (Son, Father, Spirit) seems curious at first but is in conformity with the completion of the Christian revelation: henceforth one goes to the Father through the

---

138. *TDH*, no. 9, p. 11. See Walpole, no. 5, pp. 44ff. Fontaine notes that *Deus creator omnium* was used frequently in the evening monastic office, as indicated in the *Rule* of Caesarius of Arles and that of Aurelius. This is confirmed by the rubric of the Ambrosian manuscripts, which indicates that St. Ambrose probably wrote this hymn for daily use throughout year. Later the hymn was assigned to Vespers from the Saturday preceding the first Sunday after the Octave of Epiphany to the Saturday before the first Sunday of Lent, and from the Saturday before the first Sunday in August until Advent. See Fontaine, 234 and Julian, 291.
139. *TDH*, no. 15, p. 17; *TDH*, no. 41, p. 43.
140. Walpole, no. 5, l. 29, p. 49.
141. Ambrose, *De Spiritu Sancto*, I. 119 and 152.

Son, and the Holy Spirit is received as the Spirit of the Christ, promised by Jesus, and sent by the Father at Pentecost (see Acts 16:7; Rom 8:9; Gal 4:6; Phil 1:9). The formula that designates the Spirit in line 2 is also reminiscent of that of the Hispanic *Credo* from the Third Council of Toledo in 589: *qui ex Patre Filioque procedit*.

In line 3, the phrase *unum potens per omnia* emphasizes Trinitarian unity: in *unum potens*, both words are in the accusative and give the sense of "a single power," while *per omnia*, "for ever," a frequent formulation in Ambrose, gives the line the sense of "all-powerful."[142] The formula *per omnia* is found in the Vulgate at Acts 17:2 and Hebrews 4:15. It also begins the concluding formula for collects in the Roman Rite: *per omnia sæcula sæculorum*, for ever and ever.

In line 4 of the doxology, the use of the verb *foveo* adds a note of tenderness that comes from the primary meaning of the verb, "to warm up," and from its use to designate the action of a mother who "nurtures and keeps her babies warm."[143] Here, the imperative *fove* expresses an appeal to God's grace and love. Ambrose also remembered two famous Pauline texts: "For no one hates his own flesh but rather nourishes and cherishes it, even as Christ does the church" (Eph 5:29)[144]; and "like a nursing mother taking care of her own children" (1 Thes 2:7).[145]

Qua Christus hora sítiit	29
8th c.	Ash Wednesday until Good Friday
8 8 8 8	Sext

Qua Christus hora sítiit crucem vel in qua súbiit, quos præstat in hac psállere ditet siti iustítiæ.	1. May Christ, as he ascends the Cross, consumed with thirst in noonday heat, grant those who sing the psalms this hour to grow in thirst for righteousness.
Simul sit his esúries, quam ipse de se sátiet, crimen sit ut fastídium virtúsque desiderium.	2. May hunger likewise fill their hearts, which he from his own self will sate, that they may lose all taste for sin and virtue be their sole desire.
Charísma Sancti Spíritus sic ínfluat psalléntibus, ut carnis æstus frígeat et mentis algor férveat.	3. Then may the Holy Spirit's gifts so fill the souls of those who pray, that passion in the flesh may cool and chill of mind and heart grow warm.
Christum rogámus et Patrem, Christi Patrísque Spíritum; unum potens per ómnia, fove precántes, Trínitas. Amen.	4. We ask the Father and the Son and beg the Spirit of them both: Sustain us with your loving care, who reign for ever Three in One. Amen.

---

142. See Ambrose, *De Paradiso*, 8, 16.
143. See Ovid, *Met.* 3, 450.
144. *nemo enim umquam carnem suam odio habuit, sed nutrit et fovet eam sicut et Christus ecclesiam.*
145. *tamquam si nutrix foveat filios suos.*

Text found in *TDH*, no. 99; *AH* 51, no. 65; Walpole, no. 101. Changes in *TDH*: stanza 2, 1: *Simul sit his esuries* for *Quibus sit et esuries*.

COMMENTARY

The hour of Sext recalls Christ's ascent to the Cross, and that is the single narrative event in this brief hymn. After the initial statement of the fact in lines 1 and 2, the remainder of the hymn is a *parænesis*, or moral exhortation inspired by Christ's thirst on the Cross. Of the hour of Sext Aemiliana Löhr, OSB, writes:

> The perfume of the incense that accompanied the sacrifice has dissipated, and with it the glow of morning. Several hours have passed since the Church, as a living hymn, ascended the altar to be immolated with her Lord (in the celebration of the Mass).... In the full clarity of a cosmic morning, in a mystic manner that defies comprehension, there is for her another evening and another morning—a new day. She has been plunged into the night of the death of Christ and from there elevated by the imperishable day of the glory of Christ.[146]

The hymn consists of a series of rhyming couplets that, after the initial statement of lines 1 and 2, are generally in the subjunctive mood, expressive of aspiration and the desire of those praying to engage in an authentic *imitatio Christi*, the imitation of Christ.

STANZA 1

Christ ascends the Cross and he thirsts; in this the hymn follows the gospel narrative: John 19:28–30: "After this, aware that everything was now finished, in order that the scripture might be fulfilled, Jesus said, 'I thirst.' There was a vessel filled with common wine. So they put a sponge soaked in wine on a sprig of hyssop and put it up to his mouth. When Jesus had taken the wine, he said, 'It is finished.' And bowing his head, he handed over his spirit."[147] This physical and spiritual suffering of Christ is made the source of the aspiration or thirst for righteousness on the part of those who gather to celebrate the hour of Sext. It is a trope that continues throughout the hymn.

STANZA 2

In this stanza, the thirst becomes a hunger, *simul sit his esuries*, which Christ will satisfy from himself, *quam ipse de se satiet*; see Matthew 5:6: "Blessed are they who hunger and thirst for righteousness, for they will be satisfied." With the satisfying of hungry hearts, there is then the hope that they may consequently lose their taste for sin and wrongdoing may become tedious to them, *crimen sit ut fastidium*, enabling them to become solely focused on desiring virtue, *virtusque desiderium*.

---

146. Löhr, *Il y eut un soir*, 264.
147. See also Ps 68(69):22: "and for my thirst they gave me vinegar."

STANZA 3

Thus far, all has been a preparation for an outpouring of the gifts of the Holy Spirit, filling the souls of those who are praying, *Charisma Sancti Spiritus sic influat psallentibus*. See the Vulgate text of Isaiah 11:2–3 for a list of the traditional names of the seven gifts of the Holy Spirit: "And the spirit of the Lord shall rest upon him: the spirit of wisdom, and of understanding, the spirit of counsel, and of fortitude, the spirit of knowledge, and of godliness. And he shall be filled with the spirit of the fear of the Lord.[148]" Lines 3 and 4 then outline the desired effect of the indwelling of the Holy Spirit in cooling the passion of the flesh, *ut carnis æstus frigeat*, and warming the mind and heart, *et mentis algor ferveat*. This is reminiscent of several stanzas of the great sequence of Pentecost, *Veni Sancte Spiritus*:

O lux beatíssima,	O most blessed light,
reple cordis íntima	fill the inmost heart
tuórum fidélium.	of your faithful.
Lava quod est sórdidum,	Cleanse that which is unclean,
riga quod est áridum,	water that which is dry,
sana quod est sáucium.	heal that which is wounded.
Flecte quod est rígidum,	Bend that which is inflexible,
fove quod est frígidum,	warm that which is chilled,
rege quod est dévium.	correct that which goes astray.
Da tuis fidélibus,	Give to your faithful
in te confidéntibus,	who put their trust in you,
sacrum septenárium.	sevenfold gifts.
Da virtútis méritum,	Give the reward of virtue,
da salútis éxitum,	Give the deliverance of salvation,
da perénne gáudium.	Give eternal joy.

STANZA 4

The three hymns *Dei fide qua vivimus* (H 28), *Qua Christus hora sitiit* (H 29), and *Ternis ter horus numerus* (H 30) all have the same doxology. Please see the commentary on *Dei fide qua vivimus*.

---

148. *Et requiescet super eum spiritus Domini: spiritus sapientiæ et intellectus, spiritus consilii et fortitudinis, spiritus scientiæ et pietatis; et replebit eum spiritus timoris Domini:*

	Ternis ter horis numerus	30
8th c.		Ash Wednesday until Good Friday
8 8 8 8 (LM)		None

Ternis ter horis númerus nobis sacrátus pánditur, sanctóque Iesu nómine munus precémur véniæ.	1. Three times three hours, a sacred sum, unfolds before us as we sing; in Jesus' holy name we beg the gift of pardon for our sins.
Latrónis, en, conféssio Christi merétur grátiam; laus nostra vel devótio mercétur indulgéntiam.	2. See how the thief confessed his faith and merited Christ's saving grace; let our devotion and our praise obtain his pardon and his love.
Mors per crucem nunc ínterit et post tenébras lux redit; horror dehíscat críminum, splendor nitéscat méntium.	3. Now death is ruined by the Cross and after darkness light returns; let horror brought by sin disperse and splendor shine in minds and hearts.
Christum rogámus et Patrem, Christi Patrísque Spíritum; unum potens per ómnia, fove precántes, Trínitas. Amen.	4. We ask the Father and the Son and beg the Spirit of them both: Sustain us with your loving care, who reign for ever Three in One. Amen.

Text found in *TDH*, no. 100; *AH* 51, no. 66; Walpole, no. 102. Changes in *TDH*: stanza 1, 2: *nobis sacratus* for *sacræ fidei*; 1, 3: *sanctoqu Iesu nomine* for *nunc Trinitatis nomine*; 2, 4: some manuscripts have *meretur* instead of *mercetur*. Lentini opted for *mercetur*.

COMMENTARY

Of the hour of None, Aemiliana Löhr, OSB, writes:

> The oppressive midday heat is no longer with us; we can breathe more freely. The air is growing cool, the shadows are lengthening. The sun has lost its baneful power to burn and sear. Something of the pure clarity of early morning light seems to return; and light recovers its transparency, though this is a transparency different from that of morning—the more mature, ripe clarity of eventide. Created realities are retiring once more into their domain of mystery, but for a moment they are clothed in a clear light that has about it almost nothing of the earth. This time of day is decked out with waning beauty; but this is a decline which is not experienced as decline. This is no smile before a final separation, but the mature plenitude of a life which has no fear of death itself. There is one unique death which has hallowed this hour, and it is as though this hour has received from that death that brightness of life which will remain with it for all time.[149]

149. Löhr, "Light at Eventide," trans. Chrysogonus Waddell, 53–54.

Although this hymn may be sung at any time during Lent, it has particular poignancy if sung at None during Holy Week. It is a perfect prelude and commentary on the Lord's Passion. Manuscript sources at the Biblioteca Vallicelliana in Rome ascribe the hymn to *Feria Quinta in Cena Domini*, Holy Thursday of the Lord's Supper, but other manuscripts assign it to Mondays in Lent. Although the sentiments are germane to the Christian life at any time, they are particularly appropriate during Passiontide.

STANZA 1

The hymn begins with the clever acknowledgment that None, the ninth hour, is three times three (3 x 3 = 9): *Ternis ter horis numerus*; there is also a further obvious resonance with the Blessed Trinity. The invocation of the Holy Name in Lines 3 and 4 (*sanctoque Iesu nomine munus precemur veniæ*) underlines the penitential nature of this prayer's petition. See Acts 4:12: "Neither is there salvation in any other. For there is no other name under heaven given to men, whereby we must be saved."

STANZA 2

This stanza offers a brief catechesis on the theology of merit. Luke's account of the Crucifixion records the Lord's words to the criminal crucified on his right, in chapter 24:39–43, especially the following verses (42–43): "Then he said, 'Jesus remember me when you come into your kingdom.' He replied to him, 'Amen, I say to you, today you will be with me in Paradise.'" The confession (*confessio*) of the thief unlocked the grace of pardon from the Savior (*Christi meretur gratiam*). We are exhorted to follow the example of the Good Thief and, by our devotion and praise (*laus nostra vel devotio*), merit the pardon of forgiveness (*mercetur indulgentiam*).

STANZA 3

This stanza concentrates on the effect of Christ's saving death on the Cross. Death is Satan's most powerful weapon against us. At the Cross, Christ defeated Satan on behalf of us helpless sinners: see John 12:31: "Now is the time for judgment on this world; now the prince of this world will be driven out" (see also Col 2:15). Christ has "ruined" death by his saving sacrifice of the Cross, thereby removing the "sting of death" (see 1 Cor 15:56). The verb *dehisco*, "to disperse" (line 3), is the same verb used in the Fathers to describe the opening of the Red Sea (Ex 14:16–29), and also the opening of the earth for Dathan and Abiram (Nm 16:25–35).[150] The idea seems to be that the horror of death should split open to reveal the splendor of the light of minds and hearts cleansed of sin (lines 3 and 4). See 2 Corinthians 4:6: "For God, who said, 'Let light shine out of darkness,' has shone in our hearts to give the light of the knowledge of the glory of God in the face of Jesus Christ."

---

150. See the treatment of *dehisco* in the commentary on H 27: 1, 2.

STANZA 4

The three hymns *Dei fide, qua vivimus* (H 28), *Qua Christus hora sitiit* (H 29), and *Ternis ter horis numerus* (H 30) all have the same doxology. Please see the commentary on *Dei fide qua vivimus*.

Vexílla regis pródeunt	31
Venantius Fortunatus, d. ca. 600 87 87 87	Holy Week & the Exaltation of the Holy Cross Vespers

Vexílla regis pródeunt,
fulget crucis mystérium,
quo carne carnis cónditor
suspénsus est patíbulo;

1. The banners of the King go forth,
the gleaming mystery of the Cross,
by which the Maker of all flesh
was yoked in flesh upon the wood;

Quo, vulnerátus ínsuper
mucróne diro lánceæ,
ut nos laváret crímine,
manávit unda et sánguine.

2. Where, wounded as he hung on high
by ruthless blade of sharpened spear,
there flowed forth water mixed with blood,
to wash us clean from every sin.

Arbor decóra et fúlgida,
ornáta regis púrpura,
elécta digno stípite
tam sancta membra tángere!

3. O noble tree with blood adorned,
the splendid purple of the King,
wood chosen from a worthy stock
to touch and bear such holy limbs.

Beáta, cuius brácchiis
sǽcli pepéndit prétium;
statéra facta est córporis
prædam tulítque tártari.

4. O blessed tree whose branches bore
the price and ransom of the world!
Like scales it weighed the body's worth
and bore away the spoils of hell.

Salve, ara, salve, víctima,
de passiónis glória,
qua Vita mortem pértulit
et morte vitam réddidit!

5. Hail altar, victim, sacrifice,
for glory gained through grief and death,
by which our Life endured to die
and through his death restored our life.

O crux, ave, spes única!
hoc passiónis témpore
(September 14: in hac triúmphi
  gloria)
piis adáuge grátiam
reísque dele crimina.

6. O Cross, all hail, our only hope,
in this most holy Passiontide,
(September 14: in glorious triumph
  raised on high,)
increase the grace of loving hearts
and rid the guilty of their sin.

Te, fons salútis, Trínitas,
colláudet omnis spíritus;
quos per crucis mystérium
salvas, fove per sǽcula. Amen.

7. O Triune God, let all sing praise
to you, the font of saving grace;
sustain for ever those you save
by wondrous mystery of the Cross. Amen.

Text found in *TDH*, no. 101; AH 50, no. 67; Walpole: no. 34; Roberts, ed., Fortunatus *Poems*, 80–82. Changes in *TDH*: stanzas 2, 4, and 6 are omitted, and the last two stanzas have been added since the tenth century; 4, 2: *sæcli pependit pretium* for *pretium pependit sæculi*; 7, 1: *Te, fons salutis, Trinitas* for *Te, summa Deus trinitas*.

COMMENTARY

This hymn, together with *Pange, lingua, gloriosi prœlium certaminis* (H 32 and H 33), ranks among the treasures of Latin hymnody. Venantius Fortunatus composed them at the transition from Late Antiquity to the Middle Ages.[151] Venantius was born between 530 and 540 in Treviso, Italy, and enjoyed a classical education in law and the liberal arts in Ravenna before departing to visit the tomb of St. Martin of Tours. During his travels through Gaul, he delighted secular and ecclesiastical leaders with various poems. On his journey, he also came to the royal court of Poitiers where he came to know the queen, Radegund. In her piety, she intended to request from the Byzantine Emperor Justin II a piece of the Holy Cross for her local monastery. To strengthen that petition, Venantius composed three poems in honor of the Cross.[152] The request was successful, and a splinter of the Cross was solemnly brought to Poitiers. On the occasion of the transfer of the precious relic, Venantius composed, around the year 569, the hymns *Vexilla regis* and *Pange, lingua*, still used today. He composed another poem on the Cross in thanksgiving to the imperial court in Constantinople.[153] Venantius was ordained a priest around 574 to 576 and served at Radegund's monastery. Around the year 600, he was consecrated as the Bishop of Poitiers.

STANZA 1

The *vexilla* of the King, that is, the banners of Christ, have a double meaning: On a literal level, they refer to the banners that have been carried at the head (*prodeunt*) of the procession with the relic of the Holy Cross. They "evoke the memory of the royal banners, a fitting image for the age of the Merovingian royalty."[154] On a metaphorical level, *vexilla* replaces the Greek loanword *tropæum*,[155] which early Christian writers like Justin, Hippolytus, and Tertullian used to highlight the Cross as a sign of victory.[156] Venantius himself employed *tropæum* for the Cross

---

151. For Venantius's biography see George, *Fortunatus*, 18–34; Reyellet, ed., *Venance Fortunat: Poèmes*, 1, vii–xxviii.
152. George, *Fortunatus*, 30.
153. Venantius himself put together the six poems in the second book of his collection of poems. See Masciadri, "Pange lingua", 185–223, especially 187 and Reydellet, *Poèmes* 1, 49–58. In addition to *Pange, lingua* and *Vexilla regis*, a third hymn, *Crux benedicta* (AH 50, 75) is often included in detailed commentaries. See, regarding the three hymns, Bulst, 127–29; with commentary of van Tongeren, *Exaltation of the Cross*, 236–48.
154. Szövérffy, "Venantius Fortunatus and the Earliest Hymns of the Holy Cross,", 107–22, especially 116. See also, Szövérffy *Hymns of the Holy Cross: An Annotated Edition with Introduction*, 7–20.
155. See Szövérffy, "Venantius Fortunatus", 116.
156. Reijners, *The Terminology of the Holy Cross*, 192f.

in the *Pange, lingua, gloriosi prœlium certaminis* (H 32: 1, 3). The two levels perfectly fit together as the following short main clause indicates (line 2).

Mysterium does not mean "mysterious" as might be thought, but rather, as a Greek translation of the Latin *sacramentum*, it points to the deeper reality that God is present and acting in and behind human events. Here the *crucis mysterium* expresses the redemptive power of Christ's saving Passion, which is both hidden (see 1 Cor 2:7) and still gleams through the Cross (*fulget*). Moreover, here *fulget* might reflect the splendor of the procession.

Venantius loves alliterations like *carne carnis conditor*. He highlights that the Maker (*conditor*)[157] of all flesh is hanging in his own flesh on the Cross and so is fulfilling the mystery of the Cross and Redemption (*quo* refers to *mysterium*). *Patibulum*, a Roman term for an instrument of torture for slaves and criminals, specifies the transverse beam of the Cross, which the condemned needed to carry to the place of their execution. Already in early Christian literature, *patibulum* was applied to the Cross. *Suspensus* is used in Acts 5:30 and 10:39 to refer to Christ's hanging on the Cross.

STANZA 2

In line 1, *quo* (ablative of place; meaning here: [from] where or there) refers to the Cross, where, according to John 19:34, "one soldier thrust his lance into his side and immediately blood and water flowed out." The thrust with the spear seems to have been particularly important to Venantius, because it is the only detail he mentions extensively (also in *Pange, lingua, gloriosi prœlium certaminis*). Venantius adds *mucro* (the sharp, cutting tip) of the lance to the biblical text as well as the theological explanation that this happened for the cleansing of sin. To highlight the washing, he changes the order of blood and water and uses *unda* (wave, running water) instead of *aqua* (water). Because *aqua* would have been just as possible in terms of verse meter, he apparently made the change on purpose. Remarkably, this is the only line in the whole hymn with a personal pronoun (*nos*): Christ "was pierced for *our* sins ... by his wounds we were healed" (Is 53:5).

STANZA 3

The third stanza now turns to the Cross itself. We now address it directly, "O noble tree." Calling the Cross a tree (*lignum*) is already found in Scripture (Acts 5:30; 10:39). The Vulgate here refers back to Creation and the tree of Paradise, because also in Genesis the trees are called *lignum* (principal meaning: "wood"). Venantius uses *lignum* in *Pange, lingua, gloriosi prœlium certaminis* (H 33: 2, 5) as well. In *Vexilla*, however, he calls the Cross *arbor* to emphasize its liveliness, its "living character."[158] This discreetly introduces the themes of Creation, Fall, and Redemption. Venantius had internalized the typological relationships of the Old and New Testaments, as one can see in the omitted original

---

157. *Conditor* is used in the Vulgate only in Heb 11:10.
158. Szövérffy, "Venantius Fortunatus", 117.

stanza 4, which quotes an ancient version of David's Psalm 95 (96):10, "God reigns from the wood."[159] This interpolated psalm verse inserts *a ligno* and thus allows for a Christological understanding. Already Justin had used this version, which entered the Roman Psalter.[160] However, since it is not in the original Hebrew text, "the whole beautiful stanza had to be excised."[161]

Nevertheless, the main message has been preserved: the Cross is the tree of life. It is noble (*decora*) and radiant (*fulgida*) because Christ hung on it ("chosen to bear such holy limbs") and brought about our salvation. The Cross is adorned with the purple of the King (*ornata regis purpura*). Because of the costly dyeing with the secretion of the purple snail, purple became the color of the elite. It recalls the purple cloak (*purpureum vestimentum*) with which the soldiers mocked Jesus (Jn 19:5), but which would have been owed to him as the true king (Jn 18:37). In this context, purple is especially reminiscent of Jesus's blood, which dyed the Cross red. Kingship and suffering are combined in *regis purpura*: "Christ wore the purple garment as a robe of triumph."[162]

The Cross is chosen from a worthy stock (*electa digna stipite*). *Stipes, stipitis* signifies the upright trunk of the Cross, as opposed to the transverse beam (*patibulum*) mentioned above, and thus already has a resemblance to a tree trunk. *Electa* refers to the fact that God already designated the tree of the Cross at the Fall (see *Pange, lingua, gloriosi prœlium certaminis*, H 32: 2, 5; *En acetum, fel, arundo*, H 33: 4, 1f.), which again discreetly emphasizes the link between the tree of Paradise and the Cross.[163]

STANZA 4

This stanza continues to address the Cross-tree, now especially as the place of redemption. We often take "redemption" as a word of theological vocabulary. Originally, however, it was (and still can be) one of business: *red-emptio* or *red-imere* literally means to "buy back" and was used, for instance, for buying slaves or captured soldiers back into freedom. Here the Christian understanding of redemption from sin and death is very close. The English translation of the hymn captures both meanings of redemption well by rendering *pretium sæculi* as "price and ransom." According to Mark 10:45 and Matthew 20:28, Jesus came to give

---

159. The omitted stanza reads: *Impleta sunt quæ concinit / David fideli carmine / dicendo nationibus: / Regnavit a ligno deus.* "Fulfilled are the things that David sang in his faithful song, saying to the nations: "God has reigned from the tree." The phrase "from the tree" (a ligno) is attested in manuscripts belonging to what is now called the Vetus Latina, the varied Latin versions that predate the Vulgate. See Walpole, pp. 175–76.

160. The Vulgate states: *dicite in gentibus quia Dominus regnavit.* Justin even seems to have been convinced that the interpolation belonged to the original text, but was only deleted in order to remove the basis for the Christological argument. On the Patristic testimonies see Reijners, *The Terminology of the Holy Cross*, 36f.; Prieur, "*Le Seigneur a régné*," 127–40. See also on other interpolations with Christological interest Petraglio, "Le interpolazioni," 89–109, especially 101–5.

161. Lentini, *TDH*, 104. This stanza has been retained in the German Divine Office.

162. van Tongeren, *Exaltation*, 245n60.

163. This became the starting point for the later legend, developed in the twelfth century and transmitted in the *Golden Legend*. It claimed that the wood of the Cross was in fact made from the trunk of the tree of life and that the tree of Paradise was found several times, including by the Jews before the crucifixion, so that it became wood of the Cross, which later St. Helena found again. For the Latin text see Jacobus de Voragine, *Legenda aurea*, 2, 938–42. See also Szövérffy, *Hymns of the Holy Cross*, 3n10.

his life as *redeptionem pro multis*, that is, paying the price and being the ransom for the whole world (*sæculum*). St. Paul applies the same metaphor and word that Venantius adapted: "For you have been purchased at a great price" (*pretio magno*; 1 Cor 6:20; see also 7:23). In a similar way, St. Peter declares: "you were ransomed ... not with perishable things like silver or gold but with the precious blood of Christ as of a spotless unblemished lamb" (1 Pt 1:18–19). Venantius skillfully links two biblical metaphors: Christ as the "price and ransom of the world" becomes the fruit on the tree of life.

In the following lines, Venantius goes beyond the biblical imagery when he speaks of the Cross as scales. We have to imagine a balance with two bowls: Christ, the ransom of the world, in one bowl, and fallen humanity in the other. His body hanging on the Cross has more weight and thus lifts the dead up to freedom, who had otherwise become the "spoils of hell." The extraordinary value of his sacrifice outweighs the sin of the world and bears away to safety the human race. In his explanation of the Creed, called *Expositio symboli*, Venantius unfolds this metaphor himself: "The Lord hangs on the Cross so that he as merchant weighs the price of his body in the balance for our captivity."[164]

STANZA 5

The following stanza takes the next step by greeting the Cross not only with a vocative as in stanza 4 ("O blessed tree"), but with the explicit and repeated word *salve*. Venantius calls the Cross an altar and Christ the victim, so as to emphasize the sacrificial death of Christ (as also the English translation points out plainly by adding "sacrifice"). The stanza obviously contains a reference to the Eucharist in which Christ is offering himself, being both priest and victim. The fifth preface of Easter conveys the same idea as Venantius when it states that Christ "showed himself the Priest, the Altar, and the Lamb of sacrifice."[165]

The next line, *passionis gloria*, expresses an oxymoron, an apparent contradiction. We imagine glory as very different from passion. However, the Johannine Christology emphasizes that Christ revealed his glory on the Cross (esp. Jn 17:1 and 5).[166] Since Venantius sees the suffering of Christ from its redeeming result, he can speak of the glory of Christ's Passion. He develops that contradiction further in the following relative clause by the immediate contrast of life and death: Life itself (Christ) endured death and so gave life back by his death. The chiasmus in the word order (*Vita mortem—morte vita*) not only embellishes the lines rhetorically, but also highlights the contrast that Jesus himself has emphasized in the conversation with Martha: "I am the resurrection and the life; whoever believes in me, even if he dies, will live, and everyone who lives and believes in me will never die" (Jn 11:25–26). While the first *Vita* is Christ (therefore capitalized in Latin

---

164. Reydellet, *Poèmes* 3, 108: *Dominus in cruce suspenditur, ut pro captivitate nostra pretium sui corporis mercator in statera pensaret*. See the whole explanation in Reydellet: 101–13; on the Passion in particular: 106–9. See also Stramare, "L'esaltazione della croce," 327–35, especially 334f.; van Tongeren, *Exaltation*, 245.

165. See *The Roman Missal*, Preface of Easter V.

166. The Vulgate, however, uses *clarescere* in this context and not *gloria* as Venantius.

and English), the second *vita* refers to us. Thus, Venantius visualizes what the English translation renders by adding personal pronouns: Christ's life became our life; he vitalizes us in every respect. Through his death our death perished.[167]

STANZA 6

This stanza was added to the original text of Venantius from the tenth century onward and continues the dynamic of the hymn smoothly. It continues to greet the Cross as if it were a person, using the vocative *O crux* and *ave*, obviously meaning Christ, the only hope. Lines 3 and 4 have the same structure and word order (dative, imperative, accusative), but the parallel words are exact opposites (*piis—reis; adauge—dele; gratiam—crimina*).[168] Christ may increase the grace to the *piis*, which, as well as pious or devout, can mean conscientious, upright, faithful, righteous. Therefore, the English translation with "loving hearts" captures the Latin word well. Secondly, Christ may "delete" the sins of the *reis*, which first means a party in a lawsuit, and has acquired the meaning of the guilty party, and so in a Christian context, of the sinner. Hence, the imagery underlines the salvation that Christ brought about on the Cross.

Line 2 includes a reference to the liturgical time (*passionis tempore*). By emphasizing "in *this* (*hoc*) most holy Passiontide," it could remind the faithful, now singing the hymn, that they themselves might be both the pious and the guilty. On the feast of the Exaltation of the Cross, line 2 aptly refers to the celebrated mystery, to the glory of the Cross and the victory over sin and death Christ achieved for us.

STANZA 7

This doxological stanza was also added to Venantius's composition early on, as has been done with many other hymns. Instead of returning to the quite general *Te summa Deus trinitas*, however, the Divine Office kept the version of the Roman Breviary: that the Trinity is the "font of saving grace" (*fons salutis*), which reminds us of Psalm 35 (36):10: "For with you is the fountain of life (*fons vitæ*)" and of Christ's words to the Samaritan woman at the well: "The water I shall give will become in him a spring of living water (*fons aquæ*) welling up to eternal life" (Jn 4:14). Similarly, in the book of Revelation (21:6), Christ says: *Ego sitienti dabo de fonte aquæ vitæ, gratis*: "To the thirsty I will give a gift from the spring of life-giving water."

The final stanza summarizes the whole hymn and deliberately repeats the phrase "mystery of the Cross" (1, 2). By that very mystery, the hymn asserts, Christ saves us: notice the present tense. So, it is not simply a fact of the past but remains effective today, so that we ask him to sustain us now and for ever.

---

167. See also Hos 13:14 and 1 Cor 15:54–58.
168. The *cœtus* on hymns has maintained the correction of the *Breviarium Romanum* because this "sweet and pious stanza has been so dear to the Christian faithful" and the text is not original (Lentini, *TDH*, 104). The two lines originally stated: *auge piis iustitiam / reisque dona veniam* (AH 50, 75).

Pange, lingua, gloriosi prœlium certaminis	32
Venantius Fortunatus, d. ca. 600	Holy Week
87 87 87 87	Office of Readings

Pange, lingua, gloriósi
prœlium certáminis,
et super crucis tropǽo
dic triúmphum nóbilem,
quáliter redémptor orbis
immolátus vícerit.

De paréntis protoplásti
fraude factor cóndolens,
quando pomi noxiális
morte morsu córruit,
ipse lignum tunc notávit,
damna ligni ut sólveret.

Hoc opus nostræ salútis
ordo depopóscerat,
multifórmis perditóris
arte ut artem fálleret,
et medélam ferret inde,
hostis unde lǽserat.

Quando venit ergo sacri
plenitúdo témporis,
missus est ab arce Patris
Natus, orbís cónditor,
atque ventre virgináli
carne factus pródiit.

Lustra sex qui iam perácta
tempus implens córporis,
se volénte, natus ad hoc,
passióni déditus,
agnus in crucis levátur
immolándus stípite.

Æqua Patri Filióque,
ínclito Paráclito,
sempitérna sit beátæ
Trinitáti glória,
cuius alma nos redémit
atque servat grátia. Amen

1. Sing, my tongue, of strife and contest
'mid the glory of the fray,
tell of high and noble triumph
from the trophy of the Cross,
say how Christ, the world's Redeemer,
immolated, won the day.

2. He who formed our parent, Adam,
grieved that he should fall by fraud,
by the death deceit had hidden
in the lethal fruit he ate,
then he chose the wood to rescue
from the harm that wood had wrought.

3. For this work of our salvation
fitting order had required
that he thwart the false destroyer,
foil his artifice by art:
that he might bring forth our healing
from the wound caused by our foe.

4. When, accordingly, the fullness
of the sacred time had come,
sent forth by the heavenly Father,
Son and Maker of the world,
Word in human flesh incarnate,
from the Virgin's womb he came.

5. After thirty years of living,
he had grown to man's estate,
consecrated to his Passion
—free and willing, born for this—
he was raised upon the gibbet,
he the Lamb for sacrifice.

6. Wisdom, power, and adoration
to the blessed Trinity
for redemption and salvation
through the Paschal Mystery,
now, in every generation,
and for all eternity. Amen

© Saint Gregory Institute for the Study of Latin Liturgical Texts, 1100 Connecticut Ave., Washington, DC 20036.

Text found in *TDH*, no. 102; AH 50, no. 66; Walpole, no. 33; Bulst, 128; Fortunatus, *Poems* 2, 2, ed. Roberts, pp. 70–72.

COMMENTARY

The hymn has been divided between the Office of Readings (stanzas 1–4 and 6) and Lauds (stanzas 7–10: *En acetum, fel, arundo*; see H 33). Venantius gives the *Pange, lingua, gloriosi prœlium certaminis* its structure by employing the great contexts of salvation history: the Fall in Paradise (stanzas 2–3); the Incarnation (stanzas 4–5); the Crucifixion of Christ for the redemption of humankind (6–10). The restriction to these three central aspects supports a clear line of thought and may reflect a theological development that valued these aspects above all as soteriologically significant.[169] The fifth stanza, on the Incarnation of Christ, has been omitted, although it clearly is an integral part of the hymn.[170]

Like *Vexilla regis prodeunt* (H 31), the hymn was composed by Venantius Fortunatus for the transfer of the relic of the Cross to Poitiers on November 19, 569 AD.[171] It originally comprised ten stanzas (the doxology was added later), each consisting of three long-line verses in the trochaic tetrameter catalectic (septenary; with caesura), the "meter of the old songs of Roman soldiers."[172] In the *Liturgia Horarum*, each verse has been split into two lines. Because of its lively rhythm, the hymn may have been sung during the procession to accompany the relics.[173] Whether it was immediately incorporated into the liturgy (for example, at Poitiers) beyond this occasion remains an open question;[174] but it would be possible.[175] The use in the Liturgy of the Hours during Passiontide and for the Adoration of the Cross is documented from the ninth century onward.[176] The beginning of the hymn, *Pange, lingua, gloriosi prœlium certaminis* was so popular that about eighty other hymns begin with these initial words,[177] most famously St. Thomas Aquinas's hymn for Corpus Christi (H 127). In the current liturgy, Venantius's *Pange, lingua, gloriosi prœlium certaminis* is used in the *Liturgia Horarum* during Holy Week and can be sung on Good Friday at the Adoration of the Cross, whereby text and rite mutually enrich each other.

169. See also Benini, *Liturgical Hermeneutics of Sacred Scripture*, 127.
170. Lentini gives as the main reasons *per brevità* ("for the sake of brevity") and a better connection with the following part of the hymn (*TDH*, 106). Yet Venantius had certainly included this stanza on the Incarnation, making a clear allusion to the Passion (hands and feet were bound tightly both in the manger and on the Cross).
171. See the commentaries of Alex Stock, *Lateinische Hymnen*, 148–57; van Tongeren, *Exaltation* , 238–43; Szövérffy, *Venantius Fortunatus*, 112–15; Benini, *Liturgical Hermeneutics*, 122–31.
172. Blume, *Unsere liturgischen Lieder*, 196 (author's translation).
173. See van Tongeren, *Exaltation*, 238.
174. Van Tongeren, *Exaltation*, 236, claims that the hymn had "no real liturgical role or function." However, here a modern distinction between liturgical and para-liturgical celebrations is made, but it would have been foreign to the mentality of the early Middle Ages.
175. In the biography of Radegund written by Sister Baudonivia, there are echoes of the hymns of the Cross by Venantius, which may be explained by their liturgical use; see Masciadri, "Pange lingua", 185–223, especially 194ff.
176. See AH 50, 71ff. for the ancient manuscripts.
177. See Chevalier, *Repertorium*, vol. 2, no. 14443–523; Fischer, "Pange lingua," 1311ff.

STANZA 1

Already the first word, *Pange*, sets a positive tone for the whole hymn.[178] It is all about praising the Cross, in which Christ won (*vicerit*) the combat (*prœlium*) of the glorious strife (*gloriosi certaminis*)[179] against the devil (see stanza 3). Therefore, Venantius interprets the Cross fundamentally as *tropæum*, as a victorious sign of our redemption. In this sense, the first stanza is an overture to the whole hymn and anticipates the central idea that the *redemptor orbis*, sacrificed (*immolatus*) on the Cross, is triumphant in victory.[180] The juxtaposition of *immolatus* and *vicerit*—which, put side by side, form a sharp contrast—expresses the Paschal Mystery (see 1 Cor 5:7; Jn 16:33; Rv 5:5) and reminds us of St. Augustine's concise statement: Christ is *victor et victima, et ideo victor quia victima*: "He was victor, therefore, because [he was] victim."[181] Venantius could already claim Colossians 2:14–15 as a biblical foundation for Christ's victory on the Cross: God "canceled the bond against us, with its legal claims, which was opposed to us, he also removed it from our midst, nailing it to the cross; despoiling the principalities and powers, he made a public spectacle of them, leading them away in triumph by it" ([Christus] *traduxit palam triumphans illos in semet ipso*).

Venantius further unfolds this idea with the word *tropæum*. The term was used by Roman soldiers to describe a wooden stake that, after a battle had been won, they stuck into the ground at the spot where the enemy had been put to flight, and from which they hung the captured weapons and shields as a sign of victory.[182] This metaphor was thus ideally suited to express Christ's victory over sin and death, in accordance with Colossians 2:14–15. Church Fathers such as Ambrose had already richly meditated on the Passion as triumph.[183] In art, such an understanding was reflected in the Cross being adorned with gems.[184]

For this first stanza, Venantius might have taken a hymn on Christ's life by

---

178. Szövérffy, *Venantius Fortunatus*, 112, explains that *pange* is used in Roman poetry in the sense of "to compose" a hymn, and from Prudentius onwards it means "to sing."

179. The tautology *prœlium certaminis* (two words with similar meaning) is found already in Cicero, *De re publica*, 2.13 (*prœlii certamen*). See Szövérffy, *Venantius Fortunatus*, 113.

180. Regarding the term *redemptor/redemptio* see the comment on *Vexilla regis prodeunt*, H 31, stanza 6. The Lord is referred to as *redemptor* seventeen times in the Vulgate (for example: Jb 19:25; Psalm 18 [19]:15; Isaiah 41:14; 44:6; 44:24; Lamentations 3:58). Here it is applied to Christ.

181. Augustine, *Conf.* 10.43. See also the Easter Sequence *Victimæ Paschali laudes*.

182. See Heid, "Kreuz," 1099–1148, especially 1118–21 for the Cross as sign of victory; Stock, *Hymnen*, 151.

183. See Reijners, *Terminology of the Holy Cross*, 192ff.; see also Prieur, *Das Kreuz in der christlichen Literatur*. In his commentary on Luke, Ambrose calls the whole Passion triumphal (*in Lucam*, 2, 63): *triduum triumphalis illius passionis*: "The Triduum of his triumphant Passion" as well as the elements like the crown of thorns, made of *spinis triumphalis*: "triumphant thorns" (*in Lucam*, 10, 105). But above all, the Cross is the sign of victory par excellence: *iam tropæum suum victor attollat. crux super humeros imponitur ut tropæum*: "The victor raises his trophy; He places the Cross on his shoulders as a trophy" (*in Lucam*, 10, 107 and 10, 109). See likewise his description of the finding of the Cross in the funeral oration for the emperor Theodosius: *Helena, . . . ut lignum crucis requireret, accessit ad Golgotha, et ait: ecce locus pugnæ, ubi est victoria? quæro vexillum salutis. . . . ego in aureis, et in ruinis Christi triumphus?*: "Helen went up to Gogotha in order to find the wood of the Cross, and she said: 'Behold the location of the battle. Where is the victory. I am seeking the banner of salvation: I in gold, Christ triumphant in shambles." (*De obitu Theodosii oratio*, 43). What Ambrose commented on in detail in his sermons, he summarized concisely in his hymns: (1) *Veni, redemptor gentium* (H 5; original title: *Intende, qui regis Israel*) at 5, 2: *carnis tropheo cingere*: "Gird on the trophy of [your] flesh"; and (2) *Iam surgit hora tertia* (H 48) at 5, 1: *celso triumphi vertice*: "at the high summit of [his] triumph" (stanza 5 is not included in the hymn as it is found in the *Liturgia Horarum*).

184. One thinks, for example, of the *crux gemmata* in the mosaic on the triumphal arch of the Basilica of Santa Maria Maggiore in Rome from the early fifth century. See Hack, *I mosaici*, panel 1.

Prudentius (348–413 AD) as a basis, where the eloquent Spanish poet similarly spoke of the *tropæum passionis* and the *triumfalem crucem* and animated the tongue to sing.[185]

STANZA 2

After the overture in stanza 1, Venantius now begins to delineate salvation history. The redemption became necessary because of the fall of the "first-formed parent" (note the alliteration *paréntis protoplásti* achieved by using the Greek loanword, possibly to highlight the very beginning). The bite into the noxious or lethal fruit (*pomi noxialis morsu*) led him to ruin in death (*morte corruit*). *Morte* and *morsu* are obviously juxtaposed on purpose and in the same assonance as *lignum* and *ligni*.[186] While in the Old Testament account the Fall is followed by the condemnation, the hymn skips the punishment and immediately highlights the compassion and condolence of the Creator (*factor condolens*; *con-dolens* means, literally, "sharing pain"). God grieved that Adam let himself be deceived and thus lost Paradise. The unfortunate event happened at the tree (*lignum*) of the knowledge of good and evil (Gn 2:9, 17; 3:1–7). The human being did not believe that he would die from that tree, but trusted the snake that ensnared and lured him with the false promise of godlike life.

Because it was a life-altering deception, the Creator in his mercy and compassion does not condemn his creature but thinks on a remedy by immediately marking (*notavit*) another tree to rescue the human person from the condemnation (*damna*) of the first one. This second tree, the Cross, becomes the tree of life (Gn 2:9).

Venantius transfers the Pauline theology of the parallel between Adam and Christ (Rom 5:12–21; 1 Cor 15:22ff., 45–49) poetically to a material level, to the wood of the tree of Paradise and of the Cross.[187] The materiality points indirectly to the relic of the Cross, thereby giving the theme a high measure of vividness.

STANZA 3

This stanza continues linking even more closely Paradise and Calvary. Venantius speaks of the order (*ordo*) that had required this work of our salvation (this is the only time he uses the first-person plural). As in numerous other classic hymns, "we" or "our" are very consciously employed in order to underline the relationship between the event of the Cross and the persons who pray the hymn today. Grammatically, *nostræ salutis* could belong to *ordo*; the meter, however, relates it to *opus*. The past perfect in *depoposcerat* could indicate that the plan of our salvation had already begun in Paradise.

Venantius employs a wordplay (*arte ut artem falleret*) to describe the way by

---

185. See *Cath* 9: 28, 1–3: *Solve vocem, mens sonora, solve linguam nobilem, / dic tropæum passionis, dic triumfalem crucem, / pange vexillum, notatis quod refulget frontibus.* See also Walpole, no. 33, l. 2, p. 167; van Tongeren, *Exaltation*, 238ff.

186. See also Stock, *Hymnen*, 152. The English translation uses alliterations as well: fall by fraud; death deceit; wood had wrought.

187. Venantius stands completely in the tradition of patristic interpretation. See, for instance, Ambrose, *In Ps* 35:3: *paradisum nobis crux reddidit Christi; hoc est lignum, quod Adæ Dominus demonstravit*: "The Cross of Christ restored Paradise to us; this is the tree [of life] that the Lord showed to Adam." See also Norberg, "Pange lingua," 71–79, especially 78.

which God accomplished our salvation: God applied an art (*arte*) to deceive the crafty devil. The art of the many-shaped destroyer, who cunningly had deceived the human being, has now been foiled by an even better plan. The Church Fathers developed the concept that God outwitted the destroyer,[188] who thought to have won by putting Jesus on the Cross but did not know that Christ, by that very act of his death, redeemed the world. Even on a literary level, the word *arte* (of God) is inserted in the middle of the sentence so as to demonstrate that God can interfere and thwart the devil's actions.

According to lines 5 and 6, Christ brought healing (see Mt 9:12) exactly there (*inde*) where (*unde*) the foe had wounded. Thus, the hymn contrasts the two trees again. The preface for the Exaltation of the Holy Cross does the same: "For you placed the salvation of the human race on the wood of the Cross, so that, where death arose, life might again spring forth and the evil one, who conquered on a tree, might likewise on a tree be conquered, through Christ our Lord."[189] The *lignum crucis* becomes the tree of life—or, in other words: both trees of Paradise, the one of death and the one of life, become one: "Where man failed in his own attempt to become like God, God succeeded in becoming like man until death, so that in the end his creature attained eternal life like him."[190]

STANZA 4

Stanza 4 introduces the Incarnation into the hymn.[191] When the fullness of time had come (Gal 4:4), Christ was sent *ab arce Patris*. The castle of the Father, though not a biblical image, fits well into the hymn because of its royal connotation (see *En acetum, fel, arundo*, H 33: 3, 5; and *Vexilla regis prodeunt*, H 31). The hymn thematizes the two natures of Christ, for only as fully divine and fully human could he accomplish our redemption. The Divine Son (*natus*) is at the same time the creator of the world (*orbis conditor*; Jn 1:3; Col 1:16). Venantius combines the account of the birth from the Virgin (Lk 1; Mt 1) with the prologue of John (*carne* [ablative: "in the flesh"] *factus*; Jn 1:14).

STANZA 5

Lustra is a period of five years. Thus, *lustra sex* refers to the thirty years of Jesus's hidden life (Lk 3:23). Venantius does not imply that Christ was crucified at the

---

188. See van Tongeren, *Exaltation*, 235, 240. See, for instance, Ambrose, *in Luc.* 4.12: *Sed non potuit melius conteri laqueus, nisi prædam aliquam diabolo demonstrasset; ut dum ille festinat ad prædam, suis laqueis ligaretur.... oportuit igitur hanc fraudem diabolo fieri, ut susciperet corpus Dominus Iesus, et corpus hoc corruptibile, corpus infirmum; ut crucifigeretur ex infirmitate*: "But the snare could not be better broken unless God should have shown some prize to the devil, so that while he (the devil) hastened towards the prize, he should be bound by his own snares.... It was necessary, therefore, for this fraud to befall the devil: that the Lord Jesus should assume a body, and that this should be a corruptible body, a weak body, so that he might be crucified out of weakness."

189. Roman Missal: *Qui salutem humani generis in ligno crucis constituisti, ut unde mors oriebatur, inde vita resurgeret; et, qui in ligno vincebat, in ligno quoque vinceretur* (Feast of the Exaltation of the Holy Cross, September 14).

190. Stock, *Hymnen*, 153 (author's translation).

191. Stanza 5 of the original hymn, which is not included in the hymn as it is found in the *Liturgia Horarum*, continues the theme of the Incarnation by describing the infant Christ laid in a manger and bound in swaddling clothes, a prophetic image of the Cross. The stanza reads: *Vagit infans inter arta / conditus præsepia, / membra pannis involuta / virgo mater alligat / et pedes manusque, crura / stricta pingit fascia*. "The infant cries laid within the narrow manger, his Virgin Mother binds his members in swaddling clothes; his feet, hands, and legs are adorned with tight bands."

age of thirty, but simply after (*iam peracta*) that time, that is, after his public ministry.

Tempus corporis is a poetic expression for his lifetime, similar to *in diebus carnis suæ* (Heb 5:7): "In the days when he was in the flesh." The wording *tempus implens* might allude to John 7:8 when Jesus at first said that he would not go to the feast in Jerusalem because his "time has not yet been fulfilled" (*tempus nondum impletum*). Later, however, he fulfills his lifetime on earth actively (*implens* might be a deliberate change of the passive *impletum*). Christ is ready to fulfil his life by giving it freely.

The hymn omits every detail of his public ministry and focuses only on his Passion. In concise participial constructions, Venantius highlights that: Jesus himself is willing (ablative absolute: *se volente*), he was even born for this purpose (*natus ad hoc*) and dedicated to his Passion. The English translation renders *deditus* with the stronger word "consecrated," which is, however, in line with the stanza's intention.

In this sense, Christ is called the Lamb to be sacrificed on the trunk of the Cross (*in crucis stipite*). The gerundive *immolandus* is translated well with "*for sacrifice.*" These lines recall the "lamb led to slaughter" of Isaiah 53:7 (quoted in Acts 8:32) and the exclamation of John the Baptist, "Behold, the lamb of God, who takes away the sin of the world" (Jn 1:29). They allude to the fact that Christ died at the same time that the paschal lambs were slaughtered in the temple for the Passover meal that night (see Jn 19:14) and so became the true paschal lamb (1 Cor 5:7). The verses evoke the Lamb in the book of Revelation, who is slain and glorified (Rv 5:12; 7:17; 19:7; 21:22ff.). The verb *levatur* (raised) might remind us that Christ, lifted up from the earth, will draw everyone to himself (Jn 12:32). Note that Venantius uses *immolare* twice in this hymn: in stanza 1, in combination with Christ's victory (*immolatus vicerit*), and here, with his death, thus linking both aspects of Christ's sacrifice and of the Paschal Mystery.

STANZA 6

Since the original hymn does not conclude with a doxology, this stanza has been taken from the *Breviarium Romanum*. It calls the Holy Spirit the *Paraclitus*, as Jesus had promised after the Last Supper (Jn 14:16, 26; 15:26; and 16:7). As Lentini explains, the last two lines have been changed to "add a new concept instead of repeating the previous one."[192] While the hymn mentions the Father and the Son, this stanza honors the whole Trinity and asks that its grace may redeem and preserve us. The English translation provides a slightly different doxology that is more in line with the hymn and praises the Trinity "for redemption and salvation." In addition, the doxology introduces the Paschal Mystery, a key theological term in the *Constitution on the Sacred Liturgy*, which Venantius, without using this modern term, had so eloquently praised.

---

192. *TDH*, 106 (author's translation).

En acetum, fel, arundo	33
Venantius Fortunatus, d. ca. 600	**Holy Week**
87 87 87 87	Lauds

En acétum, fel, arúndo,
sputa, clavi, láncea;
mite corpus perforátur,
sanguis, unda prófluit;
terra, pontus, astra, mundus
quo lavántur flúmine!

Crux fidélis, inter omnes
arbor una nóbilis!
Nulla talem silva profert
flore, fronde, gérmine.
Dulce lignum, dulci clavo
dulce pondus sústinens!

Flecte ramos, arbor alta,
tensa laxa víscera,
et rigor lentéscat ille
quem dedit natívitas,
ut supérni membra regis
miti tendas stípite.

Sola digna tu fuísti
ferre sæcli prétium,
atque portum præparáre
nauta mundo náufrago,
quem sacer cruor perúnxit
fusus Agní córpore.

Æqua Patri Filióque,
ínclito Paráclito,
sempitérna sit beátæ
Trinitáti glória,
cuius alma nos redémit
atque servat grátia. Amen.

1. See the reed, the gall and vinegar,
see the spittle, nails, and lance;
from the pierced and gentle body
streams of blood and water flow;
earth and sea and stars of heaven:
by this flood the world is cleansed!

2. Faithful Cross, above all others
noble tree that has no peer!
Such a tree no forest offers,
none in foliage, flower, or fruit.
Sweet the wood and sweet the burden
held on high by sweetest nail.

3. Lofty tree, now bend your branches,
ease your taught and rigid flesh,
let that rigor yield and soften,
yours by nature at your birth;
limbs of Christ, the King of heaven,
tend upon your gentle trunk.

4. You, the one alone found worthy,
bore the ransom of us all;
pilot, you prepared a harbor
for a lost and shipwrecked world;
by the Lamb you were anointed,
marked by streams of sacred blood.

5. Equal glory to the Father,
to the Son and Paraclete
everlasting praise and blessing
to the Holy Trinity,
Source of grace and loving kindness
that redeems and saves us still. Amen.

© Saint Gregory Institute for the Study of Latin Liturgical Texts, 1100 Connecticut Ave., Washington, DC 20036.

Text: This hymn is the second part of *Pange, lingua, gloriosi prœlium* (for more information see H 32).¹⁹³ Changes in *TDH*: stanza 1, 1: *En* for *Hic* to have a smoother beginning for the second half; 2, 5: *dulci* for *dulce*, changed to signify the ablative more easily; 3, 6: *miti* for *mite* for the same reason as in 2, 5; 4, 2: change in word order to *sæcli prétium* from *prétium sæculi* in order to reduce a surplus syllable.¹⁹⁴

COMMENTARY

STANZA 1

Venantius presents a summary of the Passion account in a few key words: vinegar (Jn 19:29f.), gall (Mt 27:34), reed (Mt 27:29f.), spitting (Mt 27:30), nails (see Jn 20:25), lance (Jn 19:34). These two lines make the whole account present, from the mocking by the soldiers to Jesus' death. Venantius lists the instruments of the Passion, the *arma Christi*, in the nominative, without any connective words, to speed up the enumeration and succinctly get to the heart of the narrative. He uses this rhetorical means (cumulation) quite often, for example, also in line 5.¹⁹⁵

The scene of the piercing with the lance seems to be especially dear to Venantius, so that he describes it in more detail. As he increases the contrast in *Vexilla regis* (H 31, stanza 2) with the *sharp* spear, here he does so by adding *mite corpus*, the gentle body. Again, Venantius uses *unda* (wave) and *flumine* (flood) instead of just water to highlight the cleansing effect (*lavantur*). The sacrifice of the *redemptor orbis* / *conditor orbis* (H 32: 1, 5, and 4, 4) has an impact for the whole creation: on earth (*terra*), sea (*pontus*) and stars (*astra*), on the classical threefold structure of the universe, on the whole world (*mundus*).¹⁹⁶ Christ becomes the sacrament of salvation for the entire cosmos.

Venantius has thereby recourse to patristic authors who interpreted the water that flowed from the side of Christ as the new stream of Paradise (Gn 2:10–14), which flows in baptism.¹⁹⁷ Although not explicitly stated, this idea is quite close to that of the Cross as the tree of life.

STANZA 2

Venantius then turns to the Cross itself and addresses it directly. In contrast to the deceit at the tree in Paradise, the Cross is faithful (*fidelis*). It is unique (*una*) among all other trees and noble, chosen by God himself (H 32: 2, 5). No forest of this world can compare with it in terms of flower (*flore*), foliage (*fronde*) and fruit (*germine*), because it is the new tree of life, outstanding in its freshness and vitality. The fruit is our redemption. The English alliteration "foliage, flower, or fruit" is very much in line with Venantius's text.

---

193. See also Stock, *Hymnen*, 148–57; van Tongeren, *Exaltation*, 238–43; Szövérffy, "Venantius Fortunatus, 107–22, especially 112–15; Benini, *Liturgical Hermeneutics of Sacred Scripture*, 122–31.
194. See *TDH*, 107.
195. See, for more examples, Walpole, p. 171.
196. Venantius uses this also in other parts of his poetry (Walpole, p. 171). See also, for instance, the hymn *Quem terra, pontus, æthera* (H 143).
197. See Rahner, *Symbole der Kirche*, 208; Stock, *Hymnen*, 155.

Moreover, its sweetness distinguishes this tree from all the others, as the repeated use of *dulce* or *dulci* unequivocally emphasizes. In clear contrast to the cruel instruments of the Passion, listed in the previous stanza and the bitterness of gall in particular, here only the redeeming effect matters. The wood of the Cross is sweet because it holds the sweet burden, Christ, by sweet nails (the collective singular in Latin is probably used for brevity). The faithful see both aspects together: the bitter suffering of Christ brought about the sweetness of redemption.

STANZA 3

The hymn continues addressing the Cross on Golgotha itself (with the dead Jesus hanging on it) and asks it to change from the hard wood of torture to the mild tree of life. Poetically skillful, the linguistic images of tree and Cross blend more and more.

The stanza calls for the lofty tree to bend its branches and grant relaxation to the outstretched body (*tensa viscera*) of the Crucified. Note here the contrast *tensa laxa* put side by side. The rigor/rigidity/hardness which by nature belongs to the Cross/tree (which birth has given it) should soften. As *lentescat* is the intensive form of the verb *lentere* (proceed slowly), it implies the process of softening, which the English translation expresses with the two words "yield and soften." Then the tree shall give rest to the limbs of Jesus at the gentle trunk (*miti stipite*). Though dead, Christ is still the king on high (*superni regis*).

STANZA 4

This stanza, originally the closing one, continues to highlight the uniqueness and dignity of the Cross by combining three metaphors of the biblical or patristic tradition. First, the Cross alone was worthy to bear the price of the world. Venantius also used the same biblical idea (Mk 10:45 and Mt 20:28; 1 Cor 6:20; 7:23; 1 Pt 1:18f.) in his hymn *Vexilla regis* (H 31, stanza 4; see more explanations there). Christ is himself the ransom for the world, which the English translation concretizes to "of us all." On the Cross he paid for our sins.

Lines 3 and 4 take up the patristic interpretation of the Cross as pilot (*nauta*) on the journey to the secure harbor (*portum*) in the midst of a shipwrecked world (*mundo naufrago*). A shipwreck was quite familiar to the ancient world. St. Paul experienced one three times (1 Cor 11:25), so that he used it also as a metaphor (see 1 Tm 1:19: "made a shipwreck of their faith"). The Church Fathers expanded that image to the situation of humanity in general and developed it further. Christ, the Savior, became the pilot of the ship, which stands for the Church. The Cross became its mast, on which Christ steered the faithful on their journey through life to the safe harbor of heaven.[198] Interestingly, here not Christ, but the Cross is called pilot, as the following relative clause makes clear. Venantius identifies Christ and the Cross.

The sacred blood (*sacer cruor*) anointed (*perunxit*) the Cross while pouring

---

198. See the detailed analysis in Rahner, *Symbole der Kirche*, 239–472; regarding Venantius, see 344, 352ff., 393ff.

from the body of the Lamb (*fusus Agni corpore*). Note the choice of words to emphasize the dignity of the blood of Christ: it does not simply flow down the Cross, it *anoints* the Cross. Above all, Venantius discreetly inserts a typological interpretation of the Passover Lamb in Egypt. Just as the blood marked the lintels, thus keeping the firstborn of the Israelites alive, so Christ, the true Passover Lamb (1 Cor 5:7), leads people into life, even to eternal life after death. The Church Fathers expanded on the parallel, and to this day, this is central to understanding the Paschal Mystery (SC, esp. 6–7). Venantius again relates the wood of the lintels to the wood of the Cross. The Cross is the doorpost that averts death. In each case the blood of the lamb has let salvation and liberation occur (Exodus) and so brought about redemption. Already in the first part of the *Pange, lingua*, Venantius referred to Christ as the Lamb that was sacrificed and thus became life for us (see comments on H 32, stanza 5).

STANZA 5

The doxology is the same as in *Pange, lingua* (see H 32, stanza 6).

Celsæ salutis gaudia	34
10th c. 8 8 8 8 (LM)	Palm Sunday of the Passion of the Lord Terce
Celsæ salútis gáudia mundus fidélis iúbilet: Iesus, redémptor ómnium, mortis perémit príncipem.	1. O let the faithful world cry out with joy at heaven's saving power, for Jesus has redeemed us all and overthrown the prince of death.
Palmæ et olívæ súrculos cœtus viándo déferens, "Hosánna David fílio" claris frequéntat vócibus.	2. The crowds advancing on their way are waving palm and olive boughs; they fill the air with loud acclaim: Hosanna to King David's Son!
Nos ergo summo príncipi currámus omnes óbviam; melos canéntes glóriæ, palmas gerámus gáudii.	3. So let us all run forth to meet this high exalted Prince and Lord; a song of glory let us sing and lift on high our palms of joy.
Cursúsque nostros lúbricos donis beátis súblevet, grates ut omni témpore ipsi ferámus débitas.	4. May he uphold with blessed gifts our steps that falter on the way, that we may give with grateful hearts the thanks we owe at every hour.
Deo Patri sit glória eiúsque soli Fílio cum Spíritu Paráclito, in sempitérna sǽcula. Amen.	5. To God the Father glory be, all honor to his only Son, one with the Spirit Paraclete, from age to age for evermore. Amen.

Text found in *TDH*, no. 104; *AH* 14, no. 61; see also note 199 below. Changes in *TDH*: this hymn is composed of stanzas 1, 3, 8, and 9 of an original hymn composed of ten stanzas for Palm Sunday;[199] stanza 3, 1: *nos* for *huic*; 4, 2: *sublevet* for *subleva*; 4, 4: *ipsi* for *tibi*. The original doxology has been replaced by a standard and movable doxology, in use with multiple variants during the Middle Ages and in the *Liturgia Horarum*.

COMMENTARY

This is a classic hymn carefully composed in Ambrosian quantitative iambic dimeter. Guido Dreves considers it to be a perfect metrical imitation of Ambrose.[200] The style and content is also classic for early Christian hymns, though without the layered imagery and depth of an Ambrosian hymn.[201] Instead, it is primarily an account of Christ's entrance into Jerusalem on Palm Sunday (stanzas 1–4 of the original hymn) followed by the narrative of Christ cleansing the Temple (stanzas 5–7 of the original). Stanza 4 of the original is transitional. It answers the unexpressed question: Why were the crowds following Christ with such enthusiasm and singing "Hosanna to the Son of David"? The stanza says: "Clearly, they understood that the meek Lamb would bind the savage lion in chains and return peace to the world."[202] Of the first seven stanzas of the original hymn only stanzas 1 and 3 remain, as stanzas 1 and 2 of the hymn in the *Liturgia Horarum*. In stanza 8 of the original hymn (stanza 3 of the present hymn), the narrative returns to the entrance of Christ into Jerusalem; but now, it includes the singers of the hymn, encouraging us to run (*curramus*, 3, 2) to meet our most high Prince (*summo principi*, 3, 1). In the final stanza before the doxology (stanza 9 of the original; stanza 4 of the present hymn), the singers beg Christ to uphold and steady their faltering steps, so that they may offer him due praise.

In the original hymn, the transition from exhortation in stanza 8 to direct address in stanza 9 is smooth. Lentini found it to be too abrupt in the shortened version. He changed the original verb *subleva* to *sublevet* (4, 2) and the pronoun *tibi* to *ipsi* (4, 4), thus moving the stanza away from direct address in the second person singular to the jussive subjunctive in the third person, and so remain in

---

199. See *AH* 14a, no. 61, p. 71. This volume of *AH* has the title: *Hymnarius Severianus: Das Hymnar der Abtei S. Severin in Neapel*, ed. Guido Dreves. The collection is based on two codices: Vatican City, BAV, Vat.lat. 7172 and Paris, BnF, Latin 1092. Both manuscripts contain with few exceptions the same hymns. Dreves gives an account of the manuscripts on the basis of handwriting and contents and concludes that they come from the late tenth to early eleventh centuries, p. 8.

200. Dreves comments: "This old hymn, which handles the rules of Ambrosian meter as strictly as Ambrose ..." (*Dieser alte Hymnus, der die Gesetze des ambrosianischen Metrums so strenge handhabt, wie Ambrosius ...*). Dreves, *Ein Jahrtausand*, 59–60.

201. In his commentary, Dreves also points out similarities in style and vocabulary between this hymn and Ambrose's hymns; for example, the rhetorical question of stanza 6 (not included in this hymn) echoes a similar question in Ambrose's Easter hymn, *Hic est dies verus Dei* (H 44): *quem non gravi solvit metu / latronis absolutio?* (literally: "Whom would the pardon of (granted to) the thief not release from grave fear?"; 2, 3–4).

202. *Videlicet cognoverat, / quod mitis agnus necteret / trucem leonem vinculis / pacemque mundo redderet* (4, 1–4 of the original hymn).

the narrative mode. Without the central story of the cleansing of the Temple, the hymn is simplified; but it is appropriate both in content and length for Terce on Palm Sunday, an office that immediately precedes the solemn celebration of Palm Sunday of the Lord's Passion.[203]

STANZA 1

The hymn introduces Holy Week with an invitation to joy, a joy caused by salvation that is both from on high and noble, elevated (*celsæ* means both). The juxtaposition at the end of lines 1 and 2 of *gaudia* and *iubilet* highlights the syntax. The first meaning of the Latin verb *iubilo* is "to shout"; as the *Oxford Latin Dictionary* says, "to let out whoops, to halloo"[204]; in the Psalms and in the Christian idiom, it generally means to shout for joy. Here in the hymn, *gaudia* is the direct object of the verb: "let them shout out their joy"; this captures the joyous spontaneity of that festive and noisy entry into Jerusalem, which caused such a stir in the city.[205] Using the accusative of the direct object here is vivid; it creates such a vivid image, in fact, that some later medieval copyists opted for the more usual ablative *gaudio*, signifying "cry out with joy."[206]

The verb *iubilo* appears often in the psalms. It is presented as a fundamental attitude of soul that grows out of the recognition of the gifts of God and his presence among us. Thus, it appears twice in the opening verses of the invitatory psalm:

Venite exultemus Domino,	Come, let us sing with exultation to the Lord,
iubilemus Deo salutari nostro	let us shout joyfully to God, our Salvation;
præoccupemus faciem eius in confessione	let us stand before his face in thanksgiving
et in psalmis iubilemus ei	and in psalms cry out to him with joy.
(Ps 94:1–2)	

Again, Psalm 97 (98):4 invites the earth at large to shout out, sing, exult, and "psalmodize" (four verbs in Latin). Then, at verse 6 of the psalm, lest one should take all of these verbs too figuratively, it continues: "with long trumpets and the sound of the shofar (ram's horn) shout in the presence of the King, the Lord."[207]

Finally, the subject of this sentence is unusual; it is *mundus fidelis*, the faithful world is called to rejoice. In the gospels, *mundus*, the world, is often invested with pejorative significance. It is the realm of the devil, the "prince of this world", and it represents all that stands against God and rejects his Messiah; it is often called *hic mundus*, "this world."[208] The hymn speaks of the faithful who are in the

---

203. *TDH*, 108.
204. *OLD*, s.v. iubilo.
205. In his Gospel, Matthew says: "And when he entered Jerusalem, all the city was stirred, saying, 'Who is this?' And the crowds kept saying, 'This is the prophet Jesus, the one from Nazareth of Galilee.'" (Mt 21:10–11).
206. See AH 14a, 71.
207. See the Latin text from the Vulgate: *iubilate Domino omnis terra cantate et exultate et psallite … in tubis ductilibus et voce tubæ corneæ iubilate in conspectu regis Domini* (Ps 97:4, 6).
208. See Jn 12:31 ("Now is the judgment of the world; now shall the prince of this world be cast out"). See also Jn 14:30; 16:11; Rom 5:12; 1 Cor 3:19; Eph 2:2; Jas 4:4.

world but not of it (Jn 15:19; 17:14–16); they are wheat among weeds (Mt 13:30). This contrast is brought out subtly by the visual juxtaposition at the beginning of line 2, of *mundus* linked to *fidelis* and, at the beginning of line 4, of *mortis* linked to the devil; the greatest evil in this world and the summation of all the others is death. Lines 3–4 present the stark contrast between Jesus, the Redeemer of all of creation (line 3)[209] and the prince of this world who is the prince of death (*mortis principem*; line 4).[210] On Palm Sunday we begin the commemoration of this great contrast and struggle, but we are in liturgical time: we know that Jesus has already annihilated death and the prince of death—*peremit* is past tense.

The hymn writer may have been thinking of a passage from St. Augustine that dwells at length on the contrast developed in the Gospel of John between the world as made by and then saved by God and the world as the realm of evil and death.

> The devil is not prince of heaven and earth and all things that are in them (Ps 145 [146]: 6) in the sense in which the world is understood when it is said: "And the world was made through him [Christ]" (Jn 1:10a). But the devil is prince of the world in the sense of what the Evangelist adds immediately when he says: "and the world did not know him" (Jn 1:10b); that is, unfaithful men with whom the world, over the total expanse of the globe, is full. Among these the faithful world sighs and groans [*mundus fidelis gemit*], whom he through whom the world was made has chosen out of the world (Jn 15:19). Concerning this world, he says: the Son of Man has come not to judge the world, but that through him the world might be saved (Jn 3:17). The world is condemned when he judges, the world is saved when he comes to heal; for just as a tree with foliage and fruit (Mk 11:13), and just as a field with chaff and grain (Mt 13:30), so also the world is filled with the unfaithful and the faithful.[211]

STANZA 2

Stanza 2 recounts the events of Palm Sunday. The account of the Lord's triumphal entry into Jerusalem is in all four gospels (Mt 21:1–11; Mk 11:1–10; Lk 19:28–40; and Jn 12:12–18). Line 4 captures some of the exuberant joy of the crowds. The adjective *clarus* refers to sight and to hearing; here it means "loud and clear." In line 3 the Hebrew acclamation *Hosanna* originally meant "please save us." The verb *frequentat* has as its direct object "Hosanna to the Son of David"; the fundamental idea behind the verb is one of a large number of people or things assembled or crowded together in one place. It also can mean a crowd in time; this is the sense that has come into the temporal English term "frequent." Here in line 3 it signifies that the crowds shout loud and clear again and again. It is a

---

209. The Latin *omnium* is all inclusive. This line is also classic. One finds it in many other hymns and texts. In the *Divine Office Hymnal*, see H 173: 1, 1; H 1: 1, 3; and in the variants *Christe, Redemptor omnium* in H 7: 1, 1; H 130: 1, 2; H 276: 1, 1; and *Tibi redemptor omnium* in H 40: 1, 1, etc.

210. See Heb 2:14; Wis 2:24.

211. *non enim cæli et terræ et omnium quæ in eis sunt, est diabolus princeps, qua significatione intellegitur mundus, ubi dictum est: et mundus per eum factus est; sed mundi est diabolus princeps, de quo mundo ibi continuo subiungit atque ait: et mundus eum non cognovit, hoc est homines infideles, quibus toto orbe terrarum mundus est plenus; inter quos gemit fidelis mundus, quem de mundo elegit, per quem factus est mundus; de quo ipse dicit: non venit filius hominis ut iudicet mundum, sed ut salvetur mundus per ipsum. mundus eo iudicante damnatur, mundus eo subveniente salvatur; quoniam sicut arbor foliis et pomis, sicut area paleis et frumentis, ita infidelibus et fidelibus plenus est mundus* (St. Augustine, *In Iohannis evangelium tractatus*, tract. 95.3–4).

poetic flourish added to what is essentially a paraphrase of the gospel narrative. It echoes the account in Luke: "As he was drawing near to the descent from the Mount of Olives, all the crowds of his disciples rejoicing began to praise God with a loud voice for all the mighty works that they had seen."[212]

STANZA 3

Stanza 3 introduces the prayer of those who sing. It asks that we may run to meet our most high Prince (lines 1–2). Let us liturgically and spiritually run and so participate in the Palm Sunday procession, singing a song of glory (line 3) and bearing in our hands spiritual palms of joy (line 4). The Latin *obviam* is rich in scriptural and liturgical connotations. Not only does it figure in John's account of Christ's entry into Jerusalem, but it also comes into the parable of the wise and foolish virgins in Matthew 25:1–13: "The Kingdom of Heaven shall be like ten virgins who took their lamps and went to meet (*obviam*) the Bridegroom" and "at midnight there was a cry, 'Behold, the Bridegroom comes. Go out to meet (*obviam*) him.'"[213] The wise virgin with trimmed lamp is an icon of the Christian spiritual life. It comes into the liturgy in antiphons, readings, notes to the psalms, intercessions, the Common of Virgins, and so on, throughout the liturgical year. It is even found in the *GILH*, 72, where the night Office, now called the Office of Readings, is discussed. Here in stanza 3, we are invited to run (*curramus*) as St. Paul exhorts us to run the race (1 Cor 9:24; Heb 12:1), and as the beloved in the Song of Songs runs after the Bridegroom (Song 1:3). Within the tradition, allusions to Scripture through short phrases and even single words, such as *curramus* and *obviam*, become a powerful means by which a hymn may expand its meaning and by which those who sing it may enter into the message of the hymn and the liturgical hour to which it belongs. The singing of this hymn invites us to enter into the holiest week of the year with a liturgical premonition of glory and the abiding joy that comes from the assured victory of our most high Prince, who is Prince of peace (Is 9:6) and whose first gift after the Resurrection is peace (Jn 20:19). He is "the faithful witness, the firstborn of the dead, and the prince of the kings of the earth, who has loved us and washed us from our sins in his own blood."[214]

STANZA 4

The prayer expressed by the hymn continues in stanza 4. "May Christ come to our assistance and support our faltering progress with his blessed gifts" (lines 1–2),[215] "so that we may be able to render to him the thanks we owe" (lines 3–4).

---

212. *Et cum adpropinquaret iam ad descensum montis Oliveti cœperunt omnes turbæ discipulorum gaudentes laudare Deum voce magna super omnibus quas viderant virtutibus* (Lk 19:37).

213. *Tunc simile erit regnum cælorum decem virginibus: quæ accipientes lampades suas exierunt obviam sponso et sponsæ ... Media autem nocte clamor factus est: Ecce sponsus venit, exite obviam ei* (Lk 19:37).

214. *est testis fidelis primogenitus mortuorum et princeps regum terræ qui dilexit nos et lavit nos a peccatis nostris in sanguine suo* (Rv 1:5).

215. The Latin *sublevo* literally means "raise up." It is found in the canticle of Hannah in thanksgiving for

The Latin *cursus* is the noun formed from the verb *curro*. We recognize that as we run to meet the Lord (3, 2), the danger of slipping and falling is ever-present; *lubricus* is a colorful word found in the hymns of Ambrose and Prudentius. It means "slippery, hazardous" and is associated with sin and temptation. The image is that of losing one's footing. Thus, in Ambrose's *Splendor paternæ gloriæ*, faults are described as slippery;[216] in Prudentius, the eyes are described as shifting, the visual equivalent of a lying tongue. He also uses the term in reference to the tongue to indicate something said without deliberation. Both Richardson and O'Daly translate *linguæ lubrico* as "a slip of the tongue."[217]

The phrase *grates debitas*, "due thanks," has religious connotations. The terms *gratias ago/refero* and *grates ago/refero* are synonyms. Nevertheless, *grates* means thanksgiving; *gratia* has a much wider range of senses. In his treatise on the differences between words, Isidore of Seville (d. 636) comments: "*Grates* (thanks) are rendered to God, *gratiæ* (thanks, favor, acknowledgement, etc.) are rendered to men because they can be returned. And so, that [phrase] is most appropriate to God which signifies a relation to worship."[218]

STANZA 5

The final stanza of the original hymn was a doxology.[219] Lentini does not explain his reasons for replacing it with a generic doxology. The reform of the *Liturgia Horarum*, however, seems to have envisioned a standard protocol for doxologies that both made them into a coherent unit with the other stanzas of the hymn, and made them clearly recognizable as doxologies. The doxology given here appears in exactly the same form nine times throughout the *Liturgia Horarum*. It is used in particular for the minor hours of Terce, Sext, and None in Weeks II and IV of the Four-Week Psalter, which may be the reason why it was chosen here.

Individual lines of this doxology appear multiple times throughout the *Hymnal* in various combinations. To give only one example: the last two lines appear together in twenty-six doxologies addressed to the Trinity as a whole. If the doxology begins by addressing the Son, then the mention of the Father is moved down to line 3 with the Holy Spirit: *cum Patre et almo Spiritu*. Also when the

---

the birth of Samuel in a passage that resonates with the Magnificat. Thus, the word enters into the liturgical memory of those who say the Office and emphasizes the gracious and wholly gratuitous help offered by God: *Dominus pauperem facit et ditat humiliat et sublevat*: "The Lord makes poor and makes rich, he humbles, and he exalts" (1 Sm 2:7).

216. *Splendor paternæ gloriæ* (3, 4): *culpam releget lubricam*. See also *Deus creator omnium* (7, 1): *exuta sensu lubrico*: in the context, faith is divested of shifting sensuality. See Fontaine, 256.

217. *Cath* 2: 26, 2–3: *ne lingua mendax, ne manus / oculive peccent lubrici*: "So may the whole day run its course, / that neither lying tongue, nor hand, / nor straying eyes fall into sin" (trans. Richardson, *Hymns*, 37); and *Cath* 1: 16, 1–2: *nec tale quidquam postea / linguæ locutus lubrico est*: "No more henceforth, by slip of tongue, / so base a word did Peter speak" (trans. Richardson, *Hymns* 33); and "And never after did he say / such a thing, a slip of the tongue" (trans. O'Daly, *Days Linked by Song*, 41). See also *Cath* 9: 19, 1: *pulsa pestis lubricorum milliformis dæmonum*: "banished was the plague of shifty demons in a thousand shapes"; the demons are slippery in the sense of deceitful, perfidious.

218. Isidore of Seville, *Liber differentiarum*, I: 264, 37: *Grates Deo aguntur, gratiæ vero hominibus, quoniam referri possunt. Idcirco optime Deo convenit, quod relationem significat ad latriam.*

219. *Laus sempiternæ gloriæ / Sit trinitati unicæ, / Patri, nato, Paraclito / In sæculorum sæcula.* (Literally: "Praise of/for eternal glory be to the one [unique] Trinity, to the Father, Son, Holy Spirit, for ages of ages").

doxology is addressed to the Son in the first line, the second line may be changed to fit the feast for which the hymn has been composed. Thus the hymns for the Christmas cycle generally have a doxology that begins: *Iesu, tibi sit gloria / qui natus es de Virgine* (see, for example, H 7, H 9, and H 14). The hymns for Epiphany (H 16, H 17, and H 18) have a different second line: *qui te revelas gentibus*. This pattern and others similar to it are found throughout the *Liturgia Horarum*.

O memoriale mortis Domini	35
St. Thomas Aquinas, d. 1274	**Holy Thursday**
11 11 11 11	Vespers

O memoriále mortis Dómini,	1. O sublime memorial of our Savior's death,
panis vivus vitam præstans hómini,	living bread from heaven giving us true life,
præsta meæ menti de te vívere	give my mind and spirit grace to live from you
et te illi semper dulce sápere.	and to taste you always sweet within my soul.
Pie pellicáne, Iesu Dómine,	2. Pelican most loving, Jesus Christ my Lord,
me immúndum munda tuo sánguine,	wash all my uncleanness in your holy blood;
cuius una stilla salvum	you could save the whole world by one
fácere	drop alone,
totum mundum quit ab omni scélere.	cleansing it of evil and all stain of sin.
Te cum reveláta cernam fácie	3. When at last I see you clearly face to face,
visu tandem lætus tuæ glóriæ,	joyful in the vision of your glorious light,
Patri, tibi laudes et	I shall sing your praises, joined to
Spirítui	heaven's host:
dicam beatórum iunctus cœtui.	Father, Son, and Spirit, joy of all the blest.
Amen.	Amen.

Text found in *TDH*, no. 105; AH 50, no. 389; Murray, *Aquinas at Prayer*, 239ff. Changes in *TDH*: this hymn is composed of stanzas 5–7 of the original hymn; stanza 2, 4: *quit ab* for *posset*; 3, 1–2 have elements taken from the original stanza 7 but rearranged, in order to make a doxology.

COMMENTARY

This hymn is based on the final stanzas of the *Adoro te devote* of St. Thomas Aquinas. The text is quite intricate, posing a complicated series of internal parallels and allusions that serve as a reflection on and praise of the divine mystery of the Eucharist. In order to show how the portions contained in the *Liturgia Horarum* are related to the hymn as a whole, this introduction will give an overview of the entire text before moving to a commentary on individual stanzas as they appear in the Divine Office.

The Dominican Paul Murray[220] considers the *Adoro te* to be "the finest prayer of Aquinas." Unlike the other Eucharistic poetry of the Angelic Doctor, however, this piece, which in the tradition often bears the heading *oratio*, does not appear in the office for Corpus Christi. Murray notes that only after the seventeenth century did it bear musical notation in the textual tradition; later use in the liturgy meant that it was often understood as part of the Corpus Christi compositions.[221] Murray suspects that it was used by Aquinas for his own personal devotion during Masses at which he was not the celebrant.[222] Additionally, Jan Heiner Tück tells the story, first recounted by William of Tocco in his early biography of Aquinas, that Thomas recited the prayer on his deathbed upon receiving the sacred host.[223] The inclusion of the *Adoro te* in Tocco's work and a critical edition of the text, published in 1996, corroborate other accounts of Aquinas reciting this prayer while dying.[224] The Angelic Doctor famously asked for "naught but you, O Lord" when Christ offered him any reward for his writings: this prayer gives us insight into the movements of Aquinas's mind and heart when this request was, by reception of the Eucharist and adoration of the sacred host, granted. Robert Wielockx describes the poem's themes succinctly: "The tension between faith and the sacramental order, on the one hand, and the beatific vision and resurrection, on the other, is the main theological idea involved in the overall structure of the *Adoro te devote*."[225]

While scholars, particularly the Benedictine André Wilmart, had before called into question whether this prayer was actually of Thomistic authorship, today its authenticity is considered certain.[226] Wielockx notes that, in addition to its inclusion in William's life of Thomas, forty-four manuscripts of the prayer, out of fifty-one total, bear Friar Thomas's name.[227] He dismisses concerns from Thomistic theologians that the words *in te fallitur* (not present in the *Liturgia Horarum* version of the text) could not have been written by Thomas: "the text does not contradict the continuous teaching of Thomas according to which the senses are not wrong when they judge their proper object, which, as far as the Eucharist is concerned, is only the sacramental species." Murray cites this passage from Wielockx and then continues: "When, however, it comes to the actual reality of Christ's presence in the Eucharist, our five senses simply cannot grasp the mystery. And that is surely the point St. Thomas is making.[228] Torrell, also

---

220. Murray, *Aquinas at Prayer*, 239.
221. Murray, 240–41.
222. Murray, 241.
223. Tück, *A Gift of Presence*, 230; William of Tocco, *Ystoria sancti Thome de Aquino*.
224. This story is also common in the manuscript tradition; see the apparatus in AH 50, 589.
225. Wielockx, *Christ Among the Medieval Dominicans*, 165.
226. Wilmart, *Auteurs spirituels*, 361–414; also Wilmart, "La tradition littéraire," 21–40.
227. Wielockx, *Christ Among the Medieval Dominicans*, 157.
228. Wielockx, 158, and Murray, *Aquinas at Prayer*, 242–43. The Thomistic scholar E. Hugueny argues that the hymn cannot have been written by St. Thomas because the verb *fallitur* signifies "deceive," whereas St. Thomas consistently teaches in the *Summa Theologiae* that the senses do not deceive and that "there is no

considering the contents of the poem in light of Thomas's theology, concludes that the *Adoro te* is not at odds with Thomas's thought, "but even invites us, on the contrary, to lean towards it."[229] We can securely consider the work to be by Aquinas, and its genius is certainly worthy of his theological and poetic mind.

The hymn as a whole consists of twenty-eight lines, organized into fourteen couplets.[230] It is written in lines of eleven syllables, with a break (*cæsura*) after the sixth syllable.[231] A stress accent always appears on the penultimate syllable of the first hemistich (half-line) and on the antepenult of the second in each line. Thus, in the line *Pie pellicáne, Iesu Dómine* (2, 1), the first half of the line before the comma has a strong stress accent on the second to the last syllable (*-ca-* of *pellicane*), and in the second half a strong accent on the third to the last syllable (*-Do-* of *Domine*). This gives the lines their distinctive character.

The prayer is neatly divided into two halves; the excerpts included in the *Liturgia Horarum* are drawn from the second half. The first half constitutes a meditation on the Eucharistic mystery; the second is a petition for various virtues in response to the profound reality contemplated in the first half. In this way, the hymn, while not originally designed for liturgical use, parallels the structure of liturgical prayer; collects are similarly divided into two parts, the first of which calls to mind some aspect or action of God, and the second of which is a petition. Most liturgical hymns are also similarly divided. The consistent use of the first person singular supports the notion that this composition was intended for personal use. The hymn is a work of great artistic finesse. Each line of every couplet ends in a two-syllable rhyme. Alliteration and assonance are frequent. The first seven couplets terminate in consonants while the final seven terminate in vowels in a manner that highlights the division between the two halves of the prayer.

Vespers for Holy Thursday is said only by those who do not participate in the Evening Mass of the Lord's Supper, which begins the Sacred Triduum. As such, this office is rarely celebrated. The omission of Vespers on this day dates to the reforms of Pope Pius XII in 1951, which moved the Mass of the Lord's Supper from the morning to the evening. Prior to the reforms following the Second Vatican Council, Holy Thursday Vespers did not contain a hymn. Thus, there was no historical precedent for a hymn to be used in this Hour.

---

deception in this sacrament" (*ST* III, q. 75, a. 5, ad 2). In the *Summa*, words for deceive are based on *decipere*, and related words, not on *fallere* (which can mean "deceive," but may also mean "fail to perceive, escape the notice, etc."). Note also that St. Thomas's phrase in this hymn is *visus, tactus, gustus in te fallitur* (line 5 of the original hymn); this means that sight, touch, and taste fail in their perception of *you*, Christ (*in te*), not in the perception of their proper objects, that is, things seen, touched, and tasted. It is quite possible that Thomas avoided a form of *decipere* in this poem to avoid precisely the theological issues raised by scholars like Hugueny, because while the two words, *deceptio* and *fallere*, are similar in meaning, the use of a different word allows the poet to highlight a sense that is more theologically accurate to the subject. Tück, commenting on a different passage, notes this broader expanse of poetic language: "Unlike theological conceptual work, which attempts to grasp the *intellectus fidei* and for that purpose employs definitional language, the poetic diction of the hymn involves the whole person at prayer and broadens the linguistic register" (Tück, *A Gift of Presence*, 235).

229. Torrell, *Saint Thomas Aquinas*, 1:135.
230. Wielockx, *Christ Among the Medieval Dominicans*, 157.
231. It is similar to other accentual imitations of Terentianean verse, a popular meter in the Middle Ages. See Norberg, *Introduction*, 73–74, 213.

A prayer of this level of craft and artistry, as well as theological precision, reflects a piety that prized the Eucharist as the pinnacle of all of life and demonstrates the acuity of Thomas's mind and heart in even the most private of contexts. Murray links this to a passage in Aquinas's theology (*In Quartum librum Sententiarum*, dist. 39, a. 6, ad 2),[232] in which the Angelic Doctor, discussing the role of faith in uniting the soul to God, quotes Hosea 2:20: "I will betroth you to myself in faith." According to Thomas one of the effects of the Eucharist is that it delights (*delectat*).[233] Here, we are privileged to see how Thomas himself experienced and expressed that delight.

STANZA I

In the context of its use in the office of Holy Thursday, the word *memoriale* refers not only to the Sacrament itself, but also to the institution of the Eucharist at the Last Supper. Tück states that "the hymn evokes the Lord's death, which stands at the center of the Eucharistic commemoration."[234]

Scriptural allusions in this stanza come from the Bread of Life discourse as well as the Last Supper. Line 1, *memoriale* evokes the words of institution, taken from Luke 22:19: *hoc facite in meam commemorationem*, "do this in memory of me." Line 2, *panis vivus* alludes to the Bread of Life discourse in John 6: *Ego sum panis vivus, qui de cælo descendi. Si quis manducaverit ex hoc pane, vivet in æternum*, "I am the living bread that came down from heaven; whoever eats this bread will live forever" (Jn 6:51). The participle *præstans* (line 2) and the imperative *præsta* (line 3) are common forms in the euchology of orations and doxologies, where we ask God to offer or grant a particular grace. In lines 2 and 3 of this hymn, they are used together in a highly suggestive way: God the living bread presents (*præstans*) life to mankind (line 2). Our response (in line 3) is to ask him, the living bread, to offer to our minds and hearts the grace to live from him, our spiritual bread.

This stanza is also filled with literary devices that highlight the theological message and the prayer beyond the signification of single words and phrases. For clarity, here is the stanza again with the English translation:

O memoriále mortis Dómini,	O sublime memorial of our Savior's death,
panis vivus vitam præstans hómini,	living bread from heaven giving us true life,
præsta meæ menti de te vívere	give my mind and spirit grace to live from you
et te illi semper dulce sápere.	and to taste you always sweet within my soul.

On the level of sound, the stanza has *alliteration*—repetition of a consonant at the beginning of a word (e.g., *panis, praesta*); *consonance*—the repetition of consonants at various places in the line (e.g., "m" and "r" in line 1; "p" and "v" in line 2, "m" again in line 3, and "s" in line 4); *assonance*—repetition of the same vowel

---

232. Murray, *Aquinas at Prayer*, 254.
233. *ST* III, q. 79, a. 1, corp.
234. Tück, *A Gift of Presence*, 239.

sound (e.g., "o" in line 1, "a" in line 2, and "e" in lines 3 and 4); finally two-syllable *rhyme* at the end of lines 1 and 2 and lines 3 and 4. Both good theology and prayer grow out of the relationships between words of like sound that extend the meaning of the lines and the syntax. The second line is particularly striking in this regard, as *panis vivus vitam praestans* creates a kind of chiasmus of initial alliteration. This literary device is fitting for such a hymn; as Tück says of another instance of chiasmus (formed by verses that the *Liturgia Horarum* omits): "the cross is written into the diction."[235] Here, in this stanza, the bread (*panis*) is showing and granting to us (*praestans*); what does he grant? He who is living (*vivus*) gives us life (*vitam*) drawn from his own life. In the final two lines, the prepositional phrase *de te* (line 3) creates both alliteration and assonance with *dulce* (line 4) at the same position in the line: all sweetness (*dulce*) comes from you (*de te*). Finally, the end-rhyme at the end of lines 3–4 show that to live from Christ (*vivere*) in the Eucharist is to taste (*sapere*) the bread from Heaven, of which manna in the desert was the figure; this is the bread "containing all sweetness within it" (versicle at Benediction of the Blessed Sacrament). Parallels between different words strategically placed also abound elsewhere in the stanza. The noun *mortis*, placed in the middle of line 1, is contrasted with *vitam*, in the middle of line 2. Most striking is the placement of *Domini* and *homini*. The two words not only rhyme, but they are nearly homophones. They highlight the Lord's giving of himself (*Domini*; genitive) to mankind (*homini*; dative): this is a classic example of graphic syntax. It is through the sacrificial death of the Lord that the living Bread is given to mankind.

The final word of line 4, *sapere*, elaborates on the mind's activity, creating a link between life in God (*vivere*; line 3) and knowledge of him (*sapere*). The knowledge signified by this verb is not purely intellectual; the fundamental meaning is "to taste, savor; thus, to have good taste, to be prudent, wise." Wisdom (*sapientia*) is the highest gift of the Holy Spirit (Is 11:2–3). The word *sapere* looks back at the truths conveyed in the first half of the prayer: Thomas has contemplated the Lord's Presence and now asks for a deeper understanding of it that leads to highest wisdom and that will cause him to taste and understand that the Lord is sweet (*dulce*; line 4).[236]

STANZA 2

The pelican, which begins this stanza, is a well-known medieval image, frequent in art. The bird was believed to inflict wounds on itself in order to feed its young with its own blood, hence the reference to the Blood of Christ in the following lines. The equivalence between Christ and the pelican is emphasized even further by the grammatical structure of the line. The words *pellicane* and *Domine* are in parallel positions in the line, *pellicane* before the caesura and *Domine* at the end of the line. Additionally, both words rhyme in their final syllable.

---

235. Tück, *A Gift of Presence*, 240.
236. See Ps 33:9 (34:8): *gustate et videte quoniam suavis est Dominus*.

The Blood of Christ is the dominant image of this stanza. Torrell notes the phrasing in lines 3–4 is in parallel with Thomas's other work: "this is an expression that Thomas uses twice, attributing it to St. Bernard: *una gutta sanguinis Christi fuit sufficiens pretium nostrae redemptionis*."[237] This idea is highlighted by the phonetic parallels between *immundum* and *munda* in line 2 and *mundum* in line 4: though a single drop is small, it is able to cleanse not only Thomas, but the whole world. With the repetition of the word *totum*, this stanza looks back to the opening lines of the original hymn. The Latin *totum* may be an adjective, meaning "whole" or "all," or an adverb, meaning "wholly, entirely, totally." In line 4 of this stanza, it is an adjective: *totum mundum* means "the whole world." Lines 3–4 of the original hymn are: *tibi se cor meum totum subicit, / quia te contemplans totum deficit*; "My whole heart subjects itself to you / because in contemplating you it fails completely (it is at a total loss)." In line 3, *totum* is an adjective, in line 4 an adverb. In this way, the uses of *totum* encompass nearly the whole text of the hymn and reflect the chasm between human frailty and divine generosity.[238]

The first three lines here have a pattern similar to that observed in the previous stanza, of alliteration either before or across the caesura: *pie pellicane, me immundum munda*, and *stilla | salvum*.

STANZA 3

This stanza has undergone substantial alteration in order to form a doxology, which is lacking in the original.[239] In AH, the final stanza reads:

Iesu, quem velatum nunc aspicio,	Jesus veiled and hidden whom I contemplate
Quando fiet illud, quod tam sitio,	when will that be granted which I so desire:
Ut te revelata cernens facie	that I may behold you with your face unveiled
Visu sim beatus tuae gloriae.	gazing at your glory and forever blest.

Both versions are deeply eschatological, and Lentini's reworking into a doxology maintains the rhyme scheme. The original, to use Wielockx's terminology, can be considered a "cadenza," which parallels another pair of couplets (lines 11–14) that concludes the first half of the poem.[240] Lentini's version reverses the force of Thomas's *velatum*, referring not to Christ currently veiled under the Eucharistic species, but to his being seen in fullness of glory in heaven. Tück makes this connection in writing on Thomas's original text: "It is hoped by the one praying that the body of Christ, still veiled (*velatum*) ... may one day be visible in an unveiled way (*revelatum*)."[241] The *Liturgia Horarum* text, therefore, preserves the eschatological force of this hymn even as it changes the focus of *velare*.

---

237. "One drop of the blood of Christ would have sufficed as the price of our redemption." See Torrell, *Saint Thomas Aquinas*, 1:134.
238. See Wielockx, *Christ Among the Medieval Dominicans*, 168.
239. *TDH*, 109.
240. Wielockx, *Christ Among the Medieval Dominicans*, 159. See his discussion of *sicio* (line 2 above) for *sitio*, which in the Middle Ages with would have rhymed aspicio (line 1 above).
241. Tück, *A Gift of Presence*, 243.

Christe, cælorum Domine 36

5th–6th c.
8 8 8 8

Holy Saturday
Office of Readings

Christe, cælórum Dómine,	1. O Christ, the Lord of heaven on high,
mundi salvátor máxime,	most glor*ious* Savior of the world,
qui crucis omnes múnere	who by the Cross, your gracious gift,
mortis solvísti légibus,	have freed us from the laws of death,
Te nunc orántes póscimus,	2. We beg you now with fervent prayer:
tua consérves múnera,	Preserve, O Lord, the holy gifts
quæ sacra per mystéria	you grant through sacred mysteries
cunctis donásti géntibus.	to every people, every land.
Tu agnus mitis, ínnocens,	3. As blameless, meek, and gentle Lamb,
oblátus terræ víctima,	the Victim offered for the world,
sanctórum vestes ómnium	you washed in your redeeming blood
tuo lavásti sánguine.	the robes of all your blessed saints.
Quos redemísti prétio	4. And those you ransomed with the price
tui sacráti córporis,	of your most sacred flesh and blood
cælo resúrgens ádvehis	you bring to heaven as you rise
ubi te laudant pérpetim.	where they extol you evermore.
Quorum nos addas número,	5. Include us in their number, Lord,
te deprecámur, Dómine,	we humbly pray and call on you,
qui Patri nos ex ómnibus	who, for the Father, made of us
fecísti regnum pópulis. Amen.	a Kingdom drawn from every race. Amen.

Text found in *TDH*, no. 109; AH 51, no. 8; Walpole, no. 49; Bulst, 108. Changes in *TDH*: for reasons that will become apparent below, Lentini made major changes to this text. They are listed in the following table:

Line	Original Hymn	Liturgia Horarum
1, 1	cæli	cælorum
1, 3	qui nos crucis munere	qui crucis omnes múnere
2, 3	quæ per legem catholicam	quæ sacra per mystéria
3, 1	immaculatus	mitis, ínnocens
3, 2	datus terræ victima	oblátus terræ víctima
3, 3	qui sanctorum vestimenta	sanctórum vestes ómnium
4, 1–4	—	newly composed
5, 3–4	una voce te sonamus,	qui Patri nos ex ómnibus
	unum laudamus carmine	fecísti regnum pópulis

Christe, cælorum Domine

The original hymn was composed of twelve four-line stanzas. The hymn as it stands now has twenty lines in five stanzas; twelve of the lines are different from the original, six are newly composed (all of stanza 4 and lines 3–4 of stanza 5), and six are original but edited.

COMMENTARY

The original hymn is ancient. It was composed in the fifth or sixth century and is found in the eighth-century manuscript *Vatican City, BAV, Reg. lat.* 11. It was based on the *Te Deum*, from which whole lines were taken and to which many allusions were made. The hymn seems to have been composed in couplets, each line having sixteen syllables, more or less. The number of syllables and line endings in a large number of the odd-numbered lines are defective. This seems to be due, in part at least, to the fact that the odd-numbered lines were originally the first part of a long sixteen-syllable line, instead of an entire eight-syllable iambic line. Here are a few examples, first with regard to syllable count: 1, 1: *Christe, cæli Domine* (seven syllables); 1, 3: *qui nos crucis munere* (seven syllables); 5, 1: *tibi omnes angeli* (seven syllables); 8, 1: *sanctus, sanctus, sanctus* (six syllables); 11, 1: *te multitudo beatorum* (nine syllables); in the original stanza 9, both lines 1 and 2 have only seven syllables, and so on. Second, with regard to line endings: most lines end with words of three or more syllables or with combinations forming a single metrical word. The penultimate syllable, however, is long and/or receives a stress accent in fifteen lines out of forty-eight; all of these lines are odd numbered lines: 9, 11, 13, 15, 19, 21, etc. Most of the even-numbered lines have line endings in regular iambic dimeter.[242]

Lentini and *cœtus* VII amended the hymn to make the stanzas regular enough to be sung to a standard liturgical melody.[243] Also, since hymns used in the liturgy rarely exceed a maximum of seven stanzas, and most have five or six, they shortened the hymn considerably. They retained, with modifications, stanzas 1, 2, and 10 of the original hymn. These have become stanzas 1–3 of the revised hymn. Stanza 4 of the revised hymn is entirely new, composed by Lentini and his team. Stanza 5 of the revised hymn is composed of lines 1–2 from stanza 12 of the original hymn with the addition of two newly composed lines. Thus, stanza 5 is hybrid with two ancient lines and two new lines. Lentini explains that the new stanza 4 recalls the Passion and gives a glimpse of the Resurrection in a way that is appropriate for the use of the hymn on Holy Saturday.

---

242. See Norberg, *Introduction*, 134; Norberg, *Les vers*, 37ff.

243. *C'est ainsi que deux des hymnes que nous venons d'analyser commencent par les vers* Rex æterne domine *et* Christe cæli domine *et nous avons souligné l'existence d'autres vers de 7 syllabes dans ces hymnes et dans d'autres. Chaque essai de correction de ces textes en ajoutant une syllabe est inutile* (Norberg, *Les vers*, 39): "Two of the hymns we have just analyzed begin with the line *Rex æterne domine* and *Christe cæli domine* [seven syllables each]. And we have also indicated the existence of other lines of seven syllables both in these hymns and in others. Each attempt to correct these texts by adding a syllable is ineffective." Norberg seems to imply that the lack of syllables was not an accident, but rather intentional, as part of the original composition. Whenever hymns are edited and changed, as this one has been, something is lost.

STANZA 1:

The entire hymn is filled with allusions to the Scriptures, especially to St. Paul, who provides a veritable mosaic of praise to the glorious gifts bestowed upon us in the crucified and risen Christ. The first stanza begins in direct address: "Christ, Lord of heaven and glorious Savior of the world.... " The relative clause that follows (lines 3–4) describes briefly the great labor and benefit of salvation. The Cross is a pure gift; by this gift (*munere crucis*), Christ released, unbound, set free (*solvisti*) all peoples (*omnes*) from the most serious bondage imaginable; that is, from legally binding sanctions that invariably lead to death (*legibus mortis*).

Thus, both the Cross and the Resurrection have revealed what has been true from the beginning, but which is confirmed and sealed in a New Covenant: Jesus is the sovereign Lord of heaven and earth. In his final address to the disciples, "Jesus came and said to them, 'All authority in heaven and on earth has been given to me'" (Mt 28:18). Paul says: "For he [God] has made known to us in all wisdom and insight the mystery of his will, according to his purpose which he set forth in Christ as a plan for the fullness of time, to unite all things in him, things in heaven and things on earth" (Eph 1:9–10); "that at the name of Jesus every knee should bow, in heaven and on earth and under the earth, and every tongue confess that Jesus Christ is Lord, to the glory of God the Father" (Phil 2:10–11); "for in him all things were created, in heaven and on earth, visible and invisible, whether thrones or dominions or principalities or authorities—all things were created through him and for him. He is before all things, and in him all things hold together. He is the head of the body, the church; he is the beginning, the first-born from the dead, that in everything he might be pre-eminent" (Col 1:16–18).

Jesus is also the glorious Savior of the world. St. Paul continues in his letter to the Colossians: "For in him all the fullness of God was pleased to dwell, and through him to reconcile to himself all things, whether on earth or in heaven, making peace by the blood of his cross" (Col 1:19–20). Paul tells the Romans, "For the law of the Spirit of life in Christ Jesus has set me free from the law of sin and death. For God has done what the law, weakened by the flesh, could not do: sending his own Son in the likeness of sinful flesh and for sin, he condemned sin in the flesh" (Rom 8:2–3); "Now we are released from the law of death" (Rom 7:2); Jesus Christ "abolished death and brought life and immortality to light through the gospel" (2 Tm 1:10). "[God] saved us, not because of deeds done by us in righteousness, but in virtue of his own mercy, by the washing of regeneration and renewal in the Holy Spirit, which he poured out upon us richly through Jesus Christ our Savior" (Ti 3:4–6).[244]

Like so many other Fathers of the Church, Fulgentius of Ruspe (d. ca. 527) dwells at length on the wonderful exchange initiated by Christ through his Cross. He says:

---

244. See 1 Jn 4:14; 2 Pt 1:11; Rv 5:13; and many other passages from the Old and New Testaments.

The death of the Son of God, which he incurred only in his body, destroyed each death in us, that of the soul and that of the flesh; and the resurrection of his flesh gave us the grace of spiritual and corporeal resurrection, in such a way that, justified first through faith in the death and resurrection of the Son of God, we might be resurrected from the death of infidelity—by which since we were naturally sons of wrath, like others, we were held in bondage [Eph 2:3–5]—and in such a way that, after the first resurrection, that is of our souls, which was granted to us in faith, we might also rise in this flesh in which we now live, never more to die. For no other reason did the true God and the eternal Life design to accept to be destroyed by our death, except in order that he might grant his own life that will last forever to us who believe in his resurrection. For this reason, the Lord of glory bore the shame of the cross, that he might give his own glory to his faithful ones, as he himself testified: "And I have given them the glory that you gave to me" [Jn 17:22].[245]

STANZA 2

Stanza 1 shows who Christ is and what are his gifts. In stanza 2 we pray to him and ask (*poscimus*) "that you preserve (*consérves*) the gifts you have given." The use of *te* ("you") and *tua* ("your") at the head of lines 1–2 intensifies the sense of petition. The repetition is also an echo of the *Te Deum*, in which fourteen out of twenty-one lines begin with a form of the personal pronoun *tu*, thereby creating a chain in which each affirmation leads to the next. The opening line of stanza 2, as a whole, evokes line 14 of the *Te Deum*: *Te nunc orantes poscimus* (2, 1) signals the shift in the present hymn from praise to petition. Similarly, in the *Te Deum*, *Te ergo, quæsumus, tuis famulis subveni* (14) introduces a major shift from an elaborate first section of praise to a short section in which we ask that those who have been redeemed by Christ's precious blood may be numbered among the saints in eternal glory. This same petition is found in stanzas 2–5 of the present hymn. In stanza 2, we begin by asking Christ to preserve in us the freedom from spiritual and corporeal death, so eloquently described by Fulgentius, and freedom from the web of laws (*legibus* is plural) that surrounds death and leads to it.

The original hymn had in line 3 *quæ per legem cathólicam*. For pastoral reasons, Lentini changed the line to *quæ sacra per mystéria* because, as he says, "Catholic law" would be a strange expression.[246] If we remember that this hymn was composed long before the word *cathólicam* had any association with "catholic" as a religious denomination, it is clear that *catholica* is taken in its traditional sense, transliterated from the Greek καθολικός, meaning "universal"; when said of the

---

245. Fulgentius of Ruspe, *Epistolæ*, 17 (*episcopi ad Scythos monachos*), 16, 384. *Mors autem Filii Dei, quam sola carne suscepit, utramque in nobis mortem, animæ scilicet carnisque, destruxit; et resurrectio carnis eius gratiam nobis et spiritalis et corporalis resurrectionis attribuit; ut, prius iustificati per fidem mortis et resurrectionis Filii Dei, resuscitaremur ab infidelitatis morte; qua cum naturaliter essemus filii iræ, sicut et ceteri, tenebamur obstricti, et post primam resurrectionem, scilicet animarum, quæ nobis in fide collata est, etiam ista carne in qua nunc vivimus resurgamus, numquam denuo morituri. Nec ob aliud Deus verus et vita æterna mortem nostram dignatus est accipere destruendam, nisi ut nobis in eius resurrectione credentibus vitam suam donaret sine fine mansuram. Dominus quoque gloriæ ideo contumeliam sustinuit crucis, ut gloriam suam donaret fidelibus suis, sicut ipse testatus est dicens: et ego claritatem quam dedisti mihi, dedi illis.*

246. He says, *che sarebbe oggi un po' strana determinazione*: "which [verse] would be today a rather strange designation."

Church, it has the sense of extending the preaching of the gospel to the whole of the community, or to the whole of the human race.[247] It was also used in the early Church to refer to the orthodox faith, as opposed to heresy. *Lex catholica* in lines 3–4 would refer then to the universal law by which Christ gave salvation to all nations. In his final instructions to the disciples before his Ascension, this is exactly what Christ says: "Thus it is written, that the Christ should suffer and on the third day rise from the dead, and that repentance and forgiveness of sins should be preached in his name to all nations [*cunctis gentibus*], beginning from Jerusalem."[248]

STANZA 3

Stanza 3 is stanza 10 of the original hymn, but the first three lines have been altered. Lentini explains that in line 1 and line 3 the meter was irregular. In line 2, there were only seven syllables. The sense of the stanza remains for the most part unchanged. The revised and original versions are given below:

Revised	*Original*
Tu agnus mitis, innocens,	Tu agnus immaculatus,
oblatus terræ victima,	datus terræ victima,
sanctorum vestes omnium	qui sanctorum vestimenta
tuo lavasti sanguine.	tuo lavasti sánguine.

If each version is recited simply without any particular effort to discover the meter, the revised version is significantly easier to follow. It fits rather well into a pattern of iambic dimeter. The original does not. It seems to vacillate between iambic and trochaic meter. The original version is slightly more difficult to recite or sing. In other respects, it has a vigor that is pleasing. Walpole calls it "a fine if rugged hymn."[249] Subtle differences in the sense are also inevitably introduced when changes are made. For example, the Latin *immaculatus* in the original is a clearer term, because a sacrificial victim must be without blemish, immaculate, rather than meek (*mitis*) and innocent (*innocens*).[250] Of course, these terms describe well the particular victim who is Christ.

This stanza, in either version, is filled with scriptural allusions. Christ is the Lamb of sacrifice. The Temple worship instituted in the Old Testament and based on sacrifice is prophetic of Christ; Isaiah 53:7 is a direct prophecy of his sacrifice: *oblatus est quia ipse voluit et non aperuit os suum; sicut ovis ad occisionem*

---

247. Ignatius of Antioch uses καθολικός in this sense before the year 107 AD, in his letter to the Smyrnaeans, 8. Cyprian of Carthage says: *ecclesia quæ catholica, una est* (*Ep.* 66.8: "the Church that is catholic is one"); see Blaise, *Dictionnaire*, 139.
248. *Tunc aperuit illis sensum ut intellegerent scripturas; et dixit eis quoniam sic scriptum est: et sic oportebat Christum pati et resurgere a mortuis die tertia et prædicari in nomine eius pænitentiam et remissionem peccatorum in omnes gentes incipientibus ab Hierosolyma* (Lk 24:46–47). See also Mt 24:14; Rom 1:5; Gal 3:8; Rv 7:9.
249. Walpole, p. 234.
250. "The lamb must be a year-old male and without blemish. You may take it from either the sheep or the goats" (Ex 12:5).

ducetur, et quasi agnus coram tondente obmutescet, et non aperiet os suum: "He was offered because he himself willed it, and he opened not his mouth: like a sheep led to the slaughter, he was led, and as a lamb before the shearer, he was silent and opened not his mouth" (Is 53:7). St. John the Baptist applies all of the Old Testament prophetic images to Christ, long before the Crucifixion, when he points to him as the Lamb of God (Jn 1:29 and 1:36).

In this stanza, the verb *lavasti* ("you have washed") represents an interesting shift in the usual sense of the verse from the Book of Revelation to which these lines refer. The passage in Scripture reads: *Hi sunt, qui venerunt, de tribulatione magna, et laverunt stolas suas, et dealbaverunt eas in sanguine Agni*: "These are the ones who have come from the great tribulation; they have washed their robes and made them white in the blood of the Lamb" (Rv 7:14). In the hymn, it is the Lamb himself who does the washing. Finally, notice again the *tu* with which the stanza begins. Though much of the material from the *Te Deum* is not present, the repetition of *tu* and *te* are clearly allusive.

STANZA 4

In stanza 3, Christ is the Lamb of sacrifice; here he is the price (*pretium*) paid for our freedom. The price was paid for the twofold debt we owed but could never have paid ourselves: the debt of justice to God for the offenses of sin and the price of our freedom from the tyrannical hold the devil had on us through death (cf. 1, 4). Christ's sinless blood, shed for our sake, paid the debt for our sins and destroyed the devil's power. "It was fitting that we should have such a high priest, holy, blameless, unstained, separated from sinners, exalted above the heavens. He has no need, like those [other] high priests, to offer sacrifices daily, first for his own sins and then for those of the people; he did this once for all when he offered up himself" (Heb 7:26–27). Paul tells the Corinthians: *empti enim estis pretio magno glorificate et portate Deum in corpore vestro*: "For you have been purchased at a great price; glorify and bear God in your body" (1 Cor 6:20). Later he insists: *pretio empti estis nolite fieri servi hominum*: "You have been purchased at a price. Do not become slaves to human beings" (1 Cor 7:23). When this hymn is recited, at the Office of Readings on Holy Saturday, we are in liturgical time: Christ has just paid the price; he is lying in the tomb; we know that at an unknown hour he will soon return to a greater fullness of life than any human being can imagine. In the *Exsultet*, the Church will soon cry out: "O wonder of your humble care for us! / O love, O charity beyond all telling, / to ransom a slave you gave away your Son!"

In lines 3–4, the verbs are in the indicative. The Church is stating facts: first, Christ will carry up with him to heaven those he has redeemed; second, they will praise him for ever. These lines are a discreet allusion to the Harrowing of Hell and the release of captives there (cf. 1, 4, *solvisti*). The facts apply to all, however, who welcome the gift of redemption and live by faith. At the Last Supper, Jesus reassures the Apostles: "Do not let your hearts be troubled. You have faith in

God; have faith also in me. In my Father's house there are many dwellings. If there were not, would I have told you that I am going to prepare a place for you? And if I go and prepare a place for you, I will come back again and take you to myself, so that where I am you also may be" (Jn 14:1–3).[251]

STANZA 5

The first two lines are from the original stanza 12. They are reminiscent of the *Te Deum*: *Ætérna fac cum sanctis tuis in glória numerári*: "Number them among your saints in eternal glory" (15). In line 2, *te deprecamur* also reminds us again of the insistence on *te* and the prayer in the last half of the *Te Deum*. Lines 3–4 are new; they bring the stanza within the realm of a doxology and are an allusion to the vision of heaven in the Book of Revelation: *post hæc vidi turbam magnam quam dinumerare nemo poterat ex omnibus gentibus et tribubus et populis et linguis stantes ante thronum et in conspectu agni amicti stolas albas et palmæ in manibus eorum*: "After this I looked, and behold, a great multitude that no one could count, from every nation, race, people, and tongue. They stood before the throne and before the Lamb, wearing white robes and holding palm branches in their hands" (Rv 7:9).

Salva, Redemptor, plasma tuum nobile	37
ca. 10th c. 12 12 12 12	Good Friday of the Passion of the Lord and Holy Saturday Terce
Salva, Redémptor, plasma tuum nóbile, signátum sancto vultus tui lúmine, ne lacerári sinas fraude dæmonum, propter quod mortis exsolvísti prétium.	1. Save us, Redeemer, noble creatures formed by you, sealed with the radiance from your sacred countenance; keep us uninjured by the demons' sly deceit, since for this reason you once paid the price of death.
Dole captívos esse tuos sérvulos, absólve reos, compedítos érige, et quos cruóre redemísti próprio, rex bone, tecum fac gaudére pérpetim. Amen.	2. Pity your servants held in base captivity, pardon the guilty, lift the shackled from their bonds; King, good and holy, bring to your eternal joy those whom you ransomed by your own redeeming blood. Amen.

Text found in *TDH*, no. 106; AH 51, no. 107. See also note 252 below.

---

251. See also Mt 25:34; Jn 17:24; 1 Jn 3:2; Rv 3:21; Rv 22:4.

COMMENTARY

This hymn is composed of two stanzas taken from a longer hymn under the title *Annue, Christe, sæculorum Domine*. In AH 51 (no. 107), it begins *Adnue*: both *Annue* and *Adnue* are found in the manuscript tradition, and Lentini and other modern editors favor *Annue* for ease of pronunciation. The original hymn is an early-medieval composition in a meter favored by Carolingian hymn writers, such as Paulinus of Aquileia. It is accentual, in iambic trimeter. There is always a word break after the fifth syllable. As a consequence, the stressed sixth syllable, which comes after the pause, causes the rest of the line to have a slightly trochaic feel. The lines are long, and the tone of the meter is elevated. It is well suited to solemn occasions.

Though the meter is used in other contexts, iambic trimeter in liturgical hymns is associated with the Apostles and with Christ or the Cross. It is the meter used for hymns for the Solemnity of Sts. Peter and Paul, the Conversion of St. Paul, the Chair of Peter, the Dedication of the Basilicas of Sts. Peter and Paul, as well as the Exaltation of the Holy Cross and a few other feasts. Stanzas that were original to *Aurea lucis et decore roseo*, the hymn for First Vespers on the solemnity of Sts. Peter and Paul (H 222), were taken from that hymn and added to this. Other stanzas were composed in honor of the other Apostles and added to *Annue, Christe, sæculorum Domine*, either before or after the first stanza. This practice resulted in a cluster of hymn texts mixed and matched for various feasts.[252]

The hymn as it stands is admirably adapted to Good Friday midmorning. It is the beginning of the day of all days, called "Good." When the liturgy becomes most solemn, as in the days of the Triduum, the offices traditionally simplify, as if to focus exclusively on the one matter at hand, the Paschal mystery. Here there are only two stanzas. Stanza 1 is a plea for salvation and protection against the deceit of the forces of evil. Stanza 2 is a cry for pity and absolution, and finally for communion with Christ in eternal joy. The hymn is simple and direct.

STANZA 1

Line 1 begins with the plea (*Salva, Redemptor*) that is the source from which all other prayers flow. On this day, today, Christ will redeem us by his blood. The Old Testament is filled with references to God as the Redeemer of Israel.[253] Today those Scriptures will be fulfilled in a way that far surpasses all that the Old Testament prophets saw. Christ will "purchase for God those from every tribe,

---

252. *Annue, Christe, sæculorum Domine* was in five of the extant eleventh-century hymnals from the Anglo-Saxon Church. The stanzas of the hymn are found in nos. 104–16 in Milfull, 373–87. See also AH 51, no. 188, pp. 216ff., and no. 107, pp. 121ff.; *TDH*, no.172, p. 177.

253. "You, O Lord, are our Father, our Redeemer you are named from of old" (Is 63:16); "I know that my Redeemer lives, and on the last day I shall rise and stand upon the earth" (Jb 19:25). Throughout the Old Testament there are numerous references to the Lord as redeemer (at least seventeen times) and to his redemptive action (over a hundred times) among the Israelites and the nations.

tongue, people, and nation" (Rv 5:9); that is, all of those whom he made (*plasma*) and all who are his noble work (*plasma tuum nobile*). The Latin *plasma* is taken directly from the Greek πλάσμα, "molded image, figure, something made of clay or other moldable substance," such as the *limus* (dust, slime, mud) of Genesis 2:7. It is also used in Scripture as a verb, *plasmo*.[254] In scriptural and patristic terms, *plasma* is a synonym for "creature." A common name for Adam throughout the Middle Ages was *protoplastus* or *primoplastus*, "the first one molded from clay."[255] Thus, forms of the word *plasma* appear in a number of hymns. *Precemur omnes cernui* (H 26) has: *memento quod sumus tui / licet caduci plasmatis* at 3, 1–2: "Remember we belong to you, formed by your hand, yet prone to fall." In the well-known Christmas hymn *Corde natus ex Parentis* (H 13), Prudentius uses it to describe the flesh of Adam from which Christ took his own flesh in the Incarnation:

Córporis formam cadúci,	He assumed a mortal body,
membra morti obnóxia	frail and needy, fit to die,
índuit, ne gens períret	that the race of Adam's children
primoplásti ex gérmine,	might not perish, lost in death,
mérserat quam lex profúndo	where sin's harmful law immersed them
noxiális tártaro.	in the hidden depths of hell.

Among the hymns for the days of creation for Weeks I and III of the Four-Week Psalter, the hymn that celebrates the work of "the sixth day" begins: *Plasmator hominis, Deus*: "O God, creator, [i.e., fashioner] of man" (H 92).[256] In his commentary on this hymn, Patrick Hala, OSB, mentions the scenes of creation that are depicted on the doors of the Cathedral of Chartres.[257] The days of creation are high up on the central arch of the north portal; they were made between 1194 and 1230. In each scene of the successive days of creation, God is seated performing an act that represents the day. His head is surrounded by a halo in which is inscribed a cross. It is Christ creating the world. In two separate scenes he creates Adam and Eve. As he creates Adam, Adam is partially visible rising out of the clay; his head rests comfortably on Christ's knee; Christ himself is strong, tender, and intent on the work of molding Adam's head. It is a beautiful and moving visual commentary on the opening lines of this hymn for Good Friday.

Line 2, *signatum sancto vultus tui lumine*, is a combined allusion to Genesis 1:26—"Let us make man in our image and likeness" (*faciamus hominem ad imaginem et similitudinem nostrum*)—and to Psalm 4:7—"The light of your countenance, O Lord, has been made a sign upon us" (*signatum est super nos lumen vultus*

---

254. See Jb 10:8; Ps 118(119):73; Sir 33:13–14. At Gn 3:7, the verb is *formavit*; in the context, it has the same meaning as *plasmavit*.

255. See, for example, St. Augustine: *Sanctus Irenæus dicit, antiquam serpentis plagam fide christi et cruce sanari, et quod protoplasti peccato fuimus tanquam vinculis alligati* (Augustine, *Contra Iulianum*); "St. Irenaeus says, The ancient wound of the serpent is healed by faith in Christ and by the Cross; and that we were fettered by the sin of our first parent as by chains" (PL 44, 662).

256. See also the hymn for Easter *O rex æterne, Domine*, H 43: 1, 3–4: "You formed Adam into a man according to your image": *iuxta tuam imaginem / Adam plasmasti hominem*.

257. Hala, *Louanges Vespérales*, 56.

tui Domine).²⁵⁸ The light of God's countenance upon us is his image and likeness. It is a holy light (*sancto vultus tui lumine*), the light of Christ the creator looking, as he creates, toward his own Incarnation and the Redemption he will accomplish.

In lines 3–4, we beg Christ to be mindful of the price he paid for our redemption and to save us from the fraudulent deceits of the demons. The price he paid was that of death: *mortis pretium*. St. Paul calls it "a great price": *empti enim estis pretio magno; glorificate et portate Deum in corpore vestro*: "For you have been purchased at a great price: glorify God in your body" (1 Cor 6:20).²⁵⁹ Christ paid the price for the sake of his creation, *plasma* (*quod* in line 4 is a relative pronoun, and *plasma* in line 1 is the antecedent). We ask him to remember. At the Easter Vigil, the Church gives his response; it is in essence that he has remade his creation more wonderfully than he made it in the beginning. Again, at the Easter Vigil, in the *Exsultet*, we can rightly say, "O happy fault that earned so great, so glorious a Redeemer!" In the prayers following the first reading, in which we hear once again the story of creation, we pray for the grace to understand the magnitude of the gift of redemption. The first option is as follows:

> Almighty ever-living God,
> who are wonderful in the ordering of all your works,
> may those you have redeemed understand
> that there exists nothing more marvelous
> than the world's creation in the beginning
> except that, at the end of the ages,
> Christ our Passover has been sacrificed.
> Who lives and reigns for ever and ever.²⁶⁰

The second option begins: "O God, who wonderfully created human nature and still more wonderfully redeemed it..."

Line 3 states simply and graphically the problem of evil: we have been deceived by it (*fraude dæmonum*). The devil is "a liar and the father of lies" (Jn 8:44); "by the envy of the devil, death entered the world, and they who are allied with him experience it" (Wis 2:24). We know only too well by experience and through the Scriptures the destructive and often hidden presence of the forces of evil—*dæmonum* is genitive plural—they act through deceit (Prv 12:20), wiles (Eph 6:11), snares (1 Tm 3:7). We beg Christ, who knows the cruelty and terror of Satan better than anyone, to protect us. The verb used here for the activity of the demons is *lacero*. It means "tear, mangle, mutilate, lacerate, severely damage, torture, harass, etc." Let us not be deceived and so led into the greatest possible distress. This prayer leads directly to the next stanza.

---

258. This translation follows the Septuagint and the Vulgate, the version known by the writers of the Latin hymns. The *Nova Vulgata* and modern English versions say: "Lift up the light of your countenance upon us, O Lord."

259. See also 1 Cor 7:22–23; 1 Pt 1:18–19.

260. Roman Missal 2011, Oration after the First Reading at the Easter Vigil.

STANZA 2

Stanza 2, lines 1–2 are structured around three strong imperatives: *dole* (line 1), *absolve* (line 2), and *erige* (also line 2). The verb *doleo* means "feel pain, it is said of the pangs of childbirth"; figuratively it means: "be afflicted, grieve, deplore, lament." It is not a common verb and is used only once in the Vulgate. The prophet Micah says: *dole et satage, filia Sion, quasi parturiens quia nunc egredieris de civitate* … : "Writhe and groan, O daughter of Zion, like a woman in labor, and show courage, for now you shall go out from the city …" (Mi 4:10).[261] Micah spoke to Jerusalem at the time of the captivity; the exile in Babylon was the result of sin and a sign of the greater captivity of sin. In liturgical time, on the morning of Good Friday, Christ's servants are still captive, in great need of a Redeemer. The imperative *dole* is addressed to Christ himself; he will have more pain than can be imagined on the Cross. Here we ask him to grieve with us and for us. The fruit of his pain and pity for us will be absolution (*absolve*) and our release from the bonds of sin (*erige*). Notice that *dole* and *absolve* are at the head of lines 1 and 2, a place of emphasis; *erige* is at the end of line 2, another place of emphasis. The second half of line 2 is an allusion to Psalm 145:7–8: "The Lord sets prisoners free; the Lord gives sight to the blind. The Lord raises up those who are cast down; the Lord loves the righteous."[262]

The fourth imperative comes in line 4, *fac*, "make," in the sense of causing something to happen: Bring it about, good King, that those you have redeemed may rejoice with you for ever. He has redeemed us by his own blood, *cruore proprio*. The word *cruor* signifies blood that has been shed and that may be coagulated, blood outside of the body, as opposed to *sanguis*, which is a more general term and signifies blood flowing in the veins and freshly flowing from a wound; *cruor* is more intense and far less common than *sanguis*. There is an element of pathos in this hymn that is built up by the imperatives in stanza 2 and by the vocabulary in both stanzas.

This final petition, *rex bone, tecum fac gaudere perpetim*, is the phrase that led Lentini to count stanza 2 as a doxology. Christ is all good and the King of kings (Rv 17:14). On this day he will gain for us the gift of eternal joy. This fits the beautiful antiphon from the liturgy of Good Friday in which the Church sings: *Crucem tuam adoramus, Domine, et sanctam resurrectionem tuam laudamus et glorificamus: ecce enim propter lignum venit gaudium in universo mundo*: "We adore your Cross, O Lord, we praise and glorify your holy Resurrection, for behold, because of the wood of a tree, joy has come to the whole world."

---

261. *Satago* is the word used in the Vulgate. It renders the Greek of the Septuagint: ἀνδρίζου (Mi 4:10), a middle imperative that means "act like a man." Be stouthearted, courageous, etc.

262. *Dominus solvit compeditos, Dominus illuminat cæcos, Dominus erigit allisos, Dominus diligit iustos.* Augustine comments on this Psalm: *Dominus ergo solvit compeditos, id est, ex mortalibus immortales facit.… Cecidit atque elisus est Adam: ille cecidit, Christus descendit. Quare descendit qui non cecidit, nisi ut levaretur qui cecidit?*: "The Lord, therefore, frees those in bondage; that is, out of mortals he makes immortals.… Adam fell and was dashed down: *he* fell, *Christ* descended. Why did he descend who did not fall, if not in order to raise up the one who fell?" (Augustine, *Enarrationes in Psalmos*, 145:17).

	Crux, mundi benedictio	38
St. Peter Damian, OSB Camald., d. 1072 8 8 8 8 (LM)		Good Friday of the Passion of the Lord and Holy Saturday Sext

Crux, mundi benedíctio,	1. O Cross, true blessing for the world,
spes cértaque redémptio,	our sure redemption, certain hope,
olim gehénnæ báiula,	of old you bore the curse of hell
nunc clara cæli iánua,	and now you shine as heaven's gate.
In te levátur hóstia	2. Your Victim, lifted up on high,
ad se qui traxit ómnia,	has drawn all things unto himself;
quam mundi princeps ímpetit	this world's deceitful prince attacks,
suúmque nihil ínvenit.	yet nothing finds to call his own.
Patri, tibi, Paráclito	3. May equal glory be to you,
sit æqua, Iesu, glória,	O Father, Jesus, Paraclete,
qui nos crucis victória	who give the victory of the Cross
concédis usque pérfrui. Amen.	to be our joy for evermore. Amen.

Text found in *TDH*, no. 107; *AH* 48, no. 18; Peter Damian, *L'opera poetica*, ed. M. Lokrantz, 115.

COMMENTARY

St. Peter Damian was born in Ravenna, in 1007. He received an education in liberal arts and was a teacher of rhetoric in Ravenna for a brief period before entering the clerical life and then an eremitical form of monastic life. By 1036, he was at Fonte Avellana, a monastery closely associated with the reforms of St. Romuald and later part of the Camaldolese congregation. In 1043, Peter was elected prior of the monastery and held that post until his death in 1072. From the beginning of his monastic life he was involved in the reform movement of spiritual and ecclesial life in the eleventh century. This resulted in his elevation to the rank of Cardinal of Ostia ca. 1057 and to more or less continuous work in the Roman Curia. For the rest of his life, Peter's time and heart were divided between the pressing needs of the Church and a deep-seated desire for the contemplative life.

His liturgical hymns are marked by the sobriety and the traditional, scripturally based characteristic of the genre, but in his hymns, his letters, and other writings there are flashes of an intense, personal piety centered around the person of Christ.[263] The monastery at Fonte Avellana was dedicated to the Holy Cross. The Cross was an essential element in the spirituality of Peter Damian.[264]

---

263. See, for example, Letter 66, 2, and Sermon 73, both cited by Mursell, *Bonds of Love*, 59–60, 67. Both texts apply the *Song of Songs* to the monastic life, a generation before St. Bernard.

264. See Mursell, *Bonds of Love*, 57–63; Peter Damian, *Letters*, general introduction, 3–12; Peter Damian, *L'opera poetica*, 114–16.

He wrote two hymns in honor of the Holy Cross. The present hymn was originally appointed for Lauds. It had five stanzas. Lentini chose stanzas 1 and 2 for this hymn (H 38) and stanzas 3 and 5 for the next hymn (H 39). Lentini added a new, generic doxology. Stanza 4 is conspicuously missing; it is one of those "flashes" of piety based on the *Song of Songs* that would lift the hymn out of the sobriety of traditional liturgical prayer. It begins: *odoris tui copia / cuncta vincit aromata*: "The abundance of your fragrance prevails over all perfumes and spices."

The hymn is in accentual iambic dimeter. Lines end with assonance in a pattern of aabb. Thus, in stanza 1 of this hymn the first two lines end in a two-syllable rhyme on -*tio*; the second two end in an assonance on -*a*. A clearer example of assonance, in contrast to rhyme, is found in *Per crucem, Christe, quæsumus* (H 39) at *quæsumus* (1, 1) and *præmium* (1, 2) with assonance on the vowel *u* but the beginning and end of the syllables differ.

STANZA 1

Both stanzas are heavily based on Scripture and on the teaching of the Fathers, as well as on the theology of Peter Damian, who was himself steeped in both. In line 1, the Cross is held up as the great and singular blessing for the world. In line 2, it is the sure hope of redemption. The ideas in lines 1 and 2 are closely related; the Cross is the greatest of blessings because it is the sure hope of our redemption. Hebrews 6:18–20 expresses the absolute certitude of our hope. The two "immutable things" by which God assures us are his oath to Abraham that he would be the father of nations and the oracle of Psalm 109 (110):4, with which the passage below concludes:

> so that by two immutable things, in which it is impossible for God to lie, we who have taken refuge might be strongly encouraged to hold fast to the hope that lies before us. This we have as an anchor of the soul, sure and firm, which reaches into the interior behind the veil, where Jesus has entered on our behalf as forerunner, made high priest forever according to the order of Melchizedek.[265]

St. Paul expresses the truth again and again that the Cross of Christ is the great divide of human existence. It is the blessing that has restored us to friendship with God and remade the universe. For example, he says to the Colossians:

> He is the head of the body, the church. He is the beginning, the firstborn from the dead, that in all things he himself might be preeminent. For in him all the fullness of God was pleased to dwell, and through him to reconcile to himself all things, whether on earth or in heaven, making peace by the blood of his Cross. And you who once were alienated and hostile in mind because of evil deeds he has now reconciled in his fleshly body through his death, to present you holy, without blemish, and irreproachable before him.[266]

---

265. *ut per duas res immobiles quibus impossibile est mentiri Deum fortissimum solacium habeamus, qui confugimus ad tenendam propositam spem quam sicut anchoram habemus animæ tutam ac firmam et incedentem usque in interiora velaminis ubi praecursor pro nobis introiit Iesus secundum ordinem Melchisedech pontifex factus in aeternum* (Heb 6:18–20). See also Vanhoye, *Letter to the Hebrews*, 114–15.

266. *et ipse est caput corporis ecclesiae qui est principium primogenitus ex mortuis ut sit in omnibus ipse primatum tenens quia in ipso conplacuit omnem plenitudinem habitare et per eum reconciliare omnia in ipsum pacificans per sanguinem crucis eius sive quae in terris sive quae in caelis sunt; et vos cum essetis aliquando alienati et inimici*

Addressing Christ directly in one of his Lenten homilies, St. Leo the Great says: "Your Cross is the fountain of all blessings; it is the cause of all graces, through which to those who believe power is given out of infirmity, glory out of opprobrium, life out of death."[267]

Finally, Peter Damian echoes his own hymn in his sermons and letters. Mursell comments:

> In a sermon for the Feast of the Exaltation (or Finding) of the Holy Cross, Damian describes the reversal wrought on the cross in a series of typically patristic antitheses: "Through wood [by eating the fruit of the forbidden tree in Eden] we were made slaves, through wood we were restored to our original freedom (*libertati pristinæ*); ....
> "Through wood the prince of proud servitude subdued us, through wood the author of humility called us back to the title deeds of freedom. Through wood the tyrant bound us in perpetual exile, through wood the most gentle king (*mitissimus rex*) declared us to be heirs in his kingdom. Through wood we were reduced to keeping the pigs and needing the husks they ate, through wood we were restored to our father's embraces, clothed in a robe with a ring, and received into the company of our original inheritance."[268]

Lines 3–4 are constructed in such a way as to emphasize a total contrast between the cross as an instrument of torture and the Cross of Christ as the gate to heaven for the human race. Thus, reading the two lines vertically, *olim* (formerly) matches *nunc* (now), *gehennæ* (hell) matches *cæli* (heaven), and *baiula* (bearer) matches *ianua* (gate). The expression *gehennæ baiula* (the bearer of hell) may seem surprising. *Gehenna* is the normal word for hell in the Scriptures, and the torment of those confined there is usually expressed by the verb *crucio*, "crucify, torture." Thus, The Book of Revelation describes the final state of the wicked as follows: "Fire came down from heaven and consumed them. The Devil who had led them astray was thrown into the pool of fire and sulfur, where the beast and the false prophets were. There they will be tormented (*cruciabuntur*) day and night forever and ever."[269]

Thanks to the death of Christ, the Cross has become the open gate of heaven against which evil is powerless. Christ says to Peter, "And so I say to you, you are Peter, and upon this rock I will build my church, and the gates of hell shall not prevail against it."[270]

STANZA 2

Stanza 2 is built on two statements by Christ that describe the action he will perform on the Cross and the proximate cause of his victory over Satan. First, with regard to lines 1–2, Christ says, "And if I am lifted up from the earth, I will draw

---

sensu in operibus malis, nunc autem reconciliavit in corpore carnis eius per mortem exhibere vos sanctos et inmaculatos et inreprehensibiles coram ipso (Col 1:18–22). See also Gal 6:14–16; Eph 2:14–16; Phil 2:8–11; Ti 2:11–14.

267. *Crux tua omnium fons benedictionum, omnium est causa gratiarum, per quam credentibus datur virtus de infirmitate, gloria de obprobrio, vita de morte*. Leo the Great, *Tractatus*: 59, recensio beta, line 179.

268. Mursell, *Bonds of Love*, 58–59 and note 37. Texts taken from Sermon 18:1 and 48:6. A "title deed" is a document that provides a person's right to ownership of property. This is a metaphor that Peter Damian uses, along with the image of the prodigal son, to explain our renewed status as free children of God, and so heirs of the Kingdom, by virtue of the Passion, Death, and Resurrection of Christ.

269. *et descendit ignis a Deo de caelo et devoravit eos et diabolus qui seducebat eos missus est in stagnum ignis et sulphuris ubi et bestia et pseudoprophetes et cruciabuntur die ac nocte in saecula saeculorum* (Rv 20:9–10).

270. *Tu es Petrus et super hanc petram aedificabo ecclesiam meam et portae inferi non praevalebunt adversum eam* (Mt 16:18). See also Rv 12:7–9.

all things to myself."[271] In the words of the hymn, he is lifted up as a victim (*hostia*). *Hostia* is the normal word used in Scripture for offerings in which the death of a living creature occurs. It may be combined with words signifying other types of offering (as in Heb 10:8 in reference to Ps 39:7–9 [40:6–8]).[272] In the Letter to the Hebrews, the single sacrifice of Christ is contrasted to the entire array of Old Testament sacrifices and offerings: "This one [Christ] offered one sacrifice for sins, and took his seat forever at the right hand of God."[273] Paul also says: "Christ loved us and gave himself up for us, a fragrant offering and sacrifice to God."[274]

Line 2 is a relative clause modifying *hostia*. The relative pronoun is *qui*, though from a grammatical standpoint it should be feminine, *quæ*, because *hostia*, the antecedent, is feminine, as is *crux*. Both forms are found in the manuscripts; *quæ* looks like a correction, *qui* is more expressive because the victim is known to be Christ himself.

Lines 3–4 are a paraphrase of the second statement of Christ: "I will no longer speak much with you, for the ruler of the world is coming. He has no claim on me."[275] Many of the English versions say, "he has no power over me." This is an interpretative translation of *quicquam*. The Latin *quicquam* only means "anything"; the King James Version, "hath nothing in me," is close to the mark. The English "claim" in the sense of a legal right better fits the context of Christ's solemn statement at the Last Supper. It also fits the meaning of lines 3–4; *impetit*, at the end of line 3, means "assail, attack, accuse."[276] In the Gospel of John, just before Christ says that if he is lifted up, he will draw all things to himself (Jn 12:32), he says: "Now is the judgment of this world, now shall the ruler of this world be cast out."[277] The ruler of this world is cast out not because Christ is more powerful than he is, but because Christ has no sin (1 Pt 2:22). The devil sifted Christ on the Cross but could find nothing there he could legally claim as his own; Christ was without sin.[278] This idea is heavily reinforced by the three-syllable assonance of the final words of line 3 (*impetit*) and line 4 (*invenit*).

In its current form, this hymn does not have a stanza containing a petition from the singers for graces appropriate to the mystery commemorated by the hymn. This is due to the fact that the hymn is divided. The petition comes in the first stanza of the next hymn (H 39).

STANZA 3

All evidence indicates that the doxology is new, composed according to the principles of the reform after the Second Vatican Council. In order to create a closer

---

271. *et ego, si exaltatus fuero, omnia traham ad meipsum* (Jn 12:32).

272. The psalm verse reads: *Sacrificium et oblationem noluisti, aures autem perfecisti mihi. Holocaustum et pro peccato non postulasti; tunc dixi "Ecce venio ...* : "Sacrifice and offering you have not wanted; but ears open to obedience you gave me. Holocausts and sin-offerings you do not require; then I said, 'Behold, I come ...'" (Ps 39:7–9). In a clear reference to Psalm 39 (40), the text at Heb 10:8 substitutes *hostias* for *sacrificium*; it reads is as follows: *superius dicens quia hostias et oblationes et holocaustomata et pro peccato noluisti nec placita sunt tibi quae secundum legem offeruntur*: "First he says, 'Sacrifices and offerings, holocausts and sin offerings, you neither desired nor delighted in.' These are offered according to the law." Heb 10:9 continues with the psalm: *tunc dixi, ecce venio ...*

273. *hic autem unam pro peccatis offerens hostiam in sempiternum sedit in dextera Dei* (Heb 10:12).

274. *Christus dilexit nos et tradidit se ipsum pro nobis oblationem et hostiam Deo in odorem suavitatis* (Eph 5:2).

275. *iam non multa loquar vobiscum venit enim princeps mundi huius et in me non habet quicquam* (Jn 14:30).

276. See also the following hymn (H 39), stanza 2.

277. *nunc iudicium est mundi, nunc princeps huius mundi eicietur foras* (Jn 12:31).

278. Ambrose, *De Isaac*, 6.55: *in illo solo nihil invenit qui peccatum non fecit*.

bond between the hymn and the doxology, the decision was made to address the same person there as in the hymn and then to reference the Trinity as a whole, or to name the other Persons of the Trinity. Here the hymn is addressed to the Cross, and so Christ is directly addressed in the first line of the doxology with *tibi*, "to you." Then, he is named in the second line.

The same doxology is added to the next hymn, the second half of this one, to the hymn for Vespers on Holy Saturday, *Auctor salutis unice* (H 34), and to a hymn for the Exaltation of the Holy Cross, *Signum crucis mirabile* (H 258). The absolute and astonishing victory of Christ over Satan, sin, and death is a theme that runs through the Easter hymns in the *Liturgia Horarum*. The early Church reveled in this victory.[279] The point is made in this doxology that Christ is not only powerful and victorious, he has won his victory for our sake: to give us a share in his victory and in the life and glory that follows. St. Paul says, "Thanks be to God who gives us the victory through our Lord Jesus Christ."[280] St. John adds that by faith we participate already in this life in the victory of the Cross:

> Whoever is begotten by God conquers the world. And the victory that conquers the world is our faith.... Whoever believes in the Son of God has this testimony within himself.... And this is the testimony: God gave us eternal life, and this life is in his Son.[281]

Per crucem, Christe, quæsumus	39
St. Peter Damian d. 1072 8 8 8 8 (LM)	Good Friday of the Passion of the Lord and Holy Saturday None

Per crucem, Christe, quǽsumus, ad vitæ transfer prǽmium quos ligni fixus stípite dignátus es redímere.	1. O Christ, hung high upon the wood, we beg you through your holy Cross: Be merciful, redeem us all, and bring us to the crown of life.
Tuæ legis artículus vetus cassat chirógraphum; antíqua perit sérvitus, vera libértas rédditur.	2. The finger of your law of love annuls the ancient writ of sin; the age-old bondage is undone, true, lasting freedom is restored.
Patri, tibi, Paráclito sit æqua, Iesu, glória, qui nos crucis victória concédis usque pérfrui. Amen.	3. May equal glory be to you, O Father, Jesus, Paraclete, who give the victory of the Cross to be our joy for evermore. Amen.

279. The hymn for Vespers at Easter, *Ad cenam Agni providi* (H 42), is typical: *Consurgit Christus tumulo, / victor redit de barathro, / tyrannum trudens vinculo / et paradisum reserans*: Christ rises from the tomb indeed, / triumphant Victor from the depths, / who thrusts the tyrant down in chains / and clears the way to Paradise.

280. *Deo autem gratias qui dedit nobis victoriam per Dominum nostrum Iesum Christum* (1 Cor 15:57).

281. *omne quod natum est ex Deo vincit mundum et haec est victoria quae vincit mundum fides nostra.... qui credit in Filio Dei habet testimonium Dei in se.... et hoc est testimonium quoniam vitam aeternam dedit nobis Deus et haec vita in Filio eius est* (1 Jn 5:4, 10–11).

Text found in *TDH*, no. 108. This hymn is composed of stanzas 3 and 5 of H 38, the previous hymn. The stanzas have been reversed. Stanza 5 comes before stanza 3. Stanza 4 is omitted.

COMMENTARY

For more detailed information on the sources for this hymn, for the introduction to the commentary, and for information about stanza 4, see H 38.

STANZA 1

Because the stanzas are reversed, this hymn begins with the petition that usually comes in one of the final stanzas of a hymn. Stanza 2, below, continues the narrative of stanza 2 in the original hymn (H 38). The prayer addresses Christ and asks him to bestow, through the Cross, the reward of life upon those (*quos*) whom he deigned to redeem as he was fixed with nails (*fixus*) to the gibbet of the Cross (*ligni stipite*).

In line 2, the verb *transfero* is significant. It means, "Take us from one thing or place over to another." This is made more evident by the preposition *ad*, "to." The implication here is: "Take us from the death that is our natural reward over into the reward of life (*ad vitæ præmium*)." This is the language of Christ in the gospels and of St. Paul. Christ says, "Amen, amen, I say to you, whoever hears my word and believes in the one who sent me has eternal life and will not come to condemnation, but has passed from death to life."[282] Paul gives thanks to the Father, "who has delivered us from the power of darkness and transferred us to the kingdom of his beloved Son, in whom we have redemption, the forgiveness of sins."[283] He tells the Romans: "For the law of the spirit of life in Christ Jesus has freed you from the law of sin and death."[284]

In these passages, and others like them, death and condemnation are the normal and expected end for mankind. The Cross was an astonishing rescue carried out at great cost, but it effectively transferred us out of the bondage of Satan into new life. This new life is a reward (*præmium*). We need to cooperate with the gift through faith, as St. Augustine says: "He who made you without you does not justify you without you."[285] Even faith is a gift, however: the fruit of Christ's initiative on our behalf. He came freely and graciously (*dignatus es*) to heal us and buy us back (*redimere*) from the prince of this world. In a sermon on the humility of Christ, Augustine says, "Indeed that humble physician came, he found the

---

282. *Amen amen dico vobis quia qui verbum meum audit et credit ei qui misit me habet vitam æternam et in iudicium non venit sed transit a morte in vitam* (Jn 5:24). See also Jn 11:25.

283. *qui eripuit nos de potestate tenebrarum et transtulit in regnum Filii dilectionis suæ in quo habemus redemptionem, remissionem peccatorum* (Col 1:13–14).

284. *Lex enim Spiritus vitæ in Christo Iesu liberavit te a lege peccati et mortis* (Rom 8:2). See also Rom 5:10; 2 Tm 1:10–12, etc.

285. *Qui ergo fecit te sine te, non te iustificat sine te* (Augustine, *Sermones ad populum*, Sermo 169, 374; see Boodts, "Augustine's Sermon 169," 36).

patient lying sick, he made common cause with him in his weakness, calling him to his own divinity. In his Passion, he killed the passions, and he hung on the wood of the Cross dying, in order to put death to death."[286]

STANZA 2

Stanza 2 is based on legal language. Lines 1–2 speak of an article of Christ's law (*articulus tuæ legis*), which annuls (*cassat*) the note of bondage, the handwritten record of a debt to be paid (*chirographum*). Lines 3–4 present the result of this legal invalidation of the *chirographum*: a state of inveterate (*antiqua*) servitude is abolished, and true freedom is restored.

The word *chirographum* appears in the Scriptures in the book of Tobit and in Colossians. It is the promissory note of which Tobit wrote two copies. He left one with his kinsman to whom he loaned a large sum of money twenty years before the story began. He sent Tobias, his son, with his own copy of the note, in order to receive the funds, and so the story unfolds. A *chirographum* is a legal document. Paul uses it in this sense, as a bond, debt, or ordinance that is legally binding. He tells the Colossians:

> And when you were dead in transgressions and the uncircumcision of your flesh, he brought you to life with him, having forgiven you all your transgressions, canceling the record of debt, the bond [*chirographum*] that stood against us with its legal demands; he took it from the midst of us, nailing it to the Cross. He despoiled principalities and powers and made a public spectacle of them, victorious over them in himself, leading them away in triumph.[287]

The Fathers of the Church had a keen sense of the legal aspects of the Crucifixion. Christ came to save mankind, not merely to blot out evil. Thus, although he could have conquered the devil by force, he chose a more costly route that honored the freedom he himself had given his rational creatures, and he saved us by bringing us into the power and grace of his life as man and as God. St. Ambrose and St. Augustine both speak eloquently of the legal aspects of the Redemption. Augustine says:

> The devil was holding the legal bond of our sins; he held against us the record of our debt. He possessed those he had deceived, he held those he had vanquished. We are all debtors, all were born with the hereditary debt. Blood without sin was poured out and it erased the legal bond due to sin.[288]

---

286. *Etenim venit ille medicus humilis, invenit iacentem ægrotum, communicavit cum illo infirmitatem suam, vocans illum ad divinitatem suam: factus est in passionibus occidens passiones, et moriens suspensus in ligno est, ut interficeret mortem* (Augustine, *Sermones ad populum*, 341A, 24, in *Miscellanea Agostiniania* 1, p. 314).

287. *et vos, cum mortui essetis in delictis et præputio carnis vestræ, convivificavit cum illo, donans vobis omnia delicta: delens quod adversum nos erat chirografum decretis quod erat contrarium nobis; et ipsum tulit de medio adfigens illud cruci, expolians principatus et potestates traduxit palam triumphans illos in semetipso* (Col 2:13–15). The *in semetipso* at the end signifies "in himself."

288. *Tenebatur cautio nostrorum peccatorum, tenebat contra nos chirographum diabolus; possidebat quos deceperat, habebat quos vicerat. Debitores omnes eramus, cum debito hereditario omnes nascuntur: fusus est sanguis sine peccato, et delevit cautionem de peccato* (Augustine, *Sermones ad populum*, 229E, 7, in *Miscellanea Agostiniania*).

As Ambrose compares Christ in his Crucifixion to Joseph sold into slavery in Egypt, he says:

> [Like Joseph] Christ was sold under the terms of the agreement; he was bound not by the price of a fault arising from his own sin, because he himself had not sinned. For a price, therefore, he contracted our debt, not paying with his own money, but taking upon himself our legal bond [*chirographum*], he removed the usurer and freed the debtor: alone he paid what was owed by all. We were not allowed to get out of the condition of slavery; he undertook it for us, so that he might drive away the servitude of the world, restore the freedom of Paradise, and bestow upon us, by the honor of fellowship with him, a new grace.[289]

Returning to line 1, since the hymn is addressed to Christ, *tuæ legis* must signify "your law." St. Peter Damian had a deep knowledge of the Psalms; he knew that various forms of *lex tua* return again and again in the twenty-two stanzas of Psalm 118 (119), a psalm wholly dedicated to the Law; the word *lex* is one of the building blocks of this didactic psalm. In the context of this hymn, therefore, the addition of *tua* to *lex* (*tuæ legis articulus*) strongly evokes both the Old Testament Law and Christ's fulfillment of it. *Articulus* signifies an article, clause, point, or section of the law. To which article of Christ's law does this line refer? The injunction behind the *chirographum* is the warning God gave to Adam in Paradise: *de ligno autem scientiæ boni et mali ne comedas in quocumque enim die comederis ex eo morte morieris*: "From the tree of the knowledge of good and evil you shall not eat, for in the day that you eat of it you shall surely die [die by death]" (Gn 2:17). If this is the warning that gives force and validity to the Law of the Old Testament, then the elimination of death will be the only effective means by which that Law may be annulled. We may say that for Peter Damian, the article of Christ's new Law (*tuæ legis artículus*) is written into the Incarnation itself. As man, Christ is without sin, he is the new Adam, "For as in Adam all die, so also in Christ all shall be made alive" (1 Cor 15:22), and "The first man Adam became a living being; the last Adam became a life-giving spirit" (1 Cor 15:45).[290] As God, he cannot be held by death: "I lay down my life, that I may take it again. No one takes it from me, but I lay it down of my own accord. I have power to lay it down, and I have power to take it again."[291] In his own person, therefore, Christ pays the debt, destroys the bond, and abrogates the old Law.

---

289. *venditus Christus condicionis susceptione, non culpæ peccati pretio non tenetur, quia peccatum ipse non fecit. pretio igitur nostrum debitum, non sua æra contraxit, chirographum sustulit, fæneratorem removit, exuit debitorem: unus exsolvit quod ab omnibus debebatur. non licebat nobis exire servitio. suscepit hoc ille pro nobis, ut servitutem mundi repelleret, libertatem paradisi restitueret, gratiam novam consortii sui honore donaret* (Ambrose, *De Ioseph*, 4.19).

290. *Sicut in Adam omnes moriuntur ita et in Christo omnes vivificabuntur* (1 Cor 15:22); *factus est primus homo Adam in animam viventem novissimus Adam in spiritum vivificantem* (1 Cor 15:45).

291. *Ego pono animam meam ut iterum sumam eam. Nemo tollit eam a me sed ego pono eam a me ipso; potestatem habeo ponendi eam et potestatem habeo iterum sumendi eam* (Jn 10:17–18).

STANZA 3

For the doxology, see H 38.

Tibi, Redemptor omnium 40

5th–6th c.   Holy Saturday
8 8 8 8   Lauds

Tibi, Redémptor ómnium,
hymnum defléntes cánimus;
ignósce nobis, Dómine,
ignósce confiténtibus.

1. To you, Redeemer of us all,
   we sing our hymn with tears and pray:
   Forgive us, Lord, for each offense,
   forgive the sins that we confess.

Qui vires hostis véteris
per crucem mortis cónteris,
qua nos vexíllum fídei,
fronte signáti, férimus,

2. By death upon the Cross you crushed
   the forces of our ancient foe;
   and we, with brow both signed and sealed,
   now raise the banner of our faith.

Illum a nobis iúgiter
repéllere dignáveris,
ne possit umquam lædere
redémptos tuo sánguine.

3. For ever in your kindness, Lord,
   drive far from us our enemy,
   that he may never wound again
   all those you ransomed by your blood.

Qui propter nos ad ínferos
descéndere dignátus es,
ut mortis debitóribus
vitæ donáres múnera,

4. You willed in mercy to descend
   and harrow hell on our behalf,
   that you might give the gift of life
   to all who owe a debt to death.

Tu es qui certo témpore
datúrus finem sæculo,
iustus cunctórum mérita
remunerátor státues.

5. Then at the time you have ordained
   you shall dissolve this passing world,
   the Judge who justly grants to each
   the recompense their lives deserve.

Te ergo, Christe, quæsumus,
ut nostra cures vúlnera,
qui es cum Patre et Spíritu
laudándus in perpétuum. Amen.

6. O Christ, we beg you, heal our wounds,
   who with the Father ever blest
   and with the Spirit evermore
   are worthy of eternal praise. Amen.

Text found in *TDH*, no. 110; AH 51, no. 2; Bulst, 92; Walpole, no. 42. Note that the stanzas of the original hymn have been significantly edited in order to create this version. From the original hymn, lines from stanzas 12, 9, 10, 15, and 16 have been taken with modifications, in order to configure the hymn for Holy Saturday. See the detailed notes in *TDH*.

COMMENTARY

This ancient hymn for Holy Saturday combines a petition for mercy with a request for defense from the enemy and a celebration of Christ's victory over death.[292] This version comes from the second part of the hymn *O rex æterne, Domine* (H 43), which is prescribed in the Rule of Caesarius of Arles for Sunday Matins.[293] Here Christ is proclaimed as Judge, Redeemer, and even (in the doxology) as Physician. Moreover, the Lord is supremely equitable in his distribution of gifts and "merits" (*merita*, 5, 3) to the faithful. The account of salvation thus evokes a vision of Christ as *victor* over death at the culmination of the Paschal Mystery.

In its language and style this early *Ambrosianum* resembles other imitations of Ambrose's authentic corpus. We find many terms (noted below) drawn directly from those originals as well as features such as repetition and alliteration (e.g., 4, 2: *descendere dignatus es*). By these Ambrosian features the hymn reflects early Latin hymnody's expanding application for feasts, such as Holy Saturday, that acquired distinctive status in the liturgical calendar in the fifth and sixth centuries. Moreover, the hymn's language and references include many implicit links to the traditional celebration of the initiation of catechumens at the Easter Vigil.

STANZA 1

The opening stanza presents the singers as mourning upon their Redeemer's death. The title, "Redeemer of all" (*Redemptor omnium*), appears in many hymns (see, e.g., H 1: 1, 3; H 7: 1, 1), functioning both as a title of Christ and a convenient metrical unit. Addressing Christ directly, the request for forgiveness, repeated in the same position in line 3 and line 4, adds an urgency and immediacy to the petition. As is frequent in hymns, participles highlight the present state of the petitioners, here identified as "weeping" (*deflentes*).

The opening line, which Lentini alters from a text that refers to its original setting for Vespers, adopts familiar formulas. In the Vulgate text, the Lord is referred to as *redemptor* throughout the Old Testament, as well as in the New.[294] Moreover, the hymn's invocation directly recalls the famous line of Ambrose's Christmas hymn (now used in late Advent), *Veni, redemptor gentium* (H 5). The language sets the tone for a hymn that will recall and implore the Lord's saving work.

At the same time, the opening stanza invites the congregation into a posture of penance and contrition, linking the commemoration of Christ's paschal suffering to the humbled state of the congregation. The mourning singers beseech God's mercy by repeating the imperative "forgive" (*ignosce*) at the start of lines 3

---

292. Walpole, pp. 211–12, notes the unusual form and transmission of the ancient hymn from which this hymn is largely taken. It is possible that it was originally two hymns later joined, though at an early date.

293. *TDH*, 114; there Lentini notes the singular praise that Bede gave to the original hymn.

294. See, for example, Jb 19:25: "I know that my Redeemer lives"; Is 41:14: "Fear not, you worm Jacob, you men of Israel. I shall help you, says the Lord and your Redeemer, the Holy One of Israel"; 44:24: "Thus says the Lord, your Redeemer, who formed you from the womb"; 49:26: "Then all flesh shall know that I am the Lord your Savior, and your Redeemer, the Mighty One of Jacob"; 54:8: "I hid my face from you, but with everlasting love I will have compassion on you, says the Lord, your Redeemer."

and 4. While the term itself is not common in biblical sources, the call for mercy and the request for freedom from sin appears often in the Psalms.[295] The singers are again described actively, with the participle "confessing" (*confitentibus*). The verbal root can refer not only to the confession of sins, but also to the confession of praise.[296]

STANZA 2

The hymn shifts to recount Christ's victory over the "strength" or "forces" (*vires*) of the ancient enemy. The "cross of death" (*crucem mortis*) is the tool by which the Lord achieves that victory, and which subsequently becomes the "banner" (*vexillum*) of the faithful. That same Cross is marked on the brow of believers.

The "ancient foe" (*hostis veteris*) whose strength is crushed by Christ is the devil, defeated through the Cross. The label itself recalls biblical references to Satan as the adversary who has opposed humanity from the beginning (see Gn 3:15) and the phrase itself (i.e., *hostis veteris*) appears in early Latin sources.[297] Christ's victory over the foe comes through the Cross (see Col 2:14–15). The theme of Christ's conquest of death (*mors*) is common in the earliest hymns; in *Victor Nabor Felix pii* Ambrose identifies the *mors* of the Christian as his "triumph" (line 26: *triumphus*). The language of "crushed" (*conteris*) appears in the Psalms to refer to God's destruction of his enemies and evokes the promise to Eve in Genesis, when God addresses the serpent: "She shall crush your head."[298] In the hymn, then, the Cross of Christ recalled on Holy Saturday is not simply the tool of Christ's triumph, it is also the manner by which Christ's victory resembles the way that God, who is praised in the Old Testament, achieves his victory over his foes.

The final couplet of the stanza emphasizes the congregation's participation in that victory. We are "signed" (*signati*) with the Cross on our brows. The practice of marking the believer with the Cross appears quite early in Christian sources, and eventually became linked to the enrollment in the catechumenate.[299] Given the background, the reference may resonate with the paschal celebration of initiation.

The singers also bear "the banner of faith" (*vexillum fidei*). While the celebration of the "banners" is most commonly linked to the famous hymn of Venantius Fortunatus *Vexilla regis prodeunt* (H 31), the specific phrase of our hymn appears quite frequently in early Christian writings. Ambrose uses it, for example, to indicate the distinctive mark that consecrated virginity manifests.[300] While the

295. See Ps 50 (51):1; Ps 24 (25):18.
296. A multivalence that Augustine exploits throughout his *Confessions*; see Mayer, "Confessio, confiteri," in *Augustinus-Lexikon*, 1:1122–34.
297. See Cyprian, *Ad Fortunatum*, preface 2: *Adversarius vetus est et hostis antiquus cum quo prœlium gerimus*: "The adversary is of old and the enemy ancient, with whom we wage our battle" (Cyprian, *Opera*, vol. 1).
298. *Inimicitias ponam inter te et mulierem et semen tuum et semen illius ipsa conteret caput tuum et tu insidiaberis calcaneo eius*: "I will put enmities between thee and the woman, and thy seed and her seed: she shall crush thy head, and thou shalt lie in wait for her heel" (Gn 3:15). See Walpole, p. 215, note on line 34. He also refers to Rom 16:20: *Deus ... conterat Satanam*; cf. Ps 144:20, 145:9.
299. See Tertullian, *De corona* 3, for early evidence.
300. St. Ambrose, *De virginibus* 2.2.15; see also Peter Chrysologus, sermons 12 and 11.

precise denotation of the phrase is somewhat ambiguous, "the banner of faith" probably refers not only to the subjective belief of the singers, but also to their profession of credal faith, that is, their public profession of the "faith" of the Church at the occasion of their baptism and initiation. The congregation is thus incorporated into the paschal triumph with their marks of consecration and the commitment to ecclesial doctrine.

STANZA 3

The hymn shifts to recall Christ's saving act in deigning continually (*iugiter*) to drive the evil one from the congregation. The language of wounding (*lædere*) is set in contrast to the language that evokes those redeemed by Christ's blood, a theme that appears frequently in these early hymns, and recalls the opening invocation of the "redeemer."

Through his Cross, Christ has "deigned" (*dignaveris*) to protect his people from their enemy. The same verb is repeated (in the perfect) in 4, 2, emphasizing the Word's loving "condescension" that leads him not only to take on human flesh, but to come down even further to embrace suffering and death.[301] The language of "continually / without end" (*iugiter*) draws from Ambrose's original corpus (see *Intende qui Regis Israel*, line 32) and appears often in later hymns. As with the use of the participles in lines 2 and 4, the language stresses our ongoing song and God's ongoing grace.

The devil is often described as threatening to wound (*lædere*) the faithful.[302] Moreover, the victory over the devil presented in Revelation uses the same language to indicate the protection promised to the disciple: "The victor shall not be harmed (*lædetur*) by the second death."[303] Thus, the language promises security to the baptized (or, perhaps, those preparing for baptism).

The phrase "ransomed by your blood" (*redemptos tuo sanguine*) recalls not only the saving act signaled by the opening invocation, but also refers to the ongoing effect of Christ's suffering (*ne posit umquam lædere*). The theme and the specific language appear in the earlier, influential hymn *Te Deum* (H 59: 3, 7), as well as in biblical references.[304] We are again reminded of Christ's redeeming mission.

STANZA 4

The fourth stanza extends the redemptive work beyond the living. The language of "deigned" is repeated (*dignatus es*) in recalling the saving act of the redemption of the dead. The credal reference, signaled by the phrase *ad inferos*, is explained as Christ's strategy of paying the price for life that was owed by the dead. Note the alliteration of *d-* sounds adding stress to both the debt owed to death

---

301. On condescension in patristic theology (and classical rhetoric), see Rylaarsdam, *John Chrysostom on Divine Pedagogy*, 13–54.
302. See Jerome, *Ep.*, 42.1.
303. Rv 2:11.
304. See Rv 5:9: *quoniam occisus es, et redemisti nos Deo in sanguine tuo ex omni tribu, et lingua, et populo, et natione*; see also Heb 9:12; Eph 1:7.

(*debitoribus*) and the price that Christ paid (*donares munera*) for life, for our salvation (*propter nos*).

Both phrases in line 13 have credal references: Christ's coming "on our behalf" (*propter nos*) appears in the original Nicene Creed of 325 and was retained through subsequent developments; Christ's descent "to the dead" (*ad inferos*) appears in other ancient creeds and refers to his work saving those who had died before his coming.[305] The term *descendere* in line 14 reinforces the reference to the credal *descensus* of Christ. In the stanza, then, the singers, who may include catechumens, recall the foundational faith in the Harrowing of Hell.

The theme of the debt to death appears frequently in early Christian literature, recalling Matthew 26:66: "He deserves to die" (*reus mortis*). Christ, who did not in fact deserve to die, pays off the debt owed by all those burdened with sin. The theme of the reign of "death" (*mortis*) echoes the "cross of death" in line 6. The transactional, even financial, nature of Christ's payment on our behalf is evoked with the language of "gifts" (*munera*; see Col 2:14).

STANZA 5

We move from the salvation of the dead to consider judgment. Following the credal pattern, which proceeds from Christ's saving action to the future judgment ("he will come to judge the living and the dead"), themes of divine justice and proper ordering inform this penultimate stanza. After the congregation has celebrated the expansive work of the Cross, we turn to contemplate Christ's return.

The opening couplet announces Christ's plan to give a strict "limit" (*finem*) to the world. Like many of the hymns for the canonical hours, the singers celebrate the divine divisions of time.[306] Christ has established a fixed time (*certo tempore*) for the Last Judgment. Moreover, Christ's determination indicates that the "age" (*sæculo*) will itself have an end. The pattern of ordering appears also in the final couplet. Christ is the "just one" (*iustus*) who "determines" (*statues*) the proper repayment for all. As *remunerator* Christ is instantiating the *munera* that he had granted to all in the previous stanza (4, 4). The "recompense" or "deserts" (*merita*) that the just Christ determines corresponds perfectly to the lives of those he judges (see 2 Cor 5:10; Heb 6:6; and Rv 2:23).

STANZA 6

The final doxology closely follows familiar patterns. The distinctive line 2, however, adds appropriate praise of Christ's salvific self-offering, emphasizing Christ's role as healer of wounds (*cures vulnera*).[307] Thus Christ the Redeemer is celebrated also as the Divine Physician, a role that would again be encouraging to any catechumen.

---

305. See 1 Pt 4:6. For background, see Connell, "*Descensus Christi ad Inferos*," 262–82.
306. See Dunkle, "Here We Go Again," forthcoming.
307. As Walpole, p. 217, notes, this meaning of *cures* shows the development from the classical sense of "care for" to the later sense of "cure" or "heal."

Auctor salutis unice	41

10th c.
8 8 8 8 (LM)

Holy Saturday
Vespers

Auctor salútis únice, mundi redémptor ínclite, rex, Christe, nobis ánnue crucis fecúndæ glóriam.	1. Sole Author of redeeming grace, exalted Savior of the world, O Christ, our King, grant us this day the glory of your fruitful Cross.
Tu morte mortem díruens vitámque vita lárgiens, mortis minístrum súbdolum devíceras diábolum.	2. Destroying death for us by death, bestowing life on us by life, you crushed our foe, the prince of lies and cunning minister of death.
Piis amóris ártibus somno sepúlcri tráditus, sedes reclúdis ínferi patrésque dicis líberos.	3. Consigned to sleep within the tomb by holy rites and acts of love, you opened wide the underworld, declaring righteous forebears free.
Nunc in Paréntis déxtera sacráta fulgens víctima, audi, precámur, vívido tuo redémptos sánguine,	4. O sacred Victim clothed in light, now at the Father's right enthroned, receive our humble prayers and hear those ransomed by your living blood,
Quo te diébus ómnibus puris sequéntes móribus, advérsus omnes ímpetus crucis ferámus lábarum.	5. That by it we may follow you with righteous deeds through all our days and raise the standard of the Cross against attack from every foe.
Patri, tibi, Paráclito sit æqua, Iesu, glória, qui nos crucis victória concédis usque pérfrui. Amen.	6. May equal glory be to you, O Father, Jesus, Paraclete, who give the victory of the Cross to be our joy for evermore. Amen.

Text fount in *TDH*, no. 111; AH 4, 22. Changes in *TDH*: stanza 1, 1: *unicus* has been changed to *unice*; 1, 2: *inclitus* has been changed to *inclite*; stanza 2 of the original has been removed, stanza 3 of the original is now stanza 2; 2, 1: *hinc* has been changed to *tu*; stanza 3 is new; stanza 5, 1–4 has been reconfigured; the doxology is the same as in H 38.

COMMENTARY

This hymn is found in the earliest Anglo-Saxon hymnals from the tenth century. It seems to have originated in the eastern part of the Carolingian empire.[308] It

---

308. Milfull, 23 and 41–43.

was copied into the Bosworth Psalter, also called the Canterbury Hymnal in AH 51, at the end of the tenth century.[309] The vocatives in 1, 1–2 appear to be an early variant. Lentini chose them because they prepare for the vocative *Christe* in line 3. The hymn was variously assigned to Lauds and Vespers during Passiontide. In assigning it to Vespers on Holy Saturday, Lentini suppressed the original stanza 2 on the Passion and Cross, as less appropriate for Holy Saturday. He used the original stanza 3 as stanza 2 and then composed a new stanza 3 for Holy Saturday, in order to introduce themes of the burial, the descent into hell, and the liberation of the Old Testament saints. Finally, he reconfigured stanza 5 on the grounds that the original is unclear.[310] The two versions follow:

Original
Quo te sequentes omnibus
morum processu sæculis
adversus omne scandalum
crucis feramus labarum

Liturgia Horarum
Quo te diébus ómnibus
puris sequéntes móribus,
advérsus omnes ímpetus
crucis ferámus lábarum.

STANZA 1

The hymn opens by addressing Christ as *Auctor*. He is the originator, the exemplar, and the maker of our salvation. He is unique (*unice*), the only one capable of saving us. He has accomplished this work by redeeming us from slavery to the power of evil (line 2); he is our King (line 3), and he continues to save us by granting us through the liturgy, as we sing (*annue*), a share in the fruits of his Cross (line 4). It is Holy Saturday evening; we contemplate the glory that will be the greatest fruit of all.

The letter to the Hebrews provides a beautiful commentary on the significance of *auctor* in this first stanza. At the beginning of the letter, we read; "For it was fitting that he, for whom and through whom all things exist, in leading many sons into glory, should make the author of their salvation perfect through suffering."[311] Then, toward the end of the letter: "Therefore, since we are surrounded by so great a cloud of witnesses, let us also lay aside every weight, and sin which clings so closely, and let us run with endurance the race that is set before us, looking to Jesus, the author and perfecter of our faith, who for the joy that was set before him endured the cross, despising the shame, and is seated at the right hand of the throne of God."[312] Notice that there is an inclusion here: *auctor fidei*

---

309. The shelfmark for this hymnal is London, British Library, Add. MS 37517. See AH 51, pp. xxxvi–xxxix. The hymns in this collection are some of the earliest belonging to the New Hymnal. See the historical accounts of the transition from the Old to the New Hymnal in Walpole, xi–xix; Gneuss, Latin Hymns, 408–13 and the tables on 418–21; and Milfull, 1–8.

310. If one reads the line endings vertically and if one remembers that *sæculis* refers to time as well as space, the stanza becomes clearer. Milfull translates: "so that we may follow you in all our ways, as we proceed through the world, and bear the standard of the cross against all scandal" (Milfull, 280).

311. *Decebat enim eum, propter quem omnia, et per quem omnia, qui multos filios in gloriam adduxerat, auctorem salutis eorum per passionem consummare* (Heb 2:10).

312. *ideoque et nos tantam habentes inpositam nubem testium, deponentes omne pondus et circumstans nos*

in Hebrews 12:2 corresponds to *auctor salutis* in 2:10; *consummator* in 12:2 corresponds to *consummare* in 2:10. The earlier verse refers to God the Father, the later to Christ himself. In both, it is the same sovereign power that uses the means that are fitting to the end proposed. In both verses the end sought is lasting joy for us who are saved. Christ, as Man and God, has wholly identified himself with the joy that is proposed and that will be ours tomorrow.

In line 4, the Cross is described as fruitful (*fecunda*). This line speaks to a long tradition of associating the Cross, the wood of a tree, with the tree of life in Paradise, lost by Adam and restored by Christ (1 Cor 15:22). Chromatius of Aquileia (d. 406/7) says: "What the tree of life could not offer to man then, in Paradise, the Passion of Christ has given; through the tree of the Cross; human nature has received the lost grace, which it could not regain through the tree of life." And in another sermon, he says: "And so in the Book of Revelation we read: 'To the one victor [literally: the who-is-conquering: *vincenti*] I will give the tree of life to eat, which is in the Paradise of my God' [Rv 2:7]. He says 'the victor' not 'the vanquished' [*victo*]; it is given to the righteous, not to the sinner because this fruit belongs to the righteous, which is given to those who are victorious only after their triumph. For this Christ conquered: that we might conquer."[313]

STANZA 2

Stanza 2 develops the paradox, so often expressed in the New Testament and in patristic writings: the life that dies thereby destroys death. By his physical death, the Author of life vanquished and despoiled the cunning and deceitful Satan (line 4), minister of death (line 3) who held tyrannical sway over all those who (in Adam) had forfeited their lives and fallen under his power. This theme appears throughout the long tradition of liturgical hymnody.[314] In St. Ambrose's Easter hymn, *Hic est dies verus Dei* (H 44), stanza 5 is a cry of wonder:[315]

Quid hoc potest sublimius,	What could be more sublime than this:
ut culpa quærat gratiam,	that guilt should seek the gift of grace,
metumque solvat caritas	that charity should cast out fear,
reddatque mors vitam novam?	and death should render life renewed?

---

peccatum, per patientiam curramus propositum nobis certamen, aspicientes in auctorem fidei et consummatorem Iesum, qui pro proposito sibi gaudio sustinuit crucem, confusione contempta atque in dextera sedis Dei sedit (Heb 12:1–2).

313. *Denique quod præstare homini tunc non potuit arbor vitæ in paradiso, præstitit Christi passio; et recepit amissam gratiam per arborem crucis, quam tunc per arborem vitæ recuperare non potuit* (Chromatius of Aquileia, Sermo 38, line 29); *Et ideo in apocalypsi scriptum legimus: vincenti dabo de ligno vitae edere, quod est in paradiso Dei mei. Vincenti dicit, non victo; iusto, non peccatori, quia fructus ille iustorum est, qui nonnisi post triumphum vincentibus datur. Ad hoc vicit Christus, ut nos vinceremus* (Sermo 43, line 33). For both passages, see Chromatius, *Opera*. The Roman apse mosaics from the Church of San Clemente and the Basilica of St. John Lateran show the abiding tradition of associating the tree of the Cross with the tree of life. At San Clemente, they date from the twelfth or thirteenth century. At the Lateran they span the fourth or fifth century through the thirteenth.

314. See, for example, H 204, *Iam caeca vis*, stanza 2.

315. See Rom 5:10; 6:23; 2 Tm 1:10, etc. Other examples from the *Liturgia Horarum* include H 31, 69, and the hymns for the Easter season, which have as the second line of the doxology: *qui morte victa praenites* (H 42–48 and 50).

St. Augustine says:

> The Lord Jesus Christ is life, of whom John the Evangelist says: "This is the true God and Life Eternal" [Jn 5:20]; he it was indeed who through the prophet [Hos 13:14] threatened death with death: "I shall be your death, O Death; O Hell, I shall be your sting" It is as if he were saying: "By dying I shall kill you, I shall consume you, I shall remove from you all power, I shall snatch from you all the captives you have held. I who am innocent you have wished to detain: it is just for you to lose those whom you wished to detain. Therefore, life was dead, life remained, and life rose again; and in killing death by his death, he conferred upon us life. Death, therefore, is absorbed in the victory of Christ, who is eternal life. And so, as the Apostle says, "He swallowed up death, that we might be heirs to life" (1 Pt 3:22). Through Christ, therefore, we have been made heirs to eternal life; though him we are freed from everlasting death; and we are without a doubt members of him.[316]

STANZA 3

The liturgy of Holy Saturday is marked by a deep sense of sorrow at the reality of sin and the cost of salvation, gratitude for the gift, and expectation of Easter. It is a day in which the Church in prayers, readings, and hymns recalls the suffering of Good Friday in the knowledge that Christ is truly dead; he is sleeping the sleep of death in the tomb (3, 2). We know that he will return shortly, but the disciples did not know when or how he would return. Even Our Lady, though her faith was unwavering, could not yet know experientially the joy of Easter. St. Luke seems to capture the essence of Holy Saturday when he says of the women who followed Jesus: "Then they returned [to the city] and prepared spices and ointments. On the Sabbath they rested according to the commandment."[317] They rested, but to the degree that the Sabbath commandment would allow, they engaged *piis amoris artibus*, "the holy rites and services of love" (3, 1) for burial of the dead.

St. Peter Chrysologus (d. 450) describes the frame of mind of the women who were as yet incapable of imagining anything so astonishingly wonderful as the Resurrection:

> The women hasten with feminine devotion, and they bring to the tomb not faith to one who is alive, but perfumed ointments to one who is dead; and for the one buried there they prepare services of mourning; they do not prepare for one who is risen from the dead the joys of divine triumphs. Woman, Christ accepted death, that death might die. Christ as he was killed, killed that which kills all. Christ entered

---

316. *Ipse quippe dominus Christus est vita, de quo Iohannes evangelista ait: hic est verus Deus, et vita aeterna. Ipse namque etiam per prophetam morti mortem comminatus ait: ero mors tua, o mors; ero morsus tuus, inferne. Quasi diceret: ego te moriendo occidam, ego te consumam, ego tibi omnem potestatem auferam, ego captivos quos tenuisti eruam. Innoxium me tenere voluisti: iustum est ut perdas quos tenere voluisti. Ergo et mortua est vita, et mansit vita, et resurrexit vita, et morte sua mortem interficiendo nobis contulit vitam. Absorta est itaque mors in victoria Christi, qui est vita aeterna; deglutivit ergo mortem, sicut apostolus ait, ut vitae heredes essemus. Per Christum ergo heredes vitae aeternae effecti sumus, per quem a morte sempiterna liberati sumus, cuius etiam membra nos esse non dubitamus* (Augustine, *Sermones ad populum*: 265b,9 in *Miscellanea Agostiniana*).

317. *et revertentes paraverunt aromata et unguenta et sabbato quidem siluerunt secundum mandatum* (Lk. 23:56).

the tomb intending to throw open the [gates of] Hell. The Law of Tartarus is undone, the prison of the infernal regions is destroyed, and the very power of death is annihilated. Now Christ must not be anointed as dead, but adored as Victor.[318]

As the women mourned, the soul of Christ "descended into hell" (3, 3–4). Christ's descent into hell is an article of faith found in the Apostles' Creed and in Scripture. In numbers 632–33, the *Catechism of the Catholic Church* states:[319]

> The frequent New Testament affirmations that Jesus was "raised from the dead" presuppose that the crucified one sojourned in the realm of the dead prior to his resurrection.[320] This was the first meaning given in the apostolic preaching to Christ's descent into hell: that Jesus, like all men, experienced death and in his soul joined the others in the realm of the dead. But he descended there as Savior, proclaiming the Good News to the spirits imprisoned there.[321]

> Scripture calls the abode of the dead, to which the dead Christ went down, "hell"— *Sheol* in Hebrew or *Hades* in Greek—because those who are there are deprived of the vision of God.[322] Such is the case for all the dead, whether evil or righteous, while they await the Redeemer: which does not mean that their lot is identical, as Jesus shows through the parable of the poor man Lazarus who was received into "Abraham's bosom."[323] "It is precisely these holy souls, who awaited their Savior in Abraham's bosom, whom Christ the Lord delivered when he descended into hell."[324] Jesus did not descend into hell to deliver the damned, nor to destroy the hell of damnation, but to free the just who had gone before him.[325]

In the *Summa Theologiæ*, III, q. 52, St. Thomas Aquinas gives a number of reasons why it was fitting for Christ to descend into hell.[326] He took upon himself not only the expiation of our sin but also the full reality of our death. As long as his body lay in the tomb, his soul remained in hell, like the souls of all who die, as the normal consequence of death. It was also fitting that Christ manifest his light and power in every part of the world, including the netherworld, "that at the name of Jesus every knee should bend, of those in heaven and on earth and under the earth" (Phil 2:10). Christ's descent was a descent of victory that brought the full light of truth to all those who lived before him (see 1 Pt 4:6). If they had lived holy lives, this light of truth, fulfilled in the Person of Christ, led them out of hell into the light of glory. Those who had not lived holy lives before his coming but

---

318. *Mulieres hoc loco feminea devotione discurrunt, quae non ut viventi fidem, sed ut mortuo unguenta deferunt ad sepulchrum; et sepulto parant maeroris obsequia, non ut resurgenti praeparant divinorum gaudia triumphorum. Mulier, mortem Christus, ut mors moreretur, accepit. Christus, dum occiditur, illud quod omnes occidebat occidit. Sepulchrum Christus infernum patefacturus intravit. Soluta ergo lege tartari et inferni carcere destructo et ipso mortis imperio perempto, iam Christus non est unguendus ut mortuus, sed adorandus ut victor* (Peter Chrysologus, *Sermonum Collectio*, 82).

319. The footnotes that follow are those found in the *Catechism*, which contain references to the pertinent passages from Scripture.

320. Acts 3:15; Rom 8:11; 1 Cor 15:20; cf. Heb 13:20.

321. 1 Pt 3:18–19.

322. Phil 2:10; Acts 2:24; Rv 1:18; Eph 4:9; Pss 6:6; 88:11–13.

323. Ps 89:49; 1 Sam 28:19; Ez 32:17–32; Lk 16:22–26.

324. *Roman Catechism* 1, 6, 3.

325. Council of Rome (745): DS (Denzinger) 587; Benedict XII, *Cum dudum* (1341): DS 1011; Clement VI, *Super quibusdam* (1351): DS 1077; Council of Toledo IV (625): DS 485; Mt 27:52–53.

326. What follows is a brief summary of St. Thomas Aquinas's teaching on this subject.

had rejected the light of truth, in the measure it was given to them, were confirmed by Christ's descent in their rejection of the truth, and they remain in hell eternally. Before Christ's descent into hell, the devil had power over the righteous of the Old Testament because of the punishment for original sin. When Christ made full satisfaction for our sins (see 2 Cor 5:21; 1 Pt 3:18), the penalty was lifted, and the devil was "despoiled" of his goods (see Col 2:15). The rich spiritual, literary, and artistic tradition of the Harrowing of Hell is a reflection of these theological truths. For the universal Church, East and West, Holy Saturday is a day of great triumph. At the Office of Readings on Holy Saturday we read:

> Today there is a great silence over the earth, a great silence, and stillness, a great silence because the King sleeps; the earth was in terror and was still, because God slept in the flesh and raised up those who were sleeping from the ages. God has died in the flesh, and the underworld has trembled. Truly he goes to seek out our first parent like a lost sheep; he wishes to visit those who sit in darkness and in the shadow of death. He goes to free the prisoner Adam and his fellow-prisoner Eve from their pains, he who is God, and Adam's son. The Lord goes in to them holding his victorious weapon, his cross.... And grasping his [Adam's] hand he raises him up, saying: ... "I am your God, who for your sake became your son, who for you and your descendants now speak and command with authority those in prison: Come forth, and those in darkness: Have light, and those who sleep: Rise."[327]

STANZA 4

In stanzas 4 and 5, the hymn turns to those who sing. It considers Christ as he is now (*nunc*), at the right hand of the Father (*in Parentis dextera*; line 1),[328] radiant with glory (*fulgens*) and displaying, as on that first Easter (Lk 24:40), the wounds of his sacrifice (line 2), he is still and always will be *victima sacrata*, living to make intercession for us (Heb 7:25).

We pray to him directly and humbly that he will listen to those he has redeemed by his living blood. The Latin *vividus* means literally "having life, full of life." The blood he shed for us on the Cross was filled with life; it is forever infinitely life-giving: it has formed the Church out of every race, tribe, and nation.[329] It continues to give us life now as we sing. The hymn has passed from the commemoration of the Paschal Mystery to the sacramental order of our participation in the mystery through the Eucharist and the other sacraments that are the ongoing fruit of redemption.

---

327. The author of this ancient homily is unknown. It is the second reading for the Office of Readings on Holy Saturday. The style is reminiscent of the Easter homily of Melito, Bishop of Sardis (d. 180 AD), which is read at the Office of Readings on Holy Thursday and Tuesday of the Octave of Easter.

328. Ps 109 (110):1 opens: "The Lord said to my Lord, sit at my right hand...." This psalm is an icon of the high priestly office of Christ. The Synoptics all speak of the Christ as seated at the right hand of the Father: Mt 26:64; Mk 16:19; Lk 22:69, etc.

329. "And when he [the Lamb] had taken the scroll, the four living creatures and the twenty-four elders fell down before the Lamb, every one of them holding harps and golden bowls full of incense, which are the prayers of the saints. And they sang a new song, saying, 'Worthy are you to receive the scroll and to open its seals, for you were slain, and in your blood you ransomed us for God from every tribe, language, people, and nation'" (Rv 5:8–9).

STANZA 5

In this stanza, we continue the prayer from stanza 4 (note the comma at the end of 4, 4). *Quo* (line 1) may mean "by which" referring to *sanguine* at 4, 4. Or it may express purpose and mean "in order that." Both meanings are possible here. The Latin *mores* (here; *moribus*) is the origin of the English "moral." We pray to Christ directly: that by virtue of your living blood, we may follow you (*te*) all the days of our lives, in moral integrity, and may we carry before us the standard of the Cross to protect us from all scandal (original version) and from the assaults (new version) of evil.

The term *labarum* (line 4) refers to the standard of Constantine on which he placed the monogram of Christ, the Chi-Rho, and the Cross. The name is thought to have come from the term *laureum*, that is, a *vexilla* or standard.[330] The term was in use before the time of Constantine, but it came to be identified with the Christian standard as he configured it. When, in his *Contra Symmachum*, Prudentius describes the battle of the Milvian bridge, he says: "Christ wrought in jeweled gold marked the purple *labarum*; Christ had drawn the ensigns on the shields, the Cross was gleaming added high up on the crests."[331] We also may hold aloft the victorious sign of the Cross.

STANZA 6

For the doxology, see H 38.

---

330. See Baynes, "Constantine the Great and the Christian Church," 62.
331. *Christus purpureum gemmanti textus in auro / signabat labarum, clipeorum insignia Christus / scripserat, ardebat summis crux addita cristis* (Prudentius, *Contra Symm.*, 1.486–88).

Part 4

THE SEASON OF EASTER

After the penance of Lent and after following Christ to Calvary during Holy Week, Easter joy comes to us by night, during the Vigil, as we wait for the return of the Lord. As St. John Henry Newman says, "Easter Day with the long fast of Lent, and the rigors of the Holy Week just past ... is born of Good Friday."[1] Easter joy has a depth that is not so evident in the joy of Christmas; it is filled with an understanding of the price paid for our salvation and our great personal need for redemption, and also with awe at the limitless love of Christ for us. For us, he suffered in obedience on the Cross; for us he strove with death and was victorious; for us, he rose from the tomb in resplendent glory and holiness.[2] Sin and death now have no hold on him; they are utterly powerless before him. For us, he lives now in his glorified humanity and intercedes before the throne of God, for us he seeks to lavish upon all, and at all times, the immense riches of his life and grace. Easter is the Solemnity of Solemnities, the Holy of Holies in the liturgical year.[3] The rest of the year, as it unfolds through feasts and seasons, has this unique purpose: to draw us ever deeper into Christ's risen life and holiness.

The sacraments are the primary means by which Christ imparts his life to us. In baptism, he initiates us into his own Paschal mystery: by it we die to sin and rise to new and unending life (Rom 6:3–5). This is why the Easter Vigil is a privileged moment for the sacraments of initiation. At the Vigil, catechumens are baptized and confirmed and, as newly baptized, they have their first taste of that Eucharistic food containing all sweetness within it that will bring them to the eternal life of heaven.[4] The liturgy of Easter Time dwells at length on the

---

1. Newman, *Parochial and Plain Sermons*, Bk 4, Sermon 23, 939.
2. For further reflection on these points, see Marmion, *Christ in His Mysteries*, 329–34. See also the *Liturgia Horarum*, Office of Readings for Holy Saturday, second reading: *Ex antiqua Homilia in sancto et magno Sabbato* (From an ancient homily for Holy Saturday). Note the nine repetitions of *propter te*; for example: *Propter te, ego, Deus tuus, factus sum filius tuus; propter te, Dominus, servilem tuam speciem sumpsi ...* ; "For your sake, I your God, have become your son; for your sake, I the Lord, have assumed your servile form ..." (*Antiqua Homilia*, PG 43, 451).
3. Guéranger, *Liturgical Year*, 7:1, 15.
4. See Wis 16:20. See also the liturgy for Corpus Christi: Vespers I and II, the second reading at the

sacramental significance of the Old Testament figures of the Passover Lamb, the crossing of the Red Sea, the escape from Pharaoh (Ex 12:1–15:21), and on the fulfillment of these images in Christ's sacrifice, redemption, resurrection, and triumph. In 1 Corinthians 10:1–6, St. Paul explains the symbolism of the events of the Exodus: our ancestors were baptized in the cloud, in Moses, and in the sea; they all ate the same supernatural food and drank the same supernatural drink. St. Paul is specific: these things were figures and examples for us; the Greek is τύποι (types). The whole of the liturgical year is based on what may be called the layered effect of complementary events and figures from the Old Testament and the fulfillments of them in the New. Together these prophetic figures and the underlying reality within them show the depth and power of God's saving intervention in our lives. Just as the disciples' faith was strengthened and enlightened by Christ's revelation of his mystery in the Scriptures on the road to Emmaus (Lk 24:13–32), so also are we strengthened and enlightened by the revelation that comes to us through the liturgy year after year. Nowhere is the relation between figure and fulfillment more evident than in the liturgy of Easter Time. All of this rich layering is found in the hymns.

At the Easter Vigil, the *Alleluia* returns; it punctuates all the elements of the liturgy during the season of Easter. As Dom Guéranger says, these "are days devoted exclusively to joy; every sort of sadness is forbidden; and the Church cannot speak to her divine Spouse without joining to her words that glorious cry of heaven, the *Alleluia*, wherewith, as the holy Liturgy says, the streets and squares of the heavenly Jerusalem resound without ceasing."[5] And St. John Henry Newman comments, "In such a spirit let us endeavor to celebrate this most holy of all Festivals, this continued festal Season, which lasts for fifty days, whereas Lent is forty, as if to show that where sin abounded, there much more has grace abounded."[6]

At Lauds on Easter morning, we sing the ancient and joyous *Aurora lucis rutilat*. It sings with relish of Christ's victorious Harrowing of Hell, his royal triumph over sin, the devil, and death, and his rising from the fiercely guarded tomb. Both *Aurora lucis*, at Lauds, and *Ad cenam Agni providi*, at Vespers, come from the ancient strata of liturgical hymns.[7] Together they form an Easter Diptych: while *Aurora* describes Christ's triumph, *Ad cenam* dwells on the sacramental fulfillment in Christ of the Passover Lamb, the crossing of the Red Sea, and Exodus.

Although the musical settings of the hymns of the Liturgy of the Hours are not a primary focus of this commentary, the Gregorian melody in use for *Aurora*

Office of Readings (which is from St. Thomas Aquinas), and the traditional versicle and response at Benediction of the Blessed Sacrament: "containing all sweetness within it."

5. Guéranger, *Liturgical Year*, 7:15 (see note 3 above); and see Rv. 19:6.
6. Newman, *Parochial and Plain Sermons*, Bk. 4, Sermon 23, p. 942; and see Rom 5:20.
7. Except for the hymns of Ambrose, these are the only known hymns found in the earliest collections and maintained in the later "New Hymnal" of the tenth century. The date of their composition is unknown but well before the Frankish Hymnal appeared in the late eighth to early ninth century. See Milfull, 5; Walpole, p. 349.

lucis expresses beautifully the first flush of Easter joy. One essential quality of Gregorian Chant is that the shape of the melody arises out of and is often a commentary on the text to which it is set; the chant is a cantillation of the text, a translation into a musical idiom of the sense of the text. Thus, the cumulative effect of the Easter melodies, especially of the sung Alleluias, is a subtle, pervasive exultation and joy. Hymn melodies are less closely tied to their texts because the texts are metrical, and the same melody may be used for different texts. Nevertheless, the melodic type used for this hymn fits the hour and the feast to perfection. The melody is entirely syllabic except for a melisma of five notes on the final syllable of the second line.[8] The shape of this melisma evokes the surprise, fear, and unexpected joy of the women standing before the empty tomb at dawn.

After six weeks of Easter proper, the season continues with the Ascension on the fortieth day and Pentecost on the fiftieth. The Ascension is "the supreme glorification of Christ Jesus. Holy Church calls this Ascension wonderful and glorious, and all the way through the Divine Office of this feast, she causes us to hymn the magnificence of this mystery."[9] The hymn for Lauds is particularly eloquent: the fourth stanza bursts forth: *O grande cunctis gaudium*: "O joy immense for all!"[10] Christ's victory is definitive, evident for all to see, and unassailable in the hope it brings us. He has led captivity captive;[11] and "where the Head has gone before in glory, the Body is called to follow in hope."[12] The hymn for Vespers (H 52) captures the joy that looks heavenward:

Tu esto nostrum gaudium,	Lord Jesus, be all joy for us,
qui es futurus præmium;	for you shall be our great reward;
sit nostra in te gloria	may all our glory be in you
per cuncta semper sæcula. Amen.	through endless ages evermore. Amen.

Finally, Easter closes with the Solemnity of Pentecost. At the Last Supper Christ tells his disciples that it is better for them that he go (Jn 16:7) because he will send the Paraclete (Jn 14:16); and under the Spirit's inspiration, they will do even greater things than he has done while on earth (Jn 14:12–14) since he will go to the Father and give them the greatest of gifts, the Love that is the bond between the Father and himself. Jesus, after his Ascension, seated at the right hand of the Father while still present on earth (Mt 28:20),[13] together with the Father

---

8. This melody is no. 3 in Stäblein, *Hymnen*. The medieval manuscripts in which it is found assign it to Easter hymns, but also to *Splendor paternæ gloriæ* (H 75) and to an Advent hymn. The melodic intervals vary (Stäblein identifies seven subtypes), but the overall shape of the melody is the same.

9. Marmion, *Christ in his Mysteries*, 347. See also the prayer over the gifts: *venerabili nunc ascensione* ...

10. (*Optatus votis omnium*, H 54: 4, 1).

11. See the short responsory at Lauds: R. *Ascendens Christus in altum*, * *Alleluia, alleluia*. V. *Captivam duxit captivitatem*. * *Alleluia, alleluia. Gloria Patri. Ascendens*: "Christ, ascending on high, Alleluia, alleluia, led captivity captive. Alleluia, alleluia. Glory be to the Father.... Christ ascending...."

12. Collect for the Mass of the Ascension: *quo processit gloria capitis, eo spes vocatur et corporis*.

13. Again, the hymn for Lauds (H 54: 5, 1–4) expresses it well: "May he remain the single joy / for us and those who dwell on high: / to them he gives himself in full, / from us he never shall depart" (stanza 6).

sends the Paraclete, so that throughout the ages of the Church, the Paraclete may give testimony to the work and the person of Christ, to remind the disciples, and to bring them to a greater understanding of the work of salvation.[14] With the coming of the Paraclete, all those who are baptized become temples of the Holy Spirit (1 Cor 3:16; 6:19); they are incorporated fully into the life of the Trinity.

There are seventeen hymns assigned to Easter Time. They are indicated here by the numbers found in this volume of the hymn commentary. The hymns for the Season of Easter are as follows:

No.	Name	Liturgical Hour
42	Ad cenam Agni providi	Vespers, in the Octave, Sundays before Ascension
43	O rex æterne, Domine	Vespers, Weekdays before Ascension
44	Hic est dies verus Dei	Office of Readings, in the Octave, Sundays before Ascension
45	Lætare, cælum, desuper	Office of Readings, Weekdays, before Ascension
46	Aurora lucis rutilat	Lauds, before the Ascension
47	Chorus novæ Ierusalem	Lauds, Weekdays after Octave before Ascension
48	Iam surgit hora tertia	Terce, Easter Time
49	Venite, servi, supplices	Sext, Easter Time
50	Hæc hora, quæ resplenduit	None, Easter Time
51	Iesu, redemptor sæculi	Compline, Easter Time
52	Iesu, nostra redemptio	Vespers I and II, Ascension
53	Æterne rex, altissime	Office of Readings, Ascension to Pentecost
54	Optatus votis omnium	Lauds, Ascension to Pentecost
55	Veni, creator Spiritus	Vespers, after Ascension and Pentecost
56	Lux iucunda, lux insignis	Office of Readings, Pentecost
57	Beata nobis gaudia	Lauds, Pentecost
58	Iam Christus astra ascenderat	Terce, Pentecost

---

14. Jn 14:26; Jn 15:26; Jn 16:13–14.

Ad cenam Agni próvidi 42

attributed to St. Nicetus of Remesiana, d. 414
8 8 8 8

Easter Time to the Ascension of the Lord
Vespers

Ad cenam Agni próvidi, stolis salútis cándidi, post tránsitum maris Rubri Christo canámus príncipi.	1. As we await the Lamb's high feast in snow-white robes of saving grace, we sing to Christ, our Prince and Head, for we have crossed the Red Sea tide.
Cuius corpus sanctíssimum in ara crucis tórridum, sed et cruórem róseum gustándo, Deo vívimus.	2. His holy Body, parched and seared upon the altar of the Cross, his crimson Blood, outpoured for us, we taste and so we live for God.
Protécti paschæ véspero a devastánte ángelo, de Pharaónis áspero sumus erépti império.	3. Protected on the paschal eve from devastating angel sword, we were delivered and set free from Pharaoh's harsh and bitter rule.
Iam pascha nostrum Christus est, agnus occísus ínnocens; sinceritátis ázyma qui carnem suam óbtulit.	4. And now our Pasch is Christ himself, the pure and spotless Lamb once slain, unleavened bread of truthfulness, who gives his flesh in sacrifice.
O vera, digna hóstia, per quam frangúntur tártara, captíva plebs redímitur, reddúntur vitæ præmia!	5. O worthy Victim, real and true, who rends and breaks the power of hell, the captives there have been redeemed and now enjoy the prize of life.
Consúrgit Christus túmulo, victor redit de bárathro, tyránnum trudens vínculo et paradísum réserans.	6. Christ rises from the tomb indeed, triumphant Victor from the depths, who thrusts the tyrant down in chains and clears the way to Paradise.
Esto perénne méntibus paschále, Iesu, gáudium, et nos renátos grátiæ tuis triúmphis ággrega.	7. O Jesus, be for mind and heart our everlasting paschal joy and gather us, reborn by grace, to share your triumphs evermore.
Iesu, tibi sit glória, qui morte victa prænites, cum Patre et almo Spíritu, in sempitérna sǽcula. Amen.	8. To you, Lord Jesus, glory be, who shine in victory over death, with God the Father, ever blest, and loving Spirit, ever one. Amen.

Text found in *TDH*, no. 113; *AH* 51, no. 83; Bulst, 116; Walpole, no. 109. Changes in *TDH*: stanza 1, 2: *stolis salutis candidi* for *stolis albis candidi* (only seven syllables)—Lentini suggests that originally there may have been a prosthetic "e" (*estolis*); 3, 3–4: *de Pharaonis aspero / sumus erepti imperio* for *erepti de durissimo / pharaonis imperio*; 4, 2: *agnus occísus ínnocens* for *qui immolatus agnus est*; 5, 1: Bulst and Walpole give *vera* in preference to the *vere* found in the breviaries; 5, 2–3: *per quam franguntur tartara, / captiva plebs redimitur* for *per quam fracta sunt tartara, / redempta plebs captivata*; for stanza 7, see the commentary.

COMMENTARY

This ancient Paschal hymn is one of the few hymns in the *Liturgia Horarum* that has eight stanzas. It is in accentual iambic dimeter with line endings in three-syllable words, the stress accent of which falls on the antepenult, that is, the first syllable of the word and the sixth syllable of the line.[15] It belongs to the Old Hymnal and has been in continuous use, assigned to Vespers during Easter Time; it is one of only three hymns "common to both the earlier and later hymnals."[16] It has been attributed to St. Ambrose but is never found among his hymns of more certain authorship, and the literary devices and style are not those of Ambrose. Many today attribute it to St. Nicetas of Remesiana, who was contemporary with Ambrose. Norberg places it, along with the Easter hymn for Lauds *Aurora lucis rutilat* (H 46), "at the end of antiquity" and even proposes that they may be from the same author.[17]

The hymn weaves together imagery from Revelation, Exodus, and St. Paul. The overall theme is deliverance from evil by baptism, prefigured in the deliverance of Israel from Egypt, and made possible by the sacrifice of Christ. Just as the Israelites escaped their captors by a lamb's blood, by crossing the Red Sea, and by unleavened bread, so now Christians escape the power of hell by the sacrifice of Christ, the true Lamb "who takes away the sins of the world" (Jn 1:29), by baptism, and by the Eucharist. The text of this hymn is filled with transitions: from the crossing of the Red Sea to baptism, from the Old Covenant to the New, and from death to resurrection. Imbued with liturgical and ritual images and references, it is a triumphant hymn for a triumphant Church. It is also marked by wordplay. Line endings often rhyme, although with a measure of inconsistency,

---

15. Line 3 in stanzas 1 and 5 ends irregularly with a two-syllable word or an accent on the penult. This irregularity, still visible in stanza 1, 3 (*maris Rubri*), is an indication that the later preference for an accent on the antepenult was not yet firmly established (Norberg, *Introduction*, 19 and 133).

16. Walpole, p. 349. The other two hymns are *Aurora lucis rutilat* (H 46) and *Christe, qui lux es et dies* (H 67). *Ad cenam Agni* was assigned in the Sarum and York usages to Vespers from Low Sunday to the Ascension, except on Saturdays. In the *Breviarium Romanum*, it emerged, after Urban VIII's reforms, as *Ad regias Agni dapes*, and was altered to the extent that it is essentially a different hymn. In the *Liturgia Horarum* it has been restored, with some modifications, to its more ancient form.

17. Norberg, *Introduction*, 41, 133.

even in the old manuscripts;[18] it is among the earliest hymns to rhyme. The entire piece is also highly alliterative and contains many elements of assonance.[19]

STANZA 1

Reference to the evening meal (*cena*) begins this Vespers hymn. The word has a twofold biblical connotation: it refers most directly to the heavenly banquet, as in Revelation 19:9: *beati qui ad cenam nuptiarum agni vocati sunt*: "blessed are they who have been called to the supper of the wedding feast of the Lamb."[20] This passage also appears elsewhere in the liturgy during the Easter Season and throughout the year.[21] The Church is the Bride of the Lamb at this marriage banquet: *ostendam tibi uxorem agni*: "I will show you the bride, the wife of the Lamb": (Rv 21:9). *Cena* also calls to mind the Last Supper (*Cena Domini*) and so looks back to Holy Thursday. It evokes the Lord's institution of the Eucharist on earth as well as the eternal liturgy in heaven.

Line 2 represents the first of the emendations in the *Liturgia Horarum* text of this hymn. Walpole, Milfull, Raby, and AH all give *stolis albis candidi*. As Lentini notes,[22] this does not match the meter of the rest of the hymn, as the line only has seven syllables. Some sources, such as Daniel and Chevalier (1892) have *et stolis albis candidi*. Lentini rejects this reading and substitutes the three-syllable *salutis* for *albis*.[23] Being clothed with salvation is an image common throughout Scripture, often expressed with *salutis* or a related word in the genitive.[24]

18. For a discussion of rhyme schemes, such as aaba, in this meter, see Norberg, *Introduction*, 133. Norberg sees in this rhyme scheme a possible indication of musical practice in which lines 3 and 4 would have formed a musical unit, perhaps similar to the melodic line in hymns such as "Lo, how a rose e'er blooming." The rhyme scheme of this hymn also testifies to medieval changes in Latin phonology, because the final "m" of words such as *paradisum* was lightly pronounced, and additionally the final vowels of words were fluid. Thus, pairs such as *vinculo* and *paradisum* might be considered to rhyme (Norberg, *Introduction*, 41); for the place of Christian hymnody in the emergence of rhyme, see Sedgwick, "The Origin of Rhyme," 330–46.
19. Norberg notes that while assonance was not a feature of classical poetry, it had become a common poetic device by the time this hymn was composed (*Introduction*, 32).
20. Jesus is named the Lamb throughout Scripture—see Acts 8:32 (quoting Is 53:7); 1 Pt 1:19; and Rv 5:12; 7:17; 19:7; 21:22–23. See also the comments on stanza 4 of this hymn. In Christian hymnody, the image of Christ as Lamb is taken up by Sedulius in his *Paschal Song* (e.g., 2.72, 5.140), and frequently by Venantius Fortunatus in his hymns in honor of Easter and the Cross. See, for example: 2.1.4; 2.2.18; 3.9.84. These hymns are found in Fortunatus, *Poems*.
21. For example, the passage appears at II Vespers of the Second Sunday of Easter; for the Communion Antiphon *Beati qui vocati sunt*; at the Office of Readings, Fifth Sunday of Easter; for the Common of Martyrs, of Virgins, of Holy Men, etc.
22. *TDH*, 117–18.
23. "The normalization *et stolis* (*stolisque*) distorts the construction of the hymn, since it seems obvious that *providi* (v. 1) is in agreement with *agni* (and one would be forced to consider it nominative, in the sense of "intent on") and the conjunction *et* (*-que*) would make it a poor parallel with *candidi*. Instead of the word *amicti* from the *Breviarium Romanum*, which is ultimately unusable, then, *salutis* has been added with a further connotation adapted to the mystery" (*TDH*, 117). Lentini's critiques are premised on a reading of *providi* as a genitive with *Agni* rather than referring to the crowds that would be awaiting the Lamb's supper. The Latin text is, of itself, ambiguous. The ICEL translation takes it as a nominative ("as we await"), and John Mason Neale's translation "The Lamb's high banquet we await" serves as precedent for this understanding. Julian also reads *providi* as nominative, as does Walpole (line 1, p. 350). The close verbal similarities between *providi* and *candidi*, which rhyme so closely, also guide the reader to see them in grammatical agreement. One variant (given by Daniel) has a reading *stolis in albis* which would resolve the meter and avoid Lentini's problem of putting *providi* and *candidi* in agreement.
24. See 1 Thes 5:8, *induti loricam fidei et caritatis et galeam spem salutis*: "putting on the breastplate of faith and love and the helmet that is hope for salvation"; Is 59:17, *indutus est iustitia ut lorica et galea salutis in capite*

Additionally, *salutis* adds to the assonance and alliteration of the line and creates a close connection with the robes, *stolis*.

The older reading, *albis*, carries biblical connotations. The Book of Revelation connects the white-robed crowds in heaven directly to the Lamb: "I had a vision of a great multitude.... They stood before the throne and before the Lamb, wearing white robes."[25] "The victor will thus be dressed in white."[26] Those who have come through the great tribulation "have washed their robes and whitened them in the blood of the Lamb."[27] The *Te Deum*, also believed by many scholars to be by Nicetas, refers to white-robed martyrs in heaven.[28] Julian points out that the white robes are an "allusion to those who were solemnly baptized and clothed in white garments on Easter Eve, and admitted to Holy Communion on the following day."[29] Daniel also has a note from a letter of St. Paulinus of Nola: "from there the priest obediently takes the infants from the font, white in body, heart, and dress."[30]

Thus the phrase *albis stolis*, like *cenam*, evokes the twofold image of the baptism of catechumens at Easter and the baptism of those who sing the hymn and join the heavenly crowd to which baptism unites us, first in this life and then after death. Both are signified in line 3: *post transitum maris Rubri*; Hebrews 11:29 says of the Israelites that *fide transierunt mare Rubrum*: "by faith they crossed the Red Sea." The noun *transitus* is used also in Exodus 12:11–12 for the Lord's passing over Israel's firstborn; it is used as a Latin translation of, or explanation for, the Hebrew *Pascha*: *est enim Pascha (id est Transitus) Domini et transibo per terram Ægypti nocte illa*: "It is the Lord's Passover ... on this same night I will go through Egypt." Similarly, St. Paul describes the passage through the waters of the Red Sea as a figure of baptism: "our ancestors were all under the cloud and all passed through the sea, and all of them were baptized into Moses in the cloud and in the sea."[31]

Line 4: *Christo canamus principi* is a delightfully alliterative and assonant line with the voiceless stops in *c*'s and *p*'s.[32] Walpole (l. 4, p. 350 referring to no. 31, l. 3, p. 151) notes a parallel, on the lexical level, with the third line of Sedulius's *A solis ortu cardine*, which reads *Christum canamus principem*. At Colossians 1:18, St. Paul speaks of Christ as head: "He is the head of the body, the church. He is the beginning, the firstborn from the dead."[33] Walpole also notes the use of the

---

eius: "He put on justice as his breastplate, victory as a helmet on his head"); and Is 61:10, *induit me vestimentis salutis et indumento iustitiæ circumdedit me*: "For he has clothed me with garments of salvation, and wrapped me in a robe of justice."

25. *vidi turbam magnam.... stantes ante thronum et in conspectu agni amicti stolas albas* (Rv 7:9).
26. *qui vicerit sic vestietur vestimentis albis* (Rv 3:5).
27. *laverunt stolas suas et dealbaverunt eas in sanguine agni* (Rv 7:14).
28. *te martyrum candidatus laudat exercitus* (Te Deum, 9).
29. Julian, *Dictionary of Hymnology*, 12.
30. Paulinus of Nola, *Ep.* 32.5, cited by Daniel 1:89.
31. *patres nostri omnes sub nube fuerunt et omnes mare transierunt et omnes in Mose baptizati sunt in nube et in mare* (1 Cor 10:1–2).
32. When the hymn was written, as it is so ancient, the *c* in *principi* may have still sounded similar to the *c*'s of *Christo* and *canamus*. The pattern *i* - [plosive consonant] - *i* (*-ipi*) also rhymes closely with the above lines in *-idi*.
33. *ipse est caput corporis ecclesiæ qui est principium primogenitus ex mortuis*.

word *princeps* at Revelation 1:5: John writes as a messenger from Christ, "ruler of the kings of the earth ... who loves us and has freed us from our sins by his blood."[34] *Princeps* was also a title assumed for the emperor beginning with Octavian Augustus, and so refers to the head of the entire empire: Christ is *princeps* in every sense of the word; he is head of the Church, King of kings (Rv 19:16); and, finally, he receives the homage of all those in the heavenly kingdom. Revelation depicts the one hundred forty-four thousand *singing* to the Lamb: *ecce agnus stabat supra montem Sion et cum illo centum quadraginta quattuor milia ... et cantabant quasi canticum novum ante sedem*: "there was the Lamb standing on Mount Zion, and with him a hundred and forty-four thousand who ... were singing [what seemed to be] a new hymn before the throne" (Rv 14:1, 3). The first stanza of the hymn is, thus, an exhortation (*canamus*) to join the heavenly liturgy that begins on earth with the Resurrection: *Christo canamus principem* (line 4).

STANZA 2

Line 1: *Cuius corpus sanctissimum* is another alliterative line.[35] The connecting relative (*cuius*) in a line marked by alliteration and assonance on the same sounds as the previous line (1, 4) establishes a close connection between line 4 of stanza 1 and line 1 of stanza 2. This connection signals a close association of ideas between the two stanzas: in stanza 1, baptism is presented under the image of the crossing of the Red Sea; this leads to the Eucharist, presented in stanza 2 under the image of the Paschal Lamb, whose flesh and blood we taste and so live unto God. St. Paul makes the same association in the passage from 1 Corinthians mentioned above. After saying that our fathers were baptized into Moses when they crossed the Red Sea (1 Cor 10:1–2), he continues: "All ate the same spiritual food, and all drank the same spiritual drink" (1 Cor 10:3–4).

In line 2, *in ara crucis torridum*, the liturgical imagery is expanded by a parallel between the Cross and the sacrifices of the Old Testament. "Parched and seared" translates *torridum* and refers to the act of burning a holocaust. Daniel has a note: *comparatur cum agno paschali assato* ("Christ is compared with the roasted paschal lamb"). Christ is so like the paschal lamb, that he is said to be roasted as one: see Exodus 12:9, which describes the preparation of the lamb: "Do not eat any of it raw or even boiled in water, but roasted." He is roasted on the altar of the Cross (*in ara crucis*); this phrase never occurs in the Vulgate, but it is used throughout the Middle Ages and beyond in Christian literature.[36] Given the early date of this hymn and its prominent place in the liturgy, it is possible that its usage entered into more common parlance from this hymn.

---

34. *princeps regum terræ qui dilexit nos et lavit nos a peccatis nostris in sanguine suo*. See Walpole, pp. 350–51.

35. The manuscripts offer two possibilities here: either *cuius sacrum corpusculum*, given in AH and used by Walpole (more likely the original) and *cuius corpus sanctissimum*, used by Daniel (all editions give this reading in the apparatus). Lentini explains that "*corpusculum* is not diminutive, but affectionate; however, today it would sound bad" (*TDH*, 117–18). Walpole believes that the variant, *corpus sanctissimum*, arose in the manuscript tradition from concerns similar to those of Lentini. See Walpole, note on l. 5, p. 350.

36. The phrase has become common in sermons and prayers; see also the *GILH*, 4.

Lines 3 and 4, *sed et cruorem roseum / gustando, Deo vivimus*, bring the Eucharist into full focus.[37] The blood of the lamb with which the doorposts and lintels of the Hebrews were anointed (Ex 12:7) is the blood of sacrifice that becomes the Messianic wine from which we live in the New Covenant. *Cruor* is a word rich in significance. Where *sanguis* indicates "blood" in a more general sense, flowing in the veins or having been spilled, *cruor* signifies blood flowing from a wound. It is used in poetry in the descriptions of heroic deeds, ritual sacrifice, and sacrilegious acts, and in other similar contexts. The phrase *rutilum cruorem* appears in Ovid's *Metamorphoses* 5.83, describing the death of a man slain at an altar.[38] The use of *cruor* in heroic and sacred contexts came easily into early Christian hymnody in reference to Christ and the holy martyrs.[39] Just as the Passover and the yearly commemoration of it in the Passover feast give the Israelites their defining character, so also for Christians, the Eucharist in which we eat the unleavened bread, now the Body of Christ, and drink the wine, now his precious Blood, forms us into the Church and gives us our identity as members of the Mystical Body of Christ. As we taste (*gustando*) we receive life from God (*Deo vivimus*). It is perhaps fitting that in the phrase *Deo vivimus*, *Deo* may be taken either as an ablative (we live by God, that is *from* the Eucharist received), or it may be a dative (we live *for* God).[40] Both senses apply. Lentini, who changed the line for metrical reasons to *Deo vivimus* seems to favor the ablative. Walpole, who maintains the medieval version, *vivimus Deo*, opts for the dative. He notes that forms of *vivere* with the dative appear at Luke 20:28, *omnes enim vivunt ei*; at Romans 6:10, *vivit Deo*; and at Galatians 2:19, *ut Deo vivam*. The passage from Romans is well known from the Easter liturgy. The entire verse reads: *quod enim mortuus est peccato mortuus est semel quod autem vivit, vivit Deo*: "The death that he died he died to sin, once and for all; the life that he lives he lives unto God" (Rom 6:10).

STANZA 3

Stanza 3 is a summary of and reflection on the events of the first Passover. The verb *sumus* (line 4) and the colorful vocabulary of the stanza invite us to place ourselves in Egypt and relive the scene: it is the evening of the pasch (*paschæ*

---

37. The manuscript tradition varies here, but the majority of texts have: *cruore eius roseo/gustando vivimus Deo*.

38. See also Virgil: *Georgics*, 4, 543; *Æn.*, 5.333; descriptions of combat in the last half of the *Æneid*, which serve as parallels to Homer's *Odyssey* (see *Æneid.*, 9.333 or 10.349); depictions of the Passion in epic and Iliadic terms appear also in Eudocia's Homeric centos (See Usher, *Homeric Stitchings*, 8, "Themes from the Iliad.").

39. With reference to martyrs, *cruor* appears in Ambrose: in *Amore Christi nobilis* for St. John, a martyr by faith; in *Victor Nabor Felix pii*, for the early martyrs of Milan; and in *Apostolorum passio* (H 224), for Sts. Peter and Paul); it is also found in Prudentius (*Peristeph* 3: 29, 4; 4: 21, 2; 5: 3, 4; and elsewhere). With reference to the blood of Christ, it appears in Venantius Fortunatus's hymns in honor of the Cross (*Poems*, book 2: *Hymns* 2: 1, 2, and 3: 10, 3 = H 33: 4, 4).

40. For the early Church's belief in the real presence of Christ in the Eucharistic sacrifice, see St. Justin Martyr, *First Apology*, 66.1–2; St. Cyril of Jerusalem, *Mystagogical Catecheses*, 4; Ambrose's *Splendor paternæ gloriæ* (H 75) which alludes to the Eucharist as food and drink: *Christusque nobis sit cibus, / potusque noster sit fides, / læti bibamus sobriam / ebrietatem Spiritus* (21–24): "Let Christ himself become our food,/our faith in him become our drink; / let us imbibe with deepest joy / the Spirit's sober drunkenness." See also Sedulius's *Hymn* 1.76 (*gustato Christi sanguine*); or his *Paschal Song* 5.403 (*Christus adest panis*).

vespero; 1), we are protected by the blood of the lamb on our doors (*portecti*; 1); the supremely dangerous (*devastante*; line 2) angel passes over us through the land; by his divinely mandated mission during the night, we are snatched (*erepti*; 4) out of the bitter power of Pharaoh (*aspero imperio*; 3–4). Lines 1–2, *Protécti paschæ véspero / a devastánte ángelo*, refer to Exodus 12:23: "For when the Lord goes by to strike down the Egyptians, seeing the blood on the lintel and the two doorposts, the Lord will pass over that door and not let the destroyer come into your houses to strike you down". The participle *devastante* parallels in particular the phrasing of Hebrews 11:28: *fide celebravit pascha et sanguinis effusionem ne qui vastabat primitiva tangeret eos*: "By faith he [Moses] kept the Passover and sprinkled the blood, that the Destroyer of the firstborn might not touch them."

In Lines 3–4, *de Pharaónis áspero / sumus erépti império*, the original has been altered to make the syntax clearer. The original version of line 3–4 reads: *erepti de durissimo / Pharaonis imperio*. The verb *sumus* has been added, where in the original it was implied; and in the interest of smooth liturgical delivery, one colorful word has been replaced by another: *durissimo* by *aspero*. The Latin *asper* signifies "rough, harsh, bitter"; it describes well the oppressive nature of the bondage of the Israelites in Egypt. They were treated harshly by a cruel tyrant. This is a transparent image of the suffering of the human race under the power of the devil. The use of *durissimo* (the superlative of *durus*: "hard, unyielding, severe, obstinate") in the original version, however, is a clear allusion to the text from Exodus: *induravitque Dominus cor Pharonis*: "The Lord hardened the heart of Pharaoh" (Ex 14:8).[41]

STANZA 4

Stanza 4 is essentially a versification of a text from St. Paul to the Corinthians: *etenim pascha nostrum immolatus est Christus itaque epulemur ... in azymis sinceritatis et veritatis*: "For our paschal lamb, Christ, has been sacrificed. Therefore let us celebrate the feast ... but with the unleavened bread of sincerity and truth" (1 Cor 5:7–8). The text of the original hymn is slightly different, but both versions are clearly recognizable as the iconic text used throughout Easter Time at Mass and in the Divine Office.[42] Thus, the Communion Antiphon for the Easter Vigil and for the Mass of the Resurrection during the day is: *Pascha nostrum immolatus est Christus, alleluia: itaque epulemur in azymis sinceritatis et veritatis, alleluia, alleluia, alleluia*.

Line 1, *Iam pascha nostrum Christus est*, fits the meter and brings the sacrifice of Christ into the present of liturgical time; *iam* means "now," as we sing. The Paschal Lamb is also ours (*nostrum*); he belongs to us. In line 1, *immolatus est* is conspicuously missing (see the Communion antiphon above). Line 2 supplies the

---

41. See also Sedulius's *Hymn* 1.31 and 1.32, which repeat the phrase *gens ... dura* ("a harsh people") for the crowd who put Christ to death: the Egyptians are, of course, a type of this crowd.

42. The original version of stanza 4 reads: *Iam pascha nostrum Christus est, / Qui immolatus agnus est, / Sinceritatis azyma / Caro eius oblata est*.

lack. In the original it was: *qui immolatus agnus est*. In the text for the *Liturgia Horarum*, it was changed to *agnus occisus innocens*, in order to avoid the verb *est* at the end of two consecutive lines. *Agnus occisus* evokes Revelation 5:12: "Worthy is the Lamb that was slain to receive power and riches, wisdom and strength, honor and glory and blessing."[43] Isaiah 53:7–8 and Acts 8:32 (referring to Isaiah) also speak of the *agnus occisus*. Lentini's emendation, *innocens* describes well the lamb who is Christ, but it steps outside of the metaphor. In order to be fit for use at the Passover, it makes no sense to say that the lamb is innocent; it must be fit for immolation, that is, pure in the sense of "without blemish." *Immolatus* is the right cultic term and it fits the instructions for preparation of the Passover meal in Exodus 12:21: "Taking lambs for yourselves according to your family, immolate the Passover lamb." The same language is used by God when he tells Moses what to say to Pharaoh: "... that we may offer sacrifice in the wilderness."[44]

The passage from 1 Corinthians continues in line 3 with: *sinceritatis azyma*: The word *sinceritatis* in 1 Corinthians 5:8 translates the Greek εἰλικρινείας ("judged by the light of the sun," i.e., "moral purity, integrity"). Just as the paschal lamb was without blemish (Ex 12:5, *agnus absque macula*), so Christ is the purest offering, and Christians feast on moral purity. The neuter plural *azyma* is a transliteration of Greek ἄζυμα and means "unleavened."[45] Other Vulgate appearances of the word include the Passover prescriptions for the Israelites: "for seven days you must eat unleavened bread [*azyma*]" (Ex 12:15, 13:17, 23:15, etc.), and Luke's Gospel: "now the feast of Unleavened Bread [*festus azymorum*], called the Passover, was drawing near" (Lk 22:1).[46] This third line does not rhyme with the rest of the stanza, even in the ancient text. Again, this is consonant with Norberg's observation that in hymns of this meter, the third line, which need not have an accent on the antepenult, also may not rhyme.[47]

Lines 3 and 4 together make explicit the identification of Christ with the azyma: he is the unleavened bread, free from "the old leaven of malice and wickedness" (1 Cor 5:8), who offers his own flesh as victim and food: *qui carnem suam óbtulit* (line 4). Christ as priest offers himself as victim. St. Paul tells the Ephesians: "Live in love, as Christ loved us and handed himself over for us as a sacrificial offering to God for a fragrant aroma."[48] The word *hostia* is also found in stanza 5 below.

---

43. *dignus est agnus qui occisus est accipere virtutem et divinitatem et sapientiam et fortitudinem et honorem et gloriam et benedictionem* (Rv 5:12). This text is used as a canticle at Vespers on Tuesdays throughout the year.

44. Ex 12:21: *Ite tollentes animal per familias vestras, immolate Pascha*; Ex 3:18: *ut immolemus in deserto*.

45. It is found in pre-Christian literature in medical treatises, e. g., in the Latin *Compositiones*, by Scribonius Largus (see Brepols, *LLT*, database) and Greek texts from Hippocrates and Plato (see the *Thesaurus Linguae Græcæ*, also a database).

46. The use of this word in Christian Latin indicates that *azyma* had to some degree naturalized into the religious idiom. Christine Mohrmann notes that while "the rise of Christian Latin was marked by a slow ousting of Greek," loanwords that "were already so familiar to the Christians" were retained." Mohrmann, *Liturgical Latin*, 33–34.

47. See Norberg, *Introduction*, 133.

48. *Ambulate in dilectione, sicut et Christus dilexit nos, et tradidit semetipsum pro nobis, oblationem et hostiam Deo in odorem suavitatis* (Eph 5:2).

STANZA 5

Stanza 5 is a cry of admiration. It begins: *O vera, digna hóstia*.[49] *Vera* connotes the New Covenant inaugurated by Christ's offering of himself as a victim (*hostia*) for our sins; his sacrifice surpasses, fulfills, and supersedes all the offerings of the Old Testament: "for it is impossible that the blood of bulls and goats take away sins. For this reason, when he came into the world, he said: 'Sacrifice and offering you did not desire, but a body you prepared for me.'"[50] Hebrews continues:

> then he [Christ, prefigured in the Psalm] added, "Lo, I have come to do your will" [Ps 39:8–9(40:7–8)]. He abolishes the first in order to establish the second. And by that will we have been sanctified through the offering of the body of Jesus Christ once for all. And every priest [under the Old Law] stands daily at his service, offering repeatedly the same sacrifices, which can never take away sins. But when Christ had offered for all time a single sacrifice for sins [*unam pro peccatis offerens hostiam*], he sat down at the right hand of God.[51]

Then, lines 2–4 describe the Harrowing of Hell and the reward of eternal life given to the saints held captive there, until the coming of Christ, because of original sin. The lines have been reworked but without a significant change in the sense. It is interesting to note that although the Second Vatican Council called for the removal of terms from the hymns that reflect pagan mythology or ill accord with Christian piety,[52] both *tartara* in this stanza and *barathro* in the next have been retained. This is perhaps due to the fact that there is much evidence to suggest that these words were naturalized to Christian use, similarly to *azyma* above.[53] The *captíva plebs* are the souls waiting for Christ; but, as Walpole notes, the phrase refers to all those held captive either physically or spiritually: the phrase a "captive people" appears in 1 Maccabees 15:40: ("he ... took people captive": *cœpit ... captivare populum*). St. Paul describes the old covenant as holding him captive: "another law ... taking me captive": *aliam legem ... captivantem me* (Rom 7:23).[54] The life that Christ gives to them is a pure gift, but it is also, through the riches of his mercy, a reward for their righteousness, for their

---

49. See also Rv 5:12; and Prudentius, *Peristeph*. 10: 154, 5, which refers to the tongue of a martyr that was cut out for confessing Christ: *digna est fidelis lingua quæ sit hostia*: ("worthy is the faithful tongue which would be an offering."

50. *inpossibile enim est sanguine taurorum et hircorum auferri peccata ideo ingrediens mundum dicit hostiam et oblationem noluisti corpus autem aptasti mihi* (Heb 10:4–5).

51. *tunc dixit ecce venio ut faciam Deus voluntatem tuam; aufert primum ut sequens statuat, in qua voluntate sanctificati sumus per oblationem corporis Christi Iesu in semel. et omnis quidem sacerdos præsto est cotidie ministrans et easdem sæpe offerens hostias quæ numquam possunt auferre peccata. hic autem unam pro peccatis offerens hostiam in sempiternum, sedit in dextera Dei* (Heb 10:9–12).

52. See SC 93. See also Szövérffy, "Hymnological Notes," 457–72. In his discussion of the proposal to remove references to pagan myths and concepts, Szövérffy lists two words for hell: *barathrum* and *Avernus* (471). *Barathro* is in stanza 6 of this hymn. Szövérffy does not note *tartara*, though it is easy to assume similar concerns could have applied to the word for the Greek underworld as well.

53. See note 46; also 2 Pt 2:4; Fortunatus, *Vexilla regis* (H 31: 4, 4); Prudentius, *Peristeph* 10: 95, 4 and elsewhere.

54. The original text for this line, given in AH 51, and by Walpole, and others, is *redempta plebs captiváta*, with a form of *esse* understood. This is another instance of Norberg's observation that the third line in hymns of this sort need not have the accent on the antepenult (see Norberg, *Introduction*, 133); Walpole, l. 19, p. 352.

cooperation with the graces received under the old dispensation (*vitæ præmia*; line 4).

STANZA 6

Stanza 6 is the climax of the hymn. It summarizes the details of Christ's triumph. He rises from the tomb (line 1): *consurgit* is intensive with the addition of the prefix *con-*, which adds force to the line beyond what *surgit* alone would have given. The iconic phrase from Luke 24:34: *surrexit Dominus vere* ("The Lord has truly risen") gives a sense of the intensity.

As his body lay in the tomb, however, his soul, united to his divinity, was active elsewhere, in the pit of hell (lines 2–3). He rises from the pit as a conqueror in triumphal procession accompanied by all the freed captives (*victor redit de barathro*; line 2). The concept of a Roman triumph used for Christian purposes is common in this period, particularly for martyrs. St. Paul speaks of Christ as *triumphus*: *expolians principatus et potestates traduxit palam triumphans illos in semet ipso*: "despoiling the principalities and the powers, he made a public spectacle of them, leading them away in triumph by it" Col 2:15; and *Deo autem gratias qui semper triumphat nos in Christo Iesu*: "thanks be to God, who always leads us in triumph in Christ," 2 Cor 2:14.[55]

The word *barathrum* is one of the foreign words, like *azyma* and *tartara* noted above, that remain after the revisions mandated by *Sacrosanctum Concilium*. The original βάραθρον was a pit in Athens into which "the lowest criminals were thrown." It is thus a fitting image for hell and Christ's harrowing of it.[56] The word is placed at the end of line 2, in such a way that it matches the position of *tartara* in 4, 2 and *tumulo* in line 1 of this stanza. This is graphic syntax that creates suggestive connections beyond regular syntax by the visual proximity of words and the patterns that result. While he was in the pit, Christ trod underfoot the devil, the quintessential tyrant (*tyrannum trudens vinculo*; line 3). Note the alliteration. *Tyrannus* is a loan word from the Greek τύραννος and almost universally pejorative (as in the English *tyrant*). It is said of Herod in Prudentius's hymn for the feast of the Holy Innocents (*Audit tyrannus anxius*, H 294).[57]

Finally, the freed captives are led in triumphal procession all the way up to Paradise, where the gates are opened for them, and they enter (*et paradisum reserans*; line 4). This stanza began with a reference to the tomb (*tumulo*) and to hell (*barathro*); it ends with heaven (*paradisum*). Walpole (lines 21–24, pp. 352–53) connects this line to Genesis 3:24: *et collocavit ante paradisum ... cherubim*

---

55. See Dunkle, *Enchantment*, ch. 5. See also 1 Cor 15:57: "but thanks be to God who gives us the victory through our Lord Jesus Christ": *Deo autem gratias, qui dedit nobis victoriam per Dominum nostrum Iesum Christum*.

56. Walpole, p. 352; see also in Scripture, Jgs 5:15.

57. See also Prudentius, *Peristeph*, 5: 134, 2 and 10: 104, 4. Walpole connects this line to Rv 20:2: *apprehendit draconem serpentem antiquum qui est diabolus et Satanas et ligavit eum per annos mille; et misit eum in abyssum et clausit et signavit super illum*: "He seized the dragon, the ancient serpent, which is the Devil or Satan, and tied it up for a thousand years and cast him into the bottomless pit and shut him up and set a sea upon him" (Rv 20:2–3). See also Gn 41:10. As a name for the devil, *tyrannus* is found in H 24 and H 135.

et flammeum gladium: "He expelled the man and stationed before Paradise the cherubim and the fiery revolving sword, to guard the way to the tree of life", and also to Jesus' words to the good thief in Luke 23:43: *hodie mecum eris in paradiso*: "today you will be with me in Paradise." Stanzas 5 and 6 are filled with words beginning with the prefix *re-*, which signifies "return, back." Christ has bought back (5, 3), given back (5, 4), returned (6, 2), and finally reopened (6, 4).

STANZA 7

The final two stanzas of this hymn form an extended doxology for the Easter hymns (H 42–47).[58] Stanza 7 is new, though based on the stanza found in the *Breviarium Romanum*, which is itself an Urbanite reworking of the original text. Lentini took his inspiration from the Urbanite text because, as he explains, he sought a greater emphasis on Easter joy leading to the triumph of heaven.[59] For the sake of clarity, here are the three versions of stanza 7:

Original Version
Quæsumus, auctor omnium	We beg you, Author of us all,
in hoc paschali gaudio	in this paschal joy
ab omni mortis impetu	that from every assault of death
tuum defendas populum:	you may defend your people.

Breviarium Romanum
(*Urbanite text*)
Ut sis perenne mentibus	That you may be for mind and heart
Paschale Iesu gaudium;	O Jesus, paschal joy;
a morte dira criminum	from the harsh death of our sins
vitæ renatos libera.	free those reborn to life.

Liturgia Horarum
Esto perénne méntibus	O Jesus, be for mind and heart
paschále, Iesu, gáudium,	our everlasting paschal joy
et nos renátos grátiæ	and gather us, reborn by grace,
tuis triúmphis ággrega.	to share your triumphs evermore

Speaking of the present hymn, Walpole notes that the original version of stanza 7 is always found in this hymn in medieval manuscripts; he believes it to be originally composed as a stanza in this hymn, and later adopted for use in other hymns.[60] Norberg also includes this stanza in his discussion of *Ad cenam Agni providi* and seems to assume that it is one with the rest of the text.[61] The insertion

---

58. Both stanzas 7 and 8 of this hymn appear together in H 42–47. The doxology (stanza 8 of this hymn) appears in H 42–48 and H 50–51; it is a generic doxology addressed to Christ with a second line particular to the hymns of the Easter Season before the Ascension. H 150–51, hymns for the Apostles during Easter Time, also include the same stanza as stanza 7 of this hymn; but it is followed by a doxology that differs from that of other Easter hymns.
59. See *TDH*, 116: note on lines 17ff.
60. Walpole, p. 353.
61. Norberg, *Introduction*, 41.

of the original version of this stanza before the final doxology of Easter hymns is a custom that dates to the Middle Ages, as the manuscripts attest.[62]

There is additional support, internal to the text, for the conclusion that the original version of this stanza was composed as an integral part of the hymn. It represented the classic transition, toward the end of a hymn, from praise and narrative to the needs of those who sing the hymn; this seventh stanza was a prayer that the great work of redemption from death and from the power of the Evil One be granted to those who sing. The request was made in the midst of paschal joy (*in hoc paschali gaudio*). It was also a reminder that the singers are among all of those the triumphant Lord has claimed for his own; they are *populum tuum* (line 4). This line carries overtones of the Exodus narrative referenced throughout the hymn, and so redolent of the Easter season: *dimitte populum meum*: "Let my people go" (Ex 7:16).

Lentini's reworking of the stanza differs in emphasis, though it functions in much the same way as the original stanza, as it expresses the heartfelt prayer of those who sing: "Lord, be for us always an unending Easter joy, preserve in us always the grace of our Baptism, and bring us to your triumphant glory in heaven." One is led to think of the disciples of Emmaus, whose request has become a liturgical refrain throughout the Easter season: "Remain with us, Lord, for the day is far spent."[63] For further discussion of this stanza, see notes on the same stanza in H 43 and 46.

STANZA 8

This doxology is used a total of thirty-three times throughout the *Liturgia Horarum*. It has the second line *qui natus es de Virgine* sixteen times, and *qui morte victa prænites* nine times. The other eight occasions of its use have appropriate second lines for Epiphany, Ascension, Sacred Heart, and Christ the King, among others. It is a reconfiguration of the medieval doxology that began *Gloria tibi, Domine, qui natus est de Virgine*.

The present hymn began with a clear exhortation to praise Christ for his victory over death. He is our great leader who has brought us through the Red Sea; and like Mary, the sister of Aaron and Moses (Ex 15:1–21), we have sung our canticle of praise. We conclude our hymn with a final address to Christ; here he is addressed by the familiar and loving name, *Iesu*. Having vanquished death, he shines with the light that is the natural refulgence of his divinity (*prænites*), with the Father and the Spirit, in eternal unity and joy.

---

62. See AH 51, no. 83, p. 88 (end). See also *TDH*, 116; Walpole, p. 353.

63. Lk 24:29; see also the *Liturgia Horarum*, where this verse is found at None throughout the Easter Season: V. *Mane nobiscum, Domine, Alleluia.* R. *Quoniam advesperascit, Alleluia.* Also at Vespers, it is the antiphon for the Magnificat, and elsewhere.

O rex æterne, Domine	43
5th–6th c. 8 8 8 8	Easter Time before the Ascension, Weekdays Vespers

O rex ætérne, Dómine,
semper cum Patre Fílius,
iuxta tuam imáginem
Adam plasmásti hóminem.

Quem diábolus decéperat
hostis humáni géneris,
eius et formam córporis
sumpsísti tu de Vírgine,

Ut nos Deo coniúngeres
per carnis contubérnium,
datúrus in baptísmate,
Redémptor, indulgéntiam.

Tu crucem propter hóminem
suscípere dignátus es;
dedísti tuum sánguinem
nostræ salútis prétium.

Tu surrexísti, glóriam
a Patre sumens débitam;
per te et nos resúrgere
devóta mente crédimus.

Esto perénne méntibus
paschále, Iesu, gáudium,
et nos renátos grátiæ
tuis triúmphis ággrega.

Iesu, tibi sit glória,
qui morte victa prænites,
cum Patre et almo Spíritu,
in sempitérna sǽcula. Amen.

1. O Lord, eternal King and Son,
for ever at the Father's side:
you fashioned Adam out of dust,
and in your image he was formed.

2. The devil snared him by deceit
in hatred for the human race;
so from the Virgin's womb you took
a human body, flesh and form,

3. That by your marriage with our flesh
you might unite us all to God;
Redeemer, you would pardon sin
through gift of cleansing baptism.

4. On our account you bore the Cross
and willingly you chose to die;
you gave your blood in sacrifice,
the price of our salvation, Lord.

5. Now you are risen, glorified
with glory from the Father due;
devoted minds and hearts believe
that we, through you, shall rise again.

6. O Jesus, be for mind and heart
our everlasting paschal joy
and gather us, reborn by grace,
to share your triumphs evermore.

7. To you, Lord Jesus, glory be,
who shine in victory over death,
with God the Father, ever blest,
and loving Spirit, ever one. Amen.

Text found in See Lentini, *TDH*, no. 114 (*O Rex æterne*) and no. 110 (*Tibi Redemptor*), and Walpole, no. 42; AH 51, 5; Bulst, 92. These two hymns are taken from a single ancient hymn. Through the centuries there have been many changes. For an extended discussion of the textual issues, see the sources given here, in particular *TDH*.

COMMENTARY

Celebrating Christ's victory in the Easter Season, this hymn devotes special attention to the saving effects of the Incarnation and paschal joy (see 6, 2) that is shared by the congregation. As noted below, much of the language is familiar from other hymns with a Christological focus. Lentini has excerpted, emended, and adapted the text for Easter use. In the manuscript tradition, this hymn is the first part of the hymn used for Holy Saturday (H 40), *Tibi Redemptor omnium*. Lentini's version alters the received edition significantly to improve its clarity and brevity, as well as to recover as much of the ancient original as possible.[64] Walpole considers various reasons for the eventual separation of the two hymns and maintains that the content of this hymn is not "especially suited" for the Easter season to which it is assigned.[65]

In its revised form, the hymn celebrates the resurrection joy in terms that recall the Lord's Passion and celebrate the doctrinal underpinnings to our salvation. The result is a song that is both instructional and exuberant. On the one hand, for instance, we recall the mechanism of Adam's (and our) downfall; on the other hand, we are awash in "paschal joy" (*paschale gaudium*, 6, 2).

STANZA 1

The paschal hymn opens with an invocation of Christ as both source and model for the human race. Addressing Christ as eternal King recalls the classical Ambrosian references to the Son's co-eternity with the Father. We then celebrate Christ's distinctive role in creating humanity according to his own image. By introducing Christ first as Creator, the hymn proceeds to proclaim his strategy for our recreation.

The opening title, "eternal King" (*rex æterne*), is standard in the early hymnodic lexicon. Ambrose uses similar phrasing to underscore not only Christ's role, articulated in biblical sources, as ruler, but also to stress his coeternity with the Father.[66] In contrast to the Arians, who maintained that "there was when the Son was not," the Church maintains that the Son has always (*semper*, line 2) existed in relation to the Father. The language of *æterne rex* may also hint at the claim, affirmed after the Council of Nicaea and professed in the Niceno-Constantinopolitan Creed, that the Son's "kingdom will have no end" (*regni non erit finis*).[67] It is crucial to establish the co-eternity of the Son with the Father before describing the path the eternal Son took for our salvation. Thus, the final couplet speaks of the Son as the maker of humanity (*Adam*) according to his own image. The

---

64. *TDH*, p. 119.
65. Walpole, p. 212.
66. See *Æterne rerum conditor* line 1, with commentary by Fontaine, 152–53.
67. On the insertion of this clause in response to the theology of Marcellus of Ancyra, see Joseph T. Lienhard, "Basil of Caesarea," 157–67.

language recalls Genesis 1:26, but specifies the Son as the agent of creation. The hymn says that Christ "fashioned" (*plasmasti*) Adam, using a primarily Christian Latin term that draws directly from the Greek text of Genesis.[68] Christ's creation of Adam "according to" (*iuxta*) his image indicates a dynamic intentionality to the design: Adam is fashioned not *as* the "image" (which is Christ himself, the image of the Father [Col 1:15]) but after the model.

STANZA 2

The second stanza continues the narrative introduced in the first. With the relative pronoun "whom" (*quem*, line 1) and the possessive pronoun "his" (*eius*, line 3), the stanza links immediately to the preceding mention of Adam, the first human being. After Adam's creation by Christ, he was "ensnared" (*deceperat*) by the enemy of the human race. The "enemy" (*hostis*), evoked frequently in the hymns (see, e.g., H 1: 5, 4 and H 16: 1, 1), is the cause of our downfall. Christ's response is the Incarnation, taking the form of the body (see Phil 2:7) from the Virgin.

While the title "enemy of the human race" (*hostis humani generis*) is occasionally applied to infamous human beings, it is frequently applied by Christian authors to the devil.[69] His rival is the Savior who took on Adam's form from the Virgin. Thus, a single stanza presents not only Adam's fall and redemption, but also the agents of both.

STANZA 3

Christ the Redeemer (see also H 40: 1, 1, and H 41: 1, 2) has come to be with humanity through a marital union. The union is stressed through the successive "with" (*con-*) terms that indicate the closeness of God to us through the Incarnation. In relation to our own participation, the union is received through baptism, a reference that may recall the link between the paschal season and the sacrament.

Lines 1 and 2 convey the request that Christ "unite" (*coniungeres*) us with God through the fellowship (*contubernium*) of the flesh. The distinctive term *contubernium* for "marriage" has connotations of "companionship" and even "brotherhood." Walpole notes potential connotations of both military comradeship and marriage, as well as the suggestion of "indwelling" in biblical usage.[70] The request, then, is for nothing less than deification through spousal union. The second couplet presents the sacramental mode by which we achieve this union. The reference to the forgiveness granted through baptism evokes the initiation of neophytes at the Easter Vigil. "Pardon" (*indulgentiam*) highlights God's abounding mercy.

---

68. Walpole, p. 213; see Jb 10:8.
69. See, e.g., Pliny the Elder, who speaks of Nero as the *hostis generis humani* (*Natural History* 7.46). For Christian usage, see Ambrosiaster, *Commentary on Paul's Letter to the Romans* 9.29.1.
70. Walpole, p. 214; see Wis 8:3.

STANZA 4

The stanza conveys the classic themes of the divine exchange. In virtue of his humanity, Christ takes up the Cross and deigns to offer his blood for our salvation (*salutis*). We celebrate the Lord's "condescension," that is, his kindly accommodation, to our state for our rescue. The second-person address (*Tu*) leads to a recollection of Christ's loving descent. Reprising the invocation of Philippians 2 that appears in 2, 3–4, the reference to the "Cross" (*crucem*) in line 1 recalls Paul's emphatic reminder that Christ's lowliness led to death, "even death on a cross" (Phil 2:8). In credal terms, Christ's death is "on behalf of the human being" (*propter hominem*; cf. the Creed's *propter nos homines*). The language of "deigning" (*dignatus es*) appears similarly in H 42: 4, 2, and underscores the generosity of God's self-abasement.

The final couplet presents the Passion as the mechanism of human redemption: Christ's blood is the "price" (*pretium*) that is paid. The theme appears in different forms in the New Testament, especially in Paul (see 1 Cor 6:20 and Rv 5:9), and is a frequent topic of reflection in patristic sources.[71] The hymn provides very little detail, perhaps bypassing the vexing question of precisely *to whom* the price was paid (e.g., Did God pay it to himself? to the devil?). We are not meant to be drawn into a mode of intellectual speculation, but rather collective celebration of God's bounty.

STANZA 5

The narrative moves from the Cross to the Resurrection. As Christ, again addressed as "you" (*tu*), rises from the dead, he takes up the glory that is "owed" (*debitam*) from the Father. The Resurrection then becomes an assurance of our own resurrection, which we affirm entirely.

The first couplet speaks of Christ acquiring glory through the Resurrection. The language of glory, especially the glory that is "due" (*debitam*), to him, appears often in John's Gospel and underscores the fitting reward that Christ received by rising from the dead. Christ's agency is underscored by the participle "taking" (*sumens*) in line 2: While he is given glory, he also takes it up (see Jn 10:18). The final couplet recalls that we share in the same resurrection, perhaps by reference to the baptism noted in 3, 3. The verb for Christ's Resurrection in line 1 (*surrexisti*) is applied to us in line 3 (*resurgere*). Our faith, which we profess in the Creed, is maintained with a "devoted heart" (*devota mente*), language that is reprised in the subsequent stanza. The term *mens*, common in the authentic corpus of Ambrose, is not simply a term for the intellectual faculty, but rather suggests all of our internal faculties, that is, our entire heart.[72]

---

71. See, for instance, Origen, *Homilies on Exodus* 6.9; Gregory of Nazianzus, *Oration* 45.22.
72. See in Ambrose's hymns: e.g., *Æterne rerum conditor* (H 71: 6, 2) and *Splendor paternæ gloriæ* (H 75:

STANZA 6

This stanza, along with the final doxology, appears in identical form in H 42 and H 44–47. It exhorts the "hearts" (*mentibus*) of the singers and reprises the theme of new birth signaled by the reference to baptism in 3, 3. The paschal joy should be ever present to believers. The final couplet may include a request that those reborn by grace (a grace that can refer directly to the paschal baptism) be "added" to the Lord's many triumphs, or to share in the triumphs the Lord has won.

The language of the stanza is notably similar to the vocabulary of the *ambrosiana*. The request for an "enduring" (*perenne*) good appears in Ambrose's *Splendor paternæ gloriæ* (H 75: 3, 2) and in the early *Æterna Christi munera* (H 153: 4, 4). The language of "joy" (*gaudium*) and "grace" (*gratiæ*) appear in the same hymns.[73] Last, in the *Ambrosiana* the language of "triumph" (*triumphis*), which recalls the ancient Roman celebrations of conquest over foreign lands, is often linked specifically to the victory of the Cross.[74] For more details, see the commentaries on H 46 and H 47.

STANZA 7

The final doxology departs only minimally from many familiar ones by reference to Christ who "shines out" (*prænites*) after the conquest of death (*morte victa*). While the reference to "conquered death" (*morte victa*) may have special resonance in this hymn in light of the theme of rebirth, the conclusion is identical with that of other Easter hymns, H 42–48 and H 50–51. For more details, see the commentary on H 42.

5, 1 and 7, 4). He also uses the term in the plural, as in line 21, here; see *Deus, creator omnium* (H 68: 2, 3; and H 153: 1, 4). See also Lewis & Short, "*mens.*"

73. See *Æterna Christi munera* (H 153:7, 4); *Splendor paternæ gloriæ* (H 75) has *gratia* at lines 3, 3 and 4, 4.

74. See, e.g., *Iam surgit hora tertia*, 5, 1 (not included in H 48).

Hic est dies verus Dei	44

St. Ambrose, d. 397
8 8 8 8

Easter Time to the Ascension of the Lord
Office of Readings

Hic est dies verus Dei,
sancto serénus lúmine,
quo díluit sanguis sacer
probrósa mundi crímina.

1. This is the day, true day of God,
serene with clear and holy light,
on which the sacred blood has washed
both shame and guilt from all the world.

Fidem refúndit pérditis
cæcósque visu illúminat;
quem non gravi solvit metu
latrónis absolútio?

2. In this the lost regain their faith,
the blind receive the gift of light;
can one remain in anxious fear
who sees forgiveness for the thief?

Opus stupent et ángeli,
pœnam vidéntes córporis
Christóque adhæréntem reum
vitam beátam cárpere.

3. The angels wonder at this work,
they see the body wracked with pain,
they see the thief draw near to Christ
to pluck the fruit of blessed life.

Mystérium mirábile,
ut ábluat mundi luem,
peccáta tollat ómnium
carnis vítia mundans caro,

4. How wondrous is the mystery:
that flesh should cleanse the sins of flesh,
to take away the guilt of all
and wash the world of foul decay.

Quid hoc potest sublímius,
ut culpa quærat grátiam,
metúmque solvat cáritas
reddátque mors vitam novam?

5. What could be more sublime than this:
that guilt should seek the gift of grace,
that charity should cast out fear,
and death should render life renewed?

Esto perénne méntibus
paschále, Iesu, gáudium,
et nos renátos grátiæ
tuis triúmphis ággrega.

6. O Jesus, be for mind and heart
our everlasting paschal joy
and gather us, reborn by grace,
to share your triumphs evermore.

Iesu, tibi sit glória,
qui morte victa prænites,
cum Patre et almo Spíritu,
in sempitérna sǽcula. Amen.

7. To you, Lord Jesus, glory be,
who shine in victory over death,
with God the Father, ever blest,
and loving Spirit, ever one. Amen.

Text found in *TDH*, no. 116; AH 51, no. 12; Bulst, 47; Walpole, no. 10; Fontaine, no. 9, 407ff. Changes in *TDH*: stanzas 3, 7, and 8 have been omitted.

COMMENTARY

The complex structure of this hymn combined with the editorial changes made, in order to bring the hymn into the *Liturgia Horarum*, have favored a presentation of the hymn as a whole without dividing the commentary stanza by stanza. It is a magnificent hymn worthy of the master poet and great bishop of Milan to whom it is attributed. The hymn is ancient, mentioned both by Caesarius of Arles (d. 542) and Aurelian, his successor (d. 551). Like so many hymns brought into the liturgy, the hymn has remained anonymous, though by general consensus it is included among the genuine works of Ambrose.[75]

Drawing on references to the dawn (or pre-dawn) of the first Easter morning that are found in each of the gospel narratives,[76] the opening lines (1–2) of the first stanza of this Paschal hymn proffer an image of the clear and holy light of God's "true day," for light, of course, is frequently the cardinal emblem of Christ and His Resurrection.[77] The inference in stanza 1, line 3, is that on this "true day," the sacred blood (*sanguis sacer*) shed on Good Friday has brought to completion—this is the force of the perfect tense of the verb *diluo* in this instance—a universal and definitive cleansing from sin. This lays the groundwork for the pivotal role that the repentance and salvation of the good thief will play in stanzas 2–4 in Ambrose's vision of the schema of Christ's salvation.

Apparently, in order to shape a more concise and less "harsh" association, yet one still anchored in the imagery of light and blood, of the crucifixions of Christ and the good thief, Lentini reduced to five the eight stanzas composed by St. Ambrose,[78] and it could be argued that he has succeeded in sharpening considerably the more diffuse and complex development of the original lyrical meditation on the death of death. In its fifth stanza then, the reconstituted hymn is brought to an apposite rhetorical climax with a multithreaded chiastic arrangement whose design underscores, graphically, the universal scope of a sacrifice that makes the world "more heavenly" (*sublimius*, 5, 1).

---

75. Walpole, no. 10, pp. 77–82; Hervé Savon's discussion of authorship leaves the question open (see Fontaine, 407–13). The two final stanzas that Savon would consider a later interpolation have been removed from the hymn in the *Liturgia Horarum*. See Hervé Savon, Hymne 9, *Hic est dies verus*, in Ambrose de Milan, *Hymnes*, ed. Jacques Fontaine, 407–41.

76. Mt 25:1; Mk 16:2; Lk 24:1; Jn 20:1.

77. While Malmede, *Die Lichtsymbolik* remains the most tightly focused study of the symbolism of Christian light in the context of the New Testament, more recently Katsos, *Metaphysics of Light in the Hexaemeral Literature* has attempted to develop a "luminocentric" Christian concept of light according to which the sensible properties of that substance acquire their particularly profound cosmological and theophanic significance. Moreover, in the hymn presently under consideration, given Saint Ambrose's undeniable familiarity with Cappadocian hexaemeral literature, it seems not unreasonable to suppose that his effort to approach afresh the eschatological concept of the "day of God" (see Hultgård and Norin, *Le Jour de Dieu*) hinged on the alignment of the dawning light of Easter, the "true day of God," with the cosmic spectacle—and implications—of the salvation of the good thief.

78. Lentini notes that because of a certain roughness within them (*ob earum aliquam asperitatem*), he omits the third stanza as well as the final two of Saint Ambrose's hymn (*HIBR*, no. 101, p. 97) and adds to the stanzas that remain a standard concluding doxology for Easter hymns. This addition will not be discussed here in detail because it is treated in the commentary for H 42.

In stanzas 1, 3–4, and 2, 1–2, Ambrose expands upon the power of the sacred blood: it washes away the base and shameful crimes of the world. It "pours out (generously)" faith upon lost sinners and "brings light to the blind." The second stanza concludes with the introduction of the repentant thief—the second key figure in the hymn after Christ—the *latro* of 2, 4, whose imminent admission into Paradise has been obliquely alluded to in the opening line of the hymn.

Stanza 3 of the original hymn, which has been omitted from the hymn in the *Liturgia Horarum*, develops in greater detail the conversion of the good thief: he exchanged the cross for a reward; with a "brief faith" (*brevi fide*) he found and "purchased" Jesus (*adquisit*); this was the immediate first fruit of the pouring forth of faith upon lost souls by the sacred blood (stanza 2, 1). Then, with an anticipatory step (*prævio gradu*) he preceded (*prævenit*) the righteous and entered the kingdom of God first. The stanza is an expansion of ideas introduced in the previous stanza; it is an interlude filled with the subtle irony and humor so characteristic of Ambrose. He is neither the first nor the last to take delight in the stroke of Divine Providence that led the good thief to conversion as Christ was dying on the Cross. Ambrose lets the thief remain a competent thief, who seized the faith pouring forth from the sacred blood, used it to acquire the greatest treasure, Jesus, and thereby to outstrip the just, by entering the Kingdom before them. Such is the unfathomable love of God for his creatures.

The following stanzas (3–5 of the revised hymn) present first the astonishment of the angels as they behold the twofold spectacle of Christ's death and the thief's repentance (stanza 3) and then what we might term the cosmic implications of the salvific spectacle that is created by the exchange between Christ and the thief (stanzas 4–5).

In what has now become the third stanza of the hymn, the "good thief," as Christian tradition has come to know him (and under several different names), is aptly characterized as a *reus* (specifically "convicted criminal") whose admission of guilt and recognition of Christ's innocence wins salvation for himself.[79] Particularly noteworthy here, and in keeping with the imagery of the omitted stanza, is the fact that the angels observe this "condemned criminal" "snatch" (*carpere* at 3, 4) rather than "pluck" his joyful life in Paradise, and they see that he does so, moreover, in a manner that, as the Latin participle *adhærentem* (3, 3) also suggests, includes a soupçon of subterfuge on his part.[80] The thief's repentance in the fourth stanza will point to the symbolic role (4, 1–3) of his salvation as one

---

79. The bulk of the Western (but nothing of the Russian Orthodox) traditions concerning the good thief are conveniently brought together by Merback, *The Thief, the Cross and the Wheel*, in particular chapter 2 ("The Two Thieves Crucified: Bodies, Weapons and the Technologies of Pain").

80. While Walpole (pp. 77–82) rightly observes that the phrase *Christo adhærentem* is biblical (Ps 72 [73]:28, etc.) and that Ambrose uses it elsewhere, in the present context, in particular given the additional meanings suggested by both *opus* and *carpere*, there may be detected a hint that the angelic astonishment arises from the "thieving" quality of the condemned man's attachment to Christ on Calvary. Note that Martial, *Epigrammata* 5.61.1 uses the same verb to suggest quite the opposite, i.e., that an association perceived to be proper and professional is in fact illicit in nature.

expressly emblematic of that of all those who repent: none of them inherently deserves what Christ's sacrifice will obtain for them, so that all, in a sense, may similarly be understood to "snatch" the boon. Thus, the extraordinary nature not only of the thief's prize but also of the manner in which he obtains it is a significant feature of his portrayal as a thief, a feature that has already been adumbrated through the deft choice of the word *opus* (3, 1).

Thus, the angelic spectators (3, 1), in the tradition of a kind of celestial audience in a *theatrum mundi*,[81] witness Christ's salvific work (3, 1–2), his *opus*, an allusion to Paul's phrase *opus Christi* (Phil 2:30).[82] They also cast their gaze in an equally dumbfounded manner (*stupent* at 3, 1) on the *opus* of the thief himself (3, 3–4), whose practice of his "profession"—another sense in which *opus* is commonly used[83]—is imagined to inform his repentance. With the establishment of this measure of verbal subtlety, we now may turn our attention back to the hymn's opening line, where, in pursuit of its meditation on the thief's salvation and Christ's sacrifice, a similarly subtle choice of simple but elegant wording creates a set of interlocking scriptural and literary allusions.

The deceptive simplicity of the phrase "true day" in line 1 warrants a special scrutiny. In the first place, it has long been recognized that St. Ambrose clearly had meant the phrase to allude to a well-known verse from Psalm 117 (118): *hæc est dies quam fecit Dominus; exultemus et lætemur in ea* ... : "This is the day the Lord has made; let us rejoice and be glad in it" (117 [118]:24).[84]
While, for the psalmist, "this day" (*hæc ... dies*) is that which the Lord has made for the rebuilding of the Jewish temple, for St. Ambrose "this true day / this day in truth" (*hic ... dies verus*) looks to the typological meaning of the scriptural verse, the same meaning that Christ himself had revealed (see Jn 2:19, as well as Mk 14:5; 15:29; Mt 26:61; 27:40). The "true day of God" is, of course, Easter, and the rebuilt temple an allusion to the Resurrection.[85]

There are, moreover, two further allusions that may be detected in the same phrase "this true day." The first reflects the transparent zeal of the unusually well-educated bishop of Milan for the network of revelation that is Scripture; the second is indicative of his classical learning which, although it is extensive, is applied to the hymns in a restrained manner that requires it to be teased out with care.[86]

---

81. The long-enduring Greek concept of the "world (as a) stage," adapted by St. Paul (1 Cor 4:9, etc.) but already implicit, before the advent of Athenian tragedy and comedy, in the Homeric epics (in which the gods habitually relish the spectacle of human strife), is conveniently surveyed by Minos Kokolakes, *The Dramatic Simile*, and Lynda Christian, *Theatrum Mundi*.

82. Ambrose has a long passage in his *De fide* (4.1. 5–14) describing the wonder of the Angels at the Resurrection of Christ: *Obstipuerunt et angeli cæleste mysterium* ... See also H 12, stanza 3, with commentary.

83. See OLD, s.v. *opus*.

84. See Walpole, pp. 77–82.

85. "Jesus answered them, 'Destroy this temple, and in three days I will raise it up'" (Jn 2:19).

86. Although Ambrose's more transparent citations of Virgil, for example, were brought together almost a century ago (Sr. M. Diederich, *Vergil in the Works of St. Ambrose*), the considerably restrained (and not necessarily unsubtle) expression of the broad range of Christian classical erudition among a small and elite

The first, that which is directly relevant to the theme of the hymn, is that verse in Luke's account of Calvary in which Christ himself promises salvation to the good thief "today," that is, on Good Friday: *amen dico tibi, hodie mecum eris in paradiso*: "Amen, I say to you, today you will be with me in Paradise." (Lk 23:43)

Given that the literal meaning of *hodie* in Latin, an adverb meaning "today" that represents a compression of the phrase *in hoc die*, is "on *this* day," it is reasonable to infer that the first line of the hymn also intends to allude additionally (and hardly inappropriately) to Luke's Calvary narrative, especially in view of the fact that *hodie*, i.e., Good Friday, is the day on which the salvation that is to be extended *fully* by the Resurrection on Eastern morning to all repentant sinners was *initially* bestowed upon the good thief. This proposed allusive link between these two days, then, is precisely that implied by the verb *diluit* in line 3 (see *supra*).

Yet another intertext, this one considerably more subtle and ironic from a Christian perspective, may be detected in the *iunctura* (i.e., combination of specific words) of "*dies verus*" itself, for the phrase offers a slight variation on one that was apparently coined by Horace, effectively the fountain head of the Roman lyric tradition, the genre that St. Ambrose consciously sought through his hymns to transform into a vehicle for Christian topics:

hic dies vere mihi festus atras	This day, for me truly festive, will expel
exiget curas: ego nec tumultum	my black cares; I shall have no fear
nec mori per vim metuam tenente	of civil strife or violent death while Caesar
Cæsare terras.	holds sway throughout the world.
Odes 3.14	

While "*dies verus*" (or its alternative "*dies vera*"—because the noun for "day" may be either masculine or feminine in gender—"true day / day in truth") is not an especially uncommon one in Latin, and while St. Augustine and other Christian Latin authors (for example Sts. Cyprian and Peter Chrysologus) employ the *iunctura*, as St. Ambrose does, in reference to Easter, it remains noteworthy that Horace is the *first* Latin poet—and, indeed, the first author—to bring together the very slightly altered variant (in which the adverb "*vere*" replaces the adjective "*verus /vera*") to describe the joy that *he*, Horace, experiences upon learning that Emperor Augustus, whose life had been gravely threatened by illness, is safely returned from campaign against barbarians in Spain.[87] Insignificant though such a similarity of phrasing may seem to be at first blush, in the long and rich literary

---

group in the fourth century is inevitably more elusive. M. Marin's statement, then, that "in Ambrogio, Orazio non è mai citato e viene utilizzato in misura modesta e in maniera discreta, come d'altronde gli altri *auctores*" (In Ambrose, Horace is never cited and is used in modest measure and in a discreet manner, as is the case with other authors). ("La Presenza Di Orazio", 259) begins to warrant at least some degree of revision. See also note 88, below.

87. See, e.g., Preece, *Horace's Odes*, 451ff., and Syme, "The Spanish War," esp. 310.

traditions of Greece and Rome reminiscences of an earlier author regularly turn on precisely this sort of subtle detail. It should be noted too that finely crafted allusions of this sort are by no means confined to non-Christian literature, and that, particularly in Late Antiquity, Christian authors are very much at pains to absorb and to transform in a studied manner their non-Christian literary inheritance. The echo in this present instance certainly transforms—and at the same time cleverly mocks—the sentiment expressed in the Horatian source regarding Augustus, the would-be god-emperor.[88]

The final stanzas (4–5) of the main body of the hymn further elaborate, climactically in a chiastic arrangement of the words of the text, the implications of the *mysterium mirabile* (4, 1) of the Crucifixion. The fourth stanza plays first upon the words for "world" and "cleanse" (*mundus* at 4, 2: "world"; and *mundans* at 4, 4: "cleansing"), thereby making explicit a familiar pun (already hinted at in 1, 4: *mundi*), and then in the final line (4, 4) opposing in a *chiasmus* Christ's flesh that cleanses and the sins of the flesh:

carnis vita mundans caro

This *chiasmus* introduces in turn the more elaborate interlinear *chiastic* organizations that form the climax of the hymn in the fifth stanza; a diagram of stanza 5 will be useful for the analysis of that follows:

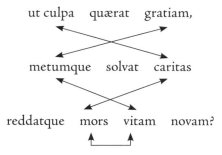

Quid hoc potest sublimius,

ut culpa quærat gratiam,

metumque solvat caritas

reddatque mors vitam novam?

---

88. While Mitsis, *Wordplay and Powerplay*, provides a recent and wide-ranging suite of studies treating of the operation of this sort of aesthetic among non-Christian authors, the series of monographs under C. Gnilka's direction, *Chrēsis: die Methode*, aims at a correctly appropriated use of classical culture by the Church Fathers.

As this schema of stanza 5 shows, the components of the question posed here, "what can be more heavenly than this?"[89] are arranged in such a way that the subject-verb-object order of line 2 is inverted to object-verb-subject in line 3. More than that, however, the sinner's guilt (line 2) corresponds syntactically (as the subject) to divine love (line 3), just as the sinner's fear (line 3) corresponds (as the object) to divine grace (line 2). Thus, with the verb in the middle of each line, a complex chiasmus is created between lines 2 and 3. In a similar manner at lines 3–4, divine love, the subject (line 3), corresponds to death, Christ's death (line 4), just as the sinner's fear, the object (line 3), corresponds to the life, the new life, that is won for the sinner through Christ's death (line 4). Thus, the transformation of earthly death into heavenly life—in response to the question "what can be more heavenly?"—which is brought about by the Crucifixion is reified rhetorically in the text itself. Moreover, the "criss-crossing" graphical arrangement of guilt and grace, of fear and love, of death and new life in this climax conclusively underscores the declaration made at the beginning of the hymn that the Resurrection, imaged by the Easter dawn, completes the sacrifice of Good Friday, completes, that is, the Pasch. Lentini's explicit inclusion of the adjective *paschale* in his sixth stanza (6, 2) highlights this twofold dimension of Easter found in the hymn; the broadly recognized twin senses of *pasch* as "crossing over" (in the original Hebrew) and "suffering" (by a false—but irresistible—Greek etymology from the verb πάσχω among Christians of Late Antiquity) are implicit in this hymn's smooth fusion of the new intersection of heaven and earth with the forgiveness of sin and transcendence of death won through the Crucifixion on Calvary.

For a discussion of the two final stanzas (6 and 7) that make the extended Easter doxology, see the commentary on H 42.

---

89. *sublimius* is translated "more heavenly"; *sublimis* means "elevating, high, lofty." See Livy, *Ab urbe condita*, 1.16.8; it also echoes *serenus* in stanza 1, 2.

	Lætare, cælum, desuper	45
8th c.		
8 8 8 8	Easter Time after the Octave to the Ascension	
	Office of Readings	

Lætáre, cælum, désuper, appláude, tellus ac mare: Christus resúrgens post crucem vitam dedit mortálibus.	1. Rejoice, O heaven, from on high and clap your hands, both earth and sea, for after death upon the Cross Christ rose again and gave us life.
Iam tempus accéptum redit, dies salútis cérnitur, quo mundus Agni sánguine refúlsit a calígine.	2. The accepted time has now returned: we see the day of saving power, on which the blood shed by the Lamb restored the darkened world to light.
Mors illa, mortis pássio, est críminis remíssio; illæsa virtus pérmanet, victus dedit victóriam.	3. His death brought agony to death and absolution from all sin; his might and power remain unharmed: the vanquished gave us victory.
Nostræ fuit gustus spei hic, ut fidéles créderent se posse post resúrgere, vitam beátam súmere.	4. This was the foretaste of our hope, so that the faithful might believe they too may rise again one day to gain the crown of blessed life.
Nunc ergo pascha cándidum causa bonórum tálium colámus omnes strénue tanto repléti múnere.	5. And filled with joy at such a gift, now, therefore, let us praise with zeal our bright, resplendent Paschal Lamb for giving us such wondrous goods.
Esto perénne méntibus paschále, Iesu, gáudium, et nos renátos grátiæ tuis triúmphis ággrega.	6. O Jesus be for mind and heart our everlasting paschal joy and gather us, reborn by grace, to share your triumphs evermore.
Iesu, tibi sit glória, qui morte victa prænites, cum Patre et almo Spíritu, in sempitérna sæcula. Amen.	7. To you, Lord Jesus, glory be, who shine in victory over death, with God the Father, ever blest, and loving Spirit, ever one. Amen.

Text found in *TDH*, no. 117; *AH* 14, no. 65; *AH* 50, no. 91; Lapidge, *Bede's Latin Poetry*, 510–11. Changes in *TDH*: stanzas 3 and 5–9 are omitted; 2, 4: *caligine* for *nigredine*; 5, 4: *tanto repleti munere* for *tantis renatis fratribus* (see below).

COMMENTARY:

This hymn is adapted from an original *Lætare, cælum, desuper* that was already known to Alcuin of York (ca. 740–804)[90] and the full text of which is preserved in two eleventh-century manuscripts from central Italy.[91] Alcuin's inclusion of the first stanza of the hymn among other hymns confidently attributed to the Venerable Bede (d. ca. 735) led Dreves (1854–1909) to attribute *Lætare, cælum, desuper* to Bede himself.[92] Later scholars have expressed varied viewpoints on this question: Fraipont included the hymn in his 1955 critical edition of Bede's hymnal,[93] while Bulst rejected Bede's authorship in an article published in 1959.[94] Anselmo Lentini was aware of Dreves's and Fraipont's attribution of the hymn to Bede,[95] but he evidently did not accept the attribution to Bede; Lentini's 1968 work refers to the hymn as "A. ignotus—Sæc. incerto" (author unknown, uncertain century) and the 1984 work refers to it as "Autore ignoto. Almeno del sec. x"(author unknown, around the tenth century).[96] Whoever may have authored the hymn, the inclusion of the first stanza in a recently identified ninth-century manuscript of Alcuin's *De laude Dei* shows that the hymn is older than Lentini supposed; the *De laude Dei* likely represents Alcuin's liturgical experience at York, which suggests that *Lætare, cælum, desuper* was circulating in England at least by the eighth century.[97] Lapidge, the editor of the most recent edition of Bede's poetry, carefully weighs the evidence for Bede's authorship and concludes that the hymn "could, on metrical grounds, have been composed by Bede himself; but there is unfortunately no evidence to prove the attribution."[98]

90. The first stanza of *Lætare, cælum, desuper* is included in the *De laude Dei* composed by Alcuin of York (ca. 740–804) and transmitted in a late ninth-century manuscript from southern France (El Escorial, Real Biblioteca de San Lorenzo, B.IV.17, fols. 134v–35r) and an early eleventh-century manuscript copied at Mainz (Bamberg, Staatsbibliothek, Misc. patr. 17 [B. II. 10], fol. 151r–v). While the Bamberg manuscript has long been known to scholars, the Escorial manuscript was first identified as a source for Alcuin in the late twentieth century by Donald A. Bullough (1928–2002) and constitutes an important confirmation of the antiquity of the hymn; see Jullien, "Les hymnes dans le milieu alcuinien," 172; for the dating of the manuscript, see Bischoff, *Katalog der festländischen Handschriften*, 252, §1193.

91. The full text of the hymn is edited in AH 14, pp. 75–76, n. 65, from two eleventh-century hymnals from Central Italy (perhaps Narni): Vatican City, BAV, Vat. lat. 7172, fols. 73r–74r and Paris, BnF, Latin 1092, fols. 86v–87r. For an overview of recent scholarship on these manuscripts, see the commentary on the Advent hymn H 4, *Verbum salutis omnium*.

92. See AH 50, pp. 97–99. Dreves provides an edition of the hymn as AH 50, pp. 113–14, n. 91 [13], drawing on the two manuscripts used in AH 14 as well as the Bamberg manuscript of Alcuin's *De laude Dei*.

93. Bede, *Opera homiletica*, 417–18. The hymn is likewise attributed to Bede in Walsh, 228–31, 464–65.

94. Bulst, "Bedæ Opera rhythmica?," 83–91, at 88–89.

95. Lentini references these two authors in the entries for the hymn in the 1968 *HIBR*, 101, and in the 1984 *TDH*, 122.

96. Lentini does not cite Bulst, but it seems likely that he was aware of his critique of Fraipont's edition. Curiously, *HIBR*, 18, §19, refers to a different hymn, *Adesto, Christe, cordibus* (H 90), as "Dubie tribuitur s. Bedæ Ven." (cf. *TDH*, 33, §31: "Attribuito, ma forse erroneamente, a S. Beda il Venerabile"). *Adesto, Christe, cordibus*, like *Lætare, cælum, desuper*, is found in Alcuin's *De laude Dei*, and was first attributed to Bede by Guido Maria Dreves, and Bede's authorship was affirmed by Fraipont and rejected by Bulst. Lapidge, *Bede's Latin Poetry*, 507–9 and 511–13, reviews the evidence and offers a similar conclusion as that reached for *Lætare cælum desuper*: "In sum, the present stanzas could, on metrical grounds, have been composed by Bede himself; but there is unfortunately no evidence to prove the attribution." The *Liturgia Horarum* includes two other hymns confidently attributed to Bede: H 293, *Hymnum canentes martyrum* for the feast of the Holy Innocents, and H 252, *Præcessor almus gratiæ* for the Passion of John the Baptist.

97. See Bullough, *Alcuin*, 177; Ganz, "De Laude Dei," 387.

98. Lapidge, *Bede's Latin Poetry*, 509–13.

The original version of the hymn includes eleven stanzas.⁹⁹ The *Liturgia Horarum* draws on stanzas 1, 2, 4, 10, and 11 from the source text, pairing them with a standard Easter stanza (*Esto perenne mentibus*) and doxology (*Iesu, tibi sit gloria*). The omitted stanzas focus on the Holy Cross and on miraculous events recounted in the gospels concerning the Passion of Christ.¹⁰⁰ The *Liturgia Horarum* version contains two further modifications from the source text. In 2, 4, *nigredine* (darkness) is replaced by *caligine* (mist, darkness, gloom). In 5, 4, *tantis renatis fratribus* (with so many brothers reborn [in baptism]) is replaced by *tanto repleti munere* (having been filled with such a great gift). In the stanzas included in the *Liturgia Horarum* assonance and rhyme are found in 2, 3–4; 3, 1–2; 4, 3–4; and 5, 1–2 and 3–4. In the omitted stanzas it is also occasionally used.

The hymn begins with an invitation to rejoice at the Resurrection of Christ (stanza 1). Then, it reflects on the Passion of Christ and the hope of the general resurrection (stanzas 2–4). It recapitulates a call to praise the Paschal Lamb (stanza 5), and finally concludes with a stanza and doxology shared with other Easter hymns in the *Liturgia Horarum* (stanzas 6–7).

STANZA 1

The opening stanza invites all of creation to join in celebrating the Resurrection of Christ. The opening word *Lætare* resonates with the command to rejoice found frequently in biblical and liturgical texts, for instance, Joel 2:21, Zephaniah 3:14, Zechariah 2:10, and liturgical chants, such as the Lenten entrance antiphon *Lætare, Ierusalem*: "Rejoice, Jerusalem" (see Is 66:10) and the Easter Compline antiphon, *Regina cæli, lætare*: "O Queen of heaven, rejoice," although this chant likely post-dates the composition of the hymn. The link of *cælum* with *desuper* recalls the Advent entrance antiphon *Rorate cæli desuper*: "Drop down dew from above, you heavens" (Is 45:8). The emphasis on heaven, earth, and sea rejoicing together evokes Psalm 95 (96):11: *Lætentur cæli, et exsultet terra; commoveatur mare et plenitudo eius*: "Let the heavens rejoice and let the earth be glad; let the sea roar and all that fills it."¹⁰¹ In line 2 *applaude* echoes Ps 46 (47): 1, *Omnes gentes, plaudite manibus* ("All peoples, clap your hands").

The participial reference to "Christ rising" imitates the grammatical form found in Romans 6:9: *Christus resurgens ex mortuis iam non moritur*: "Christ,

---

99. Two manuscripts, Vatican City, BAV, Vat. lat. 7172, and Paris, BnF, Latin 1092, include the full text of eleven stanzas and incipits for two concluding stanzas (*Quesumus auctor* and *Gloria tibi domine* [*domine* omitted in Paris]). AH 14, pp. 75–76, includes the full text of a twelfth stanza (*Quæsumus, auctor omnium*) and the incipit of a final doxology (*Gloria tibi domine*). As Bulst observes ("Bedæ Opera rhythmica?", 89), the twelfth stanza printed in AH 14 (*Quæsumus, auctor omnium*) is borrowed from *Ad cenam agni providi* and follows an accentual rhythm rather than the metrical rhythm used throughout *Lætare cælum desuper*. AH 50, pp. 113–14, n. 91 [13], and the editions of Fraipont and Lapidge omit any reference to the doxology incipits provided in the manuscript sources, providing a total of eleven stanzas. Lapidge, *Bede's Latin Poetry*, 512, observes that it is possible that the hymn originally contained other stanzas, which are not transmitted in the extant sources: "Walther Bulst thought … that it was inconceivable that Bede would allocate only eleven stanzas to a feast as important as Easter. But scribes of medieval hymnals play fast and loose with the hymns they transcribe, and it is not difficult to imagine that a scribe could have omitted five stanzas of a sixteen-stanza hymn by Bede."

100. For texts, translations, and commentary on these stanzas, see Walsh, 228–31, 464–65; Lapidge, *Bede's Latin Poetry*, 510–12.

101. This forms a poignant reversal of Jeremiah 4:28: *Lugebit terra, et mœrebunt cæli desuper*: "The earth shall mourn, and the heavens shall grieve from above."

rising from the dead, dies now no more," a text that also serves as the basis for an Easter Alleluia verse and Communion antiphon. The reference in the final line to the Resurrection giving life to mortals recalls the emphasis in 1 John 5:11 on God giving eternal life to us through Jesus.[102]

STANZA 2

Stanza 2 begins with a reference to 2 Corinthians 6:2: *Ecce nunc tempus acceptabile, ecce nunc dies salutis*: "Behold, now is the acceptable time; behold, now is the day of salvation", linking Paul's invocation of Isaiah 49:8 to the liturgical celebration of Easter.[103] The stanza continues by linking the Pauline references with the attribution of redemption to the blood of the lamb in 1 Peter 1:19: *non corruptibilibus argento vel auro redempti estis ... sed pretioso sanguine quasi agni immaculati Christi, et incontaminati*: "not by corruptible silver or gold were you redeemed ... but with the precious blood of Christ as of a spotless and unblemished lamb" and with the attribution of a whitening power to the blood of the lamb in Revelation 7:14: *dealbaverunt eas in sanguine Agni*: "They have made them white in the blood of the Lamb." Although Lentini's substitution of *caligine* (mist, darkness, gloom)[104] for the original *nigredine* (blackness, darkness) in line 4 does not fundamentally change the meaning of the text,[105] it unfortunately obscures parallel passages where the Venerable Bede associates *nigredo, nigredinis* with the overcoming of sin by baptism.[106]

STANZA 3

After the omission of a stanza focused on the Holy Cross,[107] stanza 3 focuses on the effects of the death of Christ, celebrating the paradox of Christ's victory achieved by what seemed like defeat. This stanza is redolent with Pauline language concerning the destruction of death and the granting of victory to humanity through the death of Christ.[108] The connection of the remission of sins with the

---

102. *Et hoc est testimonium, quoniam vitam æternam dedit nobis Deus: et hæc vita in Filio eius est*: "And this is the testimony: that God gave us eternal life, and this life is in his Son" (1 Jn 5:11).

103. *in tempore placito exaudivi te et in die salutis auxiliatus sum tui*: "In an acceptable time I have heard you, and in the day of salvation I have helped you" (Is 49:8).

104. Notably *caligine* appears in stanza 7 of the original version of the hymn: see Lapidge, *Bede's Latin Poetry*, 511: *Velans caput caligine / extinxit omnem lampadem, / errare noctem passus est / meridiano tempore*.

105. HIBR states that *nigredine* "non videtur placere" (does not seem to fit), and the 1984 *TDH* states the original "termine che qui è parso strano" (term is here parsed strangely).

106. See, e.g., Bede, "Expositio actuum apostolorum," 3–99, at 41 (VIII, 26): *Via vero quæ ad eandem ab Hierosolymis descendens fontem salutis aperuit Dominus Iesus Christus est qui ait; Ego sum via et veritas et vita; qui a superna Hierusalem ad nostra infirma descendit nostrique reatus* nigredinem *baptismatis unda dealbavit*: "The road that, descending to the same [Jericho] from Jerusalem, reveals the fount of salvation is the Lord Jesus Christ who says: "I am the way and the truth and the life" [Jn 14:6]; who [he] has come down from the Jerusalem on high to our infirmities and by the water of Baptism has whitened the blackness of our guilt." Bede uses this word in seven other places in texts included in the Brepols *Library of Latin Texts*.

107. Lapidge, *Bede's Latin Poetry*, 510, 512: *Crux namque sacratissima / ligni prioris vulnera / in patre nostri seminis / sanavit hostem saucians*. "For the most Holy Cross, wounding the Enemy, healed the wound made by the earlier tree [in Paradise] in the father of our seed [Adam]."

108. See Rom 6:8–9: *Si autem mortui sumus cum Christo, credimus quia simul etiam vivemus cum Christo, scientes quod Christus resurgens ex mortuis iam non moritur: mors illi ultra non dominabitur*: "Now if we have died with Christ, we believe that we will also live with him, knowing that Christ, being raised from the dead, will never die again; death no longer has dominion over him."; 1 Cor 15:21: *quoniam quidem per hominem mors, et per hominem resurrectio mortuorum*: "since indeed through one man there is death, also through one man there is

death of Christ in 3, 2 is rooted in Acts 13:38: *per hunc vobis remissio peccatorum annuntiatur*: "through him [Christ] remission of sins is preached to you" and Hebrews 9:22: *sine sanguinis effusione non fit remissio*: "without the shedding of blood there is no remission." The reference to power (*virtus*) in 3, 3 recalls references to Christ's power in Luke 6:19: *quia virtus de illo exibat, et sanabat omnes*: "for power went out from him [Christ], and he healed all", and 2 Corinthians 12:9: *Libenter igitur gloriabor in infirmitatibus meis, ut inhabitet in me virtus Christi*: "Gladly will I boast of my weaknesses, that the power of Christ may dwell in me." The rhyme in *passio* and *remissio* underlines the connection between the "agony of death" and "remission from sin," and the use of *passio*, more often applied to Christ, is ironic in the context of death itself. There is also strong alliteration of *m* in lines 1–2, and of *v* in 3–4, emphasizing the contrasts of *mors ... mortis passio* and *victus ... victoriam*.

STANZA 4

After stanza 3, five stanzas are omitted, which recount the darkening of the sun at the Passion (Mt 27:45, Mk 15:33, and Lk 23:44) and the rising of the dead from their tombs (Mt 27:52–53).[109] The omission of these stanzas has the effect of changing the referent of the current stanza 4 (the original stanza 10). In the original context, *hic* refers to the raising of the dead in Limbo, at the death of Christ, as the foretaste of our hope. In the *Liturgia Horarum* version, *hic* refers instead to Christ's death and victory. Stanza 4 focuses on the hope for resurrection and blessed eternal life that has been awakened in all the faithful by Christ's victory over death. Just as stanza 3 was rooted in the teaching of 1 Corinthians 15, that Christ's death destroyed death, so stanza 4 takes up the teaching of the same letter, that not only has Christ risen, but all the dead will one day be raised.[110] The stanza links this article of faith with our own hope for the fulfillment of what we believe. The connection of hope and immortality is already articulated in Wisdom 3:4: *etsi coram hominibus tormenta passi sunt, spes illorum immortalitate plena est*: "Though in the sight of others [men] they suffered torments, their hope is full of immortality", and the Pauline letters associate hope with the glory and second coming of Christ.[111] In addition to its literal sense in the context of the hymn as pointing to Jesus' Resurrection as a foretaste of our own resurrection, the use of

---

resurrection from the dead"; 1 Cor 15:26: *Novissima autem inimica destruetur mors*: "The final enemy that shall be destroyed is Death"; 1 Cor 15:54: *Cum autem mortale hoc induerit immortalitatem, tunc fiet sermo, qui scriptus est: Absorpta est mors in victoria*: "When the mortal shall put on immortality, then the word that is written shall come to pass: Death is swallowed up in victory."

109. Lapidge, *Bede's Latin Poetry*, 511–12: 5. *Miretur omne sæculum / crucis triumphum mysticæ. / Hæc signa congruentia / velut tropæum præsto sunt: / 6. sol namque, magnum luminar, / horas dierum permeans, / viso novo mysterio / decepit orbem, territus. / 7. Velans caput caligine / extinxit omnem lampadem, / errare noctem passus est / meridiano tempore. / 8. Finduntur et fortes petræ, / hiantur antra plurima, / defuncta surgunt corpora, / vitæ redduntur mortui. / 9. Immitis ille tartarus, / ad se trahentis omnia / præsentiam non sustinens / animasque sanctas reddidit*. "5. Let all ages marvel at the victory of the mystic Cross. These pertinent signs are at hand as an emblem: 6. for the sun, that great luminary, traversing the daylight hours, deceived the world, terrified, having seen the new mystery. 7. Covering its head in darkness it extinguished all its light: it experienced the night's advance in the midst of day. 8. And mighty rocks are split asunder and many recesses gape open; corpses of the deceased rise up; the dead are returned to life. 9. That cruel Tartarus, unable to tolerate the presence of One attracting everything to him, released its holy souls."

110. 1 Cor 15:51–52: *Ecce mysterium vobis dico: omnes quidem resurgemus, sed non omnes immutabimur. In momento, in ictu oculi, in novissima tuba: canet enim tuba, et mortui resurgent incorrupti: et nos immutabimur.*

111. See Col 1:27: *quibus voluit Deus notas facere divitias gloriæ sacramenti huius in gentibus, quod est Christus,*

the word *gustus* ("taste, foretaste") also evokes the reception of the Eucharist, in which we receive the bread that enables us to "live for ever" (Jn 6:51), "the medicine of immortality, the antidote we take in order not to die but to live for ever in Jesus Christ" (Ignatius of Antioch, *Letter to the Ephesians*, 20.2). The eternal life for which we hope will be blessed (*vitam beatam*; line 4) and filled with joy: *Gustate, et videte quoniam suavis est Dominus, beatus vir qui sperat in eo*: "O taste, and see that the Lord is sweet: happy the man who hopes in him" (Ps 33:9 [34:8]).

STANZA 5

Stanza 5 of Lentini's hymn, which was likely the final stanza of the hymn in its original form, recapitulates the invitation to praise that was articulated in the opening stanza. After recounting the victory and promise won by Christ's death and Resurrection, we are invited to give thanks for the gift we have received. The first line refers to the *pascha candidum*, to which the third line invites us (*colamus*). *Pascha candidum* may refer to Jesus Christ as the bright Paschal Lamb, or it may refer to the bright Paschal Feast. The verb *colo, colere* has a range of meanings, which include "cherish, honor, observe, and worship." It seems possible that the author of the hymn intends both meanings: we lovingly observe the Paschal Feast in which we worship the Paschal Lamb.[112] The identification of Jesus Christ as the "bright Paschal Lamb" (*pascha candidum*) takes up the identification of Christ with the Paschal Lamb found in 1 Corinthians 5:7 (*Etenim Pascha nostrum immolatus est Christus*: "For Christ our Passover lamb has been sacrificed.") and could be seen to allude to the great white throne and the one sitting upon it described in Revelation 20:11: *Et vidi thronum magnum candidum, et sedentem super eum*: "And I saw a great white throne and the one who was sitting on it."[113] Lentini changed the final line of the stanza from *tantis renatis fratribus* (with so many brothers reborn [in baptism]) to *tanto repleti munere* (having been filled with such a great gift), explaining (somewhat perplexingly) that the reference to the newly baptized no longer is relevant in its current liturgical context.[114] Lentini may have adapted the new closing line from the prayer after Communion that begins with the words *Tantis, Domine, repleti muneribus*;[115] the closing line of the hymn is identi-

---

in vobis spes gloriæ; 1 Thes 2:19: *Quæ est enim nostra spes aut gaudium, aut corona gloriæ? nonne vos ante Dominum nostrum Iesum Christum estis in adventu eius.*

112. Lapidge interprets *pascha candidum* as referring to the day of Easter itself, but strangely pairs this with translating the verb as "worship" (rather than, e.g., "observe"; see Lapidge, *Bede's Latin Poetry*, 512: "Therefore let us all now vigorously worship this bright Easter Day for the sake of such bounties, when so many of our brothers have been reborn." Walsh likewise translates *pascha candidum* as referring to the feast, but pairs it with the verb "celebrate" which seems more fitting; see Walsh, 231: "Now therefore this radiant Pasch, of our so great blessings the cause, let us all earnestly celebrate, for all our brothers now reborn." (Lapidge and Walsh are translating the original final line *tantis renatis fratribus* rather than the *Liturgia Horarum* line *tanto repleti munere*.)

113. The same theme is taken up in the fourth stanza of *Ad cenam Agni próvidi* (H 35).

114. See 1968 *HIBR*, 101: *cum relatione ad fratres noviter baptizatos; quod cum hodie non valeat*. 1984 *TDH*, 122: "con allusione ai neo battezzati: ciò che ora non vale per l'inno" (With an allusion to the newly-baptised: which now is now longer relevant)—Lentini is writing before the reintroduction of adult baptism as a normative practice at the Easter Vigil. Walsh, 465, claims that *tantis renatis fratribus* refers to "the holy ones delivered from hell," but it seems much more likely that the reference is to the newly baptized.

115. See, e.g., Mohlberg, 88, §570: *Tantis, Domine, repleti muneribus, præsta quæsumus, ut salutaria dona capiamus et a tua nunquam laude cessemus : per*: "Grant, we pray, O Lord, that, having been replenished by such great gifts, we may gain the prize of salvation and never cease to praise you." Versions of the prayer are also found

cal to the prayer, with the exception of the omission of *Domine* and the change of plural forms to the singular.

STANZAS 6 AND 7

The hymn as presented in the *Liturgia Horarum* concludes with two stanzas shared with other hymns of the Easter Season. For commentaries on these stanzas, see the commentary on H 42, above.

Aurora lucis rutilat	46
5th c.	Easter Time to the Ascension of the
8 8 8 8	Lord Lauds

Auróra lucis rútilat,	1. The morning light dawns crimson gold,
cælum resúltat láudibus,	all heaven echoes hymns of praise,
mundus exsúltans iúbilat,	the world exulting shouts for joy,
gemens inférnus úlulat,	and hell with groaning howls in grief,
Cum rex ille fortíssimus,	2. For that most strong and mighty King,
mortis confráctis víribus,	by crushing all the powers of death
pede concúlcans tártara	and trampling hell beneath his feet,
solvit caténa míseros.	has freed the wretched from their chains.
Ille, quem clausum lápide	3. Enclosed within a tomb of stone,
miles custódit ácriter,	secured by strong and zealous guard,
triúmphans pompa nóbili	the Victor rises from the grave,
victor surgit de fúnere.	in triumph nobly marching forth.
Inférni iam gemítibus	4. Now grief of hell and cries of woe,
solútis et dolóribus,	all pain and sorrow are undone;
quia surréxit Dóminus	an angel, clothed in light, proclaims:
respléndens clamat ángelus.	The Lord is risen as he said.
Esto perénne méntibus	5. O Jesus, be for mind and heart
paschále, Iesu, gáudium,	our everlasting paschal joy
et nos renátos grátiæ	and gather us, reborn by grace,
tuis triúmphis ággrega.	to share your triumphs evermore.
Iesu, tibi sit glória,	6. To you, Lord Jesus, glory be,
qui morte victa prǽnites,	who shine in victory over death,
cum Patre et almo Spíritu,	with God the Father, ever blest,
in sempitérna sǽcula. Amen.	and loving Spirit, ever one. Amen.

Text found in *TDH*, no. 112; AH 51, no. 84; Walpole, no. 111; Bulst, 114. Changes in *TDH*: stanza 1, 2: *cælum resultat laudibus* for *cælum laudibus intonat*; 3, 1–2: *Ille, quem clausum lapide / miles custodit acriter* for *Ille qui clausus lapide / custoditur sub milite*; 4, 1–2: *Inferni iam gemitibus / solutis et doloribus* for *Solutis iam gemitibus / et inferni doloribus*.

COMMENTARY

The first four stanzas of this Easter hymn are the opening section of an originally longer hymn (AH 51, no. 84). This continued with stanzas 1–4 of the hymn *Tristes erant Apostoli* (H 151), followed by stanzas 1–3 of the hymn *Claro paschali gaudio* (H 150), both for the Common of the Apostles during Easter Time. The fifth stanza of each of these hymns was added by Lentini, together with a doxology. The original hymn has usually been thought to be an early one, as in the case of the hymn *Ad cenam Agni providi* (H 42). They are both found in ancient Irish hymnaries and in other early sources.[116] Norberg actually suggested that both *Aurora lucis* and *Ad cenam Agni* could be by the same author.[117]

The underlying metrical form is the Ambrosian iambic dimeter, but the scansion is rhythmic, that is, the beat of the verse tends to coincide with the spoken stress accent, rather than following the quantitative scansion of classical verse. This is especially the case at the end of the line, where rhyme is also used. In the original text of the whole hymn some of the third lines of the stanzas are not rhymed, and one also finds a clash in some of these third lines between verse-beat and accent. It has been suggested that the third and fourth line of the stanza were treated as a single whole, and that this reflects the underlying musical structure.[118] In the text of H 46, 150, and 151, as we have them, Lentini has made some changes where accent and verse-beat do not coincide, in order to produce a smoother rhythm.

The original hymn is closely based on Matthew's narrative of the Resurrection (chapter 28). This is set in a cosmic framework. In the opening stanza the "dawning of light" on the day of Christ's rising from the dead is accompanied by the responses of heaven, earth, and hell, and toward the end (stanza 1 of H 150, or stanza 9 in the original hymn) "the sun with rays of purer light / now brightly shines with paschal joy," as the Apostles see their risen Lord. The whole hymn is filled with joy at the triumph of Christ over death and hell, and describes the effect of this and of the appearance of the risen Christ, both on the women who come to the tomb and on the Apostles, an effect that culminates in their proclamation of the Resurrection. The theme of light also runs through the hymn: the reddening light of the dawn, the splendor of the Angel (H 46: 4, 4), the sun shining with pure radiance (H 150: 1, 2), and the resplendent wounds in the flesh of Christ (H 150: 2, 1–2). Contrasted with these themes are the groans of hell (H 46: 1, 4), the crushing of death's powers, which lead to freedom for "the wretched" and an end to grief and woe for those below (H 46: stanza 2–3), and the Apostles' sadness at the brutal death of Christ and the impious cruelty of those who condemned him (H 151: stanza 1). All these negative features occur in the first five stanzas of the hymn, whereas the tone of stanzas 5–10 is wholly positive.

---

116. See AH 51, 90; Walpole, pp. 349 and 356; Walsh, 432.
117. Norberg, *Introduction*, 133–34.
118. See Norberg, *Introduction*, 133–34.

STANZA 1

All four gospels begin their accounts of the Resurrection with a reference to the time, very early in the morning, when the women (or, in John's Gospel, just Mary Magdalene) come to the tomb, although the accounts differ slightly in their description of the exact time. Matthew 28:1 has: *Vespere autem sabbati, quæ lucescit in prima sabbati*: "After the sabbath, toward the dawn of the first day of the week." (The Greek phrase τῆι ἐπιφωσκούσηι means "as it was growing light.")

In the original hymn the second line is *cælum laudibus intonat* (literally "heaven thunders with praises"). With this text all four lines end with the rhyming syllable *-at*. The other three lines have a more pronounced rhyme: *rutilat, iubilat, ululat*, and lines 2–4 are also parallel in that they all describe loud sounds of praise, joy, and despair. In lines 3–4 the words *mundus exsultans* and *gemens infernus* are in chiastic order. Thus the opening stanza has a careful and effective structure.

The first line is imitated in a later hymn, possibly by Alcuin (d. ca. 804), *lucis aurora rutilans coruscat* (H 99: 1, 2). These seem to be the only examples of the combination of *aurora* and *lucis* in classical or late Latin poetry. In the original text of line 2, *cælum laudibus intonat*, the stress accent falls on the first syllable of *laudibus*, whereas the verse-beat should normally be on the second syllable. This is why Lentini changed it. In line 3 the verb *iubilare* was used in classical Latin of the loud cries or whoops of country folk, and was originally onomatopoeic (like "yodel", perhaps). But in Christian Latin it presumably also came to be associated with the Hebrew word for a jubilee, originally a fiftieth anniversary year of emancipation and restitution, and was used of cries of joy and celebration, as for example in the Vulgate version of Psalm 99 (100):1, *Iubilate Deo, omnis terra*. In line 4 *ululare* is also an onomatopoeic word.

STANZA 2

Christ, "the most strong and mighty King," has crushed (or smashed) the powers of death. This evokes, for example, 2 Timothy 1:10, *qui destruxit quidem mortem*: "Christ Jesus, who abolished death." In lines 3–4, Christ tramples hell beneath his feet, as he releases the wretched from their chains. This describes the Harrowing of Hell, when he descends to hell and releases those holy souls who are imprisoned there. In Matthew 27:51–53, after Jesus dies, "the curtain of the temple was torn in two, from top to bottom, and the earth shook, and the rocks were split; the tombs also were opened, and many bodies of the saints who had fallen asleep were raised, and coming out of the tombs after his resurrection they went into the holy city and appeared to many." In 1 Peter 3:19 and 4:6, Peter says that after his death Christ "went and preached to the spirits in prison," and "this is why the gospel was preached even to the dead, that though judged in the flesh like men, they might live in the spirit like God." Paul likewise says, in Ephesians 4:9, "In saying, 'He ascended,' what does it mean but that he also descended into the lower parts of the earth?" This tradition is described in some versions of the apocryphal *Descent of Jesus to Hades*, and referred to by some of the early Fathers. It is included in the Apostles' Creed and the Athanasian Creed.[119]

The verb *conculcare*, from line 3, was used very frequently in the Vulgate: for example, Habakkuk 3:12 (of God) *in fremitu conculcabis terram* (you will stomp on the earth in your fury). But the description of Christ trampling hell under foot may reflect 1 Corinthians 15:25–26, "For he must reign until he has put all his enemies under his feet. The last enemy to be destroyed is death." The troparion used in the Eastern Church for Easter says:

> Christ is risen from the dead,
> By his death treading death under foot,
> And on those in the tombs
> Bestowing life.

This is most dramatically depicted in the Orthodox portrayal of the *Anastasis* (Resurrection) in art. This shows Christ actually treading on the gates of hell, as he takes Adam (or Adam and Eve) by the wrist, in order to rescue them. The gates lie in the form of a cross beneath his feet, and around them are scattered a confusion of bolts, locks, and keys.

The early Christian poets of the West also loved to describe this scene. Prudentius says in *Cathemerinon* 9, stanzas 24–25:

> What's more, he enters hell itself, the kindly one that those below may not
>   lack salvation; the door is forced, it yields,
> the bolts are wrenched back, the pivot breaks apart and falls away.
> The gate, so ready to receive those rushing in, so slow to make way for those
>   returning,
> its bolt recoils, opens—it hands over the dead.
> The law is subverted, the black doorway gapes: they can walk through again.[120]

Venantius Fortunatus, in his Easter poem for Bishop Felix (*Poems* 3.9: 59–88) describes at length Christ's vanquishing of Tartarus and his rescue of the souls held captive there. Addressing Christ directly, he says: "The cruel bonds of the infernal law gave way.... Hell, its gaping throat insatiably yawning wide, has become your captive ... the Lamb rescues his sheep from the jaws of the wolf...." Also, in stanza 5 of *Ad cenam Agni providi* (H 42: 5, 1–4), the original text runs: *o vera digna hostia, / per quam fracta sunt tartara; / redempta plebs captivata, / reddita vitæ præmia*: "O truly worthy victim / through whom hell has been broken / captive people have been redeemed / eternal life has been restored." (Walpole, no. 109, p. 352).

STANZA 3

All the gospels describe the stone with which the tomb was sealed, but Matthew is the only one who includes the narrative of the guards. The Jewish religious

---

119. See also Mt 12:40; 16:18; Jn 5:25; Acts 2:24–31; Rom 10:7; Col 1:18, and *Catechism of the Catholic Church* (1994), no. 632ff.

120. For the translation, see O'Daly, *Days Linked by Song*, 257, and Richardson, *Hymns*, 66.

leaders asked Pilate for permission to set guards at the tomb (Mt 27:62–65). They then "made the sepulcher secure by sealing the stone and setting a guard" (Mt 27:66). The guards were terrified when there was an earthquake and an angel rolled away the stone (Mt 28:2–4), and later the Jewish leaders bribed them to say that the disciples had stolen the body of Jesus (Mt 28:11–15).

In lines 1–2, the original text is *Ille qui clausus lapide / Custoditur sub milite*. Again Lentini changed this because in *custoditur* the accent would normally fall on the third syllable, whereas the verse-beat is on the second and fourth. The singular noun *miles* is used collectively of "the soldiery." In lines 3–4 the Resurrection is described in language recalling a Roman triumphal victory procession: literally "celebrating his triumph with a noble procession the Victor rises from death." Walsh suggests that *pompa nobili* may refer to the earthquake mentioned by Matthew, which accompanied the angel in his victorious descent to roll back the stone.[121] Just as nature participated in the sadness of Good Friday, when the sky was darkened and the earth quaked, so also at the Resurrection, the cosmos likewise joins the joyous procession with the angel, the women who were already at the tomb, and the terrified men. In *Pange, lingua, gloriosi prœlium certaminis* (H 32), Venantius Fortunatus has *triumphum nobilem* for the triumph of the Cross (1, 3–4), and again addressing the Cross, in his hymn *Vexilla regis prodeunt* (H 31), he has *plaudis triumpho nobili*.[122] In the hymn for Vespers on the Ascension, *Iesu nostra redemptio* (H 52), directly after a reference to his descent to hell—*Inferni claustra penetrans, / tuos captivos redimens* (3, 1–2)—Christ is hailed as *Victor triumpho nobili* (3, 3), as in stanzas 2–3 of this hymn and in the Apostles' Creed. For *nobili* in line 3 some manuscripts read *nobile*. This would give a closer rhyme, and an ablative form in *-e* is possible in later Latin. But (as explained above) not all of the third lines have an exact rhyme, and the difference is slight.

STANZA 4

The original reading of lines 1–2 is *solutis iam gemitibus / et inferni doloribus*. This is an echo of St Peter's words about Christ in Acts 2:24, *quem Deus suscitavit, solutis doloribus inferni* ("But God raised him up, having loosed the pangs of death"). This connection suggests that the primary reference here may be to Christ. But it can also have a wider reference to all who have been redeemed from death, since "Christ has been raised from the dead, the firstfruits of those who have fallen asleep" (1 Cor 15:20). Lentini objected to *inferni* on metrical grounds, because again there is a clash between the stress accent on the second syllable and the

---

121. Walsh, 432. Mt 28:2–4 reads: *et ecce terræmotus factus est magnus angelus enim Domini descendit de cælo et accedens revolvit lapidem et sedebat super eum. Erat autem aspectus eius sicut fulgur et vestimentum eius sicut nix. Præ timore autem eius exterriti sunt custodes et facti sunt velut mortui*: "And behold, there was a great earthquake, for an angel of the Lord came down from heaven and approaching, rolled back the stone, and he sat on it. His countenance was like lightning, and his clothing white as snow. For fear of him the guards were terrified, and they became like dead men."

122. Literally, addressing the Cross: "you clap your hands (rejoice) in noble triumph." (line 28 of the original hymn). This stanza is omitted in *TDH*. See Walpole no. 34, p. 177. See also H 52: 3, 3–4, *victor triumpho nobili / ad dextram Patris residens*, and Walpole no. 117, line 20, *Iesus, triumpho nobili*, of the Ascension.

verse-beat on first and third, but his replacement weakens the connection with the sentence in Acts.

Lines 3–4 echo Matthew 28:5–6: *Respondens autem angelus dixit mulieribus: Nolite timere vos: scio enim, quod Iesum, qui crucifixus est, quæritis: non est hic: surrexit enim, sicut dixit.* ("But the angel said to the women, 'Do not be afraid; for I know that you seek Jesus who was crucified. He is not here, for he has risen, as he said.'") In line 3, *quia* means "that." This use is common in Christian writers from Tertullian onward and in the Vulgate. *Resplendens* in line 4 refers to the description of the angel in Matthew 28:3 ("His appearance was like lightning, and his raiment white as snow"). The manuscripts of the hymn are divided between *splendens* and *resplendens*. It is possible that the former is original, and was pronounced as three syllables at this stage of Latin (i.e., *esplendens* or *isplendens*), with a "prosthetic" vowel.[123]

STANZA 5

This stanza was added by Lentini to the original hymn, and is used also in H 42–45 and 47. He calls it "a joyful paschal refrain" (*un gaudioso ritornello pasquale*), and says that it is derived from the *Breviarium Romanum*, "but with a greater eschatological emphasis" (*ma con maggiore accentuazione escatologica*). It is his adaptation of the seventh stanza of the hymn *Ad regias Agni dapes* in the 1961 *Breviarium Romanum*, which is itself the Urbanite revision of *Ad cenam Agni providi*. This runs:

Breviarium Romanum	Edward Caswall
Ut sis perenne mentibus	O Jesu, from the death of sin
Paschale Iesu gaudium	Keep us, we pray; so shalt Thou be
A morte dira criminum	The everlasting Paschal joy
Vitæ renatos libera.	Of all the souls newborn in Thee.

In line 3 *renatos gratiæ* presumably means "reborn to grace," as *vitæ renatos* is "reborn to life" in *Ad regias Agni dapes*. For a full discussion of this stanza, see H 42.

STANZA 6

This doxology is repeated in H 42–48 and H 50–51. It resembles, for example, the doxology for Christmas hymns, *Gloria tibi Domine* (or *Iesu tibi sit gloria*) / *qui natus es de Virgine,* / *cum Patre et Sancto* (or *almo*) *Spiritu,* / *in sempiterna sæcula*. In older versions of the whole hymn various other doxologies were used (see Walpole, p. 359). For more details, see H 42.

---

123. This is the view of Walpole, p. 357, and Norberg, *Introduction*, 133, note 11.

Chorus novæ Ierusalem 47

St. Fulbert of Chartres,
d. 1029
8 8 8 8

Easter time after the Octave of Easter
to the Ascension
Lauds

Chorus novæ Ierúsalem
hymni novam dulcédinem
promat, colens cum sóbriis
paschále festum gáudiis,

1. Now let the new Jerusalem
draw forth new sweetness from this hymn,
and let the chorus celebrate
with solemn joy this Paschal Feast.

Quo Christus invíctus leo,
dracóne surgens óbruto,
dum voce viva pérsonat,
a morte functos éxcitat.

2. For Christ, unconquered lion, comes,
the dragon crushed beneath his feet;
with living voice he cries aloud,
and, rising, wakes the dead from death.

Quam devorárat ímprobus,
prædam refúndit tártarus;
captivitáte líbera
Iesum sequúntur ágmina.

3. The prey that Satan had devoured
his nether kingdom must expel:
a crowd of captives, free at last,
now follows Jesus from the tomb.

Triúmphat ille spléndide
et dignus amplitúdine,
soli políque pátriam
unam facit rem públicam.

4. He triumphs, filled with splendid light,
in sovereign power and majesty;
he forms a single commonwealth,
one native land of heaven and earth.

Ipsum canéndo súpplices
Regem precémur mílites,
ut in suo claríssimo
nos órdinet palátio.

5. Let us entreat him with our song
as soldiers of our God and King,
that rank on rank he order us
within the splendor of his courts.

Esto perénne méntibus
paschále, Iesu, gáudium,
et nos renátos grátiæ
tuis triúmphis ággrega.

6. O Jesus, be for mind and heart
our everlasting paschal joy
and gather us, reborn by grace,
to share your triumphs evermore.

Iesu, tibi sit glória,
qui morte victa prænites,
cum Patre et almo Spíritu,
in sempitérna sǽcula. Amen.

7. To you, Lord Jesus, glory be,
who shine in victory over death,
with God the Father, ever blest,
and loving Spirit, ever one. Amen.

Text found in *TDH*, no. 118; AH 50, no. 215. Changes in *TDH*: stanza 1, 2: *hymni novam* for *novam meli*.

COMMENTARY

This hymn is the best-known poem of St. Fulbert of Chartres. It is still familiar today in the English version "Ye choirs of New Jerusalem" (published by Robert Campbell in 1850, and with some changes in *Hymns Ancient and Modern*). Fulbert taught in the Cathedral School of Chartres, and was its bishop from 1006 to 1028 (or 1029). He has been described as "the patriarch among the masters of the great cathedral schools."[124] He saw the need to integrate the study of classical and Christian culture, and as a result was able to raise the level of Latin style in both prose and poetry. His poems are composed in a range of classical meters and also accentual and rhymed ones, and show the influence of classical as well as earlier Christian writers.

The hymn is found in many manuscripts from the eleventh century (and one from the end of the tenth), and so must have soon become popular.[125] Stanzas 1–5 are from the original hymn and are in rhyming couplets. There is usually correspondence between the verse-beat and the stress accent, and this gives the hymn a very smooth and regular rhythm. As suits an Easter hymn, there is great emphasis on the triumphal character of the Resurrection, and in stanzas 3–5 the imagery is full of allusions to the military and civic aspects of imperial Rome. But the hymn as a whole also draws inspiration from the Book of Revelation. The last two stanzas are the same as in Hymns 42–46.

STANZA 1

The "new Jerusalem" comes in two passages in Revelation: "On him I will inscribe the name of my God and the name of the city of my God, the new Jerusalem, which comes down out of heaven from my God," and "And I, John, saw the holy city, a new Jerusalem, coming down out of heaven from God, prepared as a bride adorned for her husband."[126]

In line 2 the original hymn has *novam meli*. Lentini thought *meli* might be difficult to understand, and so wrote *hymni novam*. The Greek word μέλος ("song, music") is not uncommon in Latin poetry, in the forms *melos*, *melum* and *melus*. The combination *meli ... dulcedinem* suggests that Fulbert was thinking of the ancient association of the word with honey (μέλι, *mel*). The repetition of *novæ ... novam* emphasizes the notion that the new City of God must have a new and special kind of song or music. Soon after the reference to "new Jerusalem" in Revelation come the words "Behold, I make all things new."[127] The original

---

124. Southern, *The Making of the Middle Ages*, 199. On Fulbert's life and works, see also Raby, *History of Christian Latin Poetry*, 257–64; Szövérffy, *Annalen I*, 353–57; Behrends, *Letters and Poems of Fulbert of Chartres*; and Jeauneau, *Rethinking the School of Chartres*, 29–36.
125. See *AH* 50, 285, Milfull, 451–52.
126. *et scribam super eum nomen Dei mei, et nomen civitatis Dei mei novæ Ierusalem, quæ descendit de cælo a Deo meo* (Rv 3:12); and *Et ego Ioannes vidi sanctam civitatem Ierusalem novam descendentem de cælo a Deo, paratam, sicut sponsam ornatam viro suo* (Rv 21:2).
127. *Ecce nova facio omnia* (Rv 21:5).

word-order gives prominence to *novam,* and the phrase *novam meli dulcedinem* brackets the genitive between adjective and noun in a typically classical way. The phrase also has a sequence of soft consonants, which suits the idea of honeyed sweetness.

In lines 3–4, *sobriis ... gaudiis* stresses that the joyful celebration of Easter should be "sober." "Be sober and vigilant," says St. Peter. St. Paul says, "let us stay alert and sober" and "For our paschal lamb, Christ, has been sacrificed. Therefore, let us celebrate the feast, not with the old yeast, the yeast of malice and wickedness ..." More generally, he says, "let us conduct ourselves properly as in the day, not in orgies and drunkenness ... "[128]

The closest biblical equivalent to the phrase *paschale festum* is in the Vulgate version of John 13:1, *Ante diem festum Paschæ.* It was also used in the first canon of the Tenth Council of Toledo (AD 656).

STANZA 2

At his Resurrection, Christ overcomes Satan and summons the dead to life. This and the next stanza describe the Harrowing of Hell, as in the second stanza of H 46 (see the commentary on this). In line 1 *quo* refers to *paschale festum* ("the Paschal Feast, on which ..."). The reference to Christ as "unconquered lion" is another allusion to Revelation, where at 5:5 one of the elders says to St. John: "Do not weep. The lion of the tribe of Judah, the root of David, has triumphed."[129] In Genesis 49:9–10, Jacob, blessing his son Judah, called him "a lion's cub" (*catulus leonis*) and prophesied the future ascendancy of his line as rulers, in a passage that was traditionally interpreted as referring to the Messiah.[130]

To call Satan "the dragon" in line 2 also looks like an echo of Revelation 12:3–17. There the dragon (Vulgate, *draco*), who is named Satan, is cast down from heaven, and the followers of Christ are said to have conquered him by the blood of the Lamb. By contrast, in Genesis 3 he is called *serpens,* "the serpent."

Line 3 echoes the Gospel of John, where Jesus says, "'the hour is coming and is now here when the dead will hear the voice of the Son of God, and those who hear will live,'" and "'the hour is coming in which all who are in the tombs will hear his voice, and will come out.'"[131] There may also be a reminiscence of the raising of Lazarus, when Christ "cried out in a loud voice, 'Lazarus, come out!'"[132] The phrase *voce viva* in line 3 indicates the life-giving power of his voice, and *personare* is used of a loud, resounding cry. *Morte fungi* means

---

128. *Sobrii estote, et vigilate* (1 Pt 5:8); *vigilemus, et sobrii simus* (1 Thes 5:6); *Etenim Pascha nostrum immolatus est Christus. Itaque epulemur: non in fermento veteri, neque in fermento malitiæ et nequitiæ* (1 Cor 5:7–8); *Sicut in die honeste ambulemus: non in comessationibus, et ebrietatibus....* (Rom 13:13).

129. *Ne fleveris: ecce vicit leo de tribu Iuda, radix David.*

130. Daniel (*Thesaurus,* 1:222) also mentions a belief found in the early Christian work *Physiologus,* that the lion brings its cubs to life with its roar three days after birth. This was taken as an allegory of the Resurrection.

131. *venit hora, et nunc est, quando mortui audient vocem Filii Dei: et qui audierint, vivent* (Jn 5:25); *Venit hora in qua omnes qui in monumentis sunt audient vocem Filii Dei: et procedent* (Jn 5:28–29).

132. *voce magna clamavit: Lazare, veni foras* (Jn 11:43).

"to die," and so here *a morte functos excitat* is used to mean "awakes the dead from death."

STANZA 3

Improbus ("the wicked one") denotes Satan. There is again a probable reminiscence of Revelation 20:13 (in the description of the Last Judgment): "The sea gave up its dead; then Death and Hades gave up their dead."[133] In H 46 (2, 3–4), Christ tramples hell (*tartara*) underfoot and "frees the wretched from their chains" (*solvit catena miseros*). Here, in lines 3–4 the "ranks" (or "columns," *agmina*) of those who have been freed from captivity follow their leader Jesus. In view of what follows in stanzas 4–5, this suggests that they are like the troops who accompany their general in a victory procession.

STANZA 4

Christ's triumph unites earth and heaven in "a single republic." The language implies that, like a victorious Roman ruler, he brings unity and so peace by his conquest. Line 1 resembles H 46, stanza 3, 3, *triumphans pompa nobili*. In line 2 *dignus amplitudine* (literally "worthy of distinction") is a classical expression. It was used by Cicero (*Pro Murena* 16, *summa … amplitudine dignus*), and Livy (*Ab urbe condita*, 5.21.3, *dignum amplitudine tua templum*, addressing the goddess Juno). The phrase *soli polique* in line 3 is a neat way of saying "earth and heaven," as both nouns have the same metrical form (short plus long syllable) and rhyme together.

STANZA 5

The Roman military language becomes still more explicit in this stanza, which moves in typical fashion from praise to prayer, returning also to the opening theme of the song. The soldiers of Christ should ask that he will (literally) "marshal our ranks in his most glorious palace." This suggests a comparison with the special imperial troops who in the later Roman Empire were known as *palatini*, and who were the successors to the praetorian guards of the early Empire. The cavalry units known as *scholæ palatinæ* still existed in the time of Fulbert.

STANZAS 6 AND 7

For a detailed discussion of these final stanzas, see the commentary on H 42.

---

133. *et dedit mare mortuos, qui in eo erant: et mors et infernus dederunt mortuos suos.*

	Iam surgit hora tertia	48
St. Ambrose, d. 397		Easter Time until Pentecost
8 8 8 8 (LM)		Terce

Iam surgit hora tértia,
qua Christus ascéndit crucem;
nil ínsolens mens cógitet,
inténdat afféctum precis.

Qui corde Christum súscipit,
innóxium sensum gerit
votísque præstat sédulis
Sanctum meréri Spíritum.

Hæc hora, quæ finem dedit
diri vetérno críminis;
hinc iam beáta témpora
cœpére Christi grátia.

Iesu, tibi sit glória,
qui morte victa prænites,
cum Patre et almo Spíritu,
in sempitérna sǽcula. Amen.

1. Behold, the third hour rises now,
when Christ ascends the saving Cross;
our minds should think no thoughts of pride,
intent on fervor in our prayer.

2. The heart that truly welcomes Christ
brings forth a conscience free from sin;
by faithful prayer it seeks to gain
the Holy Spirit, Paraclete.

3. This is the hour that brought an end
to dire, deep-rooted, ancient sin,
and from this hour, by grace of Christ,
the time of blessing has begun.

4. To you, Lord Jesus, glory be,
who shine in victory over death,
with God the Father, ever blest,
and loving Spirit, ever one. Amen.

Text found in *TDH*, no. 119; AH 51, no. 6; Bulst, 41; Walpole, no.4; Fontaine, no. 3, 206–28. Changes in *TDH*: the text consists of stanza 1–2, stanza 3, 1–2 combined with stanza 4, 3–4, all from the original hymn; stanza 4 of the new hymn is the Easter doxology, not proper to this hymn.

COMMENTARY

This hymn for Terce, or the third hour (approximately 9 AM), during Easter Time comes directly from Ambrose of Milan. It is, therefore, the most ancient of the hymns for the "little hours," that is, the fixed times between morning Lauds and evening Vespers when the congregation gathers to praise God in light of their recollection of fixed moments in salvation history.[134] In the original version, Ambrose's hymn follows his standard length of eight stanzas. These were later abbreviated to match the expected length for the hours that were briefer than the major hours of Lauds and Vespers.[135]

---

134. See the general introduction, "The Role of the Hymn in the Divine Office."
135. On the history of its placement in the hours, see Franz, *Tageslauf und Heilsgeschichte*, 273–82.

The stanzas that remain emphasize the moment of the Crucifixion and the sending of the Holy Spirit at Pentecost. The congregation presents the saving events of the hour as happening "now" (*Iam*, 1, 1) and asks that their presentation become for them a source of purity and holiness.[136] Moreover, in the third stanza, the same moment "now" (*iam*, 3, 3) inaugurates the times of blessedness (3, 3–4).

The hymn's attribution to Ambrose is confirmed by a reference in Augustine's *On Nature and Grace*, composed in 415.[137] By quoting directly from the hymn (3, 1, discussed below), Augustine indicates that the hymn had acquired some popularity in Christian circles, including among Pelagians. The elegance, poetry, and rich biblical imagery of the hymn helps explain its widespread appeal. The sixth-century rules of Cæsarius and Aurelian both prescribe the hymn for the monastic third hour, reinforcing its influence on the subsequent tradition.[138] Yet, as Walpole notes, its place in the daily office was quickly taken over by other, slightly later hymns.[139]

The excisions made by editors to the original were necessary to match the "usual brevity" of the daytime hymns.[140] Yet this choice led also to a loss of the artistry and theological depth of Ambrose's version. The original contains an extended treatment of the conquest of death accomplished on the Cross as well as an extended and influential presentation of the mutual commendation between Mary and the Beloved Apostle (Jn 19:26–27). Moreover, Ambrose concluded his hymn with a credal formulation, which reminds us that our version was aimed ultimately to support the congregation's Nicene faith.[141] Recalling the "original" third hour at Calvary and in the Upper Room, we are confirmed in our one faith that the Word of God, born of the Father and of the Virgin, sits now at the right hand of the Father.

STANZA 1

The first stanza opens with an emphatic "Now" (*Iam*), which calls us at once to the present moment and to the past (with historical tenses, *iam* is often best translated "then"). As Mark's Gospel expresses it: "It was nine in the morning when they crucified him."[142] The very moment of Christ on the Cross is brought before our eyes, and we pray that we remain intent on its relevance to our life and holiness. The stanza, then, invites an alert and eager response to the living reality of the morning hour.

The opening "now" may serve to shock listeners from standard expectations.[143] The reference to the "hour" (*hora*) evokes Christ's announcement in the Gospel of John, "Behold the hour is coming and has already come."[144] This third

---

136. On the references to times, see Dunkle, "Mystagogy and Creed," 28–29.
137. Augustine, *De natura et gratia*, 63.74; for analysis see Dunkle, "'Made Worthy of the Holy Spirit,'" 1–12.
138. Fontaine, 210; see Cæsarius, *Regula ad virgines*, 66.
139. Walpole, p. 40.
140. Lentini's note mentions "*brevità abituale*," *TDH*, 124).
141. See Dunkle, "Mystagogy and Creed," 31–32.
142. *Erat autem hora tertia: et crucifixerunt eum* (Mk 15:25).
143. Boeft, "Æterne Rerum Conditor," 31.
144. *Ecce venit hora et iam venit* (Jn 16:32).

hour is presented to us as a singular instance of divine generosity, when Christ "ascends" (*ascendit*, 1, 2) the Cross.[145] The verbal form *ascendit* can also be perfect, in which case we recall also that this moment was historical, that is, when Christ "ascended." As commentators note, the active form of the verb *ascendit* poetically belies the account of Christ's death as imposed on him by a higher authority.[146] As we recall liturgically, Christ entered "willingly" into his Passion and, in a sense, climbed the Cross for our sake.[147] Moreover, the word itself also evokes the celebration of the Ascension, when Christ's victory over death is perfected.

Given the event we recall, our "heart" (*mens*, 1, 3) must be free of all "thoughts of pride" (*insolens*, 1, 3). Throughout the New Testament, the crucifixion marks the "height" of the Lord's humiliation (see Phil 2:8), embraced for our salvation. We furthermore adopt a "feeling of prayer" (*affectum precis*, 1, 4), a phrase that underscores the need for felt devotion, and not mere intellectual assent, to the mystery recalled. The first stanza, then, aims to effect an emotional and spiritual apprehension of the mid-morning hour, when Christ was and is crucified.

STANZA 2

The second stanza explores the subjective sense of this *affectum precis*. It is the "affect" characteristic of those who have taken up Christ interiorly and have begun to live without fault. It is also the "affect" that makes us worthy of the Holy Spirit.

Lines 1 and 2 speak of the singers' proper disposition: they "welcome" (*suscipit*, 2, 1) Christ in their heart and "bring forth" (*gerit*, 2, 2) a "faultless sensitivity" (*innoxium sensum*, line 2). The terms are deliberately evocative. We take up (*suscipit*) Christ not through a friendly greeting, but rather through an embrace; the term echoes the Lord's call to "take up our cross" and the phrasing echoes the words of Ephesians 3:17: "that Christ may dwell in your hearts."[148] The term for heart, *corde* (2, 1), complements the reference to *mens* in 1, 3, further emphasizing the need for our full, affective engagement. While *sensum* certainly suggests a moral "conscience" (2, 2), it also appears often in Ambrose's corpus to designate the full range of our sensitive faculties.[149] We are praying, then, that we perceive the cosmos around us without any blind spots.

The second couplet contains a striking reference to the blessing of the Holy Spirit. The reference is a reminder that the third hour is also the hour of the descent of the Spirit at Pentecost (Acts 2:1–4). It is by our "heartfelt" (*sedulis*, line 3) prayers that we become responsible for our worthiness for the Spirit's presence. Again, the hymn emphasizes the need for authentic, interior devotion in relation to the grace of God. Ambrose frequently uses the term *vota* for "prayers" (see, e.g., H 54: 1, 1 and H 17: 1, 3)— in both classical and Christian Latin *vota* can mean

---

145. In his treatment of the episode in his *Commentary on Luke*, Ambrose uses a very similar expression (*crucem Christus ascendit*) (*In Luc.* 10.107).
146. Fontaine, 215.
147. See Eucharistic Prayer II.
148. Fontaine, 216.
149. See Dunkle, *Enchantment*, 93–99.

anything from a vow or an obligation to a wish, a desire, or an intimate prayer, depending on the context.

There is good evidence that the second couplet of the stanza raised some questions for early singers that are relevant today. In his treatise *On Nature and Grace*, Augustine goes to some length to defend the hymn from a possible Pelagian reading, by which our own fervent prayers would somehow "earn" God's grace.[150] In Augustine's interpretation, the one who earns (*mereri*) is best understood to be Christ himself, who shows himself worthy of the Spirit by his virtue. At the same time, Augustine maintains that, even when the subject is understood as the faithful Christian, the broader context of the hymn, which refers to the "grace of Christ" (3, 4 in our version), indicates the priority of grace in the process of being worthy of the Spirit. Thus, Augustine defends the hymn against any claim that "gaining" the Holy Spirit through fervent prayer is our own achievement, apart from Christ's grace.

STANZA 3

The third stanza turns to speak of the present moment as the reversal of the world's decline. We have seen an end to the old curse of sin and now witness the age of Christ's grace. As in the opening "now," a series of indexical or pointing terms (*hæc hora*, 3, 1, *hinc iam*, 3, 3) return us to the present moment to celebrate the renewal of the age. The *hora* of line 1 recalls the *hora tertia* of the first line of stanza 1. The hymn repeatedly calls our attention to the moment in which we are singing. As in the Psalms, which proclaim often that "this is the day" (e.g., Psalm 118 [119]:24), Ambrose has repeated that this is the hour for Christ's victory. It is at 9 AM when Christ put an end to the "old age" (*veterno*, 3, 2) of the "fearful crime" (*diri criminis*, 3, 2), a phrase that evokes the decline following original sin.[151]

The new, blessed times of Christ begin "from right now" (*hinc iam*, 3, 3). Again, we are drawn back to the opening "now" and reminded that the ancient curse is behind us. As noted above, the abbreviation of the original meant a loss of some of its powerful imagery. Yet the editors' decision to conclude the predoxology stanza with the "grace of Christ" (*Christi gratia*, 3, 4) was quite wise. The placement emphasizes that any "merit" we might accrue from a life of integrity and holiness is only a result of Christ's generosity.

STANZA 4

On the final doxology, see the discussion in the general introduction and the commentary on the final stanza of H 42. The same doxology appears at the end of all the Easter hymns, H 42–H 51, except H 49. While it is neither original nor especially particular to this hymn, the reference to "conquered death" (*morte victa*, 4, 2) relates well to the theme of the immortality achieved at the moment of the crucifixion.

---

150. Augustine, *De natura et gratia*, 63.74; Dunkle, "'Made Worthy of the Holy Spirit'," 4–5.
151. On *veternus* as "lethargic," see Walpole, p. 41; Fontaine, 218.

	Venite, servi, supplices	49
5th–6th c.		Easter Time
8 8 8 8 (LM)		Sext

Veníte, servi, súpplices, et mente et ore extóllite dignis beátum láudibus nomen Dei cum cántico.	1. Come, servants, join in humble prayer with psalms and hymns of worthy praise; let mind and heart and lips extol the blest and holy name of God.
Hoc namque tempus illud est, quo sæculórum iúdicem iniústa morti trádidit mortálium senténtia.	2. For this is that dread time and hour, in which the Judge of ages stood condemned to death by false decree, unjustly judged by mortal foes.
Et nos amóre débito, timóre iusto súbditi, advérsus omnes ímpetus quos scævus hostis íncutit,	3. And we with all the love we owe, compelled by just and humble fear, seek help against our wicked foe and all his sly and fierce assaults.
Unum rogémus et Patrem Deum regémque Fílium simúlque Sanctum Spíritum, in Trinitáte Dóminum. Amen.	4. Let us implore the one true God, the Father and the Son, our King, the Holy Spirit, Paraclete, in Trinity, our God and Lord. Amen

Text found in *TDH*, no. 120; AH 51, no. 16; Bulst, 94; Walpole, no. 55. Changes in *TDH*: from the original hymn of ten stanzas, this hymn is composed of stanzas 2, 3, 8, and 9; stanza 1, 2: *et mente et ore extollite* for *mente, ore extollite*, in order to avoid hiatus; 2, 2: *quo* for *quod*.

COMMENTARY

Venite, servi, supplices is an abridged version of a prior hymn, *Iam sexta sensim volvitur*. It is composed of stanzas 2, 3, 8, and 9. The original is an ancient hymn belonging to the Old Hymnal, prescribed by Cæsarius of Arles for Sext during the Easter season.[152] The longer version is rich in references to salvific events that occurred at the sixth hour. In stanza 1 of the original hymn, the hour is described as the midpoint of the day between one night and the next. Stanza 2 invites those singing the hymn to offer worthy praise to God with their song; this is stanza 1 of the hymn in the *Liturgia Horarum*. Stanza 3 of the original hymn (stanza 2 of the current hymn) describes the moment of Christ's condemnation to death by an unjust decree. Stanzas 4–7 of the original hymn then describe events

---

152. Walpole, p. 245.

that happened at noon: Christ's moment of crucifixion when the sun hid its face (stanza 4);[153] Abraham's worship of the one God who arrived in three persons (5, 4);[154] Christ's encounter with the Samaritan woman at the well (stanza 6);[155] and finally (stanza 7), Paul's conversion on the road to Damascus.[156] Then, stanzas 8 and 9 follow; these are stanzas 3 and 4 of the current hymn. Stanza 9 of the original (4 above) may stand as a doxology. It was followed in the original hymn by a final stanza (10), a prayer begging God to keep safe those singing the hymn at the salvific sixth hour.

The more extensive *Iam sexta sensim volvitur* enumerates a greater number of events in salvation history, but the broad meaning of the hymn is retained in *Venite, servi, supplices*. The hour of noon is marked first and foremost by the beginning of the crucifixion and the saving action of God in Christ. The action is brought into the lives of the faithful by love (*amore debito*, 3, 1), by justice (*timore iusto*, 3, 2), and finally, by asking God (*rogemus*, 4, 1) to bring us to himself.

STANZA 1

The first stanza invites (*venite*) the servants of God, who are also his suppliants (*supplices*) to extol the name of God (*extollite ... nomen Dei*). The invitation *venite* is well known in the Latin tradition as a result of its use in Psalm 94 (95), the invitatory (the Psalm which opens the day's Divine Office) that begins with the line, "Come, let us praise the Lord" (*Venite, exultemus Domino*).[157] The double vocative in this hymn, *servi* and *supplices*, provides two complimentary descriptions of those who praise God. To be God's servant is to supplicate him, and those who ask good things from him are also those who serve him (consider the requests of the Lord's Prayer).

Line 2 provides a description of the way in which the supplicants praise God: both by mind and by mouth (*et mente et ore*) the servants of God extol his name in worthy praise with song. Rearranging the Latin text, it would read: *extollite et mente et ore nomen Dei dignis laudibus cum cantico*. The praise of God by mind, heart (both signified by *mens*), and mouth engages the composite nature of the human person.[158] Christians must not praise God with words only while their hearts are far from God (see Mt 15:8), but the use of words respects our embodied nature. St. Paul also joins interior prayer to vocal (and so liturgical) prayer: *Orabo spiritu, orabo et mente: psallam spiritu, psallam et mente*: "I will pray with the spirit,

---

153. This is an allusion to Prudentius, *Cath* 9: 27, 1–2: *sol refugit ... reliquit axem seque mærens abdidit*: "the sun fled in terror ... it abandoned its axis and hid in mourning."

154. *Abraham tres vidit, unum credidit* (Gn 18:1–2). See also Walpole, p. 247, who points out that this line from the original stanza 5 (*tres vidit et unum credidit*) was a commonplace among the Fathers of the Church.

155. The hour was *quasi sexta*, at about noon (Jn 4:6ff.).

156. *eunte me et adpropinquante Damasco media die subito de cælo circumfulsit me lux copiosa*: "As I was on my way and approaching Damascus, at noon, suddenly from heaven a great light shone all around me." (Acts 22:6).

157. See, for instance, Benedict, *Rule* 9–10.

158. In his *Rule*, St. Benedict exhorts his monks: *sic stemus ad psallendum ut mens nostra concordet voci nostræ*: "Let us stand to sing psalms in such a way that our mind and heart are in harmony with our voice" (*Rule* 19; see also Fry, *RB 1980*: 216–17.). This allusion to the *Rule* of St. Benedict as well as the emphasis on serving the Lord in fear (See *Rule* 7.10–30) may possibly suggest a monastic provenance for this hymn.

I will pray also with the understanding, I will sing psalms with the spirit, I will sing psalms also with the understanding" (1 Cor 14:15). To extol the name of God is, etymologically, to lift up the name of God (*ex + tollere*). The servants of God lift up his name by raising their voices and entering into prayer, which is itself defined as a "raising of the mind and the heart to God."[159]

Significantly, it is the *name* of God that is extolled. This echoes what is found throughout the Old Testament and particularly in the Psalms. In Psalm 112, we read: *Laudate, pueri, Dominum; laudate nomen Domini*: "Praise the Lord, you children; praise the name of the Lord"; the phrase "name of the Lord" or "name of God" was a substitute for the proper name no one dared to pronounce. The singular privilege of Moses to hear the Lord pronounce his name illustrates the close association between God and his name (see Ex 3:14–15; 34:5). In praising the name of God we are praising him. While this is not specified in the hymn, for the Christian, the name of God is further specified in the Incarnation with the personal name of *Jesus*.

STANZA 2

The second stanza gives the first explicit reference in the hymn to the hour of prayer. As with the hymn for None, *Hæc hora, quæ resplenduit* (H 50), the stanza opens with the demonstrative *hoc*: "this." It is at *this* time, now, as we gather for the Liturgy of the Hours, when "the unjust sentence of mortal men handed the judge of the ages over to death." The hymn for Sext during Easter Time looks backward to the moment of Christ's *hour*,[160] in order to draw those singing the hymn *through* the judgment of death to Christ's Resurrection. By being incorporated into Christ's unjust sentence of death, the Christian also receives new life in his Resurrection.[161]

The judicial terminology of this stanza is stark. While it is usually the judge (*iudex*) who passes a sentence, this stanza shows a great reversal. Here, it is the judge who is handed over by mortal men to a sentence of death. In one version of 1 Peter, we read: *tradebat autem iudicanti se iniuste*: "but he handed himself over to the one who judges unjustly."[162] While the Greek text differs in meaning, this alternative Vulgate version is instructive. Christ handed himself over to the one who judges unjustly. Christ lays down his life; they do not take it from him (see Jn 10:18). Thus, even though the structure is surprisingly inverted, Christ remains the focus of salvific action; even at the moment of his condemnation, he is the Judge of the ages (*sæculorum iudicem*).

---

159. John of Damascus, *De Fide Orthodoxa*, 3, 24.
160. See Jn 12:27.
161. *qui cum malediceretur non maledicebat cum pateretur non comminabatur tradebat autem iudicanti se iniuste*: "Who, when he was reviled, did not revile: when he suffered, he threatened not: but delivered himself to him that judged him unjustly" (1 Pt . 2:23; Douay English translation). See also Rom 6:3–11, and in particular: *si enim conplantati facti sumus similitudini mortis eius simul et resurrectionis erimus*: "For if we have been joined to him in a death like his, so also will we be united with him in a resurrection like his" (Rom 6:5).
162. The Greek has παρεδίδου δὲ τῷ κρίνοντι δικαίως: "he handed himself over," that is, entrusted himself to the one who judges justly, namely the Father. It is important to remember that the Vulgate was the version of Scripture known to the composer of this hymn.

STANZA 3

In stanza 3, we hear of the response of the faithful to this hour of Sext; line 1 begins with *Et nos*. We are defined by humility and submission (*subditi* is a substantive adjective). Because of our humility, we engage in a spiritual warfare with the enemy by means of a love that we owe (*amore debito*) and a just fear (*timore iusto*); and we are able to act in this way precisely because Christ freely submitted himself to the aforementioned judgment (stanza 2). There is a close affinity between the attacks of the enemy against us (*impetus quos scævus hostis incutit*) and the description in the previous stanza of Christ's sufferings. The terminology of conflict (*impetus, adversus, hostis*) stands in contrast to the love and justice that characterize the Christian. The idea of *owing* love may seem surprising, given the contemporary idea that love is "free," and yet, it accords with Christ's commands (the greatest commandment is to love God and neighbor);[163] and it accords with our nature. Since God is the greatest good and since the human will is drawn by good, we owe God love because he is the highest good. This in no way diminishes us or does violence to us; rather it exalts us precisely because we are made to love those things which are truly good. And what good is greater than God?

The idea of a just fear may also seem surprising. It is possible to err either by being too informal and comfortable with God or to be trepidatious before him. We must hold that "perfect love casts out fear" (1 Jn 4:18) and, at the same time, that "the fear of the Lord is the beginning of wisdom" (Prv 9:10). As Aquinas explains, there is a filial fear that comes from serving God.[164] This fear, far from being debilitating, is an expression of our reverence for the goodness of God and an aversion to evil that might offend him—not because we fear punishment, but because we fear separation from God, which is the worst evil that can befall a human person.

Stanza 3 is not a sentence; the main verb comes in stanza 4 and completes the meaning of stanza 3. The verb *rogemus* (4, 1) "let us entreat, ask" introduces how the faithful interact with the enemy. It is not our own power that is victorious; rather, we beseech help (*rogemus adversus*) from God against the blows and assaults (*impetus*) with which the wicked foe strikes (lines 3–4).

STANZA 4

The idea of stanza 3 continues in stanza 4. From whom do the faithful beseech help? It is from the One God, the Father, the Son who is the King, and the Holy Spirit—One Lord in Trinity. The descriptor of Christ as King provides a paschal note for the ending of the hymn. The aforementioned Judge who was wrongly judged is now recognized by the faithful as the King whom they beseech for help. The placement of stanza 3 between the Crucifixion and the Trinity illustrates our own status as wayfarers. It is through our humble prayer and petition that we are brought to the ultimate end of the human person—heaven with the One Triune God.

---

163. See Mt 22:36–40; Mk 12:29–31; in these passages Christ refers back to the schema of Dt 6:4–5. See also Jn 13:34–35: to love each other as Christ has loved us is the single commandment that will show the world who are Christ's disciples.

164. *ST* II-II, q. 19, a. 10, corp.

Hæc hora, quæ resplenduit	50
5th–6th c.	Easter Time
8 8 8 8 (LM)	None

Hæc hora, quæ resplénduit crucísque solvit núbila, mundum tenébris éxuens, reddens seréna lúmina.	1. This is the hour that brightly shone and rent the clouds that veiled the Cross, divesting earth of dark and gloom, restoring pure, unclouded light.
Hæc hora, qua resúscitans Iesus sepúlcris córpora, prodíre mortis líbera iussit refúso spíritu.	2. This is the hour when Jesus raised the holy bodies from their tombs; at his command they issue forth with breath of life, now freed from death.
Nováta sæcla crédimus mortis solútis légibus, vitæ beátæ múnera cursum perénnem cúrrere.	3. Believing in a world renewed where laws of death have been dissolved, we know that gifts of blessed life shall run an everlasting course.
Iesu, tibi sit glória, qui morte victa prǽnites, cum Patre et almo Spíritu, in sempitérna sǽcula. Amen.	4. To you, Lord Jesus, glory be, who shine in victory over death, with God the Father, ever blest, and loving Spirit, ever one. Amen.

Text found in *TDH*, no. 121; *AH* 51, no. 17; Bulst, 96; Walpole, no. 56. Changes in *TDH*: from an original hymn of eight stanzas, three have been taken for this hymn; stanza 3, 1: *credimus* for *credere*; 3, 3: *munera* for *munere*.

COMMENTARY

Hæc hora is composed of stanzas 3, 4, and 6 of an original hymn of eight stanzas, *Ter hora trina volvitur*.[165] The original hymn incorporated references, in stanzas 1 and 2, to Christ sending out workers into his vineyard (see Mt 20:1–16) even at the ninth hour (stanza 1) and the need to stand in readiness lest we miss the wages offered by God (stanza 2). Then, stanza 8 refers to the breaking of the fast at the ninth hour as an image of the future rewards of heaven given to faithful laborers. In stanza 7, the hymn applies the image of "late-coming workers" to the good thief hanging on a cross next to Christ. The ninth hour provides proof of the glory of the Cross because the good thief is, in a way, the first fruit of Christ's salvation: "*Today* you will be with me in Paradise" (Lk 23:43).

The hymn in its present form does not include these references, but it is still rich in content concerning the ninth hour. The emphasis on the hour (*hæc hora*, 1, 1 and repeated at 2, 1) carries Johannine overtones and highlights the cosmic and

---

165. Walpole, pp. 248–51.

definitive victory that Christ won on the Cross. Lentini's heading: *"Sconfitta la morte, cominciano nuovi secoli"* ("death having been defeated, new ages begin") fittingly summarizes the theological content of the revised hymn.

STANZA 1

The opening phrase, *Hæc hora*, begins the office of None by drawing attention to *this* hour. Those singing the Office are immediately confronted with the reality that Christ's death and Resurrection has permanent and timely relevance—the demonstrative *hæc* ("this") is used, not *ille* ("that"), thus inviting those who sing to take a personal part in the reality they commemorate as they sing. They are in liturgical time, witnessing the Crucifixion and the work of salvation through the Hour of None. The verb *resplenduit* comes from *splendere*: "to shine brightly." The addition of the prefix *re-* provides the additional nuance of shining brightly with reflected light or to shine again; in a figurative sense, it means to be illustrious with outstanding qualities, such as virtue.[166] All three senses are fitting for this hymn since, at least initially, it is cast in shadow; the light returns and it is a glorious light. Ironically, the hour (*hora*) is contrasted with the Cross (*crux, crucis*). The Cross may have overshadowed the hour, but the hour now begins to shine more brightly, precisely because it is in this hour that Christ breathed his last (see Mt 27). Christ's dying breath illumines the hour with the light of victory as the Cross begins to reflect the refulgent glory of the price of redemption. The clouds of the Cross (*nubila crucisque*) are rent (*solvit*) because Christ's death won the glory of our redemption.

It is striking that this hymn, an *Easter* hymn for None, is focused more on Good Friday than on Easter Sunday. This "backward focus" of the hymn is fitting, however. On Good Friday, Christ's Crucifixion is seen from the perspective of his death, when darkness covered the earth (Mt 27:45). When we look back from Easter Sunday, however, Good Friday takes on a new brilliance. Christians may in fact celebrate the Cross, because the earthly darkness of the Cross rends the spiritual darkness of sin and death.

The Latin verb in the formula for absolution (*Ego te absolvo* ...) has the same stem as *solvo*, used here. Thus the verb here has undertones of forgiveness. In addition, when Christ gives the keys to St. Peter, he says to Peter "Whatever you loose (*solveris*) on earth will be loosed (*erit solutum*) in heaven." The clouds that veil the Cross on Good Friday do indeed create physical darkness, but the darkness of death is pierced by the lance that pierced the side of Christ. The shadows of pain and sorrow associated with the Cross are undone by the gift of forgiveness, the fruit of the Crucifixion; forgiveness transforms suffering into radiant spiritual light.

Lines 3–4 provide further clarification for line 2. This hour is divesting (*exuens*) the world of darkness. There are two points to notice here. First, the tense of a

---

166. s.v. *resplendeo* in Blaise *Dictionnaire* 1&2.

participle is usually relative to the governing verb. Since *resplenduit* is in the perfect, the two participles in lines 3–4 (*exuens* and *reddens*) should be understood as actions contemporary with the main verb, but it is perhaps possible to give these present participles a wider theological meaning than this. Taken more broadly, these participles refer to those who sing. Now, today, this hour is still divesting the world of darkness and giving a serene, noble, and illustrious (*serena*) light. Second, prior to Christ's crucifixion, the soldiers strip him (*exuentes*) and dress him in a purple cloak to mock him. After their cruel sport, they remove the cloak (*exuerunt eum*) and put his own clothes upon him (Mt 27:28, 31). Finally, he is stripped again on Calvary. Though the Evangelists do not mention this final divesting, they all say that the soldiers cast lots for his garments.[167] Christ let himself be divested of all dignity and thereby divested the world of darkness.

STANZA 2

Stanza 2 opens with the same two words as the previous stanza, *Hæc hora*. The focus is, once again, on *this* hour. It is at this hour that Jesus descended to the dead, harrowed hell, and raised the bodies of the Old Testament saints from their tombs, as recounted in Matthew: "The tombs were opened, and many bodies of the saints who had fallen asleep were raised, and coming out of the tombs after his resurrection they came into the holy city and appeared to many."[168] As in the previous stanza, the main verb, *iussit* (2, 4), is in the perfect tense; the participle *resuscitans* indicates simultaneous action with the verb. At the hour of his death, Christ commanded (*iussit*) the bodies to come forth, free from death, with their spirits restored to their lifeless bodies.

As with stanza 1, the timing of this verse is intriguing. The focus is on the command Christ gave to the holy ones who preceded him, a command given precisely at the hour of his death. There is no recorded *verbal* command in Scripture by which Christ raised these dead. Rather, the significance of this stanza for the Hour of None in Easter Time is that it illustrates the implication and effects of Christ's death. The death of Christ immediately defeats death. Just as the good thief, who receives the effects of Christ's Passion without delay ("today [*hodie*] you will be with me in Paradise" Lk 23:43), so also the bodies of the holy ones are raised from the tomb and attest to the defeat of death. The bodies go free from death (*corpora mortis libera*); their spirit, their life's breath that God breathed into their nostrils, is fully restored to them. The focus of Eastertide is retained in this hymn precisely by looking back to the moment of Christ's death. This one stanza illustrates the hylomorphic nature of the human person. We are body and soul in this life, and so shall we be in the resurrection. Death cannot hold Christ's holy ones precisely because it cannot hold him.

---

167. Also, in the tradition of Christian piety, the tenth Station of the Cross is "Christ is stripped of his garments."

168. *et monumenta aperta sunt: et multa corpora sanctorum, qui dormierant, surrexerunt. Et exeuntes de monumentis post resurrectionem ejus, venerunt in sanctam civitatem, et apparuerunt multis* (Mt 27:52–53).

STANZA 3

Stanza 2 of this hymn was stanza 4 of the original hymn. Stanza 3 of this hymn is the original stanza 6; stanza 5 is omitted. Lentini comments that he has changed the original *credere* in line 1 of stanza 3 to *credimus* because the infinitive was dependent on the main verb in the missing stanza.[169] This seems to reflect an uncertainty in the manuscript tradition.[170] In the present configuration of the hymn, our belief (*credimus*, 3, 1) is the result of Christ's command (*iussit*, 2, 4) to the dead saints to rise and go forth. Thus, as we see the resurrection happen "before our eyes," we believe in the renewed, renovated (*novata*) ages or worlds (*sæcla*, short for *sæculum*). The Latin *sæculum* may apply both to time—ages (see Ti 1:2), lifetime, generation—and to the world (see 2 Tm 4:10), and even to the reign of an emperor.[171] This multifaceted word is a fitting expression of the object of our belief. The world to come will be the definitive reign of Christ, a timeless bliss in the new heaven and new earth (see Rv 21:1). The renewed age is also, even in this life, a new understanding of time, the world, and the reign of Christ. Line 2 specifies, by means of an ablative absolute, that the new *sæculum* is a world in which the laws of death are abolished.

Lines 3–4 provide a further description of the content of our belief. The *novata sæcla* are caused by God's gifts (*munera*) of blessed life; the gifts make the *novata saecla* such that they will run for ever in their continuous course (*cursum perennem*).[172] Etymologically, the adjective *perennem* is drawn from *per* + *annum*; the image is of an eternity that "stretches" through all the numbered years of creation. Since there is no time in heaven as it is marked on earth,[173] the experience of the blessed will be uninterrupted. Indeed, *perennem* is used to refer to the fixity of stars in their courses.[174] There is a suggestive connection here to Daniel 12:3, in which the learned or wise are compared to stars (*quasi stellæ in perpetuas æternitates*). Notice the infinitive *currere*, "run." The infinitive, *currere*, is swift; the gifts *run* their perennial course; the fact that time is surpassed is what gives eternity its "speed". The use of speed does not work against the supra-temporal but rather emphasizes it. The gift of blessed life is an active gift, it runs forever without tears or toil.

---

169. See *TDH*, 126. Stanza 5 of the original hymn dwells on the process of resurrection for the bodies long since turned to dust and the end result: that they may now see the glory of Christ. It reinforces the message of stanza 2 in the current hymn that at the moment of his death, Christ brought his saints back to life as participants in his own resurrection. The omitted stanza reads: *Redit favilla in sanguinem, / cinisque carnem reddidit, / mixtique vivis mortui / videre Christi gloriam*: "Cinders turn to blood, and ashes give back their flesh; the dead were joined to the living and saw the glory of Christ." Walpole (p. 250) suggests that this stanza may be an allusion to Jn 11:40: Before raising Lazarus, Jesus tells Martha: "Did I not tell you that if you believe, you will see the glory of God?"

170. In the omitted stanza, *videre* is not an infinitive; it is third person plural perfect. See Walpole, p. 250. Also, both Bulst and Walpole take what Lentini, following AH 51, thought was an infinitive in stanza 3 (*credere*) to be a potential subjunctive (*crederes*) meaning "You would have thought ..." Neither option seems wholly satisfactory. Although he had no manuscript precedent, Lentini in the interest of clarity removed the ambiguity by putting the verb in the present indicative (*credimus*).

171. *OLD*, s.v. *sæculum*, 4. b.

172. Walpole says that the subject of *currere* is *sæcla* (l. 24, p. 250). Walpole, Bulst, and AH 51 also read *munere* not *munera*. The *TDH* reads *munera*. My comments here presuppose that the subject is *munera*, as the *TDH* has it.

173. Rv 10:6, "... time shall be no longer," is sometimes interpreted as the total cessation of temporal progression in heaven. (See *IV Summa Contra Gentiles*, c. 97).

174. *OLD*, s.v. *perennis*.

Finally, the *munera*, the gifts, are in the plural, but the genitive of description *vitæ beatæ* is singular. There are multiple gifts in a single eternal life. The gifts of eternal life, joy, and resurrection are granted to *many*, yet all the blessed share in the one eternity of God. The Boethian definition of eternity, "the whole, simultaneous, and perfect possession of boundless life,"[175] fittingly summarizes God's eternity, but also of the blessed life of those in heaven. The blessed are made *beati* by a share in the *vita beata* of God himself. The final line of the hymn, therefore, links the final consummation of all things in heaven with *hæc hora*, the one hour in which Christ's victory was won. From this hour forward, Christ's victory will run its course forever in the fulness of the wisdom of God.

STANZA 4

For a commentary on stanza 4, see the commentaries on H 42 and H 48.

Iesu, redemptor sæculi — 51

ca. 10th c.
8 8 8 8 (LM)

Easter Time
Compline

Iesu, redémptor sǽculi,	1. Jesus, Redeemer of the world,
Verbum Patris altíssimi,	Word from the Father, God most high,
lux lucis invisíbilis,	true Light sent forth from unseen Light,
custos tuórum pérvigil:	and watchful guardian of your own:
Tu fabricátor ómnium	2. O Maker of the universe,
discrétor atque témporum,	you order all our days and hours;
fessa labóre córpora	restore our bodies, worn by toil,
noctis quiéte récrea.	with peace and silence through the night.
Qui frangis ima tártara,	3. Destroyer of the pit of hell,
tu nos ab hoste líbera,	release us from our wicked foe,
ne váleat sedúcere	that he may have no strength to lure
tuo redémptos sánguine,	the souls you ransomed by your blood.
Ut, dum graváti córpore	4. As we remain for this brief time,
brevi manémus témpore,	our weary bodies seeking rest,
sic caro nostra dórmiat	Lord, may our flesh so sleep in peace,
ut mens sopórem nésciat.	that lethargy not dull our minds.
Iesu, tibi sit glória,	5. To you, Lord Jesus, glory be,
qui morte victa prǽnites,	who shine in victory over death,
cum Patre et almo Spíritu,	with God the Father, ever blest,
in sempitérna sǽcula. Amen.	and loving Spirit, ever one. Amen.

---

175. Boethius, *Consolation* 5, prosa 6, lines 9–11.

Text found in *TDH*, no. 115; *AH*, no. 45. Changes in *TDH*: stanza 3, 1–2: Lentini reads *Qui frangis ima tartara, / tu nos ab hoste libera* for *Te deprecamur supplices / ut nos ab hoste liberes*; 4, 1: *gravati corpore* for *gravi in corpore*; 4, 4: for *soporem nesciat* a few manuscripts read *sopore nesciat, in te pervigilet*, or *in Christo vigilet*.

COMMENTARY

This hymn is found in manuscripts from the tenth to the fifteenth century and was used for Compline. In one manuscript it is adapted for Easter, with an additional stanza and doxology, and in another it is set for Advent. In the *Liturgia Horarum* it is used for Compline at Easter time, with a new version by Lentini of 3, 1–2, and a doxology to fit this context.

The structure of the hymn is simple but effective. The first six lines are an invocation of Christ, giving an unusually long series of his attributes, as Redeemer, Word of the Father, light from light, guardian of his own, Creator of all, and governor of time. This listing of divine attributes or functions is a traditional form of opening for a hymn or prayer in both classical and early Christian poetry.[176] Here, the last of the series—Christ as *discretor temporum*—leads naturally into the prayer section (2, 3–4, 4), which begins by asking for rest during the night. The next stanza prays for protection from the evil one, and the fourth stanza elaborates the previous two, contrasting physical rest with spiritual vigilance. There are many points of contact with the language and themes of the hymns of Ambrose, and also with some later hymns.

Stanzas 1–4 use rhyme (aabb), except for 1, 3–4 (*invisibilis ... pervigil*), which has some assonance. In several lines classical scansion is neglected (1, 2, *Patris*; 1, 3, *invisibilis*; 2, 3, *fessa*; 3, 4, *valeat*; 4, 3, *caro*). In the original text 4, 1 has a hiatus in *gravi in*, changed by Lentini to *gravati*.

STANZA 1

The first line is the same as the opening of H 173. See also the opening of H 7 (*Christe, redemptor omnium*), which recurs at the start of H 276, together with the commentary on this same line in H 1: 1, 3. In H 7 the following line (*ex Patre, Patris unice*) resembles line 2 here, and the first line of H 7, stanza 2 (*Tu lumen, tu splendor Patris*) is similar in theme to line 3 of this hymn. This illustrates the formulaic nature of such openings. In classical Latin *saeculum* means "generation, age, century," but from referring to the present age it came to be used, by Christian writers, of "this world," or of "worldliness." For example, James 1:27 reads *immaculata ... ab hoc saeculo* ("unstained from the world," translating ἀπὸ τοῦ κόσμου), and Prudentius *Cathemerinon* 5: 28, 1 offers *per freta saeculi* ("through the

---

176. For a discussion of this type of invocation in classical Greek hymns, see Furley, *Greek Hymns*, 52–56. In the *Liturgia Horarum*, see H 1: 1, 1–3; H 52: 1, 1–4; H 91: 1, 1–4; and for a longer list H 7: 1, 1–4 and 2, 1–2.

sea of the world"). Line 2 draws on John 1:1, "In the beginning was the Word, and the Word was with God."[177] In *Patris* the second syllable would normally be short but is scanned as long here, presumably because the sibilant "s" can easily be treated as a longer sound. Line 3 echoes the first stanza of *Splendor paternæ gloriæ* (H 75) by Ambrose:

Splendor paternæ gloriæ,	O Splendor of the Father's light,
de luce lucem proferens,	emitting glor*ious* Light from Light,
lux lucis et fons luminis,	true Light of light and source of light,
diem dies illuminans.	the Day illuminating day,

This in turn refers to the Nicene Creed: "Light from Light."[178] The epithet *invisibilis* should be taken with *lucis* rather than with *lux*, since God the Father is unseen, whereas Christ was visible in his human form. Both this and *visibilis* are rare in classical Latin but popular with early Christian poets (Juvencus, Prudentius, Paulinus of Nola). The accented third syllable of *invisibilis*, originally short, is here treated as long.

Line 4 anticipates the main themes of the hymn: as the ever-vigilant guardian of his own people, Christ is asked to keep them safe from the dangers of the night (stanza 3), and they in turn pray that their spirit will remain wakeful while their body sleeps (stanza 4).

STANZA 2

The emphatic opening word *Tu* is again a traditional feature of divine invocation in classical Latin hymns, where it is often repeated in anaphora several times.[179] Here it might be called resumptive, as it introduces two further attributes, "You (who are also) ..." *Fabricator* ("craftsman, fashioner") is an unusual word in the context of Christ as creator of the universe. It perhaps recalls the fact that people said of him, "Is not this the carpenter (*faber*), the son of Mary?"[180] It was used by Ovid (*Met.* 1.57) and Manilius (*Astr.*, 5.31) of the creator of the world, and in Christian poetry by Sedulius in his *Carmen Paschale* (1.61, *cæli fabricator ... et conditor orbis*).

The juxtaposition of Christ as Creator and as "discerner of times" in lines 1–2 is based ultimately on the account of the Creation in the opening chapter of Genesis, where God creates light, and separates the light from the darkness, calling the light day and the darkness night (Gn 1:3–5). The same combination is found in the opening stanza of Ambrose's *Æterne rerum conditor* (H 71, where line 3, *et temporum das tempora*, uses the plural "times" in a similar way. See also stanza 1 of *Sator princepsque temporum* (H 108):

---

177. *In principio erat Verbum, et Verbum erat apud Deum.*
178. *lumen de lumine* (Nicene Creed, 8).
179. Norden called this "Du-Stil" ("Thou-style") in his great work *Agnostos Theos*, 149–63. In Christian hymns see the *Te Deum*, and in the *Gloria*, *Tu solus sanctus, tu solus Dominus, tu solus altissimus Iesu Christe.*
180. *Nonne hic est faber, filius Mariæ? ...* (Mk 6:3).

Sator princepsque temporum,	Creator, sovereign Prince of time,
clarum diem laboribus	who set the hours in fixed array,
noctemque qui soporibus	you mark the light of day for work
fixo distinguis ordine.	and grant us night for sleep and rest.

The word *discretor* is first used by Christian authors (Augustine, among others).[181] Walpole's Hymn 57, 1, 1–2, reads *Deus qui certis legibus / noctem discernis et diem*, where *discernis* probably has the sense of "separation," as it does in the account in Genesis (1:4). In Walpole's introduction to his commentary on Hymn 2 (pp. 28–29) he discusses the theme of the regularity of times and seasons as created by God, which is a standard one in these hymns. The word *atque* is sometimes placed second in its phrase by classical poets, as it is here. The two lines read: *Tu fabricator omnium / discretor atque temporum*. *Atque* indicates a closer relationship than the generic *et* between the *fabricator* (maker) and the *discretor temporum* (one who orders the hours). Since Christ as both *fabricator* and *descretor*, the regular and well ordered sequence of times and seasons is entirely his to define and govern. He discerns, in every sense of the word, the depths of what he has made.

Lines 3–4 resemble Walpole, no. 59, 3, 3–4: *labore fessos diei / quietos nox suscipiat*. In *fessa labore* the second syllable of *fessa* is treated as long before the liquid consonant "l". The word order *labore fessa* would have been possible, but the author may have preferred *fessa* first as emphatic, and also because the word order *fessa labore corpora* is more classical, enclosing the ablative *labore* between the adjective and noun.

STANZA 3

Prayer for protection against the evil one is standard in these evening hymns: Ambrose includes it in his *Deus creator omnium*, 7, 3–4, in the original version: *nec hostis invidi dolo / pavor quietos suscitet* ("nor let the envious foe's deceit cause fear to stir us from our rest," tr. Walsh, 13).[182]

Lines 1–2 originally read *Te deprecamur supplices / ut nos ab hoste liberes* ("Humbly we beseech you / that you may free us from the enemy"). Lentini's lines are designed to fit the context of Easter, to which the hymn is currently assigned. For Christ as "destroyer of the pit of hell" in line 1, see *Aurora lucis rutilat* (H 46), stanza 2, with the commentary on this. In line 3 the first syllable of *valeat* is again treated as long, assisted by the liquid consonant "l". Line 4 (*tuo redemptos sanguine*) picks up the theme of the opening invocation, *redemptor sæculi*: see 1 Peter 1:18–19, "Knowing that you were ransomed ... with the precious blood of Christ."[183]

---

181. See Heb 4:12, where the word of God is *discretor cogitationum et intentionum cordis* ("discerner of the thoughts and intentions of the heart").
182. See also *Sator princepsque temporum* (H 108), stanza 2, and Prudentius, *Cath* 6, stanzas 35–37.
183. *Scientes quod.... redempti estis ... pretioso sanguine ... Christi.*

Iesu, redemptor sæculi

STANZA 4

The contrast between physical sleep and spiritual wakefulness is, again, a common theme in the hymns. Underlying this are the constant exhortations in the New Testament to be vigilant (for example, Mt 24:42; 25:13; 26:38–41; Mk 13:35; 14:4–38; 1 Pt 5:18). Ambrose prays in the original version of *Deus creator omnium* (5, 3–6, 2) that "faith may know no darkness, / and night may shine with faith," and "let not our minds succumb to sleep, / but let our sin embrace that sleep." Prudentius elaborates the theme in his "Hymn before sleep" (*Cathemerinon* 6), describing the continuing activity of the sleeping mind in good and bad dreams and visions. The closing stanza of this hymn is relevant:

Corpus licet fatiscens	Although our weary bodies
iaceat recline paulum,	may for a time lie sleeping,
Christum tamen sub ipso	yet even in our slumbers
meditabimur sopore.	our thoughts will rest in Christ.
(*Cath* 6: 38, 1–4)	

The original version of *Sator princepsque temporum* prays (stanza 3) "Let not our spirit yield to sleep, but as the body's watchful guard / let it ward off all empty fears / and put to flight deceiving joy" (tr. Walsh, 139); and stanza 4 is particularly close to the wording of lines 3–4 here:

Sed cum defessa corpora	But when our bodies wearily
Somni tenebunt gratiam,	embrace the welcome charm of sleep,
Caro quietis sit memor,	may our flesh recollect its rest,
fides soporem nesciat	but faith no slumber entertain.[184]

In line 1 the original reading was *gravi in corpore*. Lentini has removed the hiatus after *gravi*, reading the nominative plural participle *gravati* ("weighed down"). It is unclear whether the assonance in *gravi* and *brevi* in line 2 was deliberate or not.

STANZA 5

For a detailed discussion of this Easter doxology, see the commentary on H 42.

---

184. Translation from Walsh, 141. See also Walpole, no. 57 (*Deus qui certis legibus*), stanzas 3 and 5.

| | **Iesu, nostra redemptio** | 52 |

7th–8th c.   The Ascension of the Lord
8 8 8 8   Vespers I and II

Iesu, nostra redémptio   1. O Jesus, our redeeming Lord,
amor et desidérium,   our greatest love and all desire,
Deus creátor ómnium,   true God, Creator of all things,
homo in fine témporum,   true Man beyond the end of time,

Quæ te vicit cleméntia,   2. What loving mercy mastered you,
ut ferres nostra crímina,   that you should bear our grievous sins
crudélem mortem pátiens,   and suffer cruel and bitter death
ut nos a morte tólleres;   to rescue us from death's domain?

Inférni claustra pénetrans,   3. For us you breached the walls of hell
tuos captívos rédimens;   and ransomed all your captives there;
victor triúmpho nóbili   as victor at the Father's right,
ad dextram Patris résidens?   in noble triumph you preside.

Ipsa te cogat píetas,   4. May this same love compel you still
ut mala nostra súperes   to overcome our evil deeds,
parcéndo, et voti cómpotes   to pardon us and grant that we
nos tuo vultu sáties.   may gaze in wonder at your face.

Tu esto nostrum gáudium,   5. Lord Jesus, be all joy for us,
qui es futúrus præmium;   for you shall be our great reward;
sit nostra in te glória   may all our glory be in you
per cuncta semper sǽcula. Amen.   through endless ages evermore. Amen.

Text found in *TDH*, no. 122; *AH* 51, no. 89; Walpole, no. 114. Changes in *TDH*: 1, 4: *fine* for *finem*; 4, 2: *superes* for *sufferas*.

COMMENTARY

This charming and affectionate hymn addresses Christ seated at the right hand of the Father (as we hear in the Nicene Creed). Summarizing the Lord's saving mission, the lyrics are fashioned both as praise and as interrogation. We celebrate Christ's victory as we inquire about his motives for saving us.

    The style of the hymn reflects historical developments in meter and poetics. There is little attention to the natural stress of the words, but rather the words are sung according to the iambic stresses of the lines. Lentini notes the "frequent assonance," which we find from the very start of the poem in the line endings: for example, 1, 2–3: *desiderium ... omnium*.[185] Such features anticipate the developments in rhyme that reflect the changing tastes of Christian hymnodists and singers.

---

185. *TDH*, 127

STANZA 1

Addressing Jesus as our redemption, love, and desire, the hymn quotes the title of Ambrose's hymn for the evening, *Deus, creator omnium* in line 3 (see H 68). The title "God" (*Deus*) is then paired with Jesus' true humanity (*homo*) in line 4. While many hymns identify Christ as "redeemer" and even "redemption," this hymn amplifies the praise by naming him love and desire. Other hymns (e.g., H 134: 6, 2) use the term "love" (*amor*) for Christ, but the accumulated titles here heighten the degree of affection. The second couplet, celebrating Christ as God (*Deus*) and man (*homo*), condenses the Christological doctrine of the early Church. The well-known verse from Ambrose, quoted very early by Augustine, addresses God as "Creator" (*Creator*).[186] While in Ambrose's original hymn the addressee is God the Father, this hymn uses the same title for the Son, emphasizing their absolute equality.

Christ's identity as God and Creator is coupled with his identity as "man" in "the end of times" (*fine temporum*). The phrase recalls Hebrews 9:26, which states that Christ came at the "culmination of the ages" (*in consummatione sæculorum*) or Galatians 4:4, which refers to the coming "in the fullness of time" (*plenitude temporis*). The biblical expressions stress the historical fittingness of the Son's humanization.

STANZA 2

The hymn shifts from the laudatory to the interrogative. We ask Christ to explain the motive of the Incarnation. The use of the direct questioning in a hymn, while familiar from the Psalms (see Ps 23 [24]:9: "Who is the King of glory?"), is unusual in Christian hymnody. Here we ask for a direct account of Christ's merciful action on our behalf.

Lines 1 and 2 ask what sort of "loving mercy" (*clementia*) can account for Christ's voluntary assumption of our sins. The term, a classic term for the virtue of an emperor, connotes an attitude of kindly generosity, especially toward the otherwise guilty.[187] In a striking phrase, clemency is said to have "mastered" (*vicit*) Christ, who is therefore subject to mercy itself. The subjection, however, is voluntary and ordered to the forgiveness of our sins, which recalls Isaiah 53:4, *et dolores nostros ipse portavit* ("our sufferings he bore"), and 1 Peter 2:24, *peccata nostra ipse pertulit* ("He himself bore our sins").

Lines 3 and 4 express the means of this process: Christ "endures" (*patiens*) death to rescue us from death. The repetition of *mors* in successive lines, in the same metrical location (*mortem ... morte*), reflects the pattern of exchange at the heart of Christ's saving work: death is undone by death. As Paul states in 1 Corinthians 15:54: *absorpta est mors in victoria* ("Death is swallowed up in victory").

STANZA 3

This central stanza of the hymn continues the "question" of the previous stanza by speaking of the descent to the dead and of the Ascension. Drawing on classic

---

186. For Augustine's use, see, e.g., *De musica* 6.2.2, and *Conf* 10.12; 10.34.
187. See Seneca, *De clementia*.

themes of the Harrowing of Hell and credal references to Christ's "session" at the right hand of the Father, the singers ask about the heart of the day's feast. The "descent to the dead" (*descensus ad inferos*) is discussed in the commentary for H 46: 4, 1–2. Here we sing of the destruction of the "walls of hell" (*inferni claustra*) in terms familiar from the doctrinal tradition.[188] In an echo of the opening line, Christ "ransoms" (*redimens*) the captives that are "his own" (*tuos*), suggesting that they had been seized from their rightful Lord.

In terms redolent of the hymnodic tradition, Christ the victor sits with the Father. As Walpole (lines 11–12, p. 365) notes, his "noble triumph" (*triumpho nobili*) is drawn directly from the well-known hymn of Venantius Fortunatus, *Vexilla regis prodeunt*" (H 31: 7, 4; this stanza is omitted from the hymn in the *Liturgia Horarum*). The final participle, "presiding" (*residens*), expresses the credal expression that the Son is "seated at the right hand of God the Father" (*sedet ad dexteram Dei Patris*). While the prefix *re-* may simply respond to metrical demands, it may also signal the Son's "return" to his eternal seat.

STANZA 4

After inquiring after the Lord's motive for the Incarnation, the mode shifts to petition. If 2, 1 suggests that clemency compelled Christ to come to us, line 1 asks that "love" (*pietas*) compel Christ to overcome our transgressions. The ultimate aim is that Christ satisfy us with a glimpse of his face. This stanza stands out for its engagement with classical Latin poetry. In a turn of phrase that appears in the works of the Roman orator Cicero and the late classical Latin poet Lucan, we ask Christ that "devotion compel" him (*pietas cogat*).[189] Christ's "devotion" (*pietas*), that is, the love that has been celebrated in the second and third stanza, should drive him further still, to overcome our wickedness. In a clever turn of phrase, however, that "compulsion," which is also a "conquest" (*superes*, line 2), comes not through aggressive action but rather through an act of "pardoning" (*parcendo*, line 3). And it is precisely that mercy that reveals the face of God.

The language of lines 3 and 4 is somewhat elusive, but again, classical antecedents shed some light on the meaning. The ancient phrase *voti compotes* means "having gratified one's prayer" or "wish."[190] We also petition that we may be fully "satisfied" (*saties*) by the face of God.[191] Fulfillment comes from our encounter with Christ's face.

STANZA 5

The final doxological stanza sounds familiar themes, with some modifications. As in H 42, we pray that Christ's joy be ours. Here, however, our joy is Christ himself. Christ will also be our "reward" (*præmium*, line 2).

---

188. Rufinus of Aquileia, for instance, in commenting on the Creed, speaks of shattering of the walls of hell at Christ's descent (*Expositio symboli*, 14); see Maximus of Turin, *Sermo* 62: "claustra penetrat inferna."
189. See Cicero, *Ep.* 1.8.2: *me pietas … cogit*; Lucan, *Bellum civile*, 8.785–86: *cogit pietas imponere finem / officio*: "Devotion compels him to put an end to obligation."
190. See Lewis & Short, s.v. *compos*; Horace, *Ars poetica*, 76.
191. See Ps 16(17):15: *satiabor cum apparuerit gloria tua*: "I shall be satisfied (filled) when your glory appears."

	Æterne rex altissime	53
ca. 10th c. 8 8 8 8		Ascension of the Lord until Pentecost Office of Readings

Ætérne rex, altíssime, redémptor et fidélium, quo mors solúta déperit, datur triúmphus grátiæ,	1. Eternal King and God most high, Redeemer of all faithful souls, in you the power of death is crushed, and triumph shown in gifts of grace.
Scandis tribúnal déxteræ Patris, tibíque cælitus fertur potéstas ómnium, quæ non erat humánitus.	2. You mount the holy judgment seat, established at the Father's right, receiving power to rule all things, divine, not human, sovereignty,
Ut trina rerum máchina cæléstium, terréstrium et inferórum cóndita, flectat genu iam súbdita.	3. That all in heaven and on earth and in the netherworld below, the threefold universe you made, should bend the knee in tribute now.
Tremunt vidéntes ángeli versam vicem mortálium: culpat caro, purgat caro, regnat caro Verbum Dei.	4. The angels tremble as they watch the mortal order overturned: in flesh the sin, in flesh the cure, in flesh the reign of God the Word.
Tu, Christe, nostrum gáudium, manens perénne præmium, mundi regis qui fábricam, mundána vincens gáudia.	5. O Christ, you are our lasting joy, our sure, abiding recompense, who rule the fabric of this world, yet far surpass all earthly joys.
Hinc te precántes quæsumus, ignósce culpis ómnibus et corda sursum súbleva ad te supérna grátia,	6. And so with humble prayer we ask that you forgive us all our faults, and by your heavenly gift of grace lift up our hearts to you on high,
Ut, cum rubénte cœperis clarére nube iúdicis, pœnas repéllas débitas, reddas corónas pérditas.	7. That when the clouds grow red with dawn and you, the Judge, appear in light, you may remit the debt we owe and so restore the crown we lost.
Iesu, tibi sit glória, qui scandis ad cæléstia, cum Patre et almo Spíritu in sempitérna sǽcula. Amen.	8. To you, Lord Jesus, glory be, who now ascend to heaven's height, with God the Father, ever blest, and loving Spirit, ever one. Amen.

Text found in *TDH*, no. 123; AH 51, no. 88; Walpole, no. 113. Changes in *TDH*: 2, 1: *scandis* for *scandens*; 2, 2–3: *Patris tibique cælitus / fertur potestas omnium* for *Patris, potestas omnium / collata est Iesu cælitus*; 3, 3: *inferorum* for *infernorum*;

4, 4: *regnat caro Verbum Dei* for *regnat Deus Dei caro*; 5, 2: *perenne* for *Olympo*; 7, 1 *rubente* for *repente*.

COMMENTARY

Proclaiming Christ's triumphal reign in heaven, the hymn commemorates the wondrous exchange by which the one who was true God took on human flesh for our sake. With subtle wordplay as well as occasional assonance and alliteration (noted below), the hymn offers an exuberant proclamation of the Lord's magnificence and his affection for his people.

As Walpole and Lentini note, there are significant divergences in the earliest versions of the hymn. Lentini's reconstruction involves some adjustments of the version that is most widely attested. He also attempts to correct some unmetrical and doctrinally suspect verses (e.g., stanza 4, line 4). The resulting version in the *Liturgia Horarum* highlights themes of divine triumph and earthly celebration.

STANZA 1

The first stanza presents Christ as sovereign and as savior. He is the king who shares his "triumphal grace" (*triumphus gratiæ*) with the faithful. The superlative "most high" (*altissime*) and the subtle alliteration (*æterne ... altissime*; *deperit / datur*) contribute to the nobility of the stanza's register.

The opening title, "eternal king" (*æterne rex*), appears also in H 43. Ambrose uses similar phrasing to underscore not only Christ's role, articulated in biblical sources, as ruler, but also to stress his coeternity with the Father.[192] In contrast to the Arians, who maintained that "there was when the Son was not," the Church affirms the timelessness of the Son's reign. The language of *rex* may also hint at the claim, affirmed after the Council of Nicæa and professed in the Niceno-Constantinopolitan Creed, that the Son's "kingdom will have no end" (*regni non erit finis*).[193]

The Son is not only the heavenly king, but also the human redeemer. The title appears often in the hymnodic corpus.[194] By Christ (*quo*) death was "undone" (*soluta*) and "perished" (*deperit*). In Pauline terms, we celebrate the victory of Christ's death as the source of life and grace.[195] The grace here comes from the "triumph" (*triumphus*), a favorite term in the hymns, which evokes the celebratory parades of the Roman Empire. Walpole takes "grace" (*gratiæ*) as the recipient of the triumph and thus sees this final line as a celebration of grace itself as victor in the battle with death.[196]

---

192. See *Æterne rerum conditor*, line 1, with commentary by Fontaine, 152–53.
193. For background, see Lienhard, "Basil of Caesarea, Marcellus of Ancyra, and 'Sabellius,'" 157–67.
194. See note to H 7, *Christe, redemptor omnium*.
195. For example, 1 Cor 15:54.
196. Walpole, p. 362.

STANZA 2

Here we meet the central theme of the hymn: Christ's Ascension to the right hand of the Father. These lines explore the theological meaning of that moment by distinguishing the Son's heavenly power from his human power. We thus see the importance of the liturgical season for appreciating Christ's ultimate triumph.

The opening term, "you mount," (*scandis*) places us squarely in the season of the Ascension. Christ sits on his "judgment seat" (*tribunal*), a term from the Vulgate that is used not only of earthly rulers (e.g., Pilate at Mt 27:19), but also of Christ (see Rom 14:10 and 2 Cor 5:10), and at the Father's right hand (see Acts 7:55 and Rom 8:34).

Lentini notes his adjustments to lines 2 through 4. Most versions of the hymn text have a grammatically ambivalent reference to Jesus in line 3, which may render the Son as the bestower of the divine power. Lentini's version makes Jesus the recipient in heaven of the "power" (*potestas*) of rule and judgment that would not properly have been his in purely human terms.

STANZA 3

The third stanza, line 4 (*flectat genu iam subdita*) offers a poetic presentation of Philippians 2:10: *ut in nomine Iesu omne genu flectatur cælestium et terrestrium et infernorum* ("that at the name of Jesus every knee should bend, of those in heaven and on earth and under the earth"), which itself recalls Isaiah 45:23: *mihi curvabitur omne genu* ("every knee shall bow to me"). This version quotes almost directly from the Vulgate text of Paul's letter (see Phil 2:10 above), rendering in metrical form the biblical expression.

The opening of the "quotation" speaks of the threefold division of heaven, earth, and the underworld as the "triple universe" (*trina machina*). The phrase probably contains an allusion to the Spanish poet and hymnwriter Prudentius (d. ca. 413), who speaks of God's creation of the cosmos in the same terms.[197] Such a direct allusion reflects a noteworthy level of sophistication.

As Walpole notes, lines 3 and 4 highlight the contrast between the universe that was once "created" (*condita*, line 3) now "subjected" (*iam subdita*, line 4).[198] The identical endings, *-dita*, underscore the inversion of the lofty and the lowly in the Incarnation of the Word. The same themes, of course, are central to the hymn from Philippians.

STANZA 4

The inversion signaled in stanza 3 is considered further in stanza 4. An alliterative staccato characterizes the syntax and lexicon of the stanza. The angels see the "reversed order" (*videntes ... versam vicem*, lines 1–2) and "flesh sins" (*culpat caro*, line 3). By the end, we sing again of the Word's marvelous victory, and we might

---

197. Prudentius, *Cath* 9: 5, 1–2: *facta sunt / terra cælum fossa ponti trina rerum machina*.
198. Walpole, p. 363.

recognize a certain exuberance in the marching tone created by the repetitions of *caro*. Various sources speak of the "trembling" (*tremunt*, line 1) of the angels as they witness the Incarnation.[199] In Ambrose's Paschal hymn, *Hic est dies verus Dei*, the angels marvel at the Crucifixion, and Venantius Fortunatus writes of the angels who see the Ascension in awe, reciting Psalm 24: "Who is this king of glory?"[200] In the text, the awe is inspired by the reversal of human fortune: those who were destined for death are now promised true life.

The final couplet draws on traditional accounts of the fittingness of Christ's embodiment (the Incarnation and the Ascension) as a remedy for sin.[201] As Walpole notes, *culpat caro* does not necessarily mean that flesh itself sins, which would be a dualistic, perhaps Manichaean, position, but rather that it "causes sin." The logic of the stanza is that, since the body (of Adam) is the source of the Fall, so the body (of Christ) should be the source of our healing and salvation.[202] Moreover, it is in that same body that the Word of God reigns in heaven. Thus, we have a profound meditation on the fittingness of the "fleshly" means of our salvation.

STANZA 5

The hymn shifts from third-person proclamation to second-person address. In a series of alliterative and assonant verses, we celebrate Christ as our greatest joy, greater than all other joys (*gaudia*). The repetition of key vocabulary (e.g., *mundi* in line 3 and *mundana* in line 4) may itself seem somewhat unimaginative, but it may also add to the lines' appeal.

Other hymns name Christ "joy" (*gaudium*) (e.g., H 54: 4, 1; H 15: 3, 1). He is also our enduring prize. The language of line 2, chosen by Lentini, substitutes for an original reference to Mount Olympus, the classical home of the gods.[203] In this version, alliterative and Ambrosian terms (*perenne* and *præmium*) are coupled with the Johannine word "remain" (*manens*, line 2). The reference to "fabric of the world" (*fabricam mundi*, line 3) recalls the Latin term for "workshop" rather than woven material. As in a poem of the fifth-century author Sedulius, Christ is the "fabricator of heaven."[204]

---

199. See Jas 2:19, where the demons tremble before God; also Jb 26:11; Dn 6:26. See also many Patristic authors, for example: *Pavet cælum, tremunt angeli, creatura non sustinet, natura non sufficit, et una puellula sic Deum in sui pectoris capit, recipit, oblectat hospitio, ut pacem terris, cælis gloriam, salutem perditis, vitam mortuis, terrenis cum cælestibus parentelam, ipsius Dei cum carne commercium, pro ipsa domo exigat pensionem, pro ipso utero mercedem conquirat, et impleat illud prophetæ: ecce hæreditas Domini filii merces fructus ventris* (Peter Chrysologus, *Sermo* 140, line 53).

200. Ps 23 (24): 7–10. See also Ambrose, *Hic est dies verus Dei*, H 44: 3, 1–2, 14–15; Fortunatus, *Poems* 11.1 (an exposition of the Creed), line 31: *Ascendit in cælum*.

201. As Tertullian notes, "the flesh is the axis of salvation": *caro salutis cardo* (in *De resurrectione mortuorum* 8); he later cites Paul as saying "sin dwells in our body": *peccatum dixit in corpore nostro* (*De resurrectione mortuorum* 46; cf. Rom 7:20).

202. Following Rom 8:3–4: "For what the law was powerless to do because it was weakened by the flesh, God did by sending his own Son in the likeness of sinful flesh to be a sin offering. And so he condemned sin in the flesh, in order that the righteous requirement of the law might be fully met in us, who do not live according to the flesh but according to the Spirit." See Walpole, l. 15, p. 363.

203. Perhaps out of an aversion to classicizing "corruptions"; see SC, 93.

204. *Omnipotens æterne Deus, spes unica mundi, / Qui cæli fabricator ades, qui conditor orbis*, (Sedulius, *Paschale Carmen*, 1.61).

Line 4 builds on the previous lines of the stanza not only through the repetition of *mund-*, but also through the final *gaudia*, which are the "mundane" joys of this world. These should not be confused with the joy who is Christ. Christ "conquers" (*vincens*, line 4) all other joys. Again, Christ is presented as the source and summit of all our existence. We pray that he may remain our highest joy and so be a perpetual reward that surpasses all the joys of this world.

STANZA 6

As we come to the hymn's conclusion, we turn to petition and the request for mercy. Drawing us into collective prayer, the stanza uses terms that are frequent in hymnody, but also distinctive liturgical phrases and alliteration (e.g., *sursum subleva … superna*). We not only ask Christ for his pardon, but we offer him our hearts. As Walpole notes, the first word of the stanza, *hinc*, may simply mean "hence" or "and so." It may also, however, relate directly to the posture of the congregation: "from here," as in "from here on earth," we make our requests to Christ who is in heaven.[205] Our supplication, then, further emphasizes Christ's lofty height.

Line 3 includes the famous liturgical formula "lift up [your] hearts" (*sursum corda*). Augustine is quite fond of citing the phrase in his preaching to stress the active involvement of the congregation in lifting themselves up to their Lord.[206] The inclusion of the familiar phrase may integrate the verses into the Eucharistic celebration of the people. The hymn also makes clear, however, that Christ is the one who lifts up our hearts (*subleva*) by means of his "supernal grace" (*superna gratia*, line 4).

STANZA 7

The penultimate stanza brings our petitions to a close. Editors differ on minor details of the text, but this version links the singing to the approach of the new day. We hope that the "dawn of justice" is preeminently a moment of mercy. Given the traditional use of the hymn at the early morning Office of Matins, the medieval variant "reddening" (*rubente*) of the cloud points directly to the congregation's experience and expectations. The cloud is "that of the Judge" (*nube iudicis*), a reference to the gospel accounts of Christ's imminent return.[207] As in many hymns, the arrival of the sun is also the arrival of the Son of Justice.[208]

The final, rhyming couplet begs both for forgiveness and for glory. We ask Christ not only to settle our debts but also to restore our "lost crowns" (*reddas … perditas*, line 4). This final petition alludes to the command given to John in Revelation 3:11, for the church in Philadelphia: "Hold fast to what you have, so that

---

205. Walpole, p. 364.
206. See, for instance, Augustine, *Enarrationes in Psalmos* 10.3 and 132.13.
207. Mk 13:26: *Et tunc videbunt Filium hominis venientem in nubibus cum virtute multa et gloria*: "And then they will see the 'Son of Man coming in the clouds' with great power and glory"; cf. Dn 7:13.
208. See H 27, *Iam, Christe, sol iustitiæ*.

no one will take your crown." The crowning of the hymn is the ascended Christ's return to crown us in glory.

STANZA 8

The final doxology resembles the others in the collection. Lentini slightly alters the ancient version by the placement of line 2. *Scandis* refers back to the celebration of the Ascension and repeats the beginning of the second stanza, line 1.

Optatus votis omnium 54

10th c.
8 8 8 8

From the Ascension of the Lord until Pentecost
Lauds

Optátus votis ómnium
sacrátus illúxit dies,
quo Christus, mundi spes, Deus,
conscéndit cælos árduos.

1. The sacred day has dawned in light,
desired by all with fervent prayer,
when Christ our God ascends on high,
the glor*ious* hope of all the world.

Magni triúmphum prœlii,
mundi perémpto príncipe,
Patris præséntans vúltibus
victrícis carnis glóriam,

2. Triumphant in the mighty duel
that crushed the tyrant of this world,
he brings before the Father's sight
the glory of his risen flesh.

In nube fertur lúcida
et spem facit credéntibus,
iam paradísum réserans,
quem protoplásti cláuserant.

3. Borne high upon a cloud of light,
he gives to all believers hope
as he reopens Paradise,
which our first parents closed by sin.

O grande cunctis gáudium,
quod partus nostræ Vírginis,
post sputa, flagra, post crucem
patérnæ sedi iúngitur.

4. O joy profound, immense for all:
that from our Virgin came the child,
who bore derision, scourge, and Cross
and now ascends the Father's throne.

Agámus ergo grátias
nostræ salútis víndici,
nostrum quod corpus véxerit
sublíme ad cæli régiam.

5. So let us all give thanks to Christ,
our Savior and our strong defense,
since he has borne our flesh aloft
to highest heaven's royal court.

Sit nobis cum cæléstibus
commúne manens gáudium:
illis, quod semet óbtulit,
nobis, quod se non ábstulit.

6. May he remain the single joy
for us and those who dwell on high:
to them he gives himself in full,
from us he never shall depart.

Nunc, Christe, scandens æthera
ad te cor nostrum súbleva,
tuum Patrísque Spíritum
emíttens nobis cælitus. Amen.

7. O Christ, now scaling starry heights,
raise up our hearts to you on high;
send forth to us from heaven above
the Father's Spirit and your own. Amen.

Text found in *TDH*, no. 124; *AH* 51, no. 87; Walpole, no. 112. Changes in *TDH*: stanzas 2 and 8 are omitted; 3, 1: *In nube fertur lucida* for *Est elevatus nubibus*; 3, 3: *iam paradisum reserans* for *aperiens paradisum*; 6, 3: *semet obtulit* for *se præsentavit*.

COMMENTARY

Like the previous hymn (H 53), this hymn celebrates the Lord's Ascension and session with the Father. Themes of triumph through suffering and the reversal of sin are grounds for joy and thanksgiving. At the morning hour we pray in the hope that we will be united with Christ the King not only in our prayers, but also in our bodies. Stylistically the hymn abounds in alliteration and assonance. Initial *p*'s and *c*'s punctuate the lines and add a certain liveliness to the enunciation. Other stylistic features will be noted below.

STANZA I

We begin by linking the morning light with Christ's victorious ascent above the heavens. Renewing the event of the feast itself, the hymn invites the congregation to view the early hour as an image of Christ's victory. As the dawn is the hope after the night, so Christ is the hope of the world.

The repeated *o*'s of the first line seem a fitting opening to the subsequent expression of desire.[209] In a manner found already in Ambrose's hymns, the initial couplet speaks of the day of the celebration as present now.[210] At the same time, the imminent "day of the Lord," which is often invoked as a day of judgment in the Old Testament (e.g., Is 13:9; Jer 46:10; Ez 30:3–4) and the New (e.g., Rom 2:16), is here presented as a day of light and rejoicing (see Mt 24:30 and Rv 22:5). Moreover, as in Ambrose's hymn for Epiphany, the day itself "shines" forth.[211] Our prayers have longed for this day.[212]

Lines 3 and 4 condense the motive for the celebration: Christ, who is God, has scaled the "arduous heavens" (*cælos arduos*). The language suggests that his journey was a challenge, the heavens an obstacle that Christ had to overcome. We begin our day, then, with a reminder that even the Lord's glorification may involve toil. At the same time, the hymn will twice remind us that the Christ is our hope (see 3, 2). While we struggle, we are reassured.

---

209. See Marshall, *O Come Emmanuel* pp. 13–17.
210. See H 44, *Hic est dies verus Dei*. For "this day" in the Psalms, see Psalm 117 (118): 24.
211. See *Illuminans Altissimus* in Fontaine, *Hymnes* 337–59; Walpole, no. 91, pp. 314–17: *Inluxit orbi iam dies*. Walpole, p. 314, notes parallels in the classical and hymnodic tradition.
212. An alternative interpretation could imply that the day is "consecrated by the prayers" (*votis ... sacratus*).

STANZA 2

Singing of the Lord's Ascension as his victory and his conquest over the devil, the hymn presents the moment when Christ offers to the Father the flesh he used to conquer his rival. The battle (*prœlii*, 2, 1) has been won. This stanza dramatically portrays Christ's conquest as the return of the warrior with the spoils (and implements) of victory. Many of the Ascension hymns use the familiar language of *triumphus* to speak of the feast. Here the triumph is identified with the "glory of his victorious flesh" (*victricis carnis gloriam*, 2, 4). The identification is familiar: Early Christian sources speak often of the Son's humanity as the "instrument" and "trophy" of his conquest.[213]

While Christ was identified as the "hope of the world" (*mundi spes*, 1, 3) in the first stanza, here the devil is named, in scriptural terms, the "prince of this world" (*mundi principe*, 2, 2).[214] This same prince is now crushed by Christ's victory.

The striking depiction of Christ "presenting" (*præsentans*) his flesh to the face of the Father offers an account of the Son's session at the right hand. Christ is the classical champion, who displays his armor to the approving lord; Ambrose has a similar usage in referring to the "trophy of the flesh" (*carnis tropæo*).[215] The hymn recalls Colossians 2:14–15, with its reference to the triumph of the Cross, as well as Philippians 2:9–11, where Christ is raised up to the highest place in heaven. The plural *vultibus* is used here in the sense of the singular "countenance." The nineteenth-century poet Gerard Manley Hopkins offers a similar image in "As Kingfishers Catch Fire," where he states that Christ is lovely to the Father "in eyes not his / To the Father through the features of men's faces."

STANZA 3

The third stanza reprises themes of the opening stanzas. Again, Christ's Ascension gives us hope and reverses the fallen order. At the same time, the description of the feast adds subtle details to the historical account. Thus, while the first stanza presented Christ as a champion ascending the "arduous heavens" (*cælos arduos*, 1, 4), in line 1 of this stanza we proclaim that he is "borne" (*fertur*) upon a cloud. The tone is tranquil and celebratory, recalling the description of Christ's Ascension from Acts (1:2, *et nubes suscepit eum*: "and the clouds received him"). While 1, 3 identifies Christ as "hope" (*spes*), line 2 here announces that he gives hope to believers (*et spem facit credentibus*, 3, 2).[216]

The reversal is also explained in detail. This present moment (*iam*, 3, 3) recalls "the day" (*dies*) of stanza 1, 2. As in so many of the hymns, the salvific event is re-presented and actualized. Lines 3–4 refer to the Fall of Adam and Eve:

---

213. For "instrument," see Athanasius, *De incarnatione* 8.3; for "trophy," Ambrose, *Hic est dies verus Dei*, 26.
214. 2 Corinthians 4:4.
215. Ambrose, *Hic est dies verus Dei*, 7, 2; cf. *Expositio in Lucam* 2.69–70. 2.
216. 1 Tm 4:10: *quia speramus in Deum vivum, qui est Salvator omnium hominum, maxime fidelium*: "For we hope in the living God, who is the Savior of all men, especially of the faithful."

by their sin, the "first-created" (*protoplasti*) locked up Paradise (*paradisum clauserant*). In Genesis, the account of the Fall concludes: "And God cast out Adam and placed before Paradise Cherubim and a flaming sword... to guard the tree of life" (Gn 3:24). Line 3 refers to the reversal of the Fall (*paradisum reserans*). As 2 Peter states, "In this way an entrance into the eternal kingdom of our Lord and Savior Jesus Christ will be abundantly provided for you."[217] Thus, the cosmic significance of the feast is linked directly to the biblical account of humanity's Fall.

STANZA 4

Here we meet the narrative of the Incarnation in summary form. Christ's birth and Passion attain their fulfillment in his accession to the Father's right hand. The great joy of the feast, introduced with the exclamatory "O," comes in recalling not only Christ's Ascension but all his condescension for our sake. All the aspects of his life are also, in a sense, "joined" (*iungitur*, 4, 4) to the present moment.

The presentation of Christ's life and Passion uses terms that are familiar from the hymnodic lexicon. For example, in the fourth century, Ambrose had identified Christ as the "one born" (*partus*, 4, 2) of the Virgin.[218] The account of the sufferings may include a direct reference to earlier hymnography as well: as Walpole notes, one of the surviving sections from a hymn of St. Hilary of Poitiers (d. ca. 367) also names the "derision, scourge" (*sputa, flagra*, 4, 3) that Christ suffered.[219]

The stanza again hints at familiar themes of exchange and patterns of inversion: Christ is the one born of our Virgin (*nostræ Virginis*, 4, 2), yet now he takes our humanity and joins it to the seat of the Father (*paternæ sedi iungitur*, 4, 4).

STANZA 5

We turn next to exhortation: Let us give thanks. Christ's Ascension is not his alone, but draws us bodily to the lofty reign of heaven. The imagery of the opening stanza recurs here, as Christ the champion raises us up to the royal chambers.

In a striking phrase that echoes Romans 13:4 and the language of the worldly minister of justice, Christ is the "avenger" (*vindici*, 5, 2). As the frequent references to the first-person plural in these stanzas remind us, Christ's Ascension is not a solo mission. Rather he has borne us with him.[220] The language of the heavenly court is frequent in the Psalms (see, e.g., Ps 117 [118]:24). In the composition of this hymn it also mirrors the opening stanza's references to the "heavens" (*cælos*, 1, 4).

---

217. *sic enim abundanter ministrabitur vobis introitus in aeternum regnum Domini nostri et salvatoris Iesu Christi* (2 Pt 1:11).

218. See Ambrose, *Iam surgit hora tertia*, original hymn stanzas 6, 3–4. This stanza is not included in H48 of the *Liturgia Horarum*.

219. Walpole, no. 1, l. 38, p. 10.

220. See H 54: 4, 2; 5, 2–3; 6, 1 and 4; 7, 2 and 4. In all of these lines between stanzas 4 and 7, there are seven forms of the personal pronoun or adjective (*nos* / *noster*).

We thus witness a movement from the individual victory proclaimed at the start of the hymn to the collective celebration of our hope for our bodily exaltation.

STANZA 6

Central themes are repeated in the penultimate stanza, and the congregation's participation in the feast is confirmed. The joy that is Jesus Christ is shared by us on earth and those in heaven. The final, mirroring couplet (*obtulit ... abstulit*, lines 3 and 4) offers the conclusive link between the mortal and the celestial. The reference to the "heavenly" (*cælestibus*) links directly to the reference to "heaven" (*cæli*) in the previous stanza. Thus location is transferred to its inhabitants, to wit, the saints and angels. While we remain on earth, the joy (repeated here from 4, 1) of both of us can "remain" common. The Johannine theme of "remaining joy" belongs to the denizens of both realms.[221]

Lines 3 and 4 remind us that while our joy may be common, earthly and heavenly motives will be distinct. The two lines compose almost a jingle: The blessed rejoice because Christ offers himself completely to them; we rejoice because, as John's Gospel makes clear, Christ will never depart from us.[222] Thus, the careful singer will note that the reason for our "joy" (*gaudium*) has shifted: In 4, 1 we rejoice to know the Son's session at the Father's right hand; here we rejoice because he has not removed himself from us.

STANZA 7

This version of the conclusion differs from that of other versions of the hymn. The eighth stanza has been removed and an alternative doxology has been inserted. As is fitting for the liturgical season, this version revisits the feast's theme and anticipates the gift of Pentecost. As in H 53, Christ's celestial sojourn inspires the lifting of our hearts. In that hymn, the liturgical "lift up your hearts" (*sursum corda*) was included directly; here it is signaled indirectly in line 2. In yet a final reference to Christ's abode, in line 4 we ask that he send the Spirit "from heaven" (*cælitus*). And in an allusion to the *filioque*, that is, the faith that the Spirit proceeds from the Father and the Son, we name that Spirit as both the Father's and "yours" (*tuum*, 7, 3).

---

221. See, e.g., Jn 15:11.
222. Jn 14:18.

	Veni, creator Spiritus	55

attributed to Rabanus Maurus, d. 856	After the Ascension of the Lord, Pentecost Sunday
8 8 8 8	Vespers I and II

Veni, creátor Spíritus,	1. O Come, Creator Spirit blest,
mentes tuórum vísita,	come, visit souls that are your own;
imple supérna grátia,	fill all the hearts that you have made
quæ tu creásti, péctora.	with grace and blessing from on high.
Qui díceris Paráclitus,	2. For you are called the Paraclete,
donum Dei altíssimi,	the holy gift of God most High,
fons vivus, ignis, cáritas	the living wellspring, love, and fire,
et spiritális únctio.	the soul's anointing from above.
Tu septifórmis múnere,	3. In graces you are sevenfold,
dextræ Dei tu dígitus,	the Finger of God's strong right hand,
tu rite promíssum Patris	and you, the Father's promised one,
sermóne ditans gúttura.	adorn our tongues with gracious speech.
Accénde lumen sénsibus,	4. Come, fill our senses with your light,
infúnde amórem córdibus,	pour forth your love into our hearts,
infírma nostri córporis,	the weakness of our mortal frame
virtúte firmans pérpeti.	make strong with power that never fails.
Hostem repéllas lóngius	5. Drive far from us our deadly foe
pacémque dones prótinus;	and swiftly grant us lasting peace;
ductóre sic te prævio	with you to guide and lead the way,
vitémus omne nóxium.	may we avoid all harm and sin.
Per te sciámus da Patrem,	6. Now through your presence may we know
noscámus atque Fílium,	and love the Father and the Son;
te utriúsque Spíritum	and you, the Spirit of them both,
credámus omni témpore. Amen.	may we profess throughout all time. Amen.

Text found in *TDH*, no. 125; AH 50, no. 144; Walpole, no. 118; Lausberg, *Der Hymnus "Veni Creator Spiritus"*, esp. 207–12. Changes in *TDH*: stanza 2, 1: *Qui diceris Paraclitus* for *Qui Paraclitus diceris*; 3, 1: *munere* for *gratiæ*; 3, 3: *promissum* for *promisso*; 3, 4: *ditans* for *ditas*. A seventh, doxological stanza appears in some versions: Lausberg, *Veni Creator*, 212; AH 50, 194: *Præsta, pater piissime, / Patrique compar unice / Cum Spiritu paraclito / Regnans per omne sæculum.*

COMMENTARY

One of the most profound celebrations of the Holy Spirit in the Christian tradition, *Veni, creator Spiritus* has remained a fixture of the liturgy for over a millennium. Attributed to a range of authors, including Gregory the Great and Charlemagne, the hymn may be the work of the learned ninth-century theologian of the monastery of Fulda, Rabanus Maurus (d. ca. 856).[223] The earliest reference to a performance of the hymn appears at the Council of Rheims in 1049, when it was sung by the clergy upon the entrance of the pope.[224]

Since then, *Veni, creator Spiritus* has continued to inspire composers and to generate scholarly interest. Translations of the hymn appear in most modern languages, including famous German versions by Luther and Goethe; composers including Bach and Mahler have set it to music. In recent years, the renowned patrologist and papal preacher, Raniero Cantalamessa, has contributed an extended, profound meditation on the hymn's background and lyrics; the result is a commentary not only on the hymn, but also on the Holy Spirit.[225] St. John Paul II dedicated one of his Holy Thursday addresses to priests to reflections on the theology of this hymn.[226] In addition to many articles and book chapters, there is a scholarly, line-by-line investigation of the text of the hymn, by Heinrich Lausberg, which offers an exhaustive account of the hymn's sources, form, and meaning.[227] The abundant bibliography attests to the enduring appeal of this hymn.[228] It is easy to understand the interest. The hymn's stanzas and the structure are elegantly balanced and the language and theology are richly expressive. The first three stanzas of the hymn open with invocation and praise; the second three stanzas beseech the Spirit's activity in our lives.[229] Both the praise and the appeal speak of the Spirit in intimate, personal terms.

As noted below in the commentary on the stanzas, the language is indebted to the scriptural, doctrinal, and hymnodic tradition. The author chose each term to weave together links among salvation history, liturgical piety, and personal prayer. While the hymns of Ambrose constitute the remote background, the composer does not simply rework existing material, in a manner that we find in other *Ambrosiana*. The poetry rather reflects a particular and distinctive devotion to the action of the Spirit in the Christian heart.

Direct prayer to the Holy Spirit, as exemplified by the hymn, is unusual in

---

223. See Pimont, 2:127–32, for an earlier discussion of some of this background on authorship; more recently, see Heinrich Lausberg, "*Veni Creator Spiritus*," 183–85. The attribution to Rabanus rests partly on the final stanza's indirect reference to the *filioque*, which emerged as a point of contention during his lifetime.
224. Cantalamessa, *Come, Creator Spirit*, 2.
225. Cantalamessa, *Come, Creator Spirit*, 2.
226. John Paul II, "Letter to Priests, 1998," in *Letters to My Brother Priests*, 248–59; note that his letter of 1990 also contains a brief treatment of the hymn.
227. Lausberg, "*Veni Creator.*"
228. See most recently, Teresa Berger, "*Veni Creator Spiritus*," 141–54.
229. On the division, see Wilmart, *Auteurs spirituels*, 41. Lausberg, "*Veni Creator*," 26.

the early Christian tradition.²³⁰ As argued by the third-century theologian Origen in his commentary on the Our Father, both liturgical and personal prayer is typically addressed to the Father, through the Son, and in the Holy Spirit.²³¹ Early evidence suggests that Christians only rarely invoked the Spirit's aid directly. We might compare many of the other Pentecost hymns in the collection (e.g., H 57), which reflect the early custom and rarely address the Spirit directly.²³² Hence, *Veni, creator Spiritus* represents a noteworthy development in the history of Christian devotion. As True God, the Spirit is not simply one of God's activities, or God's presence in our midst, but a Person to whom we offer ourselves in praise and thanksgiving and who comes directly to our aid.

STANZA 1

The opening stanza creatively draws on traditional biblical, doctrinal, and Ambrosian material to invoke the Spirit's presence in the hearts of "your own" (*tuorum*, line 2). Some familiarity with the background of the terms sheds light on the steady progression of invocations, from "come" (*veni*) to "visit" (*visita*, line 2) and finally to "fill" (*imple*, line 3).²³³ The progress reflects our faith that the Holy Spirit, who is Creator, dwells in the hearts of the faithful and imbues them with grace.

The opening imperative, *Veni*, recalls both the invocation of the Psalms (see Ps 140 [141]) and the first line of the standard form of Ambrose's *Veni, redemptor gentium* (H 5).²³⁴ The Spirit is then addressed as "creator," evoking various associations. While the title, used for God, appears in Ambrose's hymnodic corpus (e.g., H 68, *Deus, creator omnium*) and is common in early Christian hymns (e.g., H 72, *Lucis creator optime*, and H 81, *Rerum creator optime*), it is here applied specifically to the Holy Spirit.

The Spirit's status as Creator (together with the Father and the Son) was a subject of fierce debate in the late fourth century. Ambrose's contribution to the controversy, *On the Holy Spirit*, states explicitly: "Therefore I cannot doubt that the Spirit who we know is the author of the Incarnation is the Creator."²³⁵ The theological defense of the Holy Spirit as Creator was central to the argument for the Spirit's true divinity, for God alone brings something from nothing. The opening invocation, then, is not only a generic expression of praise, but also the expression of a crucial dogmatic principle. Moreover, the title is reprised in the final line of the stanza (line 4), when we sing of the "hearts" (*pectora*, line 4) that the Spirit

---

230. See Lausberg, "Veni Creator," 56–58, on sources for addressee.
231. Origen, *On Prayer*, 14.1. On *taxis* or "order" in prayer, see Basil, *On the Holy Spirit*, 6.13–15.
232. Some later hymns, such as H 56, do address the Spirit directly.
233. On the progression from *veni* to *visita* and *imple*, see Lausberg, "Veni Creator," 25, who links the verbs to the themes of stanzas 4, 5, and 6.
234. Ambrose's hymn is also quoted directly in stanza 4, 3–4.
235. Ambrose, *On the Holy Spirit*, 2.41. For a range of witnesses, see Cantalamessa, *Come, Creator Spirit*, 25–26, who notes a related discussion on the Holy Spirit in the writings of Rabanus Maurus.

has created (*creasti*). If the reference to the Spirit's creative identity was not clear in the first line, the fourth reinforces the point. Last, the invocation also recalls Psalm 103 (104), which famously links the Spirit and creation: "Send forth your spirit, they are created" (Ps 103 [104]:30). Thus, the single term condenses a range of meanings.

We then ask the Spirit to "visit" (*visita*, line 2) the hearts of those who are "yours" (*tuorum*, line 2). The language is striking for its intimacy and affection. The invocation *visita* does not seem to occur in other early Christian hymns. It suggests the consolation of a friend, or, perhaps, the "visitation" of Mary to her cousin Elizabeth;[236] as St. John Paul II puts it, "His visit is the prerequisite for remaining in Christ's friendship."[237] We are then reminded that we belong to the Holy Spirit as "your own." Hence, we are brought face to face with our Creator. The Creator comes to our *mentes*, a term used often in hymnody to signify the heart of those at prayer.[238]

The second couplet of the stanza turns from invocation to petition, requesting the Spirit's presence as grace. While the opening line labeled the Spirit as Creator, here we consider the Spirit as sanctifier. His "celestial grace" (*superna gratia*, line 3) alludes to descriptions from both Ambrose and Augustine that speak of the virtual identity of the Spirit and saving grace from heaven; in later Scholastic terms, the Spirit is "uncreated grace."[239] The Spirit elevates the very "hearts" (*pectora*, line 4) that he created in the first place. Note the pairing of *mentes* and *pectora*: The work of the Spirit pertains not only to the spiritual *soul* but also to the much more corporeal *heart*. The hymn thus resists any facile spiritualization of the Spirit.

STANZA 2

The second stanza is a virtual catalog of traditional titles for the Spirit. Singing directly to our Creator and Sanctifier, we speak of what "you are called" (*diceris*, line 1). We then recite the many names the Spirit has been given in Scripture and tradition. Cantalamessa, then, relates the movement of the first stanza as diachronic with spatial, synchronic framing of the second stanza.[240] Following the ancient Christian practice of meditating on Christ's titles, the style of the second stanza thus makes it especially fit for contemplation.[241] Each name is a storehouse that yields its treasury only after repeated reflection.

The Spirit, then, is successively Paraclete, Gift, Living Wellspring, Fire, Charity, and Spiritual Ointment. The titles are presented in metrical sequence. In

---

236. For *visitare* in the theological tradition, see Lausberg, "Veni Creator," 60–61.
237. John Paul II, "Letter," 2.
238. For a close parallel, see Ambrose's *Deus creator omnium* (H 86), 2, 3.
239. See Peter Lombard, *Sent*. 1, dist. xvii, 18.
240. Cantalamessa, *Come, Holy Spirit*, 43.
241. See Origen, *Commentary on the Gospel of John*, 1.52–53 and 1.109–292.

John's Gospel, Jesus speaks four times of the Paraclete, a term that denotes both a "comforter" and an "advocate."[242] The label, which also appears in some early hymns, especially in doxologies (e.g., H 1 and H 57), reminds us that the Holy Spirit is not simply an elusive force or energy, but a person who works for and with us.[243]

The Spirit is also "gift," (donum, line 2) evoking the traditional link between the Spirit and grace (see Heb 10:29). Cantalamessa assembles a range of sources for the link, including a statement from Ambrose: "For how could there be grace at all, without the Holy Spirit, since every divine grace is in the Holy Spirit?"[244] The term "gift" refers back to the "celestial grace" of line 3, both ways of expressing how the Holy Spirit is always something "given" as a gift to the faithful. Moreover, the Spirit is the gift of the "most high God" (*Dei altissimi*, line 2), a title that suggests the loftiness of the gift itself.[245]

Next, the Spirit is "living wellspring" (*fons vivus*, line 3). Here we recall the links between the Holy Spirit and baptism that appear often in John's Gospel. As the Creed also affirms, the Spirit is "living" in the sense of the "giver of life." Moreover, as Cantalamessa notes, the hymn shows that the language of life expands upon reflection: "It moves from indicating only natural and physical life to indicating the life of the spirit."[246]

Although "fire" (*ignis*, line 3) lies buried in the sequence of titles of the stanza, it is surely the most likely to be linked in imagination to the feast of Pentecost, one of the typical settings for the hymn. The Spirit, of course, appears as tongues of fire on the gathered Apostles (Acts 2). In such a form, his presence recalls the many ways that the Lord appeared to his people as fire throughout the Old Testament (Ex 3:2–3; Dt 1:33).

As Augustine maintained, the Spirit is especially to be considered "love," that is, the *caritas* of line 3. The identification of the Spirit and charity is prominent in the Western tradition. In *De trinitate*, Augustine argues for the Spirit's distinctive role not only as the love between the Father and the Son, but also precisely as the love by which we love.

Finally, the Spirit is "spiritual anointing" (*spiritalis unctio*, line 4). Christ, invoking Isaiah (Is 61:1), calls on the Spirit as the one who "anointed" (*unxit*) him (Lk 4:18). The *spiritalis* refers both to the Spirit's active role and to our mode of receiving the anointing, that is, interiorly. Early theologians saw the terms of anointing as a link between Jesus and the Spirit.[247] They viewed the Spirit's role

---

242. Jn 14:16, 26; 15:26; 16:7.
243. On the Holy Spirit as a person in the hymn, see Cantalamessa, *Come, Holy Spirit*, 69–74. Note that the original, as AH suggests, may have had *Qui paraclitus diceris*, which, however, requires some manipulation of the natural stresses of the words (AH 50, 193).
244. Cantalamessa, *Come, Holy Spirit*, 49, citing Ambrose, *On the Holy Spirit*, 1.127.
245. See Ps 55 (56):3 and Lk 8:28. In performance, note the hiatus, rather than the elision, between *Dei* and *altissimi*.
246. Cantalamessa, *Come, Holy Spirit*, 98.
247. See also Acts 10:38: "God anointed Jesus of Nazareth with the Holy Spirit and power."

in chrismation as central to his cooperation with Christ (The Anointed One), in all saving acts.²⁴⁸

STANZA 3

The lofty invocations continue with the repeated address to "You" (lines 1, 2, and 3) near the heart of the hymn. Additional scripturally dense and spiritually evocative terms correspond to the Spirit's relationship to the Father. They also signal the specific ways that the Spirit is present in Christian life. As virtually all commentators note, the first line of the third stanza recalls Isaiah's references to the gifts of God.²⁴⁹ By describing the Spirit himself as "sevenfold" (*septiformis*, line 1), the composer transfers an epithet that applies properly to the gifts (since, of course, there are seven of them) to the Holy Spirit. Lausberg suggests a link between the Spirit as sevenfold and the hymn's seven stanzas (his version includes a doxology).²⁵⁰

The Spirit is also the "finger" (*digitus*, line 2) of God's right hand. The language recalls Exodus 8:19 and 31:18, which speak of the "finger" of God as the manifestation and the means of divine activity. Gospel references suggest the same link: In Matthew 12:28 Jesus indicates that he casts out demons "by the Spirit of God," while the same passage in Luke 11:20 uses the expression "by the finger of God" (*in digito Dei*). Hence, the Spirit is God's finger, an association especially appropriate for the Spirit's role in the inspiration of Scripture. The identification in the hymn, moreover, also links the Spirit and Christ, the Son of God, who is at the right hand of the Father. We are to recall the Spirit as the "point of contact" between God's action and our lives. Cantalamessa cites Augustine as a source for a further reflection on the implications for the unity and distinctions of the Trinity: "The Spirit is called 'finger of God' because 'through him the gifts of God are given to the saints and, though they are capable of diverse things, they do not depart from the harmony of charity (in the context of the human body): 'it is especially when looking at the finger that one gets the idea of a certain distinction.'"²⁵¹

Line 3 further emphasizes the Spirit's relation to the Father as the one who is promised. In contrast to some versions of the hymn, which have "by the Father's promise" (*promisso*), this version highlights the Spirit's very identity as the one who is the pledge itself. In Luke 24:49, Jesus uses the expression: "I am sending the promise of my Father" (*ego mitto promissum Patris mei*).²⁵²

---

248. See Athanasius, *Letters to Serapion*, 3.3.
249. Vulgate text with the gifts: *Et requiescet super eum spiritus Domini: spiritus sapientiæ et intellectus, spiritus consilii et fortitudinis, spiritus scientiæ et pietatis; et replebit eum spiritus timoris Domini*: "And the Spirit of the Lord shall rest upon him, the spirit of wisdom and understanding, the spirit of counsel and fortitude, the spirit of knowledge and piety, and the spirit of the fear of the Lord shall fill him" (Is. 11:2,3a).
250. Lausberg, "Veni Creator," 84.
251. Cantalamessa, *Come, Holy Spirit*, 194, citing Augustine: *quia per spiritum sanctum dona dei sanctis dividuntur, ut cum diversa possint, non tamen discedant a concordia caritatis, in digitis autem maxime apparet quædam divisio, nec tamen ab unitate præcisio* (Augustine, *De catechizandis rudibus*, 20).
252. See Acts 2:33: "Exalted at the right hand of God, he received the promise of the holy Spirit from the Father and poured it forth."

Line 4 also relates directly to the celebration of Pentecost.[253] Acts reports that when the disciples received the gift of the Spirit, those gathered in Jerusalem were able to understand what was said, each in his or her own language (see Acts 2:4). Thus, their tongues (or even their "throats" [*guttura*], a corporeal term) possessed an eloquence that they lacked before. At the same time, line 4 recalls Mark 13:11, where Christ reassures his disciples about their times of persecution: "But say whatever will be given to you at that hour. For it will not be you who are speaking but the Holy Spirit." The Holy Spirit is precisely the agent of our right speech. The sentiment is especially fitting in a song that uses words to proclaim the Spirit's identity. As we sing, the Spirit is also adorning our tongues with proper praise.[254]

STANZA 4

The fourth stanza marks the turn from praise to petition. As in the opening stanza, a series of imperatives shows a sequential involvement of the Holy Spirit in our lives: "kindle" (*accende*, line 1), "pour forth" (*infunde*, line 2), and "make strong" (*firmans*, line 4). The participle in line 4 functions virtually as a command.[255] The subtle assonance and alliteration, in addition to the direct quotation of Ambrose in lines 3 and 4, add a certain playfulness to this stanza.

The request to fill our senses (*sensibus*, line 1) with the divine light is deeply biblical. In 2 Corinthians 3:16–18 we learn that as we turn to the Lord the veil is removed and we see the Lord, "who is Spirit" (*Spiritus est*); we thereby are transformed "from glory to glory" (*a claritate in claritatem*), with the Latin term *claritas* connoting the brilliance and illumination of our faces. The language of *sensibus* is important: While the Walpole edition maintains that it means "thoughts," the language of senses should not be reduced to the intellectual.[256] Indeed, the subsequent lines stress the Spirit's agency in our hearts and our body, which are not images of abstraction.

We ask that the Spirit pour forth love into our hearts (*amorem cordibus*, line 2): as the Walpole commentator notes, Gregory the Great uses a very similar image: "The Holy Spirit casts the flames of love from himself in the hearts of his elect."[257] Having already addressed the Spirit as "charity" (*caritas*, 2, 3), we asked for a share in that love. The *homoioteleuton* (similarity of endings) of *sensibus* and *cordibus* (somewhat distinct from proper rhyme), emphasizes the parallel between our senses and our hearts.

---

253. See Lausberg, "*Veni Creator*," 94–96, on the links to the historical context.
254. For connections with *glossolalia*, or speaking in tongues, see Cantalamessa, *Come, Holy Spirit*, 220–28.
255. Cantalamessa, *Come, Holy Spirit*, 237, speaks of the verbs as "impetratives" in form "because they express a plea rather than a command."
256. Walpole, p. 376. NB: Arthur Walpole himself passed away before completing his commentary on *Veni, creator Spiritus*, and thus the notes come from the general editor, Arthur Mason. On *sensus* in Ambrosian hymnody, see Dunkle, *Enchantment*, 93–99.
257. Walpole, p. 376; Gregory, *Homily in Ezekiel* 1. 5.8.

The final couplet is drawn directly from Ambrose's Advent hymn *Veni, redemptor gentium* (H 5: 5, 3–4), and the commentary to those lines will be relevant for this hymn.[258] The insertion is hardly clumsy plagiarism; rather, the Ambrosian citation is carefully integrated into its new setting, resembling, in the analysis of Lausberg, a "collage."[259] The term *corporis* sits poetically next to *cordibus*. The sentiment, if not the specific Latin terms, recalls Ephesians 3:16: "I pray that out of his glorious riches he may strengthen you with power (*virtute*) through his Spirit in your inner being."

STANZA 5

After we have invoked the Spirit's interior presence, we turn to ask for protection from the evil one. The penultimate stanza with an apotropaic prayer that beseeches defense from hostile forces, concludes with a request for safe guidance to tranquility. Thus, the Spirit's joint role as defender and guide is emphasized.

The first term, *hostem*, refers to the evil one, the devil who is the enemy of the human race.[260] As Cantalamessa notes, the plea is more a statement of a principle than a request for a simple defense: "Where the Holy Spirit comes in, the unclean spirit goes out; the two cannot be in any place together."[261] We proceed to request the Spirit's "swift" (*protinus*, line 2) peace; the term itself also connotes both "by the same action," that is, with Satan's rejection the Spirit brings peace, and it is "lasting," as in *perpeti* in 4, 4. The link between the Holy Spirit and peace is embedded in Scripture (see Rom 8:6; 14:17; Gal 5:22–23). Note, too, the contrast, by graphic syntax, between *hostem* in the first position of line 1 and *pacem* in the first position of line 2: The pairing virtually performs the shift from the defeat of the enemy to the arrival of peace, drawing us from imagining the Spirit as a warrior to acknowledging the Spirit as the source of rest.[262]

Lines 3 and 4 conclude the petition with reference to the Spirit as guide (*ductore*, line 3). Lausberg relates the term to the hymn's use of a "metaphor of the Way" that sees the Spirit as always ahead of us on the path.[263] The image may recall the cloud of the divine presence in Exodus (see, e.g., Ex 13:21–22), which led the Israelites through the perils of the flight from their Egyptian oppressors. With the Spirit's guidance before us (*prævio*, line 3) we avoid the world's threats, but also every form of guilt (*omne noxium*, line 4).

---

258. For details of the borrowing, see Lausberg, "Veni Creator," 114–16. Also, note that in H 5, as it appears in the *Liturgia Horarum*, the lines come from stanza 5, which is stanza 7 of the original hymn.
259. Lausberg, "Veni Creator," 114.
260. Lk 10:19; 1 Pt 5:8. The hymn *Ut nox tenebris obsita* (Walpole, no. 103, l. 16, p. 306) makes almost the same request: *hostem repellat improbum*.
261. Cantalamessa, *Come, Holy Spirit*, 289.
262. Cantalamessa, *Come, Holy Spirit*, 305.
263. His terms is *Weg-Metaphor*. Lausberg, "Veni Creator," 127.

STANZA 6

Although there are versions of the hymn with concluding doxologies, the final stanza of this version contains theologically potent language. As Cantalamessa notes, we move from the "horizontal" to the "vertical."[264] We pray directly to the Spirit that through him we may know both the Father and the Son and that we may confess the *Filioque*, that is, the famous, traditionally Western, claim that the Spirit proceeds from the two other Persons of the Trinity.

The stanza represents a compressed expression of Western Trinitarian theology and pneumatology. We beg the Spirit to "grant" (*da*, line 1) that we may know both the Father and the Son, and that he is the Spirit of both (*utriusque*, line 3). The pairing of two words for "knowledge" (that is, *sciamus*, line 1, and *noscamus*, line 2) may indicate some progressive deepening of our awareness of God as Trinity.[265] This knowledge transforms our very identity: We realize that we are not orphans (see Jn 14:18), but rather children of God and brothers and sisters of Christ.

These terms for knowing culminate in the reference in the final line to "believing" (*credamus*). The term itself recalls the credal confessions that link our hymnody to our faith. Moreover, the expression of belief may relate to the specific terms of *Veni, creator Spiritus*. Studies of the hymn often stress the prominence of the controversial claim of the *filioque* here. Indeed, Lausberg dates the entire hymn to the Council of Aachen in 809 on account of the reference.[266]

Yet we should note that the specific terms of our hymn are somewhat less polemical than that particular clause. The mere claim that the Holy Spirit is the Spirit of "both" (*utriusque*, line 3) was not especially controversial in the East; many early Greek authorities make that same claim.[267] The divisive issue was the claim that the Spirit "proceeded" from both, which is neither the precise language of the original Creed nor the language Jesus uses in John 15:26. Thus, the *Veni, creator Spiritus*, which does not include a term for "procession," might be understood as in no way hostile to the Eastern developments.

---

264. Cantalamessa, *Come, Holy Spirit*, 339.
265. See the related remarks of Cantalamessa, *Come, Holy Spirit*, 349–50.
266. Lausberg, "*Veni Creator*," 140–51.
267. See H 124: 3, 3: *Sancte utriusque Spiritus*. Note that early Greek sources speak of the Spirit as the Spirit "of the Son," or as proceeding from the Father "through the Son"; on the background to the debate, see Siecienski, *Filioque: History of a Doctrinal Controversy*.

Lux iucunda, lux insignis	56
Adam of St. Victor, d. 1146 Meter: Irregular	Pentecost Sunday Office of Readings

Lux iucúnda, lux insígnis,
qua de throno missus ignis
in Christi discípulos,

Corda replet, linguas ditat,
ad concórdes nos invítat
cordis, linguæ módulos.

Consolátor alme, veni,
linguas rege, corda leni;
nihil fellis aut venéni
sub tua præséntia.

Nova facti creatúra,
te laudámus mente pura,
grátiæ nunc, sed natúra
prius iræ fílii.

Tu qui dator es et donum,
nostri cordis omne bonum,
cor ad laudem redde pronum,
nostræ linguæ formans sonum
in tua præcónia.

Tu nos purges a peccátis,
auctor ipse pietátis,
et in Christo renovátis
da perféctæ novitátis
plena nobis gáudia. Amen.

1. Light of gladness, light exalted,
from the throne as fire emitted,
sent on Christ's disciples all,

2. Filling hearts, and tongues bestowing,
bidding us to live in concord,
one in heart and gracious speech:

3. Come, O Comforter most loving,
rule our tongues, our hearts make gentle;
nothing bitter or vindictive
can before your presence stand.

4. Made again a new creation,
pure in mind and heart, we praise you,
children formerly by nature,
sealed in wrath, but now in grace.

5. You are both the gift and giver,
for the heart, sole cause of goodness;
make our hearts disposed to praise you,
form our tongues in speech and singing
for your praise and majesty.

6. You, the very source of mercy,
cleanse us of our sins and failings,
and to those reborn in Jesus
grant your gift of perfect newness,
full and everlasting joy. Amen.

Text found in *TDH*, no. 126; AH 54, no. 154; Jean Grosfillier, *Les séquences d'Adam de Saint-Victor*, 329. Changes in *TDH*: stanza 6, 1: *Tu nos purges* for *Tu purga nos*; stanzas 3–14 and 16–17 have been omitted.

COMMENTARY

The Pentecost sequence *Lux iucunda* found in the *Liturgia Horarum* is an abridged version of the original work. The structure and poetry of sequences is such that the appropriate context for a commentary upon the meanings of the stanzas that remain is most fundamentally the full poem; this provides an explanation offered by the poet himself. The original ten-stanza text was very likely written by the great twelfth-century liturgical poet, Adam of St. Victor. He was the cantor at the Cathedral of Notre Dame in Paris before taking up residence at the Augustinian Abbey of St. Victor on the left bank of the city.[268] Before he departed for the Abbey of St. Victor, Adam would have had charge of the music of the cathedral and also of its library. He was, therefore, a very learned man, and one completely steeped in the liturgy and its meanings. He belonged to the party of men who at that time desired to reform the priesthood, removing its ingrown secularity, and renewing its abilities to offer strong leadership for the Church.

The Victorines used the apostleship of the early Church as their model for rightful praise, and so the sequences Adam wrote, including this one, attempt to take the singers back to an early, Spirit-filled time. In this poem it is the time of Pentecost in the upper room of Acts 1 and 2, the place where, traditionally, the Spirit descended on the gathered disciples—including many women and Mary, the Mother of the Lord. In this commentary, the hymn as found in the *Liturgia Horarum* has been put back into the original sequence, so that Adam's meanings may be better understood.[269] Understanding the full import of the excerpted sequence depends on knowing the entirety of the hymn in all its power and richness. The adaptors of the text took the opening and closing of the original work and two half stanzas from the middle. Much of the complex scriptural commentary so prized by the poet Adam is found in the omitted stanzas.[270]

The poem praises the grace-filled light of Christ that descended on the disciples at Pentecost, the feast for which the sequence was written. This light was meant to bring the fulfillment of the meanings of all of Scripture and also to make it possible for those receiving this light to dwell in a harmonious common life, one that was both shaped and inspired by the raising up of liturgical song. The spirit is one of exuberant joy, of jubilation at the receiving of the gift, a pledge of God's promise to the Church. In many ways, the text provides Adam's greatest commentary on Ephesians and on Colossians, as it extols the coming of the fledgling Christian community into its full Jewish patrimony at the moment when the new Church was founded, on the first Pentecost so long ago. The poem is filled

---

268. The Abbey of St. Victor was founded in 1108 by William of Champeaux, Archdeacon of the Cathedral of Notre Dame, Paris. He left the Cathedral for an old, abandoned hermitage named after St. Victor, and made of it a haven for reform-minded clerics who sought to live the common life under the Rule of St. Augustine. Many among the first generations of Victorines, as they were called, came from the Cathedral with William to St. Victor. These men became Canons Regular of St. Augustine. The Abbey, with strong leadership, support from popes and kings, and a school that attracted the best minds of the first half of the twelfth century, became a center of clerical reform in the Church, of liturgical reform and innovation, and of intellectual life in the century before the rise of the universities. The Abbey influenced ecclesial life throughout Europe for the next century. Three of the greatest Victorines were Hugh of St. Victor (d. 1141), Richard of St. Victor (d. 1173), and Adam of St. Victor (d. mid-1140s), the composer of this sequence. For more detail, see Fassler, *Gothic Song*, 197–210.

269. See the full text below with the stanzas included in the *Liturgia Horarum* in bold. Except for the ICEL translations of the stanzas included in *The Divine Office Hymnal*, the English text is that of the commentator.

270. For a fuller study of this text and melody and other related Victorine sequences, readers are referred to Fassler, *Gothic Song*.

with allusions, as well, to the upper room of Acts 1 and the discussion of Pentecost found in Acts 2.

As the Christian liturgy, both of the Divine Office and of the Mass, is driven by parallel passages from both testaments of the Bible (the figure and the fulfillment), so also is the exegesis of many of Adam's sequences. *Lux iucunda* is a fine example of the interweaving of themes from both bodies of Scripture. This parallelism is clearly seen in the complete sequence. Thus, as may be seen from the text of the original, the workings of Pentecost and the coming of the Spirit are placed in parallel with the Jewish feast of Weeks (Shavuot), which celebrates the reception of the Ten Commandments by Moses. In stanzas 2 and 3 of the original, Christ sends down the fiery light on his bride, which is the Church as typified in the rock of Deuteronomy 32:13. The rock exudes first sweet honey, and then oil, and a new law of grace is put in parallel with the tablets of the Law. There are two assembled groups referenced here: those who awaited Moses at the base of Mt. Sinai and the three thousand of Acts 2:41 who were baptized by Peter after the reception of the Holy Spirit.

The sacramental power suggested by the rock in Deuteronomy that sent forth liquids continues in stanzas 4 and 5 of the original poem, with allusions to Eucharistic bread and wine. The loaves of Leviticus 23:17 are alluded to, and they then become the two sides of the cornerstone, who is the Christ of Ephesians 2:20. The jars put out to receive wine at Elisha's command in 2 Kings 4:1–7 are the jars for the new wine of Mark 2:22 and Luke 5:37–38. The new wine, too, is what the Apostles were accused of having drunk in Acts 2:13. The dew is the manna that the Lord gave the Israelites to eat in Exodus 15, a type of the Christian Bread of Life in John 6. With these exegetical parallels, the singing of the sequence prepares for the reception of Holy Communion and deepens its meanings through a host of scriptural resonances. Since the poem as a whole celebrates the founding of the Christian Church at Pentecost, it is especially fitting to give thanks for the sacraments, especially those of the Eucharist and Baptism.

Understanding the scriptural exegesis of the middle stanzas of the original sequence provides a context for the beginning and end of the abridged version. The sense that the Church itself is born on this day, so prominent in the second stanza of the original poem, helps justify the reasons for communal joy, for the emphasis on the tongues of speech that were so necessary for the building of the communal body, and for the receiving of the gift with hearts united in purpose and spirit. This refers as well to the spirit of the disciples in the upper room of Acts 1 who were "persevering with one mind in prayer with the women, and Mary the mother of Jesus, and with his brethren." The importance of communal purpose was emphasized by Jesus in John 15, when he commanded his disciples to love one another. And this command came after he had explained, in John 14, that he would indeed leave them, but that the promised Paraclete would come, the Comforter of stanza 8 of the original poem and stanza 3 of the excerpted text. The two passages from John are crucial for the understanding of how the

Comforter may be received by the assembly, and the poet underscored this powerfully in the second half of stanza 8: "Come, O Comforter most loving, rule our tongues, our hearts make gentle; nothing bitter or vindictive can before your presence stand."

The first half of the original stanza 9 continues in praise of the Paraclete and his power to sanctify the waters of baptism, the sacrament through which Christians are made new. This helps to explain the second half of this stanza, which becomes stanza 4 of the abridged sequence: the singers are made part of a new creation, a world now empowered by God's grace rather than by God's wrath.

The final stanza of the poem is broken in half, forming stanza 5 and 6 of the abridged sequence. The Comforter is both gift and giver, for he is the reward Christ gives, and he is what makes the inspired praise ring out. Those engaged in this praise hope to become part of the new creation offered through powers of the Spirit given on the feast of Pentecost, powers that continue through the sacraments of the Church.

Following is the original twelfth-century sequence with English translation.[271] The stanzas contained in the *Liturgia Horarum* are placed in bold. The numbering indicates the order of music to text. Sequences, in contrast to hymns, have melodies that are not divided into repeating verses. Rather, the melody changes over the course of the sequence; they are "through-composed." As a general rule, the melody is the same for a pair of stanzas. Then, it changes for the next pair. In the sequence given below, each pair is under one Roman numeral, and the members of the pair are designated by Arabic numerals; e.g. Stanza I.1 and Stanza I.2 both have the same melody. With Stanza II, the melody changes, and stanzas II.1 and II.2 have the same melody, which is different from stanzas I.1 and I.2. A separate rhyme scheme for the last line of each member of a pair connects the two members in the pair; for example, the last lines of III.1 and III.2 each end with a distinct two-syllable rhyme that differs from the other line endings of each member: *populo* rhymes with *cenaculo*. Thus, a double rhyme scheme is carried through the entire sequence. For more details, see the explanation after the sequence.

I.1 Lux iucunda, lux insignis, qua de throno missus ignis in Christi discipulos,	Light of gladness, light exalted, from the throne as fire emitted, sent on Christ's disciples all,
I.2 Corda replet, linguas ditat, ad concordes nos invitat cordis linguæ modulos.	Filling hearts, and tongues bestowing, bidding us to live in concord, one in heart and gracious speech:

---

271. The Latin text is the text of the manuscripts consulted.

II.1 Christus misit quem promisit,
    pignus sponsæ quam revisit
    die quinquagesima
	Christ sent whom he promised,
	a pledge to the bride to whom He returns
	on the fiftieth day;

II.2 Post dulcorem melleum
    petra fudit oleum,
    petra iam firmissima.
	after the sweet honey,
	the rock poured forth oil,
	the rock very strong at that time.

III.1 In tabellis saxeis,
    non in linguis igneis,
    lex de monte populo,
	In stone tablets,
	not in tongues of fire,
	the law came from the mountain to the people,

III.2 Paucis cordis novitas
    et linguarum unitas
    datur in cenaculo.
	the newness of heart
	and the unity of tongues
	is given to a few in the upper room.

IV.1 O quam felix, quam festiva
    dies in qua primitiva
    fundatur Ecclesia
	O how happy, how festive,
	the day on which the early
	church is founded;

IV.2 Vivæ sunt primitiæ
    nascentis Ecclesiæ,
    tria primum milia.
	The living first fruits
	of the church being born
	are the three thousand.[272]

V.1 Panes legis primitivi
    sub una sunt adoptivi
    fide duo populi.
	The loaves of the early law
	are two peoples adopted
	under one faith;

V.2 Se duobus interiecit
    sicque duos unum fecit
    lapis caput anguli.
	The Stone, the headstone of the angle,
	interposed himself between the two
	and thus made the two one.

VI.1 Utres novi, non vetusti
    sunt capaces novi musti;
    vasa paret vidua!
	The new wineskins not the old
	are filled with new must;
	let the widow prepare the jars.[273]

VI.2 Liquorem dat Elisæus,
    nobis sacrum rorem Deus,
    si corda sint congrua.
	Elisha gives a liquor,
	God gives to us a sacred dew,
	if our hearts are concordant.

VII.1 Non hoc musto vel liquore,
    non hoc digni sumus rore
    si discordes moribus.
	We are not fitting for the must
	or the liquor of the dew
	if we are discordant in customs;

VII.2 In obscuris vel divisis
    non potest hæc paraclisis
    habitare cordibus.
	This calling cannot dwell
	in darkened
	or divided hearts.

---

272. Acts 2:41.
273. 2 Kings 4:1–

VIII.1 Consolator alme, veni, linguas rege, corda leni, nihil fellis aut veneni sub tua præsentia.	Come, O Comforter most loving, rule our tongues, our hearts make gentle; nothing bitter or vindictive can before your presence stand.
VIII.2 Nil iucundum, nil amœnum, nil salubre, nil serenum, nihil dulce, nihil plenum, sine tua gratia.	Nothing joyful, nothing pleasing, nothing wholesome, nothing serene, nothing sweet, nothing complete, without your grace.
IX.1 Tu lumen es et unguentum, tu celeste condimentum aque ditans elementum virtute mysterii.	You are the light and the oil, you, heavenly seasoning, enriching the elements of water by the power of the mystery, made in a new creation.
IX.2 Nova facti creatura, te laudamus mente pura, gratiæ nunc, sed natura prius iræ filii.	Made again a new creation, pure in mind and heart, we praise you, children formerly, by nature, sealed in wrath, but now in grace.
X.1 Tu qui dator es et donum, tu qui cordis omne bonum, cor ad laudem redde pronum, nostræ linguæ formans sonum in tua præconia.	You are both the gift and giver, for the heart, sole cause of goodness; make our hearts disposed to praise you, form our tongues in speech and singing for your praise and majesty
X.2 Tu purga nos a peccatis, auctor ipse puritatis, et, in Christo renovatis, da perfectæ novitatis plena nobis gaudia.	You, the very source of mercy, cleanse us of our sins and failings, and to those reborn in Jesus grant your gift of perfect newness, full and everlasting joy. Amen.

The presentation of the sequence here shows that the structure of a sequence relates both to the poetic form and to the music of the piece. Victorine sequences fall into a traditional formal pattern, and, unlike hymns, are through-composed. This means that every successive stanza has its own music, rather than repeating music as is the case for hymns. The first stanza might well be a singleton, not part of a pair, but all the other stanzas are made up of paired versicles, so that the melody repeats twice in each case. The musical form of the original *Lux iucunda* is AABBCCDD, etc. It can be seen that the end rhymes of the individual half stanzas make the poetry line up with the repeating melodies. So, the first two stanzas of the sequence given here are actually two half stanzas. You can see that the music repeats, signified by the end rhyme of the two halves: *discipulos* and *modulos*. Stanzas 3 and 4 of the hymn as it stands in the *Liturgia Horarum* are half stanzas of two different stanzas in the original; thus, the two halves in the abridged hymn do not rhyme: *præsentia* (VIII.1 above) and *filii* (IX.2 above). Still, the redactor of the sequence in the *Liber Hymnarius* used the same melody for both, thereby keeping to the double versicle form of the Victorine sequence. The final two stanzas are indeed the two half stanzas of the final stanza of the original, and of course, they are set to the same music. Notice that the final words in each half stanza throughout the sequence have two-syllable rhyme; here in the last stanza it is *præconia* and *gaudia*.

The music itself is deeply symbolic. It is the same melody as the one originally used for the widespread twelfth-century sequence *Laudes crucis attolamus* ("Let us raise praises of the Cross"). This magnificent melody was set multiple times in the repertory at the Abbey of St. Victor, including the sequence *Lux iucunda*, thus binding the texts together, and making each chant a branch of the cosmic Cross. This melody was, in turn, used by the Dominicans as the setting for the thirteenth-century sequence *Lauda, Sion*, the sequence for Corpus Christi, usually attributed to St. Thomas Aquinas. For a community to sing this melody, with all the many poetic resonances associated with it, could have been a powerful liturgical experience. And now, when this abridged melody is sung, worshippers will still hear the first melody (AA) of the Cross sequence (and the Corpus Christi sequence), then another melody from the middle of the Cross sequence (BB), and finally, the concluding melody of the Cross sequence (CC). All of these melodies were sung with the original Victorine text of *Lux iucunda*, and the beginning and ending are the same in the *Liber Hymnarius* as in the original.

The Victorines were the greatest of the composers who used the subtle art of *contrafaction*, that is of resetting symbolically charged melodies to new texts, and writing those new texts with the original in mind to create more layers of meaning. When Adam of St. Victor wrote *Lux iucunda* he was surely thinking of the original poem set to this music, the text *Laudes crucis attollamus*. The final half stanza of that sequence is about the light that surrounded those gathered at the foot of the Cross and those contemporaries engaged in singing at the feast of the Holy Cross: "Consecrator of the Cross, hear those standing by for praise of the Cross, and after this life, take the servants of your Cross to the palace of true light." The light of the spirit that fills the Pentecost sequence is put in parallel with the light of Paradise, each unique, yet each the same.

Through a knowledge of original textual and musical context, the current sequence as it is prepared for singing in the Divine Office may offer many possible interpretations. These can change as the light changes and as the particular needs of individuals and communities themselves change, day to day, season to season, and year to year.

Beata nobis gaudia	57

ca. 10th c., but attributed to St. Hilary of Poitiers, 4th c.
8 8 8 8

Pentecost Sunday
Lauds

Beáta nobis gáudia anni redúxit órbita, cum Spíritus Paráclitus effúlsit in discípulos.	1. The running cycle of the year brings blessed joys to us once more: the day the Spirit Paraclete upon the Lord's disciples shone.
Ignis vibránte lúmine linguæ figúram détulit, verbis ut essent próflui et caritáte férvidi.	2. A fire with gleaming, flashing light, appeared as tongues and on them fell, that they might burn with charity and speak in words that flow with power.
Linguis loquúntur ómnium; turbæ pavent gentílium, musto madére députant, quos Spíritus repléverat.	3. All those the Spirit filled with gifts then spoke in every native tongue; bewildered crowds from foreign lands supposed them drunk with new-made wine.
Patráta sunt hæc mýstice Paschæ perácto témpore, sacro diérum número, quo lege fit remíssio.	4. These things were done in mystery as Paschaltide drew to a close: the sacred number of the days from which by law remission comes.
Te nunc, Deus piíssime, vultu precámur cérnuo: illápsa nobis cǽlitus largíre dona, O Spíritus.	5. Before your face, most loving God, we bow our heads and humbly pray: Bestow on us the Spirit's gifts, sent down this day from heaven above.
Dudum sacráta péctora tua replésti grátia; dimítte nunc peccámina et da quiéta témpora.	6. As once you filled those hallowed hearts with all the riches of your grace, so now forgive our sins and faults and grant us lives serene with peace.
Per te sciámus da Patrem, noscámus atque Filium, te utriúsque Spíritum credámus omni témpore. Amen.	7. Now through your presence may we know and love the Father and the Son, and you, the Spirit of them both, may we profess throughout all time. Amen.

Text found in *TDH*, no. 127; AH 51, no. 91; Walpole, no. 115; Milfull, 307. For the melody, found in medieval sources and still in use, see Stäblein, *Hymnes*, no. 64, p. 38 and 76, with notes on p. 518. Changes in *TDH*: stanza 4, 4: *legis* is a variant reading for *lege*; 5, 4, O *Spiritus* : the original text is *Spiritus* without elision; stanza 7 is taken from H 55, stanza 6.

COMMENTARY

Although the primary focus of this ICEL hymn commentary is an elucidation of the Latin texts, nevertheless, these texts are made to be sung. The relationship of text to music is one dimension of what we might call "liturgical language." An example of the close and multivalent relationships established by this liturgical language was pointed out in the commentary on H 56, the sequence *Lux iucunda*, used as a hymn for Pentecost. The original melodies for *Lux iucunda* and *Lauda Sion*, the sequence for Corput Christi, are the same. For those familiar with the genre, a connection between the texts is made as one sings. This could be a subtle art; the medieval had a name for it, *contrafactum*.

In the present hymn another aspect of the wider liturgical language is in evidence. Here, the ancient melody, still in use, fits the text and the spiritual sense of the feast to perfection. As indicated above, this hymn is assigned to Lauds on Pentecost. As such it is the first hymn of the day, properly speaking, because in the revised Liturgy of the Hours, the Office of Matins, which was traditionally said in the pre-dawn hours of the day, has been renamed and reassigned. It is now the Office of Readings, and it is no longer assigned to a fixed hour of the liturgical day. In a burst of exuberance and joy, the ancient melody for this hymn breaks forth with a rise of a fifth on the second syllable of line 1 from the tonic (the "home" tone) up to the dominant (the traditional recitation tone). It relishes this leap for joy and descends again only in the second half of the second line. At the beginning of line 3, one realizes that the melody is not just falling back to the tonic. It is actually falling down (line 3) in adoration and thanksgiving to the octave below the recitation tone. Then, in line 4, it rises again to settle back onto the tonic before beginning the next verse. The melody is a commentary that clothes the text in joy, confidence, adoration, and thanksgiving. Thus, it awakens our mind, heart, and sense to the unfathomable reality of the descent of the Holy Spirit recounted with simplicity and depth in the text of the hymn. Here is the first verse as it is found in the *Liber Hymnarius*:

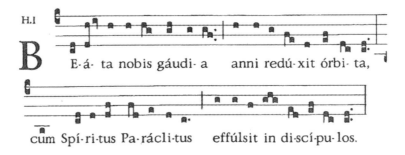

Beata nobis gaudia

The text of this fine hymn is divided into two parts. Stanzas 1–4 are in narrative mode, describing the coming of the Holy Spirit as told in Acts 2:1–13, stanzas 5–7 are a prayer for the gifts of the Holy Spirit. It has several points of contact with H 58 (*Iam Christus astra ascenderat*), though in H 57 there is usually rhyme between couplets, although not in every case, whereas H 58 uses rhyme only occasionally. The dating of H 57 is uncertain, and the ascription to St. Hilary seems to have no basis. It is preserved in manuscripts from the tenth or possibly ninth century.[274] Lentini says that it is in quantitative iambic dimeter, though there are irregularities; it moves between quantitative and accentual meter.

STANZA 1

In lines 1–2 the whole year is seen as a cycle, which comes to its blessed and joyful fulfillment at Pentecost. This idea of completion is there in Acts: "When the time for Pentecost was fulfilled."[275] This theme is taken up in stanza 4, 2, where again *Paschæ peracto tempore* indicates fulfillment of the period of Eastertide. The same notion is expressed more elaborately in stanza 2 of the original hymn from which H 58 is taken. It reads: *Sollemnis surgebat dies / quo mystico septemplici / orbis volutus septies / signat beata tempora* (literally: "The solemn day was rising on which the circuit, rolling seven times with sevenfold mystery, denotes the times of blessing").[276] In the early sixth-century hymn of Ennodius for Pentecost the feast *mysticam septemplici / ornat coronam munere*: "adorns the mystic crown with sevenfold gift", and *augmenta plenitudinis / opus ministrat divitis*: "provides the increase of rich fullness as its work."[277]

In line 3 the Holy Spirit is called *Paraclitus*. As mentioned in the commentary on H 1: 6, 3, this comes from the discourse of Christ at the Last Supper (Jn 14:16, 26; 15:26; 16:7). The Greek word παράκλητος means "advocate" or "intercessor," and has sometimes also been translated in these passages as "comforter" or "counselor." The native accent of the Greek word fell on the antepenult, but the penult had a long vowel (eta, η). When the term was brought into Latin, it seems to have yielded to Latin patterns of accentuation; the long eta (η) became a short vowel, either "e" or "i"; both spellings are found.[278]

Line 4 describes how the Spirit "shone forth" (*effulsit*) upon the disciples, appearing in the form of fire. In *discipulos* the antepenult has a short vowel, but as the stress accent falls on it, this carries the verse-beat, as again in stanza 4, 3 (*numero*).

---

274. See AH 51, 97–98; Milfull, 307–9.
275. *Cum complerentur dies Pentecostes* (Acts 2:1). In the original Greek text the verb used is συμπληροῦσθαι.
276. This stanza has been omitted from the *Liturgia Horarum*. See Walpole, no. 116; Walsh, no. 56.
277. Ennodius, Hymn 4: 27–30, *Opera Omnia*, 545.
278. Walpole points out that the hymn *Veni Creator Spiritus* (H 55) seems to be the only early hymn in which the original quantitative accentuation on the penult is observed in stanza 2, line 1: *qui Paraclitus diceris* (Walpole, no. 118, p. 375).

STANZA 2

This stanza follows Acts 2:3–4: "Then there appeared to them tongues as of fire, which parted and came to rest on each one of them. And they were all filled with the holy Spirit and began to speak in different tongues, as the Spirit enabled them to proclaim."[279] Both Walpole and Walsh take the subject of lines 1–2 as the Holy Spirit, and *ignis* as a genitive depending on *vibrante lumine*.[280] (Literally translated this would be: "the Spirit with the quivering light of fire brought down the form of a tongue"). But it seems better to take *ignis*, the emphatic opening word of the stanza, as subject. The word *detulit* usually means "conveyed," but may here have the sense of bringing down from above. Such a reading finds a parallel in H 58, stanza 3, 1–2: *De Patris ergo lumine / decorus ignis almus est*, which Walsh translates, "So downward from the Father's light / the beauteous fostering fire descends."

The effect of this second interpretation of *ignis* is twofold: it gives the disciples divine eloquence, but also makes them "burn with charity," which echoes Romans 5:5, "the love of God has been poured out into our hearts through the holy Spirit that has been given to us."[281] In Galatians 5:22 charity is the first in St. Paul's list of gifts of the Spirit. In H 55 (*Veni, creator Spiritus*): 2, 3, the Holy Spirit is called "the living spring, fire, charity" (*fons vivus, ignis, caritas*), and the hymn prays *accende lumen sensibus, / infunde amorem cordibus* (H 55: 4, 1–2).[282] Gregory the Great underlines the primacy of charity when he says that "one who does not have charity toward his neighbor should by no means take on the duty of preaching."[283]

STANZA 3

In Acts 2:5–12 all the Jews and proselytes from different parts of the world hear the disciples speaking in their own languages; they are astonished and perplexed: *multitudo ... confusa est ... stupebant ... omnes, et mirabantur....* So here in line 2 "the crowds of foreigners are afraid." Although many of them are Jews, still the word *gentilium* suggests that this is the beginning of the preaching of the gospel also to the Gentiles. The same thing is described in H 58, *Iam Christus astra ascenderat*, in stanza 6, 1–4 of the original hymn: *Ex omni gente cogitur / Græcus Latinus barbarus, / cunctisque admirantibus / linguis loquuntur omnium*: "From every race is gathered there / the Greek, Latin, barbarian, / and to the astonishment of all / they speak in universal tongues" (trans. Walsh).

---

279. *Et apparuerunt illis dispertitæ linguæ tamquam ignis, seditque super singulos eorum; et repleti sunt omnes Spiritu sancto, et cœperunt loqui variis linguis, prout Spiritus sanctus dabat eloqui illis* (Acts 2:3–4).
280. See Walpole, p. 366; Walsh, 189.
281. *caritas Dei diffusa est in cordibus nostris per Spiritum sanctum, qui datur est nobis*.
282. See the commentary on H 55: 2, 3. St. Thomas Aquinas discusses, in *ST* I q. 37, a.1, whether "Love" is a name proper to the Holy Spirit.
283. *qui caritatem erga alterum non habet, prædicationis officium suscipere nullatenus debet* (Gregory the Great, *Homiliæ in evangelia*, 1.17.1).

Lines 3–4 are from Acts: "But others scoffing said, 'They have had too much new wine.'"[284] *Mustum* is young, partly fermented wine (English "must"). The original Greek word γλεῦκος means "sweet, new wine." *Madere* (3, 3: "to be soaked") is used of heavy drinkers. Again, in H 58, *Iam Christus astra ascenderat*, stanza 7 of the original hymn expresses the reproach in a colorful and elaborate way: *Iudæa tunc incredula / vesano turba spiritu / ructare musti crapulam / alumnos Christi concrepat*: "The unbelieving crowd of Jews / being then possessed by lunacy / together shout: 'Christ's fosterlings / are belching, reeling with new wine!'" (trans. Walsh).

STANZA 4

In this stanza the period of seven weeks between Easter and Pentecost is seen as a sacred number of days, seven times seven, as noted in the more complex verses from *Iam Christus astra ascenderat*, quoted above under stanza 1. In line 1 of this stanza, *mystice* is an adverb, connoting both "in hidden mystery" and "sacramentally." The number seven was sacramental. As Walsh comments, "The Creation was completed in seven days, the gifts of the Spirit are seven, the theological and cardinal virtues combined are seven, and so forth."[285] In a similar way, in H 24: 1, 1, the forty days of Lent are said to have a mystic significance (*Ex more docti mystico*).

In lines 3–4 this period of fifty days of the Passover or Easter season (including Pentecost) is compared to the Jewish Jubilee of fifty years, which was "a year of remission" (see Nm 36:4, *annus remissionis*), when slaves were freed and lands reverted to their former owners, as prescribed in Leviticus 25:8–12. In the same way Christ's Resurrection and the sending of the Holy Spirit free us from enslavement to sin and death.[286] Ennodius, in the passage from his hymn for Pentecost quoted above, calls it a "sacred remission."[287] In line 4 of this stanza, *lege* is usually translated as "by law," but in this context one might perhaps alternatively take it as "from the Law," whose bondage is contrasted with the freedom of the Spirit. A variant reading in the manuscripts, *legis*, could also be taken in this way.

---

284. *Alii autem dicebant: Quia musto pleni sunt isti* (Acts 2:13).
285. Walsh, 451.
286. Walpole, p. 367, quotes a passage from St Ambrose, *De Apologia David et Theodosium Augustus*, 8.42, comparing the Jubilee Year to the celebration at Pentecost of remission from our debt to sin and freedom from every bond as we receive the grace of the Holy Spirit. *Hunc numerum* (50) *læti celebramus post Domini passionem, remisso culpæ totius debito, chirographoque vacuato ab omni nexu liberi; et suscipimus advenientem in nos gratiam Spiritus sancti: die Pentecostes*: "Let us celebrate this number (50) after the passion of the Lord, since the debt of all guilt has been remitted, the sentence has been annulled, and we are freed from every bond; and we receive the grace of the Holy Spirit coming in to us, on the day of Pentecost."
287. Ennodius, Hymn 4, line 25: *quot sacra nunc remissio*, Opera Omnia, 545.

STANZA 5

After the narrative section, the hymn changes to direct address to God. As the disciples were filled with his grace at Pentecost (6, 1–2), so we humbly pray that he will send the gifts of the Spirit flowing down upon us, and also grant forgiveness for sins and times of peace (stanzas 5–6). The Latin *cernuus* ("bowing forward," line 2) is often used in liturgical hymns in this context of prayer.[288] Here, we bow before God in humble prayer and gratitude for the flood of gifts that descends upon us. In line 3 *illapsa nobis cælitus* suggests that the gifts are like a stream flowing down from heaven. In line 4 the original reading is *Spiritus*, which is also read by Lentini. As such, it is a genitive dependent on *dona*. The variant O *Spiritus* would be a vocative, addressing the Holy Spirit.

STANZA 6

The double prayer that the Holy Spirit will forgive sins and also grant peace perhaps reflects John 20:19–23, where the risen Christ appears to the disciples, and after twice saying, "Peace be with you," he goes on to say, "Receive the Holy Spirit. Whose sins you forgive are forgiven them." Already in John 14:26–27 his promise to send the Holy Spirit is followed by the promise of his peace. Likewise in H 55: 5, 1–2, the Holy Spirit is asked to *Hostem repellas longius, / pacemque dones protinus*: "drive far from us our deadly foe / and swiftly grant us lasting peace."

STANZA 7

See the commentary on H 55, stanza 6, from which this is taken. It has been called "a quasi-doxology" (Walpole, p. 376). In John 16:14–15, Jesus says of the Holy Spirit: "He will glorify me, because he will take from what is mine and declare it to you. Everything that the Father has is mine; for this reason I told you that he will take from what is mine and declare it to you." Now we pray directly to the Holy Spirit: *Per te sciamus* ... : "Grant that through you we may know the Father and the Son ..."

---

288. See for example, the verse from the hymn *Pange lingua*, composed by St. Thomas Aquinas and used at Benediction of the Blessed Sacrament: *Tantum ergo sacramentum veneremur cernui*: "So great a sacrament, therefore, we venerate bowing down (in adoration)."

Iam Christus astra ascenderat	58
ca. 4th–5th c.	Pentecost Sunday
8 8 8 8 (LM)	Terce

Iam Christus astra ascénderat,	1. Once Christ ascended to the stars,
regréssus unde vénerat,	returning whence he first had come,
promíssa Patris múnera,	that from the Father he might send
Sanctum datúrus Spíritum,	the Holy Spirit, promised gift,
Cum hora felix tértia	2. Then suddenly with thunderous sound,
repénte mundo íntonat,	as his Apostles joined in prayer,
Apóstolis orántibus	that blest third hour told all the world
Deum venísse núntians.	the Spirit of our God had come.
De Patris ergo lúmine	3. Thus from the Father's light proceeds
decórus ignis almus est,	a fire of beauty, giving life,
qui fida Christi péctora	that fills with fervor for the Word
calóre verbi cómpleat.	all faithful hearts that live for Christ.
Descénde, Sancte Spíritus,	4. Come down, O Holy Spirit, come,
ac nostra corda altária	adorn our hearts with righteousness,
orna tibi virtútibus,	as altars given to your praise
tibíque templa dédica.	and temples hallowed for your use.
Per te sciámus da Patrem	5. Now through your presence may we know
noscámus atque Filium,	and love the Father and the Son,
te utriúsque Spíritum	and you, the Spirit of them both,
credámus omni témpore. Amen.	may we profess throughout all time. Amen.

Text found in *TDH*, no. 128; AH 51, no. 92; Walpole, no. 116. Changes in *TDH*: stanza 1, 3: variant readings are *promisso ... munere, promissum ... munere*; 2, 1: The *Liturgia Horarum* reads *felix* for *cunctis*; 2, 2: *mundo* for *mundus*; stanzas 2, 5–8, of original hymn are omitted.

COMMENTARY

This hymn, like *Beata nobis gaudia* (H 57), is for Pentecost. The first three stanzas of the hymn as it is found in the *Liturgia Horarum* are taken from a longer hymn (AH 51, no. 92) of eight stanzas, of which they form stanzas 1, 3, and 4. The other two stanzas of the hymn in current use are taken from elsewhere: stanza 4 appears to be newly composed, and stanza 5 is the doxology used for H 55 and 57. Stanzas 2 and 6 of the original hymn, omitted from the *Liturgia Horarum*, have been quoted in the commentary on H 57 (pp. 319, 320). In fact, these two hymns are closely related. It will be helpful to read the two commentaries together.

As it stands, hymn 58 describes the Ascension in stanza 1,[289] and the descent of the Holy Spirit on the Apostles in stanzas 2–3,[290] together with a prayer for the gifts of the Holy Spirit, stanza 4, enabling us to have knowledge of the three Persons of the Trinity, stanza 5. The rest of the original hymn corresponds to the narrative in Acts 2:4–36, ending with a stanza about St. Peter's first sermon. Again, there are a number of points of contact with H 57 (see the commentary on that hymn).

The only clear example of rhyme between couplets in the original hymn is in the first two stanzas. Several lines have a spondaic second foot (for example, in H 58: 2, 4, *Deum venisse*, where the first "e" of venisse is long).[291] The date of the composition of this hymn is uncertain, but if stanza 1, line 1 is influenced by the opening of the hymn *Iam Christus ascendit polum* of Ennodius (d. ca. 521), it would probably be no earlier than the sixth century. The whole hymn was sometimes sung in three sections at Pentecost. The reference to the third hour (2, 1) is taken from Acts 2:15, identifying the time of the events. Hence the hymn may be sung at Terce.

STANZA 1

In the present version this stanza forms a single unit with the stanza that follows: stanza 1, "Now Christ had ascended...." ends with a comma at the end of 1, 4, and is followed by stanza 2, 1 *Cum*, "when." In the original hymn, however, there is a stanza after line 4, inserted between stanzas 1 and 2. The missing stanza reads:

Sollemnis surgebat dies	The solemn day was rising
quo mystico septemplici	on which the circuit rolling
orbis volutus septies	seven times with sevenfold mystery
signat beata tempora	denotes the blessed times[292]

If this stanza were included, there would be a period at the end of the first stanza, and a comma at the end of this one, the second of the original. That is, the stanza before the stanza that begins with *cum* must end in a comma, whether the stanza is 1 or 2. This gives us some insight into the way in which editors shorten hymns considered too long for the Office for which they are intended. Something may be changed or lost, but if the cuts and edits are done well, the hymn fits seamlessly into the new place assigned to it in the Liturgy of the Hours. This particular hymn has endured many cuts and edits over the centuries.

With regard to the content of stanza 1, as mentioned earlier, line 1 resembles the first line of Ennodius's hymn *Iam Christus ascendit polum* (Walpole, no. 32,

---

289. Mk 16:19; Lk 24:51; Acts 1:9.
290. Acts 2:1–4,
291. In the original hymn, spondees are found on the second foot of lines 5, 9, 12, 19, 28, 29, etc. (Walpole, p. 368). Norberg comments that this ancient hymn and others from the same period appear to use as a deliberate technique ("une technique voulu"), a long third syllable in lines of iambic dimeter; these are at places in the line where classical meter required a short syllable. He calls iambic verses formed according to this technique "les vers lourds" or "heavy verses" (Norberg, *Les vers*, 22–24).
292. See the commentary on *Beata nobis gaudia*, H 57: 1, 1–2.

p. 160). The Latin *iam* is an emphatic opening that launches the singer into the present tense of liturgical time; we "relive" the interval of time between the Ascension and Pentecost as we wait for the coming of the Holy Spirit, and so we sing: "Now is the time when Christ had ascended ..." (stanza 1), "when suddenly ..." (stanza 2).[293]

Line 2, *regressus unde venerat*, is based on John 16:28: "I came from the Father and have come into the world. Now I am leaving the world and going back to the Father."[294] In line 3 the manuscripts have three variant readings, (1) *promissum ... munere*, (2) *promisso ... munere*, and (3) *promissa ... munera*. The first should mean "promised by the gift of the Father," in apposition to *Sanctum Spiritum*. The second is either "by the promised gift of the Father" or (less probably) literally, an ablative absolute, "the gift of the Father having been promised." With the third, the phrase "the promised gifts of the Father" is again in apposition to *Sanctum Spiritum*. In Luke 24:49 Christ says, *Et ego mitto promissum Patris mei in vos* "And I am sending the promise of my Father upon you"). The words *promissa ... munera* may have been read in order to avoid a spondaic second foot, though the plural seems less probable than the singular in this context. The word *promissum* is closest to Luke 24:49, but both Walpole and Walsh prefer *promisso ... munere*, as the more difficult reading (*lectio difficilior*), and so more likely to have been altered. Walsh translates the phrase "as promised by the Father's gift." Either reading seems possible. Christ's promise of the gift of the Holy Spirit from the Father is also mentioned several times in his discourse at the Last Supper (Jn 14:16–17, 26; 15:26; 16:7). The comma at the end of line 3 is not needed. In line 4 the future participle *daturus* means "in order to give."[295]

STANZA 2

The stanza begins with a direct reference to the scriptural text: "When the time of Pentecost was fulfilled, they were all in one place together. And suddenly there came from the sky a noise like a strong driving wind, and it filled the entire house in which they were."[296] In his speech at Pentecost St. Peter says that the Apostles cannot be drunk, because it is only the third hour of the day.[297]

Lentini took the subject of *intonat* as *hora tertia*, and read *mundo*, which is found in a few manuscripts instead of *mundus*. It seems preferable to read *mundus* and take this as the subject, with *hora tertia* in the ablative ("at the third hour"). He also replaced the original reading *cunctis* in line 1 with *felix*, although this has no manuscript authority. Walpole translates line 1 as "The world thunders

---

293. See the comments on H 48, which also uses to great effect an emphatic *iam*.
294. *Exivi a Patre et veni in mundum: iterum relinquo mundum et vado ad Patrem.*
295. Lentini opted for the third possibility: "*promissa ... munera .... quasi certamente è la lezione orig.; promissa munera è apposizione di Spiritum*": "as almost certainly the original reading; *promissa munera* is in apposition to *Spiritum*." Lentini also added the comma at the end of line 3, presumably to clarify the apposition of plural gifts to the singular Spirit.
296. *Et cum complerentur dies Pentecostes, erant omnes pariter in eodem loco: et factus est repente de cælo sonus, tamquam advenientis spiritus vehementis, et replevit totam domum ubi erant sedentes* (Acts 2:1–2).
297. *cum sit hora diei tertia* (Acts 2:15).

round them all"²⁹⁸ and suggests that there may be a reminiscence of Wisdom 1:7, "For the spirit of the Lord has filled the world, and that which contains all things has understanding of the voice."²⁹⁹ Compare also perhaps Psalm 18 (19): "Their sound has gone forth to all the earth, and their words to the ends of the world."³⁰⁰ In line 3, there may be an echo of the passage from Acts, referring to the eleven Apostles: "All these devoted themselves with one accord to prayer."³⁰¹ For line 4, Walpole (l 12, p. 369) suggests a reminiscence of Psalm 50 (49):3, *Deus manifeste veniet*: "God will manifestly come."

STANZA 3

Lines 1–2 beautifully describe the life-giving power of the Holy Spirit coming down as fire from the Father's light.³⁰² As the Letter of St. James says "Every best gift, and every perfect gift is from above, coming down from the Father of lights."³⁰³ In the *Confessions* (13.25) St. Augustine calls the tongues of fire of the Holy Spirit *ignes sancti, ignes decori*. The epithet *almus* ("fostering" or "kindly") was often applied to gods in classical Latin. For its application to God in these hymns see the discussion of *Conditor alme siderum* (H 1: 1, 1).³⁰⁴ Walpole mentions this use of *almo Spiritu* in his commentary on *Magnum salutis gaudium*, a hymn for Palm Sunday.³⁰⁵

In line 3 *fida Christi* means "trusting in Christ," with the genitive, as in Virgil, *Æneid* 12. 659, *regina, tui fidissima*. In line 4 *compleat* is in the subjunctive, indicating purpose ("so as to fill … "). The whole stanza resembles H 57, stanza 2: *Ignis vibrante lumine / linguæ figuram detulit, / verbis ut essent proflui / et caritate fervidi*: "A fire with gleaming, flashing light, / appeared as tongues and on them fell, / that they might burn with charity / and speak in words that flow with power." The phrase *calore verbi* can be translated either as "with fervor for the Word" or "with the burning heat of the word," that is, the word of God that they are to preach, as in *Beata nobis gaudia* (H 57: 2, 3). Lines 1–3 refer to all three Persons of the Trinity: Father, Holy Spirit as fire, and Christ.

STANZA 4

In this stanza, the hymn leaves behind the story of the events of Pentecost, to introduce a prayer for the descent of the Holy Spirit.³⁰⁶ This prayer alludes to the

---

298. Walpole, p. 369.

299. *Quoniam spiritus Domini replevit orbem terrarum, et hoc quod continet omnia scientiam habet vocis*. The English version above is a literal rendering of this.

300. *In omnem terram exivit sonus eorum, et in fines orbis terrarum verba eorum* (Ps 18 [19]:4).

301. *Hi omnes erant perseverantes unanimiter in oratione* (Acts 1:14).

302. As Walpole says, one can either take *decorus* and *almus* as predicates after *est*, "Beauteous and gracious is the fire proceeding from the Father's light," or else *ignis* is part of the predicate, "It is a beauteous and gracious fire …" (Walpole, notes on lines 13-14, p. 369).

303. *Omne datum optimum, et omne donum perfectum deorsum est, descendens a Patre luminum* (Jas 1:17).

304. See also *Candor æterne, Deitatis alme* (H 8: 2. 1); *Audi benigne Conditor* (H 22:2, 1).

305. See Walpole, no. 104, p. 338.

306. The hymn as a whole is presented in *HIBR*, no. 114, pp. 110–11. Included there are stanzas 1–6 of the original hymn followed by a standard doxology. By the time that *TDH* had been published (in 1984), the

famous hymn of Bianco da Siena, *Discendi, Amor Santo* (in Littledale's version, "Come Down, O Love Divine").

In 1 Corinthians, St. Paul reminds his readers that their bodies are "the temple of the Holy Spirit."[307] So here by extension the Spirit is asked (in literal translation) to "adorn our hearts as altars for you with your virtues [i.e., the gifts of the Spirit], and make them temples dedicated to you." The image of the heart as an altar for God is beautifully expressed in the opening stanza of Charles Wesley's hymn:

> O Thou who camest from above
> The fire celestial to impart,
> Kindle a flame of sacred love
> On the mean altar of my heart.

STANZA 5

See the commentaries on *Veni, creator Spiritus* (H 55), stanza 6, and *Beata nobis gaudia* (H 57), stanza 7.

---

hymn had undergone a radical change in function and form. In 1968, it was assigned to the Office of Readings on Pentecost. In 1984, it was designated for Terce. Stanzas 2, 5, and 6 had been removed and a new stanza composed, stanza 4 of the hymn as it stands in the *Liturgia Horarum*. Lentini notes that "One must sincerely admit that this hymn, although supported by a venerable tradition, seems to be destitute of almost all lyricism, and nothing more than a metrical version of the events that are narrated in Acts" (*HIBR*, p. 111). The current stanza 4 appears to have been composed by Lentini or a member of his *cœtus* as a lyrical petition added to the shortened version of the hymn appropriate for Terce.

307. *membra vestra sunt templum Spiritus sancti* (1 Cor 6:19).

BIBLIOGRAPHY

PRIMARY SOURCES

Ambrose of Milan. *Hymnes*. Edited by Jacques Fontaine, J.-L. Charlet, S. Deléani, Y.-M. Duval, A. Goulon, M.-H. Jullien, J. de Montgolfier, G. Nauroy, M. Perrin, and H. Savon. Paris: Les Éditions du Cerf, 1992.

———. *De apologia David ad Theodosium Augustus. De Helia et ieiunio. De Ioseph. De Isaac*. Edited by Charles Schenkl. CSEL, 32.2. Vienna: Hölder-Pichler-Tempsky, 1897.

———. *De fide*. Edited by Otto Faller. CSEL 78. Vienna: Hölder-Pichler-Tempsky, 1962.

———. *De institutione virginis et S. Mariæ virginitate perpetua ad Eusebium*. Edited by F. Gori. Biblioteca Ambrosiana 14/2. Turnhout: Brepols, 1989.

———. *De obitu Theodosii*. Edited by Otto Faller. CSEL 73. Vienna: Hölder-Pichler-Tempsky, 1955.

———. *De officiis*. Edited by M. Testard. CCSL 15. Turnhout: Brepols, 2001.

———. *De officiis*. Edited and translated by Ivor J. Davidson. 2 vols. Oxford: Oxford University Press, 2002.

———. *De paradiso*. Edited by Charles Schenkl. CSEL, 32.1. Vienna: Hölder-Pichler-Tempsky, 1896.

———. *De sacramentis*. Edited by Otto Faller. CSEL 73. Vienna: Hölder-Pichler-Tempsky, 1955.

———. *De Spiritu Sancto libri tres*. Edited by Otto Faller. CSEL 79. Vienna: Hölder-Pichler-Tempsky, 1964.

———. *Epistolarum liber decimus*. Edited by Michaela Zelzer. CSEL 82.3. Vienna: Hölder-Pichler-Tempsky, 1982

———. *Explanatio psalmorum XII*. Edited by Michael Petschenig and Michaela Zelzer. CSEL 64. Vienna: Österreichischen Akademie der Wissenschaften, 1999.

———. *Expositio evangelii secundum Lucam. Fragmenta in Esaiam*. Edited by M. Adriaen and P. A. Ballerini. CCSL 14. Turnhout: Brepols, 1957.

———. *Expositio psalmi CXVIII*. In *S. Ambrosii Opera*, edited by Michael Petschenig and Michaela Zelzer, Editio altera supplementis, vol. 4. CSEL 62. Vienna: Österreichischen Akademie der Wissenschaften, 1999.

———. *Traité sur l'évangile de s. Luc*. Edited and translated by Gabriel Tissot. Sources Chrétiennes 45 and 52. Paris: Les Éditions du Cerf, 1958.

Ambrosiaster. *Ambrosiaster's Commentary on the Pauline Epistles: Romans*. Edited and translated by Theodore S. de Bruyn. Writings from the Greco-Roman World 41. Atlanta: Society of Biblical Literature Press, 2017.

———. *Commentarius in epistulam ad Romanos*. Edited by Heinrich Joseph Vogels. CSEL, 81.1. Vienna: Hölder-Pichler-Tempsky, 1966.

Analecta Hymnica medii aevii. Edited by Clemens Blume, Guido Maria Dreves, and Henry M. Bannister. 55 vols. Leipzig: O. R. Reisland, 1886–1922.

Antiqua homilia in sancto et magno Sabbato. Patrologiae cursus completus, series Graeca 43. Paris: Jacques-Paul Migne, 439–64.

Apponius. *In Canticum Canticorum expositio*. Edited by B. de Vregille and L. Neyrand. CCSL 19. Turnhout: Brepols, 1986.

Athanasius. *Contra gentes and De Incarnatione*. Ed. R. W. Thomson. Oxford Early Christian Studies. Oxford: Clarendon Press, 1971.

———. *Lettres à Serapion sur la divinité du Saint Esprit*. Edited by Jean Lebon. Sources Chrétiennes 15. Paris: Éditions du Cerf, 1947.

Augustine of Hippo. *Confessionum libri XIII*. Edited by L. Verheijen. CCSL 27. Turnhout: Brepols, 1981.

———. *The Confessions*. Edited by John E. Rotelle, OSA. Translated by Maria Boulding, OSB. Hyde Park, NY: New City Press, 2012.

———. *Contra Iulianum opus imperfectum*. Edited by Ernst Kalinka and Michaela Zelzer. CSEL, 85.1–2. Vienna: Hölder-Pichler-Tempsky, 1974.

———. *De catechizandis rudibus*. Edited by William Yorke Fausset. 2nd ed. London: Metheuen & Co., 1912.

———. *De civitate Dei*. Edited by B. Dombart and A. Kalb. CCSL 47–48. Turnhout: Brepols, 1955.

———. *De doctrina Christiana*. Edited and translated by R. P. H. Green. Oxford Early Christian Texts. Oxford: Clarendon Press, 1995.

———. *De musica*. Edited by Martin Jacobsson. CSEL 102. Berlin: De Gruyter, 2017.

———. *De natura et gratia*. Edited by Karl Franz Urba and Josef Zycha. CSEL 60. Vienna: Hölder-Pichler-Tempsky, 1913.

———. *Enarrationes in psalmos*. Edited by E. Dekkers and J. Fraipont. CCSL 38–40. Turnhout: Brepols, 1956.

———. *Exposition of the Psalms*. Edited by John E. Rotelle. Translated by Maria Boulding. 6 vols. Hyde Park, NY: New City Press, 2000.

———. *In Iohannis evangelium tractatus*. Edited by R. Willems. CCSL 36. Turnhout: Brepols, 1954.

———. *Scriptorum contra Donatistas*. Edited by Michael Petschenig. CSEL 51–53. Vienna: Hölder-Pichler-Tempsky, 1908.

———. *Sermones ad populum*. Edited by Jacques-Paul Migne. Patrologiae cursus completus, series Latina 38–39. Paris: Jacques-Paul Migne, 1865.

———. *Sermones ad populum. Testi e studi pubblicati a cura dell' Ordine eremitano di s. Agostino nel XV centenario dalla morte del santo dottore*. Edited by Gabriel Morin. Rome: Tipografia poliglotta vaticana, 1930.

———. *Sermons*. Edited by John E. Rotelle and translated by Edmund Hill. The Works of Saint Augustine: A Translation for the 21st Century, 3.1–10. Hyde Park, NY: New City Press, 1990.

Basil of Caesarea. *Homélies sur l'Hexæméron*. Edited by Stanislas Giet. Sources Chrétiennes 26. Paris: Les Éditions du Cerf, 1968.

———. *Sur le Saint-Esprit*. Edited by Banoît Pruche. Sources Chrétiennes 17. Paris: Les Éditions du Cerf, 1968.

———. *Sur l'origine de l'homme: Homélies X–XI de l'Hexaéméron*. Edited by Alexis Smets and Michel van Esbroeck. Sources Chrétiennes 160. Paris: Les Éditions du Cerf, 1970.

Bede the Venerable. *Bede's Latin Poetry*. Edited by Michael Lapidge. Oxford Medieval Texts. Oxford: Clarendon Press, 2019.

———. *De arte metrica*. Edited by Ch. W. Jones, Calvin B. Kendall, M. H. King, and Fr. Lipp. CCSL 123A. Turnhout: Brepols, 1975.

———. *Libri II: De arte metrica et de schematibus et tropis: The Art of Poetry and Rhetoric*. Edited and translated by Calvin B. Kendall. Bibliotheca Germanica Series Nova 2. Saarbrücken: AQ-Verlag, 1991.

———. *Opera exegetica*. Edited by M. L. W. Laistner, D. Hurst, Roger Gryson, J. E. Hudson, and Ch. W. Jones. CCSL 119A–121A. Turnhout: Brepols, 1962.

———. *Opera homiletica. Opera rhythmica*. Edited by D. Hurst and J. Fraipont. CCSL 122. Turnhout: Brepols, 1955.

Benedict of Nursia. *The Rule of St. Benedict*. Translated by Timothy Fry. Collegeville, MN: Liturgical Press, 1981.

Bernard of Clairvaux. *Sermones in adventu Domini*. Edited by Jean Leclercq and Henri Rochais. Sancti Bernardi Opera 4. Rome: Editiones Cistercienses, 1966.

Biblia Sacra Vulgata. Editio quinta. Edited by Robert Weber and Roger Gryson. Stuttgart: Deutsche Bibelgesellschaft, 2007.

Blume, Clemens, ed. *Unsere Liturgischen Lieder: Das Hymnar der Altchristlichen Kirche aus dem Urtext ins Deutsche Umgedichtet, Psychologisch und Geschichtlich Erklärt*. Regensburg: Verlag Friedrich Pustet, 1932.

Boethius, Anicius Manlius Severinus. *Fundamentals of Music: Translation of "De institutione musica"*. Edited by Claude V. Palisca. Translated by Calvin M. Bower. New Haven, CT: Yale University Press, 1989.

———. *The Theological Tractates and The Consolation of Philosophy*. Translated by H. F. Stewart, E. K. Rand, and S. J. Tester. Loeb Classical Library. Cambridge, MA: Harvard University Press, 1973.

Britt, Matthew, ed. *The Hymns of the Breviary and Missal*. New York: Benziger Brothers, 1922.

Bulst, Walther, ed. *Hymni Latini antiquissimi LXXV, psalmi III*. Heidelberg: F. H. Kerle, 1956.

Caesarius of Arles. *Œuvres monastiques 1: Œuvres pour les moniales*. Edited by Joël Courreau and Adalbert de Vogüé. Sources Chrétiennes 345. Paris: Les Éditions du Cerf, 1988.

Cassian, John. *Conferences*. Edited by Étienne Pichery. Sources Chrétiennes 42bis, 54, 64. Paris: Les Éditions du Cerf, 1959.

Chromatius of Aquileia. *Opera*. Edited by Raymond Étaix and J. Lemarié. CCSL 9A. Turnhout: Brepols, 1974.

Chrysologus, Peter. *Sermonum collectio a Felice Episcopo parata: Sermonibus extravagantibus adiectis*. Edited by A. Olivar. CCSL 24–24B. Turnhout: Brepols, 1975.

Cicero, Marcus Tullius. *De oratore I–III*. Edited by Augustus S. Wilkins. Classic Commentaries on Latin and Greek Texts. London: Bristol Classical Press, 2002.

———. *Letters to Friends*. Translated by D. R. Shackleton Bailey. Loeb Classical Library. Cambridge, MA: Harvard University Press, 2001.

———. *On the Nature of the Gods. Academics*. Translated by H. Rackham. Loeb Classical Library. Cambridge, MA: Harvard University Press, 1933.

———. *On the Republic. On the Laws*. Translated by Clinton W. Keyes. Loeb Classical Library. Cambridge, MA: Harvard University Press, 1928.

Connelly, Joseph, ed. *The Hymns of the Roman Liturgy*. Westminster, MD: Newman Press, 1957.

Crashaw, Richard. *The Poems English, Latin, and Greek of Richard Crashaw*. Edited by L. C. Martin. Oxford: Clarendon Press, 1927.

Cyprian of Carthage. *Epistolae*. Edited by G. F. Diercks. CCSL 3B–3D. Turnhout: Brepols, 1994.

———. *Opera*. CCSL 3–3A. Turnhout: Brepols, 1972.

Cyril of Jerusalem. *The Catechetical Lectures*. Translated by R. W. Church. A Library of Fathers of the Holy Catholic Church 2. Oxford: John Henry Parker, 1838.

Daniel, Herman Adalbert, ed. *Thesaurus hymnologicus sive hymnorum, canticorum, sequentiarum circa annum MD usitatarum collectio amplissima*. Leipzig: J. T. Loeschke, 1855.

Dionysius the Carthusian. *Enarrationes piæ ac eruditæ in quatuor evangelistas: Hoc est Matthæum, Marcum, Lucam, et Ioannem*. D. Dionysii Cartusiani Opera Omnia 11. Montenegro: Typis Cartusiæ Sanctæ Mariæ de Pratis, 1900.

———. *Hymnorum aliquot veterum ecclesiasticorum pia nec minus erudita enarratio*. Opera Minora 3. D. Dionysii Cartusiani Opera Omnia 35. Montenegro: Typis Cartusiæ Sanctæ Mariæ de Pratis, 1908.

Dreves, Guido Maria, and Clemens Blume, eds. *Ein Jahrtausand Lateinischen Hymnendichtung: Eine Blütenlese aus den Analecta Hjmnica mit literarhistorischen Erläuterungen*. 2 vols. Leipzig: O. R. Reisland, 1909.

Ennodius, Magnus Felix. *Opera Omnia*. CSEL 6. Edited by W. Hartel. Vienna: C. Geroldi, 1882.

Fortunatus, Venantius. *Opera Poetica*. Edited by Friedrich Leo. Monumenta Germaniae Historica 4.1. Berlin: Weidmann, 1881.

———. *Poèmes*. Edited and translated by Marc Reydellet. Collection Des Universités de France: Série Latine 315, 346, 374. Paris: Les Belled Lettres, 1994.

———. *Poems*. Edited and translated by Michael Roberts. Dumbarton Oaks Medieval Library 46. Cambridge, MA: Harvard University Press, 2017.

Fulbert of Chartres. *The Letters and Poems of Fulbert of Chartres*. Edited and translated by Behrends Frederick. Oxford Medieval Texts. Oxford: Clarendon Press, 1976.

Fulgentius of Ruspe. *De fide ad Petrum*. Edited by J. Fraipont. CCSL 91A. Turnhout: Brepols, 1968.

———. *Epistulae*. Edited by J. Fraipont. CCSL 91–91A. Turnhout: Brepols, 1968.

———. *Liber ad Scarilam de Incarnatione Filii Dei*. Edited by J. Fraipont. CCSL 91. Turnhout: Brepols, 1968.

Furley, W., and J. M. Bremer, eds. *Greek Hymns: Selected Cult Songs from the Archaic to the Hellenistic Period*. Translated by W. Furley and J. M. Bremer. Tübingen: Mohr Siebeck, 2001.

Gregory of Nazianzus. *Oration 45: The Second Oration on Easter*. Edited by Philip Schaff and Henry Wace. Translated by Charles Gordon Browne and James Edward Swallow. Nicene and Post-Nicene Fathers: Second Series 8. New York: The Christian Literature Company, 1894.

Gregory the Great. *Homélies sur l'évangile*. Edited by Raymond Étaix, Bruno Judic, Charles Morel, and Georges Blanc. Sources Chrétiennes 485, 522. Paris: Les Éditions du Cerf, 2005.

———. *Homiliae in evangelia*. Edited by Raymond Étaix. CCSL 141. Turnhout: Brepols, 1999.

———. *Homiliae in Hiezechielem prophetam*. Edited by M. Adriaen. CCSL 142. Turnhout: Brepols, 1971.

———. *Moralia in Iob*. Edited by M. Adriaen. CCSL 143–143B. Turnhout: Brepols, 1979.

Hesiod. *Theogony*. Edited by Martin L. West. Oxford: Clarendon Press, 1966.

Hilary of Poitiers. *Traité des mystères*. Edited by Jean-Paul Brisson. Sources Chrétiennes 19bis. Paris: Les Éditions du Cerf, 1967.

Hymnodia hispanica. Edited by José Castro Sánchez. CCSL 167. Turnhout: Brepols, 2011.

Himnodia hispánica. Edited by José Castro Sánchez and Emilio García Ruiz. Corpus Christianorum in Translation 19. Turnhout: Brepols, 2015.

Hippolytus of Rome. *On the Apostolic Tradition*. Edited and translated by Alistair Stewart-Sykes. 2nd ed. Popular Patristics 54. Crestwood, NY: St. Vladimir's Seminary Press, 2020.

Horace. *Horace's Odes and Carmen Sæculare*. Translated by Simon Preece. Newcastle upon Tyne: Cambridge Scholars Publishing, 2021.

———. *Satires. Epistles. The Art of Poetry*. Translated by H. Rushton Fairclough. Loeb Classical Library. Cambridge, MA: Harvard University Press, 1926.

Ignatius of Antioch. "Letters." Edited by Michael Holmes. Apostolic Fathers: Greek Texts and English Translations, 3rd ed. Grand Rapids, MI: Baker Academic, 2007.

Isidore of Seville. *Liber differentiatum II*. Edited by M. A. Andrés Sanz. CCSL 111A. Turnhout: Brepols, 2006.

———. *Synonyma*. Edited by J. Elfassi. CCSL 111B. Turnhout: Brepols, 2010.

Jerome. *Commentarii in prophetas minores (Sophoniam, Naum, Iohel, Osee, …)*. Edited by Marc Adriaen, Roger Gryson, Sincero Mantelli, et al. CCSL 76–76Abis. Turnhout: Brepols, 2023.

———. *Commentariorum in Hiezechielem libri XIV*. Edited by Fr. Glorie. CCSL 75. Turnhout: Brepols, 1964.

———. *Commentary on Ezekiel*. Translated by Thomas P. Scheck. Ancient Christian Writers 71. New York: The Newman Press, 2017.

———. *Epistolae*. Edited by I. Hilberg and M. Kamptner. Editio altera supplementis. CSEL 54–56.2. Vienna: De Gruyter, 1996.

John of Damascus. *Expositio fidei orthodoxae*. Edited by Jacques-Paul Migne, Patrologiae cursus completus, series Graeca 94. Paris: Jacques-Paul Migne, 1864.

Josephus. *Jewish Antiquities*. Translated by H. St. John Thackeray, Ralph Marcus,

Allen Wikgren, and Louis H. Feldman. Loeb Classical Library. Cambridge, MA: Harvard University Press, 1930.

Julius Caesar. *The Gallic War Books V–VI*. Edited by Jennifer Gerrish. Liverpool: Liverpool University Press, 2024.

Justin Martyr. *The Apologies of Justin Martyr*. Edited by A. W. F. Blunt. Campbridge: Campbridge University Press, 1911.

Lactantius. "Divinae institutiones." Edited by Samuel Brandt. CSEL 19.1–19.2. Vienna: Hölder-Pichler-Tempsky, 1890.

Lentini, Anselmo. *Hymni instaurandi breviarii Romani*. Vatican City: Libreria Editrice Vaticano, 1968.

———. *Supplex Gloria: Testo, versione e commento degli inni del breviario*. Milan: Vita e pensiero, 1969.

———. *Te Decet Hymnus : L'Innario della "Liturgia Horarum."* Vatican City: Typis Polyglottis Vaticanis, 1984.

Leo the Great. *Sermones*. Edited by A. Chavasse. 2 vols. CCSL 138–138A. Turnhout: Brepols, 1973.

Leo XIII. *Leonis XIII P. M. Carmina, inscriptiones, numismata*. Edited by Joseph Bach. Cologne: J. P. Bachem, 1903.

———. *Poems, Charades, Inscriptions of Leo XIII Including the Revised Compositions of His Early Life*. Edited and translated by Hugh T. Henry. New York: American Ecclesiastical Review, 1902.

Livy. *Titi Livi ab urbe condita libri I–V*. Edited by Robert Maxwell Ogilvie. Oxford Classical Texts. Oxford: Clarendon Press, 1974.

Lombard, Peter. *Petri Lombardi sententiae in IV libris distinctae*. 3rd ed. Spicilegium Bonaventurianum. Grottaferrata: Quaracchi, 1971.

Lucan. *The Civil War*. Translated by J. D. Duff. Loeb Classical Library. Cambridge, MA: Harvard University Press, 1928. Martial. *Epigrams, Volume I: Spectacles, Books 1–5*. Edited and translated by D. R. Shackleton Bailey. Loeb Classical Library 94. Cambridge, MA: Harvard University Press, 1993.

Martial. *Epigrams, Volume I: Spectacles, Books 1–5*. Edited and translated by D. R. Shackleton Bailey. Loeb Classical Library 94. Cambridge, MA: Harvard University Press, 1993.

Maximus of Turin. *Collectio sermonum antiqua*. Edited by A. Mutzenbecher. CCSL 23. Turnhout: Brepols, 1962.

Milfull, Igne B., ed. *The Hymns of the Anglo-Saxon Church: A Study and Edition of the "Durham Hymnal."* Cambridge Studies in Anglo-Saxon England 17. Cambridge: Cambridge University Press, 1996.

Mone, Franz Josef, ed. *Lateinische Hymnen des Mittelalters*. Freiburg im Breisgau: Herdersche Verlagshandlung, 1853.

Neale, John Mason. *Collected Hymns, Sequences and Carols of John Mason Neale*. Edited by Mary Sackville Lawson. London: Hodder and Stoughton, 1914.

———. *Hymni ecclesiæ e breviariis quibusdam et missalibus Gallicanis, Germanis, Hispanis. Lusitanis desumpti*. Oxford: John Henry Parker, 1851.

Nestle, Eberhard, and Kurt Aland, eds. *Novum Testamentum Graece*. 28th ed. Stuttgart: Deutsche Bibelgesellschaft, 2012.

Newman, John Henry. *Meditations and Devotions*. London: Baronius Press, 2010.

———. *Parochial and Plain Sermons*. San Francisco: Ignatius Press, 1987.

Notker Balbulus. *The Liber Ymnorum of Notker Balbulus*. Edited and translated by Calvin M. Bower. London: Henry Bradshaw Society, 2016.

O'Daly, Gerard, ed. *Days Linked by Song: Prudentius' Cathemerinon*. Oxford: Oxford University Press, 2012.

Origen of Alexandria. *Commentaire sur saint Jean*. Edited by Cécile Blanc. Sources Chrétiennes 120 bis, 157, 222, 290, 385. Paris: Les Éditions du Cerf, 1992–2006.

———. *De oratione liber*. Edited by Jacques-Paul Migne. Patrologiae cursus completus, series Graeca 11. Paris: Jacques-Paul Migne, 1857.

———. *Homélies sur l'Exode*. Edited by Marcel Borret. Sources Chrétiennes 321. Paris: Les Éditions du Cerf, 2006.

Ovid. *The Fasti of Ovid*. Edited by G. H. Hallam. London: MacMillan, 1909.

———. *Metamorphoses*. Edited by R. J. Tarrant. Oxford Classical Texts. Oxford: Oxford University Press, 2004.

Paul the Deacon. *Carmina. Poetaeae Latini Aevi Carolini*. Edited by Ernst Dümmler. Monumenta Germaniae Historica. Berlin: Weidmann, 1881.

Paulinus of Aquileia. *L'Oeuvre poetique de Paulin d'Aquilée: Édition critique avec introduction et commentaire*. Edited by Dag Norberg. Uppsala: Almquist & Wiksell, 1979.

Paulinus of Nola. *Epistulae*. Edited by Wilhelm Hartel and Margit Kamptner. Editio altera supplementis. CCSL 29. Vienna: Österreichischen Akademie der Wissenschaften, 1999.

———. *Paulini Nolani Carmina*. Edited by Franz Dolveck. CCSL 21. Turnhout: Brepols Publishers, 2015.

———. *The Poems of St. Paulinus of Nola*. Edited and translated by Peter G. Walsh. Ancient Christian Writers 40. New York: Newman Press, 1975.

Peter Damian. *L'opera poetica di S. Pier Damiani; Descrizione dei manoscritti, edizione del testo, esame prosodico-metrico, discussione delle questioni d'autenticità*. Edited by Margareta Lokranz. Stockholm: Almquist & Wiksell, 1964.

———. *The Letters of Peter Damian*. Translated by Owen Blum and Irven M. Resnick. The Fathers of the Church: Medieval Continuations 1–6. Washington, DC: The Catholic University of America Press, 1989.

Philastrius of Brescia. *Diversarum hereseon liber*. Edited by Friedrich Marx. CSEL 38. Vienna: Hölder-Pichler-Tempsky, 1898.

Pimont, S.-G. *Les hymnes du bréviaire Romain: Études critiques, littéraires et mystiques*. Paris: Librairie Poussielgue Frères, 1874.

Plato. *Symposium*. In *The Collected Dialogues of Plato*, edited by Edith Hamilton and Huntington Cairns. Princeton, NJ: Princeton University Press, 1971.

Pliny the Elder. *Natural History*. Translated by H. Rackham, W. H. S. Jones, A. C. Andrews, and D. E. Eichholz. Loeb Classical Library. Cambridge, MA: Harvard University Press, 1938.

Plotinus. *Enneads*. Translated by A. H. Armstrong. Loeb Classical Library. Cambridge, MA: Harvard University Press, 1980.

Prudentius, Aurelius. *Against Symmachus 2. Crowns of Martyrdom. Scenes From History. Epilogue*. Translated by H. J. Thomson. Loeb Classical Library. Cambridge, MA: Harvard University Press, 1953.

———. *Carmina*. Edited by M. P. Cunningham. CCSL 126. Turnhout: Brepols, 1966.

———. *Preface. Liber Cathermerinon. Apotheosis. Hamartagenia.. Psychomachia. Contra orationem Symmachi 1*. Translated by H. J. Thomson. Loeb Classical Library. Cambridge, MA: Harvard University Press, 1949.

Quintilian (Marcus Fabius Quintilianus). *Institutio oratoria (The Orator's Education)*, vols. 1–4. Edited and translated by Donald A. Russell. Loeb Classical Library. Cambridge, MA: Harvard University Press, 2002.

Raymond of Capua. *The Life of St. Catherine of Siena*. Translated by George Lamb. Charlotte, NC: TAN Books, 2011.

Richardson, Nicholas, ed. *Prudentius' Hymns for Hours and Seasons*. New York: Routledge, 2016.

Rufinus of Aquileia. Tyrannius Rufinus. *Commentarius in symbolum Apostolorum seu exposition symboli*. Edited by Manlio Simonetti. CCSL 20. Turnhout: Brepols, 1961.

Sedulius. *Sedulius, the Paschal Song and Hymns*. Translated by Carl P. E. Springer. Writings from the Greco-Roman World 35. Atlanta: Society of Biblical Literature Press, 2013.

Seneca. "De Clementia." Translated by John W. Basore. Loeb Classical Library. Cambridge, MA: Harvard University Press, 1928.

Stäblein, Bruno, ed. *Hymnen: Die mittelalterlichen Hymnenmelodien des Abendlandes*. Monumenta monodica medii aevi 1. Kasel: Bärenreiter, 1956.

Stock, Alex, ed. *Lateinische Hymnen*. Berlin: Verlag der Weltreligionen, 2012.

Tertullian of Carthage. *De Corona. De resurrection mortuorum. Opera montanistica*. Edited by A. Gerlo, A. Kroymann, R. Willems, J. H. Waszink, et al. CCSL 2. Turnhout: Brepols, 1954.

Thomas Aquinas. *Catena aurea in quatuor evangelia*. Cura Angelici Guarienti. Roma: Marietti, 1953.

———. *Catena aurea: Commentary on the Four Gospels Collected out of the Works of the Fathers*. Translated by John Henry Newman. Oxford and London: John Henry Parker, 1841.

———. *Summa Contra Gentiles*. Leonine Edition. Rome: Typis Riccardi Garroni, 1918.

———. *Summa Theologiae*. Leonine Edition. Rome: Typographia poliglotta, S. C. de Propaganda Fide, 1888.

Tria Sunt: An Art of Poetry and Prose. Edited and translated by Martin Camargo. Dumbarton Oaks Medieval Library 53. Cambridge, MA: Harvard University Press, 2019.

Virgil. *Aeneid: Books 7–12. Appendix Vergiliana*. Translated by H. Rushton Fairclough and G. P. Goold. Loeb Classical Library. Cambridge, MA: Harvard University Press, 1918.

———. *Eclogues. Georgics. Aeneid: Books 1–6*. Translated by H. Rushton Fairclough and G. P. Goold. Revised. Loeb Classical Library. Cambridge, MA: Harvard University Press, 1916.

———. *Ecologues*. Edited by Robert Coleman. Cambridge Greek and Latin Classics. Cambridge: Cambridge University Press, 1977.

———. *Opera: Bucolica. Georgica. Aeneid*. Edited by Roger A. B. Mynors. Oxford Classical Texts. Oxford: Oxford University Press, 1969.

Voragine, Jacobus de. *Legenda aurea, Goldene Legende*. Edited and translated by Bruno W. Häptli. Freiburg: Verlag Herder, 2022.

Walpole, A. S., ed. *Early Latin Hymns*. London: Cambridge University Press, 1922.

Walsh, Peter G., ed. *One Hundred Latin Hymns: Ambrose to Aquinas.* Dumbarton Oaks Medieval Library 18. Cambridge, MA: Harvard University Press, 2012.

William of Tocco. *Ystoria sancti Thome de Aquino de Guillaume de Tocco (1323).* Edited by Clare le Brun-Gouanvic. Studies and Texts 127. Toronto: Pontifical Institute of Medieval Studies, 1997.

LITURGICAL TEXTS

Breviarium Gothicum secundum Regulam beatissimi Isidori, Archiepiscopi Hispalensis, jussu Cardinalis Francisci Ximenii de Cisneros prius editutm. Nunc opera Excelentissimi D. Francisci Antonii Lorenzana, Sanctæ Ecclesiæ Toltanæ Hispaniarum Primati Archepiscopi recognium ad usum sacella Mozarabum.. Toledo: Jachimum Ibarra, 1775.

Collection of Masses of the Blessed Virgin Mary. Approved for use in the dioceses of the United States of America. Collegeville, MN: Liturgical Press, 2012.

General Instruction on the Liturgy of the Hours. ICEL Translation, 2021, forthcoming.

Liber Hymnarius cum Invitatoriis et Aliquibus Responsoriis. Editio emendata et aucta. Sablé-sur-Sarthe: Solesmes, 2019.

Liturgia Horarum: Iuxta Ritum Romanum. Editio typica altera. Vatican City: Libreria Editrice Vaticana, 1985.

Missale Romanum. Ex decreto Sacrosancti Concilii Tridentini restitutum, summorum pontificum cura recognitum : Editio typica 1962. Civitate Vaticana: Libreria editrice Vaticana, 2007.

Missale Romanum. Ex decreto Sacrosancti Oecumenici Concilii Vaticni II instauratum. Auctoritate Pauli Pp. VI Promulgatum, Ioannis Pauli Pp. II cura recognitum. Editio typica tertia. Civitate Vaticana: Libreria Editrice Vaticana, 2002.

Mohlberg, Leo Cunibert, Leo Eizenhöfer, and Peter Siffrin, eds. *Liber Sacramentorum Romanae Ecclesiae Ordinis Anni Circuli (Cod. Vat. Reg. Lat. 316/Paris Bibl. Nat. 7193, 41/56) (Sacramentarium Gelasianum).* Rerum Ecclesiasticarum Documenta, Series Maior 4. Rome: Casa Editrice Herder, 1960.

———, eds. *Sacramentarium Veronense.* 2nd ed. Rerum Ecclesiasticarum Documenta, Series Maior 1. Rome: Casa Editrice Herder, 1966.

The Divine Office Hymnal. The United States Conference of Bishops. Chicago: GIA Publications, 2022.

The Roman Missal. Renewed by decree of the Most Holy Second Ecumenical Council of the Vatican. Promulgated by authority of Pope Paul VI and revised at the direction of Pope John Paul II. English translation according to the third typical edition for use in the dioceses of the United States of America. Totowa, NJ: Catholic Book Publishing, 2011.

DOCUMENTS OF THE MAGISTERIUM

Benedict XVI. "Spe Salvi." Libreria Editrice Vaticana, November 30, 2007. https://www.vatican.va/content/benedict-xvi/en/encyclicals/documents/hf_ben-xvi_enc_20071130_spe-salvi.html.

Catechism of the Catholic Church. Libreria Editrice Vaticana, 2018. Published by United States Catholic Conference of Bishops, 2019.

Catechism of the Council of Trent for Parish Priests: the Roman Catechism. Issued by Order of Pope St. Pius V. English translation and notes by John A. McHugh, OP, and Charles J. Callan, OP. Fitzwilliam, NH: Loreto Publications, 2023.

Christus Dominus: Decree Concerning the Pastoral Office of Bishops in the Church. Proclaimed by His Holiness, Pope Paul VI on October 28, 1965. https://www.vatican.va/archive/hist_councils/ii_vatican_council/documents/vat-ii_decree_19651028_christus-dominus_en.html

Dei Verbum: Dogmatic Constitution on Divine Revelation. Solemnly Promulgated by His Holiness Pope Paul Vi on November 18, 1965. https://www.vatican.va/archive/hist_councils/ii_vatican_council/documents/vat-ii_const_19651118_dei-verbum_en.html

Denzinger, Heinrich, and Peter Hünermann, eds. *Enchiridion Symbolorum Definitionum et Declarationum de Rebus Fidei et Morum.* Translated by Peter Hünermann. 43rd ed. San Francisco: Ignatius Press, 2012.

John Paul II. "Letter of the Holy Father Pope John Paul II to All the Priests of the Church on the Occasion of Holy Thursday, 1998." In *Letters to My Brother Priests: Holy Thursday (1979–2001)*, edited by James P. Socias. Chicago: Midwest Theological Forum, 2001.

Leo XIII. "Quamquam Pluries." Encyclical of Pope Leo XIII on Devotion to St. Joseph. August 15, 1889. https://www.vatican.va/content/leo-xiii/en/encyclicals/documents/hf_l-xiii_enc_15081889_quamquam-pluries.html

Paul VI. *Paenitemini*: Apostolic Constitution of the Supreme Pontiff Paul VI on Fast and Abstinence. February 17, 1966.. Libreria Editrice Vaticana, 1966. https://www.vatican.va/content/paul-vi/en/apost_constitutions/documents/hf_p-vi_apc_19660217_paenitemini.html

———. *Presbyterorum Ordinis* : Decree on the Ministry and Life of Priests. Promulgated by His Holiness, Pope Paul VI on December 7, 1965. https://www.vatican.va/archive/hist_councils/ii_vatican_council/documents/vat-ii_decree_19651207_presbyterorum-ordinis_en.html

Sacrosanctum Concilium: Constitutio de Sacra Liturgia. Libreria Editrice Vaticana, December 4, 1963. https://www.vatican.va/archive/hist_councils/ii_vatican_council/documents/vat-ii_const_19631204_sacrosanctum-concilium_lt.html

SECONDARY SOURCES

Albin, Célestin. *La poésie du bréviaire: Essai d'histoire critique et littéraire: Les hymnes.* Lyons: Vitte, 1899

Allen, J. H., and J. B. Greenough. *New Latin Grammar.* Edited by Anne Mahoney. Newburyport, MA: Focus Publishing, n.d.

Bibliography

Allen, W. Sidney. *Accent and Rhythm: Prosodic Features of Latin and Greek; A Study in Theory and Reconstruction*. Cambridge Studies in Linguistics 12. Cambridge: Cambridge University Press, 1973.

———. *Vox Latina: The Pronunciation of Classical Latin*. 2nd ed. Cambridge: Cambridge University Press, 1989.

Assendelft, Marion M. van. *Sol ecce surgit igneus: A Commentary on the Morning and Evening Hymns of Prudentius (Cathemerinon 1, 2, 5 and 6)*. Groningen: Bouma's Boekhuis, 1976.

Austin, Roland G. "Virgil and the Sybil." *The Classical Quarterly* 21, no. 2 (1927): 100–105.

———. "Virgilian Assonance." *The Classical Quarterly* 23, no. 1 (1929): 46–55.

Ayres, Lewis. *Nicaea and Its Legacy: An Approach to Fourth-Century Trinitarian Theology*. Oxford: Oxford University Press, 2004.

Barthold, Claudia. "Papae Poetae—Päpste Als Dichter." In *Wahrheit und Schönheit. Christliche Literatur als Einklang von Glaube und Kunst*, edited by Heinz-Lothar Barth. Mühlheim: Carthusianus Verlag, 2011.

Bastiaensen, A. A. A. R. "Prudentius in Recent Literary Criticism." In *Early Christian Poetry: A Collection of Essays*, edited by Jan den Boeft and A. Hilhorst. Leiden: Brill, 1993.

Batiffol, Pierre. *History of the Roman Breviary*. Translated by M. Y. Baylay. 3rd ed. London: Longmans, Green & Co., 1912.

Baumgartner, Alexander. *Die Lateinische und Griechische Literatur der Christlichen Völker*. Freiburg im Breisgau: Verlag Herder, 1903.

Baynes, Norman. "Constantine the Great and the Christian Church." *Proceedings of the British Academy* 15 (1931).

Benini, Marco. *Liturgical Hermeneutics of Sacred Scripture*. Translated by Brian McNeil. Verbum Domini. Washington, DC: The Catholic University of America Press, 2023.

Berardino, Angelo de, ed. *Encyclopedia of the Early Church*. Oxford: Oxford University Press, 1992.

Berger, Teresa. "Veni Creator Spiritus: The Elusive Real Presence of the Spirit in the Catholic Tradition." In *Spirit in Worship-Worship in the Spirit*, edited by Teresa Berger and Bryan Spinks. Collegeville, MN: Liturgical Press, 2009.

Billett, Jesse D. *The Divine Office in Anglo-Saxon England, 597–c.1000*. Henry Bradshaw Society Subsidia 7. London: Henry Bradshaw Society, 2014.

Bischoff, Bernhard. *Katalog der Festländischen Handschriften des Neunten Jahrhunderts (mit Ausnahme der Wisigotischen)*. Edited by Brigit Ebersperger. Wiesbaden: Harrassowitz Verlag, 1998.

Blaise, Albert. *Dictionnaire latin-français des auteurs Chrétiens*. Turnhout: Brepols, 1954.

———. *Lexicon latinitatis medii aevi—Le vocabulaire latin des principaux thèmes liturgiques*. 2 vols. Corpus Christianorum Scholars Version. Turnhout: Brepols, 2014.

Blowers, Paul M., and Peter W. Martens, eds. *The Oxford Handbook of Early Christian Biblical Interpretation*. Oxford Handbooks. Oxford: Oxford University Press, 2019.

Boeft, Jan den. "Aeterne Rerum Conditor: Ambrose's Poem about 'Time.'" In *Jerusalem, Alexandria, Rome: Studies in Ancient Cultural Interaction in Honour of A. Hilhorst*, edited by Florentino García Martínez and Gerard P. Luttikhuizen. Leiden: Brill, 2003.

Boodts, Shari, Mon Torfs, and Gert Partoens. "Augustine's Sermon 169: A Systematic Treatise on Phil. 3:3–16, Exegetical Context, Date, and Critical Edition." *Augustiniana* 59, no. 1/2 (2009): 11–44.

Bradshaw, Paul F. *Daily Prayer in the Early Church: A Study of the Origin and Early Development of the Divine Office*. Eugene, OR: Wipf & Stock, 2008.

Bradshaw, Paul F., and Maxwell E. Johnson. *The Origins of Feasts, Fasts, and Seasons in Early Christianity*. Collegeville, MN: Liturgical Press, 2011.

Bullough, Donald A. *Alcuin: Achievement and Reputation; Being Part of the Ford Lectures Delivered in Oxford in Hilary Term 1980*. Leiden: Brill, 2004.

Bulst, Walther. "Bedae Opera Rhythmica?" *Zeitschrift für deutsches Altertum und deutsche Literatur* 89, no. 2 (1959): 83–91.

Caldwell, John. "Rhythm and Meter." In *The Cambridge History of Medieval Music*. Edited by Mark Everist and Thomas Forrest Kelly. Cambridge: Cambridge University Press, 2018.

Cantalamessa, Raniero. *Come, Creator Spirit: Meditations on the Veni Creator*. Translated by Denis Barrett and Marlene Barrett. Collegeville, MN: Liturgical Press, 2003.

Carruthers, Mary. *The Craft of Thought: Meditation, Rhetoric, and the Making of Images; 400–1200*. Cambridge: Cambridge University Press, 1998.

Charlet, Jean-Louis. *La création poétique dans le Cathemerinon de Prudence*. Paris: Les Belles Lettres, 1982.

Chevalier, Ulysse. *Repertorium hymnologicum : Catalogue des chants, hymnes, proses, sequences, tropes en usage dans l'église latine depuis les origines jusqu'a nos jours*. Louvain: Imprimerie Lefever, 1892.

Christensen, Thomas. "Music Theory." In *The Cambridge History of Medieval Music*. Edited by Mark Everist and Thomas Forrest Kelly. Cambridge: Cambridge University Press, 2018.

Christian, Lynda G. *Theatrum Mundi: The History of an Idea*. New York: Garland, 1987.

Colish, Marcia L. "Why the Portiana? Reflections on the Milanese Basilica Crisis of 386." *Journal of Early Christianity* 10, no. 3 (2001): 361–72.

Combe, Pierre. *The Restoration of Gregorian Chant: Solesmes and the Vatican Edition*. Translated by Theodore Marier and William Skinner. Washington, DC: The Catholic University of America Press, 2003.

Connell, Martin F. "Descensus Christi ad inferos: Christ's Descent to the Dead." *Theological Studies* 62, no. 2 (2001): 262–82.

Crocker, Richard L. "Medieval Chant." In *The New Oxford History of Music: The Early Middle Ages to 1300*, 2nd ed. Oxford: Oxford University Press, 1990.

———. "Monophony." In *The New Oxford History of Music: The Early Middle Ages to 1300*, 2nd ed. Oxford: Oxford University Press, 1990.

Dane, Joseph A. *The Long and the Short of It: A Practical Guide to European Versification Systems*. Notre Dame, IN: University of Notre Dame Press, 2010.

Diederich, Mary Dorothea. *Vergil in the Works of St. Ambrose*. Washington, DC: The Catholic University of America Press, 1931.

Dumitrescu, Theodor. *The Early Tudor Court and International Musical Relations*. Burlington, VT: Ashgate Publishing, 2007.

Dunkle, Brian P. *Enchantment and Creed in the Hymns of Ambrose of Milan*. Oxford Early Christian Studies. Oxford: Oxford University Press, 2016.

———. "Here We Go Again: Temporal Recurrence in the Early Ambrosiana." *Journal of Orthodox Christian Studies*. Forthcoming (n.d.).

———. "'Made Worthy of the Holy Spirit': A Hymn of Ambrose in Augustine's Nature and Grace." *Augustinian Studies* 50, no. 1 (2019): 1–12.

———. "Mystagogy and Creed in Ambrose's *Iam Surgit Hora Tertia*." In *Papers Presented at the Sixteenth International Conference on Patristic Studies Held in Oxford 2011*. Edited by Markus Vinzent. Studia Patristica 69. Leuven: Peeters (2013): 25–34.

———. "Te Deum." In *Brill Encyclopedia of Early Christianity*. Edited by David G. Hunter, Paul J. J. van Geest, and Bert Jan Lietaert Peerbolte. Leiden: Brill Academic, 2024.

Emery, Gilles, and Matthew Levering, eds. *The Oxford Handbook of the Trinity*. Oxford: Oxford University Press, 2011.

Evenepoel, Willy. *Studies in the Christian Latin Poetry of Late Antiquity*. Leuven: Peeters, 2016.

Fagerberg, David W. *Theologica Prima: What Is Liturgical Theology?* 3rd ed. Chicago: Hillenbrand Books, 2012.

Fassler, Margot E. "Accent, Meter, and Rhythm in Medieval Treatises '*De Rithmis*'." *The Journal of Musicology* 5, no. 2 (1987): 164–90.

———. *Gothic Song: Victorine Sequences and Augustinian Reform in Twelfth-Century Paris*. 2nd ed. Notre Dame, IN: University of Notre Dame Press, 2011.

———. *Music in the Medieval West*. Edited by Walter Frisch. Western Music in Context. New York: Norton, 2014.

Fassler, Margot E., and Rebecca A. Baltzer, eds. *The Divine Office in the Latin Middle Ages: Methodology and Source Studies, Regional Developments, Hagiography*. Oxford: Oxford University Press, 2000.

Fischer, Balthasar. "Pange Lingua." In *Lexikon für Theologie und Kirche*, edited by Walter Kasper, 3rd ed. Freiburg im Breisgau: Verlag Herder, 1998.

Fontaine, Jacques. "Quelques vicissitudes des carmina triumphalia dans la littérature latine du haut moyen âge." *Beihefte der Francia* 16, no. 2 (1989): 349–63.

Fraenkel, Eduard. "Das Geschlecht von Dies." *Glotta* 8, no. 1/2 (1916): 24–68.

Franz, Ansgar. *Tageslauf und Heilsgeschichte: Untersuchungen zum literarischen Text und liturgischen Kontext der Tagzeitenhymnen des Ambrosius von Mailand*. St. Ottilien: EOS Verlag, 1994.

Ganz, Daniel. "Le *De laude Dei* d'Alcuin." *Annales de Bretagne et des Pays de l'Ouest* 111, no. 3 (2004): 387–91.

George, Judith W. *Venantius Fortunatus: A Latin Poet in Merovingian Gaul*. Oxford: Clarendon Press, 1992.

Gildersleeve, Basil L., and Gonzalez Lodge. *Gildersleeve's Latin Grammar*. 3rd ed. London: MacMillan and Co., 1903.

Gneuss, Helmut. *Hymnar Und Hymnen Im Englischen Mittelalter*. Tübingen: Max Niemeyer Verlag, 1968.

———. "Latin Hymns in Medieval England: The State of Scholarship and Some Tasks for Future Research." In *Chaucer and Middle English: Studies in Honor of Rossell Hope Robbins*. Edited by Beryl Rowland. London: George Allen & Unwin, 1974.

Gnilka, Christian, ed. *Kultur und Conversion*. Chrēsis: Die Methode der Kirchenväter im Umgang mit der antiken Kultur 2. Basel: Schwabe Verlag: 1993.

Gratwick, A. S. "The Origins of Roman Drama." In *The Cambridge History of Classical Literature* 2. Edited by P. E. Easterling, Bernard M. W. Knox, E. J. Kenney, and W. V. Clausen. Cambridge: Cambridge University Press, 1982.

Green, Roger P. H. *Latin Epics of the New Testament: Juvencus, Sedulius, Arator*. Oxford: Oxford University Press, 2007.

Guéranger, Prosper. *The Liturgical Year*. Translated by Laurence Shepherd. Fitzwilliam, NH: Loreto Publications, 2000.

Hack, Bernard, ed. *I mosaici della Patriarcale Basilica di Santa Maria Maggiore in Roma*. Offenburg: Reiff, 1967.

Hala, Patrick. *Louanges Matinale: Hymnes pour l'Office des laudes*. Solesmes: Les Éditions de Solesmes, 2018.

———. *Louanges Vespérales: Commentaire de hymnes de la Liturgia Horarum Vêpres, Tierce, Sexte, None et Complies*. Collection Liturgie. Solesmes: Les Éditions de Solesmes, 2008.

Hanson, Kristin. "Quantitative Meter in English: The Lesson of Sir Philip Sydney." *English Language & Linguistics* 5, no. 1 (May 2001): 41–91.

Hardie, Philip. *Classicism and Christianity in Late Antique Latin Poetry*. Berkeley: University of California Press, 2019.

Heid, Stefan. "Kreuz." In *Reallexikon für Antike und Christentum*. Edited by Georg Schöllgen. Stuttgart: Hiersemann, 2006.

Hesbert, René-Jean, ed. *Corpus aAntiphonalium Officii*. Rome: Herder, 1963.

Hildebrand, Stephen M. *The Trinitarian Theology of Basil of Caesarea: A Synthesis of Greek Thought and Biblical Truth*. Washington, DC: The Catholic University of America Press, 2009.

Hiley, David. *Western Plainchant: A Handbook*. Oxford: Clarendon Press, 1993.

Hillhorst, A., and Jan den Boeft. *Early Christian Poetry: A Collection of Essays*. Leiden: Brill, 1993.

Huglo, Michel. "Relations musicales, entre Byzance et l'Occident." In *Proceedings of the XIIIth International Congress of Byzantine Studies. Oxford 5–10 September, 1966*. Edited by Joan Meryn Hussey, 267–80. London: Oxford University Press, 1967.

Hugueny, Étienne. "L'adoro te est il de saint Thomas?" *Archivum Fratrum Praedicatorum* 4 (1934): 221–25.

Hultgard, Anders, and Stig Norin, eds. *Le jour de Dieu—Der Tag Gottes: 5. Symposium Strasbourg, Tubingen, Uppsala. 11–13 September 2006 in Uppsala*. Wissenschaftliche Untersuchugen zum Neuen Testament 245. Tübingen: Mohr Siebeck, 2009.

Hunter, David G., Paul J. J. van Geest, and Bert Jan Lietaert Peerbolte, eds. *Brill Encyclopedia of Early Christianity*. Leiden: Brill, 2024.

Jeauneau, Edouard. *Rethinking the School of Chartres*. Translated by Claude Paul Desmarais. Ontario: University of Toronto Press, 2009.

Julian, John, ed. *A Dictionary of Hymnology*. 2nd ed. New York: Charles Scribner's Sons, 1907.

Jullien, Marie-Hélène. "Les hymnes dans le milieu Alcuinien." In *De Tertullien aux Mozarabes* 2. Edited by L. Holtz, C. Fredouille, and Marie-Hélène Jullien, 171–82. Paris: Institut d'Études Augustiniennes, 1992.

Katsos, Isidoros C. *The Metaphysics of Light in the Hexameral Literature: From Philo of Alexandria to Gregory of Nyssa*. Oxford Early Christian Studies. Oxford: Oxford University Press, 2023.

Kennedy, Kathleen E., and Anna H. de Bakker. "The Charterhouse Antiphonal Fragment." *Manuscript Studies* 7, no. 1 (Spring 2022): 175–86.

Kokolakēs, Minōs. *The Dramatic Simile of Life*. Athens: Ph. Boukouri, 1960.

Lardelli, Francesco. *Dux Salutis: Prudenzio, Cathemerinon 9–10: Gli inni della redenzione*. Sapheneia 17. Bern: Peter Lang, 2014.

Latham, R. E., ed. *Revised Medieval Latin Word-List from British and Irish Sources*. Oxford: Oxford University Press, 1980.

Lausberg, Heinrich. *Der Hymnus: Ave Maris Stella*. Abhandlungen Der Rheinisch-Westfälischen Akademie Der Wissenschaften 61. Opladen: Westdeutscher Verlag, 1976.

———. *Der Hymnus: Veni Creator Spiritus*. Abhandlungen Der Rheinisch-Westfälischen Akademie Der Wissenschaften 64. Opladen: Westdeutscher Verlag, 1979.

———. *Handbook of Literary Rhetoric: A Foundation for Literary Study*. Edited by David E. Orton and R. Dean Anderson. Translated by Matthew T. Bliss and Jansen Annemiek. Leiden: Brill, 1998.

Lewis, Charlton T., and Charles Short. *A Latin Dictionary*. Oxford: Clarendon Press, 1879.

Lienhard, Joseph T. "Basil of Caesarea, Marcellus of Ancyra, and 'Sabellius.'" *Church History* 58, no. 2 (June 1989): 157–67.

Löhr, Aemiliana. *Abend und Morgen ein Tag: Die Hymnen der Herrentage und Wochentage im Stundengebet*. Regensburg: Verlag Friedrich Pustet, 1955.

———. *Il y eut un soir il y eut un matin: La prière des hymnes et des heurs*. Translated by Mère Catherine de Sienne. Paris: Éditions Saint-Paul, 1966.

———. "Light at Eventide." Translated by Chrysogonus Waddell. *Liturgy* 15, no. 3 (October 1981), 53–54.

Louth, Andrew. "Late Patristic Developments on the Trinity in the East." In *The Oxford Handbook of the Trinity*, edited by Gilles Emery and Matthew Levering. Oxford: Oxford University Press, 2011.

———, ed. *The Oxford Dictionary of the Christian Church*. 4th ed. Oxford: Oxford University Press, 2022.

Lyons, Stuart, ed. *Horace's Odes and the Mystery of Do-Re-Mi*. Oxford: Aris & Phillips, 2007.

Malmede, Hans H. *Die Lichtsymbolik im Neuen Testament*. Wiesbaden: O. Harrassowitz, 1986.

Marin, M. "La presenza di orazio nei Padri Latini: Ambrogio, Girolamo, Agostino; Note Introductive." In *Atti del Convegno Nazionale di Studi su Orazio: Torino, 13-14-15 Aprile 1992*, edited by Renato Uglione. Turin: Assessorato alla cultura, 1993.

Marmion, Columba. *Christ in His Mysteries*. Translated by Alan Bancroft. Bethesda, MD: Zacchaeus Press, 2008.

Marshall, William. *O Come Emmanuel: A Devotional Study of the Advent Antiphons*. Dublin: Columba Press, 1993.

Masciadri, Virgilio. "Pange Lingua: Überlegungen zu Text und Kontext." *Millennium* 3 (2006): 185–223.

Mayer, Cornelius Petrus. "Confessio, Confiteri." In *Augustinus-Lexikon*. Mainz: Schwabe AG, 1986–.

McNamee, M. B. "Further Symbolism in the Portinari Altarpiece." *The Art Bulletin* 45, no. 2 (June 1963): 142–43.

Menge, Hermann. *Lehrbuch der lateinischen Syntax und Semantik*. Edited by Thorsten

Burkhard and Markus Schauer. Revised. Darmstadt: Wissenschaftliche Buchgesellschaft, 2000.

Merback, Mitchell B. *The Thief, the Cross and the Wheel: Pain and the Spectacle of Punishment in Medieval and Renaissance Europe*. Chicago: The University of Chicago Press, 1999.

Messenger, Ruth Ellis. *Ethical Teachings in the Hymns of Medieval England: With Special Reference to the Seven Deadly Sins and the Seven Principal Virtues*. New York: Columbia University Press, 1930.

———. "Mozarabic Hymns in Relation to Contemporary Culture in Spain." *Traditio* 4 (1946): 149–77.

———. *The Medieval Latin Hymn*. Washington, DC: Capital Press, 1953.

———. *The Mozarabic Hymnal*. Transactions and Proceedings of the American Philological Association 75 (1944): 103–26.

Mitsis, Philip, and Ioannis Ziogas, eds. *Wordplay and Powerplay in Latin Poetry*. Trends in Classics—Supplementary volumes 36. Berlin: De Gruyter, 2016.

Mohrmann, Christine. *Liturgical Latin: Its Origins and Character; Three Lectures*. Washington, DC: The Catholic University of America Press, 1957.

Morin, Germain. *The Ideal of the Monastic Life Found in the Apostolic Age*. Translated by C. Gunning. New York: Benziger Brothers, 1914.

Murray, Paul. *Aquinas at Prayer: The Bible, Mysticism and Poetry*. London: Bloomsbury, 2013.

Mursell, Gordon. *The Bonds of Love: St. Peter Damian's Theology of the Spiritual Life*. Washington, DC: The Catholic University of America Press, 2021.

Nicolau, Mathieu G. "Les deux sources de la versification latine accentuelle." *Archivum Latinitatis Medii Aevi* 9 (1934): 55–87.

Nisbet, R. G. M., and Margaret Hubbard. *A Commentary on Horace: Odes, Book I*. 2nd ed. Oxford: Clarendon Press, 1989.

Norberg, Dag. "A quelle époque a-t-on cessé de parler latin en Gaule?" *Annales. Histoire, Sciences Sociales* 21, no. 2 (1966): 346–56.

———. *An Introduction to the Study of Medieval Latin Versification*. Translated by Grant C. Roti and Jacqueline de La Chapelle Skubly. Washington, DC: The Catholic University of America Press, 2004.

———. *Au seuil du moyen âge: Études linguistiques, métriques et littéraires publiées par ses cllègues et élèves à l'occasion de son 65e anniversaire*. Padua: Editrice Antenore, 1974.

———. *L'accentuation des mots dans le vers latin du moyen âge*. Stockholm: Almquist & Wiksell, 1985.

———. *La poésie latine rhythmique du haut moyen âge*. Stockholm: Almquist & Wiksell, 1954.

———. "La récitation du vers Latin," <u>Neuphilologische Mitteilungen</u> 66, no. 4 (1965): 496–508.

———. "Le *Pange lingua* de Fortunat pour la Croix," *Maison Dieu* 173 (1988), 71–79.

———. *Les vers latins iambiques et trochaïques au moyen âge et leurs répliques rythmiques*. Stockholm: Almquist & Wiksell, 1988.

———. *Manuel pratique de latin médiéval*. Paris: Picard, 1968.

Norden, Eduard. *Agnostos Theos: Untersuchungen zur Formengeschichte religiöser Rede*. 4th ed. Stuttgart: Verlagsgesellschaft, 1956.

Oxford Latin Dictionary. Edited by P. G. W. Glare and Roger A. B. Mynors. 2nd ed. Oxford: Clarendon Press, 2012.

Petraglio, Renzo. "Le interpolazioni cristiane del salterio greco." *Augustinianum* 28, no. 1 (1988): 89–109.

Prieur, Jean Marc. *Das Kreuz in der Christlichen Literatur der Antike*. Tradition Christiana 14. Bern: Peter Lang, 2006.

———. "'Le Seigneur a régné depuis le bois': L'adjonction Chrétienne au psaume 95, 10 et son interprétation." In *Rois et reines de La Bible au miroir des pères*. Cahiers de Biblia Patristica 6, 127–40. Strasbourg: Marc Bloch University, 1999.

Raby, F. J. E. *A History of Christian-Latin Poetry: From the Beginnings to the Close of the Middle Ages*. 2nd ed. Oxford: Clarendon Press, 1953.

Rahner, Hugo. *Symbole der Kirche: Die Ekklesiologie der Väter*. Salzburg: Otto Müller Verlag, 1964.

Raven, D. S. *Latin Metre*. Bristol: Bristol Classical Press, 1965.

Reijners, Gerard Quirinus. *The Terminology of the Holy Cross in Early Christian Literature as Based upon Old Testament Typology*. Nijmegen: Dekker & Van de Vegt N.V., 1965.

Reynal, Daniel de. *Théologie de La Liturgie Des Heures*. Paris: Beauchesne, 1977.

Rigg, A. G. *A History of Anglo-Latin Literature, 1066–1422*. Cambridge: Cambridge University Press, 1992.

Rylaarsdam, David. *John Chrysostom on Divine Pedagogy: The Coherence of His Theology and Preaching*. Oxford Early Christian Studies. Oxford: Oxford University Press, 2014.

Sarah, Robert. *The Day Is Now Far Spent*. San Francisco: Ignatius Press, 2019.

Sedgwick, W. B. "The Origin of Rhyme." *Revue Bénédictine* 36 (1924): 330–46.

Siecienski, A. Edward. *The Filioque: History of a Doctrinal Controversy*. Oxford: Oxford University Press, 2010.

Southern, R. W. *The Making of the Middle Ages*. New Haven, CT: Yale University Press, 1953.

Springer, Carl P. E. "Ambrose's *Veni Redemptor Gentium*: The Aesthetics of Antiphony." *Jahrbuch für Antike und Christentum* 34 (1991).

Stevens, John. *Words and Music in the Middle Ages: Song, Narrative, Dance and Drama, 1050–1350*. Cambridge: Cambridge University Press, 2008.

Stramare, Tarcisio. "L'esaltazione della Croce negli inni di Venanzio Fortunato." *Divinitas* 48 (2005).

Syme, Ronald. "The Spanish War of Augustus 26–25 B.C." *American Journal of Philology* 55 (1934): 293–317.

Szövérffy, Joseph. *A Concise History of Medieval Latin Hymnody: Religious Lyrics between Antiquity and Humanism*. Leiden: Classical Folia Editions, 1985.

———. "À la source de l'humanisme Chrétien médiéval: 'Romanus' et 'Barbarus' chez Vénance Fortunat." *Aevum* 45 (1971): 77–86.

———. "Crux Fidelis: Prolegomena to a History of the Holy Cross Hymns." *Traditio* 22 (1966).

———. *Die Annalen der lateinischen Hymnendichtung*. 2 vols. Berlin: Erich Schmidt Verlag, 1964.

———. "Hymnological Notes: Some Aspects of Recent Hymnological Literature and Hymns of the New Breviary." *Traditio* 25 (1969): 457–72.

———. *Hymns of the Holy Cross: An Annotated Edition with Introduction*. Medieval Classics: Texts and Studies 7. Brookline, MA: Classical Folio Editions, 1976.

———. *Latin Hymns*. Typologie des sources du moyen âge occidental 55. Turnhout: Brepols, 1989.

———. *Venantius Fortunatus and the Earliest Hymns to the Holy Cross*, 1966.

Taft, Robert. *The Liturgy of the Hours in East and West*. 2nd ed. Collegeville, MN: Liturgical Press, 1993.

Thesaurus Linguae Latinae. Deutsche Akademie der Wissenschaften zu Berlin. Leipzig: Teubner, 1900–.

Tongeren, Louis van. *Exaltation of the Cross: Toward the Origins of the Feast of the Cross and the Meaning of the Cross in Early Medieval Liturgy*. Liturgia condenda 11. Leuven: Peeters Publishers, 2000.

Torrell, Jean-Pierre. *Saint Thomas Aquinas*. Translated by Matthew K. Minerd and Robert Royal. 3rd ed. Washington, DC: The Catholic University of America Press, 2005.

Tück, Jan-Heiner. *A Gift of Presence: The Theology and Poetry of the Eucharist in Thomas Aquinas*. Translated by Scott G. Hefelfinger. Washington, DC: The Catholic University of America Press, 2018.

Usher, M. D. *Homeric Stitchings: The Homeric Centos of the Empress Eudocia*. Lanham, MD: Rowman & Littlefield Publishers, 1998.

Vanhoye, Albert. *The Letter to the Hebrews: A New Commentary*. Translated by Leo Arnold. New York: Paulist Press, 2015.

Vergine, Bibiana Carmela Pia. "The Hymns of Medieval Southern Italy: Music, Politics, and the Transformation of Local Liturgical Song." PhD dissertation, Princeton University, 2016.

White, Carolinne. *Early Christian Latin Poets*. The Early Church Fathers. London: Routledge, 2000.

Wielockx, Robert. "*Adoro Te Devote*: Zur Lösung einer alten Crux." *Annales theologici: Revista Internazionale di Teologia* 21 (2007), 101–38.

———. "Poetry and Theology in the *Adoro Te Devote*: Thomas Aquinas on the Eucharist and Christ's Uniqueness." In *Christ Among the Medieval Dominicans: Representations of Christ in the Texts and Images of the Order of Preachers*, edited by Kent Emery and Joseph Peter Wawrykow, 157–74. Notre Dame Conferences in Medieval Studies. Notre Dame, IN: University of Notre Dame Press, 1998.

Wilmart, André. *Auteurs spirituels et textes dévots du moyen âge latin: Études d'histoire littéraire*. Paris: Bloud et Gay, 1932.

———. "La tradition littéraire et textuelle de *L'Adoro te devote*." *Recherches de théologie ancienne et médiévale* 1, Janvier 1929, 21–40.

———. *Le "Jubilus" dit de saint Bernard: Étude avec textes*. Rome: Edizioni di "Storia et Letteratura," 1944.

LIST OF CONTRIBUTORS

EDITORS

Andrew Wadsworth, Cong. Orat.
Nicholas Richardson
Peter Finn
Maria Kiely, OSB

CONTRIBUTORS

Marco Benini
Lehrstuhl für Liturgiewissenschaft; Theologische Fakultät Trier,
Wissenschaftliche Abteilung des Deutschen Liturgischen Instituts

Brian Dunkle, SJ
Associate Professor of Historical Theology,
Boston College

Margot Fassler
Keough-Hesburgh Professor Emerita of Music History and Liturgy,
University of Notre Dame

Peter C. Finn
Assistant Director (1974–1985; Associate Director (1985–2020),
International Commission on English in the Liturgy

Maria Kiely, OSB
Department of Greek and Latin,
The Catholic University of America
International Commission on English in the Liturgy

Benjamin Lewis
Director of Translation Services,
International Commission on English in the Liturgy

List Of Contributors

William McCarthy
Associate Professor and Director of Graduate Studies,
The Catholic University of America

Luke Maschue
PhD Candidate, Department of Greek and Latin
The Catholic University of America

Nicholas Richardson
Emeritus Fellow, Merton College,
Oxford.

Ambrose Slama, OP
Department of Greek and Latin
The Catholic University of America

Innocent Smith, OP
Assistant Professor of Dogmatic Theology and Pastoral Studies,
Pontifical Faculty of the Immaculate Conception

Pachomius Walker, OP
Pontifical Faculty of the Immaculate Conception

Andrew Wadsworth, Cong. Orat.
Executive Director (2009–2023),
International Commission on English in the Liturgy
Director, St Gregory Institute for the Study of Latin Liturgical Texts

Andreas Weckwerth
Lehrstuhlinhaber LS Alte Kirchengeschichte und Patrologie
Theologische Fakultät, Katholische Universität, Eichstätt Ingolstadt
Translator: Gwilym Evans, FSSP

SCRIPTURAL INDEX

Old Testament

Genesis	Hymn Commentary
1:3–5	51, 2
1:20	Introduction
1:26	43, 1
2–3	9, 3
2:7	37, 1
2:8–10	12, 2
2:9	32, 2
2:10–14	33, 1
2:17	1, 2; 32, 2; 39, 2
2:23	8, 4
3:1	24, 4; 47, 2
3:1–7	32, 2
3:7	37, 1
3:15	40, 2
3:19	24, 2
3:24	54, 3
7:4	Lent
14:20	4, 5
17:5	18, 6
18:1–2	49
20:7	1, 2
22:15–18	18, 6
22:17–18	21, 1
41:10	42, 6
41:30	23, 3
49:9–10	47, 2

Exodus	
2:2–3	55, 2
3:14–15	49, 1
3:18	42, 4
7:16	42, 7
8:19	55, 3
12:1–15:21	Easter
12:5	36, 3; 42, 4
12:7	42, 2
12:9	42, 2
12:11–12	42, 1
12:21	42, 4
12:23	42, 3
13:21–22	55, 5
14:8	42, 3
14:16–29	30, 3
14:21	27, 1
15:1–21	42, 7
16:11–35	56
17:6	6, 1
19:12	1, 2
21:12	1, 2
24:18	Lent
31:18	55, 3
34:5	49, 1
34:26	24, 2

Leviticus	
17:4	1, 3
20:2	1, 2
23:17	56
23:26	24, 2
25:8–12	57, 4

Numbers	
6:25–26	13, 3
14:32–34	Lent
16–17	10, 3
16:25–35	30, 3
16:31	27, 1
17:1–11	14, 1; 18, 6
24:15–20	18, 6
24:17	3, 2
35:16	1, 3
35:21	1, 3
35:31	1, 3
36:4	57, 4

Deuteronomy	
1:31	4, 2
1:33	55, 2
9:9	24, 2
21:23	Lent
32:13	56

Judges	
5:15	42, 6
11:40	7, 4
20:26	24, 2

1 Samuel (1 Kings)	
7:6	24, 2
28:19	41, 3
31:13	24, 2

2 Samuel (2 Kings)	
2:7	34, 4
12:14	1, 2

1 (3) Kings	
3:13	23, 3
19:8	24, 2; Lent

2 (4) Kings	
1:12	24, 2
4:1–7	56
12:16–23	24, 2
22:3	15, 4

1 Chronicles

10:12	24, 2
16:35	15, 4

2 Chronicles

20:3	24, 2
28:24	4, 3

(1) Ezra

1:13–14	25, 1
8:21–23	24, 2

Nehemiah (2 Ezra)

1:4	24, 2
9:1	24, 2

Tobit

2:3	24, 2
8:19	27, 5
12:8	22, 1; 24, 2; 26, 1
12:12	22, 1; 26, 1

Judith

4:8–12	24, 2
8:6	24, 2

Esther

4:3	24, 2
4:16	24, 2
9:31	24, 2
14:2	24, 2
15:5	15, 4

1 Maccabees

3:47	24, 2
4:30	15, 4
15:40	42, 5

2 Maccabees

13:12	24, 2

Job

4:17	24, 2
10:8	37, 1
13:16	15, 4
19:25	5, 1; 7, 1; 15, 2; 32, 1; 37, 1; 40, 1
26:11	53, 4
32:22	24, 2

Psalms

2:7	Christmas
3:9	14, 4
4:7	37, 1
6	22
6:3	22, 2
6:6	41, 3
9 (9–10)	9
9:14	Introduction
10:5 (11:4)	5, 3
13 (14):6	10, 1
17 (18):47	14, 4
18 (19)	15, 2
18 (19):4	58, 2
18 (19):5	5, 4
18 (19):6	1, 3; 15, 2; Introduction; Christmas
18 (19):7	5, 4
18:6 (19:5)	5
18 (19):15	7, 1; 15, 2; 32, 1; 40, 1
21 (22):10	10, 1
22 (23):1	9, 7
23 (24):7–10	15, 1; 53, 4
23 (24):9	52, 2
24 (25):5	15, 4
24 (25):6	7, 3
24 (25):18	40, 1
26 (27):1	14, 4; 27, 4
32 (33):3	7, 6; 8, 5; 23, 5; 27, 5
33 (34)	9
33:7 (34:6)	26, 1
33:9 (34:8)	35, 1; 45, 4
34 (35):3	14, 4
34 (35):10	12, 5
34 (35):13	24, 2
35 (36):3	32, 2
35 (36):9	6, 1
35 (36):10	31, 7
37 (37):39	14, 4
37 (38)	9
37 (38):23	14, 4
39:3 (40:2)	23, 5
39:4 (40:3–4)	7, 6; 8, 5; 27, 5
39 (40):5	10, 1
39:7–9 (40:8–10)	38, 2
39:8–9 (40:9–10)	42, 5
45 (46):4	6, 1
45 (46):13	5, 3
46 (47):1	45, 1
46 (47):9–10	12, 2
49 (50):3	58, 2
50 (51)	22; 24; Lent
50 (51):1	40, 1
50 (51):4–6	22, 3
50 (51):6	14, 4
50:11–12 (51:9–10)	22, 3
50:12 (51:10)	27, 2
50:19 (51:17)	22, 4
50:20 (51:18)	22, 1
55 (56):3	55, 2
60 (61):2	7, 2
60 (61):4	10, 1
61 (62):5	15, 4
61 (62):8	10, 1
64 (65):6	10, 1
68 (69):11	24, 2
68 (69):17	22, 1
68 (69):22	29, 1
69 (70):5	4, 5
69 (70):6	12, 5
70 (71):5	10, 1
70 (71):6	20, 2
71 (72):10–11	17; 17, 3
72 (73):28	44
73 (74):12	14, 4
74 (75):8	26, 1
77 (78):35	7, 1; 15, 2; 32, 1; 40, 1
78 (79):9	26, 3
79 (80):2	7, 1
79:2–3 (80:1–2)	5
80 (81):2	14, 4
81 (82):6	7, 1
88 (89):11–13	41, 3
89 (90):49	41, 3
90 (91):9	10, 1
94 (95)	49, 1
94 (95):1–2	34, 1
94 (95):6	26, 1

Scriptural Index

Reference	Location	Reference	Location	Reference	Location
95 (96):1	7, 6; 8, 5; 23, 5; 27, 5	145 (146):5	10, 1	**Isaiah**	
95 (96):10	31, 3	145 (146):6	34, 1	1:24	26, 1
95 (96):11	45, 1	145 (146):7–8	37, 2	7:14	5, 1; 9, 3; 14, 1; Christmas
95 (96):11–12	7, 5	145 (146):9	40, 2	9:6	34, 3; Christmas
96 (97):4	25, 1	146 (147):9	9, 6	11:1	5, 2; 10, 4; 14, 1
97 (98):1	8, 5; 27, 5	148:2	4, 5	11:2–3	29, 3; 35, 1; 55, 2
97 (98):3	Christmas	148:14	Introduction	12:2	14, 4; 15, 4
97 (98):4	34, 1	149:1	8, 5; 27, 5	12:3	12, 2; 15, 4
97 (98):5	34, 1	149:4	14, 4	13:9	54, 1
97 (90):8–9	26, 1	150:6	13, 4	17:7	24, 2
97 (98):9	1, 5	**Proverbs**		17:10	15, 4
99 (100):1	46, 1	8:35	14, 4	26:19	19, 1
103 (104):30	55, 1	9:10	49, 3	30:27	Advent
108 (109):22	12, 5	12:20	37, 1	33:2	12, 4
108 (109):24	22, 4	17:5	24, 2	40:3	2, 2; Advent
109 (110):1	41, 4	31:10–31	9	40:3–4	3, 1
109 (110):3	4, 4	**Ecclesiastes**		40:11	9, 7
109 (110):4	38, 1	2:12	24, 2	41:14	7, 1; 15, 2; 32, 1; 40, 1
111 (112)	9	**Song of Songs (Song of Solomon)**		42:8	26, 3
112 (113)	9	1:3	8, 4; 34, 3	42:10	8, 5; 27, 5
112 (113):1	49, 1	4:12	1, 3	43:4	15, 4
112 (113):3	9, 1	5:2	19, 1	43:14	7, 1; 15, 2; 32, 1; 40, 1
113 (114):3	25, 3	**Wisdom (of Solomon)**		43:25	22, 3
116 (117):1	4, 5	1:1	8, 1	44:6	7, 1; 15, 2; 32, 1; 40, 1
117 (118):14	14, 4	1:7	58, 2; Advent	44:24	7, 1; 15, 2; 32, 1; 40, 1
117 (118):19–20	8, 1	2:24	34, 1; 37, 1	45:6	9, 1
117 (118):21	14, 4	3:4	45, 4	45:8	15, 4; 45, 1
117 (118):24	27, 4; 44; 54, 1; 54, 5	7:26	6, 5; 8, 1; 10, 1	45:15	15, 4
117 (118):28	14, 4	8:3	43, 3	45:23	1, 2; 53, 3
118 (119)	39, 2	16:7	15, 4	46:3	4, 2
118 (119):12	27, 4	16:20	12, 3	46:13	14, 4; Advent
118 (119):24	28, 3	16:24	24, 2	47:4	7, 1; 15, 2; 32, 1; 40, 1
118 (119):26	27, 4	**Sirach (Ecclesiasticus)**		48:11	26, 3
118 (119):49	7, 3	2:13	21, 1	48:9	22, 3
118 (119):73	37, 1	5:3	26, 1	48:17	7, 1; 15, 2; 32, 1
119 (120)	9	18:13	9, 7	49:6	8, 1
135 (136)	26, 2	24:5	2, 1	49:7	7, 1; 15, 2; 32, 1; 40, 1
136 (137):9	16	33:13–14	37, 1	49:8	25, 1; 45, 2
137:6 (138:8)	4, 5	34:31 (26)	24, 2	49:26	7, 1; 15, 2; 32, 1; 40, 1
138 (139):13–14	22, 2	51:1	15, 4	51:5	15, 4
140 (141)	55, 1				
141 (142):6	10, 1				
143 (144):9	8, 5; 27, 5				
144 (145):20	40, 2				
144 (145):21	8, 2				
145 (146)	9				

Isaiah (cont.)

51:8	14, 4
51:13	24, 2
53:4	1, 2; 52, 2
53:5	31, 2
53:7	16, 3; 32, 5; 36, 3
53:7–8	42, 4
54:5	7, 1; 15, 2; 32, 1; 40, 1
54:8	7, 1; 15, 2; 32, 1; 40, 1
53:7	3, 3; 42, 1; 42, 4
56:1	14, 4
58:4–5	24, 2
58:6	22, 4; 24, 4
58:11	12, 3
59:17	42, 1
59:20	5, 1; 15, 2
60:1–3	13, 3; 14, 4
60:5–6	17, 3
60:16	7, 1; 15, 2; 32, 1; 40, 1
60:20	6, 5; 10, 1
61:10	42, 1
62:1	15, 4
62:5	15, 2
63:8	15, 2
63:11	15, 2
63:16	7, 1; 32, 1; 37, 1; 40, 1
63:16b	15, 2
65:17–19	27, 4
66:10	45, 1

Jeremiah

3:23	14, 4
4:28	45, 1
10:7	18, 6
14:8	15, 4
17:10	22, 2
31:3	8, 4
31:10	9, 7
31:31	8, 4
36:9	24, 2
46:10	54, 1
50:4	7, 1
50:34	15, 2; 32, 1; 40, 1

Lamentations

3:58	7, 1; 15, 2; 32, 1; 40, 1

Baruch

1:5	24, 2
3:34–35	1, 2
4:24	14, 4

Ezekiel

3:18	1, 2
10:18	4, 3
30:3–4	54, 1
32:17–32	41, 3
33:11	27, 2
34:11–16	9, 7; 28, 2
36:22	22, 3
44:1–2	Introduction
44:1–3	15, 1
44:2	1, 3; 8, 1; 9, 3
44:2–3	4, 3

Daniel

2:45	15, 3
3:56–88	7, 5
6:26	53, 4
6:27	15, 4
7:13	53, 7
9:3	24, 2
12:3	50, 3
14:42	15, 4

Hosea (Osee)

2:20	35
3:14	19, 1
11:4	8, 4
13:4	15, 4
13:14	31, 5; 41, 2

Joel

2:12–13	23, 2
2:12–17	24, 2
2:13	22, 1
2:15–17	Lent
2:21	45, 1

Jonah

2:11	20, 2
3:5	24, 2

Micah

1:3	4, 4
4:10	37, 2
5:2	8, 2; 17, 4
6:9	14, 4
7:7	15, 4
7:8	6, 5; 10, 1

Nahum

1:2–8	9

Habakkuk

3:12	46, 2

Zephaniah

45, 1

Zechariah

2:10	45, 1
9:9	15, 4

Malachi

3:1	8, 2; 9, 5; Christmas
4:2	3, 2
5:2	27, 1
1:11	9, 1

Scriptural Index

New Testament

Matthew

Reference	Page
1	32, 4
1:1–17	10, 3
1:1–25	Christmas
1:18	20, 2
1:19	12, 1
1:22–23	5, 1
1:22	20, 2
1:23	14, 1; Christmas
1:34–35	5, 2
2:1	18, 3
2:2	18, 4
2:6	17, 4; 17, 5
2:9	5, 6; 16, 2
2:9–11	Christmas
2:10–11	17, 1
2:10–12	16, 2
3:1–3	3, 1; 6, 1
3:3	2, 2
3:13–17	16, 3; 20
3:14–15	20, 1; 21, 3
3:16	19, 3
3:16–17	20, 3; 21, 4
4:1–11	24, 2
4:2	Lent
4:4	6, 1
4:16	6, 5; 10, 1
4:17	Lent
4:23	1, 3
5:3	12, 5
5:21–22	1, 3
5:6	29, 2
6:2–5	Lent
6:16	Lent
6:16–18	23, 1
6:26	9, 6
6:29	12, 5
9:13	4, 5
9:17	27, 1
9:35	1, 3
11:8	12, 5
12:28	55, 3
12:40	20, 2; 46, 2
13:30	34, 1
13:33	25, 1
13:43	1, 1; 25, 1
13:52	Introduction
15:8	49, 1
16:15–16	19, 1
16:18	38, 1; 46, 2
17:2	8, 1; 27, 1
18:11	4, 5; 6, 3
20:1–16	50
20:28	15, 4; 31, 4; 33, 4
21:1–11	34, 2
21:10–11	34, 1
22:30	2, 4
22:37–40	24, 2
24:14	36, 1
24:17	3, 4
24:27	25, 1
24:42	51, 4
24:30	54, 1
25:1	44
25:1–13	34, 3
25:6	15, 2; Advent
25:10	15, 2
25:13	51, 4
25:31–46	1, 5; 2, 3; 26, 1
25:32	9, 7
25:34	36, 4
26:38–41	51, 4
26:61	44
26:64	41, 4
26:66	40, 4
27:19	53, 2
27:28	50, 1
27:29	33, 1
27:30	33, 1
27:31	50, 1
27:34	33, 1
27:40	44
27:45	45, 4; 50, 1
27:50	50, 1
27:51–52	46, 2
27:52–53	45, 4; 50, 2
27:62–66	46, 3
28:2–4	46, 3
28:1	46, 1
28:3	25, 1; 46, 3
28:5–6	46, 4
28:11–15	46, 3
28:18	36, 1
28:19	21, 1
28:20	27, 4; Christmas; Easter

Mark

Reference	Page
1:2–4	6, 1
1:3	2, 2
1:9–11	16, 3; 20; Christmas
1:10	19, 3
1:11	20, 3
2:2–4	3, 1
2:19–20	15, 2
2:20	23, 1
2:22	56
6:3	51, 2
9:4	8, 1
9:28	22, 5
10:45	31, 4; 33, 4
11:1–10	34, 2
11:13	34, 1
12:29–30	49, 3
13:11	55, 3
13:26	53, 7
13:35	51, 4
14:4–38	51, 4
14:5	44
15:23	17, 3
15:25	28
15:29	44
15:33	45, 4
16:2	44
16:19	41, 4; 58

Luke

Reference	Page
1	32, 4
1:15	20, 2
1:26–38	4, 4
1:28	15, 3
1:28–38	10, 2

Luke (cont.)

Reference	Index
1:31	20, 2
1:34	4, 3; 9, 4; 9, 5
1:35	4, 2; 9, 4; 13, 3
1:38	9, 5
1:41	9, 5; 20, 2; Advent
1:42	4, 1
1:44	20, 2
1:54–55	18, 6
1:68–72	17, 5
1:70	13, 4
1:71	14, 4
1:76	6, 1
1:76–79	3, 2
1:78	2, 1
2:7	9, 6; 14, 2
2:9	Advent
2:11	15, 4
2:12	9, 6
2:13–14	10, 3
2:13–18	9, 7
2:32	8, 1; 16, 2; 19, 3
2:7	14, 2
2:8–19	9, 7
2:8–21	4, 5
2:9	5, 6
2:9–14	8, 2
2:14	4, 5
2:21	20, 2
2:22–24	14, 3
2:25–39	Christmas
2:29–32	14, 4
2:32	7, 2; 17, 7
2:41–52	10, 6
2:51–52	12, 4
3:3–6	3, 1; 6, 1
3:4	2, 2
3:6	Advent
3:15	6, 1
3:21	16, 3
3:21–22	20
3:22	20, 3
3:23	21, 2; 32, 5
4:1–13	24, 2
4:2	23
4:18	55, 2
5:6	27, 1
5:37–38	56
6:19	45, 3
7:21	1, 3
7:24–28	3, 1
7:25	12, 5
8:26	55, 2
9:1	1, 3
9:29	8, 1
9:31	Lent
10:18	25, 1
10:19	55, 5
11:20	55, 3
12:2	2, 4
12:6	9, 6
12:49	2, 2
15:4	6, 3
15:4–6	28, 2
15:17	22, 2
16:16	24, 2
16:22–26	41, 3
17:24	25, 1
18:1	Introduction
19:10	4, 5; 6, 3
19:28–40	34, 2
19:37	34, 2
20:28	42, 2
22:1	42, 4
22:19	35, 1
22:54	12, 5
22:69	41, 4
23:43	23, 1; 42, 6; 44; 50, 2
23:44	45, 4
23:54	41, 3
24:1	44
24:13–32	Easter
24:27	4, 4; 6, 1
24:29	19, 4; 42, 7
24:34	42, 6
24:39–43	30, 2
24:40	41, 4
24:46–47	36, 2
24:49	55, 3; 58, 1
24:51	58

John

Reference	Index
1:1	12, 3; 51, 1
1:1–2	2, 1; 13, 1
1:1–18	9, 1; Christmas
1:2	20, 1
1:3	9, 2; 9, 6; 20, 1; 32, 4
1:4	19, 5; 20, 5; 21, 6
1:4–5	6, 5; 8, 1; 10, 1; 14, 4
1:5	5, 6
1:8–9	5, 6; 8, 1; 10, 1
1:10	34, 1
1:13	5, 2; 8, 2
1:14	2, 1; 4, 1; 5, 2; 7, 1; 8, 4; 12, 1; 18, 2; 19, 1; 32, 4
1:15	20, 1
1:18	2, 1; 13, 1
1:23	3, 1; 6, 1
1:29	3, 3; 16, 3; 20, 2; 21, 3; 32, 5; 36, 3; 42
1:36	3, 3; 36, 3
1:42	5, 2
2:1	20, 2
2:1–11	16, 4
2:2–5	12, 4
2:11	Christmas
2:19	44
3:16	8, 1
3:17	6, 3; 34, 1
3:20–21	3, 1
3:29	15, 2; Advent
3:30	20, 1
3:31	2, 1
4:5–42	Lent
4:6	49
4:14	12, 2; 13, 1; 31, 7
4:42	15, 4
5:2–14	1, 2
5:3	1, 2
5:7	1, 2
5:14	1, 2
5:20	41, 2
5:25	46, 2; 47, 2
5:28–29	47, 2
6:44	8, 4
6:51	35, 1; 45, 4
6:51–59	56
7:8	32, 5
7:37–38	13, 1
7:37–39	21, 4

Scriptural Index

7:38	12, 2	15:11	54, 6	2:24–31	46, 2
8:12	6, 5; 8, 1; 10, 1; 19, 3	15:12	28, 1	2:33	55, 3
		15:19	34, 1	2:41	56
8:23	2, 1	15:24	Advent	3:6	22, 3
8:44	37, 1	15:26	1, 6; 32, 6; 55, 2; 55, 6; 57, 1; 58, 1; Easter	3:15	9, 2; 14, 2; 41, 3
9:1–41	Lent			4:12	7, 4; 14, 4; 30, 1
9:5	6, 5; 10, 1				
10:1–18	9, 7	16:1	34, 1	5:30	31, 1; 31, 3
10:7–9	8, 1	16:7	1, 6; 32, 6; 55, 2; 57, 1; 58, 1; Easter	5:31	15, 4
10:17–18	39, 2			7:55	53, 2
10:18	43, 5; 49, 2			8:32	3, 3; 16, 3; 32, 5; 42, 1; 42, 4
11:25	19, 5; 20, 5; 21, 6; 39, 1	16:13–14	Easter		
		16:14–15	57, 7		
11:25–26	31, 5	16:28	5, 4; 58, 1	10:38	55, 2
11:40	50, 3	16:32	48, 1	10:39	31, 1; 31, 3
11:43	47, 2	16:33	32, 1	10:42	1, 5; 26, 1
12:12–18	34, 2	17:1	31, 5	13:23	15, 4
12:26	34, 2	17:5	13, 1; 31, 5	13:38	45, 3
12:27	49, 2	17:14–16	34, 1	16:7	28, 4
12:31	30, 3; 34, 1; 38, 2	17:22	36, 1	17:2	28, 4
		17:24	13, 1; 36, 4	22:6	6, 5; 49, 1
12:32	8, 4; 32, 5; 38, 2	18:37	31, 3	22:6–8	10, 1
		19:5	31, 3	22:16	19, 4
12:35–36	8, 1	19:14	32, 5		
12:46	6, 5; 8, 1; 10, 1	19:26–27	48	**Romans**	
13:1	47, 1	19:28–30	29, 1	1:5	36, 2
13:3–5	12, 3	19:29	33, 1	1:17	28, 1
14:1–3	36, 4	19:34	30, 2; 33, 1	2:4	27, 2
14:2	12, 6	19:37	Advent	2:16	2, 4; 54, 1
14:6	19, 5; 21, 6	19:39–40	17, 3	3:13	24, 2
14:11–30	56	20:1	44	3:24	3, 3
14:12–14	Easter	20:19	34, 2	4:11	18, 6
14:16	1, 6; 8, 1; 20, 5; 32, 6; 55, 2; 57, 1; Easter	20:19–23	57, 6	4:17	18, 6
		20:25	33, 1	4:25	27, 5
				5:2	Introduction
14:16–17	58, 1	**Acts of the Apostles**		5:5	57, 2
14:18	55, 6	1–2	56	5:10	39, 1; 41, 2
14:23	12, 6	1:2	54, 3	5:12	34, 1
14:26	1, 6; 32, 6; 55, 2; 57, 1; 58, 1; Easter	1:9	58	5:12–21	32, 2
		1:14	56; 58, 2	5:20	27, 3
		2:1	57, 1	6:3–5	Easter
14:26–27	57, 6	2:1–4	48, 2; 58	6:3–11	49, 2
14:30	34, 1; 38, 2	2:1–13	57	6:8–9	45, 3
15:1–5	6, 1	2:3–4	57, 2	6:9	45, 1
15:4	12, 6	2:4	55, 3	6:10	42, 2
15:6	12, 6	2:5–12	57, 3	6:23	41, 2
15:7	12, 6	2:13	56; 57, 3	7:2	36, 1
15:9	28, 1	2:15	28; 58, 1; 58, 2	7:20	53, 4
15:9–20	56	2:24	41, 3; 46, 4	7:23	42, 5

Scriptural Index

Romans (cont.)
8:2	29, 1
8:2–3	36, 1
8:3–4	53, 4
8:6	55, 5
8:9	28, 4
8:11	41, 3
8:27	22, 2
8:34	53, 2
8:35–39	8, 4
10:7	46, 2
12:1	Introduction
13:4	54, 5
13:11–14	3
13:13	47, 1
14:8	21, 5
14:10	53, 2
14:17	55, 5
15:4	Introduction
16:20	40, 2

1 Corinthians
1:27	22, 2
2:7	31, 1
2:8–10	38, 1
3:16	Easter
3:19	34, 1
4:5	2, 4
5:7	32, 1; 32, 5; 33, 4; 45, 5
5:7–8	42, 4; 47, 1
5:8	42, 4
6:19	58, 4; Easter
6:20	31, 4; 33, 4; 36, 4; 37, 1; 43, 1
7:22–23	37, 1
7:23	31, 4; 33, 4; 36, 4
9:24	34, 3
10:1–2	42, 1
10:1–4	42, 2
10:1–6	Easter
11:25	33, 4
12:4–6	21, 4
13:4	22, 1
13:12	36, 4
14:15	49, 1
15:20	41, 3; 46, 4
15:21	45, 3
15:22	32, 2; 39, 2; 41, 1
15:25–26	46, 2
15:26	45, 3
15:45	39, 2
15:51–52	45, 4
15:54	45, 3; 52, 2; 53, 1
15:54–58	31, 5; 38, 1
15:56	30, 3
15:57	38, 3; 42, 6

2 Corinthians
2:14	42, 6
4:4	54, 2
4:6	19, 3; 30, 3
5:10	40, 5; 53, 2
5:14–15	Lent
5:17	27, 4
5:21	41, 3
6:2	25, 1; 27, 2; Lent
6:16	5, 4
12:9	5, 5; 22, 2; 45, 3

Galatians
2:19	42, 2
3:7–14	21, 2
3:8	36, 2
4:3–4	14, 3
4:4	32, 4; 52, 1
4:6	28, 4
5:22	57, 2
5:22–23	55, 5
5:24–26	22, 4; 24, 4
6:14–16	38, 1
6:15	27, 4

Ephesians
1:7	28, 3; 40, 3
1:9–10	36, 1
2:1–2	28, 3
2:2	34, 1
2:3–5	36, 1
2:5	7, 3
2:10	19, 2
2:14–16	38, 1
2:18	Introduction
2:20	56
3:12	Introduction
3:16	55, 4
4:9	41, 3; 46, 2
4:13	Advent
4:27	24, 4
5:2	38, 2; 42, 4
5:23	15, 4
5:29	28, 4
6:11	37, 1
6:13–14	5, 5

Philippians
1:9	28, 4
2:6	5, 5
2:6–7	12, 3
2:6–8	13, 2
2:7	7, 3; 8, 4; 9, 2; 19, 2; 20, 2; 43, 1
2:8	43, 1; 47, 1
2:8–11	38, 1
2:9–10	17, 6; Introduction
2:9–11	20, 4; 54, 2
2:10	27, 5; 41, 3
2:10–11	1, 4; 36, 1
3:3–16	Lent
3:20	15, 4
3:30	44

Colossians
1:13–14	39, 1
1:16	32, 4
1:16–17	13, 1
1:16–18	36, 1
1:18	42, 1; 46, 2
1:18–22	38, 1
1:19–20	36, 1
1:27	45, 4
2:12–14	28, 3
2:13–15	29, 2
2:14	40, 4
2:14–15	32, 1; 40, 2; 54, 2
2:15	30, 3; 41, 3; 42, 6
3:1	18, 1

Scriptural Index

1 Thessalonians
2:7	28, 4
9:19	45, 4
4:3–4	24, 4
4:6	26, 1
5:6	47, 1
5:8	42, 1

1 Timothy
1:1	7, 2; 15, 4
1:19	33, 4
2:3	15, 4
2:5	Introduction
2:5–6	15, 4
2:2	15, 4
3:7	37, 1
4:10	15, 4; 54, 3

2 Timothy
1:10	36, 1; 39, 1; 41, 2; 46, 1
2:10	14, 4; 15, 4
4:8	26, 1
4:10	50, 3

Titus
1:2	50, 3
1:3	15, 4
1:4	15, 4
2:11–14	38, 1
3:4–6	36, 1
3:6–7	28, 1
2:10–11	15, 4
2:13	7, 2; 15, 4
3:4	15, 4
3:6	15, 4

Hebrews
1:1	2, 1
1:1–2	4, 1; 8, 2
1:2	1, 3; 27, 1
1:3	7, 2; 8, 1; 12, 1; 19, 5; 20, 5; 21, 6
2:3	Advent
2:10	7, 3; 9, 2; 14, 2; 41, 1
2:14	34, 1
2:24–25	39, 1
4:12	51, 2
4:12–13	2, 4
4:15	28, 4; Christmas Introduction
4:16	32, 5
5:7	40, 5
6:6	38, 1
6:18–20	41, 4
7:25	Christmas
7:25–26	36, 4
7:26–27	Introduction
8:6	8, 4
8:10	40, 3
9:12	Introduction
9:15	45, 3
9:22	42, 5
10:4–5	38, 2
10:8	42, 5
10:9–12	38, 2
10:12	8, 4
10:16	55, 2
10:29	Advent
10:37	1, 1; 22, 1
11:9–10	15, 2; 31, 1
11:10	25, 3
11:15–16	42, 3
11:28	42, 1
11:29	34, 3
12:1	41, 1
12:1–2	9, 2; 14, 2; Introduction
12:2	Introduction
12:24	41, 3
13:15	
13:20	

James
1:17	58, 3
1:18	33, 4
1:22–25	24, 2
2:10	1, 3
2:19	53, 4
4:4	34, 1
5:11	24, 2
5:9	6, 4

1 Peter
1:18–19	31, 4; 37, 1; 51, 3
1:19	16, 3; 42, 1; 45, 2
2:9	21, 1
2:22	38, 2
2:23	49, 2
2:24	52, 2
3:18	41, 3
3:18–19	41, 3
3:19	46, 2
3:22	41, 2
4:6	40, 4; 41, 3; 46, 2
5:4	6, 4; 9, 7
5:8	47, 1; 55, 5; Introduction
5:18	51, 4

2 Peter
1:11	15, 4; 36, 1; 54, 3
1:19	19, 3; 27, 1
2:4	42, 5
2:20	15, 4
3:2	15, 4
3:18	15, 4

1 John
1:5	6, 5; 10, 1
3:2	6, 6; 36, 4
3:5	20, 2
4:14	15, 4; 36, 1
4:18	49, 3
5:4	38, 2
5:10–11	38, 2
5:11	45, 1

Jude
1:25	15, 4

Revelation (Apocalypse)
1:5	34, 3; 42, 1
1:8	13, 1
1:16	27, 1
1:18	41, 3
2:7	41, 1
2:11	40, 3
2:23	22, 2; 40, 5
3:5	42, 1
3:11	53, 7
3:12	47, 1
3:20	6, 4

Revelation (Apocalypse) *(cont.)*

3:21	36, 4
5:5	31, 1; 47, 2
5:6	8, 5
5:6–7:17	3, 3
5:8–9	41, 4
5:9	27, 5; 28, 3; 37, 1; 40, 3; 43, 1
5:12	16, 3; 32, 5; 42, 1; 42, 4; 42, 5
5:13	36, 1
6:16	3, 4
7:9	36, 2; 36, 5; 42, 1
7:14	36, 3; 42, 1; 45, 2
7:17	16, 3; 32, 5; 42, 1
10:6	50, 3
12:7–9	38, 1
12:3–17	47, 2
14:1	42, 1
14:3	8, 5; 23, 5; 27, 5; 42, 1
17:14	37, 2
19:7	16, 3; 32, 5; 42, 1
19:16	42, 1
20:2–3	42, 6
20:3	47, 3
20:9–10	38, 1
20:11	45, 5
20:11–15	1, 5; 26, 1
21:1	50, 3
21:2	47, 1
21:5	47, 1
21:6	12, 3; 13, 1; 31, 7
21:9	42, 1
21:22	32, 5
21:22–23	3, 3; 42, 1
22:4	36, 4
22:5	54, 1
22:13	9; 13, 1
22:16	3, 2; 6, 5
22:22–23	16, 3

AUTHOR INDEX

Adam of St. Victor, d. 1146
56 Lux iucunda, lux insignis

Ambrose, d. 397
5 Veni, redemptor gentium
44 Hic est dies verus Dei
48 Iam surgit hora tertia

Anselmo Lentini, d. 1989
8 Candor æternæ Deitatis alme
12 Christe, splendor Patris

Fulbert of Chartres, d. 1029
47 Chorus novae Ierusalem

Gregory the Great, d. 604
22 Audi, benigne Conditor
24 Ex more docti mystico
26 Precemur omnes cernui

Hilary of Poitiers, d. ca. 367
57 Beata nobis gaudia (traditionally attributed to Hilary, but without historical evidence)

Leo XIII, d. 1903
10 O lux beata caelitum
11 Dulce fit nobis memorare parvum

Nicetus of Remesiana, d. 414
42 Ad cenam Agni providi

Peter Damian, d. 1072
38 Crux, mundi benedictio
39 Per crucem, Christe, quaesumus

Prudentius, d. ca. 405
13 Corde natus ex Parentis
17 Magi videntes parvulum
18 Quicumque Christum quaeritis

Rabanus Maurus, d. 856
55 Veni, creator Spiritus

Sedulius, d. ca. 450
9 A solis ortus cardine
16 Hostis Herodes impie

Thomas Aquinas, d. 1274
35 O memoriale mortis Domini

Venantius Fortunatus, d. ca. 600
31 Vexilla regis prodeunt
32 Pange, lingua, gloriosi proelium certaminis
33 En acetum, fel, arundo

The majority of hymns included in the Proper of Time are anonymous.

ALPHABETICAL INDEX & CONCORDANCE

Hymnal #	Commentary #	Hymn
69	19	A Patre Unigenite
35	9	A solis ortus cardine
119	42	Ad cenam Agni providi
265	106	Ad preces nostras deitatis aures
233	90	Adesto Christe cordibus
289	118	Adesto rerum conditor
361	195	Adorna Sion thalamum
235	91	Aeterna caeli gloria
609	153	Aeterna Christi munera
181	135	Aeterna imago Altissimi
201	74	Aeterna lux divinitas
A5	297	Aeterne Christe pontifex
267	107	Aeterne lucis conditor
195	71	Aeterne rerum conditor noctem
519	267	Aeterne rerum conditor qui mare
143	53	Aeterne rex altissime
639	167	Aeterne sol qui lumine
351	190	Agnes beatae virginis
377	203	Agnoscat omne saeculum
279	113	Ales diei nuntius
281	114	Amoris sensus erige
515	265	Angelum pacis Michael ad istam
489	253	Anglorum iam apostolus
583	140	Angularis fundamentum
421	220	Antra deserti teneris sub annis
429	224	Apostolorum passio
647	171	Aptata virgo lampade
171	130	Auctor beate saeculi
241	94	Auctor perennis gloriae
117	41	Auctor salutis unice
75	22	Audi benigne Conditor
579	294	Audit tyrannus anxius

Hymnal #	Commentary #	Hymn
425	222	Aurea luce et decore roseo
243	95	Aurora iam spargit polum
129	46	Aurora lucis rutilat
395	211	Aurora solis nuntia
441	230	Aurora surgit lucida
469	243	Aurora velut fulgida
383, 593	145	Ave maris stella
417	218	Barnabae clarum colimus tropaeum
653	176	Beata caeli gaudia
491	254	Beata Dei genetrix
151	57	Beata nobis gaudia
613	155	Beate (Beata) martyr prospera
473	246	Bernarde gemma caelitum
455	237	Caelestis formam gloriae
221	84	Caeli Deus sanctissime
375	202	Caelitum Ioseph decus atque nostrae
33	8	Candor aeternae Deitatis alme
555	284	Captator olim piscium
103	34	Celsae salutis gaudia (Horam Mediam PS)
23, 63, 319, 321, 323	61	Certum tenentes ordinem
131	47	Chorus novae Ierusalem
113	36	Christe caelorum Domine
541	277	Christe caelorum habitator alme
581	139	Christe cunctorum dominator alme
663	182	Christe cunctorum sator et redemptor
273	110	Christe lux vera bonitas et vita
633	161	Christe pastorum caput atque princeps
255	86	Christe precamur adnuas
17, 57, 81, 343, 345, 347	67	Christe qui splendor et dies
539	276	Christe redemptor omnium conserva tuos famulos
29	7	Christe redemptor omnium ex Patre Patris Unice
47	12	Christe splendor patris
571	290	Christus est vita veniens in orbem
601	150	Claro paschali gaudio
575	292	Cohors beata Seraphim
537	275	Commune vos apostoli
A3	296	Concinunt caeli parilique tellus
407	216	Concito gressu petis alta montis
1	1	Conditor alme siderum
207	77	Consors paterni luminis

Hymnal #	Commentary #	Hymn
173	131	Cor arca legem continens
49	13	Corde natus ex parentis
109	38	Crux mundi benedictio
523	269	Custodes hominum psallimus angelos
91	28	Dei fide qua vivimus
189	68	Deus Creator omnium
297	122	Deus de nullo veniens
291	119	Deus qui caeli lumen es
285	116	Deus qui claro lumine
617, 619	159	Deus tuorum militum
25, 65, 325, 327, 329	63	Dicamus laudes Domino
299	123	Diei luce reddita
193	70	Dies aetasque ceteris
183, 185, 187	136	Dies irae dies illa
369	199	Divina vox te deligit
641	168	Doctor aeternus coleris piusque
355	192	Doctor egregie Paule mores instrue
45	11	Dulce fit nobis memorare parvum
645	169	Dulci depromat carmine
457	238	Dulcis Iesu memoria
627	162	Dum sacerdotum celebrant fideles
445	232	Dum tuas festo pater o colende
251	99	Ecce iam noctis tenuatur umbra
505	260	Eia mater fons amoris
101	33	En acetum fel arundo
83	24	Ex more docti mystico
357	193	Excelsam Pauli gloriam
603	149	Exsultet caelum laudibus
427	223	Felix per omnes festum mundi cardines
517	266	Festiva canimus laude Hieronymum
511	263	Festiva vos archangeli
569	289	Festum celebre martyris
53	15	Fit porta Christi pervia
557	285	Fortem piumque praesulem
669	181	Fortem virili pectore
275	111	Fulgentis auctor aetheris
583	251	Fulget in caelis celebris sacerdos
287	117	Galli cantu mediante
643	170	Gaudentes festum colimus
467	245	Gaudium mundi nova stella caeli
659	178	Hae feminae laudabiles
531	273	Haec est dies qua candidae
665	177	Haec femina laudabilis

Hymnal #	Commentary #	Hymn
137, 157	50	Haec hora quae resplenduit
629	164	Hi sacerdotes Domini sacrati
125	44	Hic est dies verus Dei
293	120	Horis peractis undecim
55	16	Hostis Herodes impie
577	293	Hymnum canentes martyrum
365	197	Iam bone pastor Petre clemens accipe (Chair of St. Peter)
549	281	Iam bone pastor Petre clemens accipe (Sts. Peter and Paul)
379	204	Iam caeca vis mortalium
89	27	Iam Christe sol iustitiae
153	58	Iam Christus astra
283	115	Iam lucis orto sidere
133	48	Iam surgit hora tertia
175	132	Iesu auctor clementiae
657	175	Iesu corona celsior
649	172	Iesu corona virginum
139	52	Iesu nostra redemptio
77	23	Iesu quadragenariae
655	173	Iesu redemptor omnium
123, 147	51	Iesu redemptor saeculi
179	134	Iesu rex admirabilis
543	278	Iesu salvator saeculi
73	21	Iesus refulsit omnium
349	189	Igne divini radians amoris
159	124	Immensa et una Trinitas
681	188	Immensae rex potentiae
205	76	Immense caeli Conditor
71	20	Implente munus debitum
525	270	In caelesti collegio
465	242	In martyris Laurentii
563	288	In plausu grati carminis
651	174	Inclitos Christi famulos canamus
635	163	Inclitus rector pater atque prudens
435	227	Inter aeternas superum coronas
255	101	Ipsum nunc nobis tempus est
545	279	Iste confessor Domini sacratus
373	201	Iste quem laeti colimus fideles
127	45	Laetare caelum desuper
671	183	Laeti colentes famulum
495	256	Laude te cives superi coronant
437	228	Legifer prudens venerande doctor
359	194	Legis sacratae sanctis caeremoniis

Alphabetical Index & Concordance

Hymnal #	Commentary #	Hymn
197	72	Lucis Creator optime
259	103	Lucis largitor splendide
261	104	Luminis fons lux et origo lucis
295	121	Lux aeterna lumen potens
149	56	Lux iucunda lux insignis
439	229	Magdalae sidus mulier beata
59	17	Magi videntes parvulum
453	236	Magnae cohortis principem
229	88	Magnae Deus potentiae
21	6	Magnis prophetae vocibus
587	142	Maria quae mortalium
553	283	Maria virgo regia
547	280	Martine par apostolis
615	157	Martyr Dei qui (quae) unicum
463	241	Martyris Christi colimus triumphum
401	213	Matthia sacratissimo
247	97	Mediae noctis tempus est
387	207	Mentibus laetis tua festa Marce
479	249	Mole gravati criminum
667	179	Nobilem Christi famulam diserta
661	180	Nobiles Christi famulae diserta
263	105	Nocte surgentes vigilemus omnes
447	233	Nocti succedit lucifer
461	240	Novus athleta Domini
223	85	Nox atra rerum contegit
219	83	Nox et tenebrae et nubila
9, 37, 301, 303, 305	60	Nunc Sancte nobis Spiritus
85	25	Nunc tempus acceptabile
623	158	O castitatis signifer
621	156	O Christe flos convallium
591	144	O gloriosa Domina
43	10	O lux beata caelitum
253	100	O Lux beata Trinitas
381	205	O lux salutis nuntia
105	35	O memoriale mortis Domini
459	239	O nata lux de lumine
423, 487	221	O nimis felix meritique celsi
477	248	O quam glorifica luce coruscas
673	184	O redemptoris pietas colenda
121	43	O rex aeterne Domine
431	225	O Roma felix quae tantorum principum
209	78	O sacrosancta Trinitas
493	255	O sancta mundi domina

Hymnal #	Commentary #	Hymn
271	109	O sator rerum reparator aevi
599	148	O sempiternae curiae
385, 533	206	O vir beate Apostolis
409, 595	146	O virgo mater filia
145	54	Optatus votis omnium
521	268	Orbis patrator optime
165	127	Pange lingua gloriosi corporis
99	32	Pange lingua gloriosi proelium
187	138	Peccatricem qui solvisti
111	39	Per crucem Christe quaesumus
211	79	Pergrata mundo nuntiat
367	198	Petrus beatus catenarum laqueos
399	212	Philippe summae honoribus
237	92	Plasmator hominis Deus
535	274	Plausibus Luca canimus triumphum
A1	295	Pontifex Iesu mediator une
485	252	Praecessor almus gratiae
559	286	Praeclara custos virginum
509	262	Praeclara qua tu gloria
87	26	Precemur omnes cernui
353	191	Pressi malorum pondere
191	69	Primo dierum omnium
93	29	Qua Christus hora sitiit
411, 597	147	Quae caritatis fulgidum
451	235	Quas tibi laudes ferimusque vota
589	143	Quem terra pontus aethera
679	187	Qui lacrimatus Lazarum
433	226	Qui luce splendes ordinis
675	185	Qui vivis ante saecula
61	18	Quicumque Christum quaeritis
185	137	Quid sum miser tunc dicturus
363	196	Quod chorus vatum venerandus olim
51	14	Radix Iesse floruit
11, 39, 307, 309, 311	62	Rector potens verax Deus
529	272	Regis superni nuntia
481	250	Relucens inter principes
215	81	Rerum creator optime
245	96	Rerum Deus fons omnium
13, 41, 313, 315, 317	64	Rerum Deus tenax vigor
475	247	Rerum supremo in vertice
607	152	Rex gloriose martyrum
631	166	Sacrata nobis gaudia

Alphabetical Index & Concordance

Hymnal #	Commentary #	Hymn
167	128	Sacris sollemniis iuncta sint gaudia
107	37	Salva Redemptor plasma tuum nobile
497	257	Salve crux sancta salve mundi gloria
249	98	Salve dies dierum gloria
551	282	Salve mater misericordiae
611	154	Sanctorum meritis inclita gaudia
269	108	Sator princepsque temporum
217	82	Scientiarum Domino
499	258	Signum crucis mirabile
277	112	Sol ecce lentus occidens
227	87	Sol ecce surgit igneus
471	244	Solis O Virgo radiis amicta
199	73	Somno refectis artubus
677	186	Spes Christe nostrae veniae
203	75	Splendor paternae gloriae
503, 505, 507	259	Stabat Mater dolorosa
293	93	Summae Deus clementiae
391	209	Te Catharina maximus
683	59	Te Deum laudamus
561	287	Te dicimus praeconio
527	271	Te gestientem gaudiis
449	234	Te gratulantes pangimus
371, 397	200	Te Ioseph celebrent agmina caelitum
3, 31, 79, 337, 339, 341	66	Te lucis ante termunum
443	231	Te nostra laetis laudibus
393	210	Te pater Ioseph opifex colende
161	125	Te Patrem summum genitumque Verbum
177	133	Te saeculorum principem
213	80	Telluris ingens conditor
27, 67, 331, 333, 335	65	Ternis horarum terminis
95	30	Ternis ter horis numerus
513	264	Tibi Christe splendor Patris
115	40	Tibi Redemptor omnium
163	126	Trinitas summo solio coruscans
605	151	Tristes erant Apostoli
231	89	Tu Trinitatis Unitas
585	141	Urbs Ierusalem beata
419	219	Ut queant laxis resonare fibris
141	55	Veni Creator Spiritus
403	214	Veni praecelsa Domina
19	5	Veni redemptor gentium
405	215	Veniens mater inclita

Hymnal #	Commentary #	Hymn
135, 155	49	Venite servi supplices
15	4	Verbum salutis omnium
5	2	Verbum supernum prodiens a Patre lumen exiens
169	129	Verbum supernum prodiens nec Patris linquens dexteram
97, 501	31	Vexilla regis prodeunt
637	165	Vir celse forma fulgida
625	160	Virginis Proles opifexque Matris
573	291	Virginis virgo venerande custos
413	217	Virgo mater Ecclesiae
389	208	Virgo prudentum comitata coetum
507	261	Virgo virginum praeclara
257	102	Vita sanctorum via spes salusque
7	3	Vox clara ecce intonat